Lecture Notes in Computer Science   8729

Commenced Publication in 1973
Founding and Former Series Editors:
Gerhard Goos, Juris Hartmanis, and Jan van Leeuwen

T0212637

Preface

Following the previous six successful events of IDCS – IDCS 2008 in Khulna, Bangladesh, IDCS 2009 in Jeju Island, Korea, IDCS 2010 and IDCS 2011 in Melbourne, Australia, IDCS 2012 in Wu Yi Shan, China, IDCS 2013 in Hangzhou, China - IDCS 2014 was the seventh in the series to promote research in diverse fields related to the Internet and distributed computing systems.

The emergence of the Web as a ubiquitous platform for innovations has laid the foundation for the rapid growth of the Internet. Side-by-side, the use of mobile and wireless devices such as PDAs, laptops, and cell phones for accessing the Internet has paved the ways for related technologies to flourish through recent developments. In addition, the popularity of sensor networks is promoting a better integration of the digital world with the physical environment towards the future Internet of Things.

IDCS 2014 received innovative papers on emerging technologies related to the Internet and distributed systems to support the effective design and efficient implementation of high-performance networked systems. The audience included researchers and industry practitioners who were interested in different aspects of the Internet and distributed systems, with a particular focus on practical experiences with the design and implementation of related technologies as well as their theoretical perspectives.

IDCS 2014 received a large number of submissions (from 24 different countries), from which 23 regular papers and 15 short papers were accepted after a careful review and selection process. This year's conference also featured one invited talk, entitled "Seamless Data Communications in Space Networks", from Prof. Mohammed Atiquzzaman, Edith J. Kinney Gaylord Presidential Professor, School of Computer Science University of Oklahoma. Prof. Atiquzzaman is also editor-in-chief of the Journal of Network and Computer Applications, Elsevier.

The contributions to IDCS 2014 covered the topics of ad-hoc and sensor networks; Internet and Web technologies; network operations and management; multi-agent systems; cloud-based information infrastructures.

IDCS 2014 was held on the wonderful Tyrrenian coast of the Calabria region, Italy.

The conference organization was supported by Sensyscal S.r.l. (a spin-off of the University of Calabria whose research and development mission is directed to the development of innovative sensor-based and IoT systems in different application domains ranging from m-Health to building automation and environmental/ambient smart control) and the DIMES (Department of Informatics, Modeling, Electronics and Systems) of the University of Calabria.

Further technical co-sponsorship was provided by the Commonwealth Scientific and Industrial Research Organization (CSIRO), the national government body of scientific research in Australia, and Daily Positive (D+), a non-profit media initiative.

The successful organization of IDCS 2014 was possible thanks to the dedication and hard work of a number of individuals.

Specifically, we would like to thank Antonio Guerrieri (web chair) and Raffaele Gravina for their commendable work with the proceedings preparation and conference organization. We also express our gratitude to the general chair Giancarlo Fortino, University of Calabria, Italy, and the program chairs (Giuseppe Di Fatta, Wenfeng Li, Sergio Ochoa, Alfredo Cuzzocrea) and industry chair (Mukaddim Pathan) for their support of the conference. Last but not the least, we are thankful to all the volunteers, specifically Claudio Savaglio and Stefano Galzarano for their efforts in the conference organization during 22–24 September 2014.

September 2014

Giancarlo Fortino
Giuseppe Di Fatta
Wenfeng Li
Sergio Ochoa
Alfredo Cuzzocrea
Mukaddim Pathan

Giancarlo Fortino   Giuseppe Di Fatta
Wenfeng Li   Sergio Ochoa
Alfredo Cuzzocrea   Mukaddim Pathan (Eds.)

Internet and Distributed Computing Systems

7th International Conference, IDCS 2014
Calabria, Italy, September 22-24, 2014
Proceedings

 Springer

Volume Editors

Giancarlo Fortino
DIMES - University of Calabria (UNICAL), Rende, Italy
E-mail: g.fortino@unical.it

Giuseppe Di Fatta
University of Reading, UK
E-mail: g.difatta@reading.ac.uk

Wenfeng Li
Wuhan University of Technology, Wuhan, P.R. China
E-mail: liwf@whut.edu.cn

Sergio Ochoa
University of Chile, Santiago, Chile
E-mail: sochoa@dcc.uchile.cl

Alfredo Cuzzocrea
ICAR-CNR and University of Calabria, Rende, Italy
E-mail: cuzzocrea@si.deis.unical.it

Mukaddim Pathan
CSIRO ICT Center, Acton, ACT, Australia
E-mail: ak_mukaddim@yahoo.com.au

ISSN 0302-9743   e-ISSN 1611-3349
ISBN 978-3-319-11691-4   e-ISBN 978-3-319-11692-1
DOI 10.1007/978-3-319-11692-1
Springer Cham Heidelberg New York Dordrecht London

Library of Congress Control Number: 2014948784

LNCS Sublibrary: SL 3 – Information Systems and Application,
incl. Internet/Web and HCI

Typesetting: Camera-ready by author, data conversion by Scientific Publishing Services, Chennai, India

Printed on acid-free paper

Springer is part of Springer Science+Business Media (www.springer.com)

Organization

General Chair

Giancarlo Fortino   University of Calabria, Italy

Program Chairs

Giuseppe Di Fatta   University of Reading, UK
Wenfeng Li   Wuhan University of Technology, China
Sergio Ochoa   Universidad de Chile, Chile

Local Program Chair

Alfredo Cuzzocrea   ICAR-CNR, Italy

Web Chair

Antonio Guerrieri   University of Calabria, Italy

Publicity and Industry Chair

Mukaddim Pathan   Telstra Corporation Limited, Australia

Steering Committee - IDCS Series

Jemal Abawajy   Deakin University, Australia
Rajkumar Buyya   University of Melbourne, Australia
Giancarlo Fortino   University of Calabria, Italy
Dimitrios Georgakopolous   RMIT University, Australia
Mukaddim Pathan   Telstra Corporation Limited, Australia
Yang Xiang   Deakin University, Australia

Program Committee

Jemal Abawajy   Deakin University, Australia
Tarem Ahmed   BRAC University, Bangladesh

Table of Contents

Agent-Oriented Algorithms and Systems

Cloud Computing

Cyberphysical Systems and IoT

Parallel and Distributed Computing

Advanced Networking

Security Methods and Systems

Sensor Networks

Smart Energy Systems

Social Networks and Applications

Agent-Oriented Algorithms
and Systems

Inserting "Brains" into Software Agents – Preliminary Considerations

Maria Ganzha[1,3], Mariusz Marek Mesjasz[1], Marcin Paprzycki[1],
and Moussa Ouedraogo[2]

[1] Systems Research Institute Polish Academy of Sciences, Warsaw, Poland
`<firstname>.<lastname>@ibspan.waw.pl`
[2] CRP Henri Tudor, Luxembourg
`<firstname>.<lastname>@tudor.lu`
[3] Institute of Informatics, University of Gdansk, Gdansk, Poland

Abstract. Software agents are often seen as "intelligent, autonomous software components." Interestingly, the question of efficient implementation of "intelligence" remains open. In this paper we discuss, in some details, the process of implementing software agents with "brains." In the context of an agent system supporting decisions of glider pilots, we consider native implementation of "intelligent" behaviors, rule based engines, and semantic data processing. Based on the analysis of the state-of-the-art in these areas, we present a novel approach combining rule based engines, semantic data processing and software agents.

1 Introduction

One of the interesting issues in design and implementation of agent systems is: how to make agents "intelligent." Note that, very often, software agents are conceptualized as "intelligent, autonomous software components, which interact with each other in order to achieve goals for benefits of their users" [29, 31]. However, as illustrated below, it is not easy to find an agent platform, where a *robust* (and *flexible*) method for making agents intelligent is available.

Separately, a number of rule-based expert systems have been developed. Typically, they are based on the RETE pattern matching algorithm [24]. Implementation of RETE has been completed, among others, in C, C++ and Java, and provide user interfaces and/or definition of the API.

Finally, since the 1980's (see, [22, 30]) an explosion of research in ontologies and semantic technologies ensued. This has culminated, over the last 10 years, in rapid sprawl of ontology management tools (e.g. Protege [17]) and reasoners (with Hermit [8], Pellet [16] and Fact++ [7] being the most popular).

Let us now consider an agent-based support system for glider pilots (for more details, see [23, 27]). The idea is to aid the glider pilot in events that may occur during a flight. For instance, to detect life-threatening situations, warn the pilot and, autonomously, inform the ground station. The pilot-supporting agent runs on a tablet or a smart-phone. For the system we have selected the Android OS [1] and the JadeAndroid add-on [12] (which allows running full Jade agent container

G. Fortino et al. (Eds.): IDCS 2014, LNCS 8729, pp. 3–14, 2014.
© Springer International Publishing Switzerland 2014

on Android devices). The next step to be undertaken is to introduce "reasoning capabilities" to the *GliderAgent* agents. This provides the conceptual backdrop for the explorations reported below.

Note that we are interested in practical aspects of implementing agent systems (see, also, [26, 28]). Furthermore, we believe in open source solutions and reuse of state-of-the-art software. This gives the methodological foundation of our work. Therefore, in the next section, we summarize approaches to implementing "brains" of software agents. Specifically, we consider "native" approaches (within agent platforms), rule-based expert systems, and semantic technologies. We follow with details of the implementation of the selected approach.

2   Introducing Intelligence into Software Agents

2.1   Native Approaches

Large number of agent platforms have been written in different languages. Since we are interested in agent systems running on Android devices, we discuss those written in the Java. However, to the best of our knowledge, discussion presented here applies to majority of agent platforms in use today.

Jade [12] (Java Agent DEvelopment Framework; version 4.3.2; 2014-03-28) is written entirely in Java, with the lead developer being Telecom Italia. Jade developers provided add-ons to run it on mobile devices. JadeAndroid is an official add-on that allows to run Jade agents on Android OS. Jade agents store their knowledge in a form of *Java classes*. As a result, after Java classes are compiled, they *cannot* be changed without altering the *entire* application. Thus, an agent has to be recompiled, each time when a change is introduced into its "knowledge." Therefore, it is not trivial to introduce changes to a running Jade agent system (without taking the system down and restarting it; see [25]). Obviously, in the GliderAgent system (as well as majority of real-world multi-agent systems), a more flexible approach is desired. Namely, an intelligent agent should be able to add, modify or delete a "behavior" (related to a "knowledge fragment") on-demand (or, at least, without the need of restarting the system).

JASON [11] (version 1.4.0a; 2013-12-17) is an interpreter for an extended version of the AgentSpeak (based on the Belief Desire Intention (BDI) paradigm). It is available as an Open Source software (GNU LGPL license). JASON agents are written in AgentSpeak. Since no official version of JASON for mobile devices exists, it is unclear how easy it would be to run it on smart-phones. Furthermore, JASON requires additional infrastructure (e.g., Jade) to run it distributed over a network. Thus, one may assume that JASON *and* an additional agent platform have *both* to be ported to the Android API. This doubles the amount of required programming work, and may also result in "doubling" resource consumption.

In the JadeX agent platform [10], "intelligence" is facilitated in the form of XML-based BDI rules. However, in our context, JadeX has three disadvantages. (1) It has somewhat irregular development cycle. (2) It is evolving from a high-level BDI-agent platform to the agent-as-component model, which has much smaller granularity and, as a result, it is not clear what, if any, will be the role of the XML-demarcated BDI rules in its future releases. (3) It remains unclear how easy / difficult it would be to run JadeX on mobile devices.

JACK agents (developed by the AOS Group; [9]) use the JACK Agent Language, a super-set of Java. JACK compiler converts source code of JACK agents into pure Java. Therefore, JACK agent platform has the same limitations as Jade. Namely, agent code has to be recompiled each time when an update is required. Furthermore, as of now, JACK does not provide official support for the Android OS (or any other mobile device). Note that it may be quite difficult to port JACK to Android because JACK agents have to be translated twice: (1) from the JACK Agent Language to the Java programming language, and (2) from the Java programming language to the Android API. Since (1) is done by the JACK compiler, developers have limited control over this process. Consequently, there is a substantial risk that the resulting Java code will not work with the Android OS. Furthermore, any change in the agent system (e.g. change in agent "knowledge") would have to be done within the JACK subsystem first, and then moved to the actual system. Therefore, perspective of using JACK on mobile devices (or in a mixed mobile-non-mobile environment) is not appealing.

2.2 Rule-Based Expert Systems for Agent Systems

Let us now consider the possibility of combining a Rule-based Expert System (RES) with Jade agents running on the Android OS (however, this discussion generalizes also to other agent systems and other mobile devices). First, note that Java is not natively compatible with Android. While having the same syntax and similar interfaces, there are key differences between the Java API and the Android API. (1) Android does not use the Java Virtual Machine. Instead, it uses the Dalvik or the ART (starting from Android 4.4); two runtime environments written and maintained by Google. (2) Not all Java packages were included in the Android API; e.g. the *javax* package (Swing, XML libraries, etc.) is missing, and has to be replaced by the Android's native classes. Therefore, the RES should:

- Be an open source project (with license that permits modifications). Due to the differences between the Java API and the Android API, the RES (and its dependencies) will have to be ported (and possibly modified). Moreover, parts of the RES may need to be replaced by the Android native libraries to work and/or to achieve better performance.
- Be an "active project." Note that many open source projects are being developed by "independent" / academic teams. Therefore, the risk of selecting an unfinished or obsoleted project is high, and should be avoided. Moreover, dealing with older versions of Java may increase the amount of work needed to make the project operational.

Finally, an ideal RES should have a small number of dependencies and a simple structure. This should minimize rewriting the required libraries. Moreover, complex projects are difficult to understand and modify, without introducing errors. However, these considerations are secondary.

To compare the existing RESs, we used data found at [13]. After refreshing the information, and selecting RES's written in Java, we have summarized it in Table 2.2. For each RES (row in the table) we include: name, latest stable version (and release date), license type and website.

It is easy to notice that only three RESs (Roolie, Drools, OpenL Tablets) are of interest in the current context. The remaining ones either are significantly outdated, or have multiple licenses (depending on the type of the project / the character of the licensee), which unnecessarily complicates their use "across the board." Therefore, we provide more information about these three.

- Roolie [18] (version 1.1, 2013-12-13) is an extremely simple RES. It chains user-defined rules (stored in XML files) to create more complex rules. Due to its size (only few kilobytes) and lack of dependencies, it seems that it could be adapted to the Android API. Unfortunately, it does not include a pattern matching algorithm. Thus, an additional algorithm (e.g. RETE) would have to be implemented. Moreover, Roolie is poorly documented.
- Drools [5] (version 6.0.0, 2013-12-20) is a forward and backward chaining rule engine. From the current version, it provides its own, enhanced, implementations of the RETE algorithm, called PHREAKY. Rules are stored in a Drools native language. The entire project is very well documented. Unfortunately, while very robust, it has many external dependencies. This would make Drools difficult to port to the Android API. Furthermore, its size and scope poses question about its usability on resource-limited mobile devices.
- OpenL Tablets [14] (version 5.12, 2014-04-21) is a full-blown expert system. Its rules and policies exist as an unstructured set of Excel and Word documents. This makes rules easier to understand and change by non-technical users. Unfortunately, proprietary data formats (Excel and Word) are not well-suited for an open source type system. Furthermore, the Android API may require extra libraries to open / manage them.

2.3 Semantic Technologies for Agent Systems

Finally, to implement "brains" of software agents one could use semantic technologies. Here, facts are stored inside ontologies in a form of triples (subject, predicate, object), applications can use a reasoner to infer logical consequences from them. Statements within an ontology can be divided into: (i) a set of facts (A-box), and (ii) conceptualization associated with them (T-box). T-box defines a schema in terms of controlled vocabularies (for example, a set of classes, properties and axioms), while A-box contains T-box-compliant facts. Combination of the A-box and the T-box makes up a knowledge base. Interestingly, the Drools developers officially stated that, in the future, they will try to bring OWL Lite to Drools. This shows growing interest in combining these two technologies. Since, we are interested in open source solutions, we have considered Apache Jena and the OWL API.

Apache Jena [3] (Jena, version 2.11.1, 2013-09-18) is a, well-documented, open source framework for building semantic web and Linked Data applications.

Rule-based Engine	Developer(s)	Stable release	License	Website
Drools	Red Hat	6.0.0 / 2013-12-20	ASL 2	http://drools.jboss.org/
DTRules	Andreas Viklund	4.3 / 2011-07-05	ASL	http://dtrules.com/
Hammurapi Rules	Hammurapi Group	5.7.0 / 2009-01-11	LGPL	http://www.hammurapi.biz/
Jena rule-based reasoner	Apache Software Foundation	2.11.1, 2013-09-18	ASL 2	http://jena.apache.org/
JEOPS	Ravi Tangirala, Bob Schlicher, Jeff Carter	2.2 / 2003-09-29	LGPL	http://sourceforge.net/projects/jeops/
JLisa	Mike Beedle	0.04 / 2003-11-20	GPL	http://jlisa.sourceforge.net/
JRuleEngine	Mauro Carniel	1.3 / 2008-04-16	LGPL	http://jruleengine.sourceforge.net/
Mandarax	Jens Dietrich, Jochen Hiller, Alex Kozlenkov	1.1.0 / 2011-01-26	LGPL	https://code.google.com/p/mandarax/
Open Lexicon	OpenLexicon.org	1.0.4 / 2007-01-12	ASL	http://openlexicon.org
OpenL Tablets	OpenL Tablets	5.12 / 2014-04-21	LGPL	http://openl-tablets.sourceforge.net/
OpenRules	OpenRules, Inc.	6.3.1 / 2014-05-18	GPL / Non-GPL Licenses for Commercial Projects	http://openrules.com
Roolie	Ryan Kennedy	1.1, 2013-12-13	LGPL	http://roolie.sourceforge.net/
SweetRules	MIT Sloan and DAML	2.1 / 2005-04-25	LGPL	http://sweetrules.projects.semwebcentral.org/
TermWare	GradSoft	2.3.3 / 2011-06-16	Other	http://www.gradsoft.ua/products/termware_eng.html

It provides an API to extract data from and write to RDF, RDFS and OWL graphs. Graphs are loaded from: (i) file system, (ii) database, or (iii) the web (via URLs) and represented as abstract structures called "models." The Jena works with a) RDF, b) OWL, and c) triple store. It includes popular semantic reasoners: Fact++ [7], Pellet [16] and HermiT [8]. Furthermore, it provides its own implementation of the SPARQL 1.1 engine (the AQR). Note that, even though Jena was not designed as a rule-based engine, it implements the RETE algorithm in a general purpose rule-based reasoner. This reasoner is used for updating the loaded ontologies, when a certain rule is met. There existed two community projects aiming at running Jena on Android. (1) The Androjena [2] project supported only a subset of the Jena features and was discontinued in 2010. (2) The Apache Jena on Android [4] project tried to fully integrate Jena (with all its features) with the Android OS. Unfortunately, the latest, stable version of Apache Jena on Android was released for the outdated Jena, in version 2.7.3 released on August 7, 2012.

The OWL API [15] (version 3.50, 2014-04-07) is a Java API (and reference implementation) for creating, manipulating and serialising OWL Ontologies. It supports OWL 2.0 and offers an API to inference engines and ontology validation. Similarly to Jena, the OWL API provides interfaces for FaCT++, HermiT, Pellet and Racer (but they are not build-in). Furthermore, it features: (1) an API for OWL 2.0, (2) parsers and writers for RDF/XML, OWL/XML, OWL Functional Syntax, Turtle, KRSS, and OBO Flat. To the best of our knowledge, are no ("official" or community-driven) projects intended to port the OWL API to the Android OS (or other mobile OS).

3   Implementing Agents with "Brains" on Mobile Devices – Proposed Approach

We have considered different approaches to infuse software agents with intelligence. Despite the fact that native methods provided by agent platforms are sufficient for many scenarios, they lack flexibility. For instance, systems like the *GliderAgent* that operate in constantly changing environment (e.g. cockpit of a glider), should not relay on compiled Java classes.

Next, we have considered rule-based expert systems found at [13]. While we report only those written in Java, *neither* of them satisfied our requirements. The primary concern was related to need to re-implement the RETE (e.g. in Roolie), or porting the RES to mobile devices (e.g. Drools, OpenL Tablets).

Finally, we considered two semantic frameworks – Apache Jena and the OWL API (in Section 2.3). Here, we decided to use Jena. First, it already did run on the Android OS. Moreover, the Jena on Android creators summarized the porting process, helping us to bring the newest version of Jena (2.11.1) to the Android OS. Moreover, because Jena implements the RETE algorithm, we can take advantages of two different frameworks – RES and semantic data processing. Specifically, the system knowledge can be represented and stored in the form of an RDF / OWL ontology, while the decision making process can utilize rule-based processing.

Porting Jena to Android proceeded in two stages: (1) creating a fully functional prototype, and (2) rewriting the Java code to run on the Android OS. Note that since the prototype was created first, we were able to remove unused dependencies and, in this way, reduce the amount of work in the second stage.

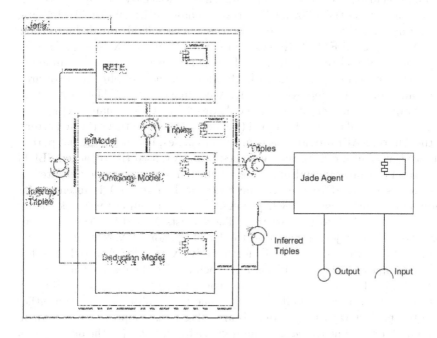

Fig. 1. The component diagram of the system

The component diagram is presented in Figure 1. There, we can see two software components: (1) Jena and (2) a Jade agent. During the initialization, a pair – an ontology and a set of rules – is loaded into Jena. They represent the knowledge base of the system. The ontology is stored as an instance of the *InfModel* class. Jade agent receives this information from the environment and analyzes it (extracts facts). Next, these facts are transformed into triples (object, predicate, subject) compliant with the loaded ontology. All triples are sent to Jena, in order to update the *InfModel*. Note that the *InfModel* is a hybrid of two different instances of the *Model* class: (i) the *Ontology Model*, and (ii) the *Deduction Model*. The *Ontology Model* stores all initial facts (loaded with the ontology) and the inserted triples (added by the Jade agent). On the other hand, the *Deduction Model* stores all facts inferred by matching rules against the ontology. When a new triple is added to the *Ontology Model*, Jena runs its implementation of the RETE algorithm. During this process, new inferred facts are added to the *Deduction Model*. Since a Jade agent is not "interested" in what it already knows (facts added to the *Ontology Model*), Jena returns new triples from the *Deduction Model*. In order to improve the system performance, these triples are combined into batches. A batch is sent when the algorithm completes the execution (all fulfilled rules were fired). Finally, the Jade agent analyses the batch and executes the appropriate behavior.

In the second stage, the system was rewritten to work with the Android API. First, it requires only a part of Jena functionality – for interacting with an ontology and executing the RETE algorithm. Thus, it was easy to empirically verify, that Jena requires the following libraries: i) jena-core, ii) jena-iri, iii) slf4j-api, iv) xercesImpl and v) xml-apis. These libraries can be roughly divided into three subsets: 1) Jena, 2) SLF4J, 3) Xerces. Here, SLF4J [19] and Xerces [20] are external projects. SLF4J (Simple Logging Facade for Java) serves as a simple abstraction for various logging frameworks. It allows the user to plug in the desired logging framework at the deployment time. According to the SLF4J website, there exists a wrapped implementation for the Android OS. Unfortunately, currently, the SLF4J is not available for download (the download site returns the 404 error). Since the Android API provides its own logger classes, it is not a crucial part of the application. Thus, during the implementation, we used the repacked SLF4J libraries from the Jade on Android project (which, however, may be outdated).

The Xerces (licensed to the Apache Software Foundation) is intended for creation and maintenance of XML parsers. It is a very important dependence in Jena and, thus, had to be rewritten. There exists Xerces for Android. This community-driven project is based on the latest version of Xerces (2.11.0) and is available for download at [21]. Unfortunately, Xerces for Android uses the *javax.** namespace to provide the missing dependencies. The *javax.** namespace is interpreted by the Dalvik (or ART) cross-compiler (as the "core" Java library), thus it is "safe" to cross-compile. To overcome this limitation, one can either compile the project with the "–core-library" flag (this suppresses the error in the compiler), or rename the *javax.** namespace to *javax2.** (as the developer of Jena on Android suggests). Overall, when SLF4J and Xerces are replaced, Jena can be repacked to be supported on the Android OS.

3.1 Testing the Solution

To test our system we proposed two scenarios. In the first scenario, an agent system runs on a device with the latest stable version of the Android OS – 4.4.4. In the first step, initial facts and rules (presented in listing 1.1) are inserted into the system. These rules were written based on the theory on psychosocial development of human beings, articulated by Erik Erikson [6]. Then, we modify the system knowledge by interacting with the Android application. Specifically, we can increase or decrease the age by one. As a result, new triples (facts about our current age) are inserted to the system. In response to user actions, the agent display short information in the form of a "toast" notification (see Figure 2). After the last triple is delivered (the number is greater than 65), the system prints out the outcome in the debug console. Each part of the result contains the following information: the current age, the current Erikson's stage of human life and two triples (one inserted into the *Ontology Model* and one inserted into *Deduction Model*). Finally, we can observe that all stages were reached by the application. Specifically, the agent properly responded to all facts and the system knowledge was correctly updated by the algorithm.

Listing 1.1. Facts and rules used in the first scenario

```
<!-- FACTS -->

<rdf:RDF
  xmlns:rdf="http://www.w3.org/1999/02/22-rdf-syntax-ns#"
  xmlns:eg="urn:x-hp:eg/" >
  <rdf:Description rdf:about="urn:x-hp:eg/Person">
    <eg:age rdf:datatype="http://www.w3.org/2001/XMLSchema#int">0</eg:age>
    <eg:stage rdf:resource="urn:x-hp:eg/Infancy"/>
  </rdf:Description>
</rdf:RDF>


<!-- RULES -->

[infancy: (?d eg:age ?a) ge(?a,0) lessThan(?a,2)
  -> (?d eg:stage eg:Infancy)]
[childhood: (?d eg:age ?a) ge(?a,2) lessThan(?a,3)
  -> (?d eg:stage eg:Childhood)]
[preschool: (?d eg:age ?a) ge(?a,3) lessThan(?a,6)
  -> (?d eg:stage eg:Preschool)]
[school: (?d eg:age ?a) ge(?a,6) lessThan(?a,12)
  -> (?d eg:stage eg:School)]
[adolescence : (?d eg:age ?a) ge(?a,12) lessThan(?a,19)
  -> (?d eg:stage eg:Adolescence)]
[young_adulthood: (?d eg:age ?a) ge(?a,19) lessThan(?a,40)
  -> (?d eg:stage eg:Young_Adulthood)]
[middle_adulthood: (?d eg:age ?a) ge(?a,40) lessThan(?a,65)
  -> (?d eg:stage eg:Middle_Adulthood)]
[maturity: (?d eg:age ?a) ge(?a,65)
  -> (?d eg:stage eg:Maturity)]
```

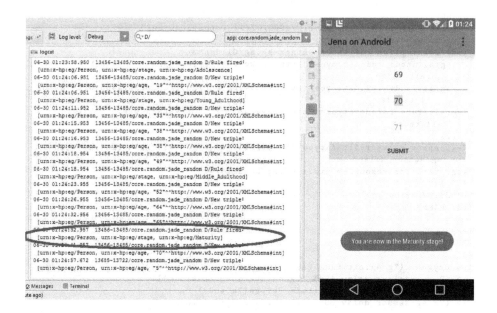

Fig. 2. The outcome of the first scenario – the application properly notify the user

In the second scenario, the rule-based decision making system is integrated
with the *GliderAgent* agent. Here, the system receives feeds from different sensors (altitude, temperature, blood pressure etc.) and, based on such information,
triggers appropriate *GliderAgent* agent behaviors. Specifically, the rules and corresponding behaviors are listed in listing 1.2. Unlike the first scenario, the system
takes autonomous actions. Specifically, for the test purposes, we used the oxygen
scenario from the initial version of the system [23]. In this scenario, we model
two types of warnings: (1) low oxygen level generated at 9842.52 ft (3000 m
above the sea level), and (2) critical oxygen level generated at 13123.36 ft (4000
m above the sea level). At the beginning of the scenario, the glider stays on the
ground at the altitude of 0 m. The position of the glider and its altitude start to
change when the scenario is executed. It is assumed that the glider is conducting
a lee-wave flight, and its altitude is increasing fast. Each time, when an agent
receives data from sensors, the *Ontology Model* is modified accordingly. Namely,
the position of the glider changes with respect to the GPS feed. Figure 3 presents
the situation when the glider reaches the altitude of 4000 m. We can see that the
XCSoar program (which observes the altitude greater than 13123.36 ft) displays
warning "Critical oxygen level". Overall, we can observe that the agent properly
identified a life-threatening situation and informed the pilot about the danger.
Thus it can be said that the new *GliderAgent* agent "has its brain in place."
This will also allow us to start building its knowledge base in form of rules and
ontologies.

Listing 1.2. Facts and rules used in the second scenario

```
<!-- FACTS -->

<rdf:RDF
    xmlns:rdf="http://www.w3.org/1999/02/22-rdf-syntax-ns#"
    xmlns:eg="urn:x-hp:eg/" >
  <rdf:Description rdf:about="urn:x-hp:eg/Glider">
    <eg:altitude rdf:datatype="http://www.w3.org/2001/XMLSchema#double">0</eg
        :altitude>
    <eg:latitude rdf:datatype="http://www.w3.org/2001/XMLSchema#double">0</eg
        :latitude>
    <eg:altitude rdf:datatype="http://www.w3.org/2001/XMLSchema#int">0</eg:
        altitude>
    (...)
    <eg:sensor_delay rdf:datatype="http://www.w3.org/2001/XMLSchema#int">300</
        eg:sensor_delay>
    <eg:state rdf:resource="urn:x-hp:eg/Normal"/>
    (...)
  </rdf:Description>
</rdf:RDF>

<!-- RULES -->

(...)
[low_oxygen: (?g eg:altitude ?a) ge(?a,3000) lessThan(?a,4000)
    -> (?g eg:sensor_delay 120) (?g eg:state eg:Cautious)]
[critical_oxygen: (?g eg:altitude ?a) ge(?a,4000)
    -> (?g eg:sensor_delay 60) (?g eg:state eg:Critical)]
(...)
```

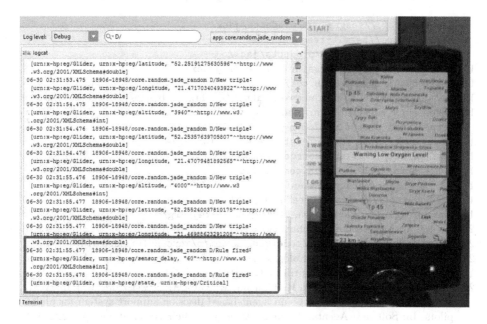

Fig. 3. The outcome of the second scenario – the GliderAgent system is running on the Android device

4   Concluding Remarks

In this paper, we considered implementation of "intelligent" software agents. Based on a analysis of possible approaches (native methods in agent platforms, rule-based expert systems and semantic frameworks), we have realized that none of them is sufficient alone, when developing agent systems for mobile devices and when agent knowledge has to be often updated. Therefore, we have combined Jade and Jena to develop a solution, which supports both rule-based and semantic technologies and tested the proposed approach on two simple scenarios. While the implemented solution is restricted to Java-based agents running on the Android OS, we believe that the presented results naturally generalize to other programming languages and operating systems.

References

1. Android os, http://www.android.com/
2. Androjena, https://code.google.com/p/androjena/
3. Apache jena, http://openl-tablets.sourceforge.net/
4. Apache jena on android, http://elite.polito.it/jena-on-android/
5. Drools, http://drools.jboss.org/
6. Erikson's psychosocial stages summary chart,
   http://psychology.about.com/library/bl_psychosocial_summary.htm

7. Fact++, http://aosgrp.com/products/jack/
8. Hermit, http://hermit-reasoner.com/
9. Jack, http://aosgrp.com/products/jack/
10. Jadex, http://sourceforge.net/projects/jadex/
11. Jason, http://jade.tilab.com/
12. Java agent development framework, http://jade.tilab.com/
13. Open source rule engines in java,
    http://java-source.net/open-source/rule-engines
14. Openl tables, http://openl-tablets.sourceforge.net/
15. Owl api, http://owlapi.sourceforge.net/
16. Pellet, http://clarkparsia.com/pellet/
17. Protege, http://protege.stanford.edu/
18. Roolie, http://roolie.sourceforge.net/
19. Simple logging facade for java, http://www.slf4j.org/
20. Xerces, http://xerces.apache.org/
21. Xerces for android, https://code.google.com/p/xerces-for-android/
22. Brodie, M.L., Fensel, D.: Ontologies: A Silver Bullet for Knowledge Management and Electronic Commerce. Springer (2003)
23. Domanski, J.J., Dziadkiewicz, R., Ganzha, M., Gab, A., Mesjasz, M.M., Paprzycki, M.: Implementing glideragent—an agent-based decision support system for glider pilots. In: Software Agents, Agent Systems and Their Applications, pp. 222–244 (2012)
24. Forgy, C.: On the efficient implementation of production systems. PhD thesis, Thesis, Carnegie-Mellon University (1979)
25. Frąckowiak, G., Ganzha, M., Paprzycki, M., Szymczak, M., Han, Y.-S., Park, M.-W.: Adaptability in an agent-based virtual organization – towards implementation. In: Cordeiro, J., Hammoudi, S., Filipe, J. (eds.) Web Information Systems and Technologies. Lecture Notes in Business Information Processing, vol. 18, pp. 27–39. Springer, Heidelberg (2009)
26. Ganzha, M., Lakhmi, J.C.: Multiagent Systems and Applicatins. A John Wiley and Sons, Ltd (2009)
27. Mesjasz, M., Cimadoro, D., Galzarano, S., Ganzha, M., Fortino, G., Paprzycki, M.: Integrating Jade and MAPS for the Development of Agent-Based WSN Applications. In: Fortino, G., Badica, C., Malgeri, M., Unland, R. (eds.) IDC 2012. Studies in Computational Intelligence, vol. 446, pp. 211–220. Springer, Heidelberg (2012)
28. Nwana, H.S., Ndumu, D.T.: A perspective on software agents research. Knowl. Eng. Rev. 14(2), 125–142 (1999)
29. Russell, S.J., Norvig, P.: Artificial Intelligence: A Modern Approach, 2nd edn. Pearson Education (2003)
30. Sowa, J.F.: Knowledge Representation: Logical, Philosophical, and Computational Foundations. Brooks / Cole (1999)
31. Wooldridge, M., Jennings, N.R.: Intelligent agents: Theory and practice. Knowledge Engineering Review 10(2), 115–152 (1995)

A Multi-agent Algorithm to Improve Content Management in CDN Networks

Agostino Forestiero and Carlo Mastroianni

CNR - ICAR
Via Pietro Bucci, 41C
87036 Rende (CS), Italy
{forestiero,mastroianni}@icar.cnr.it

Abstract. An effective solution to delivery static contents are the Content Delivery Networks (CDNs). However, when the network size increases, they show limits and weaknesses related to their size, dynamic nature, and due to the centralized/heirarchical algorithms used for their management. Decentralized algorithms and protocols can be usefully employed to improve their efficiency. A bio-inspired algorithm that improves the performance of CDNs by means of a logical organization of contents is presented in this paper. Self-organizing ant-inspired agents move and organize the metadata describing the content among the CDN servers, which are interconnected in a peer-to-peer fashion, so as to improve discovery operations. Experimental results confirm the effectiveness of the adopted approach.

Keywords: Content Delivery Networks, Bio-inspired, Peer to Peer.

1 Introduction

Content Delivery Networks are an efficient alternative to centralized storage for the delivery of static and dynamic content, such as video on-demand, TV broadcasts, media streaming services, pay-per-use software, pay-per-download music, etc. Content replication and distribution is adopted by CDNs to improve the performance of Internet-based content delivery in terms of response time and accessibility. Clusters of surrogate servers, located at the network edge, are maintained and geographically distributed in order to put content as close as possible to the users.

Nowadays, many aspects of Content Networks have been improved in aspects such as the available content, the number of hosts and servers, the kind and the number of the users and the efficiency of real time services. The best surrogate servers - that store copies of the content - are chosen to satisfy user requests. Hence, a system and a set of mechanisms able to provide contents and services in a scalable manner need to be offered. With the explosion of social networks and P2P technologies, the amount of content has increased hugely, as well as the exploitation of the Cloud Computing paradigm, in which numerous servers located in the "Clouds" manage the content and the services. However, to perform retrieval or access operations, current applications that create, modify and

G. Fortino et al. (Eds.): IDCS 2014, LNCS 8729, pp. 15–25, 2014.

manage the content, and actively place it at appropriate locations, are often insufficient. Small- or medium-sized networks can be acceptably tackled with a centralized approach. However, the CDN paradigm shows its limits in large-scale and dynamic systems. Decentralized algorithms and protocols, such as peer-to-peer (P2P) and multi agent systems, can be useful to deal with new technologies and complex paradigms [7][9].

In this paper an algorithm that exploits nature-inspired agents to organize the content in Content Delivery Networks, is presented. This approach was first introduced in [4], where a high-level description was given. Here the approach is described in more details, specifically regarding the content discovery procedure, and performance results are presented and discussed. Metadata documents that describe the content are moved and logically organized by the agents to improve information retrieval operations. In our approach, metadata documents are indexed by binary strings, obtained as the result of the application of a locality preserving hash function, which maps similar resources into similar binary strings. For example, each bit of the string may represent the absence or presence of a given characteristic of an offered service. Agents move across the CDN network through the peer-to-peer interconnections moving the metadata documents. Similar metadata, representing similar resources, are located into the same or in neighbor hosts/servers. The assignment of metadata documents to CDN servers is self-organizing and driven by probabilistic operations, and easily adapts to the dynamic conditions of the network.

The logical reorganization induced by the operations of mobile agents allows to exploit the benefits of structured and unstructured approaches adopted in peer to peer systems. The logical reorganization of the metadata documents improves the rapidity and effectiveness of discovery operations, and enables the execution of range queries, i.e., requests of content that matches some specified features. In fact, thanks to the features of the hash function, the metadata strings that differ only by a few bits will be located in neighboring regions. To measure the similarity between two binary strings the Hamming distance or the cosine of the angle between the related vectors is used.

The rest of the paper is organized as follows: Section 2 discusses related work, Section 3 describes how the bio-inspired agents replicate and logically reorganize metadata documents on the CDN network and Section 4 describes the discovery algorithm that exploits the metadata reorganization to perform simple and range queries. Finally, in Section 5 the performance analysis of the algorithm is reported.

2   Related Works

Approaches that combine CDNs and P2P methodologies have been analyzed by several studies: [12] [11] proposed the use of P2P to deliver multimedia content; [14] [10] exploit P2P overlays for surrogate cooperation while leaving the clients as regular non-cooperative entities; in [16], a collaboration between clients is proposed, but clients cannot receive data at the same time from different sources, such as from the peering community and CDN entities. Some interesting works that propose the adoption of P2P and multi agent systems in Content Delivery Networks, are collected in [7] and [8].

The dynamic nature of today's networks and the large variety of the resources make management and discovery operations very complex. Administrative bottlenecks and low scalability of centralized systems are becoming unbearable. Innovative approaches need to have properties such as self-organization, decentralization and adaptivity. Erdil et al. in [3] outline the requirements and properties of self organizing grids, where reorganization of resources and adaptive dissemination of information are applied to facilitate discovery operations. A class of agent systems which aim to solve very complex problems by imitating the behavior of some species of ants was introduced in [1]. In [6] and [5], the performance of discovery operations is improved through the creation of Grid regions specialized in specific classes of resources, and [15] proposes a decentralized scheme to tune the activity of a single agent. These systems are positioned along a research avenue whose objective is to devise possible applications of ant algorithms [1] [2]. In [13], a tree-based ant colony algorithm was proposed to support large-scale Internet-based live video streaming broadcast in CDNs. Here, differently from the traditional solutions adopted to find a path towards a target resource, an algorithm is introduced to integrate and optimize multicast trees into the CDN network.

3   Algorithm for Metadata Reorganization

The approach presented here is composed by two main algorithms, an algorithm for metadata reorganization and another for the discovery of metadata documents. The main purpose of the first algorithm is to disseminate metadata over the CDN network and at the same time achieve a logical organization of content by spatially sorting the metadata in accordance to the corresponding indexes, or binary strings. Operations of nature-inspired agents are profitably exploited to reallocate the metadata. Agents move among CDN servers, or hosts, performing simple operations. When an agent arrives to a host and it does not carry any metadata document, it decides whether or not to pick one or more documents stored in the current host. When a loaded agent arrives to a new host, it decides whether or not to leave one or more metadata documents in the local host. Probability functions drive agents' decisions. The probability functions are based on a similarity function, that is:

$$sim(\bar{m}, R) = \frac{1}{N_m} \sum_{m \in R} 1 - \frac{Ham(m, \bar{m})}{dim} \qquad (1)$$

This function measures the similarity of a metadata binary string $\bar{m}$ with all the other strings located in the local region. The length of string is assumed to be equal to dim. The local region R for each server s includes s and all the host reachable from s in a number of hops h. The value of h is set to 1 unless otherwise stated. N_m is the overall number of metadata documents located in R, while $Ham(m, \bar{m})$ is the Hamming distance between a metadata document m and $\bar{m}$. The value of the function sim ranges between 0 and 1. The probability of picking a metadata document from a server must be inversely proportional to the similarity function sim. On the other hand, the probability function of dropping a metadata must be directly proportional to the similarity function sim. In this way, an agent tends to pick metadata documents that are dissimilar to the other documents stored locally, and will move and drop them to other regions where more similar documents are stored, so improving the spatial reorganization of metadata.

According to these considerations, the probability functions of picking a metadata P_1 and the probability function of dropping a metadata P_2, are:

$$P_1 = \left(\frac{k1}{k1 + sim(\bar{m}, R)} \right)^2 \tag{2}$$

$$P_2 = \left(\frac{sim(\bar{m}, R)}{k2 + sim(\bar{m}, R)} \right)^2 \tag{3}$$

The degree of similarity among metadata documents can be tuned through the parameters $k1$ and $k2$, which have values comprised between 0 and 1, and in this work have been set, respectively, to 0.1 and 0.3, as in [1]. The flowchart showed in Figure 1 gives a high-level description of the algorithm performed by mobile agents. Cyclically, the agents perform a given number of hops among servers and, when they get to a server, they decide which probability function they must use, based on their state. If the agent does not carry metadata it computes P_1, otherwise it computes P_2.

The effectiveness of the algorithm has been evaluated by defining the spatial uniformity function, i.e. the average homogeneity of metadata documents stored in neighbor servers. The uniformity U_s of the documents stored in a local region centered in the server s is defined as:

$$U_s = dim - Avg_{m_1, m_2 \epsilon R} Ham(m_1, m_2) \tag{4}$$

where m_1 and m_2 are two metadata documents stored in the local region R. The value of the global uniformity U is obtained by averaging the values of U_s over all the servers of the network.

Simulation tests showed that the uniformity function is better increased if each agent works in two operational modes, *copy* and *move*. In the first phase of its life, an agent is required to *copy* the metadata that it picks from a server, but when it realizes from its own activeness that the reorganization process is at an advanced stage, it begins simply to *move* metadata from one host to another, without creating new replicas. In fact, the *copy* mode cannot be maintained for a long time, since eventually every host would store a very large number of metadata of all types, thus weakening the efficacy of spatial reorganization. The algorithm is effective only if each agent, after replicating a number of metadata, switches from *copy* to *move*.

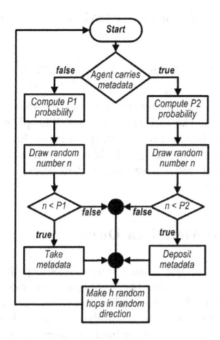

Fig. 1. The algorithm for metadata reorganization performed by agents

A self-organization approach, in some sense similar to that used in [15], enables each agent to tune its activeness, in our case to perform a mode switch, only on the basis of local information. Our approach is inspired by the observation that agents perform more operations when the system disorder is high, because metadata are distributed randomly, but operation frequency gradually decreases as metadata documents are properly reorganized. The reason for this is that the values of the functions P_1 and P_2, defined in expressions (2) and (3), decrease as metadata documents are correctly replaced and reorganized on the network.

With a mechanism inspired by ants and other insects, each agent maintains a *pheromone base* (a real value) and increases it when its activeness tends to decrease, which means that the disorder level has significantly decreased: the agent switches to the *move* mode as soon as the pheromone level exceeds a defined threshold T_h. In particular, precisely each 500 time units, each agent counts the number of times that it has evaluated the P_1 and P_2 probability functions, $N_{attempts}$, and the number of times that it has actually performed pick and drop operations, $N_{operations}$. At the end of each time interval, the agent makes a deposit into its pheromone base, which is inversely proportional to the fraction of performed operations. An evaporation mechanism is used to give a greater weight to the recent behavior of the agent. Specifically, at the end of the i-th time interval, the pheromone level Φ_i is computed with the following expression:

$$\Phi_i = Ev \cdot \Phi_{i-1} + \left(1 - \frac{N_{operations}}{N_{attempts}}\right) \tag{5}$$

The evaporation rate E_v is set to 0.9 [15], whereas ϕ_i is the amount of pheromone deposited in the last time interval. The pheromone level can assume values comprised between 0 and 10: the superior limit can be obtained by equalizing Φ_i to Φ_{i-1} and setting ϕ_i to 1. As soon as the pheromone level exceeds the threshold T_h (whose value is set to 9 in this work), the agent switches its mode from *copy* to *move*.

4 Algorithm for Metadata Discovery

The reorganization and sorting of metadata can be exploited by a discovery algorithm that allows users to find the resources or services that they need for their applications. In a CDN, users often need to locate resources with given characteristics and, after retrieving a number of them, they can choose the resources that best fit their needs. Accordingly, a query message is issued by a user to search for "target metadata", that is, for metadata documents having a given value of their binary index. The query is forwarded through the CDN network, hop by hop, so as to discover as many target metadata documents as possible. Thanks to the spatial sorting of metadata achieved by ant-based agents, the discovery procedure can be simply managed by forwarding the query, at each step, towards the "best neighbor", that is, the neighbor that maximizes the similarity between the metadata stored locally and the target metadata.

Each CDN server computes a "centroid" metadata. This metadata is a vector of *dim* real numbers comprised between 0 and 1, and is obtained by averaging all the local metadata indexes. Specifically, the value of each centroid element is calculated by averaging the values of the bits, in the same position, of all the metadata stored in the local peer. For example, the centroid metadata of a server that maintains the three metadata [1,0,0], [1,0,0] and [0,1,0] is a metadata having an index [0.67,0.33,0]. Before forwarding a query, the cosine of the angle between the query target metadata, and the centroids of all the neighbors, is computed. This value gives a hint about how much the metadata of the neighbors are similar to the target metadata. Thereafter, the query is forwarded to the neighbor that maximizes this cosine similarity index. At the next step, the target server will do the same so that, step by step, the query approaches a region of the network where it is more and more likely to discover several useful results, that is, target metadata. The search is terminated whenever it is no longer advantageous to forward the query, that is, when the best neighbor is not better than the server where the query has arrived so far. At this point, a queryHit message is issued and returns to the requesting host by following the same path, and collecting on its way all the results that it finds.

The efficient resolution of range queries is a fundamental requirement of CDN systems. A range query is defined as a query in which the bit vector of the target metadata contains one or more wildcard bits, that can assume either the 0 or the 1 value. This means that a range query can return descriptors having 2^W possible values, if W is the number of wildcard bits. Of course, the assignment of indexes to metadata must assure that the bit vectors that correspond to similar resources are also similar to one another. This can be done without losing generality by using the binary Gray code, in which two successive indexes always differ by only one bit. To select the best neighbor, the cosine similarity is still computed between the target metadata and the centroid metadata of all the neighbors, but this time these indexes are preprocessed by discarding the bits that are defined as wildcards in the target metadata. Therefore, only the centroid bits that correspond to valued bits in the target metadata are useful to drive the query message. As for simple queries, a range query terminates its journey when it is no more possible to find a better neighbor. The queryHit message will come back and collect all the metadata that match the range query. Range queries are not able to discover all the resources that would be found with the corresponding number of simple queries, but provide an efficient way to discover – in just one shot – much more results than a simple query. It can be concluded that the resource management of the algorithm actually facilitates this objective, as showed in Section 5.

5   Experimental Results

An event-based simulator, written in Java, was implemented to evaluate the performance of the algorithm. Prior to the numerical analysis, a graphical description of the behavior of the algorithm, for the case in which *dim* is set to 3, is given in Figure 2. Here, 2,500 CDN servers are arranged in a grid and each metadata is associated to a RGB color.

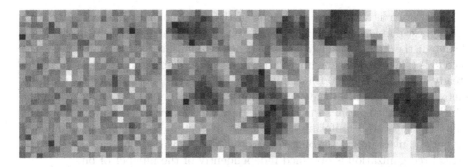

Fig. 2. Snapshots of the system showing the reorganization of metadata documents indexed by 3 bits, represented by RGB colors. The snapshots are taken when the process starts, in an intermediate state and in a steady state.

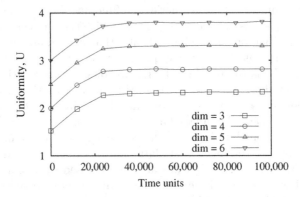

Fig. 3. Uniformity of the whole network when the number of bits of the binary string representing the content ranges from 3 to 6

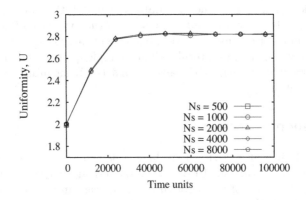

Fig. 4. Uniformity, vs. time, for different values of the number of servers

Each server is visualized by means of the RGB color of the metadata with the highest number of elements placed in it. Three snapshots of the network are depicted: the first is taken when the process is initiated (time units = 0), the second is taken 10,000 time units later, and the third snapshot is taken in a quite steady situation, 100,000 time units after the process start. Notice that similar metadata are located in the same region and that the color changes gradually, which proves the spatial sorting of metadata on the network. Figure 3 shows the value of the overall uniformity — defined in Section 3 – when the number of bits of the metadata describing the content, *dim*, is varied. We can see that the logical reorganization is obtained independently of the number of bits.

To confirm the scalability nature of the algorithm, which derives from its decentralized and self-organizing characteristics, its behavior with different numbers of servers Ns, between 500 and 8000, was analyzed and reported in Figure 4. It is noticed that the size of the network has no detectable effect on the overall uniformity index.

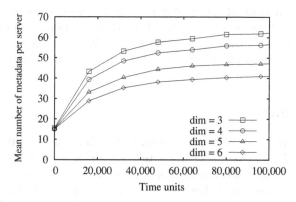

Fig. 5. Mean number of metadata documents handled by a server when the length of binary strings ranges from 3 to 6 bits

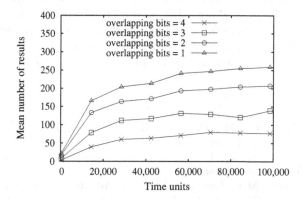

Fig. 6. Mean number of results collected by a range query when the length of the binary string representing the content is set to 4 and the number of overlapping bits ranges from 1 to 4

Figure 5 reports the average number of metadata documents that are maintained by a server at a given time. Indeed, one of the main objectives of the algorithm is the replication and dissemination of metadata. This objective is achieved: the number of metadata documents maintained by a server increases from an initial value of about 15 (equal to the average number of resources published by a server) to much higher values; the trend of this value undergoes a transient phase, then it becomes stabilized, even if with some fluctuations.

To evaluate the effectiveness of range queries, the length of binary string – *dim* – was set to 4, and queries are issued in which some bits of the target binary string are wildcard bits, while other bits are specified. The latter are called *overlapping* bits in the following. The average number of results collected by a range query, when the number of overlapping bits ranges between 1 and 4, is shown in Figure 6. It appears that, in a steady situation, the number of results increases with the number of overlapping bits, as each additional overlapping bit doubles the number of admissible results. Range queries are not able to discover all the results that would be obtained by issuing a simple query for each admissible value of the target binary index. However, range queries provide an efficient way to discover – in just one shot – much many results than a single query.

6   Conclusions

This paper presents a nature-inspired approach to build a P2P information system for CDNs. Thanks to its swarm intelligence characteristics, the proposed algorithm features fully decentralization, adaptivity and self-organization. Ant-inspired agents move and logically reorganize the metadata documents representing the content or the services. Agent operations are driven by simple probability functions that are evaluated when agents get to a new server. In this way, similar metadata documents representing similar contents are placed in the same region, that is on neighbor CDN servers. Performance analysis, achieved through event-based simulation, confirms the effectiveness of the approach and the increased efficiency of discovery operations – specifically of range queries – obtained thanks to the logical reorganization of metadata documents.

References

1. Bonabeau, E., Dorigo, M., Theraulaz, G.: Swarm intelligence: from natural to artificial systems, vol. 4. Oxford university press, New York (1999)
2. Dorigo, M., Bonabeau, E., Theraulaz, G.: Ant algorithms and stigmergy. Future Generation Computer Systems 16(8), 851–871 (2000)
3. Erdil, D.C., Lewis, M.J., Abu-Ghazaleh, N.B.: Adaptive approach to information dissemination in self-organizing grids. In: 2006 International Conference on Autonomic and Autonomous Systems, ICAS 2006, p. 55. IEEE (2006)
4. Forestiero, A.: Self organization in content delivery networks. In: 2012 IEEE 10th International Symposium on Parallel and Distributed Processing with Applications (ISPA), pp. 851–852 (July 2012)
5. Forestiero, A., Mastroianni, C., Spezzano, G.: Reorganization and discovery of grid information with epidemic tuning. Future Generation Computer Systems 24(8), 788–797 (2008)
6. Forestiero, A., Mastroianni, C., Spezzano, G.: So-grid: A self-organizing grid featuring bio-inspired algorithms. ACM Transactions on Autonomous and Adaptive Systems (TAAS) 3(2), 5 (2008)
7. Fortino, G., Mastroianni, C.: Enhancing content networks with p2p, grid and agent technologies. Future Generation Computer Systems 24(3), 177–179 (2008)
8. Fortino, G., Mastroianni, C.: Next generation content networks. Journal on Network and Computing Applications 32(5), 941–942 (2009)
9. Fortino, G., Russo, W.: Using p2p, grid and agent technologies for the development of content distribution networks. Future Generation Computer Systems 24(3), 180–190 (2008)
10. Guomin, Z., Changyou, X., Ming, C.: A distributed multimedia cdn model with p2p architecture. In: International Symposium on Communications and Information Technologies, ISCIT 2006, pp. 152–156. IEEE (2006)

11. Huang, C., Wang, A., Li, J., Ross, K.W.: Understanding hybrid cdn-p2p: why lime-light needs its own red swoosh. In: Proceedings of the 18th International Work-shop on Network and Operating Systems Support for Digital Audio and Video, pp. 75–80. ACM (2008)

12. Kang, S., Yin, H.: A hybrid cdn-p2p system for video-on-demand. In: Second In-ternational Conference on Future Networks, ICFN 2010, pp. 309–313. IEEE (2010)

13. Liu, G., Wang, H., Zhang, H.: An ant colony optimization algorithm for over-lay backbone multicast routing in content delivery networks. In: 2012 IEEE 11th International Conference on Trust, Security and Privacy in Computing and Com-munications (TrustCom), pp. 1878–1882. IEEE (2012)

14. Mulerikkal, J.P., Khalil, I.: An architecture for distributed content delivery network. In: 15th IEEE International Conference on Networks, ICON 2007, pp. 359–364. IEEE (2007)

15. Van Dyke Parunak, H., Brueckner, S.A., Matthews, R., Sauter, J.: Pheromone learning for self-organizing agents. IEEE Transactions on Systems, Man and Cy-bernetics, Part A: Systems and Humans 35(3), 316–326 (2005)

16. Xu, D., Kulkarni, S.S., Rosenberg, C., Chai, H.K.: Analysis of a cdn–p2p hy-brid architecture for cost-effective streaming media distribution. Multimedia Sys-tems 11(4), 383–399 (2006)

An Actor Based Software Framework
for Scalable Applications

Federico Bergenti[1], Agostino Poggi[2], and Michele Tomaiuolo[2]

[1] DMI, University of Parma, Parma, Italy
federico.bergenti@unipr.it
[2] DII, University of Parma, Parma, Italy
{agostino.poggi,michele.tomaiuolo}@unipr.it

Abstract. The development of scalable and efficient applications requires the use of appropriate models and software infrastructures. This paper presents a software framework that enables the development of scalable and efficient actor-based applications. Each application can be configured with different implementations of the components that drive the execution of its actors. In particular, the paper describes the experimentation of such a software framework for the development of agent-based modelling and simulation applications that involve a massive number of individuals.

Keywords: Actor model, software framework, concurrent systems, distributed systems, scalable applications, Java.

1   Introduction

Concurrency and parallelism are becoming the most important ingredients for developing applications running on nowadays computing platforms. However, one of the main obstacles that may prevent the efficient usage of such platforms is the fact that traditional (sequential) software is not the most appropriate means for their programming.

Message passing models and technologies seem be one of the most attractive solution for the programming of current computing platforms because they are defined on a concurrent model that is not based on the sharing of data and so its techniques can be used in distributed computation, too. One of the well-known theoretical and practical models of message passing is the actor model [1]. Using such a model, programs become collections of independent active objects (actors) that do not have shared state and communicate only through the exchange of messages. Actors can help developers to avoid issues such as deadlock, live-lock and starvation, which are common problems for shared memory approaches. There are a multitude of actor oriented libraries and languages, and each of them implements some variants of actor semantics. However, such libraries and languages use either thread-based programming, which facilitates the development of programs, or event-based programming, which is far more practical to develop large and efficient concurrent systems, but is also more difficult to use.

G. Fortino et al. (Eds.): IDCS 2014, LNCS 8729, pp. 26–35, 2014.

This paper presents an actor based software framework, called CoDE (Concurrent Development Environment), that has the suitable features for both simplifying the development of large and distributed complex systems and guarantying scalable and efficient applications. The next section describes the software framework. Section 3 presents its initial experimentation in the agent-based modelling and simulation of Web and social networks. Section 4 introduces related work. Finally, section 5 concludes the paper by discussing the main features of the software framework and the directions for future work.

2   CoDE

CoDE (Concurrent Development Environment), is an actor based software framework that has the goal of both simplifying the development of large and distributed complex systems and guarantying an efficient execution of applications.

CoDE is implemented by using the Java language and takes advantage of preexistent Java software libraries and solutions for supporting concurrency and distribution. CoDE has a layered architecture composed of a runtime and an application layer. The runtime layer provides the software components that implement the CoDE middleware infrastructures to support the development of standalone and distributed applications. The application layer provides the software components that an application developer needs to extend or directly use for implementing the specific actors of an application. In particular, the development of an application usually consists in the development of the actor behaviors implementing the functionalities of the application and in the definition of the configuration (i.e., the selection of the most appropriate implementations) of the components the drive the execution of such behaviors.

2.1   Actors

In CoDE an application is based on a set of interacting actors that perform tasks concurrently. Actors are autonomous concurrent objects, which interact with each other by exchanging asynchronous messages. Moreover, they can create new actors, update their local state, change their behavior and kill themselves. Finally, they can set a timeout for waiting for a new message and receive a timeout message if it fires.

An actor can be viewed as a logical thread that implements an event loop [2,3]. This event loop perpetually processes events that represent: the reception of messages and the behavior exchanges. CoDE provides two types of implementation of an actor, that allow it either to have its own thread (from here named active actor), or to share a single thread with the other actors of the actor space (from here named passive actor). Moreover, the implementation of an actor takes advantage of other four main components: a reference, a mailer, a behavior, and a state. Fig. 1 shows a graphical representation of the architecture of an actor.

A reference acts as address and proxy of an actor. Therefore, an actor needs to have the reference of another actor for sending it a message. In particular, an actor has the reference of another actor if either it created such an actor (in fact, the creation method returns the reference of the new actor), or it received a message that either is sent by such an actor or whose content enclosed its reference. In fact, a message is an object that contains a set of fields maintaining the typical header information (e.g., the sender and the receiver references) and the message content.

A mailer provides a mailbox, maintaining the messages sent to its actor until it processes them, and delivers its messages to the other actors of the application. As introduced above, a behavior can process a set of specific messages, leaving in the mailbox the messages that is not able to process. Such messages remain into the mailbox until a new behavior is able to process them and, if there is not such a behavior, they remain into the queue for all the life of the actor. A mailbox has not an explicit limit on the number of messages that it can maintain. However, it is clear that the (permanent) deposit of a large number of messages in the mailboxes of the actors may reduce the performances of applications and, in some circumstances, cause their failure.

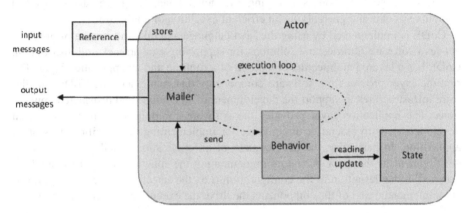

Fig. 1. Actor architecture

The original actor model associates a behavior with the task of message processing. In CoDE, a behavior can perform two kinds of tasks: its initialization and the processing of messages. In particular, a behavior does not directly process messages, but it delegates the task to some case objects, that have the goal of processing the messages that match a specific (and unreplaceable) message pattern.

A message pattern is an object that can apply a combination of constraint objects on the value of all the fields of a message. CoDE provides a set of predefines constraints, but new ones can be easily added. In particular, one of such constraints allows the application of a pattern to the value of a message field. Therefore, the addition of field patterns will allow the definition of sophisticated filters on the values of all the message fields and in particular on the content of the message.

Often, the behaviors of an actor need to share some information (e.g., a behavior may work on the results of the previous behaviors). It is possible thanks to a state object. Of course, the kind of information that the behaviors of an actor need to share depends on the type of tasks they must perform in an application. Therefore, the state of an actor must be specialized for the task it will perform.

An actor has not direct access to the local state of the other actors and can share data with them only through the exchange of messages and through the creation of actors. Therefore, to avoid the problems due to the concurrent access to mutable data, both message passing and actor creation should have call-by-value semantics. This may require making a copy of the data even on shared memory platforms, but, as the large part of the actors libraries implemented in Java do, CoDE does not make data copies because such operations would be the source of an important overhead. However, it encourages the programmers to use immutable objects (by all the predefined message content objects implementing as immutable) and delegates the appropriate use of mutable object to them.

2.2   Actor Spaces

Depending on the complexity of the application and on the availability of computing and communication resources, one or more actor spaces can manage the actors of the application. An actor space acts as "container" for a set of actors and provides them the services necessary for their execution. To do it, an actor space takes advantage of two main runtime components (i.e., the registry and the dispatcher) and two special actors (i.e., the scheduler and the service provider).

The dispatcher has the duty of supporting the communication with the other actor spaces of the application. In particular, it creates connections to/from the other actor spaces, maps remote addresses to the appropriate output connections, manages the reception of messages from the input connections, and delivers messages through the output connections. CoDE allows the use of different implementations of such a communication component. In particular, the current implementation of the software framework supports the communication among the actor spaces using ActiveMQ [4], Java RMI [5], MINA [6] and ZeroMQ [7].

The registry supports the creation of actors and the reception of the messages coming from remote actors. In fact, it has the duties of creating new references and of providing the reference of the destination actor to the dispatcher, which manages a message coming from a remote actor. In fact, as introduced in the previous section, an actor can send a message to another actor only if it has its reference. However, while the reference of a local actor allows the direct delivery of messages, the reference of a remote actor delegates the delivery to the dispatchers of the two actor spaces involved in the communication.

The scheduler is a special actor that manages the execution of the actors of an actor space. CoDE provides different implementations of such a special actor, and the use of one or another implementation represents another factor that have big influence on the attributes of the execution of an application. Of course, the duties of a scheduler depend on the type of actor implementation and, in particular, on the type of threading solutions associated with the actors of the actor space. In fact, while the Java runtime environment mainly manages the execution of active actors, CoDE schedulers completely manage the execution of passive actors.

The service provider is a special actor that offers a set of services for enabling the actors of an application to perform new kinds of actions. Of course, the actors of the application can require the execution of such services by sending a message to the service provider. In particular, the current implementation of the software framework offers services for supporting the broadcast of messages, the exchange of messages through the "publish and subscribe" pattern, the binding between names and references, the mobility, the interaction with users through emails and the creation of new actors (useful for creating actors in empty actor spaces).

2.3   Actor and Scheduler Implementations

The quality of the execution of a CoDE application mainly depends on the implementation of the actors and schedulers of its actor spaces. However, a combination of such implementations, that maximizes the quality of execution of an application, could be a bad combination for another application. Moreover, different instances of the same application can work in different conditions (e.g., different number of users to serve, different amount of data to process) and so they may require different combinations.

As introduced above, from an implementation point of view, actors are divided in active and passive actors. The use of active actors delegates their scheduling to the JVM, with the advantage of guaranteeing them a fair access to the computational resources of the actor space. However, this solution suffers from high memory consumption and context-switching overhead and so it is suitable only for applications whose actor spaces have a limited number of actors. Therefore, when the number of actors in an actor space is high, the best solution is the use of passive actors and schedulers. In this case, the scheduler implements a simple not preemptive round-robin scheduling algorithm for the execution of various actors. On the other hand, each actor provides a method that allows it to perform a piece (from here called step) of the work (i.e., the processing of some messages) in each scheduling cycle. This last solution is suitable when it is possible to distribute the tasks in equal parts among the actors. If it does not happen, heavy actors should have a priority on the access to the computational resources of the actor space. In this situation, a good solution is to provide a hybrid scheduler able to manage together active and passive actors and delegating to the active actors the heavy tasks.

However, guaranteeing a good quality of execution in different application scenarios often requires the satisfaction of some constraints that cannot be achieved by the same actor and scheduler implementations. For example, applications where actors act as proxy of real users should guarantee a fair access to the computational resources of the actor space, by limiting the number of messages that an actor can process in a single step. Heavy applications should try both to reduce the overhead of the scheduler and to offer an acceptable fair execution of the actors, for example, by extending the processing of a single step to all the messages received before the scheduling of the actor. Applications where actors mainly communicate through the exchange of broadcast messages should try to reduce the overhead of the delivery of such messages. Finally, applications that involve a massive number of actors should try to reduce the overhead of managing the inactive actors.

CoDE provides some actor and scheduler implementations that allow the improvement of the quality of execution for different types of applications, including the ones described in the previous paragraph. A large part of the implementations has few differences among them. The most particular implementations are the ones that cope with the overhead of the delivery of broadcast messages and with the overhead of the management of inactive actors.

For reducing the overhead of the delivery of broadcast messages, an actor implementation (called shared actor) uses a mailbox that transparently extracts the messages from a single queue, shared with all the other actors of the actor space, and a scheduler implementation (called shared scheduler) that has the duty of the management of such a queue. To simplify the management of the queue, the shared actors can only get the messages sent in the previous scheduling cycle and, at the end of each scheduling cycle, the shared scheduler must add an "end cycle" message at the end of the queue and then remove the messages before the previous "end-cycle" that are already processed by the actors.

For reducing the overhead of the management of inactive actors, an actor implementation (called measurable actor) offers a method providing the number of scheduling cycles from which it does not perform actions. Two scheduler implementations (called temporary and persistent schedulers) use such an information for removing actors from their scheduling list. After removing an actor, the temporary scheduler maintains the actor in the JVM memory and the persistent scheduler moves it in a persistent storage. This solution requires two different implementations of the registry component (called temporary and persistent registries) whose duty is to reload an actor, either from the JVM memory or from the persistence storage, when another actor sends a new message to it.

3   Experimentation

We experimented and are experimenting CoDE in different application domains and, in particular, in the agent-based modelling and simulation (i.e., the game of life, the prey-predators pursuit game, the flocking behavior of birds, the movement of crowds in indoor and outdoor environments, and the analysis of social networks) [8].

Our work on the modeling and simulation of social networks started some years ago when we used agent-based techniques for generating and analyzing different types of social network of limited size [9,10,11]. Now we can take advantage of the CoDE software framework for coping with very large social networks. Therefore, in a CoDE system, actors represent the individuals of the social network and maintain their information. Moreover, such actors can exhibit different behaviors, allowing both to cooperate in the measurements of the social network and to simulate the behavior of the represented individuals by performing the actions that they can perform in the social network. Of course, some additional actors are necessary, in particular, for generating the social network and for driving its measurements.

The architecture we defined for agent-based modelling and simulation is a distributed architecture based on a variable number of actor spaces (Fig. 2 shows its graphical representation). Each actor space maintains a set of measurable actors that are managed by a persistent scheduler. Moreover, the service provider takes advantage of a naming service.

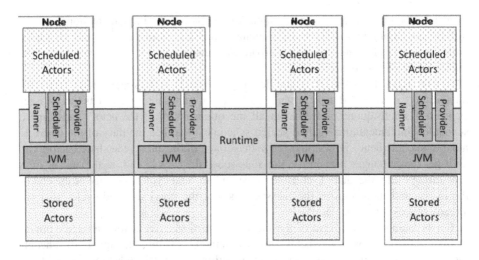

Fig. 2. Massive agent-based modelling and simulation system architecture

An important factor that simplifies the parallel construction of a social network is the availability of a universal unique identifier for each individual of the social network. Such an identifier permits to avoid the creation of actors representing the same individual in different actor spaces, thanks to the use of the naming service. In fact, the naming service allows to:

- maintain the binding between the references of the active actors with the identifiers of the corresponding individual;
- use the individual identifier to find an actor in the persistent storage;
- cooperate with the naming services of the actor spaces to decide if a new actor must be created.

We started the experimentation of such a system by modelling some social networks with a number of individuals that vary from some thousands to some millions of individuals. We built such models by using the data maintained in the "Stanford Large Network Dataset Collection" [12] and up to now, we are using them for performing some simple measures (i.e., diameter, clustering coefficient and centrality). The first tests we did compare the performances of the system with a deployment on a different number of computing nodes (from one to four). The results of the tests showed that a single actor space can manage social networks with some millions of individuals, but the use of additional actor spaces on more computing nodes gives an important improvement in the performances. In fact, the advantages on performance of the partitioning of the model of large social networks on some computing nodes are relevant for both the creation and measurement phases, because it is necessary to move a smaller number of actors from the scheduler to the persistent storage and vice versa. Of course, our experimentation is at the beginning and the results are only of qualitative level. However, we are working hard for enriching the measurement phase with new functionalities and for preparing a set of tests for acquiring a set of accurate measures of the performance of the system in its different configurations.

4   Related Work

Several actor-oriented libraries and languages have been proposed in last decades and a large part of them uses Java as implementation language. The rest of the section presents some of the most interesting works.

Salsa [13] is an actor-based language for mobile and Internet computing that provides three significant mechanisms based on the actor model: token-passing continuations, join continuations, and first-class continuations. In Salsa each actor has its own thread, and so scalability is limited. Moreover, message-passing performance suffers from the overhead of reflective method calls.

Kilim [14] is a framework used to create robust and massively concurrent actor systems in Java. It takes advantage of code annotations and a byte-code postprocessor to simplify the writing of the code. However, it provides only a very simplified implementation of the actor model where each actor (called task in Kilim) has a mailbox and a method defining its behavior. Moreover, it does not provide remote messaging capabilities.

Scala [15] is an object-oriented and functional programming language that provides an implementation of the actor model unifying thread based and event based programming models. In fact, in Scala an actor can suspend with a full thread stack (receive), or can suspend with just a continuation closure (react). Therefore, scalability can be obtained by sacrificing program simplicity. Akka [16] is an alternative toolkit and runtime system for developing event-based actors in Scala, but also providing APIs for developing actor-based systems in Java. One of its distinguishing features is the hierarchical organization of actors, so that a parent actor that creates some children actors is responsible for handling their failures.

Jetlang [17] provides a high performance Java threading library that should be used for message based concurrency. The library is designed specifically for high performance in-memory messaging and does not provide remote messaging capabilities.

AmbientTalk [2] is a distributed object-oriented programming language that is implemented on an actor-based and event driven concurrency model, which makes it highly suitable for composing service objects across a mobile network. It provides an actor implementation based on communicating event loops [3]. However, each actor is always associated with its own JVM thread and this limits the scalability of applications with respect to the number of actors for JVM.

5   Conclusions

This paper presented an actor-based software framework, called CoDE, that enables the development of scalable and efficient applications by configuring them with different implementations of its components. Moreover, such a software framework is based on a simple actor model that simplifies the development of applications. In fact, the development of application consists in the development of the actor behaviors that implement its functionalities and the definition of a configuration that choose the most suitable implementations for the components that drive the execution of the actors of the application.

CoDE is implemented by using the Java language and is an evolution of HDS [18] and ASIDE [19] from which it derives the concise actor model. CoDE shares with Kilim [14], Scala [15] and Jetlang [17] the possibility to build applications that scale to a massive number of actors, but without the need of introducing new constructs that complicate the writing of actor based programs. Moreover, CoDE has been designed for the development of distributed applications, while the previous three actor based software were designed for applications running inside multi-core computers. In fact, the use of structured messages and message patterns enables the implementation of complex interactions in a distributed application, because a message contains all the information for its delivery to the destination and then for building and sending a reply. Moreover, a message pattern filters the input messages not only with respect to their content, but also with respect to all the information they contain.

CoDE has been mainly experimented in the agent-based modelling and simulation. Such an experimentation involved the development of systems with different features (number of actors, types of communication, ratio between active and inactive actors, etc.) and demonstrated that different configurations are necessary to obtain the best performance for different types and setup of systems.

Current research activities are dedicated to extend the software framework to offer it as means for the development of multi-agent systems taking advantages of some design and implementation solutions used in JADE [20]. Future research activities will be dedicated to the extension of the functionalities provided by the software framework and to its experimentation in different application fields. Regarding the extension of the software framework, current activities have the goal of: i) providing a passive threading solution that fully take advantage of the features of multi-core processors, ii) enabling the interoperability with Web services and legacy systems [21], and iii) enhancing the definition of the content exchanged by actors with semantic Web technologies [22]. Moreover, future activities will be dedicated to the provision of a trust management infrastructure to support the interaction between actor spaces of different organizations [23], [24]. Experimentation of the software framework will be extended to the development of: i) collaborative work services [25] and ii) agent-based systems for the management of information in pervasive environments [26].

References

1. Agha, G.A.: Actors: A Model of Concurrent Computation in Distributed Systems. MIT Press, Cambridge (1986)
2. Dedecker, J., Van Cutsem, T., Mostinckx, S., D'Hondt, T., De Meuter, W.: Ambient-oriented programming in ambienttalk. In: Thomas, D. (ed.) ECOOP 2006. LNCS, vol. 4067, pp. 230–254. Springer, Heidelberg (2006)
3. Miller, M.S., Tribble, E.D., Shapiro, J.S.: Concurrency among strangers. In: De Nicola, R., Sangiorgi, D. (eds.) TGC 2005. LNCS, vol. 3705, pp. 195–229. Springer, Heidelberg (2005)
4. Snyder, B., Bosnanac, D., Davies, R.: ActiveMQ in action, Manning, Westampton, NJ, USA (2001)

5. Pitt, E., McNiff, K.: Java.rmi: the Remote Method Invocation Guide. Addison-Wesley, Boston (2001)
6. Apache Software Foundation: Apache Mina Framework. HYPERLINK, http://mina.apache.org
7. Hintjens, P.: ZeroMQ: Messaging for Many Applications. O'Reilly, Sebastopol (2013)
8. Poggi, A.: CoDE - A Software Framework for Agent-based Simulation. In: 17th WSEAS International Conference on Computers, Rhodes, Greece, pp. 50–55 (2013)
9. Bergenti, F., Franchi, E., Poggi, A.: Selected models for agent-based simulation of social networks. In: 3rd Symposium on Social Networks and Multiagent Systems (SNAMAS 2011), pp. 27–32. Society for the Study of Artificial Intelligence and the Simulation of Behaviour, York, UK (2011)
10. Franchi, E.: A Domain Specific Language Approach for Agent-Based Social Network Modeling. In: IEEE/ACM International Conference on Advances in Social Networks Analysis and Mining (ASONAM), pp. 607–612. IEEE (2012)
11. Bergenti, F., Franchi, E., Poggi, A.: Agent-based interpretations of classic network models. Computational and Mathematical Organization Theory 19(2), 105–127 (2013)
12. SNAP: Stanford Large Network Dataset Collection, http://snap.stanford.edu/data/index.html
13. Varela, C., Agha, G.A.: Programming dynamically reconfigurable open systems with SALSA. SIGPLAN Notices 36(12), 20–34 (2001)
14. Srinivasan, S., Mycroft, A.: Kilim: Isolation-typed actors for Java. In: Vitek, J. (ed.) ECOOP 2008. LNCS, vol. 5142, pp. 104–128. Springer, Heidelberg (2008)
15. Haller, P., Odersky, M.: Scala Actors: unifying thread-based and event-based programming. Theoretical Computer Science 410(2-3), 202–220 (2009)
16. Typesafe: Akka software Web site, http://akka.io
17. Rettig, M.: Jetlang software Web site, http://code.google.com/p/jetlang
18. Poggi, A.: HDS: a Software Framework for the Realization of Pervasive Applications. WSEAS Trans. on Computers 10(9), 1149–1159 (2010)
19. Poggi, A.: ASiDE - A Software Framework for Complex and Distributed Systems. In: 16th WSEAS International Conference on Computers, Kos, Greece, pp. 353–358 (2012)
20. Poggi, A., Tomaiuolo, M., Turci, P.: Extending JADE for agent grid applications. In: 13th IEEE International Workshops on Enabling Technologies: Infrastructure for Collaborative Enterprises (WET ICE 2004), Modena, Italy, pp. 352–357 (2004)
21. Poggi, A., Tomaiuolo, M., Turci, P.: An Agent-Based Service Oriented Architecture. In: WOA 2007, Genova, Italy, pp. 157–165 (2007)
22. Poggi, A.: Developing ontology based applications with O3L. WSEAS Trans. on Computers 8(8), 1286–1295 (2009)
23. Poggi, A., Tomaiuolo, M., Vitaglione, G.: A Security Infrastructure for Trust Management in Multi-agent Systems. In: Falcone, R., Barber, S.K., Sabater-Mir, J., Singh, M.P. (eds.) Trusting Agents for Trusting Electronic Societies. LNCS (LNAI), vol. 3577, pp. 162–179. Springer, Heidelberg (2005)
24. Tomaiuolo, M.: dDelega: Trust Management for Web Services. International Journal of Information Security and Privacy 7(3), 53–67 (2013)
25. Bergenti, F., Poggi, A., Somacher, M.: A collaborative platform for fixed and mobile networks. Communications of the ACM 45(11), 39–44 (2002)
26. Bergenti, F., Poggi, A.: Ubiquitous Information Agents. International Journal on Cooperative Information Systems 11(3-4), 231–244 (2002)

Cloud Computing

Semantic Representation of Cloud Services: A Case Study for Openstack

Beniamino Di Martino, Giuseppina Cretella,
Antonio Esposito, and Graziella Carta

Department of Industrial and Information Engineering,
Second University of Naples, Aversa, Italy
{beniamino.dimartino,giuseppina.cretella,antonio.esposito}@unina2.it,
graziellacarta88@gmail.com

Abstract. Thanks to its high flexibility, cost-effectiveness and availability, Cloud Computing has quickly imposed itself on the IT scenery, rapidly flooding the market with new appealing services and offers. However, the current lack of a shared standard for the description of such services can represent an obstacle to the development of interoperable and portable Cloud solutions. The approach we investigate consists in the creation of a set of interrelated OWL ontologies, which describe both Cloud Services and APIs/methods used to invoke them, together with their relative parameters. Furthermore, OWL-S is exploited to describe the internal workflow of the described services. Our representation also offers means to describe Resources Configurations, which can be compared by means of SPARQL queries, enabling users to easily choose among the different offers proposed by competing vendors. In this paper we apply the proposed semantic based representation to the description of the Openstack offer, which represents an optimal case study to test and prove its effectiveness.

Keywords: Cloud Computing, Semantic Web, Cloud Services, Cloud Resources, Ontology, OWL, Openstack, SPARQL.

1 Introduction

Cloud Computing is an emerging paradigm which is strongly conditioning the development of the IT market, overflowing it with new offers and services which are steadily updated, improved, dismissed. The scenario can be quite confusing for both standard users and more expert developers, who need to navigate in a sea of always new and changing Cloud proposals, platforms and capabilities. Furthermore, each provider tends to use its own service representation (if any) in order to differentiate from others and try to gain new pieces of the market. Such a behaviour can bring further distress to Cloud users, who fear the vendor lock-in phenomenon. Furthermore, creating new applications based on multiple Cloud platforms' services, or just making such services communicate, can be quite difficult (when not impossible) due to interoperability issues.

G. Fortino et al. (Eds.): IDCS 2014, LNCS 8729, pp. 39–50, 2014.

In this scenario, the possibility to have a machine-readable formalism describing the different Cloud services and offers, which could be easily queried in order to automatically retrieve the best resources' configuration, on the basis of the users' needing, is quite appealing. In particular, the possibility to automatically compare different Cloud services and solutions, which have been previously adequately described and annotated, can be very useful for users who need to quickly build-up their personal Cloud solution from scratch. In this paper we present a semantic based representation of a Cloud provider offer, represented by Openstack's services [3], which are used as a case study to demonstrate the effectiveness of semantic technologies in describing different Cloud services and resources, making them automatically query-able and comparable. In particular, we focus on OWL [4] based descriptions of the different services offered by the target provider, with particular attention to the resources required by each service and to default resources' configurations. This paper is organized as follows: in section 2 we provide a brief introduction to relevant works in the context of Cloud Services description and categorization; section 3 introduces the main services offered by the Openstack platform, in order to gain familiarity with the target's offering; section 4 shows how a platform's services can be semantically described through an OWL ontology, using Openstack's Neutron as an example; section 5 focuses on the semantic description of parameters used by the platform's APIs to invoke services, again referring to Neutron as a case study; subsection 5.1 offers a focus on the description of default Resources Configurations provided by vendors; an example of OWL-S description of the Openstack Neutron service is presented in section 6; section 7 reports some final considerations on the present work.

2   Related Works

In order to somehow put order in the chaos of Cloud Computing offers currently existing, many attempts have been made to categorize Cloud Services and capabilities. Remarkable is the effort made by the Opencrowd consortium, which has built an interesting Cloud Taxonomy [2] currently comprehending a good number of Cloud Platforms and Services, belonging to the different Cloud layers (IaaS, PaaS and SaaS [10]). The taxonomy also addresses a particular category called *Cloud Software*, which describes commercial and open source software supporting the development and management of Cloud Computing environments. While the resulting taxonomy is quite interesting, it lacks a machine readable version which could be automatically queried.

On the other hand, semantic based representations have proved to be particularly useful in describing Cloud resources and services, especially since they enable the use of query-able, machine readable formats. In [7] the authors present a remarkable example of Cloud services discovery system based on ontologies and matchmaking rules. In the developed system, users can identify the required Cloud services by means of three kinds of requirements: functional requirements (like programming languages for PaaS services), technical requirements (like

CPU clock or RAM for the IaaS service type) and cost requirements (like max price) as input parameters.

Another outstanding example is represented by the mOSAIC cloud ontology [11], developed for the mOSAIC [6] platform. The ontology has been built to improve interoperability among existing Cloud solutions, platforms and services, both from end-user and developer side. The ontology, developed in OWL, can be used for semantic retrieval and composition of Cloud services in the mOSAIC project and also maintains compatibility with previous works,since it is built upon existing standards.

Our research is strongly inspired by these works, in particular the mOSAIC ontology, which we have re-used and extended in order to better categorize Cloud Services and Virtual Appliances (not considered in existent efforts) and to represent API calls and relative parameters used to invoke them.

2.1   Semantic Based Representations

In the following we provide some details on the Semantic based languages we use to describe Cloud services, namely OWL and OWL-S.

The **Web Ontology Language** (OWL) [5] is a Semantic Web language designed to represent knowledge about things, groups of entities and relations between them. OWL can be reasoned with by computer programs to check the consistency of a knowledge base, or to infer new knowledge. OWL documents, also known as ontologies, can be published in the World Wide Web and may refer to or be referred from other OWL ontologies. In this way it is possible to represent complex knowledge about one or more related topics, making this representation available through the Net. **OWL-S** [8] is an ontology, within the OWL based framework for the Semantic Web, born essentially to describe Semantic Web Services. It enables users to automatically discover, invoke, compose, and monitor Web resources offering different kinds of services, under specified constraints. It can be easily used to describe work-flow of services, arranging their order of execution, using flow and decision control structures, and making it possible to annotate them against an OWL ontology. The OWL-S model defines three classes:

- **Service**: emphasizes interaction between client and service, specifying input, output, pre-conditions and results of a service. It is extended by three classes: **SimpleProcess**, used to define abstract processes; **AtomicProcess** used to describe concrete processes which cannot be split into sub-processes; **CompositeProcess**, describing processes consisting in the composition of Atomic Processes.
- **ServiceProfile**: describes what the service does in a human readable format.
- **ServiceGrounding**: specifies communication protocols and messages format users should use to interact with the service.

3   OpenStack Services Overview

Openstack is an open source Cloud operating system which provides compute, storage and networking resources together with virtualization technologies, fully accessible and manageable through a set of powerful APIs, Command Line Interfaces (CLIs) tools or Software Development Kits (SDKs) provided for different programming languages. It is also possible to leverage a graphical dashboard, which allows users to manage and monitor resources provided by the platform. Services are offered at an IaaS level. The current stable OpenStack release is named IceHouse and it has been released on April 2014. A set of Core services is accessible through RESTful APIs or Command Line Interfaces and they're representeb by:

- **Compute.** (Nova) offers on-demand computing resources, by provisioning and managing large networks of virtual machines. The architecture is designed to scale horizontally on standard hardware.
- **Object Storage.** (Swift) provides a fully distributed storage platform for data backup and archiving; it is fully integrated with applications running in the Openstack environment and expands external storage of compute instances.
- **Block Storage.** (Cinder) allows availability of persistent block level storage devices, directly connected with OpenStack compute instances.
- **Networking.** (Neutron) provides flexible networking models to support IP addresses management and traffic control. Networking allows additional functionalities such as load balancing, virtual private networks (VPN) creation and firewall configuration.

Together with Core services, Openstack also offers a set of juxtaposed Shared Services which extends the core functionalities and contribute to their integration. Such a set of services comprehends:

- **Image Service.** (Glance) providing discovery, registration and delivery services for disk and server images.
- **Identity Service.** (Keystone) offers an authentication mechanism within the Openstack operating system.
- **Telemetry Service.** (Ceilometer) allows cloud operators to consult global or individual resource relative metrics.
- **Orchestration Service.** (Heat) enables application developers to describe and automate the deployment of their Cloud infrastructure, thanks to a template language which allows users to specify both resources configurations and their workflow.
- **Database Service.** (Trove) quickly and easily provides relational database functionalities and capabilities, avoiding complex management issues.

4   The Cloud Services Ontology

In order to define a homogeneous machine readable description of Cloud Services, a classification of services offered by different Cloud providers has been

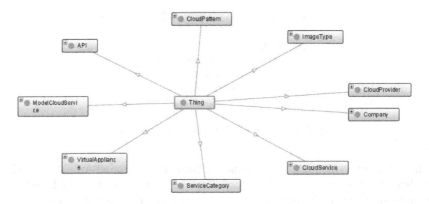

Fig. 1. The Cloud Services Ontology

realized through an OWL ontology, which identifies the most common service categories currently provided. Figure 1 offers a view of such an ontology, formally named **Cloud Services Ontology**. The structure of the Cloud Services ontology consists of different OWL classes, among which the following ones are particularly interesting:

- The **Service Category** class, used to specify the typology of the described services and better categorize them.
- The **Cloud Service** class, whose individuals represent specific Cloud services.
- The **Virtual Appliance** class, representing ready-to-use software solutions, offered by a specific company, which can be also classified alongside the described Cloud Services in this same ontology.

The most considerable object property presented in Cloud Services ontology is represented by the **aKindOf** property, whose objective is to connect Cloud Service individuals with Service Category instances. Other object properties also allow to specify, for each Cloud Service individual, the API language supported, the provider offering that specific service and the reference service model, in terms of Infrastructure, Platform or Software as a Service layers. Particularly relevant are data properties which expose Virtual Appliances architectural aspects, specifying the minimum resources necessary to instantiate a particular appliance. These properties can be exploited to match a Virtual Appliance and its minimum requirements with the default resource configurations (see section 5.1) offered by a single or multiple Cloud providers.

Further information about the Cloud Service ontology can be found in [9], where all of its classes, individuals and properties have been discussed in details. A formal, OWL based representation of this domain of interest constitutes the knowledge base from which interesting information can be inferred and extracted. By executing a SPARQL query on such an ontology it is possible to easily compare Cloud Services and/or Virtual Appliances, in order to recognize

Fig. 2. Example of Cloud Service instance

the ones that may offer the very same or similar functionalities. Within the Cloud Service ontology all of Openstack services have been described and the most important service features have been annotated. Figure 2 shows an example of Openstack Neutron service as it is described in the ontology. In particular, the object properties which have been asserted to link the *Openstack_Neutron* individual to the correct Service categories (notice the use of the *aKindOf* property) and model have been portrayed. According to our representation, Neutron belongs to different service categories, which have been all previously defined in the *Cloud Service* ontology, since it offers different functionalities.

5   The Cloud Provider Ontology

In order to semantically represent Cloud services, it is necessary to conceptually describe input and output parameters of each method and functionality such services leverage. This goal has been reached through the **Cloud Provider** ontology. For each service, the Cloud Provider ontology provides two classes:

- The first one, denoted with the suffix **Parameter**, collects individuals which define all the parameters required by each method exposed by a service.
- The second one, denoted with the suffix **Method**, defines the different methods exposed by a service.

In particular, the _Method_ class instantiates, for each method, two individuals respectively representing the input and output parameters of the described

Fig. 3. Classes in Cloud Provider ontology for conceptual representation of input and output parameters

method, linked through a object property **consistsIn** to the parameters' class. In this way, the input and output data of a method are represented as two entities, differentiated by the suffices **_Input** and **_Output**, which are in turn composed by a set of sub-parameters defined as individuals of the _Parameter_ class. The Cloud Provider ontology we have built for Openstack actually covers four services, represented through the following classes:

- **ClientParameter** describes general parameters, exploited by all services and API provided by Openstack, to identify the user invoking a particular service (like a personal ID).
- **NovaParameter/NovaMethod** represent all the methods and parameters which can be specifically used to invoke Openstack Nova services.
- **NeutronParameter/Nova** describe methods and parameters customers can use when invoking Openstack Neutron services.
- **CeilometerParameter/Method** collect parameters and methods used when user invoke Ceilometer services.
- **HeatParameter/Method** collect the parameters and methods needed to invoke the Heat services' APIs.
- **ResourceConfiguration** describes default Openstack resource configurations, which can be used to automatically instantiate a Virtual Machine with specific characteristics. Further information is provided in section 5.1.

Because of the high number of methods and parameters represented through individuals of the OWL classes listed above, for brevity we take in consideration the Neutron service only.

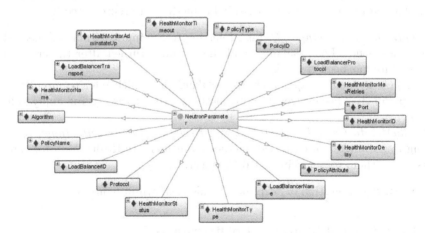

Fig. 4. Instances in NeutronParameter class for load balancing operations

Instances of the _NeutronParameter_ class are shown in figure 5 and they refer to information relative to **Load Balancer**, **Health Monitor** configurable properties and **Policy**. The Openstack services' methods represented in the Cloud

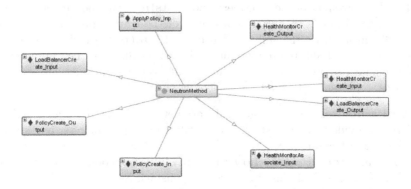

Fig. 5. Instances in NeutronMethod class

Provider ontology own a consistent number of input and output parameters: this is also true for the Neutron service and its methods. That's the main reason we preferred, in our representation, to group all these parameters through meaningful OWL individuals, instances of class **NeutronMethod**, in the form *MethodName_Input* and *MethodName_Output*. In this way, by exploiting the already mentioned object property *consistsIn*, it is possible to retrieve the set of input and output parameters of a method separately by using a simple SPARQL query. The salient methods of OpenStack Neutron service enable the creation of a Load Balancer, the setting of Policies configuration, the checking of an Openstack instance health or the association of an Health Monitor to a Load Balancer. The global parameters used by the available method are represented by:

- *LoadBalancerCreateInput/Output*, referring to the input parameters needed to create a new Load Balancer and the output returned after the creation procedure has been started.
- *PolicyCreateInput/Output* and *ApplyPolicyInput* which refer to input/output parameters needed/returned by methods called to create and apply policies.
- *HealthMonitorCreateInput/Output* and *HealthMonitorAssociateInput*, referring to parameters used to call methods which create Health Monitors and associate them to a specific Load Balancer.

A graphical representation of such individuals is shown in figure 5

5.1   Description of Resources Configurations

In our representation we dedicated particular attention to the description of predefined resources configurations offered by vendors, also referred to as "flavours" in Openstack, which can be considered as virtual machine templates. This aspect has been incorporated in the Cloud Provider ontology through the definition of the *ResourceConfiguration* class: in our example, we describe all the virtual machine

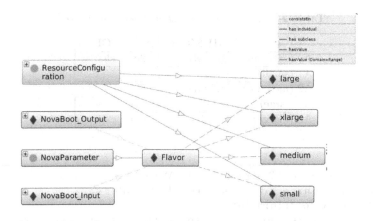

Fig. 6. Flavors available in OpenStack Nova service

sizes offered by the Openstack platform: *Tiny,Small,Medium,Large* and *Xlarge*. For each of these individuals, the configuration in terms of memory, disk and ephemeral storage size and virtual CPUs is defined by four data properties as represented in table 1. All these concepts are linked to the **Flavor** parameter, required by the *Nova boot* API and thus represented through an individual of class **NovaParameters**, thanks to the object property **"hasValue"**. Figure 5.1 graphically shows how such concepts are related in our representation. Representing these proprietary concepts might be useful to automatically compare resources configuration as they are defined by different providers. In particular, having a machine readable and easily query-able data format, such as OWL, represents a major advantage. For an instance, let's consider the Microsoft Azure Virtual Machine service [1], which also defines predefined sizes for virtual machines instances, much similarly to Openstack but using different semantics. Table 2 reports Azure's sizes and their characteristics. Clearly, having represented both these default resources configurations through our ontology, it is easy to automatically compare Openstack's and Azure's offers though a SPARQL query. As an example, consider the simple SPARQL query reported in listing 1.1.

Table 1. Virtual machine size in Openstack

	MEMORY (MB)	DISK	EPHEMERAL STORAGE	vCPUs
Tiny	512	1	0	1
Small	2048	10	20	1
Medium	4096	10	40	2
Large	8192	10	80	4
Xlarge	16384	10	160	8

Table 2. Virtual machine size in Microsoft Azure

	MEMORY	DISK	vCPUs
A0 (extrasmall)	768 MB	20	shared
A1 (small)	1.75 GB	40	1
A2 (medium)	3.5 GB	60	2
A3 (large)	7 GB	120	4
A4 (xlarge)	14 GB	240	8

```
1  SELECT ?resource   ?vendor ?CPU ?Memory
2  WHERE { ?resource rdf:type providerOntology:
       ResourceConfiguration .
3          ?resource providerOntology:hasVendor   ?vendor.
4          ?resource providerOntology:vCPUs ?CPU.
5          ?resource providerOntology:Memory ?Memory.
6          FILTER (?CPU >=3)}
```

Listing 1.1. SPARQL query

The query researches for default resources configurations which offer a minimum number of virtual CPUs (set to three). The Cloud vendor and other info about the configuration (in this case the available Memory) can be retrieved though the query. Results of the query, based on the configurations showed in tables 1 and 2 are reported in table 3.

Table 3. Results of the SPARQL query in listing 1.1

Resource Configuration	Vendor	vCPUs	Memory
xlarge	Openstack	8	16384
large	Openstack	4	8192
A3	Azure	4	7
A4	Azure	8	14

6   OWL-S Annotation of the Openstack Neutron Service

The conceptual representation of methods' parameters only represents the first step to realize a machine-readable Cloud Service description. Here we propose an OWL-S representation of the Openstack Neutron service. Neutron is here represented as an abstract Simple Process, which can be realized through one of five Atomic Processes, each corresponding to a method of the service. In this way, each method is mapped to a process expecting and returning complex messages, which can contain a variable umber of Input and Output parameters. Such parameters, thanks to the OWL-S properties **hasInput** and **hasOutput**, can be bound with concepts expressed in section 5. Bindings between atomic

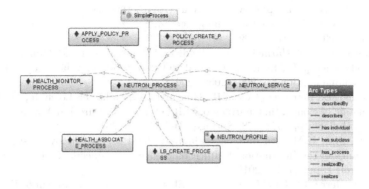

Fig. 7. Realization of a Neutron simple process starting from atomic processes

and simple processes descriptions and their relative profile and service presentations are obtained through properties defined in the OWL-S standard (here not investigated). Instead, ServiceProfile instances are linked to services described in the Cloud Service ontology through the property **presents** and its inverse **presentedBy**.

7 Conclusion

In this paper we have presented a semantic based approach to the description of both Cloud Services and the parameters needed to invoke them though APIs, together with default Resources Configurations offered by Cloud vendors. The objective is to provide a query-able machine readable formalism to support users in the comparison of different Cloud offers. Thanks to ontologies, resource configurations provided by different vendors can be easily compared, despite eventual differences in their semantics, as long as they refer to a common shared representation, here embodied by the Cloud Provider and Cloud Service ontologies. The reference query language is represented by SPARQL, which is a quite common choice when it comes to interrogate RDF and OWL representations.

Acknowledgments. This research has been supported by the European Community's Seventh Framework Programme (FP7/2007-2013) under grant agreement n 256910 (mOSAIC Project), by PRIST 2009, "Fruizione assistita e context aware di siti archeologici complessi mediante dispositivi mobili"and CoSSMic (Collaborating Smart Solar-powered Micro-grids - FP7-SMARTCITIES-2013).

References

1. Microsoft azure virtual machine service,
   http://azure.microsoft.com/en-us/services/virtual-machines
2. Opencrowd: Cloud computing vendors taxonomy,
   http://cloudtaxonomy.opencrowd.com/

3. Openstack services, http://www.openstack.org/software
4. Bechhofer, S.: Owl: Web ontology language. In: Encyclopedia of Database Systems, pp. 2008–2009. Springer (2009)
5. Bechhofer, S., Van Harmelen, F., Hendler, J., Horrocks, I., McGuinness, D.L., Patel-Schneider, P.F., Stein, L.A.: et al. Owl web ontology language reference. W3C recommendation 10, 2001–2006 (2004)
6. Di Martino, B., Petcu, D., Cossu, R., Goncalves, P., Máhr, T., Loichate, M.: Building a mosaic of clouds. In: Guarracino, M.R., et al. (eds.) Euro-Par-Workshop 2010. LNCS, vol. 6586, pp. 571–578. Springer, Heidelberg (2011)
7. Han, T., Sim, K.M.: An ontology-enhanced cloud service discovery system. In: Proceedings of the International MultiConference of Engineers and Computer Scientists, vol. 1, pp. 17–19 (2010)
8. Mark, B., Jerry, H., Ora, L., Drew, M., Sheila, M., Srini, N., Massimo, P., Bijan, P., Terry, P., Evren, S., Naveen, S., Katia, S.: OWL-s: Semantic markup for web services, http://www.w3.org/Submission/2004/SUBM-OWL-S-20041122/
9. Martino, B.D., Cretella, G., Esposito, A.: Towards an unified owl ontology of cloud vendors appliances and services at paas and saas level. In: workshop on Manuscript submitted and accepted for publication at the Semantic Web/Cloud Information and Services Discovery and Management (SWISM 2014) (2014)
10. Mell, P., Grance, T.: The nist definition of cloud computing (2011)
11. Moscato, F., Aversa, R., Di Martino, B., Fortis, T., Munteanu, V.: An analysis of mosaic ontology for cloud resources annotation. In: 2011 Federated Conference on Computer Science and Information Systems (FedCSIS), pp. 973–980. IEEE (2011)

Efficient Resource Scheduling for Big Data Processing in Cloud Platform

Mohammad Mehedi Hassan, Biao Song, M. Shamim Hossain, and Atif Alamri

College of Computer and Information Sciences
Chair of Pervasive and Mobile Computing
King Saud University, Riyadh, Saudi Arabia
{mmhassan,bsong,mshossain,atif}@ksu.edu.sa

Abstract. Nowadays, Big data processing in cloud is becoming an in-
evitable trend. For Big data processing, a specially designed cloud resource allocation approach is required. However, it is challenging how
to efficiently allocate resources dynamically based on Big data applications' QoS demands and support energy and cost savings by optimizing
the number of servers in use. In order to solve this problem, a general problem formulation is established in this paper. By giving certain
assumptions, we prove that the reduction of resource waste has a direct relation with cost minimization. Based on that, we develop efficient
heuristic algorithms with tuning parameters to find cost minimized dynamic resource allocation solutions for the above-mentioned problem. In
paper, we study and test the workload of Big data by running a group of
typical Big data jobs, i.e., video surveillance services, on Amazon Cloud
EC2. Then we create a large simulation scenario and compare our proposed method with other approaches.

Keywords: Big data, resource allocation, cloud computing, optimization.

1 Introduction

In recent time, Big data has attracted a lot of attention from academia, industry
as well as government [1] as it offers substantial value to them. However, at the
same time it poses a considerable number of challenges on existing infrastructure.
One of the most challenging issue is how to process the huge amount of data
for analysis, since it is a time-consuming and labour-intensive task and hence,
stretches existing infrastructure to its limits. Many studies [2], [1], [3], [4], [5],
[6], [7], [8] and [9] are emerging now-a-days to explore the possibility of using
cloud computing paradigm for Big data processing. Those works are driven by
a fact that the Big data processing requires scalable and parallel computing
resources rather than using on-hand database management tools or traditional
data processing applications [2].

However, for large scale BIg data analytic processing applications, conventional cloud resource management approaches are not suitable [2]. Unlike conventional applications, Big data processing applications are data or computation

G. Fortino et al. (Eds.): IDCS 2014, LNCS 8729, pp. 51–63, 2014.

intensive and the activities in the processing tasks have data or control dependencies among them. In addition, the amount of data to be transferred from one task to another is also very large. As a result, the data processing/transfer time and storage cost are higher for these type of applications. Therefore, effective resource scheduling strategies are required to efficiently manage the cost of operation or execution, and at the same time, improve the turn-around time of real-time Big data analytic services, considering the shear dynamism and heterogeneity persisted in Cloud environment [10].

Most of the existing resource management solutions [2], [1], [3], [4], [5], [6], [7], [11], [3] and [9] for cloud systems, concentrates on the efficiency of computational resource usage. They hardly consider the multiple VM resource dimensions (i.e. CPU, memory, disk I/O and network bandwidth) and overall resource utilization in the resource allocation problem which are very important for handling Big data tasks. Besides, most of these approaches focus on how the VMs are allocated over time rather than finish time based on SLA which is also very important for Big data analytic systems. In addition, few of them differentiate tasks based on their importance/priority. Hence, a cloud provider may lose the opportunity to increase profits by prioritizing Big data tasks with strict SLA, improve utilization by running low priority taks at night, or both [12].

In this paper, we tackle the aforementioned challenging allocation problem in cloud based Big data system. Specifically, we develop a cost effective and dynamic VM allocation model to handle Big data tasks. We suggest and prove that the overall resource utilization of cloud resources directly indicates the long-term service cost. Several experiments are conducted to validate the efficiency of our proposed allocation model in cloud based Big data processing platform. These experiments were conducted for different request patterns of Big data tasks in various environments. We compare our proposed algorithm with other algorithms, and present results as well as explanations in this paper.

The rest of the paper is organized as follows: Section 2 presents the detailed description of the problem formulation for resource allocation. Section 3 presents the online allocation and dynamic control situation. Section 4 shows the performance evaluation of the proposed allocation and finally section 5 concludes the paper.

2   Problem Formulation

In this paper, we consider the cloud-based resource management for big data tasks as a time-slotted task allocation problem with time slots of equal length indexed by $t = 0, 1, ...$. The actual duration of a time slot is related to the specific application (e.g., every few seconds or minutes for big data application). The major challenges regarding resource management in the proposed system are briefly described as follows.

- **Regular allocation:** We use $A(t), t = 0, 1, ...$ to denote the task allocation results by the end of each time slot. We consider that each task has its own

QoS requirements regarding resources and time. The resource requirement of a task is fulfilled by assigning it to a virtual machine having enough CPU, memory, disk I/O and bandwidth capacity. Meanwhile, each VM holding a specific task must be allocated before the task allocation deadline specified in the QoS requirement of that task.

- **Emergent task arrival:** If any emergent task arrives, the allocation decision for that task will be made immediately to handle real-time big data processing. Same as regular task, a virtual machine having enough CPU, memory, disk I/O and bandwidth resources will be created for each emergent task. Since there is no waiting time for emergent task allocation, only long-term cost reduction is considered while allocating a VM holding emergent task.

- **Loop feedback control:** As the regular allocation algorithm pursues long-term optimization goals in a dynamic environment, we propose to use a threshold variable in our on-line allocation process. Meanwhile, we define long time slots $T = 0, 1, \dots$ of equal length where the threshold value is adjusted by the end of every long time slot using a proportional-integral-derivative controller (PID controller).

- **VM migration:** VM migration can be triggered by two types of events: server overloaded event and server underloaded event. We also consider long-term cost reduction as the optimization goal for VM migration.

In the following, the modeling details of the servers and tasks are provided. We summarize the key notations in 1.

Table 1. List of notations

Parameters	
P	set of physical servers
$T(t)$	set of arrived big data tasks at time t
$V(t)$	set of VMs at time t
$pr_j(t)$	service waiting time of task t_j/VM v_j at time t
$A(t)$	allocation results at time t
C	long term cost
RW	long term resource waste
$fc_i(t)$	percentage of free CPU capacity on physical server p_i at time t
$fm_i(t)$	percentage of free memory capacity on physical server p_i at time t
$fs_i(t)$	percentage of free disk I/O capacity on physical server p_i at time t
$fb_i(t)$	percentage of free bandwidth capacity on physical server p_i at time t
$cv_i(t)$	overall resource situation on physical server p_i at time t
rc_{ij}	percentage of task t_j/VM v_j's CPU requirement on physical server p_i
rm_{ij}	percentage of task t_j/VM v_j's memory requirement on physical server p_i
rs_{ij}	percentage of task t_j/VM v_j's disk I/O requirement on physical server p_i
rb_{ij}	percentage of task t_j/VM v_j's bandwidth requirement on physical server p_i

2.1   Physical Servers and Tasks

The cloud resources consists of np physical servers defined as $P = \{p_1, p_2, ..., p_{np}\}$. In order to describe a physical server $p_i(1 \leq i \leq np)$ in general, we use c_i, m_i, s_i and b_i to represent its CPU processing capability (expressed in millions of instructions per second- MIPS), memory space (expressed in MB), disk I/O (expressed in MB/s) and network bandwidth (expressed in KB/s), respectively. At time t, let $fc_i(t)$, $fm_i(t)$, $fs_i(t)$, and $fb_i(t)$ be the percentage of free CPU processing capability, memory space, disk I/O and network bandwidth, respectively. If a physical server p_i joins a server group G where the memory or disk I/O is shared in a distributed way among the servers in G, the definitions of m_i, s_i, $fm_i(t)$ and $fs_i(t)$ are changed to represent the total resources and free resources of the server group rather than those of the individual server.

At time t, denote the set of arrived big data tasks by $T(t) = \{t_1, t_2, ..., t_{nt(t)}\}$ where $nt(t)$ is the total number of arrived tasks from time 0 to time t. For a task $t_j(1 \leq j \leq nt(t))$, let wt_j, ad_j and st_j be the waiting time, allocation deadline and service time of that task, respectively. The waiting time is counted when the task arrives and finally fixed when it is allocated on a physical machine. For any emergent task, it's allocation deadline should be specified as a distinguished value so that the allocation decision on this task will be made immediately. Meanwhile, the waiting time of any emergent task must be 0. In some cases, st_j may not be known or predictable before the processing of t_j is accomplished. Since each task may require a heterogeneous running environment, a corresponding virtual machine need to be created and deployed on a physical machine for processing. Let v_j be the virtual machine for task t_j.

As we mentioned before, we use a np-by-$nt(t)$ matrix $A(t)$ to represent the allocation results at time t where the elements are binary. For any $a_{ij}(t)$, $a_{ij}(t) = 1$ means that the virtual machine v_j has been allocated on the physical machine p_i, and vice versa. Let rc_{ij}, rm_{ij}, rs_{ij} and rb_{ij} be v_j's resource requirements on p_i regarding CPU capability, memory space, disk I/O and network bandwidth, respectively and all in percentage form. We assume that the overhead of VM creation and maintainance is also included in the resource requirements, which means rc_{ij}, rm_{ij}, rs_{ij} and rb_{ij} are the overall resource requirements for running v_j on p_i. In pratical design, the values of rc_{ij}, rm_{ij}, rs_{ij} and rb_{ij} are acquired from user-supplied information, experimental data, benchmarking, application profiling or other techniques. The following conditions must be satisfied before allocating v_j to p_i.

$$\begin{aligned} rc_{ij} &\leq fc_i(t-1) \\ rm_{ij} &\leq fm_i(t-1) \\ rs_{ij} &\leq fs_i(t-1) \\ rb_{ij} &\leq fb_i(t-1) \end{aligned} \tag{1}$$

The above conditions are crucial for the QoS guarantees in big data since the lack of processing capability, memory space, disk I/O or network bandwidth may cause severe QoS degradation. After allcating v_j to p_i, the free resources of p_i are calculated by using (2).

$$\begin{aligned}
fc_i(t-1) &\Leftarrow fc_i(t-1) - rc_{ij} \\
fm_i(t-1) &\Leftarrow fm_i(t-1) - rm_{ij} \\
fs_i(t-1) &\Leftarrow fs_i(t-1) - rs_{ij} \\
fb_i(t-1) &\Leftarrow fb_i(t-1) - rb_{ij}
\end{aligned} \tag{2}$$

When all allocation decisions have been made by the end of time slot t, the following updates are performed.

$$\begin{aligned}
fc_i(t) &\Leftarrow fc_i(t-1) \\
fm_i(t) &\Leftarrow fm_i(t-1) \\
fs_i(t) &\Leftarrow fs_i(t-1) \\
fb_i(t) &\Leftarrow fb_i(t-1)
\end{aligned} \qquad \forall i \tag{3}$$

2.2   Optimization Goal

The cost reduction is a major concern while operating a cloud-based big data system. In cloud environment, the cost is commonly associated with the number of active physical servers [11]. To be more specific, the long-term cost can be defined as the cumulative running time of all active physical servers if we assume the servers' energy consumption is homogeneous. Let $y_i(t)$ be the binary variable indicating whether a physical server p_i is active at time t ($y_i(t) = 1$) or not ($y_i(t) = 0$). The long term cost $\overline{C}$ is then expressed as

$$\overline{C} = \lim_{t \to \infty} \frac{1}{t} \sum_{i=1}^{np} \sum_{\tau=0}^{t-1} y_i(\tau) \tag{4}$$

Intuitively, the waste of resource causes the increase of long-term cost $\overline{C}$. Thus, we investigate the impacts of overall resource waste on the long-term cost reduction in Proposition 1.

Proposition 1: Assume the physical servers are homogeneous where

$$\begin{aligned}
c_\alpha &= c_\beta & rc_{\alpha j} &= rc_{\beta j} \\
m_\alpha &= m_\beta & \& \quad rm_{\alpha j} &= rm_{\beta j} & \forall \text{ Phsical Server } p_\alpha, p_\beta \\
s_\alpha &= s_\beta & rs_{\alpha j} &= rs_{\beta j} & \forall \text{ VM } v_j \\
b_\alpha &= b_\beta & rs_{\alpha j} &= rs_{\beta j}
\end{aligned} \tag{5}$$

We define the long-term resource waste function $\overline{RW}$ as

$$\overline{RW} = \lim_{t \to \infty} \frac{1}{t} \sum_{i=1}^{np} \sum_{\tau=0}^{t-1} (fc_i(\tau) + fm_i(\tau) + fs_i(\tau) + fb_i(\tau)) \times y_i(\tau) \tag{6}$$

For any task set $T(t)$, there always exists a **positive correlation** between $\overline{RW}$ and $\overline{C}$.

Based on the above definitions, we set up the optimization goal as to find an on-line allocation method that solves the following problem:

$$\min_{A(t), t=0,1,2,\ldots} \overline{C} = \frac{1}{t} \sum_{i=1}^{np} \sum_{\tau=0}^{t-1} y_i(\tau) \tag{7}$$

$$s.t., \quad fc_i(t), fm_i(t), fs_i(t), fb_i(t) \geq 0 \quad \forall t, i \tag{8}$$

$$\exists p_i : \begin{array}{l} fc_i(t) \geq rc_{ij} \\ fm_i(t) \geq rm_{ij} \\ fs_i(t) \geq rs_{ij} \\ fb_i(t) \geq rb_{ij} \end{array} \quad \forall t, j \tag{9}$$

$$t \leq ad_j | j, \sum_{i=1}^{np} a_{ij}(t) = 0 \quad \forall t \tag{10}$$

where the constraints (8) and (9) guarantee the resource sufficiency of single server and entire cloud, respectively. (10) shows that all tasks must be allocated before their allocation deadline. If (5) is satisfied, we can use the following optimization goal to replace (7) according to Proposition 1.

$$\min_{A(t), t=0,1,2,\ldots} \overline{RW} \tag{11}$$

We assume that throughout this paper the problem (5), (7)-(11) is feasible unless otherwise stated.

2.3 Problem Analysis

The optimization problem we proposed above should be solved by using an on-line allocation approach without knowing and perfectly predicting the workload parameters. The cloud-based big data system is a complex dynamical system because of the following reasons. At any time t, future task set $T(t + \varepsilon), \varepsilon > 0$ is not able to be obtained. For the allocated tasks, the st_j may not be known or perfectly predictable before the processing of t_j is accomplished. It is also possible that the resource requirements $rc_{ij}, rm_{ij}, rs_{ij}$ and rb_{ij} may differ from their original settings during running time. Therefore, the possible solutions can only achieve near-optimal results for this allocation problem.

The computational complexity of the online allocation algorithm is another important issue that need to be analyzed. To this end, we consider a possible workload pattern where the allocation decision made at any time t is independent with the previous allocation status. Then we are able to analyze the complexity of the problem in Proposition 2.

Proposition 2: Assume the allocation deadline and service time of any task satisfies

$$ad_j = t, st_j = 1 | t_j \in T(t) - T(t-1) \quad \forall t \tag{12}$$

meaning all tasks must be allocated in the same time slots when they arrive, and the processing of any task can be finished within next time slot. By taking this assumption, we can prove that the allocation problem at any time t is a NP-complete problem.

Proof: The optimization goal of the allocation is

$$\min_{A(t),t=0,1,2,...} \bar{C} = \lim_{t\to\infty} \frac{1}{t} \sum_{i=1}^{np} \sum_{\tau=0}^{t-1} y_i(\tau) \tag{13}$$

Furthermore, the allocation decision made at time t is independent with previous and future decisions. Thus, the allocation problem at time t can be again simplified as

$$\min \quad \sum_{i=1}^{np} y_i(t) \tag{14}$$

The above problem can be mapped to the multi-dimensional bin-packing problem [13]. The goal of this problem is to map several items, where each item represents a tuple containing its dimensions, into the smallest number of bins as possible. As the multi-dimensional bin-packing problem is a well-known NP-complete problem, it is proved that the allocation problem in our senario is also a NP-complete problem at any time t. More specifically, the size of this NP-complete problem depends on the number of arrived tasks during $t-1$ to t, which can be expressed as $nt(t) - nt(t-1)$.

3   Online Allocation and Dynamic Control

In this section, we first describe the key parameters used in our online allocation process. After that, the entire online allocation process are presented. The updating method for dynamic controller is explained at the end of this section.

3.1   Key Parameters

As we proved in Proposition 1, the long-term service cost of cloud is related to the overall resource usage. By taking this as the starting point, we define the following parameters to represent the overall resource utilization condition of physical server. Given a physical server p_i, The first parameter is the mean of resource usage $\mu_i(t)$ at time t.

$$\mu_i(t) = \frac{fc_i(t) + fm_i(t) + fs_i(t) + fb_i(t)}{4} \tag{15}$$

$\mu_i(t)$ provides a direct view showing how efficiently the resources of p_i are utilized at time t. However, there is another parameter which indicates the overall resource utilization condition implicitly. We use $\sigma_i(t)$ to denote the situation of resource balance.

$$
\begin{aligned}
temp_1 &= (\mu_i(t) - fc_i(t))^2 \\
temp_2 &= (\mu_i(t) - fm_i(t))^2 \\
temp_3 &= (\mu_i(t) - fs_i(t))^2 \\
temp_4 &= (\mu_i(t) - fb_i(t))^2 \\
\sigma_i(t) &= \frac{\sqrt{temp_1 + temp_2 + temp_3 + temp_4}}{2}
\end{aligned}
\tag{16}
$$

It can be seen intuitively that a better overall resource utilization will occur when $\mu_i(t)$ increases and $\sigma_i(t)$ increases. Thus, we combine these two parameters into a single parameter $cv_i(t)$. The definition of $cv_i(t)$ is

$$cv_i(t) = \sigma_i(t) \times \nu_i(t) \qquad (17)$$

Since the actual value of the $cv_i(t)$ is independent of the unit in which the measurement has been taken, it also has the potential to be applied on heterogeneous or inconsistent physical servers where (5) is not fully satisfied.

3.2   Online Allocation

We first introduce Min-Min heuristic algorithm [13] and modify it by changing the metric and adding a threshold. Based on Min-Min heuristic, we explain our proposed online allocation process step-by-step.

The metric in Min-Min heuristics are defined as $cv_i(t)$. We also introduce a dynamic threshold value $\xi(t)$. If a candidate allocation $a_{ij}(t) = 1$ satisfies $cv_i(t) \leq \xi(t)$, it is considered as an approved allocation. At time t, a regular task t_j can not be allocated when there does not exist any physical server p_i satisfies $cv_i(t) \leq \xi(t)$.

The original Min-Min attempts to map as many VMs as possible to the first choice resource. Among all VM/server pairs, the modified Min-Min heuristic selects the one that produces the overall minimum metric value. If the VM/resource pair is approved according to the threshold value, the VM in that pair will be allocated to the corresponding server. This process continuously repeats until all of the VMs have been allocated or until no VM/server pair has a value below the threshold. If any VM cannot be allocated, the corresponding task will be put into the waiting list for future allocation.

We provide the detailed steps of allocation process as follows.

Step 1: The allocation process starts at time $t = 0$. The initial threshold value is defined as $\xi(0) = +\infty$, which means the threshold is not adopted. For any physical machine p_i, we have $fc_i(0) = fm_i(0) = fs_i(0) = fb_i(0) = 100\%$. The task set is an empty set, i.e., $T(0) = \emptyset$. The initial selected heuristic is Min-Min. In fact, the initial selection of threshold value is not an important issue. It will be changed at the end of first long-period $T = 1$.

Step 2: During a short time slot t, the urgent allocation requests may arrive. To handle them, we use the modified Min-Min and remove the constraint of threshold from it. As each urgent request is executed individually and immediately, the actual metric is $cv_i(t)$.

Step 3: At the end of a short time slot t, the regular allocation requests need to be handled. The modified Min-Min heuristic with threshold value is used.

Step 4: Repeat Step 2 and Step 3 until the end of a long-period T. If the time is also the end of a short time slot, finish Step 3 before starting this step. According to the pre-defined conditions, choose the VMs that need to be migrated first. Try to allocate the VMs use modified Min-Min heuristic, and check whether the condition is eliminated or not. If so, then execute the allocation.

Step 5: At this step, the threshold value for next long-period are determined. The method is to adopt different threshold values in each heuristic to find the offline allocation results for the past period. We use (11) to judge which is the optimal threshold value The optimal threshold value passes PID controller which generates the threshold value that can be used in next long-period.

4 Performance Evaluation

In this section, we first explain the simulation setup and then illustrate the results from the simulations in details.

4.1 Setup

To generate the big data workload, we focus on four typical video surveillance paradigms: video streaming and monitoring, face detection, video encoding/ transcoding and video storage. Video streaming and monitoring tasks represents the basic functionality of cloud-based video surveillance system. To understand the characteristics of our video surveillance workloads, we analyze their runtime statistics collected while running the applications on AMAZON cloud EC2. We rent a M1 Small VM having 1 Intel(R) Xeon(R) E5430 @2.66GHz CPU unit, 1 CPU core, 1.7GiB memory, 1Gbps bandwidth and 30G hard drive with Microsoft Server 2008 Base 64-bit. We use the performance monitor of Windows to record the resource utilization of CPU, memory, storage and network bandwidth. We download videos from PETS (Performance Evaluation of Tracking and Surveillance) where each video consists 1000-5000 frames taken at 1000-5000 time instants. Each frame is a 720 by 576 JPEG photo. We use open-source software for face detection and video encoding. The following are the observed results of our workload test in cloud environment. Table 2 clearly illustrates the inter-workload diversity of workload.

Table 2. Summary of workload

Workload	CPU/Memory	CPU/Disk I/O	CPU/Net
Face detection	72.13%	184.57%	37.63%
Monitoring	59.89%	136.06%	24.42%
Storage	4.76%	1.37%	9.22%
Transcoding	250.06%	765.97%	564.29%

To create static and dynamic workload, we generate the aforementioned four groups of tasks with different arrival rates. The arrival rate of each service request is fixed in the static workload. For dynamic workolad, the task arrival rate of each service request is changed every 100 time-slots. The Total duration of task arrival is between time-slot 0 and 1000. 30% of service request has be allocated immediately, and the allocation deadline of the remaining tasks is randomly generated from 0 to 1000 time-slots after arriving to the system. The service time of each task is randomly generated from 50 to 1000. The physical servers are homogeneous and sufficient. The exact resource requirements of each task is generated based on Table 2

4.2 Simulation Results

In our simulation, we implemented five approaches: Fisrt Come First Serve (FCFS), single-resouce-Min-Min heuristic (CPU), multi-resource-Min-Min heuristic (CPU+memory+disk I/O+bandwidth), Min-Min heuristic with proposed metric, and Min-Min heuristic with proposed metric plus dynamic threshold. We first present the results of total cost in terms of cumulative machine hours in Figures 1 and 2. As we can see from these figures, FCFS has the worst performance among five approaches. Single-resource-Min-Min heuristic is slightly better than FCFS in static environment, but also has the worst performance in dynamic environment. The multi-resource-Min-Min heuristic, since it considers overall resource utilization, performs better than FCFS and single-resource-Min-Min heuristic. With proposed metric, the efficiency of Min-Min heuristic again increases. However, the improvement is not magnificent without applying dynamic threshold. The best approach is the Min-Min with proposed metric plus dynamic threshold, which saves more than 20% cost comparing with other approaches. Now we provide the resource utilization of CPU, memory, disk I/O and bandwidth while running the dynamic workload. The percentage value in each sub-figure represents how much resource on the physical machines have been reserved by the VMs averagely. As we can see from Figure 3, our proposed appraoch can fully utilize all resources from time-slot 100 to 900 while other approaches only maintain high utilization from time-slot 100 to 400. Thus, this figure clearly indicates the efficiency of proposed approach.

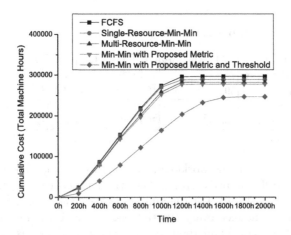

Fig. 1. Total cost of running static workload

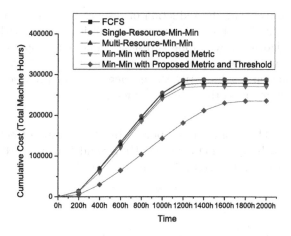

Fig. 2. Total cost of running dynamic workload

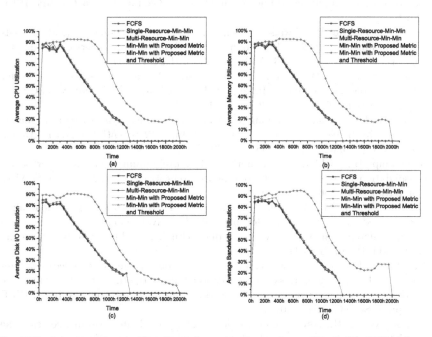

Fig. 3. Realtime resource utilizations of running dynamic workload. (a) CPU. (b) memory. (c) disk I/O. (d) bandwidth.

5 Conclusion

In this paper, we provide a dynamic cloud resource provisioning method to handle QoS-aware big data processing. We address the challenging issue of incorporating the comprehensive QoS demand of big data with cloud while minimizing the total cost. We prove that the reduction of resoure waste has a direct relation with cost minimization. Thus, we propose an efficient metric with modified Min-Min heuristic algorithm by adding threshold value. Our approach can find cost minimized dynamic resource allocation solutions for the above mentioned problem. Our simulation results verify the efficiency of our proposed approach in both static and dynamic workload environment.

Acknowledgment. This work was supported by the Research Center of College of Computer and Information Sciences, King Saud University, Project No: RC1303109. The authors are grateful for this support

References

1. Demchenko, Y., Zhao, Z., Grosso, P., Wibisono, A., de Laat, C.: Addressing big data challenges for scientific data infrastructure. In: 2012 IEEE 4th International Conference on Cloud Computing Technology and Science (CloudCom), pp. 614–617. IEEE (2012)
2. Ji, C., Li, Y., Qiu, W., Awada, U., Li, K.: Big data processing in cloud computing environments. In: 2012 12th International Symposium on Pervasive Systems, Algorithms and Networks (ISPAN), pp. 17–23. IEEE (2012)
3. Guo, S., Xiong, J., Wang, W., Lee, R.: Mastiff: A mapreduce-based system for time-based big data analytics. In: 2012 IEEE International Conference on Cluster Computing (CLUSTER), pp. 72–80. IEEE (2012)
4. Zhang, G., Li, C., Zhang, Y., Xing, C., Yang, J.: An efficient massive data processing model in the cloud – a preliminary report. In: 2012 Seventh ChinaGrid Annual Conference (ChinaGrid), pp. 148–155 (2012)
5. Speitkamp, B., Bichler, M.: A mathematical programming approach for server consolidation problems in virtualized data centers. IEEE Transactions on Services Computing 3(4), 266–278 (2010)
6. Guo, J., Zhu, Z.-M., Zhou, X.-M., Zhang, G.-X.: An instances placement algorithm based on disk i/o load for big data in private cloud. In: 2012 International Conference on Wavelet Active Media Technology and Information Processing (ICWAMTIP), pp. 287–290 (2012)
7. Kaushik, R.T., Nahrstedt, K.: T: a data-centric cooling energy costs reduction approach for big data analytics cloud. In: Proceedings of the International Conference on High Performance Computing, Networking, Storage and Analysis, p. 52. IEEE Computer Society Press (2012)
8. Mo, X., Wang, H.: Asynchronous index strategy for high performance real-time big data stream storage. In: 2012 3rd IEEE International Conference on Network Infrastructure and Digital Content (IC-NIDC), pp. 232–236. IEEE (2012)
9. Jung, N.G., Gnanasambandam, Mukherjee, T.: Synchronous parallel processing of big-data analytics services to optimize performance in federated clouds. In: 2012 IEEE 5th International Conference on Cloud Computing (CLOUD), pp. 811–818 (2012)

10. Rahman, M., Li, X., Palit, H.: Hybrid heuristic for scheduling data analytics workflow applications in hybrid cloud environment. In: 2011 IEEE International Symposium on Parallel and Distributed Processing Workshops and Phd Forum (IPDPSW), pp. 966–974. IEEE (2011)
11. Ferreto, T.C., Netto, M.A.S., Calheiros, R.N., De Rose, C.A.F.: Server consolidation with migration control for virtualized data centers. Future Gener. Comput. Syst. 27, 1027–1034 (2011)
12. Jain, N., Menache, I., Naor, J., Yaniv, J.: Near-optimal scheduling mechanisms for deadline-sensitive jobs in large computing clusters. In: Proceedings of the 24th ACM Symposium on Parallelism in Algorithms and Architectures, pp. 255–266. ACM (2012)
13. Kou, L.T., Markowsky, G.: Multidimensional bin packing algorithms. IBM J. Res. Dev. 21, 443–448 (1977)

High Performance Cloud: A MapReduce and GPGPU Based Hybrid Approach

Beniamino Di Martino, Antonio Esposito, and Andrea Barbato

Department of Industrial and Information Engineering,
Second University of Naples,
Via Roma 29, Aversa
beniamino.dimartino@unina.it, antonio.esposito@unina2.it,
and.barbato@gmail.com

Abstract. High Performance Computing systems typically require performant hardware infrastructures, in most cases managed and operated on-premises by single organizations. However, the computing power demand often fluctuates in time, resulting into periods where allocated resources can be underused. The pay-as-you-go and resources-on-demand approach provided by Cloud Computing can surely ease such problem, consequently reducing the upfront investment on enterprise infrastructures. However, a common approach to support software migration to the Cloud is still missing. Here we propose a methodology to recognize design and algorithmic characteristics in sequential source code and, thanks parallel Compilers and Skeletons, to support the parallelization and migration of existing software to the Cloud, guided in the process by the parallel programming paradigm represented by MapReduce. In addition, by leveraging the virtualization capabilities of the Cloud, it is possible to further parallelize specific sections of code by means of virtual GPUs, which can take advantage of the parallel data transmission capabilities offered by multiple Cloud nodes.

1 Introduction

Cloud Computing allows users to exploit a virtually unlimited pool of resources in an on-demand and pay-as-you-go fashion, attracting organizations strongly interested in reducing their investment in ICT infrastructures. This is even more true if we consider High Performance Computing, where powerful (and expensive) computing infrastructures are needed. However, migrating an application from an on-premises enterprise server to a cloud environment can be rather complicated because of the differences between the original and target environments. The lack of standards in programming models and interfaces provided by Cloud vendors surely worse the problem. According to the approach we propose, it is possible to identify algorithmic and design features of an application by examining its sequential source code and to use such characteristics to determine a mapping between application elements and Cloud Platforms' components. The necessary code re-factoring is obtained by means of Parallel Skeletons, which can

G. Fortino et al. (Eds.): IDCS 2014, LNCS 8729, pp. 64–73, 2014.

be used as a template to create a parallel version of the input program. In particular in this paper we show how, considering a specific parallel programming paradigm, represented by the MapReduce framework, and having recognized peculiar algorithmic characteristics in source code, it is possible to automatically refactor an application to make it work in a Cloud environment. Also, we propose to leverage the Clouds virtualization capabilities to provide a second level of parallelization through virtual GPUs. In this work we present a prototype implementation of such approach, obtained through a tool which receives a source code, let the programmer select portions of sequential code through a graphical interface and then automatically performs a parallel transformation. The paper is organized as follows: in section 2 we provide an inside of the technologies involved in our approach; in section 3 we present a prototype of the proposed tool; sections 3.2 and 3.1 describe the Skeleton based approach and the code analysis method we use; section 4 describes an application of the MapReduce paradigm, using matrix multiplication as an example; section 4.1 shows the application of GPU parallelization to the same matrix multiplication example; section 5 reports some final consideration and provides hints for future work.

2   State of Art

2.1   Parallel Skeletons

Algorithmic Skeleton, also referred to as Parallel Patterns, are a high-level parallel programming model which can be used to support applications design and implementation for parallel and distributed computing. Skeletons allow the declaration of high order functions as a program or procedure 'template', which specifies the overall structure of a computation, with gaps left for the definition of problem specific procedures and declarations [1]. One of the main advantages deriving from the use of Skeletons is that orchestration and synchronization of the parallel activities are implicitly defined and hidden to the programmer. This implies that communication models are known in advance and cannot be modified by programmers who, in turn, are less prone to introduce errors and bugs since they are 'guided' in writing their code. Different frameworks and libraries have been defined to assist programmers through Skeletons: a survey of these tools is provided in [2].

2.2   MapReduce

The processing of large amounts of data is a central topic for industries working in the IT field: the main reason lies in a phenomenon commonly known as Data Deluge (or Data Flood) or Big Data revolution. Huge volumes of data are continually being produced, analysed, transformed and transmitted, often iteratively and with time limits. Since dealing with such data requires intensive computation, the application of parallelization techniques and the use of Clusters, Grids or Cloud architectures seems the best solution. Nevertheless, this implies a logical separation of computational and storage resources, together with the necessity to create communication channels to share data among computing nodes. The MapReduce framework, originally introduced by Google developers [3], represents a good solution to this problem, since it promotes data locality and reduces communication overheads. MapReduce organizes computation tasks according to data distribution among computing nodes so that storage, not computational resources, lead the analysis. Data are processes in parallel by *Map* procedures, performing filtering, sorting and distribution tasks, while results are summarized by *Reduce* procedures. Since data locality limits the parallelization in order to reduce communications among nodes, the framework gives best results when working with huge data sets. In particular, a MapReduce round can be divided into three phases:

- The Map phase works on the input data directly. A map function is invoked on the data-set and it produces key/value pairs which are used to mark the distributed data and make it possible to recollect the results of the single computation.
- During the shuffle phase all the key/value pairs are grouped by key, obtaining multiple sub-sets of data.
- Every sub-set is then reduced during the Reduce phase, which produces the partial results of the computation: the output of the computation is obtained by recombining these partial results.

2.3   GPU and CUDA

CUDA is a parallel computing platform and programming model created by NVIDIA and implemented by the graphics processing units (GPUs) that they produce. Using CUDA, the GPUs can be used for general purpose processing, an approach known as GPGPU [4]. Cloud platforms can virtualize one or more GPU nodes [5], therefore CUDA may be introduced into applications produced for Cloud environments. The NVIDIA CUDA programming model, shown in figure 1, is composed of a host (traditionally a CPU) and one or more compute devices, generally massive data parallel coprocessors. All CUDA device processors support the Single-Program Multiple Data (SPMD) model, in which a set of parallel threads executes the same program on different data. CUDA programming use keywords provided as extensions to high-level programming languages like C/C++, that designate data-parallel functions, called Kernels, and their associated data structures. A kernel is organized as a hierarchy structure in which threads are grouped into blocks, and blocks into a grid. Threads in the same block are executed on a single multiprocessor, share their data and synchronize their actions through built-in primitives. Instead, threads in different blocks may be assigned to concurrent multiprocessors. When the CUDA developer calls a kernel function, he must specify the size of the grid and blocks in the hierarchy. Efficient CUDA programs isolate components that are rich in data parallelism, in order to launch many threads and blocks to keep the GPU full and amortize memory-transfer costs.

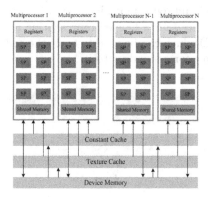

Fig. 1. CUDA programming model

3   Overview of the Prototype Tool

Our main objective is to develop a tool which, once a parallelizable portion of code has been identified and selected, either by a human operator through the provided GUI or automatically, is able to produce a parallel Cloud deployable version of the input source. In order to reduce the users involvement in the selection phase it could be possible to use parallel compilers which, during the compilation process, would analyse the program and determine which parts of it are eligible for parallelization. However, leaving the selection of parallelizable portions of code to automatic procedures only is not always possible and, in some cases, could also be inefficient, due to the impossibility to detect all control and data dependences during compile time. What we propose is to support the user by suggesting her which parts should be executed in parallel. In this way the programmer is only responsible of the validation of the code selections made by the tool, still being free to modify and correct the automatic guesses.

3.1   Analysis of the Source Code

In order to suggest the user which parts should be selected for parallelization, we need to analyse the source code. This can be done through a source to source compiler which parses the source code through a front-end and then realizes a representation of it using an Abstract Syntax Tree (AST). This intermediate representation can be used to automatically analyse control dependencies in source code for parallelization purposes. All code selections are automatically reflected in code transformations which alter the AST produced from the source code. An unparser will generate the new source code directly from the AST, regardess pf the chosen target language. As of now, the automatic analysis and selection of the code has not been realized yet in our prototype tool, but we let the user determine the portions of code to parallelize. In order to better support the user in his decisions, the tool doesnt show a graphical representation of the AST: we prefer to use a Program Dependence Graph (PDG) which can be used to describe both control and data dependency in a program. Figure 2 shows an example of a PDG produced for a C code representing a matrix multiplication. Each node reports an ID which can be used to trace the code line and the relative control or data structure corresponding to it.

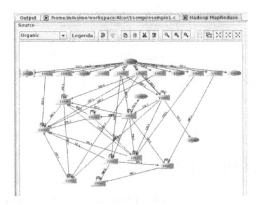

Fig. 2. Example of Program Dependence Graph

3.2   A Skeleton Based Approach

Using Skeletons can greatly reduce the users responsibilities, but this approach implies that it is possible to parallelize only sequential algorithms which present themselves in a specific form. The parallel structure of most programs can be classified in a limited number of categories, representing the basic models of organization for parallel computing. However, even when the algorithm belongs to a well specified category, the Skeleton choice can depend on minor aspects related to data distribution or algorithm structure, which become relevant in terms of performance. In our tool a set of Skeletons is presented to the user according to the target programming framework, here represented by MapReduce. Such Skeletons differ in the distribution and communication models they implement, which can be chosen according to the target distributed platforms characteristics, requirements or limitations (maximum number of computing nodes, storage services, networking capabilities and so on). When the user selects one of the available Skeletons, the tool shows a preview of how data will be distributed among reducer nodes by the mapping procedure. Figure 3 shows the panel that a user can use to select a Skeleton, set some optional configuration parameters, and have a preview of the data-set distribution. The user can also choose to further parallelize reducers code through GPUs. In our example, matrices involved in a multiplication are divided in blocks: the user can set the blocks dimensions each reducer will receive, or let the Skeleton choose the configuration based on the matrices dimensions. If a GPU parallelization is chosen, other parameters are needed to correctly set-up data distribution to the GPUs grids and blocks. After clicking on the Transform Code button, the AST of the code is modified

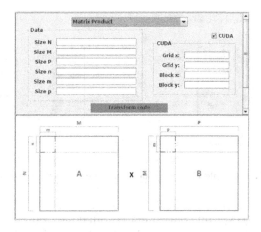

Fig. 3. Skeleton choosing and distribution preview

according to the chosen Skeleton and parameters, then it is unparsed to generate the target code written in a preselected programming language.

4   Application of MapReduce

In our work we focus on algorithms involving operations on mono-dimensional and bidimensional arrays, which can be represented by linear algebraic expressions involving an undefined number of arrays elements or matrix products. Being the matrix multiplication the most complex operation we considered, we report here an example of code transformation operated by means of Skeletons. In particular, here we consider the product of two matrices A and B, having dimensions NxM and MxP, resulting in a matrix C of dimensions NxP, as executed through the pseudo-code in figure 4. The Skeleton we propose for the matrix product is based on the Hadoop MapReduce model [6], which is quite common in Big Data analysis. Such Skeleton maps the matrix multiplication algorithm into two MapReduce rounds. During the first round, matrices are decomposed in blocks (Map phase) and key/value pairs are produced to keep trace of the elements each node works on and to determine how the Reduce phase has to be executed: using such pairs, reducers operate by multiplying the sub-matrices they have been assigned to (Reduce phase). Once all multiplications have been executed, the second round begins: matrix blocks are re-assigned to

```
for i = 1 to N
  for j = 1 to P
    Cij = 0;
    for k = 1 to M
      Cij = Cij + Aij * Bij;
```

Fig. 4. Pseudo-code for matrix multiplication

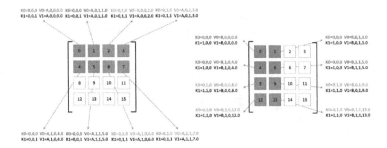

Fig. 5. Example of key/value pairs generation for round 1

reducers, using new key/value pairs, and the final sum operation of the partial results is executed. Key/value production for the two MapReduce rounds can be quite complex, as shown in figure 5 for step 1 (step 2 is simpler and not shown here for brevity). The code relative to round one is shown in figure 6. Two classes are created: The MyMapper class, which is an instance of Mapper, is used to generate the key/value pairs needed to correctly execute the reduce procedure. Since the Skeleton used is based on a Hadoop based implementation of MapReduce, theres no explicit communication since all accesses will happen on a shared, distributed file system. The two loops present in the code generate the key/value pairs needed for the matrices to multiply. The MyReducer class, instance of Reducer, executes a partial matrix multiplication on the blocks

```
class MyMapper : public Mapper {
    void map(MapContext& context) {
    string line = context.getInputValue();
    vector<string> indicesAndValue = splitString( line, "," );
    int subColA = N/n;
    int subRowB = P/p;
    if(indicesAndValue[0].compare("A")==0) {
      int i = toInt(indicesAndValue[1]);
      int j = toInt(indicesAndValue[2]);
      for(int index=0; index<subRowB; index++) {
        string key = toString(i/n) + "," +
          toString(j/m) + "," + toString(index);
        string value = "A." + toString(i%n) + "," +
          toString(j%m) + "," + indicesAndValue[3];
        context.emit(key, value);}
    } else { int j = toInt(indicesAndValue[1]);
        int k = toInt(indicesAndValue[2]);
        for (int index=0; index<subColA; index++) {
          string key = toString(index) + "," +
            toString(j/m) + "," + toString(k/p);
          string value = "B," + toString(j%m) +
            "," + toString(k%p) + "," + indicesAndValue[3];
          context.emit(key, value);
    }}}};
```

```
class MyReducer : public Reducer {
    void reduce(ReduceContext& context) {
    while (context.nextValue() ) {
      string line = context.getInputValue();
      vector<string> indicesAndValue = splitString(line, ",");;
      int i = toInt(indicesAndValue[1]);
      int j = toInt(indicesAndValue[2]);
      float value = toFloat(indicesAndValue[3]);
      if(indicesAndValue[0].compare("A")==0)
        A_h[i*m+j] = value;
      else
        B_h[i*p+j] = value;}
    for(int i=0; i<n; i++) {
      for(int j=0; j<p; j++) {
        C_h[i*p+j] = 0;
        for(int k=0; k<m; k++)
          C_h[i*p+j] += A_h[i*m+k]*B_h[k*p+j];}
    string key = context.getInputKey();
    vector<string> blockIndices = splitString(key, ",");
    for(int row=0; row<n; row++)
      for(int col=0; col<p; col++) {
        int i = toInt(blockIndices[0])*n + row;
        int j = toInt(blockIndices[2])*p + col;
        string ii = toString(i);
        string jj = toString(j);
        string value = toString(C_h[row*p+col]);
        context.emit(ii+","+jj+",", value);}}};
```

Fig. 6. Matrix Multiplication: first MapReduce round

```
class MyMapper : public Mapper {
    void map(MapContext& context) {
    string line = context.getInputValue();
    vector<string> indicesAndValue = splitString( line, "," );
    string key = indicesAndValue[0] + "," + indicesAndValue[1];
    string value = indicesAndValue[2];
    context.emit(key, value);
    }};
```

```
class MyReducer : public Reducer {
    void reduce(ReduceContext& context) {
    float result = 0.0;
    while ( context.nextValue() ) {
      string value = context.getInputValue();
      result += toFloat(value);}
    context.emit(context.getInputKey(), toString(result));
    }};
```

Fig. 7. Matrix Multiplication: second MapReduce round

identified in the Map phase. Two arrays are used, together with the keys generated by the Mapper procedure, to determine which elements of the input matrices the Reducer procedure needs to process. The recollection of partial results from Reducers is not explicitly shown, since the Hadoop implementation hides such details. The code produced for round 2 is much simpler, as shown in figure 7. As before, two classes are produced: A MyMapper class, instance of Mapper, generates the key/value pairs to distribute data among reducers. The MyReducer class, instance of Reducer, executes the sum operations needed to complete the Matrix Multiplication task. The resulting product matrix is automatically reconstructed through the shared file system and no communications are needed.

4.1 Applying GPU Parallelization

The computation of each Reducer in the first round consists again in a matrix product, row by column, between sub-matrices of small dimension. However, depending on the size of the original matrices and on the number of nodes at disposal, the sub-matrices can be wide enough to require a consistent processing time: in this scenario it is possible to reduce processing time by moving the computation on a GPU, according with the CUDA model. This way a second level of parallelization is achieved, in which each thread on the GPU calculates a single element of the resulting matrix as shown in figure 8. This approach allows each reducer to run thousands of concurrent threads on the GPU, being it

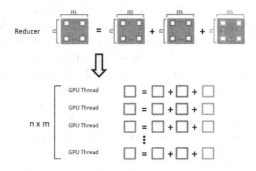

Fig. 8. Second level of parallelization through GPGPUs

```
float *A_d;
float *B_d;
float *C_d;
cudaMalloc( (void**)&A_d, (n)*(m)*sizeof(float) );
cudaMalloc( (void**)&B_d, (m)*(p)*sizeof(float) );
cudaMalloc( (void**)&C_d, (n)*(p)*sizeof(float) );
cudaMemcpy( A_d, A_h, (n)*(m)*sizeof(float), cudaMemcpyHostToDevice );
cudaMemcpy( B_d, B_h, (m)*(p)*sizeof(float), cudaMemcpyHostToDevice );
dim3 dimBlock( DIM_BLOCK_X, DIM_BLOCK_Y );
dim3 dimGrid( DIM_GRID_X, DIM_GRID_Y );
multiply_matrix<<<dimGrid, dimBlock>>>(A_d, B_d, C_d, n, m, p);
cudaMemcpy( C_h, C_d, (n)*(p)*sizeof(float), cudaMemcpyDeviceToHost );
cudaFree( A_d );
cudaFree( B_d );
cudaFree( C_d );
```

Fig. 9. Cuda code generated for the Reducer

a many-core machine with multiple SIMD multiprocessors, and simultaneously reduces the cost of data transfers to GPU, because all the reducers concurrently move their own data sub-set on GPU. For this purpose we developed a Skeleton that includes the CUDA functions allowing each reducer to allocate and transfer their sub-matrices on the GPU memory, run the kernel, recover the results and deallocate the memory of the GPU. The remaining computational parts of the two rounds follow the previous Skeleton plan. Figure 9 shows the CUDA instructions used to allocate memory on the GPU, create blocks and grids and transfer data back and forth from the it. The kernel code multiply matrix just executes the sub-matrix multiplication on the GPU and is not shown here.

5   Conclusion and Future Work

In this paper we presented a prototype tool which implements a Skeleton based approach for the parallelization of sequential code and its deployment to the Cloud. In particular we showed our results in the application of a Skeleton for the refactoring of serial code executing a matrix multiplication, based on the Hadoop MapReduce reference model, and we also showed a further level of parallelization by means of GPGPUs. The users contribution is needed to determine which parts of the source program have to be parallelized. The user also chooses the Skeletons to apply and provides further information to support data distribution among computing nodes when needed. Being our main objective the automatic refactoring of sequential code, we need to define means to accurately recognize algorithmic characteristic in source code or attached documentation to automatically annotate programs or to efficiently suggest users which portions of code can be executed on parallel computing nodes. Existing studies made on algorithmic Pattern recognition in source code, like those presented in [7] and [8], or Design Pattern recognition in UML documentation, like the ones presented in [9] and [10], can be considered as a starting point to determine the necessary methodology and a relative implementation. New Skeletons need to be defined in order to support different transformations. Also, an approach to exploit Cloud Patterns descriptions [11] [12] [13] [14] could be very useful to define mappings to different Cloud Platforms and to better support applications migration.

Acknowledgment. The research leading to these results has received funding from the European Communitys Seventh Framework Programme (FP7/2007-2013) under grant agreement n 256910 (mOSAIC Project), and has been supported by PRIST 2009, Fruizione assistita e context aware di siti archeologici complessi mediante dispositivi mobili and CoSSMic (Collaborating Smart Solar-powered Micro-grids FP7-SMARTCITIES-2013).

References

1. Cole, M.I.: Algorithmic skeletons: structured management of parallel computation. Pitman London (1989)
2. González-Vélez, H., Leyton, M.: A survey of algorithmic skeleton frameworks: high-level structured parallel programming enablers. Software: Practice and Experience 40(12), 1135–1160 (2010)
3. Dean, J., Ghemawat, S.: Mapreduce: simplified data processing on large clusters. Communications of the ACM 51(1), 107–113 (2008)
4. Nvidia cuda parallel programming and computing platform, http://www.nvidia.com/object/cuda_home_new.html
5. Aws gpu instances, http://docs.aws.amazon.com/AWSEC2/latest/UserGuide/using_cluster_computing.html
6. Borthakur, D.: The hadoop distributed file system: Architecture and design. Hadoop Project Website 11, 21 (2007)
7. Di Martino, B.: Algorithmic concept recognition support for skeleton based parallel programming. In: Proceedings International Parallel and Distributed Processing Symposium, p. 10. IEEE (2003)
8. Di Martino, B., Cretella, G.: Semantic and algorithmic recognition support to porting software applications to cloud. In: Joint Workshop on Intelligent Methods for Software System Engineering (JIMSE 2012), pp. 24–30 (2012)
9. Di Martino, B., Esposito, A.: Automatic recognition of design patterns from uml-based software documentation. In: Proceedings of International Conference on Information Integration and Web-based Applications & Services, p. 280. ACM (2013)
10. Zhu, H., Bayley, I., Shan, L., Amphlett, R.: Tool support for design pattern recognition at model level. In: 33rd Annual IEEE International Computer Software and Applications Conference, COMPSAC 2009, vol. 1, pp. 228–233. IEEE (2009)
11. Cloud computing patterns, http://cloudcomputingpatterns.org
12. Cloud patterns, http://cloudpatterns.org
13. Windows azure application patterns, http://blogs.msdn.com/b/jmeier/archive/2010/09/11/windows-azure-application-patterns.aspx
14. Aws cloud design patterns, http://en.clouddesignpattern.org

A Trust-Based, Multi-agent Architecture Supporting Inter-Cloud VM Migration in IaaS Federations

Fabrizio Messina[1], Giuseppe Pappalardo[1], Domenico Rosaci[2],
and Giuseppe M.L. Sarné[3]

[1] DMI, University of Catania, Italy
{messina,pappalardo}@dmi.unict.it
[2] DIIES, University Mediterranea of Reggio Calabria, Italy
domenico.rosaci@unirc.it
[3] DICEAM, University Mediterranea of Reggio Calabria, Italy
sarne@unirc.it

Abstract. The success of inter-cloud VM migration depends on several different factors for which a good estimate should be made in advance by Cloud providers. In this context, the ability of the counterparts in performing related measures and appropriate evaluations will affect the success of the migration to be performed. We argue that the risks due to errors made in the evaluations above can be classified into two different classes: *i)* a direct (negative) consequence on the reputation built towards the client customer, and *ii)* additional costs due to waste of resources. In this work we propose a trust-based, multi-agent architecture on which software agents assist providers in taking decisions about VM migration, by performing an evaluation of the different risks discussed above. We envision a first class of software agents that computes trust information by means of a model that considers the critical concerns to take into account in advance for the VM migration process. A second class of software agents is employed to assist the decisional agents in performing measures about VMs and measuring errors in front of previous VMs migrations. Moreover, they are also employed to disseminate trust information by means of a gossip-based protocol, in order to provide fault tolerance, efficiency and redundancy.

1 Introduction

As pointed out in [26], virtualization technology for mainframe was developed in the late 1960s in order to provide the necessary functionalities to manage resources efficiently, since hardware was expensive. Today consolidation techniques are based on virtualization technologies [2,8] which in turn are managed by cloud middlewares [1,9]. Such software stack is allowed to run on commodity hardware and provides several benefits as isolation, security, efficiency. As a consequence there is not anymore a one-to-one relationship for the tuple {applications, OS, hardware}, as companies run multiple *isolated* applications

G. Fortino et al. (Eds.): IDCS 2014, LNCS 8729, pp. 74–83, 2014.

on a single shared resource. Furthermore, as Cloud Data Centers are becoming increasingly larger, VM migration [5] has allowed Cloud Providers to consolidate physical servers [22,24], therefore costs can be reduced and customers can acquire more resources and/or obtain a higher level of QoS at the same cost. A further interesting step is the development of Cloud Federations [4,14,16] which enables cloud providers to address the complex requirements of the recent applications [18]. Indeed federated providers can rent resources from other providers in response to demand variation and complex application requirements. In the context above performing inter-Cloud VM migrations, i.e. moving customers' virtual machines from a data center to another one, represents an opportunity to get more efficiency, and, possibly, consolidate servers.

Given the premises above, in this paper we propose a trust model specifically designed to assist Cloud providers in taking decisions about inter-Cloud VM migration, i.e. in order to select a suitable "partner", such that risks can be evaluated in advance. We also present a multi-agent [3] architecture in order to assist Cloud providers in evaluating factors to be considered for a VM migration, and eventually take decisions about inter-Cloud VM migration. In the proposed architecture a second class of agents, which reside on each physical machine, helps the former class of agents to get measures and estimate errors in the physical infrastructure.

The paper is structured as follows. In Section 2 we discuss the scenario on which this work is based, a well as some detailed motivations, while in Section 3 we present the trust model to support the selection of appropriate partners to perform inter-cloud VM migrations. Section 4 describes the decentralised solution we designed to employ the trust model discussed in Section 3 and some details about the different responsibilities of the software agents. Section 5 presents some related work and, finally, in section 6 we draw our conclusions and present future work.

2   Motivating Scenario and Basic Architecture

When a Cloud provider negotiates with a customer for IaaS resources, it might not have all the resources needed to satisfy the requests. Therefore, to guarantee the negotiated SLA [15], it might be forced to (i) give up the negotiation or (ii) to cancel some of the services already running. In either way it will lose a revenue and, possibly, part of the reputation with the customer. Moreover, an IaaS provider may have unused resources which could be used by other providers. The cases discussed above can be addressed by means of Cloud Federations [4]. By joining a Cloud Federation a provider may assign unused resources to other providers for a fee, so that the cost of the infrastructures could be better sustained, helping the counterparts to address the under-provisioning problem stated above. In the scenario above, *inter-Cloud VM migration* may help provider in dealing with the issues above: some VMs are moved from a data center of a provider to another one. We remark that the *opportunity* to migrate one or more VMs has to be evaluated by the parties and the migration process must be properly managed.

Multi-agent Architecture for Inter-Cloud VM Migration. In this work we assume that software agents [3] assist providers in activities related to VM migration process.

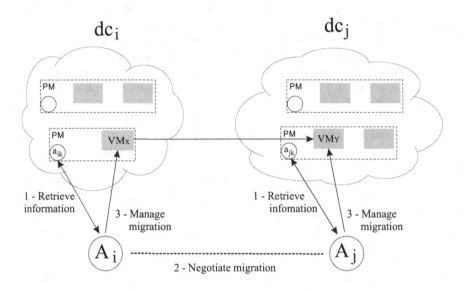

Fig. 1. Inter Cloud VM migration managed by Software Agents

As shown in Figure 1, we envision two different classes of software agents, the former (e.g. A_i in Fig. 1) is responsible of the whole data center (dc_i), it maintains trust information (see Section 3) in order to take decision about a VM migration. It has also the responsibility of retrieving and evaluating the information needed to take such decision (point 1), negotiating VM migrations with its own counterparts (point 2) and eventually manage VM migrations (point 3). As shown in Figure 1, a second class of software agents (e.g. a_{ik}) will reside on a each physical machine (PM), in order to retrieve information (measures, errors, state of physical machines, etc) from the VMM (Virtual Machine Monitor) and the Cloud middleware [9], to make them available to agents A_i. We discuss the complete list of tasks performed by agents A_i and a_{ik} in Section 4.

Factors Affecting Inter-Cloud VM Migration. We report in Table 1 a sample of the factors (column 1) to be evaluated by the generic agent A_i in order to take decisions about VM migrations, and the potential impacts (see columns 2 and 3, e.g. resource expenses, SLA violations, etc.) of the errors made when evaluating them. We argue that the success of the second and third phases shown into Fig. 1, i.e. negotiation and management of VM migration, strongly depends on the *reliability* of the information collected by software agents into their own Cloud infrastructure (cf. Table 1), and their ability in performing correct evaluations basing on these information. Basically, through Table 1, we want remark that making errors in such evaluations may impact in different manners: *i*) *additional costs* sustained by the provider, and/or *ii*) SLA violations which may also involve in additional costs but, more important, can also affect the provider reputation (*loss of reputation with the customer*).

In order to provide a concrete example, we would mention the case on which some errors have been made in the evaluation of VM hosting requirements (see Table 1). This will cause some faults during the preparation of the customer's VM in the destination, without affecting the performance of the customer VM which is still running services into the source physical machine. I.e. it causes additional costs but, as the SLA of the customer will not be violated, there will not be loss of reputation with him. In order to provide a different example, we would mention the case on which some errors on VM workload characterisations are made by agent A_i or A_j or both. In this case the performance of the customer VM(s) may be affected; therefore, once the VMs have migrated, a violation of the SLA might occur for the migrated VMs and for the VMs already running into the physical hosts of the data center dc_j. As indicated in the third column of Table 1, this will affect the reputation that the provider has built towards the customers.

Table 1. VM migration factors. Effects and impact.

Factor	Potential effects of evaluation errors	Potential impact
VM Hosting requirements	Time/resource expenses	Add. Cost
VM(s) workload characterisation	SLA violation	Reputation
VM(s) bandwidth consumption	SLA violation	Reputation
VM(s) transfer requirements	Time/bandwidth expense	Add.Cost
Expected downtime	SLA violation	Reputation
Expected slowdown	SLA violation	Reputation
VM Consolidation model/algorithm	SLA violation, faults, resource expenses	Reputation, Add. cost

3   The Trust Model for Inter-Cloud VM Migration

In order to deal with the issues discussed in the last part of previous Section (see table 1), we present a trust model designed to support software agents assisting their providers in taking decision about VM migration. Our proposal is based on the concept of trustworthiness [7] on which the truster will compute the final trust by means of two different measures: *reliability*, that is a *direct measure* derived by the direct experience of the truster with the trustee, and the *reputation*, which is an *indirect measure* based on the opinions that the other agents have about the trustee.

Given the generic Cloud IaaS Federation, as depicted in Figure 1, i.e. a set of data centers dc_i assisted by software agents A_i, let E_{j,f_k} be the error made by agent A_j in the evaluation of the factor f_k (see Table 1), and $C(E_{j,f_k})$ a real and positive number representing the cost sustained by the provider i due to the error E_{j,f_k}. Let also $R_{ij}(E_{j,f_k})$ be a mapping assuming real values in $[0 \ldots 1]$, that quantifies the (negative) impact, due to the error E_{j,f_k}, on the reputation built towards A_i customers. Note that, in the notation above, agent A_j, i.e. the agents which made the error E_{j,f_k}, may represent the origin data center (dc_i in Figure 1), or the destination (dc_j in Figure 1).

Reliability. In order to compute the *reliability* of an agent we consider the agent's *ability to perform reliable evaluations and accurate measurements* with respect to the critical factors such as those sampled in the Table 1. We assume that each agent A_i will compute a degree of reliability of another agent A_j by calculating two different values, Γ_{ij} (additional cost) and Θ_{ij} (loss of reputation), as follows:

$$\Gamma_{ij} = \frac{1}{l} \sum_{k=1}^{l} F_c^{(i)}(C_{ijk}) \qquad C_{ijk} = 1 - C_{ij}(E_{j,f_k})$$

$$\Theta_{ij} = \frac{1}{l} \sum_{k=1}^{l} R_{ijk} \qquad R_{ijk} = 1 - R_{ij}(E_{j,f_k})$$

where $F_c^{(i)}(\cdot)$ is a suitable function selected by the agent A_i, that maps the cost C_{ijk} in a real number in $[0...1]$. The reliability RL_{ij} is defined as:

$$RL_{ij}^{(t)} = \alpha\{\omega_\Gamma \Gamma_{ij} + (1 - \omega_\Gamma)\Theta_{ijk}\} + (1 - \alpha)RL_{ij}^{(t-1)} \qquad (1)$$

with $\alpha, \omega_\Gamma \in \mathbb{R}$, $\ 0 \leq \gamma, \omega_\Gamma \leq 1$. The real parameter α is used to weight the new value of reliability (left part of the sum in equation 1) and the old one ($RL_{ij}^{(t-1)}$), while parameter ω_Γ is used to weight the additional cost Γ with the loss of reputation Θ. Finally, since the impact of additional costs (C_{ijk}) is highly dependent on several factors which may have subjective nature, we used the generic function $F_c^{(i)}$ which must be freely chosen by the agent A_i.

Reputation and Overall Trust. The reputation of an agent A_j is an indirect measure of reliability, and it is based on the opinion of some other agents. As our choice has been to take into account the different impact of costs (Γ and Θ) separately, we also suppose that when an agent A_k is requested to send its opinion to an agent A_i about another agent A_j, it will send a vector $[\Gamma_{kj}^*, \Theta_{kj}^*]$, where Γ_{kj}^* and Θ_{kj}^* respectively represent the opinion of agent A_k about agent A_j concerning its ability to not incur into additional costs and loss of reputation. The agent A_i, once received Γ_{kj}^* and Θ_{kj}^*, combines them as follows:

$$RP_{ij}^{(t)} = \beta\{\omega_\Gamma RP_{\Gamma,ij}^{(t)} + (1 - \omega_\Gamma)RP_{\Theta,ij}^{(t)}\} + (1 - \beta) \cdot RP_{ij}^{(t-1)}$$

$$RP_{\Gamma,ij}^{(t)} = \frac{1}{l} \sum_{k=1}^{l} (cs_{\Gamma,i,kj}^{(t)} \cdot \Gamma_{kj}^*) \qquad RP_{\Theta,ij}^{(t)} = \frac{1}{l} \sum_{k=1}^{l} (cs_{\Theta,i,kj}^{(t)} \cdot \Theta_{kj}^*)$$

where parameter $\beta \in \mathbb{R}$, $0 \leq \beta \leq 1$ gives a similar contribution of parameter α in Equation 1. Factor $cs_{i,kj}^{(\Gamma)}$ ($cs_{i,kj}^{(\Theta)}$) measures how similar is the computation made by agents A_j and agent A_k of additional cost Γ (vs Γ^*) and loss of reputation Θ (vs Θ^*):

$$cs_{\Gamma,i,kj}^{(t)} = 1 - E_{\Gamma,i,kj}^{(t)} \qquad E_{\Gamma,i,kj}^{(t)} = \frac{1}{l} \sum_{k=1}^{l} \left| \Gamma_{i,kj}^{(t-1)} - \Gamma_{i,kj}^{*(t-1)} \right|$$

$$cs_{\Theta,i,kj}^{(t)} = 1 - E_{\Theta,i,kj}^{(t)} \qquad E_{\Theta,i,kj}^{(t)} = \frac{1}{l} \sum_{k=1}^{l} \left| \Theta_{i,kj}^{(t-1)} - \Theta_{i,kj}^{*(t-1)} \right|$$

Finally, the overall trust is computed as:

$$\tau_{ij}^{(t)} = \gamma \cdot RL_{ij}^{(t)} + (1 - \gamma) \cdot RP_{ij}^{(t)} \qquad (\gamma \in \mathbb{R}, \ 0 \leq \gamma \leq 1)$$

4   Maintaining and Disseminating Trust Information

As discussed into Section 2, we envision a layered multi-agent architecture to assist Cloud provider in VM migration. Software agents A_i reside on each data center dc_i, while agents a_{ik} reside on each physical machine and collaborate with agents A_i as specified below:

- collect, from their own physical machines, all the runtime information needed to evaluate the factors listed in Table 1;
- as a consequence of VM migrations concerning their own physical machines, compute the errors E_{j,f_k} made in the evaluation of the factors f_k as those mentioned in Table 1;
- periodically send the errors E_{j,f_k} to agents A_i;
- disseminates the measures $[\Gamma_{kj}^*, \Theta_{kj}^*]$ received by its own peers a_{lm}, as we will discuss in section 4.1.

Each agent A_i is involved in the following activities:

- collects the errors E_{j,f_k} computed by the agents a_{ik} and updates Γ_{ij}, Θ_{ij} as specified into Section 3.
- each time a vector $[\Gamma_{kj}^*, \Theta_{kj}^*]$ (i.e. reputation) is received from the trust network, it updates the trust index τ_{ij} associated to the agent A_j, as detailed in section 3;
- each time trust information about one or more agent A_j changes, it sends the correspondent reputation vector $[\Gamma_{kj}^*, \Theta_{kj}^*]$ to one of the agents a_{lm} in order to spread these information to its own peers A_k. As we discuss in Section 4.1, these information are spread into its own data center (agents a_{ik}) and the others (agents a_{lm} not belonging to the Data Center dc_i) of the Cloud Federation.

4.1   The Trust Network

In the proposed model, trust information are spread within the Cloud federation by agents a_{ik}. In order to perform this task, a simple *gossip protocol* can be used, such that the information can be spread in a way similar to those used in online social networks [21,12,13]. Gossip-based protocols are used for a wide range of problems, and provides several benefits [27]:

- *fault tolerance*: a communication failure of the agent A_i will not affect the transmission of trust information, once it has been transmitted to the network of agents a_{ik};
- *redundancy*: trust information are stored by agents a_{ik} until a fresh version will overwrite the old one;
- *efficiency*: agent A_i does not have to send trust information to all its own peers A_k, it only has to send it to an agent a_{ik} of its own data center.

The gossip-based protocol we propose in this section is reported in listing 2. Its behavior is based on the "probability" that any message is forwarded from an agent a_{ik} to another agent a_{lm}. The aspect above is tuned by the threshold $v \in \mathbb{R}, 0 \leq v \leq 1$. When v is closest to 1, the message will propagate approximately to the whole neighborhood. As a consequence, the "hubs" of the network will generate, in average, too many messages. Conversely, in order to reach most of the nodes, the threshold v should not be too low. Moreover, a TTL (Time-To-Live) and a cache storing the most recent messages are used to stop the process in a few steps.

```
int gossipTrust(msg, v){        /* msg is the received message; v is a threshold */
    if !(gossip_msg(msg))
        return 0;
    if (in_cache(msg) || msg.ttl == 0)          /* dissemination stops here */
        return 0;
    else{                                       /* disseminate the information */
        put_in_cache(msg);
        M=new_msg(msg);
    }
    for(i=1; i<l; i++)          /* neighbours are agents of other physical servers */
        if(random_uniform(0,1)) < v             /* threshold will limit the number */
            send_msg(M, neighbour(i));          /* of generated messages */
    return 1;
}
```

Fig. 2. Gossip protocol to disseminate trust (reputation) information

5   Related Work

VM migration has been mainly addressed by considering technical aspects [5] and those related to energy consumption, especially by means of server consolidation, which is based on VM migration and represents a critical issue when managing Data Center. Server consolidation is one of the main reason driving Cloud providers to negotiate inter-cloud VM migration. In particular, VM migration for server consolidation has been studied even before the massive advent of virtualization for commodity hardware [26], and there are a lot of studies in the literature focusing on server consolidation, especially for energy saving on data center. For instance, in [25] the authors present a detailed analysis of an enterprise server workload aiming at finding characteristics for server consolidation and designed two novel consolidation methods to achieve significant power savings and to contain the risks of consolidation in terms of performance.

In another study presented in [24], the problem of energy-aware consolidation has been addressed by studying the relationships between energy consumption, resource utilisation, and performances of consolidated workloads. As a consequence, some trade-offs were found and optimal operating points revealed. The authors modelled the consolidation problem as a modified bin packing problem [6]. A recent work [23] contains an analytical approach on which the authors describe a decision model, based on a set of real-world constraints, to assist the allocation of virtual servers. As in the approach described above, the problem is established to be NP-hard, therefore the author introduce a heuristic to address server consolidation. Experiments were conducted on large set of server real load data have shown that a saving of about 30 percent can be achieved by means of the described heuristics. Authors of [10] focused on the problem of energy-aware task consolidation by means of task migration which is supported by the virtualization technology. The proposal is based on the fact that energy consumption scales linearly with CPUs utilisation, therefore the authors designed two energy-aware task consolidation practices aiming at maximising resource utilisation by taking into account both active and idle energy consumption. By means of these heuristics each task is assigned to the resource on which the energy consumption can be minimised without degrading the performance. Another interesting approach is presented in [11], on which the authors proposed a fully decentralised algorithm for VMs consolidating in large Cloud data centers. The central part of the solution is that the initial allocation of VMs is "random", but the subsequent allocations are performed by a simple gossip protocol which is well known to hold desired characteristics as efficiency and scalability, eventually reaching the one which maximises the number of idle hosts, i.e. that minimise the consumption.

6   Conclusions and Future Work

In this paper we presented a trust-based, multi-agent architecture to assist Cloud providers in taking decisions about VM migration. The trust model allows the software agents assisting their providers to separate the evaluation of the different impacts, i.e. additional cost or loss of reputation with the customer, which are caused by the errors made by the counterparts when evaluating factors affecting VM migration. The multi-agent architecture is layered, i.e. composed by two classes of software agents. The former is composed by those agents whose responsibility is of computing trust information and negotiating VM migration with their own peers, while the latter is composed by a set of software agents which reside into the physical machines of the data centers. The second class of software agents assist those of the former class in taking measures about VMs and measuring errors derived from previous VM migrations. They also disseminate trust information by a gossip-based protocol that can provide fault tolerance, efficiency and redundancy of trust information. As future work we will perform a wide set of experiments by simulating a typical and detailed scenario by means of a general purpose, parallel simulator[17,19,20].

Acknowledgements. This work is a part of the research project **PRISMA**, code **PON04a2_A/F**, funded by the Italian Ministry of University within the **PON 2007-2013** framework program.

References

1. Armbrust, M., et al.: A view of cloud computing. Communications of the ACM 53(4), 50–58 (2010)
2. Barham, P., et al.: Xen and the art of virtualization. ACM SIGOPS Operating Systems Review 37(5), 164–177 (2003)
3. Bradshaw, J.M.: Software agents. MIT Press (1997)
4. Buyya, R., Ranjan, R., Calheiros, R.N.: InterCloud: Utility-oriented federation of cloud computing environments for scaling of application services. In: Hsu, C.-H., Yang, L.T., Park, J.H., Yeo, S.-S. (eds.) ICA3PP 2010, Part I. LNCS, vol. 6081, pp. 13–31. Springer, Heidelberg (2010)
5. Clark, C.: et al. Live migration of virtual machines. In: Proceedings of the 2nd conference on Symposium on Networked Systems Design & Implementation, vol. 2, pp. 273–286. USENIX Association (2005)
6. Coffman Jr., E.G., Garey, M.R., Johnson, D.S.: Approximation algorithms for bin packing: A survey. In: Approximation Algorithms for NP-Hard Problems, pp. 46–93. PWS Publishing Co. (1996)
7. Grandison, T., Sloman, M.: Trust Management Tools for Internet Applications. In: Nixon, P., Terzis, S. (eds.) iTrust 2003. LNCS, vol. 2692, pp. 91–107. Springer, Heidelberg (2003)
8. Hirt, T.: Kvm-the kernel-based virtual machine. Red Hat Inc. (2010)
9. Jackson, K.: OpenStack Cloud Computing Cookbook. Packt Publishing Ltd (2012)
10. Lee, Y.C., Zomaya, A.Y.: Energy efficient utilization of resources in cloud computing systems. The Journal of Supercomputing 60(2), 268–280 (2012)
11. Marzolla, M., et al.: Server consolidation in clouds through gossiping. In: WoW-MoM, International Symposium, pp. 1–6. IEEE (2011)
12. Messina, F., Pappalardo, G., Rosaci, D., Santoro, C., Sarné, G.M.L.: A distributed agent-based approach for supporting group formation in P2P e-learning. In: Baldoni, M., Baroglio, C., Boella, G., Micalizio, R. (eds.) AI*IA 2013. LNCS, vol. 8249, pp. 312–323. Springer, Heidelberg (2013)
13. Messina, F., Pappalardo, G., Rosaci, D., Santoro, C., Sarné, G.M.L.: HySoN: A distributed agent-based protocol for group formation in online social networks. In: Klusch, M., Thimm, M., Paprzycki, M. (eds.) MATES 2013. LNCS, vol. 8076, pp. 320–333. Springer, Heidelberg (2013)

14. Messina, F., Pappalardo, G., Rosaci, D., Santoro, C., Sarné, G.M.L.: A trust model for competitive cloud federations. In: Complex, Intelligent, and Software Intensive Systems (CISIS), pp. 469–474. IEEE (2014), doi:11.1109/CISIS.2014.67
15. Messina, F., Pappalardo, G., Rosaci, D., Santoro, C., Sarné, G.M.L.: An agent based negotiation protocol for cloud service level agreements. In: 23th IEEE International Workshops on Enabling Technologies: Infrastructure for Collaborative Enterprise, pp. 161–166. IEEE (2014), doi:10.1109/WETICE.2014.12
16. Messina, F., Pappalardo, G., Rosaci, D., Sarné, G.M.L.: An agent based architecture for vm software tracking in cloud federations. In: Complex, Intelligent, and Software Intensive Systems (CISIS), pp. 463–468. IEEE (2014)
17. Messina, F., Pappalardo, G., Santoro, C.: Complexsim: An smp-aware complex network simulation framework. In: 2012 Sixth International Conference on Complex, Intelligent and Software Intensive Systems (CISIS), pp. 861–866. IEEE (2012), doi:10.1109/CISIS.2012.102
18. Messina, F., Pappalardo, G., Santoro, C.: Integrating cloud services in behaviour programming for autonomous robots. In: Aversa, R., Kołodziej, J., Zhang, J., Amato, F., Fortino, G. (eds.) ICA3PP 2013, Part II. LNCS, vol. 8286, pp. 295–302. Springer, Heidelberg (2013)
19. Messina, F., Pappalardo, G., Santoro, C.: Exploiting gpus to simulate complex systems. In: 2013 Seventh International Conference on Complex, Intelligent, and Software Intensive Systems (CISIS), pp. 535–540. IEEE (2013), doi:10.1109/CISIS.2013.97
20. Messina, F., Pappalardo, G., Santoro, C.: Complexsim: a flexible simulation platform for complex systems. International Journal of Simulation and Process Modelling 8(4), 202–211 (2013), doi:10.1504/IJSPM.2013.059417
21. Mislove, A., Marcon, M., Gummadi, K.P., Druschel, P., Bhattacharjee, B.: Measurement and analysis of online social networks. In: Proceedings of the 7th ACM SIGCOMM Conference on Internet Measurement, pp. 29–42. ACM (2007)
22. Murtazaev, A., Oh, S., et al.: Sercon: Server consolidation algorithm using live migration of virtual machines for green computing. IETE-Technical Review 28(3), 212 (2011)
23. Speitkamp, B., Bichler, M.: A mathematical programming approach for server consolidation problems in virtualized data centers. IEEE Transactions on Services Computing 3(4), 266–278 (2010)
24. Srikantaiah, S., Kansal, A., Zhao, F.: Energy aware consolidation for cloud computing. In: Proceedings of the 2008 Conference on Power Aware Computing and Systems, San Diego, California, vol. 10 (2008)
25. Verma, A., et al.: Server workload analysis for power minimization using consolidation. In: USENIX Annual Technical Conference, p. 28. USENIX Association (2009)
26. Vogels, W.: Beyond server consolidation. Queue 6(1), 20–26 (2008)
27. Wuhib, F., Stadler, R., Spreitzer, M.: A gossip protocol for dynamic resource management in large cloud environments. IEEE Transactions on Network and Service Management 9(2), 213–225 (2012)

Cyberphysical Systems and IoT

A Cyber-Physical System for Distributed Real-Time Control of Urban Drainage Networks in Smart Cities

Andrea Giordano[1], Giandomenico Spezzano[1], Andrea Vinci[1],
Giuseppina Garofalo[2], and Patrizia Piro[2]

[1] CNR – National Research Council of Italy
Institute for High Performance Computing and Networking (ICAR)
Via P. Bucci 41C - 87036 Rende (CS), Italy
{giordano,spezzano,vinci}@icar.cnr.it
[2] Department of Civil Engineering of the University of Calabria
Via P. Bucci - 87036 Rende (CS), Italy
{garofalo,piro}@unical.it

Abstract. This paper focuses on a distributed real time control approach applied to drainage networks. The increasing of urbanization and climate change heightens the challenge for new technologies to be developed for drainage networks. Higher runoff volume, produced by the increase in impervious surfaces and intense rain events, overwhelms the existing urban drainage systems. Recent technical improvements have enabled the exploitation of real-time control on drainage networks. The novelty in this paper regards the use of a totally decentralized approach based on a proper combination of a Gossip-based algorithm, which ensures a global correct behaviour even if local faults occur, and a classic controlling technique (PID) used for local actuations.

1 Introduction

The magnitude and the frequency of sewer flooding are likely to increase due to climate change (causing higher intensity of rainfall) and expanding urbanization (which results in an increase of impermeable areas and hence, in an increase of surface runoff) [13]. As a consequence, existing urban drainage systems become drastically overloaded during rainy events, especially when the presence of obstructions and blockages in conduits and catch basins, often caused by infrequent maintenance, strongly reduces their hydraulic capacity. Given the potential risk to human life, economic assets and the environment, measures need to be adopted to cope with stormwater volumes and prevent urban areas from sewer flooding.

In recent years, research on embedded systems has been moving towards the integration of computational resources within the physical system under monitoring and control, leading to the so-called Cyber-Physical systems (CPS) [12], i.e., complex networks of interconnected embedded devices tightly integrated with the physical process under control. Examples of CPS use are found in such fields as energy systems, traffic control, medical systems, smart buildings and so on.

G. Fortino et al. (Eds.): IDCS 2014, LNCS 8729, pp. 87–98, 2014.

CPS vision can be even applied effectively in the drainage network scenario. In this context, the network of interconnected devices can be properly exploited to realize a real time control (RTC), where the devices monitor and regulate the functionality of the water network in real-time according to the maintenance conditions and the rainfall events. This approach can be a valuable solution for dynamically and effectively managing urban flood risks [4].

The employment of an RTC, though, raises several issues due to the large amount of data to be read, managed and processed. Using a typical centralized monolithic approach (see SCADA model [11]), all sensed data are sent to a central unit that elaborates a suitable strategy based on a comprehensive network model thus producing commands for the actuation part. This approach has certain drawbacks: it requires a complex mathematical model of the network and results in execution and communication times too long to correctly capture dynamic changes on the physical part. In addition, a centralized strategy requires all physical parts (sensors and actuators) to be connected with and reachable by the central unit.

In this study, an RTC based on a distributed system of sensors and actuators is set up on an urban drainage system. In particular, we instrument the urban drainage system with a series of moveable gates, functioning as actuators, and sensors which monitor water level and, hence, the degree of filling in each conduit. Using the information acquired by the sensors, the gates are dynamically regulated in order to utilize the full storage capacity of the pipeline by accumulating the excess stormwater volume in the less overloaded conduits thus preventing water from overflowing from the sewer systems to the sidewalks and street paving.

A certain number of computing nodes are spread throughout the drainage network and connected to sensors and gate actuators. Each computing node can communicate only with its neighbourhood, i.e. sensors, actuators and other nodes it can reach through wired or wireless connection. An optimization algorithm, executed on computing nodes in a distributed fashion, aims to distribute equally the degree of filling of the conduits thus preventing overcharge phenomena as far as possible. The algorithm exploits Gossip-based aggregation for dealing with the global aspect of the drainage network while a PID controller is locally used in each gate.

Preliminary experiments were carried out using SWMM software [5] which emulates the behaviour of a typical urban drainage network regulated by moveable gates during severe rainy events. The Real Time Control was added by means of customizing SWMM software permitting it to real-time communicate with a separate multi-agent Java controller implemented using Rainbow architecture [6]. The results have demonstrated that our proposal provides positive effects on the overall hydraulic performance of the network as it is able to prevent (or delay) flooding events that would occur in the original (not instrumented) network.

The rest of this paper is structured as follows: Section 2 discusses problems about drainage network control and describes the ideas underlying the proposed approach; Section 3 supplies details about algorithm implementation and running. Section 4 demonstrates the benefits of the approach where some experimental results are given; finally, conclusions are discussed with an indication of ongoing and future work.

2   Drainage Network Optimization

At first, a drainage network can be formally seen as a graph (V, E) of nodes $v \in V$ connected by edges $e \in E$. More specifically V comprises *Junctions* $j \in J$, *Inlets* $l \in L$ and *Outlets* $o \in O$. E is made up of *Conduits* $c \in C$. Junctions are just intersection points for conduits. Inlets are nodes where runoff enters into the system. Outlets are the points of the network where water is discharged into a river, lake, reservoir and so forth. Conduits are pipes of different cross-sectional shapes where the storm water flows [7]. Actually, there are some other features inherent to drainage networks that allow us to further refine the model so as to simplify achieving the proposed goal. Firstly, in a typical urban scenario, the whole drainage watershed can be broken down into several, not connected, networks in which each network comprises only one outfall. In addition, each network is likely to be modelled by a tree structure. Indeed, we can see a network as a main channel, ended by the only outlet, into which recursively defined sub-networks discharge. Finally, it can be assumed that inlets are located in the "leaves" of the tree. A very simple drainage network is outlined in Figure 1(a).

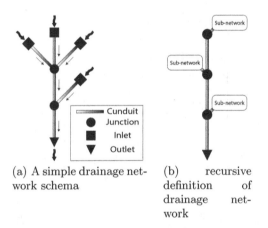

(a) A simple drainage net-work schema

(b)   recursive definition   of drainage   network

Fig. 1. Sub-networks in a realistic case

On the basis of the previous considerations we formally define a drainage network as follows. Firstly, we define *Most Simple Drainage Network* ($MSDN = (c, l)$) as a network only made up of one conduit c ending with inlet node l. Then, we define a drainage network DN as either just an $MSDN$ or a couple (M, S) where M represents the main channel and S a set of DNs. A main channel M is an ordered set of conduits in which each conduit is linked with the next one through a junction. The last conduit optionally ends with an outlet node. Figure 1(b) shows graphically this recursive definition. Figure 2(a) and 2(b) show respectively: a case of realistic network and the sub-networks, surrounded by dashed lines, as results from the above definition. We also define *Degree* of a *DN* as a natural number D that is 0 for an *MSDN* and $1 + max(Deg(s))$ for a $DN = (M, S)$ where $s \in S$ and $Deg(s)$ is the degree of s.

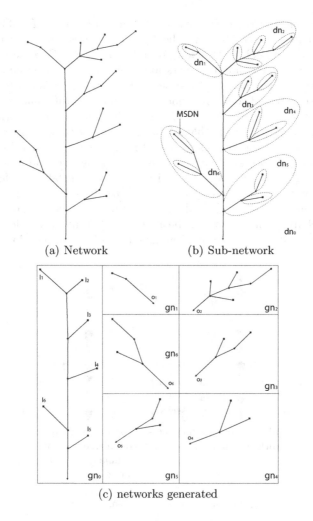

(a) Network   (b) Sub-network

(c) networks generated

Fig. 2. Sub-networks in a realistic case

The recursive definition of a drainage network permits us to exploit an optimization strategy, conceived for simple networks (such as the one shown in Figure 1(a)), even in more complex scenarios. Basically, we split the complex network in a set of more simple networks. Given a *DN*, we firstly define $nets(DN)$ as the set of all networks of *DN* as follows:

$$nets(DN) = \begin{cases} \emptyset, & \text{if } DN \text{ is a } MSDN \\ \{DN\} \cup \bigcup_{s_i \in S} nets(s_i), & \text{if } DN = (M, S) \end{cases}$$

Then, starting from a generic drainage network DN, with $DN^* = nets(DN) = \{dn_i\}$ and $dn_i = (M_i, S_i)$, we generate a set $GN = \{gn_i\}$, with $Degree(gn_i) = 1$ in which each $gn_i = (M'_i, S'_i)$, is given by the following formulas:

$$M'_i = \begin{cases} M_i, & \text{if } i = 0 \\ M_i \cup o_i, & \text{elsewhere} \end{cases}$$

$$S'_i = \{msdn_k = (c_k, l_k) : \exists dn_k \in S_i\} \cup \{msdn_x : msdn_x \in S_i\}$$

The intuitive idea concerns replacing all the sub-networks $dn_k \in S_i$ with an MSDN $msdn_k = (c_k, l_k)$ in S'_i. M'_i is M_i plus o_i outlet node except for $i = 0$, since the top level sub-network already hosts an outlet node. The idea underlying this decomposition consists in running the optimization algorithm detailed below for all generated sub-networks at the same time so as to achieve a global optimum for the original network. The incoming flow of the generated inlet nodes l_k shall be the outcoming flow of the corresponding outlet nodes $o_{i=k}$, i.e. the outlet nodes of the "replaced" sub-networks gn_k, while the generated conduits c_k are just "dummy" conduits that link the inlet nodes l_k to the main channels. Figure 2(c) show the networks generated starting from the network of figure 2(a).

Basically, the idea consists in balancing water level throughout the conduits of the network so as to reduce water level in the more overloaded conduits. In order to achieve the proposed goal, the network needs to be instrumented by: (i) *sensors*, (ii) *computational nodes*, (iii) *"smart" gates* as detailed in the following.

- Sensors measure the level of water in each conduit;
- computational nodes are made from single-board computers such as *Raspberry pi* [10] or *Beagleboard* which can be effectively spread inside the network because they have low energy consumption and small size;
- smart gates are electronically adjustable gates made up of mobile plates rotating around a horizontal hinge. The gate is completely closed when the plate rotates in a perpendicular position with respect to the flow direction. Conversely, the gate is fully open when the plate is parallel to the flow.

The computational nodes read data from sensors and collectively elaborate the acquired information in order to trigger suitable actuations on the gates. The collective computation of the network of nodes supplies the gates with an "intelligent" behaviour.

Smart gates are located at the points of the network where sub-networks are connected to a main channel. Figure 3(a) shows the logical places for inserting the gates, while figure 3(b) shows the gates insertion in a case of a realistic network.

Each computational node has a partial view of the network as it reads only from sensors located in its spatial neighbourhood, i.e. the sensors it can physically reach. In the same way, it can actuate only on its neighbour gates. On the basis

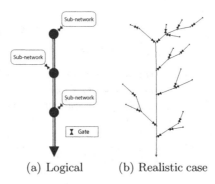

(a) Logical   (b) Realistic case

Fig. 3. Gates positions

of the previous considerations our proposal lies in using a *distributed agent-based* architecture [8]. The agent paradigm has several important characteristics:

Autonomy. Each agent is self-aware and has a self-behaviour. It perceives the environment, interacts with others and plans its execution autonomously.

Local views. No agent has a full global view of the whole environment but it behaves solely on the basis of local information.

Decentralization. There is no "master" agent controlling the others, but the system is made up of interacting "peer" agents.

Through these basic features, multi-agent systems make it possible to obtain complex *emergent* behaviours based on the interactions among agents that have a simple behaviour. Examples of emergent behaviour could refer to the properties of adaptivity, fault tolerance, self-reconfiguration, etcetera. In general, we could talk about *swarm-intelligence* [1] when an "intelligent" behaviour emerges from interactions among simple entities.

In the case of drainage networks, the property of fault tolerance is particularly useful since the system needs to continue to operate properly even if unexpected conditions occur, such as obstructions and blockages, which may reduce the hydraulic capacity of the system.

Regarding hardware, computational nodes are spread throughout the network in order to cover all the points of interest, i.e. the sensors and the gates. Regarding software, our proposal considers one agent per gate. Each *gate-agent* runs on one of the computational nodes covering the specific gate, it can perceive the local water level and communicate with the neighbouring gate-agents in order to elaborate a proper actuation strategy for its gate. Another agent is logically associated with the outlet node, it behaves the same as other agents except for the actuation part, indeed, it is not associated with any gate. Figure 4 gives an intuitive idea of the agents' role in the generated networks. For each generated network, the algorithm consists in real-time balancing the water level perceived by the agents.

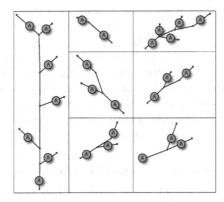

Fig. 4. Agents in generated networks

This water balance is achieved by means of agents continuously executing two tasks:

Task 1. figuring out the average of the water level in the network.
Task 2. triggering specific gates in order to bring the water level closer to that average.

Given that an agent has no global knowledge of the water level throughout the network, the *Task 1* is accomplished by exploiting a gossip-based algorithm summarized in 2.1. This kind of algorithm also supplies the previously mentioned fault-tolerance. As regards *Task 2*, even if we knew the optimal water level to set, we would not know how to tune the gate so as to achieve it. Indeed, the relationship between the actuation upon the gate and the actual change of water level depends on the structure of the entire network and the dynamics of the water flowing through the system, so it is very hard or even impossible to deduce a tractable mathematical model for it. For this reason a *PID* controller is used as explained in 2.2.

2.1   Task 1: Gossip-Based Aggregation

In a Gossip-Based Algorithm [2] there are many nodes interconnected through a network. Each node possesses some numerical values and can exchange information only with a limited set of peer nodes (i.e. its neighbourhood). The goal of this kind of algorithm concerns estimating global aggregate values such as average, variance, maximum and so forth, despite only local communication being possible.

Basically, in the case of average aggregated value, each agent maintains its current measured value and its local average (initially set to the measured value). The algorithm consists in continuously exchanging local averages among neighbour nodes. Each time a node receives the average of a neighbour node, it updates its local average (just applying average operator). Values exchanges and local computations are done continuously for enough *steps* so as to ensure that each local average, computed at every node, converges to the actual global average (the algorithm convergence is proved in [2]).

When the algorithm converges, the average value is exploited by each gate-agent for tuning its gate so as to bring water levels closer to that average. Whenever the convergence is reached, the algorithm is executed taking as input the new measured values at node level thus reaching the convergence again. Running this process continuously ensures adaptivity properties as the algorithm dynamically converges to the new global average even if an unforeseen event dramatically changes some node values.

2.2   Task 2: Tuning Gates through PID Controllers

Once an agent knows the global water level through the previously described "gossip-based aggregation", there remains the problem of appropriately tuning its gate so as to reach that "desired" level.

This issue is addressed using the well-known controlling technique called Proportional Integral and Derivative (PID) control [9] which, indeed, is particularly suitable when you do not know an exact mathematical model of the system you want to control.

A PID controller is a control loop feedback mechanism where an error value is computed as the difference between a measured output of a process and the desired value (setpoint) (see figure 5). The controller tries to minimize this error, appropriately tuning the actuator device.

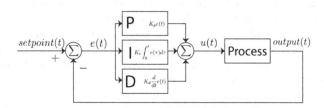

Fig. 5. PID controller

The setting of the actuator device depends on three effects, suitably tuned by three parameter: the proportional one (P), the integral one (I) and the derivative one (D). P depend on present error, i.e. the absolute error computed at the current evaluation. D measures the foreseen error, i.e. the expected error in the next step, computed deriving the error signal, while the I represent the integral effect, a measures of the historical behaviour of the error signal. The following equation defines a general time-continuous PID controller.

$$u(t) = K_p e(t) + K_i \int_0^t e(\tau)d\tau + K_d \frac{d}{dt} e(t)$$

Where $e(t) = setpoint(t) - output(t)$; $u(t)$ is the controller output at time t, i.e. the actuation signal; K_p, K_i, K_d, three constants which refer at the proportional, integral and derivative effects.

In the case of this study, each gate of the drainage network is controlled by a PID, thus u represents the degree of opening of a gate, while *output* is the actual water level of its related conduit and *setpoint* is the "desired" water level, that is the average computed by *Task 1*.

3 Implementation

To validate the approach, we have exploited the Storm Water Management Model (SWMM) software [5] which is a dynamic rainfall-runoff simulation model for predicting hydrological and hydraulic behaviour of urban drainage systems and watersheds. Developed by the United States Environment Protection Agency, the SWMM sofware is widely used by the scientific community and engineers for planning, analysis and design related to stormwater runoff, combined and separated sewers, and other drainage systems in urban areas.

SWMM simulates any kind of rainfall event. It also includes a routing module that simulates the transport of rainfall water through a system of pipes, channels, storage/treatment devices, pumps, regulators and so on.

SWMM relies on a time stepped simulation, where the model advancement is carried out step by step by numerically solving the flow routing equations (dynamic wave).

SWMM software also allows setting some simple rules to emulate some kind of control upon the network, anyway, this feature is not enough to develop complex/collective behaviour such as the one proposed in this work. For this reason we have customized SWMM in order to make it able to exchange information with an external controlling part, i.e. which runs in a different process with respect to SWMM.

More specifically, the software has been extended with a module that uses a tcp/ip connection for real-time sending and receiving information to/from the controlling part during the advancement of the simulation.

This module also permits to choose where the sensors are located inside the network, i.e. the physical quantities of interest for the controlling part. At each pre-defined time interval all values of interest are gathered and sent to the controlling part which, in turn, replies with the collectively computed actuations. An actuation is an update in a network parameter (e.g. the opening degree of a gate).

The controlling part is the multi-agent software which implements the approach described above.

4 Experimental Results

The experiments were carried out using a network which consists in a main channel of 1 m diameter and a total of 35 pipes inside the sub-networks. The network delivers the stormwater flow to a final reach, represented by a receiving water body or a treatment plant. All pipes have circular shape section with a slope of 2%. In the drainage system the connections between the main channel and the secondary pipes (junction nodes) are made of 1.5 m tall catch basins, closed on top. The inlets, i.e. the connections between the urban watershed surfaces (roads and street paving) with the pipes, are made of open catch basins which collect surface runoff and deliver it into the sewer system.

In the following two kinds of experiment are shown . The first has the purpose to graphically show how the proposed technique affects the behaviour of a drainage network in terms of conduits water load.

The second kind of experiment shows the effectiveness of our approach using the reduction of the overload time as quantitative index of performance.

Experiment 1. For this experiment, we use a 40 minute-rainfall/runoff event with a fixed flow rate of $0.20m^3/s$ for each inlet node.

The results are shown in Figures 6(a) and 6(b), where the degree of filling of conduits, represented by values between 0 and 1, are plotted versus time. In the uncontrolled case (a), the degrees of filling of the less charged conduits are much lower than the degree of filling of the most charged one. As a consequence a conduit results overcharged while the other ones result undercharged. This means that the network does not properly exploit the residual water capacity of the undercharged conduits.

When the proposed technique is applied (b) the behaviour is completely different. The load curves are much closer to each other as the load on the entire

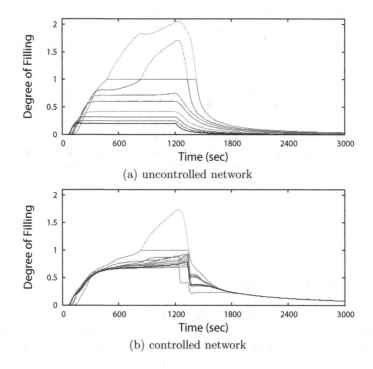

(a) uncontrolled network

(b) controlled network

Fig. 6. Degree of filling of conduits versus time. Overflowed water level is shown using a dashed line.

network is more balanced. The latter implies an improvement in the behaviour of the critical conduit that reaches the overcharge condition later.

Experiment 2. As previously mentioned, the reduction of overload time (the duration of the overcharge phenomena observed at the most charged conduit) between the controlled/uncontrolled scenarios is used as quantitative index of the effectiveness of the approach. It is easy to see that this index is related to the delay in reaching the maximum value as shown in the previous section. Indeed, the more time is needed to reach the maximum level the less time the network is full of charge. Also, even in the case of a heavy rain event, if the duration is short enough, i.e. delay time is greater than this duration, the system can be able to ensure no overcharge at all.

The experiment consists in running the algorithm using 40 minute-rainfall/ runoff events with a flow rate spanning from $0.16m^3/s$ to $0.20m^3/s$ for each inlet node. Each rainfall event is characterized by having a constant flow rate value during all the event duration.

Figures 7(a) and 7(b) show, respectively, (i) a comparison of the delays in reaching the maximum level in controlled/uncontrolled scenarios and (ii) the ratio between these delay times. It can be noted that the delay times in the controlled network are almost ever double with respect to the uncontrolled one thus demonstrating the effectiveness of our methodology.

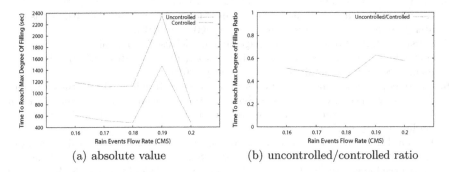

(a) absolute value   (b) uncontrolled/controlled ratio

Fig. 7. Time to reach maximum degree of filling. Controlled vs uncontrolled comparison.

5   Conclusions

This paper presents a methodology to control an urban drainage network by adopting a fully distributed and decentralized real-time approach. Each gate of the instrumented drainage network is represented by a software agent that communicates only with a limited number of "peer" agents, i.e. its neighbours. The entire network is broken down into a set of more simple sub-networks where a Gossip-based algorithm runs continuously to balance water levels. Each gate is locally controlled by a classic PID controller so as to maintain its related water level as close as possible to the "suggested" value computed by the Gossip-based algorithm.

Preliminary experiments were carried out using the SWMM simulation software which was properly customized in order to allow an external module to real-time control the simulated network. The experimental results witness a significant reduction of the overload times hence demonstrating the effectiveness of the approach.

Future works will focus on extending the algorithm and validating the approach in real drainage networks.

Acknowledgments. This work has been partially supported by RES-NOVAE - "Buildings, roads, networks, new virtuous targets for the Environment and Energy" project, funded by the Italian Government (PON 04a2_E).

References

1. Bonabeau, E., Dorigo, M., Theraulaz, G.: Swarm Intelligence: From Natural to Artificial Systems. Oxford University Press, New York (1999); Santa Fe Institute Studies in the Sciences of Complexity, Paper: ISBN 0-19-513159-2
2. Jelasity, M., Montresor, A., Babaoglu, O.: Gossip-based aggregation in large dynamic networks. ACM Transactions on Computer Systems 23(3), 219–252 (2005)
3. Piro, P., Carbone, M., Garofalo, G.: Distributed vs. concentrated storage options for controlling CSO volumes and pollutant loads. Water Practice & Technology 5, 3 (2010)
4. Campisano, A., Cabot Ple, J., Muschalla, D., Pleau, M., Vanrolleghem, P.A.: Potential and limitations of modern equipment for real time control of urban wastewater systems. Urban Water Journal 10(5), 300–311 (2013)
5. Rossman, L.A.: Storm water management model user's manual, version 5.0. National Risk Management Research Laboratory, Office of Research and Development, US Environmental Protection Agency (2010)
6. Giordano, A., Spezzano, G., Vinci, A.: Rainbow: An Intelligent Platform for Large-Scale Networked Cyber-Physical Systems. In: Proceedings of 5th International Workshop on Networks of Cooperating Objects for Smart Cities (UBICITEC), Berlin, pp. 70–85 (2014)
7. Dotsch, F., Denzinger, J., Kasinger, H., Bauer, B.: Decentralized Real-Time Control of Water Distribution Networks Using Self-Organizing Multi-agent Systems. In: Proceedings of the 2010 Fourth IEEE International Conference on Self-Adaptive and Self-Organizing Systems, pp. 223–232 (2010)
8. Wooldridge, M.: An introduction to multi-agent systems. John Wiley & Sons, Ltd. (2002)
9. Åström, K.J., Hägglund, T.: PID Controllers: Theory, Design, and Tuning. ISA: The Instrumentation, Systems, and Automation Society (1995)
10. RaspBerry online, http://www.raspberrypi.org/
11. Daneels, A., Salter, W.: What is SCADA. In: International Conference on Accelerator and Large Experimental Physics Control Systems, pp. 339–343 (1999)
12. Lee, A.: Cyber Physical Systems: Design Challenges. In: Proceedings of the 2008 11th IEEE Symposium on Object Oriented Real-Time Distributed Computing. IEEE Computer Society, Washington, DC (2008)
13. Carbone, M., Garofalo, G., Tomei, G., Piro, P.: Storm tracking based on rain gauges for flooding control in urban areas. Procedia Engineering, 256–265 (2014)

Coordination in Situated Systems: Engineering MAS Environment in TuCSoN

Stefano Mariani and Andrea Omicini

Alma Mater Studiorum–Università di Bologna
via Sacchi 3, 47521 Cesena, FC, Italy
{s.mariani,andrea.omicini}@unibo.it

Abstract. Multi-agent systems (MAS) provide a well-founded approach to the engineering of *situated systems*, where governing the *interaction* of a multiplicity of *autonomous*, distributed components with the *environment* represents one of the most critical issues. By interpreting situatedness as a *coordination* issue, in this paper we describe the TuCSoN coordination architecture for situated MAS, and show how the corresponding TuCSoN coordination technology can be effectively used for engineering MAS environment.

1 Coordination and Situatedness in MAS

Agents are not the only fundamental bricks for multi-agent systems (MAS): since MAS provide a well-founded approach to situated systems [1] – such as sensor networks [2] –, *environment* is an essential abstraction for MAS modelling and engineering [3], which needs to be suitably represented and related to agents. This is the core of the notion of *situated action* [4], as the realisation that coordinated, social, intelligent action arises from strict interaction with the environment.

Essentially, this means that in a MAS things happen not just as a result of agent *actions*, but also because of *environment change*—and, these are the two sources of *events* for a MAS. Following [5], *dependencies* – here, both agent-agent and agent-environment ones – are one of the main sources of system complexity: so, both *social* and *situated* interactions make MAS complex. Since *coordination* is essentially *managing dependencies* [5], it could be used to deal with both social and situated dependencies in a uniform way—so that coordination artefacts could be exploited to handle both social and situated interaction [6].

In this paper, we focus on the TuCSoN coordination middleware [7], and show how it supports *environment engineering* in MAS, by providing *coordination artefacts* [8] to handle situated interactions. After an overview of the TuCSoN event-driven architecture (Section 2), we focus on situatedness by describing the steps a MAS designer should follow to effectively engineer computational environments supporting agents situated action in TuCSoN (Section 3).

G. Fortino et al. (Eds.): IDCS 2014, LNCS 8729, pp. 99–110, 2014.

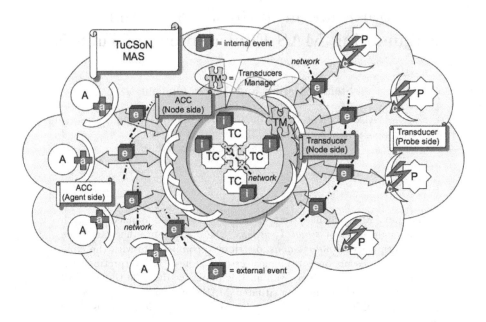

Fig. 1. In TuCSoN, both social (agent-agent) and situated (agent-environment) interactions are *mediated* by ReSpecT tuple centres. The unifying abstractions in TuCSoN are ACC and transducers (as *boundary artefacts*), the TuCSoN *event model*, and ReSpecT tuple centres (as *coordination artefacts*).

2   TuCSoN Architecture

TuCSoN [7] is a tuple-based coordination model for open, distributed MAS, providing *tuple centres* [9] as its coordination artefacts. Tuple centres are *programmable* coordination abstractions, which can encapsulate the law of MAS coordination expressed in the ReSpecT first-order logic language [9].

TuCSoN is available as a Java-based middleware[1], and is shaped upon an *event-based architecture* handling both social and situated interaction in a uniform way. Inspired by the A&A meta-model [10], the TuCSoN architecture provides two sorts of abstractions: *boundary artefacts*, to handle both agent activity and environment change within the MAS; and *social artefacts*, to govern both agent-agent and agent-environment interaction. While TuCSoN social artefacts are ReSpecT tuple centres, boundary artefacts have a twofold nature, accounting for the diverse nature of agent actions and environment change: TuCSoN individual agent interactions are handled by *agent coordination contexts* (ACC) [11], whereas *transducers* [12] deal with individual environmental resources.

The overall architecture of the TuCSoN coordination middleware is depicted in Fig. 1. Its main components are the following:

---

[1] http://tucson.unibo.it

agents — Any computational entity willing to exploit TuCSoN coordination services is a TuCSoN *agent*. In order to do so, an agent should request and obtain an ACC (see below) from the TuCSoN node it is willing to interact with. Any action from any agent towards the MAS – either social or situated – is then mediated by its associated ACC. Since TuCSoN deals with agent observable behaviour only, the inner structure and dynamics of individual agents is of no concern for the TuCSoN coordination model and middleware.

ACC — *Agent coordination contexts* [11] are TuCSoN boundary artefacts devoted to agents. ACC both enable and constrain agents interactions through an API including only the *admissible operations*: in particular, ACC map every agent operation into *events*, dispatching them to the target tuple centre. As depicted in Fig. 1, the implementation of ACC is actually split in two:

- the *agent side* is responsible for filtering admissible operations then generate events accordingly, dispatching them to its *node side* sibling;
- the *node side* of the ACC listens for its sibling requests, dispatching them to the target tuple centre then waiting for the outcome of the coordination process to send the reply back to the agent side.

The resulting bi-directional communication channel decouples agents from MAS in control, reference, space, and time.

probes — Environmental resources in TuCSoN are called *probes*. They are dealt with either as sources of perceptions (aka *sensors*) or makers of actions (aka *actuators*), or even both, in a uniform way. In fact, actions over probes are called *situation operations*, and are operated by transducers (see below): in the same way as agents, probes do not directly interact with the MAS, but through their associated transducer mediation.

transducers — Analogously to ACC for agents, TuCSoN *transducers* [12] are the boundary artefacts devoted to probes. Each probe is assigned to a trans-

Table 1. ReSpecT situated *event model*

$$\langle Event \rangle ::= \langle StartCause \rangle , \langle Cause \rangle , \langle Evaluation \rangle$$
$$\langle StartCause \rangle , \langle Cause \rangle ::= \langle Activity \rangle \mid \langle Change \rangle , \langle Source \rangle , \langle Target \rangle , \langle Time \rangle , \langle Space{:}Place \rangle$$
$$\langle Source \rangle , \langle Target \rangle ::= \langle AgentId \rangle \mid \langle CoordArtefactId \rangle \mid \langle EnvResId \rangle \mid \bot$$
$$\langle Evaluation \rangle ::= \bot \mid \{ \langle Result \rangle \}$$

Table 2. ReSpecT *triggering events*

$$\langle Activity \rangle ::= \langle Operation \rangle \mid \langle Situation \rangle$$
$$\langle Operation \rangle ::= \texttt{out}(\langle Tuple \rangle) \mid (\texttt{in} \mid \texttt{rd} \mid \texttt{no} \mid \texttt{inp} \mid \texttt{rdp} \mid \texttt{nop}) (\langle Template \rangle [, \langle Term \rangle])$$
$$\langle Situation \rangle ::= \texttt{getEnv}(\langle Key \rangle , \langle Value \rangle) \mid \texttt{setEnv}(\langle Key \rangle , \langle Value \rangle)$$
$$\langle Change \rangle ::= \texttt{env}(\langle Key \rangle , \langle Value \rangle) \mid \texttt{time}(\langle Time \rangle) \mid$$
$$\texttt{from}(\langle Space \rangle , \langle Place \rangle) \mid \texttt{to}(\langle Space \rangle , \langle Place \rangle)$$

ducer, which is specialised to handle events from that probe, and to act on probes through situation operations. Like ACC, transducers are split in two run-time components: the probe side monitors resources for changes – to be mapped into events, then dispatched (*sensor mode*) – and listens to its node side counterpart for action requests—to be actually carried out on the probe (*actuator mode*); the node side of the transducer listens for its sibling notifications – dispatching them to the target tuple centre (sensor mode) – and monitors the tuple centre for action requests—dispatching them to the probe side for execution (actuator mode). Hence, another bi-directional communication channel is established, decoupling in control, reference, space, and time probes from tuple centres.

events — TuCSoN adopts and generalises the ReSpecT [9] *event model*, depicted in Table 1: events are the run-time data structure represent both agent- and environment-related in a uniform way—as depicted in Table 2. In particular, TuCSoN events record: the *immediate* and *primary* cause of the event, its outcome, who is the source of the event, who is its target, when and where the event was generated. As depicted in Fig. 1, ACC and transducers translate external events into TuCSoN events that tuple centres can handle to implement the policies required for MAS coordination.

tuple centres — ReSpecT *tuple centres* [9] are the TuCSoN architectural component implementing coordination artefacts, thus in charge of managing dependencies. As such, they are meant to *govern* interactions – thus enacting coordination – while *decoupling* (in control, reference, space, and time) dependencies between agent actions and environment changes—in other words, both social and situated interactions [6]. By adopting ReSpecT tuple centres, TuCSoN relies on *(i)* the ReSpecT language to program coordination laws, and *(ii)* the ReSpecT situated event model to implement events.

In particular, ReSpecT tuple centres are *programmable* (first-order) logic tuple spaces [9] based on the tuProlog[2] engine for logic-based reasoning and knowledge representation. As such, they allow MAS designers to program custom *coordination laws*, by associating *events* generated by agent actions as well as by environment changes to (logic-based) computations. The association is implemented by means of *reaction specification tuples*, a special kind of first-order logic tuples whose structure is `reaction(E,G,R)`, where: E is the *triggering event* causing reaction scheduling, G is the conjunction of *guard predicates* to fine-select reactions for execution, R is the *reaction* to execute, that is, the computations to be carried out in response to the selected event.

Summing up, TuCSoN tackles the issue of coordination in situated system with a uniform and coherent set of components: ACC and transducers represent coordinated entities (agents as well as the environment) in the MAS, then translate activities and changes coming from them in a common event model (ReSpecT situated event model); tuple centres coordinate both social and situated dependencies by allowing the management of such events to be programmed.

---

[2] `http://tuprolog.unibo.it`

3 Environment Engineering in TuCSoN: A Case Study

By adopting the designers standpoint to focus on TuCSoN architectural components providing support to environment engineering, in the following we show how to deal with situated systems using TuCSoN. Thus, in the remainder of this section we discuss how to implement probes and transducers, how to make the TuCSoN middleware aware of them, and how to program TuCSoN tuple centres to inspect and manipulate TuCSoN situatedness-related events.

Generally speaking, designing a situated MAS with TuCSoN would amount at dealing with the following tasks:

1. Implementing the probes—sensor probes and actuator probes. Typically, this does not require implementing, e.g., the software drivers for the resources: designers can simply wrap existing drivers in a Java class interacting with TuCSoN transducers, implementing the ISimpleProbe Java interface (Fig. 2).
2. Implementing the transducers associated to the sensor and actuator probes by extending the TuCSoN AbstractTransducer Java class (Fig. 4).
3. Interacting with the *transducer manager* singleton entity (Fig. 1) to request its services, which is responsible for probes and transducers association in TuCSoN. The transducer manager listens to incoming requests for probes (de)registration and transducers (de)association, booting and setting up the two sibling sides of the transducer—the node and probe sides.
4. Programming TuCSoN tuple centres with ReSpecT in order to implement the coordination policies that, along with TuCSoN agents, represent the logic of the application.

As a running example, we refer to the simple scenario implemented in package alice.tucson.examples.situatedness within TuCSoN latest distribution[3]: its simplicity allows us to clearly describe design and implementation issues without losing in completeness.

There, a situated, "intelligent" thermostat (Thermostat.java) is in charge of keeping a room temperature between 18 and 22 degrees. To this end, it interacts with a sensor (ActualSensor.java) and an actuator (ActualActuator.java): the former is queried by the thermostat to perceive the temperature, whereas the latter is prompted to change the temperature upon need. Both the sensor and the actuator, as probes, interface with the MAS (which, in this simple case, is represented by the thermostat TuCSoN agent alone) through one transducer each (respectively, SensorTransducer.java and ActuatorTransducer.java).

According to the TuCSoN architecture depicted in Fig. 1, in order to promote distribution of the application logic the transducers and the thermostat are associated each with their own tuple centre (tempTc for the thermostat agent, sensorTc for the sensor transducer and actuatorTc for the actuator transducer), suitably programmed through ReSpecT reactions (sensorSpec.rsp for the sensor transducer and actuatorSpec.rsp for the actuator transducer) that handle the specific interaction with the MAS. Finally, the core logic of

---

[3] TuCSoN-1.10.5.0208, available at http://tucson.unibo.it.

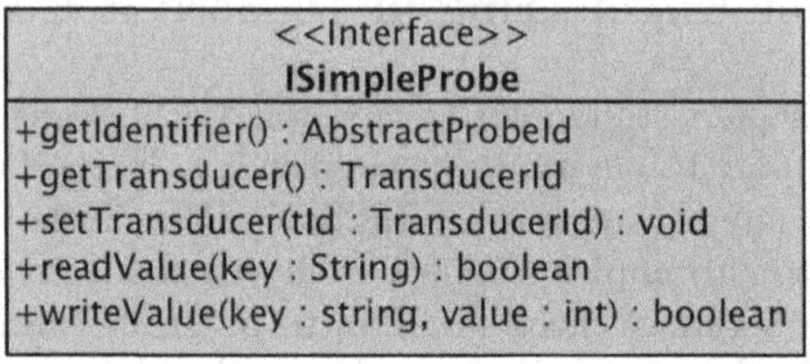

<<Interface>>
ISimpleProbe
+getIdentifier() : AbstractProbeId
+getTransducer() : TransducerId
+setTransducer(tId : TransducerId) : void
+readValue(key : String) : boolean
+writeValue(key : string, value : int) : boolean

Fig. 2. Interface to be implemented by probes

```
1  @Override
   public boolean readValue(final String key) {
3      // field 'tid' stores transducer's id
       if (this.tid == null) {
5          // no transducer associated yet!
           return false;
7      }
       // field 'transducer' stores transducer's reference
9      if (this.transducer == null) {
           this.transducer = TransducersManager.INSTANCE.getTransducer(
11                            this.tid.getAgentName()
                           );
13     }
       try {
15         // probe's interaction logic
           ...
17         this.transducer.notifyEnvEvent(
               key, value, AbstractTransducer.GET_MODE // sensor
19         );
           ...
21         return true;
       } catch (...) {
23         return false;
       }
25 }
```

Fig. 3. Stripped-down version of the code from `ActualSensor.java`. Method `writeValue` in `ActualActuator` class is similar, thus not reported here.

the application is implemented through the `Thermostat` Java class in package `alice.tucson.examples.situatedness`.

More specifically, task 1 just requires MAS designers to implement the five methods of the `ISimpleProbe` interface (Fig. 2) as a non-abstract Java class—in our example, classes `ActualSensor.java` and `ActualActuator.java`:

`getIdentifier` — retrieving this probe ID
`getTransducer` — retrieving this probe associated transducer—if any
`setTransducer` — to associate an existing transducer to this probe
`readValue` — to *perceive* the resource—mandatory for sensors
`writeValue` — to *act* on the resource—mandatory for actuators

Whereas the probe ID is assigned by the programmer at construction time, its association with the transducer occurs dynamically at run-time—hence the

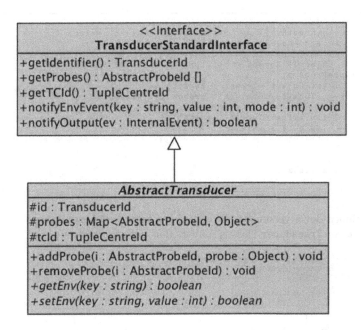

Fig. 4. Class to be extended by custom transducers and its interface

setTransducer method is usually called by the TuCSoN middleware. To operate on the probe, the methods readValue and/or writeValue (depending on whether the probe can behave as a sensor, an actuator, or both) should implement the logic required to interact with the actual probe—either a simulated environmental resource, or a real-world object. By completing task 1, the probe side of the transducer is partially implemented, as depicted in Fig. 1.

Since the transducer logic is fixed – in particular, capturing events from both probes and tuple centres – an abstract Java class is provided for extension by the TuCSoN middleware for task 2: AbstractTransducer implementing TransducerStandardInterface—as depicted in Fig. 4. Therefore, only two methods have to be implemented:

getEnv — to *sense* an environmental property change—usually, implemented by transducers assigned to sensors
setEnv — to *effect* an environmental property change—usually, implemented by transducers assigned to actuators

Both methods are automatically called by the TuCSoN middleware whenever an event generated by an environmental property change is raised either by the associated probe (the notifyEnvEvent method in TransducerStandardInterface—see Fig. 3) or by the associated tuple centre (the notifyOutput method in TransducerStandardInterface automatically called by the TuCSoN middleware in response to ReSpecT primitives such as getEnv—see Fig. 9). Such methods have

```
1   @Override
    public boolean setEnv(final String key, final int value) {
3       boolean success = true;
        // field 'probes' stores this transducer's probes
5       final Object[] keySet = this.probes.keySet().toArray();
        ISimpleProbe p;
7       for (final Object element : keySet) {
            p = (ISimpleProbe) this.probes.get(element);
9           // try to effect the property change
            if (!p.writeValue(key, value)) {
11              success = false;
                break;
13          }
        }
15      return success;
    }
```

Fig. 5. Stripped-down version of the code from `ActuatorTransducer.java`. Method `getEnv` in `SensorTransducer` class is similar, thus not reported here.

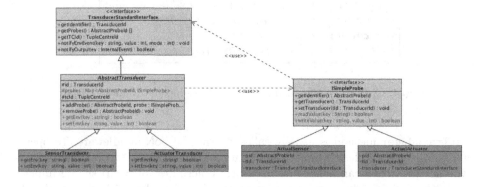

Fig. 6. Dependencies among transducers and probes. Transducers dispatch to probes the requests to undertake the situation actions issued by agents (`AbstractTransducer` methods in red font), whereas probes rely on transducers to notify the outcome of a situation operation back to agents (`ISimpleProbe` methods in red font).

to be implemented so as to actually dispatch to the probes the command to either sense an environmental property (method `getEnv`) or change it (method `setEnv`)—the simplest possible implementation is shown in Fig. 5 in the actuator case. Fig. 6 sums up the dependencies existing between transducers and probes.

Tasks 1, 2 complete the implementation of the transducer probe side, also automatically achieving part of the transducer node side (see Fig. 1). Once both probes and transducers are implemented, MAS designers should exploit TuCSoN services in order to register such components and to associate them through the transducer manager, which exposes the following API (Fig. 7):

`createTransducer` — to create a new transducer associated to the given probe and bound to the given tuple centre

| <<enumeration>> |
| TransducersManager |
| -probesToTransducersMap : Map<TransducerId, List<AbstractProbeId>> |
| -transducersList : Map<TransducerId, AbstractTransducer> |
| -transducersToTupleCentresMap : Map<TupleCentreId, List<TransducerId>> |
| +createTransducer(className : string, id : TransducerId, tcId : TupleCentreId, probeId : AbstractProbeId) : boolean |
| +addProbe(id : AbstractProbeId, tId : TransducerId, probe : ISimpleProbe) : boolean |
| +removeProbe(probe : AbstractProbeId) : boolean |
| +getTransducer(tId : string) : TransducerStandardInterface |
| +stopTransducer(id : TransducerId) : void |

Fig. 7. The transducer manager

addProbe — to attach a probe to a given transducer

removeProbe — to detach a probe from its transducer

getTransducer — to retrieve a transducer reference given its id

stopTransducer — to destroy a given transducer

Such methods are usually exploited by the agent in charge of configuring the MAS—in our case, the Thermostat class. It is worth to notice that in order to enable dynamic and distributed addition/removal of transducers and probes, as well as dynamic change of their associations, all the services are also available via TuCSoN coordination operations. In particular, TuCSoN agents may benefit from transducer manager services also by emitting special tuples in the built-in '$ENV' tuple centre, available in any TuCSoN node—the syntax of such tuples can be found in TuCSoN official guide[4]. This is, e.g., the choice of the Thermostat class as shown in Fig. 8, which establishes the communication channel depicted in Fig. 1 between the transducer probe side and its node side sibling. Furthermore, a tuple centre is chosen as the coordination medium programmed to effectively enable situated interactions between agents and the tuple centre associated transducer.

The last development task MAS designers have to undertake so as to correctly exploit TuCSoN situated coordination services is to connect the agents and the environment – technically, the probes – by means of the TuCSoN tuple centres, programmed via the ReSpecT language. In fact, as described in Section 2, agents and probes – or better, ACC and transducers – do not directly interact: all the interactions happen through coordination operations provided by the TuCSoN middleware—in particular, by TuCSoN tuple centres. Therefore, focussing on situation operations, whenever agents need to interact with a probe, they perform a coordination operation on the tuple centre bound to the transducer responsible for that probe. This is what makes it possible to reify situation operations into ReSpecT events, which are to be managed by ReSpecT reactions—and thus govern the overall event-driven MAS [6].

In the case of our thermostat scenario, taking into account the situated interaction with the sensor (ActualSensor.java), the ReSpecT specification tuples

---

[4] http://www.slideshare.net/andreaomicini/
the-tucson-coordination-model-technology-a-guide.

```
2    public static void main(final String[] args) {
         ...
4        final TucsonTupleCentreId configTc =
             new TucsonTupleCentreId(" '$ENV'" , Thermostat.DEFAULT_HOST,
6                Thermostat.DEFAULT_PORT);
         ...
         // tuple reifying createTransducer method call
8        final LogicTuple sensorTuple = new LogicTuple(
             "createTransducerSensor",
10           new TupleArgument(sensorTc.toTerm()), // the transducer's tuple centre
             new Value( // the class implementing it
12               "alice.tucson.examples.situatedness.SensorTransducer"),
             new Value("sensorTransducer"),
14           new Value( // the class implementing its probe
                 "alice.tucson.examples.situatedness.ActualSensor"),
16           new Value("sensor"));
         acc.out(configTc, sensorTuple, null);
18       ...
```

Fig. 8. Stripped-down version of the code from `Thermostat.java`. Insertion in `'$ENV'` tuple centre of the tuple built in lines 9 − 17 is equivalent to call method `crateTransducer` on the transducer manager. Nevertheless, this allows the exploitation of the services of a given TuCSoN node from a remote location—in fact, `configTc` may store the id of a remote tuple centre, deployed on another node of the network w.r.t. the caller.

```
reaction(
2    in(sense(temp(T))), // agent request
     (operation, invocation),
4    sensor@localhost:20504 ? getEnv(temp, T) // perception ''request''
).
6  reaction(
     getEnv(temp, T), // perception ''reply''
8    (from_env, completion), // environment filter
     out(sense(temp(T)))
10 ).
```

Fig. 9. Stripped-down version of the code from `sensorSpec.rsp` in package `alice.tucson.examples.situatedness` within current TuCSoN distribution (`TuCSoN-1.10.5.0207`). `'sensor'` is the probe ID of the probe target of the situation operation request: the id of its transducers is automatically retrieved by TuCSoN middleware at run-time, hence transducer mediation is transparent to the ReSpecT programmer.

in Fig. 9 have to be put in the tuple centre associated to the sensor transducer (`'sensorTc'`, bound to `TransducerSensor.java` which is responsible for `'sensor'` probe).

Although the code shown in Fig. 9 is taken from our specific example, the ReSpecT program is quite general, since it implements a pattern that is basically valid for any situated interaction:

- reaction 1−5 maps agents coordination operations requests (external events) into situation operations commands (internal events)
- reaction 6−10 maps situation operation replies (from probes, external events) into coordination operations outcomes (internal events)

```
2      /* Start perception-reason-action loop */
       LogicTuple template;
       ITucsonOperation op;
4      int temp;
       LogicTuple action = null;
6      for (int i = 0; i < Thermostat.ITERS; i++) {
          /* Perception */
8         template = LogicTuple.parse("sense(temp(_))");
          op = acc.in(sensorTc, template, null); // see line 2 in Fig.9
10        if (op.isResultSuccess()) {
             temp = op.getLogicTupleResult().getArg(0).getArg(0).intValue();
12           /* Reason */
             if ((temp >= Thermostat.LOW) && (temp <= Thermostat.HIGH)) {
14              continue;
             } else if (temp < Thermostat.LOW) {
16              action = LogicTuple.parse("act(temp(" + ++temp + "))");
             } else if (temp > Thermostat.HIGH) {
18              action = LogicTuple.parse("act(temp(" + --temp + "))");
             }
20           /* Action */
             // 'act' ReSpecT reactions are similar to those in Fig.9
             acc.out(actuatorTc, action, null);
22        }
       }
24     }
```

Fig. 10. Stripped-down version of the code from `Thermostat.java`. Notice the thermostat interacts solely with TuCSoN tuple centres, being transducers (thus probes) interactions transparently delegated to the TuCSoN middleware—through the ReSpecT reactions in Fig. 9.

By completing task 4 through ReSpecT reactions programming, MAS designers explicitly exploit the ReSpecT event model – in particular its triggering events listed in Table 2 – to support situatedness, binding together events coming from the agent through its ACC with events going toward the environment through its transducer (Fig. 9, reaction $1-5$)—and, dually, from the environment toward the agents (Fig. 9, reaction $6-10$). Technically, this last step in MAS design using TuCSoN links the node side of ACC with the node side of transducers, enacting the very notion of situatedness.

The last code snippet in Fig. 10 is meant to show how the application logic – the thermostat aimed at keeping temperature between LOW and HIGH thresholds – is linked to the "situatedness machinery"—sensor and actuator probes as well as their transducers. In particular, line 10 shows TuCSoN coordination operation invocation causing ReSpecT reactions in Fig. 9 to trigger, leading to stimulate `ActualSensor` through its transducer `SensorTransducer`—transparently to the designer of the application logic. Conversely, line 27 shows how `Thermostat` interacts with `ActualActuator` (through its transducer `ActuatorTransducer`) to properly command the needed temperature adjustments—again, transparently.

The same sort of transparency is provided to ReSpecT programmers – as they have no need to know the internal machinery of probes, but just transducer API – as well as to probes programmers—since they only deal with `ISimpleProbe` and `TransducerStandardInterface` API. This promotes and supports a clear *separation of concerns*: application logic (agent) programmers, coordination (ReSpecT) programmers, and environment (probes and transducers) programmers each may focus on their task, just relying on others adhering to TuCSoN API.

4 Conclusion

In this paper we describe how the TuCSoN coordination middleware can be effectively used to handle environment interaction in situated systems modelled and engineered as MAS [1]. In particular, we first present the TuCSoN event-driven architecture, overviewing TuCSoN main architectural abstractions, then we discuss how to exploit them for engineering MAS environment, by illustrating a simple example of situated MAS based on the TuCSoN middleware.

References

1. Fortino, G., Garro, A., Mascillaro, S., Russo, W.: Using event-driven lightweight DSC-based agents for MAS modelling. International Journal of Agent-Oriented Software Engineering 4(2), 113–140 (2010)
2. Aiello, F., Bellifemine, F.L., Fortino, G., Galzarano, S., Gravina, R.: An agent-based signal processing in-node environment for real-time human activity monitoring based on wireless body sensor networks. Engineering Applications of Artificial Intelligence 24(7), 1147–1161 (2011)
3. Weyns, D., Omicini, A., Odell, J.J.: Environment as a first-class abstraction in multi-agent systems. Autonomous Agents and Multi-Agent Systems 14(1), 5–30 (2007)
4. Suchman, L.A.: Situated actions. In: Plans and Situated Actions: The Problem of Human-Machine Communication, pp. 49–67. Cambridge University Press, New York (1987)
5. Malone, T.W., Crowston, K.: The interdisciplinary study of coordination. ACM Computing Surveys 26(1), 87–119 (1994)
6. Omicini, A., Mariani, S.: Coordination for situated MAS: Towards an event-driven architecture. In: Moldt, D., Rölke, H. (eds.) International Workshop on Petri Nets and Software Engineering (PNSE 2013). CEUR Workshop Proceedings, vol. 989, pp. 17–22. Sun SITE Central Europe, RWTH Aachen University (August 6, 2013)
7. Omicini, A., Zambonelli, F.: Coordination for Internet application development. Autonomous Agents and Multi-Agent Systems 2(3), 251–269 (1999)
8. Omicini, A., Ricci, A., Viroli, M., Castelfranchi, C., Tummolini, L.: Coordination artifacts: Environment-based coordination for intelligent agents. In: Jennings, N.R., Sierra, C., Sonenberg, L., Tambe, M. (eds.) 3rd international Joint Conference on Autonomous Agents and Multiagent Systems (AAMAS 2004), vol. 1, pp. 286–293. ACM, New York (2004)
9. Omicini, A., Denti, E.: From tuple spaces to tuple centres. Science of Computer Programming 41(3), 277–294 (2001)
10. Omicini, A., Ricci, A., Viroli, M.: Artifacts in the A&A meta-model for multi-agent systems. Autonomous Agents and Multi-Agent Systems 17(3), 432–456 (2008)
11. Omicini, A.: Towards a notion of agent coordination context. In: Marinescu, D.C., Lee, C. (eds.) Process Coordination and Ubiquitous Computing, pp. 187–200. CRC Press, Boca Raton (2002)
12. Casadei, M., Omicini, A.: Situated tuple centres in ReSpecT. In: Shin, S.Y., Ossowski, S., Menezes, R., Viroli, M. (eds.) 24th Annual ACM Symposium on Applied Computing (SAC 2009), vol. III, pp. 1361–1368. ACM, Honolulu (2009)

Experimental Evaluation of the CoAP, HTTP and SPDY Transport Services for Internet of Things

Laila Daniel[1], Markku Kojo[1] and Mikael Latvala[2]

[1] Department of Computer Science, University of Helsinki, Finland
[2] Mosa Consulting, Finland
{ldaniel,kojo}@cs.helsinki.fi,
mikael.latvala@mosa-consulting.com

Abstract. Internet of Things (IoT) seeks to broaden the scope of the Internet by connecting a variety of devices that can communicate with the Internet. Transport services for IoT are crucial in enabling the applications to communicate reliably and in a timely manner while making efficient and fair use of the potentially scarce network resources. The communication with IoT devices is often implemented using HyperText Transfer Protocol (HTTP) or a specifically designed protocol such as Constrained Application Protocol (CoAP) that is a specialized web transfer protocol for constrained nodes and networks. In this paper we discuss various options for modifying or adapting HTTP to offer better transport service for IoT environments. We consider HTTP, SPDY that has been developed to speed up HTTP in general, IoT-HTTP and IoT-SPDY that are adaptations of HTTP and SPDY for IoT, and CoAP as transport services for IoT and experimentally evaluate their performance. The results of our experiments show that CoAP has the lowest object download times and the least number of bytes transferred compared to the other four transport services. IoT-HTTP and IoT-SPDY have around 50% shorter object download times and smaller number of bytes transferred compared to HTTP and SPDY.

1   Introduction

Internet of Things (IoT) refers to an emerging scenario in which a variety of Things (devices, appliances, sensors) equipped with Internet connectivity are embedded in various settings such as automobiles, buildings, homes, forests, etc. and can be used to collect data, communicate and make decisions with or without human intervention [1]. This scenario is interesting and has a wide range of applications in a variety of fields including environment monitoring, surveillance, emergency and rescue, and health care.

To extend the Internet services to IoT devices, a suitable transport service is needed. As the IoT devices have limited resources in terms of computation, communication, radio and battery life, the transport services should be simple, scalable, robust, efficient in making near-optimal use of resources, easy to maintain and deploy and also customisable to the need of the applications.

HyperText Transfer Protocol (HTTP) [12] is the de facto standard for information transfer in the Internet. It operates in a request-reply mode in a client-server environment on top of the Transmission Control Protocol (TCP) [19]. HTTP is often used to

G. Fortino et al. (Eds.): IDCS 2014, LNCS 8729, pp. 111–123, 2014.

implement the communication with IoT devices as it enables the IoT devices to connect to the Internet easily and directly. The main problems in using HTTP in an IoT environment are the lengthy HTTP headers and the need to establish TCP/IP sessions for each request-reply data transfer.

SPDY [5, 9] is a transport service developed by Google to speed up HTTP. It multiplexes several HTTP transactions with priorities over a single TCP connection and employs header compression to reduce data volume of the HTTP headers. Even though SPDY uses header compression, SPDY has the 'verbose' headers of HTTP in addition to the need to establish a TCP connection for data transfer.

Constrained Application Protocol (CoAP) [22] is a transport service designed specially considering the requirement of constrained devices such as sensors and IoT devices. As CoAP has a short binary header, the header overhead in transferring data can be kept at very low level. On the other hand, a CoAP-HTTP proxy is needed to connect a CoAP client to an HTTP server or vice-versa. The IETF RFC on CoAP [22] defines a basic mapping between HTTP and CoAP. In addition, deploying proxies can have scalability issues.

In this paper we examine whether HTTP and SPDY can be adapted to favourably compare with CoAP as they can directly connect the IoT devices to the Internet without the need for proxies. In order to have comparable performance with CoAP in terms of object download time and total bytes transferred to fetch an object, we propose minimizing the HTTP and SPDY headers along with TCP enhancements. We use an extension to TCP known as TCP Fast Open [10, 20] to reduce the object download time. We refer to the enhanced HTTP and SPDY proposed here as IoT-HTTP and IoT-SPDY. The results of our experiments show that by using IoT-HTTP and IoT-SPDY there is at least 50% reduction in object download time and bytes transferred compared to HTTP and SPDY. However, we note that CoAP still has at least 50% lower download time and needs fewer bytes to fetch an object compared to IoT-HTTP and IoT-SPDY respectively.

The organisation of the rest of the paper is as follows. Section 2 describes the related work and Section 3 describes the proposed transport services IoT-HTTP and IoT-SPDY in detail. Section 4 presents an experimental evaluation of different transport services in an IoT environment. Section 5 discusses some additional enhancements to IoT-HTTP and IoT-SPDY that need further evaluation and study. Section 6 concludes the paper.

2   Related Work

Relatively few studies are available in the literature on the comparison with CoAP and HTTP in wireless sensor networks. A comparative study of CoAP and HTTP in terms of mote's (wireless sensor node) energy consumption and response time carried out using simulations and experiments in real sensor networks is given in [11]. The simulation results on energy consumption by motes show that energy consumed by CoAP is about half that of HTTP in processing packets while in transmitting packets CoAP consumes only one fourth. The experiments in real sensor networks show that CoAP's response time is nine times lower than the response time of HTTP. CoAP and HTTP are evaluated in a use case of an intelligent cargo container that transmits information such as temperature, humidity of fruits and meat inside a container during land or sea

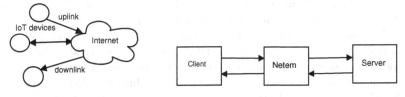

Fig. 1. Typical IoT Topology   **Fig. 2.** Experimental Setup

transportation [16]. The results show that CoAP transfers smaller number of bytes and that it features shorter retrieval times compared to HTTP. The authors also compare CoAP/UDP with HTTP/TCP and HTTP/UDP and the results show that HTTP/TCP has longer retrieval times compared to UDP based protocols due to the initial TCP connection establishment. Paper [18] evaluates HTTP/TCP, HTTP/UDP with TinyCoAP, a CoAP implementation in TinyOS [6]. It shows that for transferring small objects, HTTP/UDP is a better choice than TinyCoAP while for transferring large payloads TinyCoAP has the best performance in terms of latency and energy. Analysis of CoAP and HTTP in IoT environments using the total cost of ownership (TCO) model is given in [17]. The paper shows that CoAP is more cost-efficient than HTTP when smart devices communicate frequently with each other. Also CoAP is found to be economically preferable when the charging of the communication is based on the volume of transferred data. The survey paper [14] gives a detailed description on the IETF Standardization in the field of the Internet of Things (IoT) and also compares HTTP and CoAP as the transport services in IoT environments.

In presenting our work, we are not aware of any previous studies that evaluate CoAP, HTTP and SPDY in a comparative manner.

3   Transport Services for IoT

In this section we describe briefly the requirements for an IoT transport service and discuss the five transport services we consider in this paper.

The IoT transport service should provide easy connectivity to the Internet. In this study we are focusing on the IoT topology as shown in Figure 1 where the IoT devices are directly connected to the Internet. The IoT devices may also be connected to a gateway or to a base station that has a connectivity to the Internet. To connect the IoT devices to the Internet, the transport service should be compatible with TCP/IP protocol suite, should be an open standard and proven to be scalable. So in our study we only consider transport services based on HTTP, SPDY or CoAP that are Internet Engineering Task Force (IETF) specified.

The transport services should provide congestion control to regulate the data flow that applications may send to the network and achieve some sort of fairness in sharing the scarce network resources. Even though reliable data transfer is not always a requirement, the transport service should provide reliable data delivery if the application needs it. Congestion control and reliable data delivery may be the functions of the underlying transport protocols. If these functions are not provided by the underlying transport protocol, they may need to be implemented at the upper layers. The congestion control and the reliability mechanisms needed depend on the mode of data transfer between the IoT devices and the Internet. In push data and request-reply modes of data transfer where a small amount of data from the IoT devices are to be transferred, simple congestion control and reliability mechanisms are needed. On the other hand as data volume increases as in continuous data transfer like imaging data from a habitat, more advanced mechanisms to enforce congestion control and reliability are called for.

As HTTP [12] is the de facto standard of information transfer in the Internet, the main advantage of using HTTP as a transport service is that any device with HTTP can be directly connected to the Internet. Another advantage of using HTTP is that TCP which is the transport protocol for HTTP provides congestion control and reliability. HTTP operates in a request-reply mode in a client-server environment. The client request is called the GET request and the reply for the GET request from the server is known as the ACCEPT message. The header overhead associated with GET and ACCEPT messages is quite large for transferring data in push data and request-reply modes, when only a small amount of payload bytes are to be transferred from the IoT devices to the Internet. As HTTP uses TCP, the connection establishment takes at least one round-trip time(RTT) before the actual data transfer can take place. So for short transfers like in push data and request-reply modes, the connection establishment time may be longer than the time taken for actual data transfer.

SPDY [5, 9] is a transport service developed by Google to make HTTP faster i.e., to reduce the latency of applications that use HTTP. SPDY can be placed at the session layer in the OSI model where the application layer protocol is HTTP. To speed up the HTTP requests and responses, SPDY allows many concurrent HTTP requests in a single SPDY session over a single TCP connection. These concurrent requests are called streams that are bi-directional flows of bytes across a virtual channel in a SPDY session. Using a SYN_STREAM control frame, a stream can be created and a stream ID is associated with each stream. In the SYN_STREAM frame, additional information such as upload bandwidth, download bandwidth, round-trip time, initial window size can be sent through the HEADER block's name/value pairs. The name/value pairs, also known as ID/value pairs in the header block are usually compressed. After the SYN exchange, client and server send a SETTINGS frame that contains the configuration data and this data can be used for future connections from the same IP address and from the same TCP port. SPDY compresses HTTP headers resulting in fewer packets and fewer bytes to be transmitted thereby reducing the bandwidth used by HTTP. SPDY enables the server to initiate the communications with the client and push data to the client whenever possible. SPDY also uses the SSL protocol for security. Google claims that with SPDY around 50% reduction in pageload time can be achieved [5].

CoAP [22] is a transport service for use with constrained devices (devices with low power, small memory and lossy links) and constrained networks. CoAP operates in a request-response mode and its transport layer protocol is UDP. As CoAP has a short binary header of four bytes, the small header overhead in transferring a request-response type of messages suits well for IoT environments. There is no connection establishment phase as CoAP operates over UDP which is a connectionless datagram protocol. CoAP supports optional reliability with exponential backoff for messages. Many issues are associated with using CoAP as a transport service for IoT devices. To directly connect the IoT devices to the Internet, a CoAP-HTTP proxy is needed and the scalability of proxies is always a concern. The IETF RFC on CoAP [22] defines a basic mapping between CoAP and HTTP. As this RFC is very recent, future changes in CoAP may pose challenges to the mapping between CoAP and HTTP. CoAP supports optional reliability with exponential retransmission timeout backoff to implement a simple congestion control mechanism.

In this paper we propose IoT-HTTP and IoT-SPDY in which we seek for adapting HTTP and SPDY, respectively, to make them better suit as transport services for IoT. In IoT-HTTP and IoT-SPDY, we minimize the headers associated with HTTP GET request and ACCEPT message and also enhance TCP with TCP Fast Open [10, 20], a mechanism that reduces the connection establishment time for successive TCP connections between two end points. In IoT-HTTP and IoT-SPDY, TCP SACK option and TCP timestamps option are disabled. By disabling TCP timestamps option, 12 bytes can be saved with every TCP segment.

For IoT-HTTP, we have implemented a simple web server and client to minimize the HTTP headers associated with GET request and ACCEPT message. When a legacy browser is used as the Web client for HTTP and SPDY, the GET request includes the GET method itself, and the details of the operating system, date and time, accepted data types, encoding schemes, encryption schemes, etc., whereas IoT-HTTP GET request adds only the protocol name as HTTP and the IP address of the server. In IoT-HTTP, the ACCEPT message contains only the protocol name HTTP with version, a short server name and the content type. Thus in IoT-HTTP, the Web client has thinned down the headers significantly. In IoT-SPDY, to minimize the headers, spdy-python [13] is used as the SPDY client and spdyd [23] is used as the SPDY server. In addition to reducing header data volume for IoT-HTTP and IoT-SPDY, we employ TCP Fast Open (TFO) [10, 20] with IoT-HTTP and IoT-SPDY.

TCP Fast Open (TFO) [10, 20] is an enhancement to TCP in which data transfer is allowed during TCP's initial handshake, i.e., during the SYN exchange so as to decrease the delay experienced by short TCP transfers. Usually data exchange is allowed after the SYN exchange, i.e., after one Round-trip time (RTT) and this latency is a significant portion of the latency of a short flow. TFO protocol proposes secure data transfer during SYN exchange thereby reducing the latency for HTTP transfers considerably. The security issues that arise due to the data transfer with the SYN is mitigated by a server-generated Fast Open cookie.

Figure 3 gives the TFO protocol overview. The client sends a request to the server for a Fast Open cookie with a regular SYN packet. The cookie generated by the server authenticates the client's IP address. The server sends the Fast Open cookie to the client in the SYN-ACK. The client caches this cookie and uses it for future TCP connections. Both the cookie request from the client and the issue of the cookie by the server are implemented using TCP options. Once the client gets a cookie from the server, it can use this cookie for opening new TCP connections. For new TCP connections, the client sends the SYN with TFO cookie and data. If the server finds that this is a valid cookie it sends SYN-ACK acknowledging both SYN and data, then it delivers the data to the application. The TFO Internet draft [10] states that the server may also send data with the SYN-ACK before the handshake completes if the TCP congestion control allows.

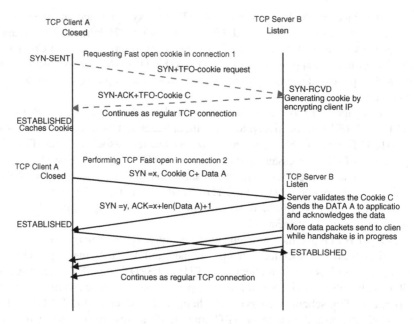

Fig. 3. TCP Fast Open protocol [10, 20]

Typically the server sends the SYN-ACK without any data and starts sending the data in subsequent packets even before the acknowledgement for SYN-ACK from the client arrives at the server. If the cookie is not valid the server drops the data and sends back a SYN-ACK, thus following the usual TCP 3-way handshake (3WHS).

In IoT scenarios where the devices have a small amount of data to be transferred reliably and quite frequently, TFO allows data transfer during the TCP SYN exchange thereby saving up to one RTT compared to standard TCP that requires a 3-way handshake which takes one RTT to complete before the data transfer.

4   Experimental Evaluation of CoAP, HTTP, SPDY, IoT-HTTP and IoT-SPDY

In this section we evaluate the transport services CoAP, HTTP, SPDY, IoT-HTTP and IoT-SPDY that are described in Section 3.

4.1   Experimental Setup

The experiments are carried out over an emulated IoT environment. The initial set of experiments are of request-response type between a client and server that communicate over an emulated link of data rate 20 Kbps, one-way link-delay of 20 ms and Maximum Transmission Unit (MTU) of 128 bytes. The above data rate, delay and MTU size roughly correspond to the data rate, latency and packet size of Zigbee [7] and is

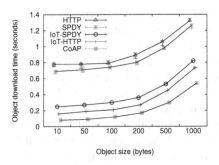
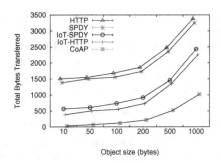

Fig. 4. Object download times for different object sizes and transport services CoAP, HTTP, SPDY, IoT-HTTP and IoT-SPDY

Fig. 5. Total bytes transferred to download objects of different sizes (includes all headers)

emulated using the network emulator, Netem [4]. Netem is a network emulator functionality in Linux that enables to emulate links of different delays, data rates, packet loss and reordering, etc. Netem is controlled by the command line tool 'tc' that allows to show/manipulate traffic control settings. In our experimental set up, shown in Figure 2, the client, server and the network emulator are hosted by x86_64 GNU/Linux machines. The client runs Ubuntu 3.8.0 and the server and emulator run Debian 3.12.2.

In our experiments, Google Chrome and Apache server are used as the client and the server with HTTP and SPDY. As the SPDY server, Apache server enabled with the module mod-spdy [3] is used. As explained in Section 3, we use a simple Web client and Web server, and we enable TCP TFO in the Linux TCP/IP stack. The IoT-SPDY client is spdy-python [13] and the IoT-SPDY server is spdyd [23]. For both IoT-SPDY client and server, TCP is enabled with TFO. Linux kernels (versions from 3.6 onwards) now support TFO. Some small modifications are needed to the client and the server to employ TFO [15]. We use the standard TCP implementation in Linux with the SACK and the timestamp options disabled. The libcoap implementation which is a C implementation of CoAP [2] is used as the CoAP server and the client.

In our test environment, the client fetches from the server a single object of size that varies from 10 bytes to 1000 bytes over an error free channel. The metrics used in the experiments are the object download time and the total bytes transferred in the request-response communication. The object download time is the duration between the time the client initiates the request for the object to the time the last byte of the object arrives at the client. In the cases of HTTP, SPDY, IoT-HTTP and IoT-SPDY, we take the time difference between the SYN request from the client to the arrival of the final byte of the object requested. We calculate these times from the tcpdumps collected at the client while running the experiments.

4.2   Results

Figure 4 shows the object download times for different object sizes when using the different transport services CoAP, HTTP, SPDY, IoT-HTTP, and IoT-SPDY. We observe from Figure 4 that the object download times increase with the size of the object requested in all the five cases. CoAP has the lowest object download times as the protocol overhead for CoAP is quite small. It can be clearly seen that TFO decreases the object download times for IoT-HTTP and IoT-SPDY. The object download time is decreased also due to the minimized headers for IoT-HTTP and IoT-SPDY. There is at least 50% reduction in object download time for IoT-HTTP and IoT-SPDY compared to HTTP and SPDY. It can be noticed from the Figure 4 that the reduction with smaller object sizes is substantially more. For example, in downloading a 10-byte object, IoT-HTTP achieves around 75 % reduction in object download time compared to HTTP.

Figure 5 shows the total bytes transferred including all headers when objects of different sizes are requested by the client from the server when using the different transport services CoAP, HTTP, SPDY, IoT-HTTP and IoT-SPDY. The amount of total bytes are calculated at the client summing up all IP packets from the first packet sent to the arrival of the last packet carrying the last byte of the object requested. As the protocol overhead is minimum for CoAP it transfers the lowest number of bytes for each object compared to that of HTTP and SPDY. SPDY's header compression accounts for the slight reduction in object download time compared to HTTP. The minimized headers and TFO are responsible for the reduction in total bytes transferred for IoT-HTTP and IoT-SPDY compared to SPDY and HTTP.

4.3   Detailed Analysis of the Results

Next we present a detailed analysis of object download time and bytes transferred for fetching an object of size 10 bytes by describing the message sequence chart (MSC) that shows the different phases of the data transfer. The message sequence chart also shows the packet types and the bytes transferred in this process.

Figure 6 shows the message sequence for HTTP when fetching an object of size 10 bytes from the server. The object download time is 790 ms. The SYN exchange phase takes about 99 ms. The size of SYN segment is 48 bytes that includes the negotiation for maximum segment size (MSS). The GET request of size 588 bytes is sent in four 128 bytes packets plus one 76 bytes packet as the MTU of the link is 128 bytes. The ACCEPT message together with the data is 502 bytes in size and is sent as four packets from the server to the client. A total number of 20 packets including the ACK packets

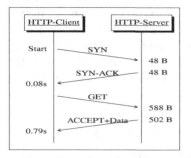

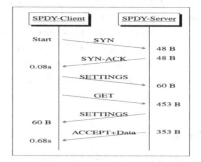

Fig. 6. Message Sequence Chart (MSC) for object download with HTTP

Fig. 7. Message Sequence Chart (MSC) for object download with SPDY

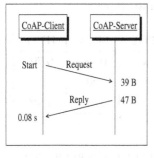

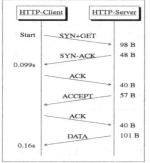

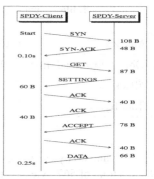

Fig. 8. MSC for object download with CoAP

Fig. 9. MSC for object download with IoT-HTTP

Fig. 10. MSC for object download with IoT-SPDY

are used and 1546 bytes including IP and TCP protocol headers are transferred to fetch an object of size 10 bytes.

Figure 7 shows the message sequence for SPDY when fetching an object of size 10 bytes from the server. It takes 680 ms to fetch an object of size 10 bytes from the server. There are two SETTINGS frames, each 60 bytes in length, transferred both from client to server and from server to client. The GET request is of size 453 bytes and is sent as four packets, while the ACCEPT message together with the data is of 353 bytes and is sent as three packets. The total number of packets transferred in this process is 20 including the ACK packets and a total of 1382 bytes are transferred including IP and TCP protocol headers. SPDY header compression accounts for the reduction of 164 bytes compared to that of HTTP transfer.

Figure 8 shows the message sequence when an object of size 10 bytes is downloaded using CoAP. CoAP takes 80 ms to download the object. CoAP uses only two packets, one request packet sent from the client to the server and one response packet from the server to the client. CoAP transfers 86 bytes including IP and UDP protocol headers.

Figure 9 shows the message sequence for IOT-HTTP to fetch an object of size 10 bytes. The object download time is 160 ms and for this process 384 bytes are transferred in six packets. Compared to the time taken when HTTP or SPDY is used to fetch an object of 10 bytes, this shorter object download time for IoT-HTTP is due to two factors, namely, the use of TFO and the reduced size of the HTTP GET request. With the use of TFO, the GET request is transferred with the SYN segment causing a reduction of one RTT. Google Chrome GET request is of size 588 bytes while in the case of IoT-HTTP, the client sends a single packet of only 98 bytes in size carrying both TCP SYN and HTTP GET request.

Figure 10 shows message sequence for IoT-SPDY taking 250 ms to fetch an object of size 10 bytes. The SYN packet contains SYN, TFO cookie and part of GET request and it has a length of 108 bytes. One SETTINGS frame of 60 bytes in length is transferred from the server to the client. The packet carrying the second part of the GET request is 87 bytes in size and the ACCEPT message with object data is carried in two packets

Table 1. Summary of the analysis of downloading a 10-byte object

Metrics	CoAP	IoT-HTTP	IoT-SPDY	SPDY	HTTP
Object download time	0.08s	0.16s	0.25s	0.68s	0.79s
#Packets	2	6	9	20	20
TotalBytes	86	384	567	1382	1546

being 78 and 66 bytes in size. The total number of packets transferred in this process is 9 and a total of 567 bytes are transferred including IP and TCP protocol headers.

Table 1 summarises the analysis of downloading a 10-byte object using the five transport services. From the above table, we observe that IoT-HTTP and IoT-SPDY have object download times closer to that of CoAP than HTTP and SPDY. With IoT-HTTP and IoT-SPDY, the object download time reduces from 50% up to 75% compared to that of HTTP and SPDY.

5   Analysis of Protocol Overhead and Discussions on Additional Enhancements

In our experiments reported in Section 4, IoT-HTTP and IoT-SPDY use TFO and minimized HTTP headers. TCP header compression and a reduced set of TCP congestion control may further improve IoT-HTTP and IoT-SPDY in IoT environments. In this section we carry out in detail the analysis of the protocol overhead involved and discuss additional enhancements to improve the performance of IoT-HTTP and IoT-SPDY.

Figure 11 shows another way to compare CoAP, IoT-HTTP and IoT-SPDY based on the protocol overhead associated with them when fetching objects of sizes 10 bytes and

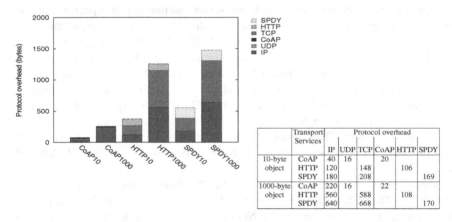

Fig. 11. Protocol overhead for downloading objects of sizes 10 bytes and 1000 bytes with CoAP, IoT-HTTP and IoT-SPDY

1000 bytes. The x-axis labels CoAP10 and CoAP1000 refer to COAP that downloads 10-byte and 1000-byte objects. Similarly, HTTP10 and HTTP1000 refer to IoT-HTTP and SPDY10 and SPDY1000 refer to IoT-SPDY that download a 10-byte and a 1000-byte objects. In the case of CoAP, out of the total 86 byes transferred to fetch a 10-byte object, IP uses 40 bytes, where UDP and CoAP use 16 bytes and 20 bytes, respectively. The TCP/IP overhead for IoT-HTTP and IoT-SPDY are 268 bytes and 388 bytes, respectively. The HTTP overhead in IoT-HTTP and the SPDY overhead in IoT-SPDY are 106 and 169 bytes, respectively.

When it comes to fetching a 1000-byte object, the object has to be divided into 11 TCP segments for IoT-HTTP and IoT-SPDY as the MTU of the emulated link is 128 bytes. For downloading the 1000-byte object, 28 IP packets are needed for IoT-HTTP including the SYN, SYN-ACK, data and acknowledgements whereas for IoT-SPDY, 32 IP packets are needed. The TCP/IP header overhead for IoT-HTTP and IoT-SPDY are 1148 bytes and 1308 bytes respectively. The HTTP and the SPDY overheads are 108 bytes and 170 bytes for IoT-HTTP and IoT-SPDY respectively. In the case of fetching the 1000-byte object using CoAP, the object is fragmented into 10 fragments and a total of 11 packets are transferred including one CoAP request and 10 CoAP reply data packets. The protocol overhead in this transfer consists of 22 bytes for CoAP, 16 bytes for UDP and 220 bytes for IP. The above analysis shows that HTTP protocol overhead in IoT-HTTP and SPDY protocol overhead in IoT-SPDY are quite large compared to CoAP. It can also be seen that TCP/IP overhead in IoT-HTTP and IoT-SPDY is much larger than UDP/IP overhead in CoAP.

Even though, SPDY has built-in header compression, the above analysis suggests that it is worth investigating the possibility to further reduce the overhead associated with SPDY. The TCP/IP overhead can be reduced significantly by using TCP header compression schemes like RObust Header Compression protocol (ROHC) [21] and thereby reducing the total bytes transferred in fetching an object.

TCP uses a sliding window mechanism that allows to send a number of TCP segments in succession without getting an acknowledgement for each segment. TCP's sliding window mechanism uses 32-bit sequence numbers and 32-bit arithmetic to implement this. In IoT scenarios where data transfer is either push mode or request-reply mode, a small number of TCP segments are sent. So instead of using the TCP sliding window mechanism, we can use TCP as a stop and wait protocol where a new segment is sent only after the sender gets the acknowledgement for the previous segment. This eliminates the processing time and the memory requirements for implementing the sliding window mechanism.

In IoT scenarios where the data transfer is either push mode or request-reply mode, we can go for the simplest congestion control mechanism of retransmission timeout (RTO). The simplified reliability and congestion control mechanisms allow a small footprint for TCP. However in bulk transfer or in continuous data flow mode of data transfer between IoT devices and base station, TCP sliding window mechanisms and congestion control mechanism based on duplicate acknowledgements (dupack) and retransmission timeout [8] can be used.

6 Summary and Future Work

In this paper we evaluated the performance of transport services HTTP, SPDY, CoAP, IoT-HTTP, and IoT-SPDY in an emulated IoT environment. HTTP, SPDY and CoAP are well-known transport services in the Internet whereas IoT-HTTP and IoT-SPDY are adaptations of HTTP and SPDY to make them better suited for IoT environments. The adaptations include minimization of the HTTP/SPDY headers, using TCP Fast Open to lower latency by reducing the TCP connection establishment time, and disabling TCP SACK and timestamps options.

The transport services are compared on the basis of object download time, the total amount of transferred bytes, and the introduced overhead. The experiments are performed in an emulated setup using Netem emulator with Zigbee-like settings and in the context of a simple request-response scenario.

As expected, our experiments show that CoAP has the lowest object download times and the least number of bytes transferred compared to that of HTTP and SPDY due to the header overhead in HTTP and the TCP connection establishment. With our proposed schemes, IoT-HTTP and IoT-SPDY, we observe that IoT-HTTP and IoT-SPDY have around 50% shorter object download times and smaller number of bytes transferred compared to HTTP and SPDY. As SPDY has built-in header compression, we suggest IoT-SPDY as a good candidate for IoT transport service. In addition, we intend to investigate the possibility to further reduce the overhead associated with SPDY and TCP. Possible targets for additional enhancements include improving SPDY's header compression scheme and RObust Header Compression (ROHC) scheme with TCP.

Acknowledgements. This work was supported by TEKES as part of the Internet of Things DIGILE (Finnish Strategic Centre for Science, Technology and Innovation in the field of ICT and digital business). We thank the anonymous reviewers for their constructive comments on our paper.

References

[1] ICT SHOK IoT programme, http://www.internetofthings.fi/
[2] libcoap: C-Implementation of CoAP,
    http://sourceforge.net/projects/libcoap
[3] mod_spdy: Apache spdy module, http://code.google.com/p/mod-spdy
[4] Netem: Network Emulator, http://manpages.ubuntu.com/
    manpages/raring/en/man8/tc-netem.8.html
[5] SPDY: An Experimental Protocol for a Faster Web,
    http://www.chromium.org/spdy/spdy-whitepaper
[6] TinyOS, http://www.tinyos.net/
[7] Zigbee, http://en.wikipedia.org/wiki/ZigBee
[8] Allman, M., Paxson, V., Blanton, E.: TCP Congestion Control. Internet RFCs, RFC 5681 (September 2009) ISSN 2070-1721
[9] Belshe, M., Peon, R.: SPDY Protocol. Internet draft "draft-mbelshe-httpbis-spdy-00", Work in progress (February 2012)
[10] Cheng, Y., Chu, J., Radhakrishnan, S., Jain, A.: TCP Fast Open. Internet draft "draft-cheng-tcpm-fastopen-09.txt", Work in progress (June 2014)

[11] Colitti, W., Steenhaut, K., De Caro, N., Buta, B., Dobrota, V.: Evaluation of Constrained Application Protocol for Wireless Sensor Networks. In: Proceedings of the 18th IEEE Workshop on Local and Metropolitan Area Networks (LANMAN), pp. 1–6 (2011)

[12] Fielding, R., Gettys, J., Mogul, J., Frystyk, H., Masinter, L., Leach, P., Berners-Lee, T.: HyperText Transfer Protocol - HTTP/1.1. Internet RFCs, RFC 2616 (June 1999) ISSN 2070-1721

[13] Gupta, A.: spdy-python: A SPDY Library in Python, https://github.com/ashish-gupta-/spdy-python/

[14] Ishaq, I., Carels, D., Teklemariam, G.K., Hoebeke, J., Abeele, F., Poorter, E., Moerman, I., Demeester, P.: IETF Standardization in the Field of the Internet of Things (IoT): A Survey. Journal of Sensor and Actuator Networks 2(2), 235–287 (2013)

[15] Kerrisk, M.: TCP Fast Open: Expediting Web Services, http://lwn.net/Articles/508865/

[16] Kuladinithi, K., Bergmann, O., Pötsch, T., Becker, M., Görg, C.: Implementation of CoAP and its Application in Transport Logistics. In: Proceedings of the workshop on Extending the Internet to Low power and Lossy Networks (IP+SN) (2011)

[17] Levä, T., Mazhelis, O., Suomi, H.: Comparing the cost-efficiency of CoAP and HTTP in Web of Things applications. Decision Support Systems 63, 23–38 (2014)

[18] Ludovici, A., Moreno, P., Calveras, A.: TinyCoAP: A Novel Constrained Application Protocol (CoAP) Implementation for Embedding RESTful Web Services in Wireless Sensor Networks Based on TinyOS. Journal of Sensor and Actuator Networks 2(2), 288–315 (2013)

[19] Postel, J.: Transmission Control Protocol. Internet RFCs, RFC 793 (September 1981) ISSN 2070-1721

[20] Radhakrishnan, S., Cheng, Y., Jerry Chu, H.K., Jain, A., Raghavan, B.: TCP Fast Open. In: Proceedings of the Seventh Conference on Emerging Networking EXperiments and Technologies, CoNEXT 2011, pp. 20:1–20:12 (2011)

[21] Sandlund, K., Pelletier, G., Jonsson, L.-E.: RObust Header Compression (ROHC) Framework. Internet RFCs, RFC 5795 (March 2010) ISSN 2070-1721

[22] Shelby, Z., Hartke, K., Bormann, C.: The Constrained Application Protocol (CoAP). Internet RFCs, RFC 7252 (June 2014) ISSN 2070-1721

[23] Tsujikawa, T.: spdylay:The experimental SPDY protocol version 2, 3 and 3.1 implementation in C, http://tatsuhiro-t.github.io/spdylay/

An Effective and Efficient Middleware
for Supporting Distributed Query Processing
in Large-Scale Cyber-Physical Systems

Alfredo Cuzzocrea[1], Jose Cecilio[2], and Pedro Furtado[2]

[1] ICAR-CNR and University of Calabria, Italy
[2] CISUC/DEI, University of Coimbra, Portugal
cuzzocrea@si.deis.unical.it, {jcecilio,pnf}@dei.uc.pt

Abstract. *Large-scale Cyber-Physical Systems* (CPS) represent the new frontier for distributed computing and, in particular, *Cloud computing*. In such systems, there is a tight need for effective and efficient *distributed query processing tasks*, which may be implemented within the core layer of conventional *middleware*. In particular, *autonomous embedded devices* (also known as *motes*) and *wireless sensor networks* appear to be the most convenient computational infrastructures to implement and deploy CPS effectively and efficiently. Within this so-delineated research context, in this paper we propose architecture and functionalities of *StreamOperation* (**StreamOp**), a middleware for supporting distributed query processing via a novel paradigm that lies on the *autonomous database management metaphor* to be implemented on each mote of the system. We also provide experimental analysis and assessment which clearly validate our research even from a performance-oriented point of view, beyond the conceptual point of view ensured by our main contributions.

1 Introduction

Large-scale Cyber-Physical Systems (CPS) (e.g., [26,27,28]) represent the new frontier for distributed computing and, in particular, *Cloud computing* (e.g., [29,30]). In such systems, there is a tight need for effective and efficient *distributed query processing tasks*, which may be implemented within the core layer of conventional *middleware*. During the last decade, a lot of progress has happened in the field of *autonomous embedded devices* (also known as *motes*) and *wireless sensor networks*. In this context, we envision next-generation systems to have *autonomous database management functionalities* on each mote, for supporting *easy management of data on flash disks*, *adequate querying capabilities*, and *ubiquitous computing* with no-effort. Following this major vision, in this paper we describe application scenarios, middleware approach and data management algorithms of a novel system, called *StreamOperation* (**StreamOp**), which effectively and efficiently realizes the depicted challenges. In particular, **StreamOp** supports *heterogeneity*, i.e. it works on top of different platforms, *efficiency*, i.e. it returns responses quickly, and *autonomy*, i.e. it saves battery power. We show how **StreamOp** provides these features, along with some experimental results that clearly validate our main assumptions.

G. Fortino et al. (Eds.): IDCS 2014, LNCS 8729, pp. 124–135, 2014.
© Springer International Publishing Switzerland 2014

Motes are *embedded devices* that are small, compact and are characterized by a set of features that make them autonomous. Examples include *TelosB*, *Arduino* and *Raspberry-PI*. Motes can (*i*) interact with the physical world through their incorporated *ADC/DAC interfaces*, (*ii*) compute tasks, (*iii*) communicate via *wireless connections*, (*iv*) store large amounts of data in their *flash disks*, and (*v*) work autonomously over extended periods of time thanks to battery power. These special features allow motes to be capable of collecting data autonomously over extended time periods, while later-on the data are aggregated and processed for query processing purposes. Some of those devices are also quite limited in computational capabilities (e.g., *TelosB* exposes a 48 KB code memory and a 10 KB data memory). *Wireless sensor networks* (WSN) can be built *in an ad-hoc manner* by placing a bunch of motes anywhere (or, alternatively, they can even be thrown!), being just after these motes collecting data and talking to each-other automatically. Also, in order to globally collect data from motes for analysis purposes, one or more *sink nodes* interface with a computer, e.g. via USB or WIFI, and route collected data into its storage layer. Individual nodes or a whole WSN may stay autonomous collecting data that are requested later-on.

For many common sensing and processing (and possibly actuation) applications over those devices, *coding in low-level languages can be replaced by declarative configurations over a middleware*. The advantage is for application domain experts to deploy and run such systems without specific programming skills, beyond to defining scalable environments. Nevertheless, since platform and application requirements vary over time, a good configuration system should have a set of characteristics to be set. Among those, it should handle heterogeneous subsystems, node-wise operation, offer operation expressive power, and support data exchanges. Even more importantly, if we install appropriate data management functionalities in motes and a middleware to query them, the resulting system can be used in the most diverse application scenarios easily. On the other hand, the system should also fit into constrained devices, be efficient and save battery power. Inspired by this evident trade-off need, in this paper we focus on *supporting data management and query functionalities over sensor network streams efficiently*, and describe application scenarios of this context, *a middleware approach* and the data management algorithms that convey in the proposal *StreamOperation* (StreamOp), a novel system supporting the described features.

2   Data Management Within the Node

The data management system is defined by a set of mechanisms: organization of data storage, stream relational algebra and corresponding algorithms, *time-ordered Group-by* for aggregating over time intervals, and the *generic Group-by* for grouping by an attribute that is not pre-sorted. Finally, we also provide an algorithm for joining arbitrary datasets, although we did not test it. It is developed as part of the *Stream Management Engine* (SME) that is installed into each node for the system to work.

SME is installed in nodes and implements a query processor over ram and flash, and data exchanges between nodes. A stream has a metadata structure that is stored in flash or ram memory and defines attributes. Streams stored in memory are arrays of tuples, while flash-resident streams are stored in files (each stream is stored in one file). One typical use scenario is to log a stream of sensor data into flash and retrieve it later using queries. Another scenario is to acquire sensor data into a window in memory and to send the data to the PC when the window fills-up.

Physical storage on flash has two main possible organizations: constant- and variable-sized tuples. Fig. 1 shows the metadata and data corresponding to both alternatives. Although SME can handle both, we focus on the simpler constant-sized tuples for our implementations on motes with small code and data memory.

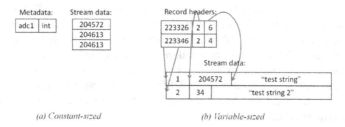

(a) Constant-sized   (b) Variable-sized

Fig. 1. Metadata and Data: Constant and Variable-Sized

If desired, it is possible to store one timestamp value per stream row. However, for streams representing periodic acquisitions (e.g., every minute) it is enough to store the pair (starting timestamp, acquisition rate). The timestamp of every tuple is determined from those. If the stream stops execution and restarts later, a new pair needs to be added. This timestamp information of a stream is stored in a companion file that is called the timestamp index. In the case of variable-sized tuples, a b-tree index is used over the timestamp.

The sensor network is a distributed system with at least one SME in a sensor node and a SME with catalog and a Java console application in one PC. The catalog maintains all information on node configurations and status. Queries are submitted through the console. The query is pre-parsed into a query bytecode and nodes run the query and return the result to the caller. In the case of a stream with a window, when the window fills-up the query is ran and results forwarded to registered consumers (other streams). The constrained SME version should occupy very small amounts of code and data memory, we will describe its query processing algorithms.

The base query-processing algorithm of Fig. 2 works on a row-by-row fashion, retrieving one tuple at a time, applying selection and projection restrictions on the row and outputting the results if the row is not excluded by evaluated conditions. The clause *select* contains a set of expressions (e.g., stream attributes, parameters, constants, function calls such as *todate()*, aggregation functions applied to attributes, or simple expressions). These are pre-parsed in the console application into a bytecode that represents the select fields to be interpreted by the mote. Examples of node parameters that can be included in queries include *nodeID* or sensor identifiers. Where conditions are either *operand operator operand* expressions (binary) or *operand operator* expressions (unary). Operands are (simple) expressions, and operators are a set of possible operators (e.g. ">","<","=","!=",">=","<="). Multiple where conditions can be *anded* or *ored*.

In Fig. 1, the temporary aggregation structure A maintains additive quantities (sum s, square sum ss, maximum, minimum and number of tuples processed n) that allow aggregations to be computed after all the tuples were processed. For instance, the maximum and minimum are given directly from the current maximum and minimum in the structure, the average is a sum divided by the number of tuples, and the variance can be derived according to: $(ss-(s*s)/n)/n$.

The query processing algorithm shown in the figure requires only a minimal amount of memory. It needs one tuple for input stream data, about 100 B for keeping metadata for each stream, few bytes for local variables used during query processing, space for the aggregation structure A (less than 50 B), and space for the output buffer O that holds result tuples. This buffer is flushed into network messages as soon as there are enough tuples to fill a packet payload, to be sent to the destination computer. This way, O needs only a packet payload size (about 100 B in *TelosB*). We show results on the memory space that was consumed in the experimental section.

```
O= temporary tuple space for output tuples;
A=Aggregation structure, a temporary structure for computing
aggregations;

1. Scan stream, tuple-by-tuple:
For each tuple,
   Apply selection operations (early-select) (where clause conditions)
   If selection operations evaluate to false (tuple will not contribute
to output),
   go to step 2 with next tuple
For each select clause field,
   If field is a constant, output it to a temporary output tuple space
O;
   If the field is attribute, copy its value in current tuple to O;
   If the field is a function applied to an attribute, call the
function with the attribute value of current tuple, output the result to
O;
   If the field is an aggregation (e.g. sum, count, avg, max, min),
the attribute value of the current tuple updates A, a temporary
aggregation computation structure for that attribute (an aggregation
hashmap);
   If (0 already fills a network packet), fill the packet and send the
results, emptying O)

2. End of query:
If the query is an aggregation, compose final output from aggregation
structure.
```

Fig. 2. Base Query Processing Algorithm

The objective concerning Constrained group aims at devise efficient solutions that may be run entirely in very small amounts of data memory (e.g., [24]), and the code should fit into the code memory of motes.

Sensor data is stored in stream format in monotonically increasing timestamp order, and it is very frequent to aggregate by time units. Therefore, we take advantage of the timestamp-order to define a simple *Group-By Time* approach with minimal memory requirements that is based on ordered aggregation. Only for the more generic case when the group-by attributes are not ordered we apply an external sort prior to using the same ordered aggregation algorithm. In this section we describe the algorithms, which are evaluated in the experimental section.

How to efficiently retrieve time-interval files? Consider a query retrieving logged data for a time interval. Since the stream data is time-ordered and the stream has a timestamp index, the appropriate offset in the stream is calculated from the index and the query timestamp interval start. Tuples are then read until the timestamp interval end is reached. In our proposal, this is implemented by the so-called file seek index.

The objective of algorithm *Group-By Time* together with the time-interval file seek is to run fast, save battery and to use the minimum possible amount of data memory, so that the algorithm can run efficiently in 2KB or less of data memory. The algorithm keeps a single aggregation computation structure (*A*) in data memory and is useful for grouping into time-intervals and to aggregate all the dataset. It is also used as the second step of the all-purpose group-by algorithm given in the next sub-section.

Consider an acquisition stream, that is, a stream that results from acquiring sensor data periodically. The time granularity of the stream is given by the sensor-sampling rate (or the rate at which it receives data from another stream), and time-aggregated queries aggregate into some other time granularity. The *Group-By Time* algorithm of Fig. 3 executes when a time argument is used in the group by clause. If the where

```
timeF: the time format string used in the query groups
('DD-MON-YY,HH' in the above example);
timeG: the current group identified as a string;
aggregationStructure: A(timeG, s=0,ss=0,max=-1,min=MAXVAL,n=0);
                      (sum s, square sum ss, maximum max, minimum min,
       and number of tuples processed n)
GBTime Algorithm:
0. timeG="";

1. If a time interval specified in the where clause restricts the
interval that must be considered,
   Seek the position on flash corresponding to the start of the time
interval specified in the where clause.

2. Scan the tuples one-by-one while the tuple timestamp is lower than
the upper bound on time interval or the end of the dataset is met.
Evaluate where conditions on the tuple, if tuple is excluded continue
(2.) with next tuple;
   if todate(timestamp, timeF) for the tuple equals timeG
      update aggregation structure variables by adding the value(s) from
the tuple;
   else // ended computing group aggregation for timeG
      compute select aggregations and expressions from A and output to
O;
      if O fills packet, send packet and empty O;
      reset A structure for next group;
      timeG= new timeF;

3. Send O;

4. End.
```

Fig. 3. Group-By-Time Algorithm

clause contains a time interval condition (alone or *anded* with other conditions), the file seek index is used to avoid full table scans. Then the algorithm simply scans the dataset tuples within the time interval specified in the where condition, while updating the aggregation computation for the current group. When the group changes (group time boundary is passed), the group aggregation is computed and it switches to compute the next group.

Group-By Time is evaluated in the experimental section and its performance and energy consumption is compared with alternatives. Resources used are: (*i*) I/O (flash): n = number of tuples in dataset, nI in time interval; (*ii*) Constant-sized = nI (Variable-sized = $logn + nI$); (*iii*) Minimum data memory: $sizeOf(A) + sizeOf(Tuple) + sizeOf(O)$, where O is the temporary output buffer that can be flushed whenever needed.

An *all-purpose Group-By* is given for processing aggregations over generic non-stream-ordered attributes. A *Sort-Group By* algorithm is so-determined. Similarly, an *all-purpose Join* is given with the *Sort-Merge-Join algorithm*. These will be slower when temporary flash-space is needed, but will handle generic aggregation and join operations. Fig. 4 shows the *Sort-Group By* algorithm that was implemented. In Step 1 (external sort), the data set is sorted by the group-by attributes using an external sort (flash memory). Step 2 (re-)uses the *Group-By Time* algorithm, replacing time attribute values by the group-by attribute values in the algorithm. This way, the grouping of the sorted data can be done with small amounts of data memory, and re-utilizes the aggregation algorithm of *Group-By Time*.

We denote as *GB-fts* the *Group-By Time* algorithm doing a full-table scan and *GB-idx* a version using the timestamp index when one exists and a where clause restricts retrieval over a time interval.

```
GB-fts and GB-idx Algorithms:

Step 1. External Sort (simplified for the sake of brevity):
S= Sort buffer, should fit in memory, S=empty initially
For all tuples of dataset
    Apply where conditions, if tuple excluded by where conditions,
continue (1.) with next tuple;
    Project attributes and add remaining tuple values to S;
    If S full, apply in-mem sort algorithm, store as runfile and empty S;
For each input tuple from all runfiles
    Output next tuple in sort order and read next tuple from the runfile
of the chosen tuple;
    Output tuples are flushed to flash when output buffer fills up,
emptying the buffer;
```

Fig. 4. Sort-Group By Algorithm

In the case of the Join algorithm shown in Fig. 5, for the sort-merge join both datasets need to be sorted. The same external sort algorithm is used, then the algorithm reads sequentially tuples from both datasets simultaneously, outputting matches.

```
Sort-Merge-Join of datasets A and B

Run External Sort on A and on B to order by join attribute(s), resulting
in sortedA and sortedB (external sort Algorithm given above)
While there are input tuples from sortedA or sortedB
   If join attribute values for sortedA and sortedB match,
        Compose output tuple to O, from the sortedA and sortedB tuples;
        If O fills a packet, compose the packet and send it, then empty O.
        Retrieve next sortedA and sortedB tuples;
   Else
        Retrieve next tuple from either sortedA or sorted, by getting the
smallest of the two based on the sort order. Replace the corresponding
input tuple;
```

Fig. 5. Sort-Group By Algorithm

Resources used are: (*i*) IO (flash): n = number of tuples in dataset, σ is where selectivity; (*ii*) IO(sort A) + IO(sort B) + $\sigma A n A$+ $\sigma B n B$; (*iii*) Minimum data memory: $sizeOf(S)$ for sorts, then $sizeOf(A) + sizeOf(B) + sizeOf(O)$.

3   StreamOp Architecture

StreamOp is an application-level middleware that views one or more networks as a distributed system, where every computing device is a stream engine with a common set of computation, storage and data exchange functionalities, and the whole distributed system is a distributed stream processing system. Fig. 6 is an example of a distributed system, where the same operating component exists in a computer, an Arduino with a *WiFly* communications shield and in *TelosB* nodes running *Contiki* operating system and proprietary (*Rime*) communications stack. The stream engine handles acquisition, computation, storage and data exchange. Since the computer, any node within the *TelosB* network and the *Arduino* all have the same component and that component defines uniform computation, storage and exchange primitives, all nodes are made to process and talk to each-other easily through easy remote configurations. In the system of Fig. 6, another relevant component is the *Remote Config Component*, a Java application. The *Operating Component* is the proper StreamOp. As long as that component already exists for each of the platforms where it is supposed to run, and the gateway also exists for non-IP sub-systems, all that is needed to setup a system is to install the StreamOp in each platform and to start configuring the system to operate.

Interaction with the distributed system is through the following components: a *Remote Configuration Component* offers both an application programming interface (API) and an SQL console for SQL commands. Nodes are configured to run using this interface. External applications receive streamed data from the system by subscribing published streams and insert data into the system through the API or SQL interface.

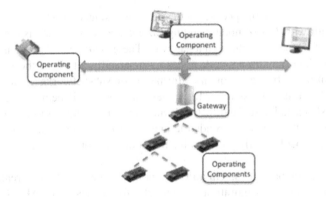

Fig. 6. Heterogeneous Sensor Network

The node *Operating Component* – **StreamOp** – organizes the data as streams. Network messages arriving at the node may either be commands or data. Commands are parsed and executed, while data is stored in streams. According to configuration commands, the component also arms timers and responds when they fire, by operating on the data or acquiring new sensor values, depending on the command.

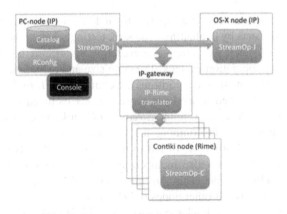

Fig. 7. Components of the Middleware

Fig. 7 shows the components of the middleware. Every node that is to run in the system only needs to install a **StreamOp** component and be turned on. This component is written for the node platform and abstracts the platform details into a common operations model. Every device capable of running a *Java Virtual Machine* (JVM) simply installs the *StreamOp-J* version for Java on the JVM. In Fig. 7 both the PC and the OS-X nodes run a JVM and *StreamOp-J* (e.g., OS-X node can be a *RaspBerry* platform running *Linux*). Nodes running different OSs, different network protocols and no JVM, install a platform-specific **StreamOp** component (e.g., *TelosB* running *Contiki* and *Rime* install a *StreamOp-Contiki* component).

All nodes are automatically assigned IP addresses as soon as they plug into the network. Nodes running protocols other than IP must be in a sub-network under a gateway and have protocol-specific addresses. For instance, a whole wireless sensor network is built with *TelosB* nodes running *Contiki* and *Rime*, which is then interfaced with the rest of the network through a gateway. The gateway is plugged-in to the main network first, then the sub-network nodes automatically attach to the gateway. The catalog shown in the figure maintains information on sub-networks (nodes under each gateway) and address translations for nodes with protocol-specific addresses. The gateway translates addresses and forwards messages. For a node to send a message to a node in some sub-network, it sends the message to the appropriate gateway, which retrieves the protocol specific address for the node and forwards the message to that node.

The *RConfig* component runs in a PC and controls queries, stream creation, stream dropping and other configuration commands for nodes. An API (web-service interface) is used by a console application and other clients to submit requests through *RConfig*. *RConfig* is linked to a **StreamOp** that handles *RConfig* requests to target nodes. Each node has a **StreamOp** component, which configures the node, handles communication and handles all details of operation.

4   Experimental Results

In this section, we assess the approach and show results from testing it experimentally. We start by evaluating code size, testing whether the code fits even in constrained devices. Then we compare aggregation algorithms in terms of runtime. Finally we test other operation timings. The code size and operation timings are taken for different platforms, while the algorithms are compared in *TelosB* running *Contiki*.

The testbed that we used to evaluate these metrics included one wireless sensor network with 16 *TelosB* nodes running *StreamOp-Contiki*. One of the *TelosB* was a sink node connected to a PC running the Gateway component for *Contiki*. Each *TelosB* device has 48KB of ROM, 10 KB of data memory, 1024 B of flash and 2 AA 800 mAh batteries; the setup also included an *Arduino Mega device* for which we developed *StreamOp-Arduino*. This Arduino had a *WiFly* shield, so that it talked directly with *RConfig* and all other nodes (CPU ATmega1280, Flash Memory 128 KB of which 4 KB used by boot-loader, SRAM 8 KB, EEPROM 4 KB, Clock Speed 16 MHz). The setup also included a *Raspberry-PI* device running *Debian Linux ARM* distribution and a JVM over which we deployed *StreamOp-Java*. This device was connected directly to the Ethernet cable. (CPU ARM1176JZF-S (armv6k) 700 MHz, memory 512 MB). Finally, there were two PCs (2.53 GHz Intel Core 2 Duo, 4 GB 1067 MHz DD33 memory) running *Windows 7* and a JVM with **StreamOp** running on it. One of the PCs was running *RConfig* and a console, to allow us to submit commands. The other one, which we denote as "control station" was receiving and displaying the data from the embedded devices.

Fig. 8 shows the time spent for aggregating 100 tuples over a memory-resident stream and a flash-resident stream in milliseconds. Aggregation operations such as *avg()*, *max()*, *min()* are computed by visiting all the tuples in the stream window once, computing corresponding aggregations additively. That is the reason why all aggregation operations take the same time. The operation denoted as VALUE in the figure corresponds to just retrieving the values, without the need to do any computations on them. Finally, the percentile operation is a bit more time consuming, since it needs to order the data that it gathers in order to return the desired percentile. Fig. 9 shows the time taken to compute an average operation versus the size of the window, both in memory and in flash storage.

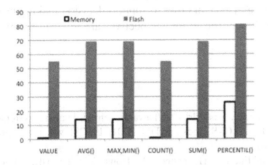

Fig. 8. Times for Flash vs Memory Operation (ms)

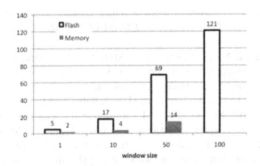

Fig. 9. Time vs Window Size for AVG Operation (ms)

5   Conclusions and Future Work

In this paper we described a system developed to help configure and run heterogeneous distributed control systems that include wireless sensor networks with programmable nodes. The approach allows very different configurations to be done without a single line of code, and operates perfectly within a complex heterogeneous distributed systems environment. It includes capabilities to allow it to work in many different modes, as described in the use cases section. Users can define what to do and query or configure streams of acquired or exchanged data, as they can also configure streams to send data to consumer streams elsewhere, including consumer control stations or indeed any other node outside the sensor network. We have shown, by means of experimental evaluation, that the approach results in code that fits constrained devices, is able to run heterogeneous devices (we tested a system with

TelosB, PCs, *Arduino, Raspberry-PI*) and evaluated performance of the approach. In the future, this kind of models and programming approaches will ease the job of deploying sensor networks in real applications, resulting in more widespread applications.

As future work, we plan (1) to enhance our framework by means of *data compression paradigms* (e.g., [22,23]) as to further magnify the efficiency of StreamOp routines, and (2) to integrate our framework with *analysis and visualization tools* (e.g., [25]), in order to support decision making processes on top of which our framework may run. Both perspectives are relevant for emerging *Big Data paradigms.*

References

1. Bonnet, P., Gehrke, J., Seshadri, P.: Towards sensor database systems. In: Tan, K.-L., Franklin, M.J., Lui, J.C.-S. (eds.) MDM 2001. LNCS, vol. 1987, pp. 3–14. Springer, Heidelberg (2000)
2. Madden, S., Franklin, M., Hellerstein, J., Hong, W.: TinyDB: an acquisitional query processing system for sensor networks. ACM Transactions on Database Systems 30(1), 122–173 (2005)
3. Yoneki, E., Bacon, J.: A survey of wireless sensor network technologies: research trends and middleware's role. Technical report UCAM-CL-TR-646, University of Cambridge (2005)
4. Wang, M.-M., Cao, J.-N., Li, J., Dasi, S.K.: Middleware for wireless sensor networks: a survey. Journal of Computer Science and Technology 23(3), 305–326 (2008)
5. Mottola, L.: Programming wireless sensor networks: from physical to logical neighborhoods. PhD Thesis, Politecnico di Milano, Italy (2008)
6. Aberer, K., Hauswirth, M., Salehi, A.: Infrastructure for data processing in large-scale interconnected sensor networks. In: Proceedings of MDM, pp. 198–205 (2007)
7. Shneidman, J., Pietzuch, P., Ledlie, J., Roussopoulos, M., Seltzer, M., et al.: An infrastructure for connecting sensor networks and applications. Technical Report TR-21-04, Harvard University (2004)
8. Franklin, M., Jeffery, S., Krishnamurthy, S., Reiss, F., Rizvi, S., et al.: Design considerations for high fan-in systems: the HiFi approach. In: Proceedings of CIDR, pp. 290–304 (2005)
9. Gibbons, P.B., Karp, B., Ke, Y., Nath, S., Seshan, S.: IrisNet: an architecture for a world-wide sensor web. IEEE Pervasive Computing 2(4), 22–33 (2003)
10. Gummadi, R., Gnawali, O., Govindan, R.: Macro-programming wireless sensor networks using Kairos. In: Prasanna, V.K., Iyengar, S.S., Spirakis, P.G., Welsh, M. (eds.) DCOSS 2005. LNCS, vol. 3560, pp. 126–140. Springer, Heidelberg (2005)
11. Bakshi, A., Prasanna, V.K., Reich, J., Larner, D.: The abstract task graph: a methodology for architecture-independent programming of networked sensor systems. In: Proceedings of EESR, pp. 19–24 (2005)
12. Levis, P., Culler, D.: Maté: a tiny virtual machine for sensor networks. In: Proceedings of ACM ASPLOS X, pp. 85–95 (2002)
13. Levis, P., Gay, D., Culler, D.: Active sensor networks. In: Proceedings of ACM NSDI, vol. 2, pp. 343–356 (2005)
14. Whitehouse, K., Sharp, C., Brewer, E., Culler, D.: Hood: a neighborhood abstraction for sensor networks. In: Proceedings of MobiSys, pp. 99–110 (2004)

15. Shen, C.-C., Srisathapornphat, C., Jaikaeo, C.: Sensor information networking architecture and applications. IEEE Personal Communications Magazine 8(4), 52–59 (2001)
16. Srisathapornphat, C., Jaikaeo, C., Shen, C.-C.: Sensor information networking architecture. In: Proceedings of International Workshop on Parallel Processing, pp. 23–30 (2000)
17. Li, S., Son, S.H., Stankovic, J.A.: Event detection services using data service middleware in distributed sensor networks. In: Zhao, F., Guibas, L.J. (eds.) IPSN 2003. LNCS, vol. 2634, pp. 502–517. Springer, Heidelberg (2003)
18. Boulis, A., Han, C.-C., Srivastava, M.B.: Design and implementation of a framework for efficient and programmable sensor networks. In: Proceedings of MobiSys, pp. 187–200 (2003)
19. Tsiftes, N., Dunkels, A.: A database in every sensor. In: Proceedings of ACM SenSys, pp. 316–332 (2011)
20. Furtado, P., Cecilio, J.: Sensor streams middleware for easy configuration and processing in hybrid sensor network. In: Proceedings of ACM SAC, pp. 1499–1504 (2013)
21. Furtado, P.: TinyStream sensors. In: Quirchmayr, G., Basl, J., You, I., Xu, L., Weippl, E. (eds.) CD-ARES 2012. LNCS, vol. 7465, pp. 218–232. Springer, Heidelberg (2012)
22. Cuzzocrea, A., Serafino, P.: LCS-Hist: taming massive high-dimensional data cube compression. In: Proceedings of EDBT, pp. 768–779 (2009)
23. Cuzzocrea, A.: Providing probabilistically-bounded approximate answers to non-holistic aggregate range queries in OLAP. In: Proceedings of DOLAP, pp. 97–106 (2005)
24. Cuzzocrea, A., Furfaro, F., Masciari, E., Saccà, D., Sirangelo, C.: Approximate Query Answering on Sensor Network Data Streams. In: Stefanidis, A., Nittel, S. (eds.) GeoSensor Networks, pp. 53–72. CRC Press (2004)
25. Cuzzocrea, A., Mansmann, S.: OLAP Visualization: Models, Issues, and Techniques. In: Wang, J. (ed.) Encyclopedia of Data Warehousing and Mining, 2nd edn., pp. 1439–1446. IGI Global (2009)
26. Munir, S., Stankovic, J.A.: DepSys: Dependency aware integration of cyber-physical systems for smart homes. In: Proceedings of ACM ICCPS, pp. 127–138 (2014)
27. Medhat, R., Kumar, D., Bonakdarpour, B., Fischmeister, S.: Sacrificing a little space can significantly improve monitoring of time-sensitive cyber-physical systems. In: Proceedings of ACM ICCPS, pp. 115–126 (2014)
28. Hunter, T., Das, T., Zaharia, M., Abbeel, P., Bayen, A.M.: Large-Scale Estimation in Cyberphysical Systems Using Streaming Data: A Case Study with Arterial Traffic Estimation. IEEE Transactions on Automation Science and Engineering 10(4), 884–898 (2013)
29. Dean, J., Ghemawat, S.: MapReduce: Simplified Data Processing on Large Clusters. Communications of the ACM 51(1), 107–113 (2008)
30. Armbrust, M., Fox, A., Griffith, R., Joseph, A.D., Katz, R.H., Konwinski, A., Lee, G., Patterson, D.A., Rabkin, A., Stoica, I., Zaharia, M.: A View of Cloud Computing. Communications of the ACM 53(4), 50–58 (2010)

A Framework of Adaptive Interaction Support in Cloud-Based Internet of Things (IoT) Environment

Noura Alhakbani, Mohammed Mehedi Hassan, M. Anwar Hossain,
and Mohammed Alnuem

College of Computer and Information Sciences,
King Saud University, Riyadh, 11543, Saudi Arabia
{nhakbani,mmhassan,mahossain,malnuem}@ksu.edu.sa

Abstract. This paper discusses the Internet of Things (IoT) within the cloud computing concepts and architectures. We review different frameworks of combined IoT architecture with cloud being in the center. Then we investigate adaptive interaction support concept. Finally, we propose a novel framework that incorporates and supports adaptive interaction of the user with the IoT cloud architecture based on the quality of context information and quality of services. The propsed framework increases user satisfaction and reduces user annoyance towards the IoT cloud environment.

Keywords: Internet of Things (IoT), Cloud Computing, Adaptive Interaction Support, Context Awareness.

1 Introduction

These days many of the devices we use and encounter daily are smart devices starting from our phones, and T.V.s to our cars and even ovens. With the advancement and widespread use of the internet and specifically wireless technologies all of the smart devices are wirelessly and seamlessly connected to the internet. This leads us to the Internet of Things concept which is semantically defined as "a world-wide network of interconnected objects uniquely addressable, based on standard communication protocols" [1]. The idea of Internet of Things (IoT) stems from the pervasive and ubiquitous nature of internet connected things or objects around us in everyday life. Nowadays these smart things use the cloud to communicate amongst each other to provide the user with smarter environments. The IoT uses the cloud to leverage its processing powers due to its need to greater processing than that provided by the miniature sensors and things. Yet there are some challenges to the IoT cloud such as interoperability amongst different smart things which are created by different manufacturers. Communication errors and security threats are also valid concerns. Our concern is adaptive interaction with the IoT cloud architecture. Many studies have presented frameworks and architectures that combine the internet of things with the cloud [2], [3]. But little has been done to support the user interaction with such smart environments.

G. Fortino et al. (Eds.): IDCS 2014, LNCS 8729, pp. 136–146, 2014.

The following scenario shows the need to adaptive interaction within the IoT cloud framework. Let's say Sarah is living in a house where she has her smart things - Television, coffee machine, air condition, lights, car, blinds, and towel heater - set up and connected to the cloud all the time. Sarah has her smart things work automatically according to her daily schedule and awareness of her location and status. The smart things communicate her status amongst each other. She wakes up every weekday at 6:00 am by her alarm and the blinds are set to be fully opened at the same time as well. When Sarah starts exercising at her home gym, the towel heater rack turns on to heat the towels for her to use after shower. When she is done with exercising her bathroom lights are automatically turned on. When she starts her shower the coffee machine starts preparing her coffee to be ready at 7:00 am. At 7:30 am she leaves to work and the air conditioning will automatically turn off. At 5:00 pm the air conditioning checks her calendar to see if she has any appointments after work, and then communicates with her car navigator to find her destination. If the destination is home, the air conditioning will switch on to cool the house. The light turn on automatically when it senses that her car is parked in the garage. And this can go on to turn the television to her favorite channel and lights are turned on and off according to her location in the house. This is a perfect scenario of sensing Sarah's status and acting accordingly. But in reality our lives don't follow precise schedules, communication of the smart things amongst each other allows for such flexibility, yet these things are not always accurate and error free due to many reasons such as their small processing powers, errors in perceiving or understanding the status or communication failures. That's why we need these smart things to adapt their communication with the users especially if they are not able to get the accurate status. The system should give the user more control on these things without turning things on and off automatically which might cause user annoyance. So, our main goal is to design the architecture of the adaptive interaction support in IoT cloud environment. There are some adaptive interaction support architectures [4] provided, but not specifically designed for, the IoT cloud environment. The IoT cloud framework has its own architectures, framework and limitations that need to be addressed specifically when designing adaptive interaction support.

In our proposed approach, the interaction is adapted based on the quality of context and quality of services provided to the user. This dynamic adaptation gives the user more control at times of less quality of information communicated. This reduces irrelevant or annoying actions taken by the system [5].

The remainder of the paper is organized as the following: First, within the literature review, we review Internet of Things and cloud computing. Then, we review Internet of Things and cloud architectures, and then we review interaction support within the IoT cloud environment. Next, we propose our framework where we incorporate the IoT cloud architecture with the adaptive interaction capability. Finally, we present our conclusion.

2   Literature Review

2.1   Internet of Things (IoT) and Cloud Computing

Recent research proposed the cloud as a unifying framework for the IoT to achieve smart environment. In terms of this view IoT is defined as "Interconnection of sensing and actuating devices providing the ability to share information across platforms through a unified framework, developing a common operating picture for enabling innovative applications. This is achieved by seamless ubiquitous sensing, data analytics and information representation with cloud computing as the unifying framework" [6].

Cloud computing definition provided by the National Institute of Standards and Technology (NIST) [7] states that, "cloud computing is a model for enabling ubiquitous, convenient, on-demand network access to a shared pool of configurable computing resources (e.g., networks, servers, storage, applications and services) that can be rapidly provisioned and released with minimal management effort or service provider interaction."

The aforementioned definition demonstrates how cloud computing and internet of things when mentioned, configurable computing resources, lend themselves naturally to be merged and then utilized with minimal effort. The traditional view on cloud computing structure consists of four layers the hardware-datacenter layer, which is responsible for managing the physical resources of the cloud; the infrastructure layer as a service (IaaS) known as the virtualization layer which is responsible for partitioning the physical resources using virtualization technologies; the platform layer as Service (PaaS) its purpose minimize the burden of deploying applications directly into VM containers, and the application layer also known as software as a service (SaaS) which consists of the actual cloud applications [8].

On the other hand, cloud computing is defined as "both the applications delivered as services over the Internet and the hardware and systems software in the data centers that provide those services. The services themselves have long been referred to as Software as a Service (SaaS)." This definition aggregates IaaS and PaaS and adds them to the software as a service layer (SaaS), since they believe that the differences between IaaS and PaaS are not well established [9].

2.2   IoT Cloud Architecture

With regard to the Internet of Things architecture, there is no clear or well established effort. Borrowing the internet architecture which was designed in the 70s is not the optimal solution for the current Internet of Things applications. The nature of the internet has shifted from its early vision - where the internet was basically connected to personal computers. The internet now is connected to all sorts of things starting from mobile phones to watches and cars. A well-tailored architecture to the new vision of the internet is much needed to support the Internet of Things concept.

One of the first architectures proposed for the Internet of Things was composed of 4 layers starting from the bottom with RFID/Sensor Network, then Access Gateway through different Access Networks such as the internet, then the middleware where different services are offered such as directory services, context modelling and management, and content management. In this proposal the RFID and Sensor Network were explicitly mentioned technologies, since the definition at that time had these technologies as hard wired to the concept [10].

Interoperability issues appeared between different applications in the proposed architectures so a coordination layer is added to facilitate communication between different applications. The proposed architecture constitutes of five layers: The first one consists of Edge technology layer, access Layer, and existed application systems. The second layer is backbone network layer, then they added the coordination layer, middleware layer and finally the application layer [1].

Internet of things could be viewed from different perspectives or visions. "Things" oriented visions, "Internet" oriented Visions, and "Semantic" oriented visions [11]. Or alternatively, could be classified into two categories the first having the internet as the center part or the second having the data as the center part. A framework was proposed adopting the first category, where the internet is at the center, but here they substituted the internet with the cloud and presented cloud centric internet of things framework. The benefits from such frameworks are the scalability and cost effectiveness. The cloud will offer its services to all connected parties where they can benefit and utilize them as needed [6]

Integrating the cloud computing and internet of things has been presented in many researches. One proposed framework is under the name CloudThings architecture. They studied a Things-enabled scenario, and designed a Cloud-based Internet of Things platform – the CloudThings architecture, which accommodates IaaS, PaaS, and SaaS for developing, deploying, running, and composing Things applications. The implemented prototypes establish the fundamental developments for approaching CloudThings architecture [3].

Another proposal that adopted the cloud things concept as well and proposed generic architecture that enables objects to exchange information through the internet to achieve nonintrusive behavior and Service Level Agreement (SLA) on an open source cloud platform. And noted the key components to interoperable cloud based systems are the open APIs. [12].

Different architectures for the IoT cloud are presented, and some modifications suggested overcoming some challenges such as interoperability. In the next section we will present adaptive interaction depending on different quality attributes.

2.3   Interaction Support in IoT Cloud Platform

One of the IoT cloud architecture framework challenges is the interaction support. In the following section, adaptive interaction support within context aware systems are presented. To explain the context interaction concept, we first define context as any information which is relevant to the interaction between the user and the application and modeled using ontologies. Time and date, location, temperature, light, noise and activity can be considered as contextual information [13].

Contextual information can be modeled, as well using semantic language, describing the environment information and connections residing between the concepts [14].

Context is divided into set of elements context provider such as sensors, context consumer or context aware services, and context broker. These elements are added to a context provisioning framework, where the interaction amongst these elements follows a specified pattern as shown below in Fig. 1, where the context consumer asks for information from a context provider through context broker. The context broker requests context information from different services on the cloud. The context information has varying levels of Quality of Context (QoC) and Quality of Service (QoS). QoC refers to information and not the process nor the hardware component. Examples of QoC parameters are location, probability of correctness and freshness [15] . While QoS indicators may be availability, response–time, and perceived quality [16]. The context broker delivers appropriate context information in terms of desired quality levels to context consumers. This context provisioning model is best suited to be implemented in the SaaS and it could be accessed through API [17], [18].

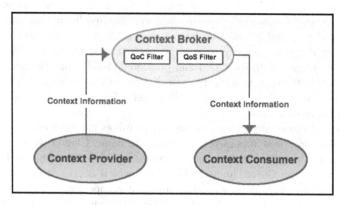

Fig. 1. Context Interaction

Interaction between the system and the user is classified into

- Explicit interaction mode - where the user initiates the interaction.
- Implicit interaction mode - where actions are performed automatically by the environment, based on the knowledge of the user's situation or the context.
- Mixed-initiative interaction - which combines explicit interaction with implicit interaction to facilitate joint interaction between user and environment.

Different modes of interaction are suggested based on the quality of information (QoI) of the context. The suggested modes are full automation, action suggestion, simple notification or null action. More automation is selected with higher (QoI) and more user control is provided as the (QoI) decreases. [4].

The aforementioned proposed framework [18] studied context provisioning but did not study adaptive interaction in terms of such context aware systems. The later [4] studied adaptive interaction support. In the proposed framework we would like to study adaptive interaction in the IoT cloud framework taking context provisioning into account.

3   Proposed Interaction Support Framework

As we can see from the literature the framework of cloud centric IoT has been proposed and used as a base in many central papers [3], [6], [12]. Then again adaptive interaction in context aware systems has been discussed in the literature [4]. Our proposal incorporates both concepts into one framework and uses the quality of context and quality of service levels to base the adaptive interaction mode with the user.

3.1   Inceptions

The IoT cloud centric architecture elements communicate through the cloud. The basic adopted architecture has the cloud in the center between the IoT smart environment and the user as presented in Fig. 2 below. The sensors are set in smart IoT

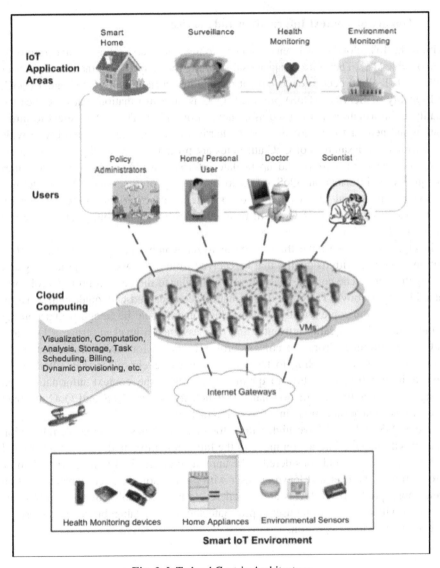

Fig. 2. IoT cloud Centric Architecture

environments within different application areas, environmental sensors are set for environmental monitoring purposes, sensor enabled home appliances are fixed in smart home environments, and health monitoring devices are set for health monitoring purposes, etc... These sensor enabled devices from different application areas send the gathered data to the cloud where it is processed then the reaction or feedback is sent to the concerned users through the sensors interfaces'. Such smart environments require intensive information processing which is done in the cloud rather than exhausting the miniature sensors' processors.

3.2   Quality of Context Information and Services

Within the IoT cloud centric environment context or users' situation uncertainty is unavoidable [13]. Therefore our proposal supports the adaptive interaction of the user with the IoT cloud centric environment depending on the Quality of Context (QoC) and Quality of Services (QoS) provided. QoC is any information that describes the quality of information that is used as context information. Thus, QoC refers to information and neither to the process nor the hardware component that possibly provide the information. Examples of QoC attributes are precision, probability of correctness, trust-worthiness, resolution, and up to date information [15]. While QoC describes the quality of information, QoS refers to the quality of a service. QoS is defined by the nonfunctional characteristics of a system, affecting the perceived quality of the results. Examples of QoS attributes are timeliness, reliability, and perceived quality [16].

In Fig. 3 below we have the context analyzer which analyses the context information combined with its quality that is received from the raw context processing and aggregation unit. The context analyzer role is similar to the context broker's role presented in Fig. 1 above. The context information accompanied with quality information is passed on to the context analyzer where the context could be categorized according to the values of the quality attributes and then assigned a level in terms of QoS and QoC. The difference from the context broker is that it forwards the context information categorized according to the various quality levels rather than filtering the context information according to quality. It forwards the context information and rating to the adaptive interaction handler which maps both QoS and QoC attribute levels to the appropriate mode in terms of interaction.

If the QoS and QoC have high values for their attributes the adaptive interaction handler will map the interaction mode to the full automation mode. On the other hand if the levels are low and considered to be unreliable or erratic it will select to display information to the user and leave the user with the freedom to select whatever action seems appropriate. If the levels are considered to be acceptable but not totally trustworthy it will suggests to the user appropriate action to be taken but again the user is able to override the suggestion.

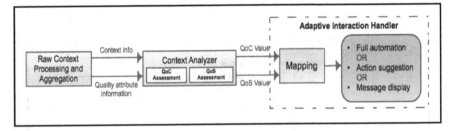

Fig. 3. Context Interaction in the IoT cloud Centric Environment

3.3   Motivation for Interaction Support

Our novel contribution is designing an IoT cloud centric framework that supports adaptive interaction with the user according to the level of quality in terms of context and service. Our framework indicates that the better the quality of both the context and the service (QoS) and (QoC) the more automation the system provides and the less the quality or certainty of context information the more control is given to the user. Therefore adaptive interaction enables more automation with better quality of context information and services provided and on the other hand give the user more control with decreased quality levels which reduces the annoyance with wrong automation [5]. This adaptive interaction mode take into consideration the unavoidable uncertainty [13]   instead of ignoring it and pretending to have a perfect scenario which is far from realistic at the time being with the current technological capabilities.

3.4   The Proposed Framework for Adaptive Interaction in the IoT Cloud Centric Environment

The IoT cloud framework incorporates adaptive interaction as presented in Fig. 4 below. The context information is aggregated from the sensors distributed in the environment and connected to the cloud/ SaaS. We specify SaaS in particular since it is the most suitable for such processing as mentioned by [9]. Their quality attributes are gathered as well. The context information, accompanied with quality information, is passed on to the context analyzer, where the context could be later categorized according to the values of the quality attributes, and then assigned a level in terms of QoS and QoC. According to the calculated levels of both QoS and QoC, the interaction handler will decide to interact with the user and IoT smart environment, choosing from different interaction modes. The modes are full automation, which is chosen when high level of QoC and QoS are provided or action suggestion mode, where the smart environment will suggest action to be taken according to the context information provided where the associated level of QoS or QoC are not ideal. Finally, a message or information would be displayed on the user interface for the user, and the user needs to take explicit interaction with reduced level of QoS or QoC or both of them.

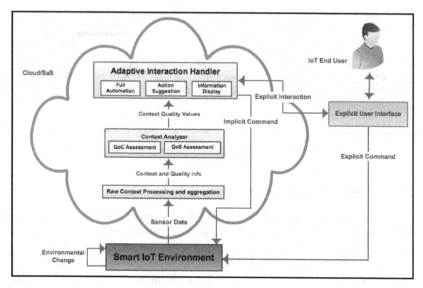

Fig. 4. Adaptive Interaction Support in IoT cloud Centric Environment

The process of selecting a suitable interaction mode according to varying levels of QoC and QoS is presented in mathematical notation as the following. This process is carried out in the cloud. Let us assume, C_x is a context of a certain situation x.

$$\forall C_x \rightarrow \exists \{QoC_j (C_x), \ QoS_k (C_x)\} \tag{1}$$

For every context situation there exist quality of context attributes QoC_j (Cx) and quality of service attributes QoS_k (Cx) for such context such that j and k are j $\in\{1,2,...,m\}$ and k $\in\{1,2,...,h\}$ where m and h are the numbers of quality of context or quality of service attributes respectively.

$$\forall QoC_j (C_x) \rightarrow \exists L_{Qc} \tag{2}$$

$$\forall QoS_k (C_x) \rightarrow \exists L_{Qs} \tag{3}$$

For every quality of context or service attribute there is associated level L_{Qc} and $L_{Qs.}$ $L_{Qc} \in$ {good, acceptable, poor} and $L_{Qs} \in$ {good, acceptable, poor}

$$\forall C_x \rightarrow \exists A_i (Cx) \tag{4}$$

For every context there is list of possible actions represented as Ai, where $A_i (C_x) \subseteq$ {A1, A2, . . . , An}, $1 \leq i \leq n$ is the subset of actions to be performed in any context Cx and n is the total number of listed actions permitted in the environment.

$$\forall A_i(C_x) \wedge \exists \{QoS_j (C_x) \wedge QoC_j (C_x)\} \rightarrow \exists Y \tag{5}$$

For every context and permissible associated actions to be taken compound with the level of quality of context and quality of service associated with such context there exists Y where Y $\in$ {full automation, action suggestion, message display}.Y is calculated by mapping the QoS_j and QoC_j levels for each context C_x and then finding the appropriate automation level. Then the appropriate action is chosen from $A_i(C_x)$ depending on the level of Y.

Below the process of choosing a particular interaction mode is presented in a high level algorithm.

```
Algorithm Adaptive Interaction
Input: {Context Information C_x, QoC(C_x), QoS(C_x)}
BEGIN
1: Identify context C_x
2: Determine quality attributes QoC(C_x) and QoS(C_x)
3: Assign values L_Qc and L_Qs for each QoC(C_x) and QoS(C_x)
4: Map C_x, QoC(C_x), QoS(C_x) and their respective L_Qc and L_Qs
to the appropriate automation level {full automation, ac-
tion suggestion, message display}
5: Invoke the actions (A_i) for a given context C_x based on
the selected automation level
END
```

3.5   Limitations of the Proposed Framework

Our proposed framework focuses on the idea of providing dynamic or adaptive interaction framework for the IoT cloud Integration according to (QoS) and (QoC) rather than identifying exact actions to be performed with certain quality levels. The choice of specific action or action mode criteria is left to the system designer. Our framework aggregates context information and gathers quality information according to each system's requirement in terms of different quality context and services attributes. More or less number of attributes and acceptable levels to each attribute is modified according to different systems' requirements. The degree of confidence in QoS or QoC are not decided in our framework, it is left to each system designer to adjust it to the specific level of quality requirements.

4   Conclusions

The purpose of the proposed framework is to include adaptive interaction support to the IoT cloud framework. The quality of context and services determines the level of automation or user control. A high level algorithm is presented to show how the mapping between the QoS and QoC attribute values for each context and automation level is performed. Further research should be done to investigate the appropriate metrics or attributes to be included in the framework and what the quality threshold levels that affect the interaction are and decreases the automation level with respect to different fields. An important benefit to this study is to give the user more control when context information is unreliable - which will decrease the level of annoyance with the smart environment.

References

1. Internet of Things in 2020, Roadmap for the future (2008)
2. Distefano, S., Milano, P., Merlino, G., Puliafito, A.: Towards the Cloud of Things Sensing and Actuation as a Service, a key enabler for a new Cloud paradigm (2013)
3. Zhou, J., Leppänen, T., Harjula, E., Yu, C., Jin, H., Yang, L.T.: CloudThings: a Common Architecture for Integrating the Internet of Things with Cloud Computing, pp. 651–657 (2013)
4. Hossain, M.A., Shirehjini, A.A.N., Alghamdi, A.S., Saddik, A.: Adaptive interaction support in ambient-aware environments based on quality of context information. Multimed. Tools Appl. 67(2), 409–432 (2013)
5. de Vries, P., Midden, C., Bouwhuis, D.: The effects of errors on system trust, self-confidence, and the allocation of control in route planning. Int. J. Hum. Comput. Stud. 58(6), 719–735 (2003)
6. Gubbi, J., Buyya, R., Marusic, S., Palaniswami, M.: Internet of Things (IoT): A vision, architectural elements, and future directions. Futur. Gener. Comput. Syst. 29(7), 1645–1660 (2013)
7. Computer, N., Division, S.: The NIST Definition of Cloud Computing Recommendations of the National Institute of Standards and Technology (2011)
8. Zhang, Q., Cheng, L., Boutaba, R.: Cloud computing: state-of-the-art and research challenges. J. Internet Serv. Appl. 1(1), 7–18 (2010)
9. Armbrust, M., Fox, A., Griffith, R., Joseph, A., Katz, R.H.: Above the clouds: A Berkeley view of cloud computing. Univ. California, Berkeley. Tech. Rep. UCB, pp. 07–013 (2009)
10. Furness, P.A.: A Framework Model for The Internet of Things. In: A Framework Model for The Internet of Things (2008)
11. Atzori, L., Iera, A., Morabito, G.: The Internet of Things: A survey. Comput. Networks 54(15), 2787–2805 (2010)
12. Suciu, G., Halunga, S., Vulpe, A., Suciu, V.: Generic platform for IoT and cloud computing interoperability study. In: Int. Symp. Signals, Circuits Syst., ISSCS 2013, pp. 1–4 (July 2013)
13. Truong, B.A., Lee, Y.-K., Lee, S.-Y.: Modeling Uncertainty in Context-Aware Computing, pp. 676–681 (2005)
14. Gouin-vallerand, C., Abdulrazak, B., Giroux, S., Dey, A.K.: A Context-Aware Service Provision System for Smart Environments Based on the User Interaction Modalities 5, 47–64 (2013)
15. Buchholz, T., Axel, K., Schiffers, M.: Quality of Context: What It Is And Why We Need It, pp. 1–14 (2003)
16. Rveys, I.S.U.: A Survey of Quality of Service in Mobile Computing Environments, pp. 2–10 (1999)
17. Klein, A., Mannweiler, C., Schneider, J., Schotten, H.D.: Access Schemes for Mobile Cloud Computing. In: 2010 Eleventh International Conference on Mobile Data Management, pp. 387–392 (2010)
18. Badidi, E.: A Cloud-based Approach for Context Information Provisioning 1(3), 63–70 (2011)

Including Cyberphysical Smart Objects into Digital Libraries

Giancarlo Fortino[1], Anna Rovella[2], Wilma Russo[1], and Claudio Savaglio[1]

[1] DIMES, Università della Calabria
Via P. Bucci, cubo 41C, 87036 Rende (CS), Italy
{g.fortino,w.russo}@unical.it, csavaglio@si.dimes.unical.it
[2] DLISE, Università della Calabria
Via P. Bucci, cubo 20B, 87036 Rende (CS), Italy
anna.rovella@unical.it

Abstract. Digital libraries are distributed software infrastructures that aim at collecting, managing, preserving, and using digital objects (or resources) for the long term, and providing specialized services on such resources to its users. Service provision should be of measurable quality and performed according to codified policies. Currently, modern digital libraries include a wide range of conventional digital objects: text document, image, audio, video, software, etc. In the emerging domain of the Internet of Things (IoT), cyberphysical smart objects (or simply smart objects) will play a central role in providing new (smart) services to both humans and machines. It is therefore challenging to include smart objects, the newest type of digital objects, into digital libraries as novel first-class objects to be collected, managed, and preserved. However, their inclusion poses critical issues to address and many research challenges to deal with. This paper aims at paving the way towards such a novel inclusion that will enable effective discovery, management and querying of smart objects. In particular, our approach is based on a metadata model purposely defined to describe all the cyberphysical characteristics (geophysical, functional, and non-functional) of smart objects. The metadata model is then used for a seamless integration of smart objects into digital libraries compliant with the digital library reference model proposed by the DL.org community. The proposed approach is also exemplified through a simple yet effective case study.

Keywords: Internet of Things, Cyberphysical Smart Objects, Digital Libraries, Metadata.

1 Introduction

Digital Libraries (DLs) have undergone a considerable evolution, becoming complex entities, able of managing and preserving different types of digital material [1]. They offer a variety of services that can be pervasive and ubiquitous and can be heterogeneous in characteristics, objectives and functions. Since the 1990s librarians first and researchers belonging to different fields later have elaborated different theories and

G. Fortino et al. (Eds.): IDCS 2014, LNCS 8729, pp. 147–158, 2014.

applications and for this reason the definition of DL presents a polysemy of meanings that reflects different visions and approaches. The concept of DL has therefore evolved, moving from a system for the retrieval of static information (primarily books and digitalized textual documents) to a tool useful for the collaboration and interaction between researchers and users, regarding domain-specific topics. Currently, DLs include a wide range of digital objects: text document, image, audio, video, software, etc.

In the emerging domain of the Internet of Things (IoT) [2], a novel type of digital resource is the cyberphysical smart object (SO). An SO is a daily life physical object augmented with sensing/actuation, processing, storing, and networking capabilities, in order to provide a set of physical and digital services to its users (both humans, machines, or digital systems) [3, 4]. During their lifecycle, SOs can produce continuous streams of geolocalized and contextual data also related to their use and their surrounding environment. Moreover, SOs may evolve to provide new/different cyberphysical services to their users.

The aim of this paper is to propose an approach for the inclusion of SOs into DLs which would enable effective discovery, querying and management of SOs based on typical DL tools and facilities. To the best of our knowledge, this approach represents the first research effort towards the integration of SOs into DLs.

In particular, the approach is based on a well-defined metadata model for SOs able to describe all the cyberphysical characteristics (geophysical, functional, and non-functional) of SOs. The SO metadata model is used for the inclusion of SOs into DLs compliant with the digital library reference model [5] proposed by the DL.org community [6].

The remainder of this paper is organized as follows. Section 2 discusses work related to operational and non-operational metadata models for SOs. In Section 3, we define the proposed SO metadata model in detail whereas in Section 4, a case study is presented to exemplify all concepts of the SO metadata model. Section 5 provides an articulated discussion about the inclusion of SOs into DLs. Finally, conclusions are drawn and future research efforts are anticipated.

2   Related Work

SOs will represent the basic intelligent entities constituting the future IoT and its related IoT applications [2]. There is therefore a need to define a reference metadata model for SOs that can facilitate their management from different perspectives (e.g. internal status, provided services, distributed discovery, and interaction with the physical world, the user and other systems) and their inclusion in highly dynamic and complex ecosystems (e.g. IoT, Internet of the Future, and next-generation DLs).

In the literature, many works are available, in which the SO definition and the consequent inclusion in existing architectures is very differently argued. Among these, it is possible to recognize operational and non-operational SO metadata models.

Models proposed in [7] and [2] belong to the non-operational models. In [7], an SO classification according to the concepts of creator and purpose is defined. In particular, the creator can be either an individual creating SOs for a personal purpose (e.g. personal use) or an industrial company that creates SOs for business. The former SOs are called self-made whereas the latter ones are named ready-made. The purpose of an SO may be to play a role in a specific application/system or to be reused in a wide range of different applications. The former is defined specific, while the latter open-ended. However, such a classification considers only two dimensions (creator and purpose) that are not related to the cyberphysical characteristics of the SOs. Thus, such classification cannot be used in an operational way within an IoT system. In [2] authors classify SOs in activity-aware, policy-aware, and process-aware. Each SO type is characterized by three design dimensions: (i) awareness, which is the ability of SOs to understand (environmental or human) events of the SO surrounding context; (ii) representation, which refers to the programming model of the SO; and (iii) interaction, which defines the communication with users. Such classification is oriented to the design of SOs within an application domain and can be usefully exploited during IoT systems development. However, such contribution is not operational as it can only be used to classify SOs according to design dimensions.

We are indeed interested in operational classifications that are the base to build up SO discovery services and management systems. In [8] the operational SO classification is based on two documents: Smart Object Description Document (SODD) and Profile Description Document (PDD). SODD contains the meta-information of the SO: name, vendor, and list of profiles. PDD specifies a profile that can be either a detector or an actuator. A detector contains information about a specific sensing device according to the Sensor Modeling Language (SML), whereas an actuator is modeled through the Actuator Modeling Language (AML). The proposed classification is specific to the SO implementation and management supported by the FedNet middleware [8]. In [9] two main concerns are addressed through a conceptual technological agnostic model: (i) the interactions between the User (human or not) and the SO, (ii) the synergy between the Physical Entity and the Digital counterpart. In this direction the Digital Proxy - which is the representation of a given set of aspects (or properties) of the Physical Entity - plays the crucial roles of SO identifier and bridge between the real and the virtual world. In fact, the functionalities of sensing and actuation are delegated to the Devices, which therefore realize the effective interaction with the physical reality. Concepts such as aggregation between SOs (which can be logically grouped in a structured, often hierarchical way) and the relationship between Services and Resources provide flexible guidelines for an SO modeling that ensures interoperability with and openness to functional and technological developments not entirely predictable. In [10] and [11], a metadata model to represent functional and non-functional characteristics of SOs in a structured way is proposed. The metadata model is divided into four main categories: type, device, services, and location. The type is the SO type (e.g. smart pen, smart table, etc.). The device defines the hw/sw characteristics of the SO device. Services contain the list of services provided by the SO; in particular, a service can have one or more operations implementing it. The location represents the position of the SO. This metadata model, which is more general than the one proposed in [9], is currently implemented in a discovery framework (named SmartSearch) for SO indexing, discovery and dynamic selection [10, 11].

3   A Metadata Model for CyberPhysical Smart Objects

The proposed metadata model is an extension of the model proposed in [10, 11] and also borrows some concepts from the other models discussed in Section 2. The metadata model is portrayed in Figure 1 according to the UML class diagram formalism. In particular, the proposed model defines a set of metadata categories that can characterize an SO in any application domain of interest (e.g. Smart Cities, Smart Factories, Smart Home, Smart Grid, Smart Building, etc.). The metadata represent the SOs static parameters, while the related dynamic parameters can be retrieved through operations associated to the available services or from the smart object status (usually through basic SO status services). In our metadata model, an SO, which could aggregate other SOs according to the aggregation relationship, is a composition of the following main metadata categories:

- **Status:** is characterized by a list of variables, given as pairs <name, value>, that capture the SO state.
- **FingerPrint:** contains the following basic and immutable SO information:
  - **Identifier:** represents the identifier (or Id) of the SO, which allows its unique identification within the IoT or an IoT subsystem;
  - **Creator:** represents the SO creator, which can be either an individual creating the SO for personal use, an industrial company that creates it for business, or an academic research laboratory implementing it for research purposes;
  - **Type:** represents a primary type of SO (e.g. a smart pen, a smart chair, a smart office). Moreover, secondary SO types can also be given that contain, for instance, information about the SO design classification as proposed in [2];
  - **QoSParameter:** defines a QoS parameter associated to the SO. Different QoS parameters may be defined such as trustness, reliability, availability, etc.
- **PhysicalProperty:** represents a physical property of the original object without any hardware augmentation and embedded smartness.
- **Service:** models a digital service provided by the SO. A service has a name, a description, the type (sensing, actuation, SO status), input parameters, and the return (primitive or complex) parameter type. Each Service is characterized by one or more **Operations** that implement the service itself and by zero or more **QoSIndicators** whose associated values are provided. In particular, an **Operation**, which defines the individual operation that may be invoked on a service, is equipped with a set of input parameters necessary for its invocation, the return (primitive or complex) parameter type and a description.
- **Device:** defines the hardware and software characteristics of a device that allows to augment the physical object and make it smart. Device can be specialized into one of the following three categories:
  - **Computer:** represents the features of a processing unit of the SO (e.g. PC, embedded computer, plug computer, smart-phone);
  - **Sensor:** models the characteristics of a sensor node belonging to the SO;
  - **Actuator:** models the characteristics of an actuator node of the SO.

- **Location:** represents the geophysical position of the SO. It can be set in absolute terms, specifying the coordinates (latitude and longitude), and/or in relative terms through the use of location tags.
- **User:** identifies the entity using the services provided by the SO. In particular, users of an SO can be of three types:
  - **Human:** represents the classical man-object usage relationship;
  - **SmartObject:** represents a less conventional use relationship, in which the SOs take advantage of services exposed by other ones and vice versa;
  - **DigitalSystem:** represents a generic digital entity, like a Web Server, a software agent, a robot or even more complex systems.

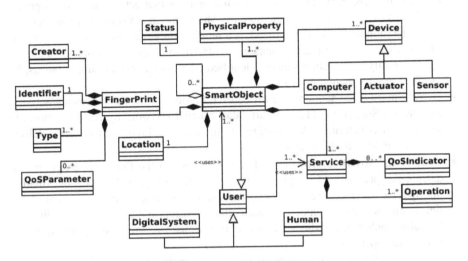

Fig. 1. The SO Metadata Model

4   A Case Study: Smart Office

The objective of this section is to show the instantiation of the SO metadata model introduced in Section 3 with respect to a case study referring to the SO "SmartOffice" defined in [10]. The SmartOffice, on the basis of the information gathered and a set of inference rules, supports office users during their daily working activity by providing suggestions (e.g. warnings that it would be appropriate to take a break after a long session of work by sitting, or indicating how to adjust the screen brightness based on the room luminosity showing such information on the screen closest to the user) and performing smart actuations (e.g. turning the lights and/or the projector off while not used in order to avoid energy wastage). In particular, the SmartOffice provides services obtained by the cooperation of multiple heterogeneous (but at same time independent) SOs located in the office area. The SmartOffice model, which is obtained by instantiating the SO metadata model, can be partitioned into six parts (see Figure 2):

- *Smart Object Core*: SmartOffice contains the current status information about the SmartOffice itself (temperature, humidity, presence, and light variables). Moreover, the UML aggregation and *uses* relationships underline respectively that Smart Office aggregates and uses three SOs and interacts with different users (see below).
- *Basic Features*: information related to the categories FingerPrint, Location, and PhysicalProperty (see Figure 1), finds place here. In particular, the Smart Office is a room of dimensions 500x700x230 (cm), located at DIMES-Unical, Cube 41 c, 4th floor. Its fingerprint shows that the Smart Office was created by the "SenSysCal" company, is identified with the name "Office1" and has a trustness score of 0.95.
- *Devices*: the laptop Host1, provided with a monitor that acts as actuator, supports the SmartOffice application logic and also shows messages sent by the aggregated SOs. The monitor Actuator1, instead, is a monitor only used as message visualizer. Moreover, a presence sensor (identified as Sensor1) and a light/humidity/temperature sensor (identified as Sensor2) gather simple but useful in-office environmental information.
- *Users*: SmartOffice supports the office user Antonio in his daily working activity, and the SO SmartBody [12]. In particular, SmartBody worn by Antonio allows to recognize user activities like standing, sitting, walking, laying down, and to deliver such information to the SmartOffice.
- *Services*: SmartOffice provides different services: (i) the PresenceService, which detects the presence of people inside the office, and provides such information through the GetPresence operation; (ii) the LightService, which informs if the lights are switched on/off through the GetLightStatus operation; (iii) the VisualizationService, which shows notifications on the display through the SetDisplay operation.
- *Aggregated SOs*: SmartOffice aggregates the following SOs: (i) SmartDesk, which provides a presence service able to detect whether or not the user is at desk; (ii) SmartProjector, which provides services to query the projector status and to control it; (iii) SmartWhiteboard, which provides a detection service able to recognize its exploitation by a user. Such SOs are used to implement the SmartOffice services.

5   SO Inclusion According to the Digital Library Reference Model

The inclusion of SOs into DLs is carried out according to the Digital Library Reference Model (DLRM) [5], which is currently the main reference model for architecting DLs. As the DLRM is structured into six domains (Content, User, Functionality, Policy, Quality, and Architecture), the SO is contextualized in each of such domains by discussing matching and implications of its inclusion with respect to the adopted SO metadata model, and providing meaningful examples related to the case study proposed in Section 4. In the following, we reuse the specific terminology of the DLRM [5]; in particular, the DLRM terms are reported in italics.

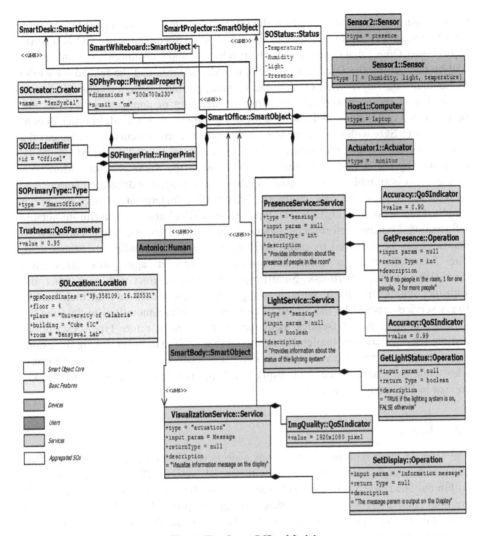

Fig. 2. The SmartOffice Model

An SO, as compliant with the definition (and also rationale) provided in the DLRM [5], can be straightly included as *Resource* in a DL and uniquely identifiable through the *Resource ID*. It could be easily accessed, queried and managed by the DL entities as long as it complies with the *Resource Format* defined in the proposed SO metadata model. Moreover, SOs play both the roles of *Actors* and *Information Objects*, as discussed in the following subsections.

5.1   Content

The *Content Domain* represents the various aspects related to the modeling of information managed in the DL universe to serve the information needs of the *Actors*. The main *Resource* of *Content Domain* is the *Information Object*, which is an information item that seamlessly provides data to the DL *Actors*. Specifically, the SO is a novel *Information Object* that contributes to the production and consumption of content that will be handled by the DL *Actors* through the SO Services and the related (possible) SO annotations. *Information Objects* can be grouped into *Collections* concept, a specialization of the *Resource Set*, for some management or application purpose. The proposed SO metadata model allows a logical grouping of this kind, in order to convey different SOs within an aggregated entity which complements and enhances the Services of the various components SO. The content requested to the SO could be monitored by the *Action Log* over time so allowing the *Actor profiling*. Moreover, such content is suitable for being contextualized or displayed in different *Views*.

With reference to the case study, the SmartOffice fingerprint includes its creator (SenSysCal), its unique id (Office1), type (Smart Office) and other useful immutable information. Dynamic information about current SmartOffice status (e.g. current temperature) can be retrieved by using basic accessory services hiding the status field. The SmartOffice is a composite entity, because it aggregates other SOs (SmartWhiteboard, SmartDesk, SmartProjector) which interact with each other and with the SmartOffice itself, without losing their independence or alter their nature. Every service exposed by the SmartOffice presents useful annotations to describe the expected content output (service id, requested parameters, return type, description) and the list of operations implementing the service itself. Moreover, taking the example of the `PresenceService`, the SmartOffice could maintain the list of the users, who requested such service, and display such information in an aggregate weekly *view* or in a monthly average *view*.

5.2 User

The *User Domain* represents the various aspects related to the modeling of entities, either human or machines, interacting with any DL system. The SOs play a dual role within the DL reference model, and specifically in the *end-user domain*: in fact, SOs are both *content creators*, because they produce or update data and information, and *content consumers*, as it often happens that they are themselves users of other SOs or *Resources* in general. The proposed SO metadata model contemplates both of these occurrences, together with the possibility that other *Actors*, humans or in a broader sense digital systems (such as web server, robot, etc.), can play the role of consumer of SO-generated content. Other *Roles* envisaged in the DL reference model (DL Managers and DL Software Developers) fall outside the proposed SO metadata model.

Regarding the case study, the SmartOffice plays both the role of: (i) content creator, in order to provide services like the `LightService` to the human user (e.g. the employee in the Smart Office) or even to general digital systems (e.g. a remote web service or software agent); (ii) content consumer, even exploiting data generated by other SOs like the SmartDesk through the `PresenceService`.

5.3 Functionality

The *Functionality Domain* represents the various aspects related to the modeling of facilities/services provided in the DL universe to serve *Actor* needs. A *Function* is a particular operation that can be realized on a *Resource* upon an *Actor* request. With reference to the SO, for which the main operations pertain the discovery, querying and configuration, functions can be specialized in two classes: the *Access Resource Function* and the *Manage Function*. The first family of functions aims at finding *Resources* compliant to certain (static or dynamic) features (*Discovery*), querying them (*Search-Browse*), retaining the content retrieved through specific mechanisms (*Acquire*) and finally displaying it (*Visualize*). The *Manage Function*, instead, supports the production (*Create*), publication (*Publish*), updating (*Update*), configuration (*Personalize*) and other basic operations related to the Resource lifecycle. It should be noted that these functionalities are not provided directly by the SO but by the DL, on the basis of information structured in the proposed SO metadata model.

Considering the case study, when a *User* of the DL searches for a specific service (e.g. the LightService) through the *Discovery Function*, this will query the metadata generated by the *Resources* contained in the DL, among which the SmartOffice. The SmartOffice matches the search criteria, so the User will fulfill a list of parameters contained in the *Personalize Function* (e.g. which *View* to be adopted) before proceeding to the query. Based on such information, the DL will interact with the SmartOffice LightService to carry out the requests through the *Visualize Function*.

5.4 Policy

The *Policy Domain* represents a set of guiding principles designed to organize actions in a coherent way and to help in decision making. The proposed SO metadata model is neutral with respect to the concept of *Policy*. Few changes to the SO metadata model could be carried out to regulate the interactions between the SO user and the SO services, according to what is present in the reference DL model respectively with the *User Policy* and *Content Policy*. In particular, one could implement the concept of *Policy* by directly associating it to the SO User or SO Service entity, or binding it outside of the SO metadata model, at the level of the DL.

As an example related to the case study, referring to the *User Policy*, it could be stated that the LightService could be accessed only by a few trusted users (the ability to close the lights remotely can have undesirable consequences in case of abuse from malicious users) while the VisualizationService could be used by everyone present in the SmartOffice. In this direction, the definition of a user's level of reliability could be a facility for the implementation of the *User Policy* (see subsection 5.5 next entry, *User Quality Parameter*).

5.5 Quality

The *Quality Domain* captures the aspects that permit considering DL systems from a quality point of view, with the goal of judging and evaluating them with respect to specific facets. It represents the various aspects related to features and attributes of *Resources* with respect to their degree of excellence. The proposed SO metadata model already contains two elements that refer to the SO quality (QoS Parameter) and the quality of the SO Services (QoS Indicator), in full agreement with the DL reference model that provides *Quality Parameters* on the *Resources* (*Generic Quality Parameter*) and on the *Information Object* (*Content Quality Parameter*). Regarding the *User*, the DLRM presents a *User Quality Parameter* that could be easily imported into the SO metadata model, for example by assigning each SO User a reliability value, on the basis of which it is possible to define *Policy* and granting special rights or access privileges to the SO Services.

For instance, the SmartOffice has a high trustness value (*Generic Quality Parameter*) because it exploits carefully designed and maintained hardware and software components; the PresenceService, in turn, has a high accuracy (*Content Quality Parameter*) because the percentage of false positives and false negatives is extremely low.

5.6   Architecture

The *Architecture Domain* represents the various aspects related to the software systems that concretely realize the DL universe. The inclusion of a SO within the DL architecture presented in the DLRM may involve (i) the insertion of an architectural *Running Component*, which represents a running instance of a *Software Component* active on a *Hosting Node*, suitably designed, based on the SO characteristics and equipped with specific interfaces, or (ii) the creation of a new component, currently not present in the reference architecture, delegated to the SO virtualization [13].

As opposed to traditional *Resources* that can be acquired and placed directly into DLs (such as documents, videos, etc.), the SmartOffice belongs stably to an external system and is associated to other SOs (SmartDesk, SmartProjector, SmartWhiteBoard) that are also part of the same external system. Therefore, there is the need for a proxy that virtualizes the SmartOffice [13] and makes it look "physically" integrated into the DL as other more traditional *Resources*.

6   Conclusion and Future Work

In this paper we have proposed an approach for the inclusion of SOs into DLs compliant with the DLRM defined by DL.org [6]. The inclusion is based on a metadata model for SOs purposely defined to fully characterize all SO properties (both physical and cyber) as well as their interactions with other human, digital and cyberphysical actors. The approach has also been exemplified through a case study concerning a smart office environment. In particular, the SO metadata model has been instantiated with respect to the case study, and the resulting SmartOffice model has been used to exemplify the main SO inclusion concepts.

Such an inclusion would enable, from one perspective, to effectively support discovery, querying and management of SOs through tools and facilities provided by modern DLs and, from another perspective, to extend currently available DLs with a new type of object to collect, manage and preserve. To the best of our knowledge, our proposal is the first research aiming at this inclusion that would pave the way towards the development of cyberphysical DLs.

Future work will be mainly twofold: (i) addressing interoperability and trust issues of cyberphysical DLs [14]; (ii) implementing the proposed approach in a real DL management system such as Fedora [15] and/or DSpace [16].

Acknowledgement. This work has been partially supported by DICET INMOTO Organization of Cultural Heritage for Smart Tourism and REal Time Accessibility (OR.C.HE.S.T.R.A.) project funded by the Italian Government (PON04a2 D).

References

1. Ross, S.: Digital library development review: Final report. National Library of New Zealand (2003)
2. Kortuem, G., Kawsar, F., Fitton, D., Sundramoorthy, V.: Smart objects as buildingblocks for the internet of things. IEEE Internet Computing 14(1), 44–51 (2010)
3. Fortino, G., Guerrieri, A., Russo, W., Savaglio, C.: Middlewares for Smart Objects and Smart Environments: Overview and Comparison. In: Internet of Things Based on Smart Objects: Technology, Middleware and Applications. Internet of Things: Technology, Communications and Computing, pp. 1–27. Springer (2014)
4. Fortino, G., Guerrieri, A., Russo, W.: Agent-oriented Smart Objects Development. In: IoT and Logistics Workshop jointly held with 16th IEEE International Conference on Computer Supported Cooperative Work in Design (CSCWD 2012), pp. 907–912. IEEE, Wuhan (2012)
5. Candela, L., et al.: The Digital Library Reference Model. Report (2010),
   http://www.dlorg.eu/index.php/outcomes/
   reference-modeloutcomes/reference-model
6. Dl.org - Digital Library Interoperability, Best Practices and Modelling Foundations,
   http://www.dlorg.eu/
7. Uckelmann, D., Harrison, M., Michahelles, F. (eds.): Architecting the Internet of Things. Springer (2011)
8. Kawsar, F., Nakajima, T., Park, J.H., Yeo, S.S.: Design and implementation of aframework for building distributed smart object systems. J. Supercomput. 54(1), 4–28 (2010)
9. Serbanati, A., Medaglia, C.M., Ceipidor, U.B.: Building blocks of the internet of things: State of the art and beyond. In: Turcu, C. (ed.) Deploying RFID-Challenges, Solutions, and Open Issues. InTech (2011)
10. Fortino, G., Lackovic, M., Russo, W., Trunfio, P.: A discovery service for smart objects over an agent-based middleware. In: Pathan, M., Wei, G., Fortino, G. (eds.) IDCS 2013. LNCS, vol. 8223, pp. 281–293. Springer, Heidelberg (2013)

11. Fortino, G., Russo, W., Rovella, A., Savaglio, C.: On the Classification of Cyberphysical Smart Objects in Internet of Things. In: In:International Workshop on Networks of Cooperating Objects for Smart Cities 2014 (UBICITEC 2014), vol. 1156, pp. 76–84 (2014)
12. Fortino, G., Guerrieri, A., Lacopo, M., Lucia, M., Russo, W.: An agent-based middleware for cooperating smart objects. In: Corchado, J.M., Bajo, J., Kozlak, J., Pawlewski, P., Molina, J.M., Julian, V., Silveira, R.A., Unland, R., Giroux, S. (eds.) PAAMS 2013. CCIS, vol. 365, pp. 387–398. Springer, Heidelberg (2013)
13. Fortino, G., Guerrieri, A., Russo, W., Savaglio, C.: Integration of Agent-based and Cloud Computing for the Smart Objects-oriented IoT. In: IEEE Computer Supported Cooperative Work in Design (CSCWD 2014), Taiwan (2014)
14. Innocenti, P., Vullo, G., Ross, S.: Towards a digital library policy and quality interoperability framework: the DL.org project. New Review of Information Networking 15(1), 29–53 (2010)
15. Fedora Project, http://www.fedora-commons.org/about
16. DSpace, http://www.dspace.org

Parallel and Distributed Computing

Static Data Race Detection for Java Programs with Dynamic Class Loading

Noriaki Yoshiura and Wei Wei*

Department of Information and Computer Sciences, Saitama University,
255, Shimo-ookubo, Sakura-ku, Saitama, Japan
{yoshiura,weiwei}@fmx.ics.saitama-u.ac.jp

Abstract. Multi-thread programs are likely to have bugs in mutual exclusion among threads. Data race is one of the problems that occur in wrong mutual exclusion. There are two kinds of methods of data race detection: dynamic analysis detection and static analysis detection. Dynamic analysis detection is to detect data race by analyzing the results or processes of program executions. Static analysis detection is to detect data race by analyzing source codes of programs. A method of static analysis detection of data race for Java programs has been proposed, but this method cannot handle dynamic class loading. This paper proposes a method of static analysis detection of data race for dynamic class loading and implements this method. This paper also evaluates the implementation by experiments using Java programs that have dynamic class loading. This experiment shows that the proposed method detects data races that cannot be found by the previous data race detection method. The result of experiment shows advantages of the proposed method.

1 Introduction

In multi-thread programs, mutual exclusion among threads is one of the important things. Failure of mutual exclusion would bring troubles in execution of the programs. One of the problems of mutual exclusion is data race. Data race is a trouble that occurs when two threads access the same data and at least one of them writes the data. In multi-thread programs, the access order of data is not decided and depends on the schedule of thread execution. Some access orders of the same data would bring program behaviors that the program creators do not desire. However, detection of data race in programs is difficult[7]. There are two kinds of methods of detection of data race: static analysis method and dynamic analysis method. Dynamic analysis method detects data race by analyzing information that is obtained in program executions[12,11,1,9,10]. Static analysis method detects data race by analyzing program codes without executing programs[7,3]. Naik et al. proposed static data race detection method for Java programs[7]. The experiment in [7] shows that the method is more effective than other methods, but the method ignores dynamic class loading in Java

---

* Now, Wei Wei works at a company in China.

G. Fortino et al. (Eds.): IDCS 2014, LNCS 8729, pp. 161–173, 2014.

programs[5]. Dynamic class loading is that Java programs start loading class files at the first time when the class files are required. In dynamic class loading, Java programs can load class files via the Internet. Because many Java programs use dynamic class loading, static data race detection method with ignorance of dynamic class loading fails to find critical data races.

This paper proposes static data race detection method that can handle dynamic class loading. The locations of class files that Java programs load are expressed by URLs. The proposed static data race detection method requires to obtain the location URLs of class files without executing Java programs, but all the URLs are not found without executing Java programs and the URLs may change according to executions of programs. Thus the detection method proposed in this paper computes the candidates of URLs of class files, loads all class files from the candidates of URLs, decompiles all class files and obtains source files of the class files. Next, the proposed method combines Java programs with the source files of class files and analyzes the combined Java programs to detect data race by the method in [7]. This paper also implements the proposed method and evaluates the implementation by experiments. In the experiments, the implemented method detects several data races in Java programs. These data races cannot be found by the method in [7].

There are several researches that are related with this paper. The paper of [14] focuses on wrong using of dynamic class loading and reports that many Java programs do not use dynamic class loading rightly; the paper proposes the method of resolving the wrong usages of dynamic class loading. The method proposed in this paper uses dataflow analysis to compute the location URLs of class files. There are several researches that are related with dataflow analysis[15,16]. The method proposed in this paper is related with several researches that have already been published, but dataflow analysis has not been used for static data race detection for dynamic class loading.

This paper is organized as follows: Section 2 explains static data race detection. Section 3 explains Java dynamic class loading. Section 4 proposes a static data race detection method for dynamic class loading. Section 5 shows the experiment of implementation of the proposed detection method. Section 6 concludes this paper.

2   Static Data Race Detection

The static data race detection method in [7] consists of five steps as shown in Figure 1. The five steps are OriginalPairs computation, ReachablePairs computation, AliasingPairs computation, EscapingPairs computation and UnlockedPairs computation. The method is incomplete; all of the data race that the method detects in Java programs are not true data races. The method detects the candidates of data races and cannot detect data races accurately. The features of this detection method are as follows:

- Apache commons-pool is a component of object pool implementations. The static data race detection method in [7] found 17 data races in the compo-

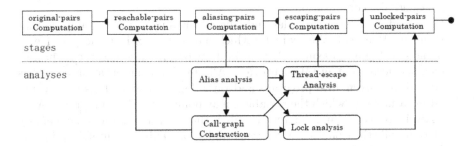

Fig. 1. Overview of static detection of data race

nent. Five data races among the 17 data races are really data races. Probability of wrong detection of the method is lower than that of the other methods of data race detection.

- The method can handle Java programs of about 650,000 lines. It follows that the method can handle large scale projects.
- The method can handle synchronized, wait and notify methods in Java programs.
- The method does not handles libraries.
- The method can output the examples of Java program behaviors that take data race.

2.1 Algorithm of Static Data Race Detection

The method in [7] consists of the following steps.

- OriginalPairs computation
  By Soot tool[13], OriginalPairs computation picks up all memory access pairs that have possibilities of accessing the same memory places simultaneously. The set of all the memory access pairs is called OriginalPairs. OriginalPairs includes the pairs in which one element writes a variable and the other element reads or writes the same variable. Soot tool[13] analyzes Java programs: analyzing class files, null pointer, control flow and dataflow. OriginalPairs also includes the memory access pairs that do not take data race. The following steps remove, from OriginalPairs, the memory access pairs that do not take data race.
- ReachablePairs computation
  The first step of ReachablePairs computation creates call graph[4], which is a directed graph expressing call relations among subroutines in Java programs. The call graph is used to remove, from OriginalPairs, memory access pairs whose element is not reached from the main methods in Java programs because memory access pairs that take data race must be reached from the main methods. The result of ReachablePairs computation is called ReachablePairs.

- AliasingPairs computation

  Let x and y be local variables and f be an instance variable. Suppose that ReachablePairs contains (x.f,y.f), which means that x in f and y in f may be accessed simultaneously. If x=y in Java programs is executed, the two memory accesses may take data race. AliasingPairs computation uses alias analysis[6]. Given Java programs and variable x.f, alias analysis returns the set of variables to which the variable x may point in the Java programs. Alias analysis enables to find different variables that may access the same memory place by substitution, call by reference and so on. This computation removes, from ReachablePairs, the memory access pairs that are not included in the result of alias analysis because the memory access pairs never access the same memory place simultaneously. The result of AliasingPairs computation is called AliasingPairs.

- EscapingPairs computation

  EscapingPairs computation uses thread-escape analysis to remove, from AliasingPairs, memory access pairs whose both elements are not executed by several threads simultaneously. Thread-escape analysis finds the objects that are shared by several threads. In Java programs an object may be shared if it is reachable from arguments of methods starting threads or if it is reachable from some static fields in objects.

  Figure 2 shows an example of shared objects. In the figure, x and y are arguments of the method starting threads and may be shared by several threads that are started by Thread1(x,y).start() and Thread2(x,y).start().

```
Main() {
  Object x,y;
  Thread1(x,y).start();
  .......
  Thread2(x,y).start();
  .......
}
```

Fig. 2. Thread-escape analysis

In addition to thread-escape analysis, EscapingPairs computation uses aliasing analysis again to find the memory that may be shared by several threads. As a result, EscapingPairs computation obtains a set of memory access pairs that may be shared by several threads. Finally, the EscapingPairs computation removes, from AliasingPairs, the memory accesses that are not in a set of memory access pairs that may be shared by several threads. The result of EscapingPairs computation is called EscapingPairs.

- UnlockedPairs computation

  UnlockedPairs computation uses lock analysis to remove the memory access pairs that have the same lock. In Java programs, lock is used for mutual

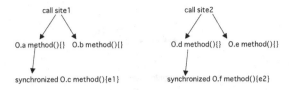

Fig. 3. UnlockPairs Computation

exclusion; the memory access pairs that have the same lock do not take data race.

By searching all path in the call graph and checking whether each memory access pair has the same lock, lock analysis finds memory access pairs whose elements do not have the same lock. In Figure 3, suppose that call site1 and call site2 are the methods starting threads, O is an object and e1 and e2 are memory accesses. In the call graph, the path call site1, O.a method(), synchronized O.c method() and the path call site2, O.d method(), synchronized O.f method() have the same lock. UnlockPairs computation removes, from EscapingPairs, the memory access pairs that have locks. The result of UnlockPairs computation is called UnlockedPairs.

Figure 4 shows the relation among the sets of pairs. The static data race detection method in [7] supposes that UnlockedPairs is a set of candidate memory access pairs that take data race. However, all elements of UnlockedPairs do not take data race. Manual check is necessary to decide whether each element of UnlockedPairs really takes data race.

2.2   Problems of Static Data Race Detection Method

There are several problems in the static data race detection method[7].

1. The alias analysis that is used in AliasingPairs computation is may-alias analysis but not must-alias analysis. This fact decreases the correctness of data race detection.
2. Analysis of data race in class libraries requires to prepare methods of calling the class libraries. There is a possibility of failure of detecting data race in class libraries because how to call the class libraries depends on Java programs that use the class libraries and because all kinds of calling the class libraries cannot be considered in static data race detection.
3. The method cannot detect data races that occur in initializers, constructors and finalizers that typically lack synchronization and seldom contain data races but cause many false alarms without a method-escape analysis.
4. The method ignores the effects of reflection and dynamic class loading.

Many Java programs use dynamic class loading. Especially, in distributed systems, dynamic class loading loads class files in a lot of places via the Internet

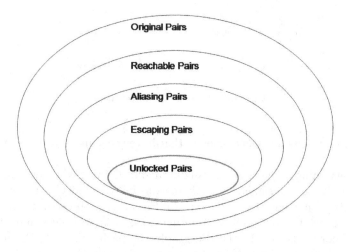

Fig. 4. Relations of several sets of pairs

or local area networks. Thus, it is important to deal with dynamic class loading in data race detection. This paper proposes static data race detection method for dynamic class loading.

3   Java Dynamic Class Loading

In Java programs, three class loaders that are used in Java virtual machine[5]: bootstrap class loader, extended class loader and system class loader.

Bootstrap class loader loads standard libraries (java.* packages and javax.* packages), extended class loader loads the class files in the extended directory (<JRE_HOME>/lib/ext), and the system class loader loads class files from JAR files or the directories that are specified by the variable "CLASSPATH". Extending and using system class loader enables to load class files from the Internet.

Dynamic class loading is that Java programs load class files at the first time when they are required to be executed. In executing Java programs Java virtual machine can load class files from servers via the Internet by class loader that is defined by program users.

The locations of the class files are expressed by URLs in user defined class loaders; HTTP protocol, FTP protocol and local file name can be used. The location URLs depend on user inputs, the configuration file of Java, property files, or the computation in the processes of Java program executions. The static data race detection method in [7] analyzes source codes of Java programs to detect data race without executions. Thus, the method ignores dynamic class loading because some locations of the class files can be found only in Java program executions.

4 Method for Dynamic Class Loading

4.1 Conversion of Programs

Detection of data race in Java programs for dynamic class loading requires to compute location URLs of class files. There are four patterns of computing location URLs in execution of programs; URLs depend on user inputs, variables, profiles or configurations. The method that is proposed in this paper constructs dataflow graphs of variables and computes the candidate values of location URLs as many as possible. To ease constructing dataflow graphs, the proposed method converts repetition statements, exception handling, method calling and arrays.

- Conversion of repetition statements
  The proposed method removes repetition statements in Java programs before computing location URLs of class files; the method handles for-statement, while-statement and do-while-statement. For-statements are converted into several statements that are repeated in for-statements. If the number of repetition is a constant, repetition statements are converted into the constant time repeated statements. If the number of repetition depends on variables whose values are computed in the processes of the program executions, the number of repetition is set up as a prepared number. The prepared number can be defined by users of the data race detection method. In the experiment of this paper, the prepared number is one to five.
  Regarding while-statement, as shown in Figure 5, while-statements are converted into several if-then-else statements. The condition of if-then-else statement is that of while-statement. The number of repetition is set up as a prepared number. The prepared number can be defined by users of the data race detection method. In the experiment of this paper, the prepared number is one to five. Do-while statements are handled similarly to while-statements.

```
                            if (Cond) {
                              Body;
                              if (Cond) {
  while (Cond)                  Body;
  Body;        ⟹              if (Cond) {
                                ......
                              }
                            }
                          }
```

Fig. 5. Conversion of while sentence

- Conversion of exception handling
  Errors in execution of Java programs are handled as exception; try-catch statements are used for exception handling. If computation of location URLs requires analysis of try-catch, try-catch statements are converted into if-then-else-statements.

– Conversion of method call

   If computation of location URLs requires analysis of method call, caller places are replaced by copied callee methods. If callee methods return values, caller places are converted into substitution statement of copied callee methods. This conversion increases source codes of programs, but it becomes easy to compute location URLs. Because methods may be called recursively, the proposed method limits the number of copying callee methods.

– Conversion of arrays

   If computation of location URLs requires to handle arrays, the proposed method converts arrays. In the case that the index of an array is fixed, the array is replaced by the value of array of the fixed index. In the case that the index of an array is not fixed, the array is replaced by each element of array. The proposed method checks source codes of programs for each replaced element of array.

4.2   Data Race Detection Method

The proposed data race detection method consists of two steps: computation of location URLs of class files and static data race detection for Java programs with class files that may be loaded dynamically in executions of the programs.

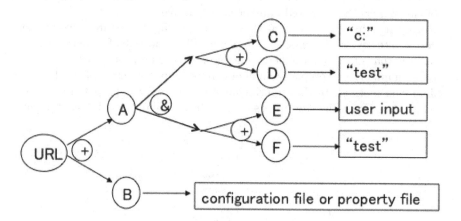

Fig. 6. Dependency relation of variables for URL

Computation of Location URLs. The proposed method requires location URLs that may be fixed in the processes of program executions. If location URLs are constants, it is easy to load class files by the constant URLs and combine Java program source codes with the source codes of class files. If location URLs are not constants, the following procedure computes the candidate values of location URLs by using converted program source codes.

   The procedure that computes the candidate values of location URLs constructs dataflow graphs from converted program source codes. Figure 6 shows the example of dataflow graphs. In this graph, & means that all elements are necessary to compute the dependent element, and + means that each one of elements is sufficient to compute the dependent element. The dataflow graphs are constructed as follows;

- Find variables expressing location URLs
- Repeatedly search other variables that the variables depend on
- Stop searching variables until the values of the variables are user inputs or fixed, or depend on configuration files or profiles

Some variables may depend on the same variables because some methods are called recursively. Thus, the procedure limits the number of tracing variables in constructing dataflow graphs. This limitation may make dataflow graphs incomplete and dataflow graphs do not find all candidate values of location URLs. Even if dataflow graphs are constructed completely, the procedure do not always find all candidate values of location URLs because the variables that depend on user inputs cannot be found without program executions. However, the procedure finds many candidate values of location URLs without executing programs.

Data Race Detection. After finding the candidate values of location URLs, the method that is proposed in this paper downloads all class files whose location URLs are found and decompiles the class files because class files are in JAR file format. It is possible to decompile JAR files into Java source codes except optimization of operation of constants. The method combines Java program source codes with Java source codes of class files and applies the detection method in [7]. Because one location URL has several candidate values, the method that is proposed in this paper applies the detection method in [7] to Java program source codes for each candidate value of location URLs.

4.3 Implementation

This paper implements the static data race detection method that is proposed in this paper. This implementation is written in Java and uses Chord[2] that is implementation of the method in [7].

5 Experiment

The experiment of this paper applies the implementation to three Java programs that use dynamic class loading. In the environment of the experiment, CPU is AMD Athlon(tm)64 Dual Core Processor 2.0GHz, memory size is 2GB and OS is Windows XP. The three Java programs are "fileStream", "weatherService" and "examSystem".

"fileStream" is file transfer software. In this software, the class files that are dynamically loaded check types and sizes of transferred files. "weatherService" is software that checks weekly weather of date and location that the users input. In

Table 1. Target Software

Software	class	dynamic class loading files	line
fileStream	5	1	638
weatherService	18	2	1598
examSystem	35	2	6653

Table 2. Data race detection without dynamic class loading

Project	Time	Original Pairs	Reachable Pairs	Aliasing Pairs	Escaping Pairs	Unlocked Pairs	Datarace Pairs
file Stream	5s	456	28	15	15	4	0
weather Service	19s	1762	117	87	74	19	1
exam System	52s	3725	220	106	104	8	1

this software, the class files that are dynamically loaded display weekly weather clearly. "examSystem" is software for examinations. The users of this software input ID and password to this software, select and answer examination questions, and check their answers. In this software, the class files that are dynamically loaded tell each user the subjects that the user is good or bad at and the subjects that the user should study to improve examination scores. The class files display a line chart of each subject score. This line chart enables to compare average scores and user's own scores. Table 1 shows the features of the three kinds of software.

5.1   Result of Experiment

The experiment applies the method in [7] to the three Java programs to compare the methods in this paper and in [7]. Table 2 is the result of the method in [7] and Table 3 is the result of the method proposed in this paper.

Each table shows the time it takes for the methods to construct UnlockPairs, the number of elements for OriginalPairs, ReachablePairs, AliasingPairs, EscapingPairs and UnlockedPairs, and the number of memory access pairs (DataracePairs) that really take data race. Notice that all elements of UnlockedPairs do not take data race. To construct DataracePairs requires to check manually whether each element in UnlockedPairs takes data race. DataracePairs enables to compare the correctness or detection ability between the method in [7] and the method in this paper. Comparison of two tables shows that the proposed method detects new memory access pairs that take data race. The new memory access pairs in "weatherService" and "examSystem" are related with class files of dynamic class loading. This result shows efficacy of the proposed method.

Table 3. Data race detection with dynamic class loading

Project	Time	Original Pairs	Reachable Pairs	Aliasing Pairs	Escaping Pairs	Unlocked Pairs	Datarace Pairs
file Stream	17s	526	46	32	29	9	0
weather Service	47s	2062	185	137	122	23	3
exam System	157s	4465	323	253	247	12	2

5.2 Discussion

The method proposed in this paper detects new memory access pairs that take data race. The memory access pairs cannot be detected by the method in [7]. However, the execution time of data race detection method increases. In "examSystem", the execution time of the proposed method is three times as much as that of the method in [7]. The 80% of increased time of execution in weatherService or examSystem is used for computation of location URLs. To compute location URLs takes more time than to analyze program source codes to detect data race. It is inferred that the larger source codes are, the more time it takes to compute location URLs. It follows that the fast computation of location URLs is necessary for improvement of the proposed data race detection method.

Let us discuss the number of elements of OriginalPairs, ReachablePairs, AliasingPairs, EscapingPairs, UnlockedPairs and DataracePairs. In weatherService, the element number of UnlockedPairs changes from 19 to 23, but the element number of DataracePairs increases only two. In examSystem, the element number of UnlockedPairs changes from 8 to 12, but the element number of Datarace-Pairs increases only one. As compared with increase of the elements of Unlocked-Pairs, the memory access pairs that take data race are not detected effectively.

In weatherService, the proposed method increases OriginalPairs by 1.17 times, ReachablePairs by 1.58 times, AliasingPairs by 1.54 times, EscapingPairs by 1.65 times and UnlockedPairs by 1.2 times. In examSystem, the proposed method increases OriginalPairs by 1.2 times, ReachablePairs by 1.46 times, AliasingPairs by 2.39 times, EscapingPairs by 2.38 times and UnlockedPairs by 1.5 times. In fileStream, the proposed method also increases the element number of each pairs. Increasing ratio of AliasingPairs and EscapingPairs are more than that of UnlockPairs. The element numbers of AliasingPairs and EscapingPairs are not so different both in weatherService and in examSystem; the EscapingPairs computation do not remove, from Aliasing pairs, many memory access pairs that do not take data race. It follows that omitting EscapingPairs computation is one of the ways of reducing execution time of the data race detection method.

6 Conclusion

This paper proposed static data race detection method for Java programs and implemented the method in Java. The proposed method handles dynamic class loading. This paper also evaluated the proposed method by experiment and showed that the proposed method detected the new memory access pairs that take data race. The pairs cannot be detected the method in [7], which the proposed method is based on.

There are several future works; one of them is to improve computation of location URLs of class files. Another is to construct algorithm of removing, from UnlockedPairs, the elements that do not take data race.

References

1. Agarwal, R., Sasturkar, A., Wang, L., Stoller, S.: Optimized run-time race detection and atomicity checking using partial discovered types. In: Proceedings of the 20th IEEE/ACM International Conference on Automated Software Engineering (ASE 2005), pp. 233–242 (2005)
2. Chord: A Versatile Program Analysis Plathome for Java, http://pag.gatech.edu/chord/ (October 01, 2011)
3. Engler, D., Ashcraft, K.: RacerX: Effective, static detection of race conditions and deadlocks. In: Proceedings of the 19th ACM Symposium on Operating Systems Principles, pp. 237–252 (2003)
4. Grove, D., DeFouw, G., Dean, J., Chambers, C.: Call graph construction in object-oriented languages. In: Proceedings of the ACM Conference on Object-oriented Programming, Systems, Languages, and Applications, pp. 108–124 (1997)
5. Liang, S., Bracha, G.: Dynamic Class Loading in the Java Virtual Machine. In: Proceedings of the 13th ACM SIGPLAN Conference on Object-oriented Programming, Systems, Languages, and Applications, pp. 36–44 (1998)
6. Milanova, A., Rountev, A., Ryder, B.: Parameterized object sensitivity for points-to analysis for Java. ACM Transactions on Software Engineering Methodology 14(1), 1–41 (2005)
7. Naik, M., Aiken, A., Whaley, J.: Effective Static Race Detection for Java. In: Proceedings of the ACM SIGPLAN Conference on Programming Language Design and Implementation (PLDI 2006), pp. 20–29 (2006)
8. Pratikakis, P., Foster, J., Hicks, M.: LOCKSMITH: Context-sensitive correlation analysis for race detection. In: Proceedings of the ACM SIGPLAN Conference on Programming Language Design and Implementation (PLDI 2006), pp. 320–331 (2006)
9. Praun, C., Gross, T.: Static conflict analysis for multi-threaded object-oriented programs. In: Proceedings of the ACM SIGPLAN Conference on Programming Language Design and Implementation (PLDI 2003), pp. 115–128 (2003)
10. Praun, C., Gross, T.: Object race detection. In: Proceedings of the ACM SIGPLAN Conference on Object-Oriented Programming, Systems, Languages and Applications, pp. 70–82 (2003)
11. Ronsse, M., Bosschere, K.: RecPlay: A fully integrated practical record/replay system. ACM Transactions on Computer Systems 17(2), 133–152 (1999)
12. Schonberg, E.: On-the-fly detection of access anomalies. In: Proceedings of the ACM SIGPLAN Conference on Programming Language Design and Implementation (PLDI 1989), pp. 285–297 (1989)

13. Vallee-Rai, R., Co, P., Gargnon, E., Hendren, L., Lam, P., Sundaresan, Y.: Soot - a Java optimization framework. In: Proceedings of the 1999 Conference of the Centre for Advanced Studies on Collaboratives Research, pp. 125–135 (1999)
14. Sawin, J., Rountev, A.: Improved Static Resolution of Dynamic Class Loading in Java. Automated Software Engineering 16(2), 357–381 (2009)
15. Christensen, A.S., Moller, A., Schwartzbach, M.: Precise Analysis of String Expressions. In: Cousot, R. (ed.) SAS 2003. LNCS, vol. 2694, pp. 1–18. Springer, Heidelberg (2003)
16. Chugh, R., Voung, W.J., Jhala, R., Lerner, S.: Dataflow analysis for concurrent programs using datarace detection. In: Proceedings of the 2008 ACM SIGPLAN Conference on Programming Language Design and Implementation, pp. 316–326 (2008)

Rule Based Classification on a Multi Node Scalable Hadoop Cluster

Shashank Gugnani, Devavrat Khanolkar, Tushar Bihany, and Nikhil Khadilkar

BITS Pilani K.K. Birla Goa Campus,
Goa - 403726, India
shashankgugnani@gmail.com

Abstract. Hadoop framework is one of the reliable, scalable framework for the big data analytics. In this paper we investigate the Hadoop framework for distributed data mining to reduce the computational cost for the exponentially growing scientific data. We use the RIPPER (Repeated Incremental Pruning for Error Reduction) algorithm [5] to develop a rule based classifier. We propose a parallel implementation of RIPPER based on the Hadoop MapReduce framework. The data is horizontally partitioned so that each node operates on a portion of the dataset and finally the results are aggregated to develop the classifier. We tested our algorithm on two large datasets and results showed that we can achieve a speed up of as high as 3.7 on 4 nodes.

Keywords: Hadoop, Distributed Data Mining, Data-intensive computing.

1 Introduction

Computational power is increasing with time. However, the requirements to process the everyday generated data are still challenging. Moreover, the data is distributed all over the globe. Silicon based architectures have almost reached upper limits in terms of processing capabilities (clock speed). Significant technological advancements have paved way for cost-effective parallel computing systems. Hence, there is a sudden increase in the importance of parallel and distributed computing.

Apache Hadoop [1] is an open-source framework which allows users to store and process huge datasets in a distributed environment. Today, it is used by most of the top corporates viz. Yahoo, Facebook, etc. The framework of Apache Hadoop is composed of the following modules:

1. Hadoop Common - contains libraries and utilities needed by other Hadoop modules.
2. Hadoop Distributed File System (HDFS) [4] - a distributed file-system that stores data on the commodity machines, providing very high aggregate bandwidth across the cluster.

G. Fortino et al. (Eds.): IDCS 2014, LNCS 8729, pp. 174–183, 2014.

3. Hadoop YARN - a resource-management platform responsible for managing compute resources in clusters and using them for scheduling of user's applications.
4. Hadoop MapReduce - a programming model for large scale data processing.

Apache Hadoop uses **MapReduce** to process large datasets in parallel and on thousands of nodes in a reliable, fault-tolerant manner. Initially, Hadoop MapReduce job divides the input data into chunks (default size is 64MB). These independent chunks are then processed by the Map tasks on different nodes in a completely parallel manner. The outputs are passed on after sorting to the reduce tasks which does the job of collating the work and combining the results into a single value. Monitoring, scheduling and re-executing the failed tasks are the responsibility of MapReduce.

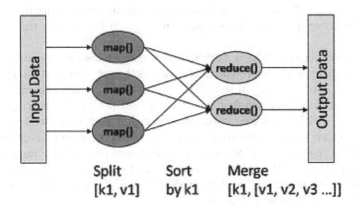

Fig. 1. Map-Reduce Framework

In this paper we present the parallel implementation of Rule-Based Classifier on Hadoop. We use **RIPPER** (Repeated Incremental Pruning for Error Reduction) algorithm for rule generation. Proposed by William Cohen, RIPPER employs a general-to-specific strategy to grow rules and FOILs (First Order Inductive Learning) information measure to choose the next conjunct to be added into the rule. In this paper we propose an implementation of RIPPER on Hadoop by using a data parallel model and then give the results of our experiments.

The rest of the paper is organized as follows. In Section 2 we discuss related work, Section 3 presents the standard RIPPER algorithm and its parallel implementation on Hadoop. Section 4 gives the complexity analysis of our algorithm, Section 5 shows the experimental results and finally in Section 6 we conclude our paper.

2 Related Work

Classification in data mining is a kind of mapping that maps items in a collection to target categories. But for this mapping one needs to process datasets which can be very large. To handle the problem of processing large datasets, the processing model of MapReduce is taken into consideration. The embedded features like parallelization across large scale clusters, handling node failures and effective communication among machines have made this model pretty demanding. Dean and Ghemawat [6] have expressed their ideas towards this model and have designed simple pseudo codes for mapper and reducer functions. Another illustration was given by Mackey et al. [9] on Hadoop MapReduce implementation and they also broadcasted their ideas about Hadoop Distributed File System (HDFS). Dean and Ghemawat [7] hailed MapReduce as a flexible data processing tool in their publication concerning the advantages of MapReduce over other parallel databases. Nguyen et al. [10] implemented the complex computation problem called the N-body problem using map reduce. The N-body problem simulates the movement of particles under gravitational or electrostatic forces. Zhou et al. [12] have used the Hadoop MapReduce framework to show how parallel implementing Nave Bayes algorithm is much faster than the standard algorithm.

A rule based classification is a technique used for classification using a collection of conditional rules. A general idea of rule based classification algorithm was shared by Qin et al. [11] in their URULE algorithm which also includes the criterion for growing and pruning the rules. More specifically the ripper algorithm is most widely used rule induction algorithm and works well with even noisy datasets as it uses validation set to prevent over fitting. Further ideas on RIPPER were elaborated by Basu and Kumaravel [3] and they implemented RIPPER algorithm (JRIP). The model for fast and effective rule algorithm using RIPPER was formulated and implemented by Cohen [5] in his IREP (Incremental Reduced Error Pruning) algorithm.

Ishibuchi et al. [8] have proposed an island model to build a fuzzy rule based classifier. They divide the data equally among each island (node) and regularly shift the data to the adjacent node. For each set of data, a classifier is built. The classifier which performs the best out of all the sets, is selected as a member of the final ensemble classifier. Even though the accuracy of the ensemble classifier is better than the individual classifiers, the total accuracy never reaches beyond 90%. Also, the classifiers built on each island only represent a locally optimum solution and may not be the best solution of the problem.

3   Rule Based Classification Using RIPPER

3.1   The RIPPER Algorithm

RIPPER is a widely used rule induction algorithm. It scales linearly with the number of training records used and is suited for building models with imbalanced class distribution. In addition, it uses a validation set to prevent model over-fitting.

RIPPER orders the classes according to their frequencies. If $(y_1, y_2, ..., y_c)$ are the class labels and y_1 is the least frequent and y_c the most frequent, then, RIPPER first builds rules for y_1 taking remaining class records as negative records. Next, RIPPER extracts rules for y_2. This process is repeated until y_c is left, which is labeled as the default class.

For rule growing, RIPPER uses a general to specific strategy, where initially each rule is empty and then it is built by adding conjuncts to it serially. It uses FOIL's information gain to add conjuncts to the rule. Suppose we have a rule $R : A \rightarrow class$ that covers p_0 positive records and n_0 negative records. After adding a new conjunct B, the rule $R' : A \wedge B \rightarrow class$ covers p_1 positive records and n_1 negative records. Then, the FOIL's information gain can be calculated as

$$\text{FOIL's information gain} = p_1 \times \left(\log \frac{p_1}{p_1 + n_1} - \log \frac{p_0}{p_0 + n_0} \right) \qquad (1)$$

Conjuncts are added until the rule starts covering negative examples. The rule is then pruned based on its performance on the validation set using the following metric $(p - n)/(p + n)$, where p is the number of positive records covered by the rule in the validation set and n is the number of negative records covered by the rule in the validation set. If the value of the above mentioned metric increases after removing a conjunct, then the rule is pruned.

Upon generating a rule, all records covered by the rule are eliminated. The algorithm then continues with building a new rule. Rules are built as long as the rule set doesn't violate the Minimum Description Length (MDL) principle and the error on the validation set is less than 50%.

3.2   Why Is Parallelizing RIPPER Important?

RIPPER is an iterative algorithm, and in each iteration it has to go over the complete dataset. Thus, for datasets of order $10^6 - 10^8$, it would take forever to complete even one iteration of the algorithm. It is important to parallelize the work done in an iteration, and develop an algorithm to distribute work among the parallel cluster nodes.

3.3   RIPPER Implementation on Hadoop

We implemented RIPPER in Java using Hadoop Java libraries. The dataset was partitioned horizontally to support the Hadoop MapReduce framework and ensure parallel execution of the code. Three sets of mapper-reducer functions were used, one each for rule building, rule pruning and calculating accuracy. Hence, each mapper executes its code on a portion of the dataset and the reducer aggregates over the output of mapper to produce one common output.

For rule building, the mapper-reducer functions calculate the value of p_1 and n_1 values for computing the FOIL's information gain (the p_0 and n_0 values are the p_1 and n_1 values for the old rule respectively). For adding a conjunct, every possible value for all attributes are considered as conjuncts to be added to the rule. The FOIL's information gain for each of these values is calculated, and the value for which the information gain is maximum is added as a conjunct to the rule.

The rule pruning is done using the validation set as reference. The mapper-reducer functions for pruning calculate the p and n values for the metric $(p - n)/(p + n)$. Depending on the value of the metric, the rule is pruned and added to the rule set.

After all rules have been built the rule set needs to be validated on the test records. The accuracy mapper-reducer functions calculate the number of positive and negative records covered by each rule and the whole rule set. These values are then used to calculate the accuracy of each rule and the overall accuracy as well.

The algorithm is briefly described below and the pseudo code is given in Figure 2:

1. Rule Growing Stage
   The rule is initialized as an empty rule, i.e., it covers all records. After that, conjuncts are added one by one to the rule. The conjunct to be added is selected by the value of FOIL's information gain measure. The parameters of the measure are calculated using a MapReduce function and the <key, value> pairs have the values of p_0, p_1, n_0 & n_1. Conjuncts are added to the rule as long as it does not cover negative records.
2. Rule Pruning Stage
   The rule generated in 1. is then pruned using the $(p - n)/(p + n)$ metric. To calculate the parameters p & n of this metric a Map-Reduce function is called in which the <key, value> pairs have the values of p & n.
   Stage 1. and 2. are repeated until adding a new rule violates the Minimum Description Length (MDL) principle.
3. Model Evaluation Stage
   After the rule set has been generated, the rules are used to classify the test records. A Map-Reduce function is called to classify the records and calculate the accuracy of the model. The <key, value> pairs in the function contain the value of the total positive and negative records covered by the model.

The code returns the pruned rule set and the accuracy of the rules and the rule set on the test records.

4   Complexity Analysis

We now calculate the time complexity for the sequential as well as the parallel implementation of RIPPER. Let the total number of training records be N, the total number of attributes in a record be A, the average of the number of possible values for each attribute be V and the number of nodes in the Hadoop cluster be K. Since the data is partitioned among each node, the total records in each node will be N/K.

4.1   Sequential Implementation

For adding each conjunct to the rule, we calculate the FOIL's information gain for all values of all attributes. For calculating gain we must iterate over all

Algorithm 1: RIPPER(Dataset D)

```
Input: Labeled Dataset D
Output: Rule Set R
1.   NR = New Rule
2.   R = Rule Set
3.   FIG: FOIL's Information Gain
4.   Max FIG: Maximum FIG among all conjuncts
5.   A = Accuracy
6.   Max Rules: Maximum Possible Rules (MDL)
7.   P: Pruning Metric
8.   While loop number < Max Rules do
9.        Initialize new Rule NR to empty
10.       While Max FIG != 0 do
11.           MapReduce 1(Train): Calc. FIG for all possible conjuncts
12.           compute Max FIG
13.           Add conjunct having Max FIG to NR
14.       End While
15.       While Old P < New P do
16.           MapReduce 2(Pruning): Calculate P
17.           if Old P < New P then
18.               Prune last conjunct in NR
19.           End if
20.       End While
21.       Add NR to R
22.  End While
23.  MapReduce 3(Accuracy): Calculate A
24.  Return R, A
```

Fig. 2. Algorithm 1

records in the dataset. The total conjuncts that can be added overall is limited by the Minimum Description Length (MDL). Hence, the time complexity of the sequential implementation is $O(A \cdot V \cdot N \cdot MDL)$.

4.2   Parallel Implementation

The runtime of the Mapper and Reducer functions are as follows:

1. *Mapper:* In each mapper we calculate the FOIL's information gain for all possible values for all attributes. Each Mapper runs for N/K records. Hence, time taken for each mapper to execute is $A \cdot V \cdot N/K$.

2. *Reducer:* In each reduce task, we simply shuffle the <key, value> pairs to the appropriate nodes and aggregate the results. Each node has N/K records. Hence, each node may send out at most N/K records to other nodes. Assuming a completely connected network, the time to shuffle the <key, value> pairs is N/K. We generate one key-value pair per record, hence the time

taken for aggregating the key values is N/K. The total time taken for the reducer is $O(N/K)$.

Since RIPPER uses a Minimum Description Length (MDL) as a stopping condition, the number of conjuncts added are limited to constant. Each time MapReduce is called, a conjunct is added to the Rule. Hence, the MapReduce function will only be called a maximum of MDL times. Hence, the total time complexity of the algorithm is $O(A \cdot V \cdot N \cdot MDL/K + MDL \cdot N/K)$. We now know that the execution time of the algorithm is proportional to $1/K$. Hence, by increasing the number of nodes in the Hadoop cluster, the execution time decreases.

4.3   Speed Up

We define the **speed up factor** of the Hadoop cluster as the ratio of time taken for the sequential algorithm and the time taken to execute the parallel algorithm on K nodes. We represent this factor as $S@K$. Using the time complexity calculated above, we can calculate the speed up as

$$S@K = \frac{A \cdot V \cdot N \cdot MDL}{\frac{A \cdot V \cdot N \cdot MDL}{K} + \frac{MDL \cdot N}{K}} = \frac{A \cdot V}{A \cdot V + 1} \times K = CK, \qquad (2)$$

where C is a constant.

We now see that the speed up we achieve on a Hadoop cluster is linear in the number of nodes in the cluster (K).

4.4   Cost Optimality

The **cost** of a parallel algorithm is the number of processors used times the time taken to execute the parallel algorithm (T_p). A parallel algorithm is **cost optimal** if the cost of the parallel algorithm is equal to the time taken by the sequential algorithm (T_s).

$$Cost = K \cdot T_p = O((A \cdot V + 1) \cdot N \cdot MDL) = O(A \cdot V \cdot N \cdot MDL) = T_s$$
$$[\text{Assuming } A \cdot V >> 1]$$

Since $Cost = T_s$, our parallel RIPPER algorithm is cost optimal.

5   Experimental Results

5.1   Experimental Environment

We setup a Hadoop Cluster with four nodes to test the algorithm. Tables 1 and 2 show the configuration of the cluster.

Table 1. Configuration of each node

SNo.	Software/Package
1	Ubuntu 13.04
2	Hadoop 1.1.2
3	sun java6-jdk
4	100 Mbps Ethernet

Table 2. Configuration of cluster

Node	No of cores	RAM	Clock Speed
Master	2	4GB	2.1GHz
Slave1	2	8GB	2.1GHz
Slave2	2	4GB	2.2GHz
Slave3	2	4GB	1.8GHz

5.2 Datasets Used

To test the accuracy of our algorithm on Hadoop we used two datsets; one randomly generated dataset of 100 million records with 22 categorical attributes, each attribute having an average of 6 values, the other dataset was extracted from the SDSS (Sloan Digital Sky Survey) Server [2]. We used only a subset (6) of the attributes from the SDSS dataset and considered records for two classes only ('STAR' and 'GALAXY'). The total records extracted amounted to about 2.5 million. Table 3 gives the description of the datasets used.

Table 3. Description of datasets

Dataset	No of records	No of attributes
Randomly generated	100 million	22
SDSS	2.5 million	6

5.3 Speed Up

To evaluate the performance of our algorithm, we calculated the speed up ($S@K$) by varying the number of nodes for both the datasets. The results are shown in Figures 3 and 4. For the randomized dataset we achieve a speed up of almost 3.7 on 4 nodes.

One can see that the speed up of the algorithm increases almost **linearly** with the number of nodes as predicted by the complexity analysis. This shows that

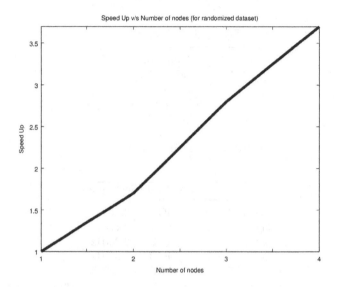

Fig. 3. Change in Speed Up Factor by varying number of nodes in the Cluster for randomly generated dataset

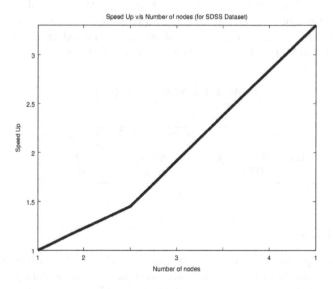

Fig. 4. Change in Speed Up Factor by varying number of nodes in the Cluster for SDSS dataset

our parallel implementation of RIPPER is very efficient and scalable. Also, the final classifier built is a globally optimum solution and the model is independent of number of nodes and distribution of data.

6   Conclusion and Future Work

We studied the Hadoop framework for reducing the computational cost of the exponential growing scientific data using a rule based classifier. The results shows that the efficiency of the parallel execution algorithm of RIPPER is higher than the standard implementation of the algorithm. Experimental results shows that by using the MapReduce framework on multiple nodes the computation time is reduced. In future we will implement our algorithm in General-Purpose computation on Graphics Processing Units and will compare the result with the CPU implementation.

References

1. Apache hadoop, http://hadoop.apache.org/
2. Sloan Digital Sky Survey Data Release 10,
   http://skyserver.sdss3.org/dr10/en/home.aspx
3. Basu, S., Kumaravel, A.: Classification by rules mining model with map- reduce framework in cloud. International Journal of Advanced and Innovative Research 2, 403–409 (2013)
4. Borthakur, D.: The hadoop distributed file system: Architecture and design. Hadoop Project Website (2007)
5. Cohen, W.W.: Fast effective rule induction. In: Proceedings of the 12th International Conference on Machine Learning (ICML 1995), pp. 115–123 (1995)
6. Dean, J., Ghemawat, S.: Mapreduce: simplified data processing on large clusters. Commun. ACM 51, 107–113 (2008)
7. Dean, J., Ghemawat, S.: MapReduce: A flexible data processing tool. Communications of the ACM 53(1), 72–77 (2010)
8. Ishibuchi, H., Yamane, M., Nojima, Y.: Ensemble fuzzy rule-based classifier design by parallel distributed fuzzy gbml algorithms. In: Bui, L.T., Ong, Y.S., Hoai, N.X., Ishibuchi, H., Suganthan, P.N. (eds.) SEAL 2012. LNCS, vol. 7673, pp. 93–103. Springer, Heidelberg (2012)
9. Mackey, G., Sehrish, S., Bent, J., Lopez, J., Habib, S., Wang, J.: Introducing mapreduce to high end computing. In: 3rd Petascale Data Storage Workshop, PDSW 2008. 3rd, pp. 1–6 (2008)
10. Nguyen, T.-C., Shen, W.-F., Chai, Y.-H., Xu, W.-M.: Research and implementation of scalable parallel computing based on map-reduce. Journal of Shanghai University (English Edition) 15(5), 426–429 (2011)
11. Qin, B., Xia, Y., Prabhakar, S., Tu, Y.-C.: A rule-based classification algorithm for uncertain data. In: Ioannidis, Y.E., Lee, D.L., Ng, R.T. (eds.) ICDE, pp. 1633–1640. IEEE (2009)
12. Zhou, L., Wang, H., Wang, W.: Parallel implementation of classification algorithms based on cloud computing environment. Indonesian Journal of Electrical Engineering 10(5), 1087–1092 (2012)

Consistent Management of Context Information in Ubiquitous Systems

Gabriel Guerrero-Contreras, José Luis Garrido, Sara Balderas-Díaz,
and Carlos Rodríguez-Domínguez

University of Granada
Software Engineering Department, E.T.S.I.I.T.
C/ Periodista Daniel Saucedo Aranda s/n, Granada, Spain
{gjguerrero,jgarrido,carlosrodriguez}@ugr.es, sarabd@correo.ugr.es

Abstract. In context-aware systems, where the context information
tends to be distributed and/or replicated, can be decisive to maintain the
correctness of this information, owing to the decisions in context-aware
systems are taken on the basis of it. In ubiquitous environments, new
challenges are emerging, which can affect to the consistent management
of the distributed context information. For instance, the dynamism is a
feature that directly affects the availability of the resources deployed in
the network, among other quality features, and it implies additional design and development efforts from software engineers. Service Oriented
Architecture (SOA), together with replication techniques may help to
improve resource availability and strengthen the system against node
disconnections, nevertheless, additional techniques must be applied to
ensure the consistency of the distributed/replicated resources. In this
paper, an approach to support, from the software design stage, the synchronization and consistency management of context information is introduced. This approach follows the SOA model, and provides a common
basis for the synchronization of distributed/replicated resources. A case
study, related with an ubiquitous system deployed in a hospital where
context-aware services can be found, will be described in order to show
the feasibility of the proposal.

Keywords: Distributed resources, context-awareness systems, ubiquitous and pervasive computing, Service Oriented Architecture (SOA).

1 Introduction

Context-aware systems are defined as those which *"use context to provide relevant information and/or services to the user"* [2]. These provides a new approach in Human Computer Interaction (HCI), where the system adapts to the
user and his/her environment. Ubiquitous environments, which are conceived
as a distributed computing power in the environment, make use of the techniques and methods adopted by context-aware systems to provide a natural and
unconscious interaction with the computational system to the user.

G. Fortino et al. (Eds.): IDCS 2014, LNCS 8729, pp. 184–193, 2014.
© Springer International Publishing Switzerland 2014

In context-aware systems is decisive to maintain the correctness and the quality of context information [1], owing to the decisions of the system is based on this information and, therefore, if it is incorrect, the behaviour of the system will be incorrect. However, along with ubiquitous computing, new challenges are emerging, which can affect to the consistent management of the context information, such as [11]: (1) *uneven conditioning*, caused by the heterogeneous nature of the environment, where different devices with different capabilities exist, and also, some resources or features may not be always available; (2) *localized scalability*, related with certain limitations in the use of resources, e.g., to prevent to send information beyond the local environment where it makes sense, in order to avoid communication network overload; and (3) a *dynamic network topology*, caused by users' mobility, which could imply unstable connections producing disconnections and network partitions.

The Service Oriented Architecture (SOA) model [8], together with replication techniques, may help to address some of these challenges. SOA provides the basis to obtain a reusable, scalable and interoperable system, through the service encapsulation and the use of standards, while replication is recommendable to obtain high-availability and good performance in distributed systems. However, in dynamic environments additional techniques must be applied to ensure the consistency of the distributed/replicated resources. For instance, if a user changes his/her availability to busy for a certain hours, by a meeting, through his/her smartphone, and in that moment there is no connection available, this change will not be reflected in the copy of the agenda of the office. If meanwhile, in the office, another meeting is concerted for the same hours, an inconsistency will be generated, as a consequence of it the user will not able to attend to the two meetings at the same time.

In this paper, an approach to support, from the software design stage, the synchronization and consistency management of distributed context information is introduced. This approach is based on the SOA model and provides two main services (Monitoring and Synchronization) for the synchronization of replicated resources [5]. In turn, a Context Manager service will turn out to be built from the specialization of the Synchronization service. This service will be able to work in a dynamic environment under a distributed setting, thus facilitating the development of context-aware systems.

The rest of this paper is structured as follows. Section 2 presents related work which have tried to provide several proposal at architectural level to facilitate the development of context-aware systems; Section 3 proposes an approach for a consistent management of replicated context information; Section 4 shows the feasibility of the proposal through a case study in an ubiquitous environment; and finally, conclusions and future work are summarized in Section 5.

2   Related Work

Several research works have addressed main challenges on context management in distributed environments. CASS [3] and SOCAM [4] propose middleware-based technologies. These technologies provide an architecture specifically designed in order to facilitate the development of context-aware mobile applications. Both of them propose a similar architecture, in which a centralized context manager is provided. This manager will receive context data from several distributed context providers, such as sensors. Additionally, the CASS middleware allows caching context information in mobile devices, in order to overcome device disconnections.

Korpipää et al. [7] propose an architecture for the context management in mobile devices. Its architecture is based in a hierarchical infrastructure, which consists of the following main services/components at system level: the Resource server, the Security component, the Context Recognition and Change Detection services. These entities are grouped into the context manager, which provides context information to the client applications. While the resource servers and the context recognition services are distributed, the context manager is actually a centralized entity managing all the context information.

The Hydrogen project [6] is a framework to context acquisition in mobile environments. This framework distinguishes between local and remote context information. The local information is about the device, while the remote information relates to the information which has been obtained from the communication with nearby devices, under a peer-to-peer communication scheme. Its architecture is divided into three layers: the lower layer, which collects the information from the device's sensors; the intermediate layer, which manages, and allows the access to, the information collected; and the upper layer, in which the context-aware applications are developed.

The work presented in [12] is based on a SOA approach to manage the data consistency in heterogeneous systems. In that context, there are several applications with different local data models. The models are different, however, they refer to the same data. The main objective of the work is that the modifications in a local model are automatically disseminated to the other local models. The proposed architecture is based on two specific services: the Directory service serves to link between local data models and the Synchronization service in intended to solve possible inconsistencies.

However, these works follow a centralized approach (at least partially). This makes the system weakest against device disconnections and network partitions (which are frequent in dynamic environments), although it facilitates the synchronization of the context information.

3   Consistent Management of Context Information

In this section, an approach for a consistent management of distributed and/or replicated context information is presented. The Figure 1 shows the model in which the approach is based. This model provides a common basis for the management of shared resources (which may be replicated or distributed) in a dynamic environment. As mentioned, in this kind of environments, the shared resources are susceptible to the emergence of inconsistencies between their different copies. The following subsections describe in detail the proposal. For the sake

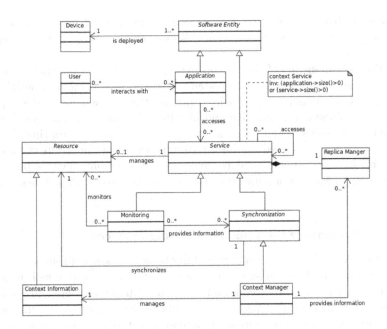

Fig. 1. A model for a consistent management of distributed/replicated context information

of a more structured description of the model, the main entities are grouped as follow: (1) the *Service* Entity and the *Replica Manager*; (2) the *Synchronization* and *Monitoring services*; and (3) the *Context Manager*.

3.1 The Service Entity and Replica Manager

The Service entity is an abstract class which brings together the common relations for all the system services. A service may be being accessed by one or more applications (which interact with the user), and by one or more services (i.e., service composition). By definition [8], a service should enable access to one or more capabilities, a service which is not accessed for any customer becomes meaningless. Therefore, in the diagram of the Figure 1 a restriction is introduced: a service must be accessed at least by an application or a service. Both the service and the application are *Software Entities*, which are deployed on a hardware device (server or personal computer, sensor, mobile device, among others). Also, the service can manage a kind of shared resources (e.g., a document repository service manages a set of text documents).

Moreover, the approach aims to support the deployment of software in distributed systems with dynamic network topology, therefore, each service is composed by a Replica Manager (RM) entity. The objective of this decision is to avoid central controls and strengthen the system against node disconnections and network partitions. Note that this is a model addressing a logical architecture viewpoint for services and, consequently, the entity Service is represented as an service, irrespective of its real implementation, which it may be carried out through a set of service replicas (in this case, each replica will have a replica of the RM entity).

The RM is responsible of the synchronization of the operations performed on the different service replicas in the system. However, in this model, the RM will also encapsulate the adaptation logic, regarding the deployment of this replica, in order to provide a self-adaptive and distributed solution to the dynamic deployment of the services and thus improving its availability in run-time. To this end, the RM entity will need the information provided by the Context Manager service (for instance, it will need to know when the mobile device's battery is running low) to know when and how to change the current deployment of the service.

3.2   The Synchronization and Monitoring Services

Nowadays, in the absence of standardized methods for the synchronization of the shared resources replicas, most of the proposed solutions are planned in an ad-hoc manner. By taking into account an increasing number of users and resources to be managed, this entails a higher complexity in the correct synchronization of these resources. Thus, this approach is intended to provide a common basis for the consistent management of the shared resources in context-aware systems. To this end, the Synchronization and Monitoring services are provided (Figure 1).

It is not possible to provide a general service for the synchronization, owing to the synchronization algorithms are dependent of the resource type and its specific nature and usage. For this reason, and regarding the goal of providing a reusable service, the Synchronization service is an abstract service, which must be specialized according to each particular resource to be synchronized. This abstract service uses the Monitoring Service. It is a basic service which stores all kind of information about changes on the different replicas of the shared resources. This information seeks to serve several purposes, e.g., version control. In the synchronization case, this information is required by the specific synchronization algorithm to be applied.

In this way, the common part related to manage the resource synchronization is identified and assigned to the abstract service and its composition with the Monitoring Service. The Synchronization service, according to the information received from the Monitoring service, can detect the actions that have been applied to other replicas of the resource but not in its associated replica, that is, the information would be in an inconsistent state. Once the inconsistencies are detected, they should be resolved in the specialization of this service, and it will depend on the particular requirements of the resource.

3.3   The Context Manager

The importance of maintaining the consistency of context information in context-aware systems needs to be emphasized, as the decisions in context-aware systems are taken on the basis of this information. The context information can be considered a shared resource, which is constantly modified by the user actions (e.g., a user enters in a room), changes in the environment (e.g., the temperature in the room has changed) and explicit information provides by a user (e.g., changing a meeting in an electronic agenda). This context information can be distributed and/or replicated, e.g., information about user's agenda may be located in his/her personal smartphone and the public information of the agenda can be replicated also in a server in his/her office building.

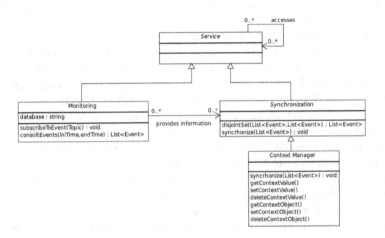

Fig. 2. The Context Manager service as a result of the specialization of the Synchronization service

In this approach, through of the specialization of the Synchronization service, a Context Manager which can address these context inconsistencies at the service level is provided (Figure 2). The Context Manager will implement the *'synchronize'* abstract method, where it will should add the specific synchronization algorithms for manage the context data resource. Also, the Context Manager will implement the specific methods to provide functionality to its customers. Note that this implementation follows a Event-Driven Approach (EDA), where the actions performed on the shared data are represented through events. In this way, through the events dissemination, a low coupling between components of the system is achieved.

4 Case Study

In this section, a case study is described in order to try to show the usefulness of the approach. We assume a hospital and its emergency service, which form part of an ubiquitous environment. In this system different context information need to be managed, such as the location of the medical staff, the availability of the medical resources, the profile of the patients, etc. Certain of this information can be partially replicated. For instance, a doctor's mobile device may host information about his/her patients, but not about the work routine of the nurse staff. The Emergency service, just in case of an emergency, will look for the the most appropriate specialist doctor to attend the emergency. It will take into account information such as: who is the family doctor of the patient, the type of emergency and if the doctor can be immediately available, i.e., it is an context-aware service. Therefore, it is important to know where is the doctor. The location of the staff is obtained through the use of RFID readers, which are placed in the doors of the doctor's offices, patient rooms, and in other different areas of the building.

However, the following specific scenario depicted in Figure 3 can arise. The doctor has left the hospital to examine a patient at home as consequence of a emergency call, however, he/she has forgotten his/her identification card in his/her office. Therefore, the Context Manager replica service deployed at the hospital assumes that the doctor is still in his/her office. This is caused because (at time T) the Context Manager service received an event from the Positioning service which indicated that the doctor became to his/her office, but the doctor forgot his/her identification card, and the Positioning service cannot inform about the event of leaving the office/building.

While the doctor goes to the patient's house, he/she interacts with his/her mobile device, in order to consult the patient profile (at the time T+1). This device hosts another replica of the Context Manager service, and it manages replicated context information, such as the medical history of the patient and another information about the activities that the doctor is performed, such as *'inquiry of the medical history of the patient'* or *'request for an operating room'*. Through this interaction, the Context Manager updates the location of the doctor, he/she is not longer in the hospital, he/she is now out of the hospital, particularly traveling by an ambulance.

At this point, the replicated context information (the information about current location of the doctor) is in an inconsistent state. The doctor can be located in two places at the same time. This has a negative impact on the functioning of the Emergency service, which has been mentioned previously, owing to it cannot find the correct information about the real doctor location. However, thanks to the approach provided, the Context Manager service is based in the Synchronization and Monitoring services (Figure 2), and therefore, these inconsistencies can be detected and resolved at the service level, preventing its propagation to the upper layers of the architecture. The inconsistency will be resolved through the implementation of the abstract method *'synchronize'*, which is shown partially below. In this case, the synchronization of the Event 2 (Figure 3) may be considered relatively straightforward, as the timestamp of this event is upper than the last modification performed in the *location* of the doctor. However, more complex inconsistencies can be found, in which may be involved several events. For example, if a doctor requests for a specific operating room while he/her is in an emergency and his/her local context information is not updated, this operating room will may be already busy. Therefore, when the Context Manager starts

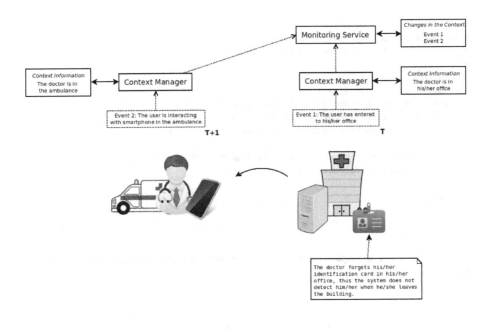

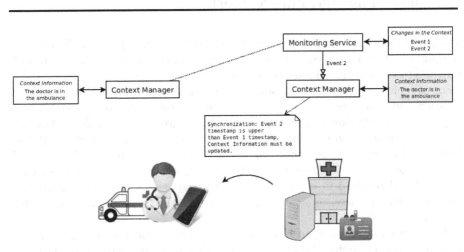

Fig. 3. Example scenario of the case study. A doctor has left the hospital to examine a patient at home owing to an emergency, however, he/she has forgotten his/her identification card in his/her office and therefore the system assumes that the doctor still is in his/her office.

the synchronization and detects this inconsistency, it can decide to automatically make a request for a similar operating room.

```
/**
 * @param list: a list of events obtained from the
 *                'disjointSet' method
 */
void synchronize(List<Events> list){
  foreach(Event evt in list){
    evtName = evt.getMemberValue("object").GetString();
    evtValue = evt.getMemberValue("value").GetString();
    evtTime = evt.getMemberValue("timestamp").GetInt64();
    [...]
    if(this.getContextObject(evtName).getTimestamp() < evtTime){
      this.setContextValue(evtName, evtValue);
    }
    [...]
  }
}
```

(Example of a C# implementation of the *'synchronization'* method of the Context Manager.)

5 Conclusions and Future Work

The presented approach in this paper stems from the application of a distributed computation techniques to service-based architectural design. The devised model provides to the software engineers the basis for a correct and consistent management of replicated/distributed resources. This is achieved through the Synchronization and Monitoring services. This model also contemplates the adaptation logic of the replication of services in run-time, through the Replica Manager entity. In this model a Context Manager service has been also provided. It has been build from the Synchronization service, which facilitates the detection of inconsistencies in the context information owing to the inconsistencies can be detected and resolved in design time. In this way, this service will be able to work in a dynamic environment, such as context-aware system, thus facilitating their development.

Regarding future work an implementation of the model in a real scenarios similar to the presented in this paper, together with an analysis of the more convenient technologies to implement the context information models will be performed. Additionally, an analysis about the different configuration parameters and the behavior of different service replication techniques will be carried out. Finally, we plan to study the composition between the herein presented services and other high level self-adaptive services [10], all of them will be deployed on a middleware [9] for ubiquitous systems, in order to provide a full implementation in real scenarios.

Acknowledgment. This research work has been funded by the Ministry of Economy and Competitiveness of the Spanish Government with European Regional Development Funds (FEDER), and by the Andalusian Regional Government, through the research projects TIN2012-38600 and P10-TIC-6600, respectively.

References

1. Buchholz, T., Küpper, A., Schiffers, M.: Quality of context: What it is and why we need it. In: Proceedings of the Workshop of the HP OpenView University Association, vol. 2003 (2003)
2. Dey, A.K.: Understanding and using context. Personal and Ubiquitous Computing 5(1), 4–7 (2001)
3. Fahy, P., Clarke, S.: Cass–a middleware for mobile context-aware applications. In: Workshop on Context Awareness, MobiSys. Citeseer (2004)
4. Gu, T., Pung, H.K., Zhang, D.Q.: A middleware for building context-aware mobile services. In: 2004 IEEE 59th Vehicular Technology Conference, VTC 2004-Sprin, pp. 2656–2660. IEEE (2004)
5. Guerrero-Contreras, G., Garrido, J.L., Rodríguez-Domínguez, C., Noguera, M., Benghazi, K.: Designing a service platform for sharing internet resources in manets. In: Canal, C., Villari, M. (eds.) ESOCC 2013. CCIS, vol. 393, pp. 331–345. Springer, Heidelberg (2013)
6. Hofer, T., Schwinger, W., Pichler, M., Leonhartsberger, G., Altmann, J., Retschitzegger, W.: Context-awareness on mobile devices-the hydrogen approach. In: Proceedings of the 36th Annual Hawaii International Conference on System Sciences, 2003, p. 10. IEEE (2003)
7. Jani, M., Kela, J., Malm, E.J., et al.: Managing context information in mobile devices. IEEE Pervasive Computing 2(3), 42–51 (2003)
8. MacKenzie, C.M., Laskey, K., McCabe, F., Brown, P.F., Metz, R., Hamilton, B.A.: Reference model for service oriented architecture 1.0. OASIS Standard 12 (2006)
9. Rodríguez-Domínguez, C., Benghazi, K., Noguera, M., Garrido, J.L., Rodríguez, M.L., Ruiz-López, T.: A communication model to integrate the request-response and the publish-subscribe paradigms into ubiquitous systems. Sensors 12(6), 7648–7668 (2012)
10. Ruiz-López, T., Rodríguez-Domínguez, C., Ochoa, S., Garrido, J.L.: Mdubi: A model-driven approach to the development of self-adaptive services for ubiquitous systems. Sensors, 1–25 (in press, 2014)
11. Satyanarayanan, M.: Pervasive computing: Vision and challenges. IEEE Personal Communications 8(4), 10–17 (2001)
12. Svensson, E., Vetter, C., Werner, T.: Data consistency in a heterogeneous it landscape: a service oriented architecture approach. In: Proceedings of the Eighth IEEE International Enterprise Distributed Object Computing Conference, EDOC 2004, pp. 3–8. IEEE (2004)

Dynamic Deployment of Software Components for Self-adaptive Distributed Systems

Jingtao Sun and Ichiro Satoh

National Institute of Informatics,
The Graduate University for Advanced Studies,
2-1-2 Hitotsubashi, Chiyoda-ku, Tokyo, Japan
{sun,ichiro}@nii.ac.jp

Abstract. This paper proposes a novel approach to adapting applications, which are running on one or more computers. The key idea behind the proposed approach is to introduce the policy-based relocation of components to define functions between computers as a basic mechanism for adaptation on distributed systems. It is constructed as a middleware system for Java-based general-purposed software components. This paper describes the proposed approach and the design and implementation of the approach with several applications, e.g., adaptive data replication between primary backup and chain replication approaches.

1 Introduction

Distributed systems are complicated and dynamic by nature because their structures and applications tend to dynamically change. Computers and software components of which an application consists may be added to or removed from them, and networks between computers may be connected or disconnected. The complexity and dynamism of distributed systems are beyond our ability to build and manage systems through conventional approaches, such as those that are centralized and top-down. Distributed systems should adapt themselves to such changes to solve these problems.

Distributed systems, on the other hand, need to support availability, dependability, and reliability, because they are often used for mission-critical purposes. Nevertheless, several existing approaches to dynamic adaptation, e.g., genetic algorithm and programming and swarm intelligence, assume random or speculative adaptation, which may seriously affect the targets of distributed systems and consume their computational resources. Therefore, we believe that our adaptation should be predictable and save computational resources as much as possible.

This paper proposes an approach to adapting distributed systems to such changes. The key idea behind the approach is to introduce the policy-based relocation of software components as a basic adaptation mechanism. We assumed that a distributed application would consist of one or more software components, which might have been running on different computers through a network. When changes in a distributed system occurred, e.g., in the requirements of the application and the structures of the system, its software components would automatically be relocated to different computers according to their policies to adapt it to the changes.

G. Fortino et al. (Eds.): IDCS 2014, LNCS 8729, pp. 194–203, 2014.

The relocation of software components may seem to be simple but it makes their applications resilient. In fact, there have been many different approaches to solve the same problems. For example, *primary-backup* and *chain replication*, which are widely used in distributed systems, including cloud computing, consistently support replication mechanisms with consistency on distributed systems. Nevertheless, the latter has been designed to improve throughput rather than latency in comparison with the former. They should be dynamically selected according to the requirements of applications, which may often change. The main purpose of our approach was to enable distributed systems to adapt themselves to various changes. We are constructing a middleware system that will be used for building and operating adaptive distributed systems.

2   Approach

As the requirements of applications and the structures of systems may often change in distributed systems, the applications need to adapt themselves to such changes. Our approach introduces the relocation of software components to define functions at other computers as a basic adaptation mechanism.

2.1   Requirements

Distributed systems are used for multiple purposes and need abilities to adapt them to various changes results from their dynamic properties. Our adaptation has five requirements.

- *Resiliency:* Distributed systems cannot avoid network connection/partitioning in addition to system failures. Even when nodes may meet or separate other agents, software running on the nodes should continue to provide their applications as much as possible. Centralized management may be simple but can become a single point of failures. Therefore, our adaptation should be managed without any centralized management for reasons of avoiding any single points of failures and supporting scalability.
- *Self-adaptation:* Distributed systems essentially lack no global view due to communication latency between computers. Software components, which may be running on different computers, need to coordinate them to support their applications with partial knowledge about other computers. They should be managed in a manner of self-adaptation.
- *General-purpose and adaptation-independency:* There are various applications running on distributed systems are various. Therefore, the approach should be implemented as a practical middleware to support general-purpose applications. All software components should be defined independently of our adaptation mechanism as much as possible. As a result, developers should be able to concentrate on their own application-specific processing.
- *Reusable adaptation:* There have been many attempts to provide adaptive distributed systems. However, the approaches and parameters in most of them these strictly and statically depended on their target systems, so that they would need to be re-defined overall to be reused in other distributed systems. Our adaptation should be abstracted away from the underlying systems for reasons of reusability.

- *Limited resources and networks:* Computers on distributed systems may have limited resources, e.g., processing, storage resources, and networks. Our approach should be available with such limited resource, whereas many existing adaptation approaches explicitly or implicitly assume that their target distributed systems have enriched resources. The bandwidth of networks on several distributed systems tend to be narrow and their latency cannot be neglected. The approach should support such networks.

2.2   Policy-Based Adaptation

Our approach separates software components from their policies for adaptation, although components have their own policies.

Deployable Software Component: This approach assumes that an application consists of one or more software components, which may be running on different computers. Each component is general-purpose and is a programmable entity. It can be deployed at another computer according to its deployment policy, while it have started to run. It is defined as a collection of Java objects like JavaBeans component in the current implementation.

Deployment Policy for Adaptation: Each component can have one or more policies, where each policy is basically defined as a pair of information on where and when the component is deployed. Before explaining deployment policies in the proposed approach, we need to discuss policies for adaptation in distributed systems. Our approach introduces the these concepts:

- The approach does not support any adaptation inside software components. Instead, it introduces the dynamic deployment of components as a basic mechanism in its adaptation. When more than one dimension must be considered for adaptation, representing the policies and choices between policies tends to be too complicated to define and select policies. Therefore, we intend to support at most one dimension, i.e., the dynamic deployment of components.
- Each component has one or more policies, where a policy specifies the relocation of its components and instructs them to migrate to the destination according to conditions specified in the policy. The validation of every policy can be explicitly configure to be one-time, within specified computers, or permanent within its component.
- Each policy is specified as a pair of a condition part and at the most one destination part. The former is written in a first-order predicate logic-like notation, where predicates reflect information about the system and applications. The destination part refers to another components instead of the computer itself. This is because such policies should be abstracted away from the underlying systems, e.g., network addresses, so that they can be reused on other distributed systems. The policy deploys its target component (or a copy of the component) at the current computer of the component specified as the destination, if the condition is satisfied.

Since components for which other components have policies can be statically or dynamically deployed at computers, the destinations of policies can easily be changed for reuse by other distributed systems.

3   Design

The proposed approach dynamically deploys components to define application-specific functions at computers according to the policies of the components to adapt distributed applications to changes in distributed systems.

Our middleware system consists of two parts: a *component runtime system* and an *adaptation manager*, where each of the systems are coordinated with one another through a network. The first part is responsible for executing and duplicating components at computers and also exchanging components and messages in runtime systems on other computers through a network. The second part is responsible for managing policies for adaptation. It consists of an interpreter for policies written in our proposed language and a database system to maintain the policies.

3.1   Component Runtime System

Each runtime system allows each component to have at most one activity through the Java thread library. When the life-cycle state of a component changes, e.g., when it is created, terminates, duplicate, or migrates to another computer, the runtime system issues specific events to the component. To capture such events, each component can have more than one listener object that implements a specific listener interface to hook certain events issued before or after changes have been made in its life-cycle state. The current implementation uses the notion of dynamic method invocation studied in CORBA so that it can easily hide differences between the interfaces of objects at the original and other computers.

Each runtime system can exchange components with other runtime systems through a TCP channel using mobile-agent technology. When an component is transferred over the network, not only the code of the component but also its state is transformed into a bitstream by using Java's object serialization package and then the bit stream is transferred to the destination. The component runtime system on the receiving side receives and unmarshals the bit stream.

Even after components have been deployed at destinations, their methods should still be able to be invoked from other components, which are running at local or remote computers. The runtime systems exchanges information about components that visit them with one another in a peer-to-peer manner to trace the locations of components. The runtime system can forward messages to co-partner components after it has migrated to another computer through a network.

3.2   Adaptation Manager

The policy-based deployment of components is managed by adaptation managers, where each manager is running with a component runtime system on each computer, without a centralized management server. Each component runtime system periodically advertises its address to the others through UDP multicasting, and these computers then return their addresses and capabilities to the computer through a TCP channel.[1]

Each policy is specified as a pair of conditions and actions. The former is written in a first-order predicate logic-like notation and its predicates reflect various system and network properties, e.g., the utility rates and processing capabilities of processors, network connections, and application-specific conditions. The latter is specified as a relocation of components. Our adaptation was intended to be specified in a rule-style notation. However, existing general-purpose rule-based systems tend to be unwieldy because they cannot express necessary adaptation expertise or subtleties of adaptation in distributed systems.

name {	(Name of policy)
$predicate_1, \cdots, predicate_n$	(Condition of policy)
relocation ($component_{id}$)	(The destination of relocation)
validation	(Validation of policy)
}	

where *relocation* in the syntax is provided with built-in or user-defined policies. Our adaptation has three built-in policies:

- When a component has a *pushing* policy for another component, if the condition specified in the policy is satisfied, the policy instructs the the former to migrate to the current computer of the latter.
- When a component has a *duplicating* policy with another component, if the condition specified in the policy is satisfied, the policy makes a clone of the former and instructs the clone to migrate to the current computer of the latter.
- When a component has an *extinct* policy, if the condition specified in the policy is satisfied, it terminates.

For example, when the condition of the *pushing* policy is the movement of the co-partner component, the target component follows the movement of the co-partner (Figure 1). This is useful when the two components need to interact frequently and/or require heavy data-transfer on each interaction yet they cannot be programmed inside a single component. When the condition of the *extinct* policy is that the target component and specified component are at the same computer, it reduces the number of components. Excess components result in overloads. The same functions must be distributively processed to reduce the amount of load and information.

4   Implementation

This section describes the current implementation of a middleware system based on the proposed approach.

---

[1] We assumed that the components that comprised an application would initially be deployed at computers within a localized space smaller than the domain of a sub-network.

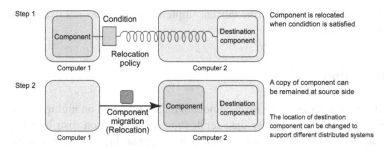

Fig. 1. Conditional relocation for adaptation

Each component is a general-purpose programmable entity defined as a collection of Java objects and packaged in the standard JAR file format like JavaBeans. It can migrate and duplicate itself between computers. Our runtime system is similar to a mobile agent platform, but it has been constructed independently of any existing middleware systems. This is because existing middleware systems, including mobile agents and distributed objects, have not supported the policy-based relocation of software components. The system is built on the Java virtual machine (JVM), which can abstract away differences between operating systems.

The current implementation basically uses the Java object serialization package to marshal or duplicate components. The package does not support the capture of stack frames of threads. Instead, when a component is duplicated, the runtime system issues events to it to invoke their specified methods, which should be executed before the component is duplicated or migrated, and it then suspends their active threads. We also introduce our original remote method invocation between computers instead of Java remote method invocation (RMI), because Java RMI does not support message forwarding to moving objects.

The adaptation manager is running on each computer and consists of three parts: an interpreter, a database for policies, and an event manager. The first is responsible for evaluating policies, the second maintains the policies that components are running on the computer, and the third receives events from the external systems to notify changes in the underlying system and applications and then forwards them to the first.

We describe a process of the relocation of a component according to one of its policies. (1) When a component creates or arrives at a computer, it automatically registers its deployment policies with the database of the current adaptation manager, where the database maintains the policies of components running on its runtime system. (2) The manager periodically evaluates the conditions of the policies maintained in its database. (3) When it detects the policies whose conditions are satisfied, it deploys components according to the selected policies at the computer that the destination component is running on.

Two or more policies may specify different destinations under the same condition that drive them. The current implementation provides no mechanism to solve conflict between policies. We assumed that policies would be defined without any conflicts between policies. The destination of the component may enter divergence or vibration modes due to conflicts between some of a component's policies, if it has multiple deployment policies. However, the current implementation does not exclude such divergence or vibration.

5 Application

This application is for adaptive management in data replication on multiple computers. Although there have been many data replication approaches on distributed systems, the *primary-backup* approach is one of the most typical [1]. A client only sends an update request to one designated primary server. The server updates its replica and then forwards the request to one or more backup servers to update the replica and waits for responses from the backup servers before responding to the client. The *chain replication* approach is a replication protocol to support large-scale storage services, e.g., key-value stores, to achieve high throughput and availability while providing strong consistency guarantees [11]. A client sends update requests to the backup server with the maximum number (head) to update its replica, while forward the request to update the replica of the server with the next lowest number until it reaches the server with the minimum number (tail). The tail server responds to the client.

Both the approaches have advantages and disadvantages. For example, the primary backup approach must wait for acknowledgements from the backups for prior updates, whereas the chain replication approach can execute sequencing requests before prior updates have not been completed. Chain replication is at a disadvantage for reply latency to update requests since it disseminates updates serially, compared to primary-backup, which disseminates updates in parallel. Therefore, the approaches should be selected according to the requirements of applications.

The proposed approach enables the two approaches to be easily transformed into each other. As shown in Fig. 2, the application consists of three kinds of components: a client, a server, and a replica manager. The first receives update requests from the external system. The second has polices for one of either the primary backup or chain replication approaches. The third component is statically deployed at a computer that keeps the replica, is assigned with its own number, and is responsible for updating the replica on behalf of server components.

- In the primary backup approach, the client component first creates a server component after receiving a update request and then deploys at computers with the minimum number and block itself until the server returns to it. The server component creates its clones and deploys them at computers that have the other replica components. Each server component asks the replica component to update the replica at its destination and then it returns to the computer that has the parent server component. The parent waits for all its clone components to arrive and then migrates to the computer that has the client component.
- In the chain replication, the client component first creates a server component after receiving a update request and waits for the next update request. Next, the server component migrates to the computer that has the replica component with the maximum number. After asking the replica component at the destination, it migrates to the computer that has the replica component with the next lowest number until

it reaches the computer that has the replica with the minimum number. The server component migrates to the computer that has the client component.

The server component in the former follows the *duplicating* policy and the *pushing* policy, in the latter as was discussed in Section 3. By changing policies of the server component, the whole system can adapt itself to one of either of the primary-backup or chain replication approaches. This application means that our approach can enable a distributed system to be adapted in its architecture level between *primary-backup* and *chain replication*. It has no centralized management system so that it is useful in providing scalable and dependable distributed systems, as was discussed in Section 2.

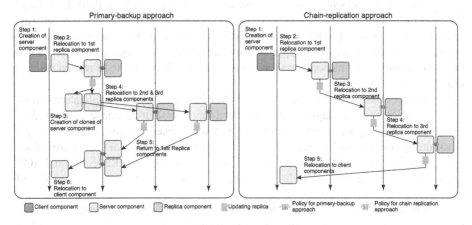

Fig. 2. Adaptive consistency for data replication

6 Related Work

The notion of adaptation is rapidly attracting attention in the area of distributed systems. There have been several attempts to develop adaptive distributed systems. Most of them have aimed at managing balance computational loads or network traffic.

The most typical self-organization approaches have included genetic computation, genetic programming [9], and swarm intelligence [2,4]. Although there is no centralized control structure dictating how individual agents should behave, interactions between simple agents with static rules often lead to the emergence of intelligent global behavior. Most existing approaches have only focused on their target problems or applications but they are not general purpose, whereas distributed systems are. Our software adaptation approach should be independent of applications. Furthermore, most existing self-organization approaches explicitly or implicitly assume a large population of agents or boids. However, real distributed systems have no room to execute such large numbers of agents.

There have been several attempts to support software adaptation in the literature on adaptive computing and evolution computing. Jaeger et al. [8] introduced the notion of self-organization to an object request broker and a publish/subscribe system. Georgiadis et al. [5] presented connection-based architecture for self-organizing software components on a distributed system. Like other software component architectures, they intended to customize their systems by changing the connections between components instead of the internal behaviors inside them. Like ours, Cheng at al. [3] presented an adaptive selection mechanism for servers by enabling selection policies, but they did not customize the servers themselves. They also needed to execute different servers simultaneously. Herrman et al. proposed the bio-inspired deployment of services on sensor networks [6]. Unlike ours, their work focused on the deployment and coordination of services, instead of the adaptation of software itself to provide services. Nakano and Suda [10,14] proposed bio-inspired middleware, called Bio-Networking, for disseminating network services in dynamic and large-scale networks where there were large numbers of decentralized data and services. As most of their parameters, e.g., energy, tended to depend on a particular distributed system, so that they may not have been available in another system. Our approach was designed independently of the capabilities of distributed systems because adaptive policies should be able to be reused in other distributed systems.

Separation of concerns enables the separate development of an applications functional behavior and its adaptive behavior involving crosscutting concerns. A widely used technique is aspect-oriented programming (AOP), where the code implementing a crosscutting concern, called an *aspect*, is developed separately from other parts of the system and woven with the business logic at compile- or run-time. Reflective and AOP approaches are primitive so that they do not directly support adaptation for distributed systems.

Existing mobile agent platforms have been designed for solving problems in distributed systems, e.g., the reduction of network latency and fault tolerance, instead of adaptation. There have been a few attempts to introduce the policy-based relocation of software components or agents. The FarGo system introduced a mechanism for distributed applications dynamically laid out in a decentralized manner [7]. This was similar to our relocation policy in the sense that it allowed all components to have their own policies, but it only supports a simple relocation corresponding to our *pushing* policy, and could not specify any conditions for their policies, unlike ours. Satoh [12] proposed other relocation policies for relocating components based on policies that other components moved to. However, these policies did not have the conditions that select and execute them unlike the approach proposed in this paper. One of the authors proposed an adaptation mechanism for distributed systems [13]. However, the mechanism was aimed at adapting functions of software components, which are statically located at computers, by using the notion of differentiation instead of their locations.

7   Conclusion

This paper proposed an approach to adapting distributed applications. It introduced the relocation of software components between computers as a basic mechanism for adaptation. It separated software components from their adaptations in addition to underlying systems by specifying policies outside the components. It was simple but provided various adaptations to support resilient distributed systems without any centralized management. It was available with limited resources because it had no speculative approaches, which tended to spend computational resources. The relocation of components between computers was useful to avoid network latency. It was constructed as a general-purpose middleware system on distributed systems instead of any simulation-based systems. Components could be composed from Java objects like JavaBean modules. We described several the approaches with practical applications.

References

1. Alsberg, P.A., Day, J.D.: A principle for resilient sharing of distributed resources. In: Proceedings of 2nd International Conference on Software Engineering (ICSE 1976), pp. 627–644 (1976)
2. Bonabeau, E., Dorigo, M., Theraulaz, G.: Swarm Intelligence: From Natural to Artificial Systems. Oxford University Press (1999)
3. Cheng, S., Garlan, D., Schmerl, B.: Architecture-based self-adaptation in the presence of multiple objectives. In: Proceedings of International Workshop on Self-adaptation and Self-managing Systems (SEAMS 2006), pp. 2–8. ACM Press (2006)
4. Dorigo, M., Stutzle, T.: Ant Colony Optimization. MIT Press (2004)
5. Georgiadis, I., Magee, J., Kramer, J.: Self-Organising Software Architectures for Distributed Systems. In: Proceedings of 1st Workshop on Self-healing Systems (WOSS 2002), pp. 33–38. ACM Press (2002)
6. Herrman, K.: Self-organizing Ambient Intelligence. In: VDM (2008)
7. Holder, O., Ben-Shaul, I., Gazit, H.: System Support for Dynamic Layout of Distributed Applications. In: Proceedings of International Conference on Distributed Computing Systems (ICDCS 1999), pp. 403–411. IEEE Computer Society (1999)
8. Jaeger, M.A., Parzyjegla, H., Muhl, G., Herrmann, K.: Self-organizing broker topologies for publish/subscribe systems. In: Proceedings of ACM symposium on Applied Computing (SAC 2007), pp. 543–550. ACM (2007)
9. Koza, J.R.: Genetic Programming: On the Programming of Computers by Means of Natural Selection. MIT Press (1992)
10. Nakano, T., Suda, T.: Self-Organizing Network Services With Evolutionary Adaptation. IEEE Transactions on Neural Networks 16(5), 1269–1278 (2005)
11. van Renesse, R., Schneider, F.B.: Chain replication for supporting high throughput and availability. In: Proceedings of 6th Conference on Symposium on Opearting Systems Design & Implementation, OSDI 2004 (2004)
12. Satoh, I.: Self-organizing Software Components in Distributed Systems. In: Lukowicz, P., Thiele, L., Tröster, G. (eds.) ARCS 2007. LNCS, vol. 4415, pp. 185–198. Springer, Heidelberg (2007)
13. Satoh, I.: Evolutionary Mechanism for Disaggregated Computing. In: Proceedings of 6th International Conference on Complex, Intelligent, and Software Intensive Systems (CISIS 2012), pp. 343–350. IEEE Computer Society (2012)
14. Suda, T., Suzuki, J.: A Middleware Platform for a Biologically-inspired Network Architecture Supporting Autonomous and Adaptive Applications. IEEE Journal on Selected Areas in Communications 23(2), 249–260 (2005)

Modelling and Analysis of Parallel/Distributed Time-dependent Systems: An Approach Based on JADE

Franco Cicirelli and Libero Nigro

Laboratorio di Ingegneria del Software
Dipartimento di Ingegneria Informatica Modellistica Elettronica e Sistemistica
Universitá della Calabria
87036 Rende (CS) - Italy
f.cicirelli@dimes.unical.it, l.nigro@unical.it

Abstract. The work described in this paper develops a control framework for modelling and analysis of parallel/distributed time-dependent multi-agent systems. The approach centres on a minimal computational model which separates agent behaviours from schedulable actions which model activities which have a time duration and require specific processing units. Different control strategies ranging from pure concurrent to time sensitive (real-time or simulated-time) can be considered and applied as a plug-in to a multi-agent system. The control framework is tailored to the JADE distributed agent infrastructure, which lacks of any built-in solution for developing time-dependent applications. This paper focusses on the achievement of control strategies for schedulability analysis of embedded real-time systems designed to execute on a multicore/distributed context. As a case study, a real-time tasking set is modelled and analyzed through simulation, which requires flexible computational resources.

Keywords: multi-agent systems, control framework, real-time constraints, schedulability analysis, parallel/distributed simulation, actors, JADE.

1 Introduction

JADE [1, 2] is a representative agent framework which permits the development of general, untimed, distributed multi-agent systems [3]. JADE is widely used and open source, it adheres to FIPA communication standards [4] which favour application interoperability, it is based on Java. JADE rests on a multi-threaded agent model and on asynchronous message-passing. An agent encapsulates a behaviour and a data status. The behaviour specifies in which way the data status gets modified by the arrival of messages. Messages are buffered into a mailbox owned by the recipient agent from which they are extracted, one at a time, by the control thread of the agent, and eventually processed. When the mailbox is empty, the agent goes into sleep waiting for new incoming messages.

G. Fortino et al. (Eds.): IDCS 2014, LNCS 8729, pp. 204–214, 2014.
© Springer International Publishing Switzerland 2014

The multi-threaded control structure of a multi-agent system is felt sufficient to ensure the basic agent abilities [5], namely autonomy, proactivity, adaptivity to the surrounding environment, sociality, mobility, and so forth.

This work argues that in order to widen/tailor the applicability of multi-agent systems to specific application domains, it is important to adapt the basic control structure of agents so as to ensure, e.g., a time-sensitive behaviour, the fulfilment of dependency/precedence constraints, and so on. This paper proposes an original and flexible control framework for distributed multi-agent systems. The approach is prototyped in JADE and makes it possible to transparently aggregate a specific control module to a multi-agent system, so as to regulate its evolution, e.g. according to a chosen time notion (real-time or simulated-time) and to the availability of processing units.

Whereas some JADE based simulation tools are described in the literature (e.g. [6–9]), the proposed control framework purposely depends on a minimal computational actor model [10–13] which simplifies the use of JADE built-in agent behavioural structure, and permits the design of application specific control structures. The actor model actually used in this paper is novel with respect to the preliminary version described in [13] in that it now hosts a notion of *actions* [14]. Actions are well suited to model activities whose execution consumes time and requires computational resources not owned by actors in an exclusive way (e.g. shared CPUs in a computing system). Actions can abstract operations which need to be reified when switching from model analysis to real execution. They do not affect/trigger actor behavior, i.e. the business logic of a model remains expressed in terms of message processing only. The framework hides and makes orthogonal all the aspects related to action scheduling and their dispatching on the available computational resources thus simplifying modelling activities.

This paper focusses on modelling and analysis, through simulation, of embedded real-time systems with timing constraints, executed on top of a parallel/distributed context [15]. The modelling phase, similarly to Preemptive Time Petri Nets (PTPN) [16, 17], allows one to specify the control flow of each real-time task, e.g. to be activated periodically or sporadically, competing for the access to shared data guarded by locks, and composed of computational steps which have timing constraints, e.g. non deterministic execution time, and scheduling parameters, e.g. a fixed priority, deadline, and specific processing unit to execute. Exhaustive verification of such systems is known to be undecidable in the general case and it is unfeasible for large models. In the Oris tool [18], which supports PTPN and Fixed Priority (FP) scheduling only, the analysis of a model is assisted by a posteriori phase of cancellation of false behaviours in the enumerated state classes of a model. In [19] PTPN were mapped onto Uppaal [20, 21] for model checking. As in [21], the approach permits either FP or Earliest Deadline First (EDF) scheduling. However, the use of stopwatches, necessary to properly implement task preemptions, forces model checking to depend on over-approximation [21] in the generation of the state graph zones. As a consequence, some properties can be checked but only with some uncertainty.

In this paper, a control strategy is presented which is based on simulation, therefore it can show a deadline miss in a multicore based model, but obviously cannot guarantee deadlines are always met. Nevertheless, the approach is of practical value in that it allows to flexibly adapt the scheduling algorithm, and to check system behaviour under general conditions. The use of the achieved control framework is demonstrated by a case study concerned with the schedulability analysis of a preemptive multiprocessor real-time tasking set.

The remainder of this paper is organized as follows. Section 2 describes the assumed computational model. Section 3 proposes the control framework design in JADE. Section 4 summarizes a library of achieved control strategies. Section 5 reports about the chosen case study. Finally, conclusions are drawn in section 6 together with an indication of on-going and future work.

2   A Computational Model Based on Actors and Actions

A minimal computational model easily hosted by JADE is adopted, which makes it possible to introduce control aspects modularly separated from the application logic but reflectively governing the evolution of the application itself. Main concepts are communicating actors and schedulable actions. Actors [10–12] hide some internal data variables and have a behaviour (finite state automaton) for responding to messages. The communication model relies on asynchronous message passing. An actor is a reactive entity which answers to an incoming message on the basis of its current state and received message. Message processing is carried out in the handler(msg) method of the actor, which implements actor behaviour and makes data/state transitions. During a message processing, one or multiple actions can be activated. An action encapsulates a basic timing consuming activity of the actor. Action execution requires a computational resource (processing unit) for it to be carried out. Actors are mapped onto JADE agents (see also Fig. 1). Basic mechanisms like naming, setup, message-passing, migration etc. are borrowed from JADE. Basic operations of actors are the following:

- *newActor*, for creating a new actor
- *become*, for changing the behaviour (state) of the actor
- (non-blocking) *send* for transmitting messages to acquaintance actors (including itself for proactive behaviour). The send operation carries a message with a timestamp which specifies when the message has to be delivered to its recipient
- *do* action, for scheduling the execution of a given action. The *do* operation can specify also if the requesting actor wants to receive a completion message when the action terminates
- *abort* action, for aborting a previously scheduled action.

An action is a black box mainly characterized by a set of input parameters, a set of output parameters and an execution body. Actions have no visibility to the actor internal data variables. At action termination, the informed actor can retrieve the output parameters from the action object and update its internal

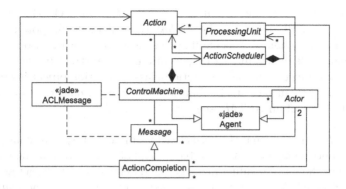

Fig. 1. Basic classes of the control framework in JADE

data variables. It is useful to point out the different roles played by messages and actions. Messages mainly serve to maintain sociality relationships among actors (communication), and to trigger actor behaviour. Actions, on the other hand, express execution concerns, i.e. tasks to be accomplished and which affect the temporal evolution of actors. Message processing is atomic. Action execution, instead, can be suspended and subsequently resumed.

A subsystem of actors (Logical Process or LP) is assigned to an execution locus (i.e., a JADE container) and it is regulated by a control machine (CM). The control machine hides a specific control strategy for administering sent messages and submitted actions. Action execution ultimately depends on a collection of parallel processing units (PUs), hosted by the CM and administered by an action scheduler (AS) (see Fig. 1). A control machine can be in charge of managing a time notion (real-time or simulated-time) regulating actor behaviour.

3   A Control Framework in JADE

The actor model described in the previous section was embedded into JADE as shown in Fig. 1. As one can see in Fig. 1 control machines too are mapped onto JADE agents. Both actors and control machines communicate to one another by exchanging *ACLMessages*. Basic roles of the control framework are assigned to the following abstract classes:

- *Message*, which owns the involved sender/receiver actors and a timestamp information. This is the base class from which all the applicative messages derive. A message is designed to be embodied as a serialized object content in an *ACLMessage*.
- *Action*, which contains the submission time, two free slots for hosting respectively the input and output parameters (array of serializable Objects), the deadline, the action priority and an indication about the PU to use for its execution. In the case no information is provided, the action can be executed on any PU. For an action it is possible also to express if the indicated

PU is the *preferred* one or if it is the *mandatory* one. On the base of the above rules, a PU is said to be *exploitable* if it could be potentially used to execute an action. A specific flag can be set to indicate also if an action is pre-emptable or not during its execution. The abstract method *execute()* must be redefined in a concrete action class. An action object is created by an actor and (transparently) submitted to a control machine as a serialized content object of an *ACLMessage*.

– *ControlMachine*, which is the base class for application-specific control strate-gies. A control machine repeats a basic loop: at each iteration one message is selected in the set of pending messages, and delivered to its target actor for it to be processed. At each message processing termination, the activated actor replies the control machine by an explicit *ACLMessage* containing the set of the messages and the set of actions generated by the activated actor. On re-ceiving such a reply, the new messages are added to the pending set whereas the submitted actions are delivered to the action scheduler. The behaviour of a time-sensitive control machine can require, before a pending message can actually be delivered, a synchronization phase with a time server (see Fig. 2) for achieving the necessary grant to proceed with the message.

– *ActionScheduler*, which imposes the application-specific execution policy for the actions. An action scheduler governs a set of processing units. On the basis of the adopted execution policy, a scheduler can (i) assign the action to a free processing unit, (ii) assign the action to a busy processing unit by firstly preempting the ongoing action and saving its execution status or (iii) add the action to a pending set for its subsequent execution. Preempted actions are added to the pending set too and marked as *suspended*.

– *ProcessingUnit*, which abstracts an actual action executor able to process one action at time. It could be, in a case, an instance of a thread in a pool, which maps onto a physical core of the underlying hardware. The use of PUs allows naturally to take into account the computational capabilities of a multi-core architecture both during analysis (i.e. simulations) and real execution. Basic methods offered by a PU are *start*, *preempt* and *stop*. An *ActionCompletion* message is used to state that an action has terminated its execution.

– *Actor*, which serves as a common ancestor for applicative actors and provides all the basic operations. The JADE behaviour hidden in the Actor class re-ceives an *ACLMessage* from a control machine, extracts from it the Message content (deserialized) object, and starts the message processing by invoking the *handler()* method. At the handler termination, all the newly generated messages and actions get collected and sent back to the control machine as a part of an *ACLMessage*. An actor is bound to the control machine of the hosting JADE container. Actor migration is supported by a redefinition of the *afterMove()* method which is in charge of adjusting the binding to the local control machine according to the destination container.

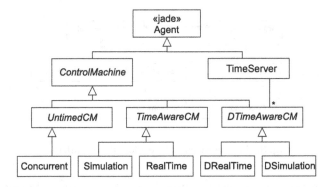

Fig. 2. The hierarchy of developed control machines

4   A Library of Control Forms

A library of reusable control structures was prototyped as depicted in Fig. 2. Other control mechanisms can be added as well. A common design principle of all the control machines in Fig. 2 concerns the *handler* methods of actors which are always executed one at time in an interleaved way (co-operative concurrency) in a given container. Actions are instead executed in parallel according to the configured number of processing units which in turn mirrors the assumed parallel degree of the model. The way actions are ultimately executed is determined by the adopted implementation of the action scheduler. A library of reusable schedulers, along with the implemented kinds of processing units, was prototyped as reported in Fig. 3. Other schedulers can be added too. A description of the available control forms is provided in the following.

4.1   Prototyped Control Machines

Three families of control machines can be identified in Fig. 2. The UntimedCM family groups control structures which do not manage an explicit time notion. This kind on control machines can be naturally used both in a centralized or in a parallel/distributed scenario where an actor model is partitioned among multiple JADE containers. The TimeAwareCM collects control machines which manage time but in a not distributed context, that is the actor model cannot be partitioned into multiple JADE containers. The DTimeAwareCM control machines, on the other hand, can be used in the case a time-sensitive model requires to be handled in a parallel/distributed scenario. In particular, a TimeServer is required in order to ensure a coherent time notion gets used in the participating control machines. Concurrent implements an untimed parallel control structure which rests on a FIFO message queue as the message pending set. Simulation manages a virtual time notion of a classical discrete-event simulation schema, and processes messages in timestamp order.

An actor model can be split into multiple JADE containers each equipped with a control machine. Containers can run on different cores of a same CPU

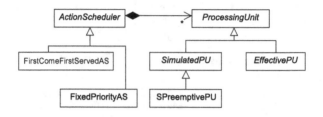

Fig. 3. The hierarchy of developed schedulers

or they can be assigned to distinct processors of a distributed system. In the case the application is time sensitive, it can be necessary a time server to ensure a global time notion (simulated-time or real-time). `DSimulation` in Fig. 2 differs from `Simulation` only because time advancement is now negotiated (i.e., a conservative control structure is adopted) among the various control machines, through the use of a specialization of the `TimeServer`. Before processing the next timed message whose timestamp is greater than current simulation time, a control machine asks the time server a grant to advance to the next time. The time server collects all the proposals of time advancement and the minimum of those proposals is furnished as grant to relevant control machines. Of course, the time server can generate the grant provided no in-transit messages exist in the system. Towards this a distinct counter for the sent and received messages [22] related to each actor/agent, are kept by the control machines and furnished as accompanying information to proposal messages to the time server. These fine-grain counters are necessary for taking into account actor migration and then the fact that a same actor can be handled, dynamically, by different control machines.

`Realtime` is useful for applications based on real-time execution. It rests on a real time notion achieved on top of Java `System.currentTimeMillis()` service. `DRealTime` control machine is analogous to `RealTime` but it is suited for parallel/distributed execution. A description of the control machines based on a real-time notion is beyond the scope of this paper.

4.2   Action Schedulers

Prototyped schedulers (see Fig. 3) immediately put into execution a newly scheduled action on a idle *exploitable* PU (if there are any), otherwise, different scheduling strategies can be adopted. In the case no such idle PUs exist, the `FirstComeFirstServerAS` scheduler organizes actions in a pending list. The list is ordered by using the time an action is scheduled. Each time a PU becomes idle, the pending list is iterated and the first action for which the PU is exploitable is removed from the list and assigned to the PU. The PU remains idle in the case it is not exploitable by any of the actions in the list.

The `FixedPriorityAS` scheduler uses action priority to keep ordered the pending list. Action execution is priority driven and preemptive. The duration of a preempted action is shortened by the time the action was running. It is worth noticing that switching from simulation to real execution, implies only a redefinition of PUs. For simulation purposes, the `SPreemptivePUs` can be used which are passive objects without internal threads. When an action is assigned to a PU, an action completion message is scheduled to occur at the time obtained by summing the current virtual time to the action duration. This provision (i) permits the virtual time to grow accordingly to the time needed to simulate the execution of the action, (ii) allows the scheduler to be informed that a previously busy processing unit is now ready to be used again, (iii) notifies action completion to the originator actor in the case it expressed the willingness of receiving such notification. In the case an action is preempted, the related action completion message is simply descheduled (see the association between `ProcessingUnit` and `ControlMachine` in Fig. 2).

5   A Case Study

The control framework was put into practice in a case by studying the schedulability analysis of a tasking set (see Fig. 4) designed, for demonstration purposes, to run under static priority preemptive scheduling over a multi-processor architecture. The example is made up of two periodic processes ($P1$ and $P2$ with period T_{P1} and T_{P2} respectively) and a sporadic one ($P3^s$ with minimal interdistance between two consecutive occurrences of the triggering event being T_{P3^s}) all having non-deterministic execution times. Task durations are supposed to include the scheduling algorithm costs. The three tasks are supposed to be ready at time 0, i.e. the first task instances (jobs) arrive at time 0. In addition, the relative deadlines coincide with task periods. Process $P1$ has the highest priority (i.e. 3) whereas process $P3^s$ has the lowest one (i.e. 1). An intermediate priority is assigned to process $P2$ (i.e. 2). Mutual exclusion, based on a *mutex* semaphore, is required between processes $P1$ and $P2$ to regulate access to some shared data. Each process task is split in two sub-tasks t_{xy} each allocated to a different CPU. The computation time of a sub-task is denoted in Fig. 4 by C_{txy}. Three CPUs, namely $cpu1$, $cpu2$ and $cpu3$, are assumed for task execution. The $cpu1$ and $cpu2$ in particular are supposed to be hosted by a same multi-core machine MA whereas $cpu3$ resides on a dedicated computer MB.

It is worth noting that the analysis of one such tasking model is not covered by the classical scheduling theory. In addition, the use of a multi-processor context opens, in general, to possible scheduling anomalies [23, 16, 19]. The case study, though, is intended to address basic problems and to highlight the achieved programming style.

The following kinds of agents were developed. A *Generator* agent is in charge of generation of task instances on the basis of task periods. A *SubTask* agent models sub-tasks. The acquaintance relationship among sub-task agents mirrors the precedence schema of the task model. Coordination among sub-task executions is achieved by exchanging *Next* messages. One such a message informs a *SubTask* agent that the previous sub-task completed thence its sub-task can be

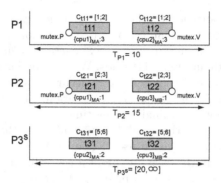

Fig. 4. A task set model

scheduled. Each *SubTask* agent models its assigned sub-task as an activity. A *Semaphore* agent is introduced to manage mutual exclusion. The *Acquire* and *Release* messages are used to negotiate semaphore acquisition and its subsequent release. Two specializations of sub-task agents are implemented, namely the *SubTaskWithAcquire* and *SubTaskWithRelease*, which model respectively the case a sub-task requires to acquire/release the semaphore. Finally, an *Oberver* agent in used to gather data about the start-time and completion-time of any task instance in order to evaluate the maximum and minimum response times of tasks. When a job of a given task begins before the completion of the previous one, the observer notifies the task model is not schedulable.

The following reports the *handler* method (behaviour) of the *SubTaskWith-Release* agent, which confirms simplicity of the resultant programming style. As one can see, the code completely hides all the issues related to the scheduling policy, execution, preemption etc. of actions.

```
public void handler(Message m) {
  if (m instanceof Next) {
    double subTaskDuration = random.nextSample(minDuration,maxDuration);
    MyAction subTask = new MyAction(subTaskDuration, cpu, priority);
    do(subTask, true);
  } else if (m instanceof ActionCompletion) {
    Observer.End end = new Observer.End(observerAID, subTaskName);
    end.setTimestamp(now()); send(end);
    Mutex.Release release = new Mutex.Release(semaphoreAID);
    release.setTimestamp(now()); send(release);
    if (nextAgentExists){
      Next next = new Next(nextAgentAID);
      next.setTimestamp(now()); send(next);
    }
  }
}//handler
```

The model was partitioned in two JADE containers, one simulating the machine *MA* and the other simulating *MB*. The model was configured by using

`DSimulation` for the control machines, `FixedPriorityAS` for the action schedulers and `SPreemptivePU` for the processing units. Two PUs were assigned to the container simulating MA and one PU to the container simulating MB.

Simulation experiments were carried out using a time limit of 10^6, on a Win 7, 12GB, Intel Core i7, 3.50GHz, 4 cores workstation. It emerged that the original model in Fig. 4 is not schedulable due to a priority inversion problem occurring for the task $P1$ which misses its deadline in the case the sub-task $t22$ is executing but gets preempted by the sporadic task $P3^s$. By raising the priority of $t22$ to 3 (which is the priority of $P1$), i.e. by (partly) emulating a priority ceiling protocol, the task model appears to be schedulable and the estimated response times (after five runs) of $P1$, $P2$ and $P3^s$ were found to be respectively $[2.002; 9.907]$, $[4.006; 9.875]$ and $[10.014; 16.815]$.

6   Conclusions

This paper proposes a control framework in JADE which makes it possible to develop time-dependent multi-agent systems. In particular, the achievement of a distributed simulation control strategy is presented for the schedulability analysis of real-time embedded systems designed to run on top of a multiprocessor architecture.

Prosecution of the research is aimed to:

- extending the library with other real-time schedulers, e.g. based on Earliest Deadline First (EDF);
- supporting adversary simulators [24] for large sporadic task models, to evaluate global fixed-priority over multiprocessors;
- specializing the approach so as to support a different scheduling algorithm [19] for each distinct CPU;
- experimenting with the use of the control structures in the analysis and implementation of complex agent-based models, e.g. time-constrained workflow modelling, analysis and enactment, virtual environments etc.

References

1. Bellifemine, F., Caire, G., Greenwood, D.: Developing multi-agent systems with JADE. John Wiley & Sons (2007)
2. Jade, `http://jade.tilab.com` (accessed on June 2014)
3. Agha, G.: Actors: a model of concurrent computation in distributed systems. MIT Press, Cambridge (1986)
4. Fipa, foundation for intelligent physical agents, `http://www.fipa.org` (accessed on June 2014)
5. Wooldridge, M.: An introduction to multi-agent systems, 2nd edn. John Wiley & Sons (2009)
6. Carzaniga, A., Picco, G.P., Vigna, G.: Agent.gui: A multi-agent based simulation framework. In: Proc. of FedCSIS 2011, pp. 623–630 (2011)

7. Gianni, D., Loukas, G., Gelenbe, E.: A simulation framework for the investigation of adaptive behaviours in largely populated building evacuation scenarios. In: Proc. of OAMAS, pp. 1–15 (2008)

8. Wang, F., Turner, S.J., Wang, L.: Agent communication in distributed simulations. In: Davidsson, P., Logan, B., Takadama, K. (eds.) MABS 2004. LNCS (LNAI), vol. 3415, pp. 11–24. Springer, Heidelberg (2005)

9. Pawlaszyk, D., Strassburger, S.: A synchronization protocol for distributed agent-based simulations with constrained optimism. In: Proc. of ESM 2009, pp. 337–341 (2009)

10. Cicirelli, F., Furfaro, A., Nigro, L.: An agent infrastructure over HLA for distributed simulation of reconfigurable systems and its application to UAV coordination. Trans. of SCS SIMULATION 85(1), 17–32 (2009)

11. Cicirelli, F., Giordano, A., Nigro, L.: Efficient environment management for distributed simulation of large-scale situated multi-agent systems. In: Concurrency and Computation: Practice and Experience (2014), doi:10.1002/cpe.3254

12. Cicirelli, F., Furfaro, A., Nigro, L.: Modelling and simulation of complex manufacturing systems using statechart-based actors. Simulation Modelling Practice and Theory 19(2), 685–703 (2011)

13. Cicirelli, F., Nigro, L., Pupo, F.: Agent-based control framework in JADE. In: 28st European Conf. on Modelling and Simulation, Brescia, pp. 25–31 (May 2014)

14. Cicirelli, F., Nigro, L.: A control framework for model continuity in JADE. In: Proc. of the IEEE/ACM 18th Intl. Symp. DS-RT (to appear, 2014)

15. Brekling, A.W., Hansen, M.R., Madsen, J.: Models and formal verifications of multiprocessor system-on-chips. The J. of Logic and Algebraic Prog. 77, 1–19 (2008)

16. Bucci, G., Fedeli, A., Sassoli, L., Vicario, E.: Timed state space analysis of real-time preemptive systems. IEEE Trans. on Soft. Eng. 30(2), 97–111 (2004)

17. Carnevali, L., Ridi, L., Vicario, E.: Putting preemptive time petri nets to work in a v-model sw lifecycle. IEEE Trans. on Soft. Eng. 37(6), 826–844 (2011)

18. Bucci, G., Carnevali, L., Ridi, L., Vicario, E.: Oris: a tool for modeling, verification and evaluation of real-time systems. Int'l J. Software Tools for Technology Transfer 12(5), 391–403 (2010)

19. Cicirelli, F., Angelo, F., Nigro, L., Pupo, F.: Development of a schedulability analysis framework based on PTPN and Uppaal with stopwatches. In: Proc. of 16th IEEE/ACM Intl. Symp. DS-RT 2012, pp. 57–64 (2012)

20. Behrmann, G., David, A., Larsen, K.G.: A tutorial on Uppaal. In: Bernardo, M., Corradini, F. (eds.) SFM-RT 2004. LNCS, vol. 3185, pp. 200–236. Springer, Heidelberg (2004)

21. David, A., Illum, J., Larsen, K.G., Skou, A.: Model-based framework for schedulability analysis using Uppaal 4.1. In: Model-Based Design for Embedded Systems, ch. 3, pp. 93–120. CRC Press (2009)

22. Fujimoto, R.M.: Parallel and distributed simulation systems. John Wiley (2000)

23. Andersson, B., Jonsson, J.: Preemptive multiprocessor scheduling anomalies. In: Proc. of the 16th IEEE Int. Parallel and Dist. Proc. Symp., pp. 12–19 (2002)

24. Silva de Oliveria, R., Carminati, A., Starke, R.A.: On using adversary simulators to evaluate global fixed-priority and FPZL scheduling of multiprocessors. The Journal of Systems and Software 86, 403–411 (2013)

Advanced Networking

A Basic Study on High Bandwidth Streaming in Realtime over Multipath Using LDPC-IRA Codes

Masahiko Kitamura, Hiroyuki Kimiyama,
Tsuyoshi Ogura, and Tatsuya Fujii

NTT Network Innovation Laboratories, Yokosuka, Kanagawa 239-0847, Japan

Abstract. This paper describes a distributed video streaming system using widely disparsed storages, in which each storage hosts send chunked video packets to single receiver through multipath network. By adding parity packets by forward error correction (FEC) along with source video data in each storage hosts, this system enables realtime video streamings even if there are unbalance between those hosts. In this paper, we introduce a model of this unbalance and its effect to the amount of needed packet sending, then discuss how to design redundancy rate in FEC. The result are shown to have a trade off among the range of balancing and the additional amount of sending packet needed for stable video streaming.

Keywords: network virtualization, multipath routing, realtime streaming, forward error correction, IRA codes.

1 Introduction

Networking Innovations of Software Defined Network(SDN) [1] and network virtualization [2] have been making networks more flexible and extensible for application such as video streamings and big size data handlings. Along with such advanced networking architectures, one can control network behavior as a generalized programmings, e.g. a flow controller on OpenFlow switches, while it's basically impossible to do so on conventional network switches.

Thanks to these emerging network structures, huge-bandwidth applications like video production that needs high bandwidth networking are emigrating to cloud from locally deployed computing resources [3]. Apart from comercial video on-demand services, high definition and quality are highly required in video production, so that these services have to arrange equivalent bandwidth on network, e.g. uncompressed video streaming in High Definition is equal to 1.5 Gbit/s. Keeping such a huge bandwidth is substantially too difficult, which results in a limit of these applications.

On the other hand, from an aspect of data storage in cloud, data redundancy framework such as the redundant arrays of inexpensive disks (RAID) is widely applied for fault tolerance and load balancing. However, these simple duplication approach for huge sized data comes at a cost. For instance, content delivery

G. Fortino et al. (Eds.): IDCS 2014, LNCS 8729, pp. 217–226, 2014.

network services are one of current solution for load balancing to the access request. This approach incurs linear increase of storage size to a content to be delivered although it can be implemented in a simple structure. Therefore, huge sized data such as video materials in movie production cannot be handled in this conventional framework.

From these perspective, some distributed streaming systems over multipath from distributed storage are proposed. These systems bring a high fault tolerance, efficient networking usage and load dispersion on storage hosts. In [4], a streaming system from two distributed sender is proposed for video delivery in realtime. This system focuses on how to control the sending rate so as to avoid the player's stall caused by the lack of receiving packets to be played back. In [5], this streaming system introduces Reed-Solomon codes (RS coes) of forward error correction to avoid packet loss in network. However, with this system still difficult to handle huge sized data because deciding process takes much time in RS codes as the code length, which is proportion to data size, grows because RS codes exploit Galois field in its calculation. In addition, RS codes is not flexible for data size and pakcet size on network in general because of Galois field's calculation.

In this paper, we propose a distributed streaming system using low-density parity-check irregular repeat-accumulate (LDPC-IRA) codes, which is also one of the forward error correction scheme, for high bandwidth video handling on networks that aggregate the bandwidth in multipath to make virtual high bandwidth for video streaming. As well as the fault tolerance and load balancing to user request, proposed system provides this virtual aggregation by sending parity packet in paths with high available bandwidth to compensate the packets that cannot be sent because of lack of bandwidth in a path. The LDPC codes, in particular IRA codes, provides not only the high performance decoding at a receiver side, but also the load balancing in sending rate in each sender to match their available bandwidth. This paper focuses on how to control and distribute the sending rate for each host so as to perform a streaming system for high bandwidth data streaming in realtime as a whole.

The rest of this paper consists of following sections. In Section 2 we discuss the feature of distributed streaming system on multipath with forward error correction codes so as to clarify the advantages against the conventional streaming approaches. In Secrion 3 we review the forward error correction code, in particular IRA codes, and extend the codes to construct the multipath streaming from distributed storage host. By constructing models for the load balancing of bandwidth between multipath, we finally introduces a principle to determine the main parameters of IRA codes for the system. Section 4 concludes these discussion.

2   Distributed Streaming System with IRA Codes

This section goes through a distributed streaming system on multipath using IRA codes, a family of error correcting codes, to make unbalanced bandwidth

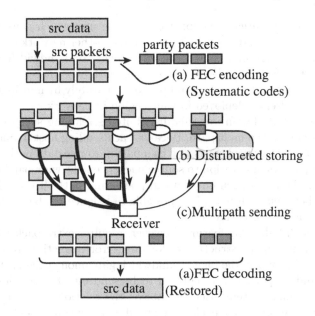

Fig. 1. The overview of distributed streaming system on multipath using forward error correction codes

aggregation. This system consists of three component — a) forward error correction, FEC, b) widely distributed storage, and c) distributed streaming over multipath of unbalanced bandwidth(see Figure 1). The FEC component generates redundancy data packets, parity packets, from source data packet by systematic error correction codes. Then, these source and parity packets are put on the distributed storages. At the distributed streaming component, each storage host starts streaming of packets as soon as user's request is received. Finally, FEC decoding process restores the original source data from received packet that is not lost in network. In this restoring process, original source data can be restored by only re-ordering if all sent packet are received. If some packets are lost and doesn't reach, the original source data is to be recovering by FEC decoding.

These components brings some advantages to the distributed streaming system. First, the distributed data storing exploiting forward error correction benefits fault tolerance to the failure of storage media ranging from disk media to disaster in a data center. In addition to the tolerance to storage media troubles, forward error correction makes streaming system more robust if sent packets are lost caused by network traffic congestion. In this system, the forward error correction is applied as a single framework from distributed storing to multipath streaming, so that it is unnecessary to encode twice at the time of sending on each storage hosts.

Second, dispersibility of usage rate of bandwidth in network is an another benefit that comes from structure of distributed storing and multipath streaming. In the single path streaming of high bandwidth video in a conventional system, network resources are largely occupied by a single use, which causes the local burst in network usage and imposes a limitation on other network services. This dispersibility attribution makes high efficient network on bandwidth where such a video streaming service can be provided along with other network services. In the distributed system, it's easy to send packets separately by multipath because these packets are already deployed in wide region in network.

Finally, the another feature of this distributed streaming system is sending rate balancing among the multipath. Because each sending host, namely storage host, has a part of parity packets as well as a part of source data packets, sending some of parity packets in addition to source packets on the wide band path helps to make up for the lack of sending data in poor band path. If there is variance of bandwidth between each path, it is possible to balance the bandwidth in this manner by forward error correction.

This bandwidth balancing feature, however, requires extra packet sending as a whole system due to the structure of forward error correction. In fact, as described later in this paper, the bigger bandwidth gap among each path becomes, the more redundant packets are required to be send out. For the design of the distributed streaming system discussed above, the relation between bandwidth gap and the amount of parity packets required is a key component if the paths and its bandwidth are given. This paper shows this relation from the aspect of forward error correction codes by evaluating actually IRA codes.

3   Multipath Realtime Streaming with IRA Codes

This section describes on the IRA codes, a family of Low-density Parity-cehck (LDPC) codes, then discuss its extension to the distributed multipath streaming.

3.1   LDPC and IRA Codes

LDPC codes is one of forward error correcting codes in block code form whose parity check matrix is very sparse [6]. The approaches to construct LDPC codes are proposed in several ways. In particular, the irregular repeat-accumurate (IRA) codes [7] take an approach of coupling sparse matrix and staircase matrix to generate a parity check matrix. Because of this simple construction, IRA codes can encode and decode in linear time, and can obtain the generator matrix immediately from parity check matrix. The IRA codes are a family of systematic codes, where source data are included in a encoded data, so that it is easier to handle data on actual implementation since source data can be stored separately from parity data.

In our system, source data was chopped and packetized into source packets $s = (s_1, s_2, ..., s_k)$, then IRA encoder generates relevant parity packets $p = (p_1, p_2, ..., p_m)$ from source packets. These two types of packets act as coding symbols in the forward error correcting codes. An IRA code of code length $n = k + m$ has sparse matrix S of $(m \times m)$ and staricase matrix T of $(m \times k)$ in its parity check matrix. By the definition of forward error correcting codes,

$$H(s \quad p)^{\mathrm{T}} = (S|T)(s \quad p)^{\mathrm{T}} = Ss^{\mathrm{T}} + Tp^{\mathrm{T}} = \mathbf{0}. \tag{1}$$

An example of parity check matrix of IRA code is as follows.

$$H = (S|T) = \begin{pmatrix} 1 & 1 & | & 1 & & & \\ & 1 & & 1 & | & 1 & 1 & & \\ & 1 & 1 & | & & & 1 & 1 & \\ & & 1 & 1 & | & & & 1 & 1 \end{pmatrix}. \tag{2}$$

In this example, the size of matrix is too small to have sparse matrix. In general, because parity check matrix with very large size, at least $n > 10000$, should be taken, the matrix S become sparse. The degree of column, which is the number of '1's in a column, is uniformly 2 in this matrix.

In the discussion of forward error correction codes, coding rate $r = k/n$ is widely used to measure redundancy degree. However, this paper adopts redundancy rate $R = n/k = 1/r$ because the size of parity packet to that of data packet is more intuitive in terms of system design. In the example above, it is found that the number of source packet is $k = 4$, the number of parity packet is $m = 4$, and redundancy date is $R = 2$. With IRA codes, decoding process should be done in linear time for code length n by using message passing algorithm (MPA). In our system, decoding process takes MPA approach for high bandwidth streaming in real-time.

3.2   Design of IRA Codes for Multipath Streaming

In our system, source packets and parity packets are divided into N blocks respectively, then they are placed on distributed storage hosts $S_i(i = 1, 2, .., N)$. Let the data size of source packets and parity packets be l_{srci} and l_{prtyi}, the original data size of source data and parity data can be described by $L_{src} = \sum_i l_{srci}$ and $L_{prty} = \sum_i l_{prtyi}$.

The target of our system focus on the real-time streaming of stored content in advance, in which the data size to be sent in a unit of time, denoted by streaming rate, is determined by streaming content. In this paper, for simplicity, we define the source data size L_{src} as the streaming rate. Additionally, available bandwidth from a storage host S_i to a receiver R is denoted by b_i, while the actual sending rate is denoted by $x_i(0 \leq x_i \leq b_i)$. Although detecting actual available bandwidth is another issue in general, we assume the network is closed and managed such as that in a data center in which it is possible to obtain available bandwidth in each path.

The design of multipath streaming system from distributed storage with IRA codes can be divided into two types of problem — data size distribution problem and streaming rate distribution problem. The data size distribution problem is on how to make group of source packets and parity packets to meet the condition of storage capacity in each host. The streaming rate distribution problem is on how to assign the sending rate to meet the condition for restoring original source data at a receiver. Although these two problem are mutually related in general, it is difficult to determine the data size distribution because available bandwidth could be variable each time. Consequently, our system divides source packets and parity packets equally and distributes to each storage host. In this case, the data size of source packets and parity packets on host S_i should be $l_{srci} = L_{src}/N$ and $l_{prtyi} = L_{prty}/N$.

On the other hand, in streaming rate distribution problem, it should be considered by feature of IRA codes. In systematic codes including IRA codes, the more source packets are received, the higher success probability in decoding become, thus source packet should be sent out prior to parity packets. Therefore, when the path has an enough bandwidth to send determined sending rate of source packets l_{srci}, $b_i > l_{srci}$, corresponding storage host should send out all source packets, whereas it should send as many source packets as possible in the other case. In the latter case, where the path doesn't have enough capability to send source packets, some source packets not sent out due to lack of bandwidth are repaired by the parity packets sent by another paths with redundant bandwidth in our system.

For the whole system, the amount of source packets $\bar{L}_{src}$ is given as

$$\bar{L}_{src} = \sum_{i'} (l_{srci'} - b_{i'}), \qquad (i' = i | b_i < l_{srci}). \tag{3}$$

Then, the amount of parity packets to be sent is equivalent to the number of parity packet that can restores the lack of source packets $\bar{L}_{src}$. From aspect of forward error correction codes, considering the error probability of source packets and parity packets, denoted by P_e^{src} and P_e^{prty}, the streaming rate distribution problem comes down to a problem to determine the maximum error probability of parity packet $\hat{P}_e^{prty} = \max P_e^{prty}$ that can afford to recover the source packets with error probability $P_e^{src} = \bar{L}_{src}/L_{src}$.

As a consequence, the packets sent out in this system consists of the source packets excluding not sent packet because of inadequate bandwidth and the parity packet sent out additionally for compensating the lack of source packet. The amount of this sent packet L_{sent} can be obtained as

$$L_{sent} = (L_{src} - \bar{L}_{src}) + L_{prty}(1 - P_e^{prty}). \tag{4}$$

Note that the packet sending increase is invoked by only the set of hosts with inadequate bandwidth path. To avoid the redundant packet sending system should be designed to make the sending rate distribution on each path not to exceed the data sets on each storage host S_i. The rest of this paper discusses the correlation between the set of path with inadequate bandwidth path S_i' and the increase of packet to be sent out $\bar{L}_{src}$.

Figure 3 illustrates an example of load balancing on bandwidth between paths with abundant bandwidth and paths with inadequate bandwidth. In this example, the size of each source packet are 5 Mbit each, and there are three paths of abundant bandwidth and two paths of inadequate bandwidth to the source packets to be sent. From this model, we obtain the lack of source packet sending caused by inadequate bandwidth $P_e^{src} = \bar{L}_{src}/L_{src} = 4 / 25 = 0.16$. Recall that packet sending increase depends on only $\bar{L}_{src}$, this multipath streaming model can be transformed to an equivalent form as shown in Figrue 3-b.

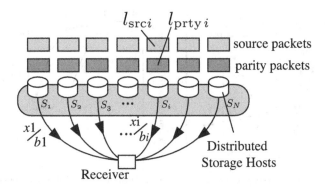

Fig. 2. Network model of multipath streaming from distributed storage hosts

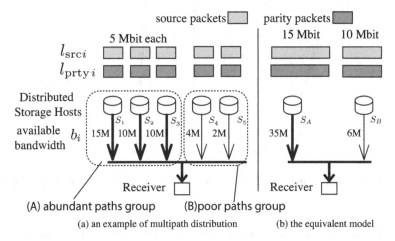

Fig. 3. Model of bandwidth load balancing between multipath

3.3 Evaluation of Redundant Packet Sending and System Design

In this section, we evaluate redundant packet increase required for balancing bandwidth over multipath by introducing actual IRA codes and its parity check matrices. Before the generating actual parity check matrices, it is required to specify the number of source packet k in IRA codes, redundancy rate R and packet size l_{pkt} to match actual data size to be sent. In terms of implementation of system, packet size l_{pkt} should be match the maximum transmission unit (MTU) that is about 1500 bytes in conventional Ethernet/IP network. If the size of data L_{src}, i.e. the bitrate of content data to be sent, is 560 Mbit/sec, IRA codes with $k = 5 \cdot 10^4$ and $l_{pkt} = 1400$ bytes are acceptable. As to redundancy rate R depends on how the system should cover the range of unbalanced bandwidth between multipath. High redundancy rate R is needed to cover wide range of unbalancing bandwidth because the system needs to send more parity packets as the lack of source packet increases. We use $R = 2$, 1.5 and 1.25 here to compare the efficiency in this system.

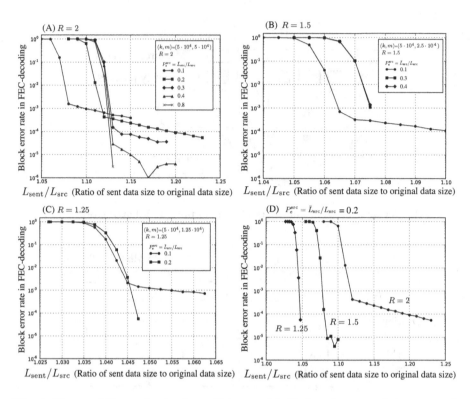

Fig. 4. The capability and redundant efficiency with H of random raw choice approach

In terms of construction of actual parity check matrix H, firstly we take random raw choice approach for simplicity. In this approach, the sparse matrix S in H is generated by placing '1's of D_c randomly in each column. This construction may make loops of '1' in the matrix that degrades the recovering capability because the position of '1' in a column is determined independently to other columns. The capability and redundant efficiency with this H are shown in Figure 4. Figure 4 - A–C shows the error probability of decoding to the redundant efficiency on sending packet for each redundancy rate of IRA codes R. It is indicated that more parity packet sending are needed as the lack of source packet sending due to inadequate bandwidth, denoted as $P_e^{\mathrm{src}} = \bar{L}_{\mathrm{src}}/L_{\mathrm{src}}$, grows. Indeed, under the IRA code of $R = 2$ and $k = 5 \cdot 10^4$, 10% extra packet sending to original source data size is required to satisfy the error probability $P_e^{\mathrm{prty}} = 10^{-3}$ at $P_e^{\mathrm{src}} = 0.1$ as shown in Figure 4-A. This additional packet sending can be considered as an overhead for virtual bandwidth aggregation.

As to coverage of bandwidth unbalance, P_e^{src} becomes limited as redundancy rate R decreases. In fact, in case of $R = 1.25$, the system supports up to $P_e^{\mathrm{src}} \simeq 0.2$ as illustrated in Figure 4-C.

On the other hand, Figure 4-D illustrates the difference between redundancy rate R at the same P_e^{src}. The maltipath streaming with lower R is lean in the

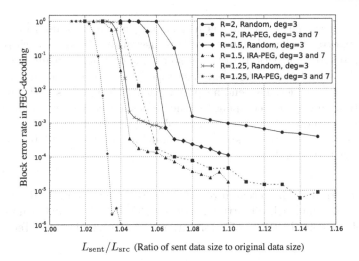

$L_{\text{sent}}/L_{\text{src}}$ (Ratio of sent data size to original data size)

Fig. 5. The capability and redundant efficiency with H of IRA-PEG approach

sense that sending fewer extra packets satisfy the lower error probability in decoding, whereas its coverage become limited. This denotes a tradeoff between coverage of unbalanced bandwidth and efficiency of sending packet to original source data size exists.

In some cases in the figure, there is a region that the error probability in decoding is not improved if extra packets are sent. This is referred as the error floor that caused by stopping set in the MPA decoding process. In order to avoid this degration, another approach to generate sparse matrix S in parity check matrix H of IRA codes should be introduced. To this end, we exploit progressive edge growth (PEG) [[8]] approach to construct parity check matrix. For IRA codes construction, PEG should be applied after placing staircase matrix T in H.

Figure 5 shows the equivalent performance with parity check matrix H generated by IRA-PEG approach with $D_c = 3, 7$ and $R = 2$, 1.5, and 1.25. As a result, the error floor is improved n all cases, while there are still error floor degration in $R = 2$ and 1.5. Moreover, the amount of required sending packet is also improved. In the case of $R = 2$, required extra sending packet ratio to original source data is improved from 1.068 to 1.043 at decoding error rate of 10^{-3}.

For the design of multipath streaming system with distributed storage using IRA codes, as we discussed above, it is necessary to determine a range of lack of source packet sending $\bar{L}_{\text{src}} = \sum_{i'} (l_{\text{src}i'} - b_{i'})$ first, then determine the minimum redundancy rate R so that can recover the source packets under this condition. With the higher R, the system is able to cover range of load balancing on transmission rate between multipath, whereas the required additional packet sending increases that results in degration of transmission efficiency.

4 Conclusion

In this paper, we discussed a multipath streaming system with distributed storage that supports the load balancing of trasmission rate between each path by using forward error correction. In this system, the original transmission source data are split and placed in distributed storage hosts along with parity packets generated by IRA codes. By sending parity packets from hosts with abundant path, the streaming system compensates the lack of source packet sending caused by inadequate bandwidth at the receiver. We also discussed on how to design IRA codes for this streaming system by modeling of these load balancing of bandwidth with IRA codes.

Acknowledgment. The research resutls have been achieved by "Robust data transmission over multi-sliced virtual networks: ROMSNET", the Commissioned Research of National Institute of Information and Communications Technology (NICT).

References

1. McKeown, N., et al.: OpenFlow: enabling innovation in campus networks. ACM SIGCOMM Computer Communication Review 38(2), 69–74 (2008)
2. Nakao, A.: Network virtualization as foundation for enabling new network architectures and applications. IEICE Transactions on Communications 93(3), 454–457 (2010)
3. Sony Media Cloud Services, https://www.sonymcs.com
4. Nguyen, T., Zakhor, A.: Distributed video streaming over Internet. In: Proc. of Multimedia Computing and Networking (MMCN 2002) (2002)
5. Nguyen, T., Zakhor, A.: Distributed video streaming with forward error correction. In: Packet Video Workshop, vol. 2002 (2002)
6. Gallager, R.: Low-density parity-check codes. IRE Transactions on Information Theory 8(1), 21–28 (1962)
7. Jin, H., Khandekar, A., McEliece, R.: Irregular repeat-accumulate codes. In: Proc. 2nd Int. Symp. Turbo Codes and Related Topics (2000)
8. Hu, X.-Y., Eleftheriou, E., Arnold, D.-M.: Progressive edge-growth Tanner graphs. In: IEEE Global Telecommunications Conference, GLOBECOM 2001, vol. 2. IEEE (2001)

Resolving Fallback and Path MTU Problems Caused by Denying ICMP Packets in IPv6

Noriaki Yoshiura and Keita Omi*

Department of Information and Computer Sciences, Saitama University
255, Shimo-ookubo, Sakura-ku, Saitama, Japan
{yoshiura,komi}@fmx.ics.saitama-u.ac.jp

Abstract. Denying ICMP packets in IPv6 causes two problems. One is a problem of fallback in IPv4/IPv6 Dual-Stack environment and the other is that of Path MTU Discovery. Each of the problems delays communications. This paper creates a system that shortens this communication delay. The system runs on the gateway of a network and chapters the IPv6 traffic of the nodes in the network and checks IPv6 communications between the nodes in the network and outside of the network. If the system notices failure of the IPv6 communication, the system sends ICMP packets to the node of IPv6 communications to prompt fallback of IPv6/IPv4 or adjustment of packet length for path MTU problem. This paper evaluates the performance of the system by experiment, which shows that the system can shorten communication delay that is caused by the fallback problem.

1 Introduction

On the Internet, IPv4 addresses are exhausted and change from IPv4 to IPv6 or using IPv6[13] address starts. The goal of IPv6 is that the Internet uses IPv6 addresses and remove IPv4 addresses. Now, IPv6 addresses increase[6] in the Internet because IPv4 addresses are short and some countries recommend usage of IPv6[1]. Several surveys also show that IPv6 users increase and IPv6 infrastructure has been deployed[2,5,3,7] However, change from IPv4 to IPv6 and using IPv6 instead of IPv4 are uneasy because of technical problems and cost. All the IPv4 addresses cannot be changed to IPv6 addresses in the Internet at one time and it is necessary to change IPv4 to IPv6 with using IPv4 and IPv6 addresses concurrently.

IPv6 uses ICMP (Internet Control Message Protocol), which complements TCP/IP communications by sending and receiving error or control messages. However, in some networks, ICMP packets are blocked by firewall because of security reason; ICMP packets can be used for detection of PCs, portscan and DoS attacks. ICMP packets are used when some troubles happen in networks. For example, if packets do not arrive at the destinations, then routers in the routes of packets send ICMP packets to the sources of the packets to let the

---

* Now, Keita Omi works at Internet Initiative Japan.

G. Fortino et al. (Eds.): IDCS 2014, LNCS 8729, pp. 227–236, 2014.

sources know that packets do not arrive at the destinations. The sources of the packets can take countermeasures after they receive ICMP packets.

In IPv6, blocking ICMP packets causes fallback problem and Path MTU problem. This paper proposes a system that resolves the two problems. If blocking ICMP packets causes these problems, the system creates and sends ICMP packets instead of blocked ICMP packets to resolve the problems.

Fujisaki pointed out fallback problem and proposed a solution[8]. Fujisaki also discussed the relation between fallback problem and blocking ICMP packets. However, Fujisaki do not use ICMP packets to resolve fallback problem because some operating systems do not occur fallback even if they receive ICMP packets. This paper resolves fallback problems by using ICMP packets and implements a system that resolves fallback problem and Path MTU problem. This paper also evaluates the system by experiment.

2   Problems in IPv6 by Blocking ICMP Packets

2.1   Fallback Problem

Blocking ICMP packets in IPv6 causes fallback problem and Path MTU problem. Fallback problem occurs in dual stack of IPv4 and IPv6. Changing IPv4 to IPv6 requires concurrent usage of IPv4 and IPv6 because it is impossible to change IPv4 to IPv6 at one time. On the Internet, PCs use DNS (Domain Name Service) to obtain IP addresses of destinations before they try to communicate with other PCs, servers or so on. Dual stack of IPv4 and IPv6 enables PCs to use both IP addresses. Fig.1 shows fallback in dual stack of IPv4 and IPv6. If the leftside PC in Fig.1 tries to send packets to the rightside PC, the leftside PC can send packets by IPv4 or IPv6. Whether PCs select IPv4 or IPv6 depends on PCs. In Fig.1, the leftside PC select IPv6 first. If IPv6 communications fails, the leftside PC sends packets by IPv4. This mechanism is called fallback. In this mechanism, PCs must notice whether IPv4 or IPv6 communications fails. PCs use ICMP packets to find that IPv4 or IPv6 communications fails; if a router on the way from a source PC to a destination PC cannot send packets to a destination because the router does not have routing information for the destination, the router cannot deal with IPv6 packets or so on, the router sends ICMP message "destination unreachable" to the source PC to notify the source PC of failure of communications. Thus, blocking ICMP packets prevents this notification. If the source PC cannot receive ICMP packets, the source PC does not have occasion to run fallback and the source PC waits for timeout of receiving the reply packets from the destination PC.

2.2   Path MTU Problem

MTU (Maximum Transmission Unit) is a maximum packet size that can be transmitted to next network equipment[9]. Path MTU is a minimum packet size between a source and a destination of communication. In IPv4, packets can

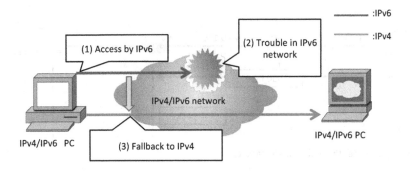

Fig. 1. Path MTU Discovery

be fragmented in network equipment on the way of a route. However, in IPv6, packets cannot be fragmented and the source PC must know Path MTU of a route to a destination because if the source PC sends packets whose size is more than Path MTU, the packets are dropped in network equipment on the route. PCs can use Path MTU Discovery[12], which is a method of finding Path MTU. Path MTU Discovery is based on ICMP message "Packet to Big"[11]. Fig.2 shows Path MTU Discovery; first, the source PC sends the destination PC a packet whose size is MTU of the source PC. If the size of the packet exceeds the MTU of some network on the route to the destination PC, the network equipment of the network sends ICMP message "Packet to Big" to the source PC. This ICMP message includes MTU of the network equipment that sends the ICMP message and the source PC sends a packet whose size is the MTU that is included in the ICMP message. The source PC repeats this procedure until the source PC receives a reply packet from the destination.

If ICMP packets are blocked on the way between the source PC and the destination PC, Path MTU Discovery is unavailable. The source PC cannot find Path MTU of the way between the source PC and the destination PC and transmission of packets is delayed.

3 Overview of the Proposed System

Blocking ICMP packets is reasonable because ICMP packets are used for cyber attack. However, blocking ICMP packets causes troubles in IPv6 and it is difficult to compel all networks to permit ICMP packets. This paper proposes a system that resolves fallback and Path MTU problems that are due to blocking ICMP packets.

The proposed system runs on gateway routers and can also run on network stubs such as PCs. The system had better run on gateway routers because the system collects information on blocking IPv6 ICMP packets and the PCs under the gateway router share the information. Sharing the information improve delay

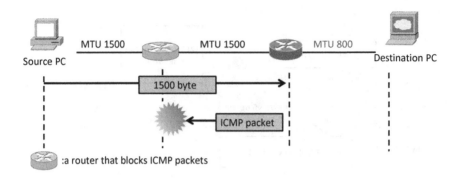

Fig. 2. Fallback

that occurs because of blocking IPv6 ICMP. Moreover, the system does not require to be installed on each PC if the system runs on the gateway router.

The system always checks packets that pass on the gateway router. The system works for fallback problem as follows; if some packets for IPv6 or IPv4 pass on the gateway router, which does not find reply packets, the gateway router notice that it is impossible to send packets for IPv6 or IPv4 to the destination. If the gateway router finds some packets of IPv6 or IPv4 to the same destination, the gateway router drops the packets and sends ICMP message "destination unreachable message". the source PC of the packets takes fallback and sends packets to the destination by IPv4 or IPv6 respectively. The proposed system works for Path MTU problem similarly; the proposed system checks packets of IPv6 on the gateway router. If the gateway router does not find reply packets, the gateway router sends ICMP message "Packet too big" to the source PC.

3.1   Work Flow of System

The proposed system has the following functions.

- Capture of packets
- Analysis of communications
- Construction and Transmission of ICMP packets
- Storage of processing information for destination IP addresses

Fig.3 shows a flowchart of the system. First, the system captures packets on the gateway router and saves information such as source IP address, destination IP address and so on. The behavior of the system depends on information of packets. Fig.4 shows that the system on the gateway router analyzes packets between source PC and destination PC and checks whether communications between them succeed or not. If the system notices that communications between source PC and destination PC fails, the system sends ICMP packets to the source PC. After that, the system analyzes packets between source PC and

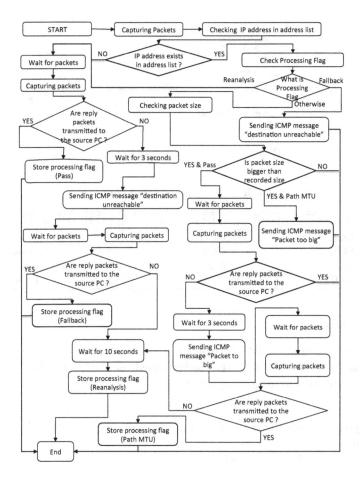

Fig. 3. System flowchart

destination PC again. By repeating analyses, the system obtains many results for communications between many source PCs and many destination PCs. The system makes and saves the best processing for each pair of source PC and destination PC from the results.

3.2 Capture of Packets

The system always captures packets and obtains information from the packets. Table 1 is an example of saved data. The system obtains source and destination IP addresses and packet size from a packet and save them.

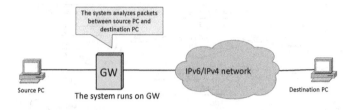

Fig. 4. Analysis of communications

Table 1. Example of saved data

Source IP address	Destination IP address	Path MTU	Processing flag
ABCD	YYYY	1280	Path MTU
EFGH	XXXX	78	Fallback
IJKL	ZZZZ	400	Reanalysis
MNOP	WWWW	1440	Pass

3.3 Processing Flag

If source and destination IP addresses of a captured packet are in the list in Table 1, the system deals with the packet based on processing flag. There are four kinds of processing flags as follows;

- Pass
  The system passes the packets whose processing flags are "Pass".
- Reanalysis
  The system analyzes the packets whose processing flags are "Reanalysis".
- Fallback
  The system sends ICMP message "destination unreachable" to the source PC if the processing flag of the packet is "Fallback".
- Path MTU
  The system sends ICMP message "Packet too big" to the source PC if the processing flag of the packet is "Path MTU".

3.4 Analysis of Communications

The system analyzes communications and checks whether communications succeeds or not. In order to find whether communications between a source PC and a destination PC succeeds or not, the system captures packets from outside networks in specified time. If the system finds packets from the destination PC among the captured packets, the system decides that communications between the source PC and the destination PC succeeds. Otherwise, the system decides that communications between the source PC and the destination PC fails because of fallback problem or Path MTU problem.

The system deals with fallback problem and Path MTU problem. The countermeasures for fallback problem and Path MTU problem are different. Thus, the system must find which the troubles of communications are based on fallback problem or Path MTU problem. Regarding TCP communications, the system checks three way handshake and if three way handshake fails, the system decides which the troubles of three way handshake are based on fallback problem or Path MTU problem.

Detection of Fallback Problem. When fallback problem occurs, a source PC and a destination PC cannot communicate by IPv6. In three way handshake, the source PC sends SYN packet to the destination PC. If IPv6 cannot work between the source and destination PCs, SYN packet does not arrive at the destination PC and SYN+ACK packet does not arrive at the source PC from the destination PC. The proposed system uses this feature; after the system detects SYN packets, the system checks whether SYN+ACK packets arrive at the source PCs of SYN packets. The system decides that fallback problem occurs if SYN+ACK packets do not arrive at the source PCs of SYN packets.

Detection of Path MTU Problem. Path MTU problem occurs when too big packets are used in communications. The packets in three way handshake are small and Path MTU problem does not occur in three way handshake. Thus, Path MTU problem occurs after three way handshake finishes and TCP connection is established. It is a different point between fallback problem and Path MTU problem. The proposed system checks a reply packet from the destination PC after the source PC sends a big packet. If the proposed system cannot find a reply packet for the big packet from the source PC, the proposed system decides that Path MTU problem occurs. The system creates and sends ICMP message "Packet too big" to the source PC. This message should have a possible size of packet. The proposed system decides the possible size of packet based on analysis of the previous communications.

3.5   Creating and Sending ICMP Packets

There are two kinds of ICMP: ICMPv4 and ICMPv6. The proposed system creates and sends ICMPv6 packets to source PCs. The packet of ICMPv6 includes "Type", "Code" and "Message Body". "Type" presents the type of ICMP message, "Code" presents presents additional information in ICMP message and "Message Body" is different according to Type and Code. The proposed system creates the same ICMPv6 packets that are created on the routers on the way to destination PCs. The created packets obey RFC documents that are related with ICMP[10,11].

To let source PCs process fallback, ICMP message for fallback problems must be "Destination unreachable". To create the ICMP message, the proposed system obtains IP headers and TCP headers on packets that are sent from the source PCs. The ICMP messages that are created by the proposed system include these

IP headers and TCP headers. To deal with Path MTU problem, ICMP message must be "Packet too big". The ICMP messages that are created by the proposed system must include a size of packet. First this size is set to 1280 byte, which is a minimum size of MTU in IPv6. If the proposed system finds that over 1280 byte packets can be transmitted to the destination PC, the proposed system sets over 1280 byte in ICMP message as a minimum size of MTU.

3.6   Decision of Success of Fallback

The system analyzes communications and finds which each communication succeeds or not. As Subsection 3.4 describes, The system checks all packets and obtains destination IP addresses. If the system finds reply packets from the destination PC, the system decides that communications succeeds. In the case of Path MTU problem, after the system sends ICMP message to source PCs, IPv6 is used between source and destination PCs. Thus, the system checks only IP addresses in reply packets to find that communications succeeds. However, in the case of fallback problem, a protocol that is used in communications changes from IPv6 to IPv4. Finding whether communications succeeds requires obtaining IPv4 addresses of source and destination PCs after fallback. Moreover, the systems must know IPv6 addresses and IPv4 addresses of the source and destination PCs and correspondence between IPv6 and IPv4 addresses for each PC. The proposed system obtains IPv4 addresses and correspondence between IPv4 and IPv6 addresses by using DNS data; the system finds PTR records from IPv6 addresses to obtain host names and obtains IPv4 addresses of the host names.

4   Implementation and Experiment

This paper implements the proposed system on the Linux PC router, which has Intel Core 2 Duo 1.06GHz as CPU and 2Gbyte memory. The implementation uses raw socket to obtain all packets and is described in C programming language. For experiment, this paper prepares network environment where fallback problems and Path MTU problems occur. The experiment in this paper compares the cases with and without the proposed system. In the experiment, a PC tries to access web pages by IPv6 and 60 web pages are accessed.

To cause fallback problem, the experiment prepares obstacles on the experiment network. These obstacles can deal with IPv4 but not IPv6 and do not send ICMP packets. To cause Path MTU problem, the experiment prepares the network obstacles that have small MTUs.

4.1   Result of Experiment

Table 2 shows the result of experiment for fallback problem. In some cases, the system cannot find that fallback succeeds because the system cannot have all correspondences between IPv4 and IPv6. The system obtains the correspondences

Table 2. Results of experiment for fallback

	Without the system	With the system
Average	205.29 sec	3.96 sec

by using DNS PTR records, but PTR records of all IPv6 addresses are not registered on DNS and the system does not work well in all cases. The proposed system does not obtain PTR records of 36 web pages in 60 web pages.

Table 3 shows the result of experiment for Path MTU problem. This paper cannot find the web pages whose access causes Path MTU problems. Thus, the experiment prepares the network where Path MTU problems occur.

Table 3. Results of experiment for Path MTU

	Without the system	With the system
Average	52.94 sec	3.52 sec

5   Discussion

The result of experiment shows that the proposed system is useful for fallback problems and Path MTU problems that are caused by blocking ICMP. In the result of the experiment, it takes 3.96 second to perform fallback in the proposed system because the proposed system waits for 3 second to check whether the communications succeeds and sends ICMP packets to source PCs. Efficiency of resolving fallback problems in the proposed system depends on waiting time. This paper does not confirm that 3 second waiting is optimum and therefore it is a future work to find optimum time to check whether communications succeeds.

The experiment also shows that the proposed system does not detect completely whether communications succeeds. The reason of this incompleteness is that PTR records of many IPv6 addresses are not registered. Some researches focus on IPv6 of DNS[4], but this paper does not hope that PTR records of all IPv6 addresses are registered on DNS. Thus, this paper requires another method of obtaining correspondences between IPv4 and IPv6 addresses.

6   Conclusion

This paper proposed the implemented system that resolves fallback problems and Path MTU problems in IPv6. The cause of these problems is blocking ICMP packets. As a future work, this paper plans to construct new method of obtaining correspondences between IPv4 and IPv6 addresses that are used in one PC. Another future work is to decide optimum time for which the system waits for reply packets to decide whether communications succeeds or not.

References

1. Claffy, K.: Tracking IPv6 evolution: data we have and data we need. SIGCOMM Computer Communication Review 41(3), 43–48 (2011)
2. Colitti, L., Gunderson, S.H., Kline, E., Refice, T.: Evaluating IPv6 adoption in the internet. In: Krishnamurthy, A., Plattner, B. (eds.) PAM 2010. LNCS, vol. 6032, pp. 141–150. Springer, Heidelberg (2010)
3. Zander, S., Andrew, L.L.H., Armitage, G., Huston, G., Michaelson, G.: Mitigating Sampling Error with Measuring Internet Client IPv6 Capabilities. In: Proceedings of the Intenet Measurement Conference, pp. 87–100 (2012)
4. Arthur, B., Nicholas, W., Robert, B., Larry, C.: Internet Nameserver IPv4 and IPv6 Address Relationships. In: Proceedings of the 2013 Conference on Internet Measurement Conference, pp. 91–104 (2013)
5. RIPE NCC, World IPv6 Day Measurements, `http://v6day.ripe.net` (last access June 14, 2014)
6. Huston, G.: IPv6 BGP Statistics (2013), `http://bgp.potaroo.net/v6/as2.0/` (last access June 14, 2014)
7. ISOC, World IPv6 Day (2012), `http://www.worldipv6launch.org`
8. NTT Information Sharing Platform Laboratories, Deploying IPv6: Problems and Solutions (2011),
   `http://wiki.nttv6.net/cgi-bin/wiki.cgi?page=FrontPage&file=`
   `pub_v6fix-en-v1.2.1.pdf&action=ATTACH` (last access June 14, 2014)
9. RFC 791, Internet Protocol Darpa Internet Program Protocol Specification,
   `http://tools.ietf.org/html/rfc791`
10. RFC 792, Internet Control Message Protocol,
    `http://tools.ietf.org/html/rfc792`
11. RFC 4443, Internet Control Message Protocol (ICMPv6) for the Internet Protocol Version 6 (IPv6) Specification,
    `http://tools.ietf.org/html/rfc4443`
12. RFC1981, Path MTU Discovery for IP version 6,
    `http://tools.ietf.org/html/rfc1981`
13. RFC2460, Internet Protocol, Version 6 (IPv6) Specification,
    `http://tools.ietf.org/html/rfc2460`
14. RFC2923, TCP Problems with Path MTU Discovery,
    `http://tools.ietf.org/html/rfc2923`

Using a History-Based Approach to Predict Topology Control Information in Mobile Ad Hoc Networks

Pere Millán[1], Carlos Molina[1], Roc Meseguer[2], Sergio F. Ochoa[3], and Rodrigo Santos[4]

[1] Department of Computer Engineering, Universitat Rovira i Virgili, Tarragona, Spain
[2] Department of Computer Architecture, Universitat Politècnica de Catalunya, Barcelona, Spain
[3] Department of Computer Science, Universidad de Chile, Santiago, Chile
[4] Department of Electrical Engineering, Universidad Nacional del Sur, Bahia Blanca, Argentina
{pere.millan,carlos.molina}@urv.net, meseguer@ac.upc.edu,
sochoa@dcc.uchile.cl, ierms@uns.edu.ar

Abstract. Several social computing participation strategies, such as crowdsensing and crowdsourcing, use mobile ad hoc or opportunistic networks to support the users activities. The unreliability and dynamism of these communication links make routing protocols a key component to achieve efficient and reliable data communication in physical environments. Often these routing capabilities come at expenses of flooding the network with a huge amount of topology control information (TCI), which can overload the communication links and dramatically increase the energy consumption of the participating devices. In previous works the authors have shown that predicting the network topology in these work scenarios helps reduce the number of control packets delivered through the network. This saves energy and increases the available bandwidth. This paper presents a study that extends the authors' previous works, by identifying the impact of predicting the TCI generated by routing protocols in these networks. The prediction process is done following a history-based approach that uses information of the nodes past behavior. The paper also determines the predictability limits of this strategy, assuming that a TCI message can be correctly predicted if it appeared at least once in the past. The results show that the upper-bound limit of the history-based prediction approach is high, and that realistic prediction mechanisms can achieve significant ratios of accuracy. Mobile collaborative applications and routing protocols using mobile ad hoc or opportunistic networks can take advantage of this prediction approach to reduce network traffic, and consequently, the energy consumption of their devices.

Keywords: Network Topology Prediction, History-Based Prediction, Routing Protocols, Mobile Ad Hoc Networks, Mobile Collaboration.

1 Introduction

Mobile computing and wireless networks are part of our life. Everyday more and more people are becoming a part of collaborative networks to share several information, such as the status of the vehicular traffic in an area, the security level of a city zone, or the location of interesting places to visit while performing touristic activities.

G. Fortino et al. (Eds.): IDCS 2014, LNCS 8729, pp. 237–249, 2014.

In many scenarios, the networks of these applications are wireless and ad hoc, and the provision of the applications' services makes sense only if the consumer (i.e. the end-user) is localized near to the service provider. For instance, during lunch time the restaurants located in a promenade area can deliver special offers to the smartphone of the passers-by, motivating them to take lunch in those places. If the service providers (i.e. the restaurants) use WiFi to irradiate these messages to the people, then this process will need to use message routing to reach the devices of potential clients that are located to more than one-hop of distance from the provider. This means more than 80-100 meters in open areas or more than 30-25 meters in build areas.

The routing protocols used in these mobile collaboration scenarios must be simple, efficient, reliable and they have to quickly adapt themselves to changes in the network topology [1, 2, 3, 4]. Moreover, these protocols should minimize the delivery of topology control information (TCI) to avoid consuming too much energy of the passers-by' devices. Link-state proactive-routing protocols could be used in these scenarios to support interaction among devices, since they have low latency when sending data through ad hoc networks. The latency is low because these protocols utilize an optimized and known data-path for delivering messages to the destination nodes [5]. However, this advantage comes at the cost of periodically flooding the network with TCI that negatively impacts the energy consumption of the nodes.

Medina et al. [6] and Meseguer et al. [7] show that the traffic generated by OLSR (Optimized Link State Routing protocol [5]) for different nodes densities, grows almost exponentially with the number of nodes. Therefore, for a large number of nodes, a huge amount of TCI should be delivered through the network. This not only overloads the communication links, but also increases the energy consumption of the nodes. The authors have also shown that the problem of delivering much control information through the network can be addressed using predictions [6, 8]. Particularly, the OLSRp (OLSR with prediction) protocol was proposed to eliminate redundant control information, and thus, to reduce CPU and energy consumption in mobile ad-hoc networks. This prediction mechanism is based on the assumption that the last TCI send by a node will probably be repeated during the next round of information delivery. The results of this prediction strategy show that this simple algorithm can reduce considerably the number of control packets (CP) transmitted through the network, saving computational processing and energy consumption, without affecting the routing capability of the protocol.

However, this prediction process sometimes introduces additional complexity to routing protocols, because additional hardware, software, or both of them, must be devoted to make a prediction, and possibly to validate it. Moreover, the prediction can also introduce additional time-penalties to the system, mainly when the rate of mispredictions is high. On average, if the percentage of right predictions is high enough, the overall performance of the routing protocols can be significantly improved at a reasonable hardware/software cost. The same concerns can be extended to computer networks, as they also have been aware of prediction techniques in several ways, such as energy-efficient routing [9, 10], nodes sleeping-state scheduling [11, 12], reliability [13, 14], link-quality tracking [15, 16] and routing-traffic reduction [6, 7, 8].

This paper extends the proposal described in [2, 4], by presenting and evaluating a new strategy for predicting TCI in mobile ad hoc and opportunistic networks. This new prediction approach uses a time window, in which the historical TCI of a node is considered to predict the next TCI. By using simulations, this proposal determines the performance of the history-based prediction in several mobile scenarios. The scenarios used in these simulations are representative of some everyday life activities, where people freely move around a certain area, and eventually interact with other people in these places. The obtained results help designers of both, routing protocols and mobile collaborative systems, to conceive more efficient ways to manage the TCI in these scenarios.

2   Predicting TCI Using Past Information

Although it seems to be a good idea to use historical TCI to make predictions of the next control packets [8], it is important to determine the performance and limits of this approach. Only after that, it would be possible to determine in which mobile computing scenarios this proposal can provide a real benefit.

The history-based prediction (HBP) approach considers that each node keeps updated locally (in a table) the recent history of the TCI received from its neighbors. The prediction process performed in such a node takes this information as input, and produces a prediction of TCI for each neighbor. Thus, it tries to guess the network topology without delivering control information. The prediction that a node makes for a TCI of a neighbor can be done whenever the recently TCI received from such a neighbor, matches with the previously TCI stored by that node. It is important to notice that the HBP approach is focused on predicting a state that has already appeared in the past.

In order to understand the performance of the HBP approach, we performed several simulations using unbounded tables with historical information. These unbounded tables give more flexibility to identify patterns in the nodes' movements, and thus to try guess the next topology of the network. This pattern identification can be done analyzing the tables with historical information that each node keeps for such a purpose. Each movement pattern corresponds just to a sequence of TCI packets (one or more), that the node making the prediction has seen in the past (and it has registered in its local table). Attached to every pattern stored in the table there is a list of all the packets that appeared after such a pattern. These packets could be predicted depending on the prediction strategy used by the node.

The table with historical information also records some statistical information that helps the prediction process to select one option among several candidate node mobility patterns; i.e., to determine which is the most suitable candidate (pattern) to match with the next TCI packet in the current prediction scenario. In short, an entry of the table will be composed by an input (TCI packets representing the pattern), an output (a list of control packets that appeared after each particular pattern) and statistical information (related to every output, which helps predict the next control packet). For every entry, it is maintained a list of all CPs that appeared after the pattern that is under consideration by the prediction process. The statistics attached to the table establish both, the most frequent and the last packet of the pattern.

In order to analyze properly the usefulness of this historical information for the prediction process, we have defined the *history depth* (HD) metric. This metric can be calculated as the number of TCI packets that compose a movement pattern. In our study, the HD can assume values from 0 to 5. If we consider for instance a table with HD=1, this means that the number of packets that identify each pattern is one. Therefore, there will be one entry in the table for every control packet (CP) that appeared in the past. We believe that high HD means more accurate predictions, but few opportunities for predicting, because the packets sequences are long. Contrarily, low HD means more opportunities for predicting, but less accuracy in the predictions.

Based on the information stored in this table, we use and analyze the performance of three different flavors of the HBP approach: *last value* (it uses the last packet of the pattern to make the predictions), *most-frequent value* (it uses the most-frequent packet for predicting the next TCI) and *random value* (it uses any packet from the list, which is randomly selected). For instance, the OLSRp mechanism [6] assumes a last-value policy and HD=0 for predicting the next control packet with TCI. Probably, this is the most simple prediction mechanism, as just one control packet has to be stored and no statistics have to be maintained. Even this simple strategy has shown to be useful for reducing the traffic of TCI and energy consumption in mobile ad hoc networks [7, 8].

The different flavors of the HBP approach must not only succeed in their predictions, but also not predict when this success is not guaranteed. In our scenario, success reduces the network traffic and saves energy consumption, but incorrect predictions can skew the network topology map, and therefore decrease the reliability of the process. In this paper, we include a confidence mechanism to determine the likelihood that a prediction done using the HBP approach is correct. This could help both, maximize right and minimize wrong predictions. We assume a simple confidence mechanism, which determines if every packet of the output data list of a pattern was already predicted. If so, a counter is incremented by 1. Otherwise, it is decremented by 1. The counter is initialized as 1, and it can assume values in the range from 0 to 3. We consider that a prediction is confident, if the counter is equal or higher than 2.

Although this confidence mechanism can helps us improve the prediction accuracy, if we assume a fixed HD, the opportunities for predicting TCI packets remain fixed. Therefore, in this article we analyze an additional flavor of the HBP approach, in which the HD is not initially fixed. We call this strategy as *prediction tree*. This strategy predicts the TCI assuming the maximum HD. Every time that it is not possible to do such an assumption (e.g. because there is not an entry or enough confidence), the HD will be decreased by 1. After that, the prediction tree attempts to make a new prediction, but using a shorter pattern. This will be repeated until the HD metric reaches 0. We analyze this approach with and without a confidence mechanism.

Finally, we quantify the repetition of TCI over time, in order to help understand predictability and prediction opportunity limits of this proposal. In one side, we determine the maximum prediction accuracy that these flavors of the HBP approach can reach, by counting if a certain TCI packet has ever appeared in the past. If it has appeared once, we assume that it could be correctly predicted. Moreover, we also quantify the incorrect prediction of a pattern for each particular HD that could be correctly predicted as the correct prediction was in the list of control packets related to that pattern. Therefore, this information can help us identify the limits of the HBP approach, and also determine how far a particular prediction approach is from the best prediction performance. On the other side, this article also analyzes the representativeness of the most-frequent packets, respect to whole set of packets received by a node over time. This will give us a first understanding about how difficult is to make right predictions, and which is the amount of data (historical information) that must be tracked to make these predictions.

3   Experimental Framework

In order to determine the performance of the HBP approach, we designed and simulated several interaction scenarios using the NS-3 simulator [17]. This tool allowed us to model these scenarios, collect statistics, define initial network topologies, configure wireless network interfaces, and set the mobility-patterns of the nodes. Every simulation performed in this study lasted 14,400 seconds (4 hours).

In these simulations we used the Optimized Link State Routing (OLSR) protocol, which is a well-known protocol for routing messages in ad-hoc networks [5]. The nodes of these networks periodically exchange control information to maintain a local map of the network topology. In order to do that, OLSR uses two types of control messages: HELLO and Topology Control (TC). HELLO messages allow a node to discover its neighbors, and determine the quality of the links between them. TC messages allow a node to disseminate topology information with its neighbors. The simulations considered the delivery of a HELLO message every 2 seconds, and a TC message every 3 seconds.

The physical place available for interactions was a square open area of 300×300 meters, that could represent a beach or a park, where people are free to move throughout the whole space, and eventually interact with other people (e.g., friends, relatives, or service providers). In these scenarios, the people can remain stationary (e.g. during a picnic), or walking with or without a clear direction. A mobile collaborative application, that detects the presence of related people in a physical area, can be eventually used to promote face-to-face encounters among them, as proposed in [18].

The simulations considered devices using Wi-Fi to detect other nodes, and exchange control information among them. Using these interfaces, mobile networks composed of 10, 20, 30, and 40 nodes were simulated. The nodes were randomly deployed in the open area, and their behavior alternate between some stationary periods, and others in which they move up to 1 m/s (walking), 2 m/s (trotting), 4 m/s (running), and 6 m/s (bicycling).

The node movements can follow one of the following mobility models: *Random Walk*, *Nomadic*, or *Self-similar Least Action Walk* (SLAW) [19, 20]. These mobility models are quite representative of the movement patterns of a person or a group that performs outdoor activities. The node mobility was implemented using the BonnMotion simulator [21]. The Random Walk model considers people moving randomly in terms of direction and speed within a certain area; e.g. people in a park, where each person can move via walking, running, or riding a bicycle without using formal paths. The Nomadic model considers people moving in groups, from one location to another. This is representative of guided tours, e.g. at a city downtown. This model considers a particular node per group (i.e., a reference node) that determines the next target point to be visited, and also a reference path and speed to reach such a place. This role can be played by the tour guide. Finally, in the SLAW model people move quite randomly, but they consider their previous movements (speed and direction) to determine the new ones. This is similar to the movements of people that use the walking paths in a park. This model is also effective to model casual encounters among community members; e.g., students at the university campus, or friends in a theme park. Unlike other models, the speed in this model cannot be parameterized, and it assumes a default value of 1 m/s (walking speed).

Finally, we have assumed that all nodes are similar, and their capabilities are equivalent to an iPhone 4. These devices have an effective WiFi range of approximately 80 meters in open areas. In such range, we can expect quite stable ad-hoc communication among devices, and a bandwidth of at least of 50 Kbps, which is appropriate to support reliable interactions among mobile nodes.

4   Analysis of Obtained Results

4.1   Predictability Limits

In order to determine the upper-bound limit achievable by the HBP approach, we have assumed unbounded memory for the nodes, and also tracking if a TCI packet has ever appeared in the past. Figure 1 shows how the three mobility models behave when considering several nodes densities (from 10 to 40 nodes) and a similar average mobility speed (1 m/s) for the nodes in every model. Notice that for the scenario with 10 nodes, about 80% of the times the control packet to be predicted has already appeared in the past. This upper-bound limit is extremely high; therefore, the potential of predicting correctly the TCI is also high.

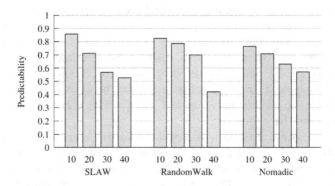

Fig. 1. Predictability limits

Besides that, we can see that there are no significant differences among the prediction capability in the three mobility models. This would indicate that the prediction capability of the HBP approach does not depend on the mobility model being used by the nodes. In fact, we could expect similar results even in scenarios where the nodes use several mobility patterns.

The results also show that the prediction limits decreases when increases the node density. This is a result that can be expected, since a high-density network has many communication links that need to be correctly predicted; therefore, an important amount of control packets must delivered through the network, and a fewer number of patterns (in percentage) are identifiable by the nodes.

In order to determine the role that the speed of nodes is playing in the obtained results, we established maximum speeds to the nodes. The nodes can randomly assume a certain speed (1 m/s, 2 m/s, 4 m/s, or 6 m/s) for a short time period, and then make a new assumption for the next period. The obtained results have shown that the nodes' speed does not affect the prediction upper-bound limit of the HBP approach. Therefore, we can say that this limit always ranges between 50% and 80%. Moreover, the predictability limit decreases when the node density increases, and there is not a significant difference among the mobility models used by the nodes.

4.2   Frequency of the Observed Control Packets

Concerning the control packets that appear most frequently in the history kept by the nodes, Figure 2 shows a curve illustrating the results. The curve considers, from left to right, the most frequent packets. The X-axis indicates (in percentage) the number of different packets that appear more frequently, respect to the total number of observed packets (i.e. packets that were recorded in the historical information of the nodes). For instance, in the scenario with 30 nodes, there are a 30% of different the control packets that represent 70% of the (total) observed packets. Notice that Y-axis and X-axis are both normalized.

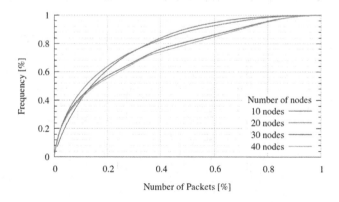

Fig. 2. Frequency of the observed control packets

The most important result shown in Figure 2 is that there is a small subset of packets that are representative of most packets delivered by the nodes through the network. In other words, the control packets belonging to this small subset traverse the network many times, therefore they have high representativeness. Although it seems that the combination of multiple nodes will produce a huge number of possibilities, in reality only with a few number of packets we can obtain most of the packets that a network produces. Notice that this result does not depend on the node density in the network.

Although the values shown in Figure 2 were obtained considering a SLAW mobility model, and a speed of 1 m/s, the simulations done using the other mobility models have shown the same distribution for the results. Summarizing, these results and the predictability limits shown by the HBP approach are highly encouraging, as it provides many opportunities for predicting TCI packets, and these predictions would be focused on a small subset of the total packets delivered through the network.

4.3   History-Based Prediction

In order to perform a more comprehensive evaluation of the prediction performance, we have used several flavors of the HBP prediction approach. Moreover, we have identified four typical cases to analyze when making a prediction: (1) *nopred*, (2) *hit*, (3) *missNoPred*, and (4) *missPred*. In the first case (*nopred*), there is no prediction because there was no table entry that matches the current pattern. This would be the case with the lowest occurrence probably, as it only occurs the first time that a pattern appears. The second case (*hit*) means that there is a prediction (i.e., the pattern is in the table) and it is correct (i.e., the packet associated to that entry is the next expected packet). The third case (*missNoPred*) means that there is a prediction, and it is not correct, but it is impossible to do a correct prediction, as the next expected packet never appeared in the past with that pattern. Finally, the fourth case (*missPred*) means that there is a prediction, and it is not correct, however the packet could be correctly predicted, as the next expected packet appeared with that pattern at least once in the past.

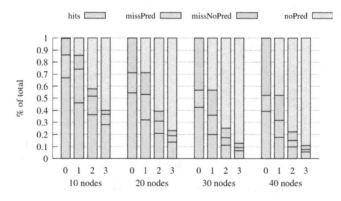

Fig. 3. History-based prediction using a SLAW mobility model and last value policy

Figure 3 shows the HBP performance considering these prediction cases in a scenario with a SLAW mobility, and node density ranging from 10 to 40 nodes. The HBP approach assumes the last-value policy as the selected prediction mechanism, and a HD in the range from 0 to 3.

These results indicate that the largest percentages of *hits* are achieved with HD=0, but these cases also present important percentages of *misses* (i.e. *missPred* and *missNoPred*). The results also show the effects of the predictability limits (already seen in Figure 1), which reduces the number of *hits* and *misses* when the node density increases. The equivalence of *missNoPred* (*HD=0*) and *noPred* (*HD=1*) can be explained because for *HD=1* the mechanism cannot predict the first time that a packet appears; i.e., this is *missNoPred* for *HD=0*.

Figure 4 shows the effect of using different prediction policies with a SLAW mobility model, for a network with 10 nodes. For this analysis we have considered three different sizes of history windows, corresponding to 1, 2, and 3 rounds of TCI delivery (X-axis). These windows sizes establish the amount of historical information used to identify the patterns.

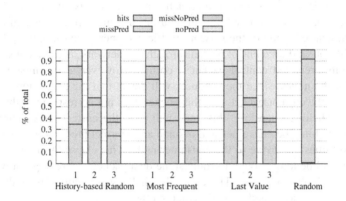

Fig. 4. History-based prediction using different prediction policies

When using pure Random policy it is always possible to make a prediction (even without history information), but most predictions are *missPred*. The use of historical information clearly allows achieving better results, even using a history-based Random strategy. This can be considered as the baseline, and demonstrates the importance of utilizing the historical information to make more and accurate predictions.

Finally, Figure 5 shows the effect of using different mobility models with a speed of 1 m/s, for a network with 10 nodes. For this analysis we have considered three different sizes of history windows (1, 2, and 3). We can observe that the behavior of the 3 mobility models is quite similar (less than a 10% of difference), with a significant increase in *noPred* cases for large history values. These results confirm that there are no significant differences among the prediction capability in the three mobility models, as outlined in the analysis of predictability limits.

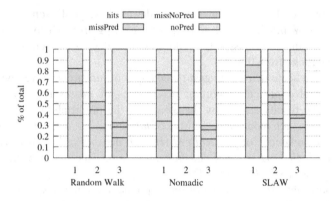

Fig. 5. History-based prediction using different mobility-models

4.4   History-Based Prediction Using a Confidence Mechanism

Notice also that in all the analyzed approaches a prediction is always done (besides the *noPred* case), and this prediction can be a hit or a miss. In the case of a hit, the direct benefit is a reduction of the network traffic and energy consumption, due to the producer will not send the control packet through the network, and the consumer will assume that its predicted control packet is correct. However, every miss prediction has a cost for the nodes, since the producer will detect that the prediction is not correct (due it has the current packet, and this packet does not correspond to the one that returns the predictor). Therefore, this node will send the correct packet through the network. Meanwhile, the consumer will assume an incorrect prediction, as long as the correct packet does not arrive to the consumer node. This elapsed time would not be long, but it could be long enough to route some data packets, assuming a low accuracy of the network topology map. Therefore, the challenge to address is to always predict in certainty scenarios, and do not predict in other cases.

This strategy can be implemented by including a mechanism that adds two more cases to the previous four. Now a prediction is made if the predictor has enough confidence. In other case, the prediction would be a hit (*noConfidence/hit*) or a miss (*noConfidence/miss*). Our aim is to maximize *noConfidence/miss* with a minimum *noConfidence/hit*. Figure 6 shows the behavior of this confidence mechanism, considering the 6 cases (four of them consider no confidence). The results were obtained using a Nomadic mobility model, in a network with 10 nodes, which had a maximum speed of 1 m/s. A last-value strategy was chosen to perform the predictions.

The results indicate that there are few predictions when using confidence; however, most of them are hits, and there are few misses (the miss ratio is minimized). On the other hand, the most of the predictions were not made because there were not enough confidence (*noConfidence/miss* with little *noConfidence/hit*). This indicates that using a confidence mechanism we can minimize prediction errors.

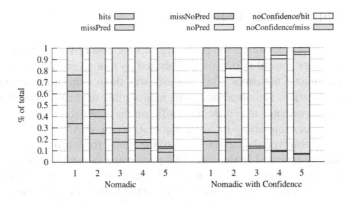

Fig. 6. History-based prediction using a 2-bit confidence-mechanism

4.5   Dynamic History-Depth

With the aim of improving the total number of hits, we relaxed the condition of fixed history-depth patterns, in order to have more opportunities to correctly predict the next TCI packet. When a pattern has no previous history and/or not enough confidence, we decrease in 1 the history depth, and we check again if a prediction can be made (with the same selection policy), as a way to minimize *noPred* cases. We call this method *Dynamic History-Depth* (or *Tree*).

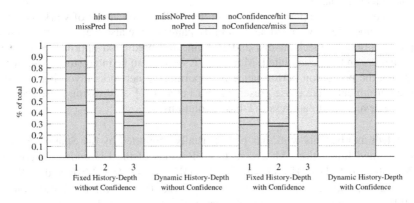

Fig. 7. Fixed History-Depth versus Dynamic History-Depth (Tree)

Figure 7 shows the results of using *Fixed* versus *Dynamic History-Depth* with and without confidence (using SLAW mobility, 10 nodes, 5 as maximum HD, maximum speed 1 m/s, and the last-value policy). We can see that the Tree method minimizes *noPred*. Therefore, for the same percentage of hits, the total number of hits increases significantly. When we include a confidence mechanism (right side of Figure 7), Fixed History-Depth shows a decrease in number of hits and misses. However, Tree with Confidence achieves better results, maximizing hits and minimizing misses.

5   Conclusions and Future Work

In this work, we have analyzed the performance of a history-based strategy for predicting the topology control information generated by routing protocols for mobile ad hoc and opportunistic networks. This analysis was done simulating several mobile collaboration scenarios. The obtained results indicate that the history-based prediction (HBP) strategy contributes to reduce the traffic on these networks, and saves energy in the mobile devices supporting mobile collaborative activities.

First, we have observed that around 80% of the times, for low densities of nodes, a packet has already appeared in the past. This percentage falls to 50% when considering a network with a higher node density. This demonstrates that the upper bound limits of the HBP strategy remain high for an ample variety of interaction scenarios, which make us expecting important benefits for mobile collaborative applications that use these networks as communication support. Second, the results also show that few packets contribute significantly to the total percentage of packets delivered through the network. This means that there is a high opportunity for predicting the TCI, and this prediction can be just focused on a small subset of packets. Finally, we have identified the role played by different history-depth patterns, prediction policies, confidence mechanisms, and the combination of several approaches at the same time after analyzing the behavior of history-based prediction mechanisms under several scenarios. Considering all these issues and a worst-case scenario (with high density of nodes), we can correctly predict at least 30% of the control packets, minimizing the percentage of errors and getting an upper-bound limit of predictions that is close to 50% in such an scenario.

As a future work, we plan to analyze in detail all combinations of work scenarios, considering node density, speed, and mobility patterns. We also want to develop more complex confidence mechanisms, and combine the prediction approaches to see if their benefits can be accumulated. Moreover, it would also be interesting to analyze in a next step the prediction performance in opportunistic networks involving heterogeneous environments, like those presented by Li et al. [22]. Addressing these scenarios will allow developers to address IoT-based solutions.

Acknowledgments. This work has been partially supported by the Spanish Ministry of Science and Innovation (MCI) and FEDER funds of the EU under the contracts TIN2013-44375-R, TIN2013-47245-C2-1-R, TIN2013-47245-C2-2-R and TIN2012-37171-C02-02, and also the Community Networks Testbed for the Future Internet (CONFINE) Large-scale Integrating Project: FP7-288535, and also by the Generalitat de Catalunya as a Consolidated Research Group 2014-SGR-881, and also by Fondecyt (Chile), Grant No 1120207.

References

1. Spyropoulos, T., et al.: Routing for Disruption Tolerant Networks: Taxonomy and Design. Wireless Networks 16(8) (2010)
2. Zeng, Y., et al.: Directional Routing and Scheduling for Green Vehicular Delay Tolerant Networks. Wireless Networks 19(2) (2013)

3. Vasilakos, A., et al.: Delay Tolerant Networks: Protocols and Applications. CRC Press (2012)
4. Youssef, M., et al.: Routing Metrics of Cognitive Radio Networks: A Survey. IEEE Communications Surveys and Tutorials 16(1) (2014)
5. Clausen, T., Jacquet, P.: Optimized Link State Routing Protocol (OLSR). IETF RFC 3626 (October 2003)
6. Medina, E., Meseguer, R., Molina, C., Royo, D.: OLSRp: Predicting Control Information to Achieve Scalability in OLSR Ad Hoc Networks. In: Pentikousis, K., Agüero, R., García-Arranz, M., Papavassiliou, S. (eds.) MONAMI 2010. LNICST, vol. 68, pp. 225–236. Springer, Heidelberg (2011)
7. Meseguer, R., et al.: Reducing Energy Consumption in Human-Centric Wireless Sensor Networks. In: Procs. IEEE Int. Conf. on Systems, Man, & Cybernetics (October 2012)
8. Meseguer, R., et al.: Energy-Aware Topology Control Strategy for Human-Centric Wireless Sensor Networks. Sensors Journal 14 (February 2014)
9. Maleki, M., Dantu, K., Pedram, M.: Lifetime Prediction Routing in Mobile Ad Hoc Networks. In: Wireless Communication& Networking, pp. 1185–1190. IEEE Press (2003)
10. Kim, D., et al.: Routing Mechanisms for Mobile Ad Hoc Networks Based on the Energy Drain Rate. IEEE Trans. on Mobile Computing (April 2003)
11. Chen, B., et al.: Span: An Energy-Efficient Coordination Algorithm for Topology Maintenance in Ad Hoc Wireless Networks. Journal of Wireless Networks 5 (2002)
12. Ye, F., et al.: Peas: A Robust Energy Conserving Protocol for Long-Lived Sensor Networks. In: Proc. of the 23rd Int. Conf. on Distributed Computing Systems (May 2003)
13. De Rosa, F., et al.: Disconnection Prediction in Mobile Ad Hoc Networks for Supporting Cooperative Work. IEEE Pervasive Computing (2005)
14. Su, W., Lee, S.J., Gerla, M.: Mobility Prediction and Routing in Ad Hoc Wireless Networks. International Journal of Network Management 11 (2001)
15. Millan, P., et al.: Tracking and Predicting Link Quality in Wireless Community Networks. Tech. Report UPC-DAC-RR-2014-10. DAC-UPC, Spain (June 2014)
16. Koksal, C.E., Balakrishnan, H.: Quality-Aware Routing Metrics for Time-Varying Wireless Mesh Networks. J. Selected Areas in Communications (2006)
17. NS-3, A Discrete-Event Network Simulator for Internet Systems, http://www.nsnam.org/
18. Vergara, C., Ochoa, S.F., Gutierrez, F., Rodriguez-Covili, J.: Extending social networking services toward a physical interaction scenario. In: Bravo, J., López-de-Ipiña, D., Moya, F. (eds.) UCAmI 2012. LNCS, vol. 7656, pp. 208–215. Springer, Heidelberg (2012)
19. Camp, T., Boleng, J., Davies, V.: A Survey of Mobility Models for Ad Hoc Network Research. Wirel. Commun. Mob. Comput. (2002)
20. Lee, K., Hong, S., Kim, S.J., Rhee, I., Chong, S.: Slaw: A New Mobility Model for Human Walks. In: Proceedings of INFOCOM 2009 (April 2009)
21. Aschenbruck, N., et al.: BonnMotion: A Mobility Scenario Generation and Analysis Tool. In: Procs. 3rd Int. ICST Conf. Simulation Tools & Techniques (March 2010)
22. Fu, X., Li, W., Fortino, G.: A utility-oriented routing algorithm for community based opportunistic networks. In: Proc. of the 2013 IEEE 17th International Conference on Computer Supported Cooperative Work in Design (CSCWD 2013), June 27-29, pp. 675–680 (2013)

Testing AMQP Protocol on Unstable and Mobile Networks

Jorge E. Luzuriaga[1], Miguel Perez[2], Pablo Boronat[2],
Juan Carlos Cano[1], Carlos Calafate[1], and Pietro Manzoni[1]

[1] Department of Computer Engineering
Universitat Politècnica de València, Valencia, Spain
jorlu@upv.es,{jucano,calafate,pmanzoni}@disca.upv.es
[2] Universitat Jaume I, Castelló de la Plana, Spain
mperez@icc.uji.es,boronat@uji.es

Abstract. AMQP is a middleware protocol extensively used for exchanging messages in distributed applications. It provides an abstraction of the different participating parts and simplifies communication
programming details. AMQP provides reliability features and alleviates
the coordination of different entities of an application.

However, implementations of this protocol have not been well tested in
the context of mobile or unstable networks. This paper is the starting point
of an experimental evaluation of AMQP protocol in such kind of scenarios. Our goal is to identify the limits of applicability of this middleware,
assessing its the capacity in terms of message losses, latencies or jitter,
when wireless devices are interrupted and reconnected. This evaluation is
of interest for the upcoming applications in which personal devices and
vehicles will collaborate, forming part of large complex systems.

Keywords: client-server systems, performance evaluation, AMQP, advanced message queuing protocol, Mobile communication, Mobile
Computing.

1   Introduction

With current expectations around the *Internet of Things* (IoT) there is a need
to build and extend what is known as *intelligent spaces*. The idea behind these
spaces is to connect computing elements such as sensors and actuators through
a distributed network. The computing elements interact cooperatively in order
to offer services to users. The network is usually a MANET or the mobile phone
system (i.e. 3G, 4G) due to easy deployment. The massive use of smartphones or
even On Board Units (OBU) in vehicles are favouring the development of these
kinds of systems and applications.

The cooperation of the computing elements makes it easier to identify situations and then to provide data or to react when confronted with a set of stimulus.
Intelligent spaces are highly dynamic due to the spontaneity with which elements

G. Fortino et al. (Eds.): IDCS 2014, LNCS 8729, pp. 250–260, 2014.

connect or disconnect to the network. A flexible way to communicate the computing elements are message queuing middlewares such as the *Java Message Service* (JMS) or the emerging *Advanced Message Queuing Protocol* (AMQP).

AMQP is an application layer protocol which takes into account Message-oriented middleware (MOM) standards [1]. AMQP has been used in challenging applications, including Autonomous Computing [2], Cloud computing [3] or in security aspects related to the Internet of Things [4].

AMQP is designed to facilitate the dialogue among the components of a system, by making easy the exchange of messages independently of their underlying platforms. There are libraries available for most popular programming languages, and there are implementations for most of common operating systems. In addition, AMQP cares about security and confidentiality issues without affecting significantly the communication's performance.

In AMQP the messages are self-contained and data content in a message is opaque and immutable. The size of a messages in not limited. It can either support a 4 GByte message or a 4 KByte one. For message delivering, several possibilities are possible, as it can be *point-to-point, store-and-forward* or *publish-and-subscribe*. For instance, when a message is sent to an AMQP broker, actually it is sent to a queue, and after it is delivered to all subscribed customers to this queue as a push notification [1]. With AMQP the number of subscribers is unbounded.

This work is a starting point to test the behaviour of AMQP protocol over unstable networks. We call *unstable networks* those in which links can be frequently modified or broken without control. Examples of unstable networks could be mobile networks or wireless networks in urban environments, which suffer channel interferences, as occurs in community networks. Our goal is to determine whether AMQP provides satisfactory service, depending of the applications' load needs, in terms message size and communication rates. We detect the extreme working values at which message losses starts, as well as the effect of network changes on the messages' jitter.

In the present paper we introduce the first results in which we test the effect of a mobile producer which changes from one WiFi access point (AP) to another in the same IP network. We have developed a synthetic load generator which we call *amqperf*. This program sends messages with a sequence number to detect losses or messages delivered in different sending order. The size of messages and the frequency in which they are send by the producer can be modified. In the results we use a simple scenario with just one producer and one consumer.

The rest of the article is organized as follows: Section 2 presents a literature review related to the topic. In Section 3 there is a description of the methodology used in this work, showing how measurements have been done in order to be reproducible. The Section 4 presents the results and, finally, Section 5 provides some conclusions and the next steps to follow in this research line.

2   Related Work

There are several works in which the AMQP protocol is evaluated. In [5] the performance of AMQP is assessed using Infiniband and Gigabit Ethernet networks with Qpid as AMQP middleware. Five simple synthetic benchmarks modeled after the OSU Micro-benchmarks for MPI were used. They exercise the number of Publishers, the number of Consumers, and the Exchange type. Each benchmark measures performance for data capacity (the amount of raw data in MegaBytes per second), message rate (the number of discrete messages transmitted), and speed (average time one message takes to travel from the publisher to the consumer).

In [6] it is shown a way to evaluate the performance of AMQP by using an adapted version of the well-known *SPECjms2007* and *jms2009-PS* benchmarks. This would allow to compare AMQP with other messaging systems such as *JMS* (Java Message Service), in terms of performance, stability and scalability.

In [7] a performance comparison between AMQP and RESTful *web services* is presented. Three different tests are performed, which consist of several client applications sending messages during 30 minutes to the broker or the web server respectively; once the messages arrive to the server they are stored in a database. Then, the average number of messages per second that have been sent is compared to the total number of messages stored in the database. They conclude that, when the AMQP protocol is used to exchange messages, a larger number of messages per second is supported.

A study about MQTT, a "light weight" publish-subscribe based messaging protocol, is presented in [8]. The correlation between the end-to-end latency and loss of system messages is studied. Three different QoS levels with different sizes of payload (from 1 to 16 Kbytes) are tested on a real world scenario with both wired and wireless clients using 3G. They prove that there is a strong correlation between these two variables.

However, few studies are focused on the effectiveness of AMQP over unstable networks.

3   Methodology of the Experiments

In the set of experiments we present in this paper we use a *producer* which, at a given frequency, sends messages of a prefixed size to an AMQP broker. The AMQP broker automatically creates a queue to the exchange of *fanout* type. Finally, a *consumer*, connected to the same broker is always ready to get messages. The producer is connected to a WiFi access point to reach the broker. The broker and the consumer are executed in the same computer. This scenario can be seen in Figure 1 and a picture can be seen in Figure 2.

The consumer records the sending (timestamped by the producer in each message) and reception time and the sequence number in a log file. There is not a strict synchronization between the producer and consumer clocks. When there are changes in the producer link, the regularity in the reception of messages is

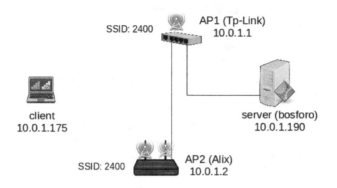

Fig. 1. Schema of the network

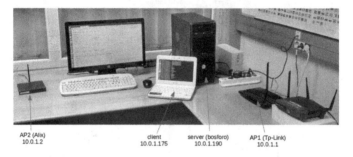

Fig. 2. A picture of the scenario

affected. The inter-message times is modified, bursts of messages can be delivered to the consumer and even the sending order can be changed.

Message losses are produced when the hand-off time is too important with respect the load parameters of the test. Current implementations of AMQP use TCP connections to the broker in order to enhance reliability. If the producer connection is interrupted, the producer's AMQP client has to stock the messages until it can send it to the broker. If the sending buffer is full, messages will be lost. But this is not the only reason for losing sequence numbers. In the producer part, we create a thread to produce and send each message. Thus, in some extreme tests, the amount of threads exceeded the operating system limit. We have not tuned this parameter given that the workload in these circumstances is far from reasonable; for instance, bigger than high definition video streaming.

A testing application, which we call *amqperf* has been developed to generate a workload for the message queuing system in the part of the producer. Amqperf uses the RabbitMQ library [9], which is an AMQP implementation. An schema of amqperf can be seen in Figure 3.

In the experiments, we perform tests of 20 seconds because we are interested in the AP migration of the producer. We checked whether there were message

connection	start tune open
channel	open
exchange	declare

producer	consumer
| ```
while (test_duration){
  thread{ publish(message) }
  sleep Period

  if (exception)
    reOpenConnection()
}
``` | ```
while(true){
  read message with a timeout
  if (message!=NULL)
    treat_message
  else
    endtest=true

  if(endtest)
    treat_test
}
``` |

| channel | close |
| connection | close |

Fig. 3. Schema of amqperf

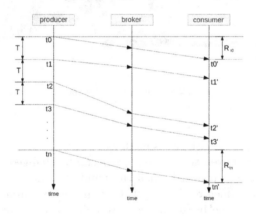

Fig. 4. Times involved in the experiments

losses or if messages arrive out of order. The nth message jitter of inter-arrival times is computed with the following equation:

$J_n = t'_n - t'_{n-1} - T$, where t'_n is the arrival time of message n to the consumer and T is the (fixed) period between messages produced by the producer. T is one of the variables fixed for each experiment. Note that with this formula we are not concerned by a possible asynchrony between the producer and the consumer, which are executed in different computers. A simplification of the times involved in the experiments can be seen in Figure 4.

The values we used in the test were decided considering the bandwidth needed by high definition video streaming, which is about 5 Mbps. We obtain this value by transmitting 12500 byte messages every 0.02 seconds or 625000 byte messages each second. In any case, we have made some tests to detect the point at which messages start being lost in both cases: if there is a migration of access point is produced or without interruption in the WiFi network. These values are detailed in the following section.

The AMQP broker was created on a server with an AMD 8-core processor and 16Gb of RAM memory. The client had an Atom N450 processor and 1Gb of RAM memory. Both of them were running Ubuntu 12.04 operating system. For the wireless network we have used the OpenWRT operative system with Attitude Adjustment version on a Alix PC-Engines (alix2d2) and a Tplink (TL-WDR3600) routers. And the test were run on a dedicated LAN with no other traffic.

4 Results

In this section we present the results of the first set of experiments in which a wireless producer migrates from access point but remaining in the same IP network. In these tests, the TCP connection between the producer and the AMQP broker is maintained. Each combination of message production frequency and message size is repeated 100 times and we analyse the distribution function of the maximum jitter for each one of the tests.

4.1 Behaviour during Access Point Transition

For the experiments, we have used a completely dedicated network without external traffic. If there is not any interruption in the wireless link of the producer, a very limited jitter is observed for reasonable workloads, for instance, less than 5 Mbps.

In order to see a typical behaviour with an AP migration, we provide Figures 5 and 6. These figures shows the jitter for each message received by the consumer. In these figures, the positive peak corresponds to the hand-off, and the negative values are due to the reception of a burst of messages which the producer have retained during this communication's interruption.

In 5, the small oscillations after the handoff peak are produced because the messages in the interruption burst are delivered in the inverted order (like in a LIFO queue).

As expected, the number of messages with negative jitter can be approximated by the peak positive jitter divided by the message producing period. For instance, in figure 6b, it is $4000/500 \approx 8$ messages.

4.2 Workload Boundary

Without performing an exhaustive delimitation of the workloads producing message losses, we have made some tests to provide hints about the applicability of AMQP. Note that these "extreme" workloads can be dependent on the platform

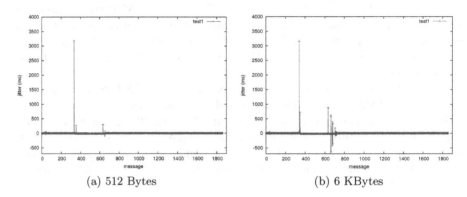

(a) 512 Bytes   (b) 6 KBytes

Fig. 5. Behaviour of jitter with migration of access point. Both tests producing a message each 10 ms and with messages sizes: a) 512 Bytes and b) 6 KBytes.

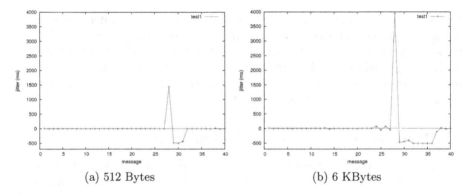

(a) 512 Bytes   (b) 6 KBytes

Fig. 6. Behaviour of jitter with migration of access point. Both tests producing a message each 500 ms and with messages sizes:a) 512 Bytes and b) 6 KBytes.

used, and even the configuration of these platforms. These experiments have been conducted without access point migration, in order to know the capacity of the system.

Figure 7 shows an approximation of the capacity of the system in terms of message size and production frequency. For loads above the red line, the system is saturated and not all produced messages arrive to consumers. The limits are around to 20 Mbps. This bandwidth is close to that we obtain with the *iperf* tool using the TCP test.

4.3   Jitter Analysis

We analyse the jitter of the messages arriving to the consumer when the producer makes an AP migration using the maximum jitter's distribution function after repeating 100 times the same scenario (the same combination of messages production frequency and size). We know that the maximum jitter in our tests is

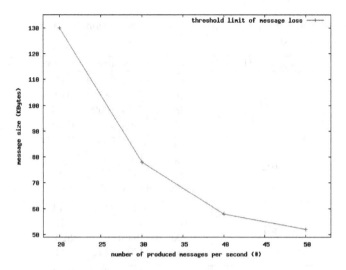

Fig. 7. Threshold limit of message losses for different message production frequency and message size

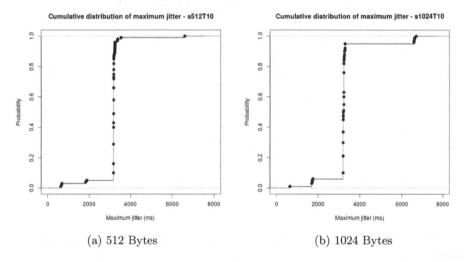

(a) 512 Bytes   (b) 1024 Bytes

Fig. 8. Distribution function of the maximum jitter using a period of 10 ms for the production of messages and two message sizes: a) 512 Bytes and b) 1024 Bytes

due to access point migration given that the network has not external traffic and that the workloads used in these tests do not saturate the system (no message losses are observed).

In Figure 8 it can be seen the distribution function of the maximum jitter using a period of 10 ms for message production and two message sizes: a) 512 Bytes and b) 1024 Bytes. In both cases, the jitter is concentrated around 3 s.

Table 1. Statistical values of maximum jitter distribution for messages sent with different size and period

message size (Bytes)	period (ms)	max	mean	sta. dev.
	10	6594	3132	587
512	100	7361	1879	950
	500	7043	1660	1006
	1000	3367	1363	1010
	10	6711	3285	876
1024	100	4104	1931	818
	500	6346	1576	809
	1000	3404	1375	875
	10	6552	4437	1714
3072	100	3105	1599	587
	500	4045	1672	823
	1000	3701	1441	934
	10	6579	4708	1854
6144	100	6402	1739	786
	500	6426	1696	949
	1000	3915	1272	949

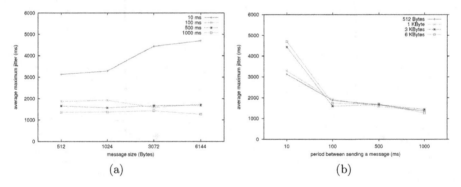

(a)   (b)

Fig. 9. Evolution of maximum jitter as function of (a) message's size, or (b) message production period

In Table 1 it is shown the maximum, mean and standard deviation of the maximum jitter in 100 tests for different combinations of message size (from 0.5 KByte to 6 KByte) and message production periods (10, 100, 500 and 1000 ms).

To see the jitter evolution depending on each of the two parameters we use in the workload, we present the mean values in Table 1 in two ways: as a function of the message size (Figure 9a) or as function of the message production frequency (Figure 9b).

In Figure 9 it can be seen that, concerning the jitter, the sending period is more relevant than the size of messages. This is clearly shown in Figure 9(a) for the line corresponding to 10 ms.

Also the combination of both parameters seems to have an important and non linear influence, as it can be seen by the proximity of lines corresponding to message sizes 3 and 6 KBytes and the difference between the 1 and 3 KBytes in Figure 9 (b).

5   Conclusions and Future Work

In this paper we presented our first results concerning how jitter is affected when using AMQP in unstable networks. AMQP is a middleware protocol which facilitates the development of applications based on producer-consumer or publish-subscribe models and make them platform independent. We have checked a simple workload model of one producer and one consumer in the presence of access point migration in an extended wireless network (i.e. several access points conforming a same Service Set). We have observed that the messaging system is robust and guarantees message delivery without losses. The occurrences of message losses are found when the load is higher than the system buffer capacity in the producer side; but the transfer rate requirement for what is considered a heavy traffic load, such as high quality video streaming across wireless networks, is below the covered area under the curve of the threshold limit of message loss.

We can conclude that, in a simple and controlled scenario with roaming between two access points, we observe jitters between 3 and 4.7 seconds, with peaks of 7 seconds appearing only for high transmission rates (e.g., 100 messages per second) which is a considerable rate for monitoring systems running on a general purpose network. Also, using off-the-self inexpensive hardware, we have tested extreme workloads from which message losses are detected.

As a follow-up of this work, we are planning more complex scenarios in which a roaming producer switches between different IP networks and not only between access point, thereby causing the TCP connection to be reset. Also, a deeper analysis about the relation between jitter, message size and message production rate is needed in order to provide a good characterization which will help developers to decide whether protocols such as AMQP fit their requirements.

References

1. O'Hara, J.: Toward a Commodity Enterprise Middleware. Communications Magazine (2007)
2. Gusmeroli, S., Piccione, S., Rotondi, D.: IoT@Work automation middleware system design and architecture. In: IEEE International Conference on Emerging Technologies and Factory Automation, ETFA (2012)
3. Foundation OpenStack. AMQP and Nova (2014)
4. Corporation IMatix. Security and Robustness (2014)

5. Subramoni, H., Marsh, G., Narravula, S., Lai, P., Panda, D.K.: Design and evaluation of benchmarks for financial applications using advanced message queuing protocol (AMQP) over infiniband. In: 2008 Workshop on High Performance Computational Finance, WHPCF 2008 (2008)
6. Appel, S., Sachs, K., Buchmann, A.: Towards benchmarking of amqp. In: Proceedings of the Fourth ACM International Conference on Distributed Event-Based Systems, pp. 99–100. ACM (2010)
7. Fernandes, J.L., Lopes, I.C., Rodrigues, J.J.P.C., Ullah, S.: Performance evaluation of RESTful web services and AMQP protocol. In: IEEE ICUFN, pp. 810–815 (2013)
8. Lee, S., Kim, H., Hong, D.K., Ju, H.: Correlation analysis of MQTT loss and delay according to QoS level. In: International Conference on Information Networking, pp. 714–717 (2013)
9. Inc. Pivotal Software. Messaging that just works (2014)

Security Methods and Systems

Modelling and Simulation of a Defense Strategy to Face Indirect DDoS Flooding Attacks

Angelo Furfaro[1], Pasquale Pace[1], Andrea Parise[2], and Lorena Molina Valdiviezo[1,3]

[1] Dipartimento di Ingegneria Informatica, Modellistica, Elettronica e Sistemistica
Università della Calabria,
Via P. Bucci 41C, 87036 Rende (CS), Italy
{a.furfaro,ppace,l.molina}@dimes.unical.it
[2] Open Knowledge Technologies s.r.l.
Piazza Vermicelli
I-87036, Rende (CS) – Italy
andrea.parise@okt-srl.com
[3] Faculty of Engineering
National University of Chimborazo
Riobamba – Ecuador
lmolina@unach.edu.ec

Abstract. Distributed Denial of Service (DDoS) flooding attack is one of the most diffused and effective threat against services and applications running over the Internet. Its distributed and cooperative nature makes it complicated to prevent and/or to counteract. *StopIt* is a robust, filter-based defence mechanism which is able to deal with various types of massive DDoS flooding attacks but which fails when the DDoS is achieved indirectly, *i.e.* by congestion of a link shared with the victim. This paper introduces an extension of *StopIt* which makes it able to cooperate with capability-based mechanisms for defeating indirect attacks. The enhanced version of the protocol has been implemented into the ns-3 simulator and its effectiveness has been evaluated under different scenarios.

1 Introduction

In recent years, issues related to *Cyber Security* aspects, mainly focused on the security of computer systems and the services they offer, have gained considerable importance. Many aspects of the daily people lives, companies and even national governments, are incessantly affected by these issues to ensure the integrity of information systems and data managed and transmitted through communication networks [16,2]. In addition, open and accessible networks such as the Internet, are particularly suitable to the widespread of malwares able to exploit vulnerabilities in connected systems with the aim of launching targeted attacks to undermine security. For these reasons, a careful and accurate analysis of the most common attacks in both wired and wireless communication networks, is crucial to design more effective defence mechanisms.

Among all possible security attack types, one of the most interesting and sophisticated attack technique that is still not easily be contained, is represented by the DDoS (Distributed Denial of Service) which is very difficult to detect and to deal with because

G. Fortino et al. (Eds.): IDCS 2014, LNCS 8729, pp. 263–274, 2014.

of its distributed nature. Usually, DDoS attacks are carried out by a *Botnet* consisting of widely scattered and remotely controlled computers called *zombies*, able to send a big amount of service requests and data traffic to the target victim in constant and simultaneous fashion. In particular, the attack can be launched both to network/transport (*i.e.* by exhausting bandwidth, router processing capacity or network resources) or application level (*i.e.* by exhausting the server resources such as memory, CPU, sockets) thus causing a considerable slowdown of responses from the target system or even a complete crash.

Starting from this challenging and modern communication scenario, the paper shows how to configure and extend the well known ns-3 network simulator [14,4] for testing different network communication scenarios during DDoS attacks; moreover, a new strategy to improve the performance of a standard hybrid defence mechanism, is also proposed and validated. The main contribution can be summarized as follow:

1. we recall the operation of the standard *StopIt* mechanism to face DDoS security attacks and we show its performances and limitations by implementing a specific simulation model;
2. we propose an extension of that technique by taking advantage from the integration of the *DiffServ* architecture, typically used to guarantee specific quality of service levels within a communication network;
3. we have implemented our proposal and we have tested it throughout simulations in order to demonstrate the extreme reactivity and adaptability to different network traffic conditions.

The rest of the paper is organized as follows. Section 2 introduces related works on different types of DDoS security attacks. Section 3 describes the main features of the reference *StopIt* mechanism by also discussing few limitations of this technique. A novel solution, to overcome some of those limitations, is presented in Section 4. Section 5 validates the goodness of our proposal by showing results obtained throughout several simulation campaigns in different network conditions. Finally, section 6 concludes the paper by offering few future research directions.

2   Related Work

In the last few years DDoS attacks have been the subject of various surveys that analize them from different viewpoints [21,8,15,19]. In particular, the authors of [21] discussed about the growing need of a comprehensive, collaborative and distributed defence approach after they categorized the different DDoS flooding attacks and classified existing countermeasures according to the ability to prevent, detect, and respond to DDoS flooding attacks. In [8], the coordinated nature of the DDoS attack is explained by recalling that an effective defence strategy for these attacks should also be designed in a collaborative fashion; thus, all the routers need to work collaboratively by exchanging their caveat messages with their neighbours. For this reason, hybrid defence mechanisms are more effective than centralized ones because their components are distributed over multiple locations such as source, destination or intermediate networks by implementing cooperative behaviours among the deployment points.

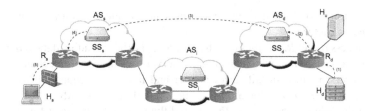

Fig. 1. *StopIt operation*

Few famous hybrid DDoS defence strategies are based on the following mechanisms:

- *Throttling / filtering* and *Hybrid packet marking* [12,5] consisting into the installation, by the victims side, of a router throttle at upstream routers several hops away with the aim of limiting the forwarding packets data rate; nevertheless, these defence strategies only limit the rate of malicious packets.
- *Capability-based* [1] consisting into a short-term authorization from the receivers by adding specific stamps on their packets. In this way, the recipients explicitly authorize the traffic it would like to receive.
- *Active Internet Traffic Filtering (AITF)* [3] consisting into the default acceptance of all the traffic and the explicit refusal of that traffic identified as undesirable. According to this filtering scheme, the main limitation is the need of a bounded amount of filtering resources from participating ISPs.
- *StopIt* [11] which will be extensively detailed in the next section to address its main limitation with respect to an indirect DDoS attack.

3 The *StopIt* Mechanism

Since the main contribution of this paper is the proposal of a new strategy to improve the performance of a widely used hybrid filter-based mechanism named *StopIt* [11], this section summarises the features of this reference defence technique also highlighting few limitations to be addressed in our study. In particular, the *StopIt* technique consists in the installation of a specific network filter able to block the received undesirable traffic by using Passport [10] as secure source authentication system to prevent source address spoofing. It is worth to note that, this technique does not aim at the detection of an attack, but it implements an effective mechanism to face the problem in a quick and completely automatic way.

Figure 1 shows the operation of the *StopIt* mechanism applied to a general communication architecture consisting of more Autonomous Systems (AS) connected throughout secure connections in order to avoid the address spoofing; moreover, each specific server who wants to activate the *StopIt* has to be equipped with an algorithm to detect an attack. Each AS owns a *StopIt* server within its domain and all the *StopIt* servers use IGP [18] to exchange data with their AS and BGP [13] to learn the presence of other *StopIt* servers in the neighbourhood. Going into more details, we briefly recall the operation of the *StopIt* scheme as described in the following steps:

1. The victim host H_d detects the attack and send a request of source blocking toward its access router R_d
2. The access router R_d verifies that the source H_s is really sending data to the server to avoid the situation in which an attacked server uses the *StopIt* mechanism to block legal users; then, it installs a local filter and it sends a request of flow blocking $< source - server >$ to the *StopIt* server SS_d within its own AS
3. Once the *StopIt* server SS_d authenticated the received request, it forwards the request toward the *StopIt* server belonging to the sourcing AS by using the BGP protocol.
4. The *StopIt* server SS_s within the sourcing AS, once received the request, notifies the blocking request to its access router R_s
5. Finally, the access router within the sourcing AS installs the filter to block the flow $< source - server >$ for a certain period and it sends a request to the attacking source. After receiving this request, a compliant host H_s installs a local filter to stop sending to H_d. If H_s does not stop, it will be punished by its own access router R_s.

More details about the operation of the *StopIt* mechanism can be found in [11].

3.1 Security Aspects

The *StopIt* mechanism previously described supports different security features by addressing the following security issues:

- *Spoofing* - The *StopIt* architecture does not allow to use spoofed addresses because it is coupled with the Passport [10] system to implement a robust inter and intra domain security support.
- *Compromised Server* - To avoid the activation of the *StopIt* mechanism by a compromised server to block a legal use, the access router within the victim's AS has to verify that the source to be blocked is really sending data traffic; thus, the access router first checks the actual sending of data toward the server in a recent time interval; then, it sends a traffic interruption request to the server by using a specific request message called *End-To-End StopIt* request.
- *Filter exhaustion* - An attacker who attempts to bypass the defence system could aim at saturating the filters available to a router. To limit this strategic attack, the routers have to follow few strategies such as *Filter Aggregation* and *Random Filter Replacement*, to wisely install the filters.

3.2 Limitations

In the last years, the *StopIt* mechanism has been validated and tested in different communication scenarios demonstrating its effectiveness respect to various types of massive DDoS flooding attacks; however, it fails when the DDoS attack is achieved in an indirect way by congesting a link shared with the victim. With reference to Figure 1, if the DDoS attack is conducted against a host H_u belonging to AS_d, the server H_d within the same AS, experiences a high performance decrease because it shares the same link with the victim.

4   The Proposal

Starting from the analysis conducted [11], we can argue that *StopIt* overcomes filter-based mechanisms such as AITF, and it provides non-interrupted communication under a wide range of DDoS attacks; however, *StopIt* does not always outperforms capability-based mechanisms if the malicious traffic congests a link shared by the victim instead of directly reaching the victim. In such situations, a standard capability-based mechanism (*e.g. TVA* [20], *TVA+*[11]) is more effective but it has few drawbacks mainly due to *i)* the accuracy and reliability of the attack detection strategy implemented by the receiver, *ii)* the high processing and memory costs due to the notable amount of per flow state information to be maintained at each router. In particular, in case of indirect attack, the behaviours of *TVA+* and *StopIt* are opposite: *StopIt* experiences an increase of the data transfer time with the growth of data traffic and *TVA+* does not complete the data transfer if the bandwidth is not high enough. The best solution, to get the advantages of both defence mechanisms, would consist into the merge of the two hybrid techniques so as to obtain the benefits of both. However, the merging of those two techniques is not trivial because it would consist into the creation, from scratch, of a new hybrid mechanism having an high complexity with consequent impacts on the actual feasibility of the system; thus we propose to make the *StopIt* system able to activate a priority-based strategy, already available within the AS routers, with the aim of offering privileges to traffic with destination towards the server that is experiencing a degradation of its performance.

Starting from this intuition, we propose an *"uncommon"* use of the *DiffServ* [7] model for IP traffic differentiation as a simple, but effective, technique to make the *StopIt* more robust against the indirect flooding attacks. In this way, the *StopIt* mechanism will face an indirect DDoS attack by using a technology already supported by the access routes and designed to provide a specific QoS level within the network.

DiffServ has been already used against DDoS attacks. In particular, it was employed to attenuate the effect of DDoS flooding attacks [9] by adopting a bandwidth allocation policy which assigns to the normal traffic a priority higher than the one assigned to suspicious traffic. Incoming packets are analysed and classified through a suitable anomaly detection module. On the contrary, the solution proposed in this paper does not extend the *DiffServ* model but simply exploits it as a standard tool to implement an effective capability-based mechanism.

In the next subsections first, we briefly recall the main features of the *DiffServ* model, then we explain the dynamic integration of that model with the *StopIt* mechanism.

4.1   DiffServ for Traffic Management

The *DiffServ* is a *coarse-grained, class-based* mechanism for traffic management and QoS differentiation. It has been designed to make a differentiation among IP traffic in order to determine traffic relative priorities on a per-hop basis. Thanks to the *DiffServ* model, traffic is first classified by taking into account a specific priority; then, it is forwarded according to one of three per-hop behaviour (PHB) mechanisms defined by IETF and referring to different priority queues. By following this approach, the traffic with similar service characteristics can be handled with similar guarantees across multiple networks, even if the presence of multiple networks does not ensure the same service at the same way. The *DiffServ* model replaces the first bits in the standard ToS (Type of Service) byte with a differentiated services code point (DSCP) that is then mapped to the PHB. This specific technique allows service providers to control how the DSCP code points are mapped to PHBs, and each time a packet enters a network domain it may be re-marked. Most common networks use the following generally defined PHBs:

- *Assured Forwarding (AF)* that gives assurance of delivery under prescribed and stringent conditions (Premium Service)
- *Expedited Forwarding (EF)* dedicated to low-loss, low-latency traffic
- *Default Behaviour (BE)* typically used for best-effort traffic

4.2   StopIt-DiffServ Cooperation

In case of an indirect DDoS attack where the flooding traffic is sent to a normal host H_u sharing a link with a DNS Server H_d, the dynamic activation of the *DiffServ* support by the server H_d, experiencing a performance degradation, is implemented according to the following assumptions within the communication network:

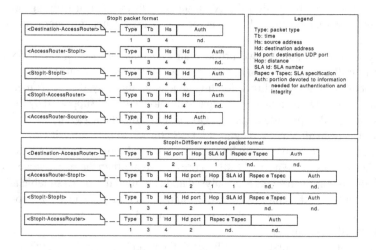

Fig. 2. *StopIt* packet format for *DiffServ* activation

- At least one *StopIt* server is present within each AS;
- Each AS corresponds to a *DiffServ* domain;
- In each *DiffServ* domain, the packets coming from the *StopIt* server are managed throughout the highest priority Assured Forwarding (AF) queue;
- The *DiffServ* system is able to install new Service Level Agreements (SLAs) at run time;
- The server H_d experiencing a performance degradation is able to detect anomalous traffic conditions by using a specific detection algorithm that is out of the scope of this work.

To support the integration between *StopIt* and *DiffServ*, we extended the standard packet format exchanged among different network entities by adding specific fields such as the Hop counter, the SLA identifier, the Rspec and Tspec representing traffic and request specifications respectively. Figure 2 shows the comparison between the standard *StopIt* packet format and the extended version.

Once the server H_d detects a decrease in its performance, mostly due to traffic anomalies, it starts the activation of the jointly *StopIt-DiffServ* defence mechanism by executing the following steps:

1. H_d sends a temporary *DiffServ* activation request toward the access router R_d within its AS by respecting the packet format defined in Figure 2;
2. R_d forwards the request to the *StopIt* server after filling the packet with the information about all the interfaces connected to the AS;
3. The *StopIt* server installs the specific SLA for a certain time T_b, then it decreases by one the hop limit field and forwards the request to all the neighbour ASs
4. The other *StopIt* servers, once received the request packet, repeat the actions from point 2 until the hop limit field reaches zero.

At the end of this procedure, the ASs in which the SLA has been installed, will give priority to traffic destined to H_d so that it is not affected by the attack any more. It is worth to note that, the proposed technique for packet diffusion is similar to the selective flooding strategy used by the OSPF [6] routing protocol; thus it can be easily implemented as well.

5   Simulation Analysis and Results

In this section we describe the modelling and simulation of the *StopIt* mechanism and of the proposed enhancements by using the ns-3 discrete-event network simulator specifically designed to test and validate the performances of wireless and wired IP network systems. In particular, ns-3 is one of the fastest and efficient network simulators freely available on the web in which the simulation time discretely moves from one event to another. Events are scheduled at a specific simulation time and they will wait until that time to be executed. To perform a simulation, the network topology is first setup and configured with the desired attributes such as link bandwidths, propagation delays and traffic sources. We developed the proposed strategy by integrating a freely downloadable *DiffServ* model for ns-3 simulator [17] with the standard operation offered by the *StopIt* mechanism in order to generate a unified simulation framework. In particular the *StopIt* implementation has been made under the following assumptions:

- IP addresses cannot be spoofed because *StopIt* deployment in a real network subsumes the use of Passport;
- The only network elements corrupted are the hosts belonging to the botnet;
- Strategic attacks directed to filter exhaustion are not taken into account;
- Only IPv4 networks are considered;
- *StopIt* servers are already aware of their peers at start-up;
- Access routers play also the role of edge routers and are able to install/remove *DiffServ* SLAs at runtime.

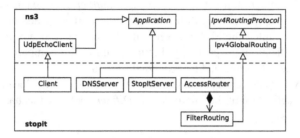

Fig. 3. *StopIt* class hierarchy

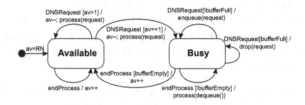

Fig. 4. DNS server behaviour

5.1   Modelling with ns-3

In order to simulate in ns-3 a DDoS attack scenario in presence of the *StopIt* defense mechanism, we implemented the needed components by introducing suitable classes, that inherit from the ns-3 `Application` base class, which respectively reproduce the behaviour of a DNS server (the victim), *StopIt* servers, routers supporting packet filtering and DNS clients (see Fig. 3). The DNS server, whose behaviour is specified by the finite state automaton shown in Fig. 4, is modelled by the `DNSServer` class as a multithreaded application which is able to process up to n requests in parallel. In particular, if the DNS server is in the *Available* state, it handles incoming requests as soon as they arrive; on the contrary, when there are no more available processing resources, the server switches to the *Busy* state and stores the incoming requests into a limited buffer. If the buffer gets filled, incoming requests are dropped. Service time is assumed to follow an exponential distribution with mean 5 *ms*.

As stated before, *StopIt* needs the support of an attack detection algorithm. For simulation purposes, we model the presence of such an algorithm by using a detection function which is parametrized with respect to the probability of detecting a malicious address and the time employed to recognize an attack since the arrival of the first malicious packet. A *StopIt* server is modelled by the `StopItServer` class which reproduces the behaviour described in Sections 3 and 4. The `AccessRouter` class implements the router application which is in charge of packet filtering, dispatching of *StopIt* requests and *DiffServ* policy enforcement.

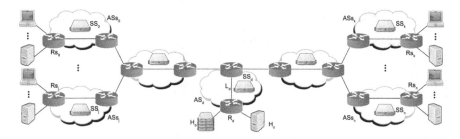

Fig. 5. Network topology

5.2 Simulation Scenario

In order to evaluate the effectiveness of the proposed mechanism we simulated both direct and indirect DDoS attacks against a DNS server. The network topology that has been considered is represented in Figure 5. The network is split up into three zones as in [8]. The first zone contains ten ASs, each made up of 50 hosts, where the traffic sources are located in. The 50% of such ASs is corrupted and belongs to the botnet. The second zone represents the intermediate network and the third zone contains only the victim's AS. To evaluate the behaviours of the defence mechanisms in a realistic scenario we introduced different types of traffic sources. We included 24 VoIP sources (using the ilbc_mode_30 codec at 13.33kbps), 230 HTTP sources and 230 DNS sources. During normal network operation, *DiffServ* handles both DNS and HTTP sources as Best Effort traffic and VoIP sources as Assured Forwarding. To face an indirect DDoS attack, DNS traffic is handled as coming from high priority sources. Since the simulated attacks aimed at exhausting the available capacity of the link L_d, we measured its bandwidth occupation.

Table 1. Simulation parameters

Links		DNS Service		Legal DNS traffic		Malicious traffic	
Bandwidth	10 Mbps	Resources	8	Packet size	26 bytes	Packet size	78 bytes
Delay	1 ms	Buffer size	200	Packet rate	1 pkt/s	Packet rate	100 pkt/s
		Mean service time 5 ms					

Direct Flooding Attack. Figure 6(a) shows the effectiveness of *StopIt* in the case of direct attack. The black curve is the total used bandwidth, the purple line represents the HTTP traffic, the blue line is the VoIP traffic and the green one the DNS traffic (both legal and illegal). In the simulated scenario, the attack begins at $t = 20\ s$ and it is detected after $3\ s$.

During the time interval between the begin of the attack and the *StopIt* response, the DNS traffic increases and saturates the available bandwidth at expense of the HTTP packets. As can be seen in the details reported in Figure 6(b), during this period the DNS traffic is almost totally made of malicious packets. After the filters are successfully installed, the botnet traffic is blocked (100% of malicious sources identified) and

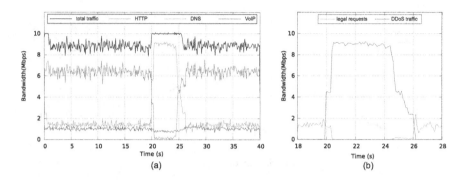

Fig. 6. (a) Direct DNS DDoS attack (b) Detail of legal and malicious DNS traffic

the normal situation is restored. It is worth noting that the VoIP traffic remains almost unaffected due to the priority ensured by the *DiffServ* policy.

Shared Link Flooding Attack. Figure 7(a) depicts a scenario where the attack is achieved indirectly by flooding a host that belongs to the same AS of the victim with the aim of exhaust the available bandwidth of a shared link. In this case, the victim does not known the IP addresses of the zombies, so it can only become aware of the attack because its incoming traffic falls under the expected value for a long time. It can be seen that *StopIt* is not able to face the attack while the VoIP traffic remains unaffected as in the previous scenario.

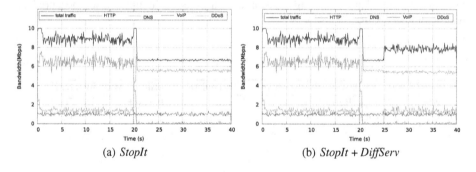

Fig. 7. Indirect DDos attack

Figure 7(b) shows how the proposed defence strategy, by exploiting the cooperation of *StopIt* and *DiffServ*, re-insures the necessary bandwidth to the DNS server after the time needed to detect the anomalous behaviour and to dispatch the *StopIt* requests.

Of course, the data traffic generated by the DDoS attack (orange curve) is still present in the network causing a decrease in terms of performances to the HTTP connections that experience a very low throughput. This issue is out of the scope of this work and it will be investigated in a future research.

6 Conclusion

This paper proposed and validated the integration of the *DiffServ* model within the *StopIt* mechanism to overcome the main limitation of this standard filter-based technique with the aim of facing both direct and indirect DDoS attacks. The cooperation between *DiffServ* and *StopIt* has the great advantage to be easily implemented in common routers since it is based on widely available technologies. The results, obtained throughout a self developed extension of the ns-3 simulator, have confirmed this initial intuition. However, the proposed solution cannot be considered as final because, even if the main services are guaranteed, the illegal sources still continue to overload the network. As future work we plan to extend our research by designing suitable detection algorithms that may directly run on edge network devices and exploit *StopIt* features to block illegal sources also in the case of indirect attacks.

Acknowledgements. This work has been partially funded by the project "Cybersecurity –P2" (PON03PE_00032_2/06), financed by the Italian Ministry of Education, University and Research (MIUR) within the PON Project - Research and Competitiveness 2007-2013.

References

1. Anderson, T., Roscoe, T., Wetherall, D.: Preventing internet denial-of-service with capabilities. SIGCOMM Comput. Commun. Rev. 34(1), 39–44 (2004)
2. Angelini, M., Arcuri, M.C., Baldoni, R., Ciccotelli, C., Di Luna, G.A., Montanari, L., Panetta, I.C., Querzoni, L., Verde, N.V.: Italian cyber security report: Critical infrastructure and other sensitive sectors readiness. Technical report, Research Center of Cyber Intelligence and Information Security, University of Rome Sapienza (December 2013)
3. Argyraki, K., Cheriton, D.R.: Scalable network-layer defense against internet bandwidth-flooding attacks. IEEE/ACM Trans. Netw. 17(4), 1284–1297 (2009)
4. Carneiro, G., Fontes, H., Ricardo, M.: Fast prototyping of network protocols through ns-3 simulation model reuse. Simulation Modelling Practice and Theory 19(9), 2063–2075 (2011)
5. Chen, R., Park, J.-M., Marchany, R.: Track: A novel approach for defending against distributed denial-of-service attacks. Technical report, Technical Report TR-ECE-06-02, Dept. of Electrical and Computer Engineering, Virginia Tech. (2006)
6. IETF. Rfc 2328: Ospf - open shortest path first. Technical report (1998), https://www.ietf.org/rfc/rfc2328.txt
7. IETF. Rfc 2475: An architecture for differentiated services. Technical report (1998), http://www.ietf.org/rfc/rfc2475.txt
8. Kumar, P.A.R., Selvakumar, S.: Distributed denial-of-service (DDoS) threat in collaborative environment - A survey on DDoS attack tools and traceback mechanisms. In: IEEE International Advance Computing Conference, IACC 2009, pp. 1275–1280 (March 2009)
9. Lai, W.-S., Lin, C.-H., Liu, J.-C., Huang, H.-C., Yang, T.-C.: Using adaptive bandwidth allocation approach to defend ddos attacks. International Journal of Software Engineering and Its Applications 2(4), 61–72 (2008)
10. Liu, X., Li, A., Yang, X., Wetherall, D.: Passport: Secure and adoptable source authentication. In: Proceedings of the 5th USENIX Symposium on Networked Systems Design and Implementation, NSDI 2008, pp. 365–378. USENIX Association, Berkeley (2008)

11. Liu, X., Yang, X., Lu, Y.: To filter or to authorize: Network-layer DoS defense against multimillion-node botnets. In: Proceedings of the ACM SIGCOMM 2008 Conference on Data Communication, pp. 195–206. ACM, New York (2008)
12. Mahajan, R., Bellovin, S.M., Floyd, S., Ioannidis, J., Paxson, V., Shenker, S.: Controlling high bandwidth aggregates in the network. SIGCOMM Comput. Commun. Rev. 32(3), 62–73 (2002)
13. Medhi, D., Ramasamy, K.: Network Routing: algorithms, protocols and architectures. Morgan Kaufmann (2007)
14. nsnam. Ns-3 documentation, http://www.nsnam.org/ns-3-19/documentation/
15. Peng, T., Leckie, C., Ramamohanarao, K.: Survey of network-based defense mechanisms countering the DoS and DDoS problems. ACM Comput. Surv. 39(1) (April 2007)
16. PwC. UK cyber security standards research. Technical report, Department for Business, Innovation & Skills Cabinet Office (2013)
17. Ramroop, S.: A diffserv model for the ns-3 simulator (2011), http://www.eng.uwi.tt/depts/elec/staff/rvadams/sramroop/index.htm
18. Sendra, S., Fernández, P.A., Quilez, M.A., Lloret, J.: Study and performance of interior gateway ip routing protocols. Network Protocols and Algorithms 2(4), 88–117 (2010)
19. Thing, V.L., Sloman, M., Dulay, N.: A survey of bots used for distributed denial of service attacks. In: Venter, H., Eloff, M., Labuschagne, L., Eloff, J., Solms, R. (eds.) New Approaches for Security, Privacy and Trust in Complex Environments. IFIP International Federation for Information Processing, vol. 232, pp. 229–240. Springer, Boston (2007)
20. Yang, X., Wetherall, D., Anderson, T.: A dos-limiting network architecture, vol. 35, pp. 241–252. ACM, New York (2005)
21. Zargar, S.T., Joshi, J., Tipper, D.: A survey of defense mechanisms against distributed denial of service (DDoS) flooding attacks. IEEE Communications Surveys & Tutorials 15(4), 2046–2069 (2013)

Towards a Reference Architecture for Service-Oriented Cross Domain Security Infrastructures

Wen Zhu[1], Lowell Vizenor[2], and Avinash Srinivasan[3]

[1] Alion Science and Technology, Vienna, VA, USA
wzhu@alionscience.com
[2] National Center for Ontological Research, Reston, VA, USA
[3] George Mason University, Fairfax, VA, USA
asriniv5@gmu.edu

Abstract. Today's Cross Domain Communication (CDC) infrastructure largely consists of guards built to vendor specifications. Such an infrastructure often fails to provide adequate protections for CDC workflows involving Service Oriented Architectures. Focusing on the transport layer and oblivious to the context of the information exchanges, the guards often rely on rudimentary filtering techniques that require frequent human intervention to adjudicate messages. In this paper, we present a set of key requirements and design principles for a Service Oriented Cross Domain Security Infrastructure in form of a CDC Reference Architecture, featuring domain-associated guards as active workflow participants. This reference architecture will provide the foundation for the development of protocols and ontologies enabling runtime coordination among CDC elements, leading to more secure, effective, and interoperable CDC solutions.

Keywords: Cross Domain Communications, Security Guard, Workflow, Service Oriented Architecture, Reference Architecture, Ontology, Protocol.

1   Introduction

A common network security practice is to separate computer systems into secure domains or enclaves based on the classification and sensitivity of data stored and processed by these systems. Within each domain, a certain level of trust among systems is assumed. The domains are protected by Cross Domain Communication (CDC) infrastructures, which largely consist of security guards placed at the network links between two domains. These guards are responsible for enforcing security policies by inspecting and filtering information that flows between domains. However, information needed to support a mission often cut across two or more security domains. Currently, CDC flows are impeded by time-consuming release procedures that require frequent human intervention. While there have been research efforts in this area, most of them address particular aspects of CDC [1][2][3]. The lack of a comprehensive CDC framework to provide a systematic examination of CDC issues, a necessary step toward standardization, contributes to issues mentioned above.

G. Fortino et al. (Eds.): IDCS 2014, LNCS 8729, pp. 275–284, 2014.
© Springer International Publishing Switzerland 2014

The wide adaption of Service Oriented Architectures (SOA), and web service technologies in particular, has presented both new challenges and new opportunities in the area of CDC. It is now possible to accomplish complex workflows, carried out at the application layer across organizational boundaries with security implications. At the same time, service description metadata [4] could be used to understand the context and semantics of service interactions, and automate the enforcement of policies.

The alignment of CDC infrastructures with SOA will help extend SOA across the boundaries of security domains. In this paper, we propose a reference architecture to delineate responsibilities among various CDC participants, and describe how they interact with one another.   It addresses the many facets of CDC:

1. From a workflow perspective, what role does the CDC infrastructure play in an application workflow and business process management (BPM) in particular?
2. From an information perspective, how does the CDC infrastructure interpret and act upon the information carried in CDC messages and web services in particular?
3. From a network perspective, how does the CDC infrastructure fit into the transport protocols' stack and the web services technology stack in particular?

The rest of this paper is organized as follows. We will start with a survey of current CDC solutions and highlight the key issues we seek to resolve. Then in sections 3 and 4, we introduce the reference architecture and discuss how a security ontology based on such an architecture enables coordination among CDC participants and between security domains. Section 5 identifies opportunities for standardizing CDC interactions in the forms of protocol candidates. Finally, we conclude our discussion and evaluation of an implementation approach.

2   Background and Issues

2.1   Cross Domain Solutions Today

A survey of current cross-domain security solutions revealed a number of critical issues related to application design and network infrastructure. From the perspective of mission applications design [5], current CDC solutions require mission application programs to design and implement their own individual solutions around particular guard designs, resulting in vendor lock-ins. Even then, the solutions are limited to simple cases without full-duplex architectures. Current CDC offerings include email integration, file transfer, chat, and browse down capabilities. Yet, an application workflow is likely to involve more complex interactions and different transport mechanisms, which are difficult to implement with current, inflexible CDC solutions.

From the perspective of enterprise security infrastructure, existing CDC solutions use a Transport-Oriented Guard (TOG), associated with the links between domains. TOGs monitor traffic on the links rather than at nodes. While most guards today understand XML formats and HTTP protocol, they make security decisions solely based on the bytes over the wire, without the benefit of application context.   TOG creates several issues. First, the guard is required to have the highest security privilege to inspect the information flow and prevent confidentiality breach. Consequently, the guard may have to be (pre-)loaded with cryptographic keys and other sensitive information. Contrary to the best security practices, such models of CDC make the guard a target for attack. Furthermore, this design implies that the same security terminology is required at both domains connected by the guard. For example, the same set of security labels have to be used. Such an assumption is not always true, especially when the information exchange is across organizational boundaries. Second, associating the guards with the links often fails to scale as the network grows in size. The number of guards required grows exponentially as the number of interconnected security domains increases, commonly known as the "n-squared" problem. Finally, CDC guards often have limited configurability and vendor-specific API, resulting in locked-in stacks, increased development cost and the lack of flexibility to support mission requirements.

2.2   CDC in the Context of SOA

The need for aligning CDC with services and their supporting infrastructure has become increasingly evident as organizations adopt SOA. For example, the US Intelligence Community has developed a set of service specifications, including XML schemas and REST [6] API, for content discovery and retrieval across multiple repositories and potential different security domains[7]. While these specifications identify required services, CDC concerns are notably absent. Leaving the alignment of CDC infrastructure to service infrastructure to the interpretation of their perspective developers could result in inconsistent and potentially non-interoperable implementations.

We should note that the industry has developed innovative CDC solutions for specific service implementations despite of the lack of a CDC reference architecture. For example, XDDS [3] is a cross domain service discovery solution designed to work with existing guards. In this solution, a Local Discovery Agent (LDA) is deployed in a domain to intercept service discovery requests using Universal Description Discovery and Integration protocol (UDDI) [8]. It coordinates with LDA instances in other domains to locate appropriate services for the request. When the security policy requires the service provider's identity be masked, the solution uses a Global Discovery Service (GDS) for anonymization. Since the GDS is aware of all LDAs across all domains, the GDS will need the highest security privilege. There are several interesting obversations. First, this solution introduces a new infrastructure component (LDA) to address a particular CDC need (service discovery). Add-hoc components like LDA will be needed for other CDC usecases without an overall framework to address CDC concerns. Second, even though the security guards are considered transparent to the mission applications, the LDAs are not. The mission applications need to address UDDI requests to the LDA for local domain. This inconsistency calls for a convention on CDC infrastructure's role in application workflows. Finally, UDDI is an application layer protocol. There is clearly a need for the guards to understand the context of application-level interactions in order to make more intelligent security decisions.

2.3   Relevant Security Ontology Work

Current CDC solutions also require excessive amounts of human intervention, mainly due to the lack of a standard and flexible framework for describing information exchanged. Many guards use a dirty word list or some rudimentary rules expressed in eXtensible Stylesheet Language Transformations (XSLT) to filter information passing through them. These techniques often fail to take into account the context of messages and the meaning of the words, leading to high error rates, i.e., false positives and negatives. Human review is often required to adjudicate ambiguities.

In order to build applications that can more precisely analyze information flows across domains, we argue that the security community should adopt a standard security ontology. A standard security ontology would provide the community with a common set of concepts around which they could form a shared understanding to advance the theory and practice of security, privacy, and trust of Web-based applications. A number of security ontologies have been developed and are currently in use. Some notable examples are the DAML Services Security and Privacy ontology[1], the Navy Research Lab (NRL) Security ontology[9] and SecOnt[2,3], which is based on the security relationship model described in the National Institute of Standards and Technology (NIST) Special Publication 800-12. These security ontologies focus on the areas of assets, threats, vulnerabilities, and countermeasures. Examples of how security ontologies are being applied include: the use of formal representations of policies in ontology and algorithms in order to support machine-aided reason about the policies [10] and the use of ontologies to annotate generic resources from simple documents to interactive services with security-related metadata and not just Web services.

Our review identified a number of relevant security ontology work but they are not specific to CDC [11]. We believe more ontology work needs to be done in this area.

3   Cross Domain Security Reference Architecture (CDC-RA)

3.1   Overview

CDC-RA is a key to CDC standardization. It provides: 1) a common framework and vocabulary to describe CDC mechanisms; 2) the abstract interaction patterns among CDC participants (basis for standardization through protocols); and 3) CDC infrastructure design patterns in the form of protocol constraints and assumptions.

We are primarily concerned with standardized interfaces for products whose primary responsibility is to facilitate secure cross-domain communications. A security guard is one such product, and perhaps the most important. However, CDC is a shared responsibility between the CDC infrastructure and the mission application taking advantage of such an infrastructure. We should not lose sight of the critical role that mission applications play. As illustrated in Fig. 1, we separate the CDC concerns into two categories: Application Aspects and   Infrastructure Aspects.

The Application Aspects of CDC address the following:

- Architecture Concerns: We believe it is reasonable to assume that mission applications are aware of the fact that they interact with systems in other security domains, and therefore presence of the security guards. Application is responsible for properly handling the cases where a message is rejected by the guard.

---

[1] http://www.daml.org/services/owl-s/security.html

[2] http://www.securityontology.com

[3] http://www.ida.liu.se/~iislab/projects/secont/

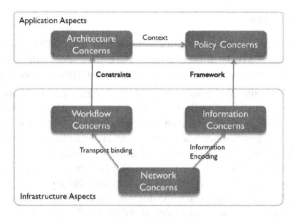

Fig. 1. Cross Domain Security Concerns

- Policy Concerns: Security attributes for application messages need to be defined so that proper security policies can be enforced by the infrastructure. We consider this an application specific concern since the security attributes associated with individual data elements are processed by that application.

The Infrastructure Aspects of CDC address the following:

- Network Concerns: We would like to address the concerns of how a guard interacts with the network, including how the CDC-specific communications are carried in the network protocols, for instance, in a SOAP message for web services-based communications or in the HTTP header for web traffic. Doing so may require extensions to existing protocols such that security-specific information could be added to the messages. A particular aspect of integrating guard with network protocol is a mechanism to handle end-to-end encryption and authentication. For example, if a mission application encrypts payload using WS-Security [12], the guard would not be able to inspect the message content unless the message is addressed to the guard (instead of the target system) and encrypted using the guard's key(s).
- Information Concerns: We would like to address how guards interact with the information flowing through them as part of the information concerns. There needs to be a convention for determining how application-specific messages are interpreted and acted upon by the guards, to enable automation and interoperability.
- Workflow Concerns: We would like to address how guards interact with other participants of the workflow, i.e. mission application and other guards. Compared to others, there hasn't been an extensive research on this aspect of CDC. Much less discussion exists about how existing standards such as Business Process Modeling Notation (BPMN) [13] and WS-BPEL [14] languages can be leveraged for CDC. One important workflow consideration is whether or not the guard is an active participant in the workflow, and if so, how the guard acts as a service intermediary.

Standards like BPMN and WS-BEPL allow complex workflows to be defined, but their use in CDC has been limited because guards have been largely absent in workflow definitions. As an active workflow participant, the guards will be able to enforce policies based on models expressed in BPMN and WS-BEPL. Guard vendors may even include BPMS functionality in their products to manage cross-domain workflows.

3.2   CDC Participants

With the CDC concerns cataloged, we need to discuss how CDC participants address these concerns collaboratively in order to determine their roles and responsibilities. As illustrated in Fig. 2, cross-domain solutions include the following four key participants:

i. Security Domain: We assume that, for a single security domain, there is a consistent security vocabulary for all actors, activities, and information. Examples include a single information classification hierarchy (Top Secret, Secret, FOUO). Furthermore, a security domain may have one or more Security Guards to enforce policies, described using the domain's security vocabulary.

ii. Mission Application: For the purpose of CDC, mission applications associate mission-specific concepts with the security vocabulary.

iii. Security Monitor (Optional): A domain may utilize a centralized security management and monitoring system. With the Security Monitor, the domain security administrator can define consistent security policies for communication with other domains using the domain's security vocabulary. A Security Monitor may communicate with the Security Guard at runtime.

iv. Security Guard: A security guard enforces security policy defined by the mission application, and may act as a policy enforcement point for the domain. A guard may coordinate with other guards, in the same or different domains, to enforce the security policies.

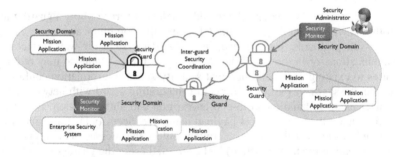

Fig. 2. CDC Participants

Deviating from the existing TOG approach of CDC security, we advocate associating security guards with domains instead of the links. Domain-Oriented Guards (DOG) would operate at the same security level as the associated domain, without unnecessary privilege. In addition, the same security monitor will be able to manage both the domain and the guard, avoiding policy conflicts and duplication. The number of guards required for securing inter-connected domains increases linearly with the number of domains unlike TOG where the increase is exponential in nature. The implication is that, for any communication path, there will be at least two guards, hence the need for inter-guard coordination. Because the guards need to trust each other without necessarily revealing mission information, the issues of identity and trust must be addressed in the context of inter-guard coordination/ synchronization. We envision a CDC protocol could require mutual authentication between guards through a mechanism such as Public Key Infrastructure (PKI) while assuming mutual trust to be established out of band, e.g. through a white list distributed among the guards.

3.3 Guards as Active Workflow Participants

In many CDC solutions, guards are considered transparent to the mission applications. In reality, a well-designed application must be aware of the fact that certain communications involve systems in other domains in order to handle the unique nature of CDC. For example, CDC communications may be blocked by the guards or delayed due to pending human review. Without the knowledge of the guards' existence along with a feedback mechanism, an application could silently fail in the background.

Our reference architecture assumes mission applications are aware of the guards. As such, we see security guards as active paticipants in CDC workflows. By having the guard as an active participant in the workflow, it becomes possible to define a notification mechanism. The notification mechanism enables the mission application to be informed in case the guard blocks an application message, for security reasons, thereby allowing the mission application to take appropriate remedial actions. Having a guard as an active participant in the workflow also solves another otherwise difficult issue: end-to-end encryption. Without a message being explicitly addressed to the guard, encryption will prevent the guard from inspecting the message due to lack of cryptographic keys at the guard. It is now possible for the guards to encrypt the message on behalf of the application after taking appropriate security actions (redaction for example) and forward the message on to its ultimate destination.

For separation of business and security concerns, it may be possible to design an application workflow in a CDC-independent way using BPMN. When the process is deployed in a CDC environment, security guards are injected into a business process through such approaches as Object Management Group's (OMG) Model Driven Architecture® (MDA) [15], as shown in Fig. 3.

A guard-aware workflow opens up other possibilities as well. For example, the guard could also act as brokers for cross domain service discovery. It could also proxy the service provider and consumer to avoid unnecessary disclosure of system identity, while eliminating the needs for ad-hoc CDC infrastructure components as described in [3]. An implication of this approach is that the guard may have to expose the same interface as the invocation target, an issue that CDC protocol design needs to take into account. For example, to proxy web service, the guard may have to implement the same service interface as defined in Web Service Description Language (WSDL) [16].

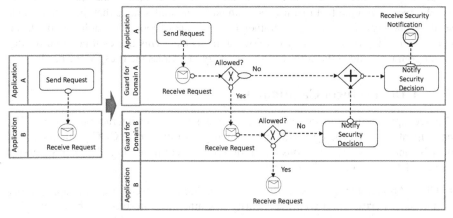

Fig. 3. Transformation of CDC Workflow

4   Security Ontology

The security community has begun to recognize the need for controlled vocabularies, taxonomies, and ontologies to make progress toward a science of (cyber) security [17]. In 2010, DOD sponsored a study to examine the theory and practice of security, and evaluate whether it is possible to adopt a more scientific approach [18]. In the context of CDC, the use of a security ontology would reduce the need for humans to adjudicate CDC messages, a problem exacerbated by the use of user-defined labels and keywords without precise meanings. These labels and keywords make it difficult for computer agents to analyze information flows without human intervention.

We envision a number of distinct, yet related ontologies to mediate the vocabularies and policies among different security domains. This will reduce the need to standardize on a single set of security policies across all domains. In addition, these ontologies will enable machine-to-machine communication, minimizing the need for human review. A community supported security ontology can be used to support the semantic annotation of generic resources such as documents, enterprise architectures, business process models and web service with security-related metadata. Semantic annotation is the act of associating an ontology term with a resource or some part of resource. More precisely, this means embedding a Uniform Resource Identifier (URI) within an information resource. Semantic annotation differs from user-generated tags in that the meaning of the metadata is defined in an external ontology that can be used disambiguate the metadata and supports the automatic discovery of resources.

The security ontology would also provide the capability to use reasoning to match mission requirements with service capabilities. Different domains may use different security vocabularies, making the discovery of services across domains difficult. The security ontology would help to harmonize the differences in security terminology and make it possible for agents to use a domain specific vocabulary and discover resources described using a different vocabulary. In [19], we described a semantic mediation infrastructure that uses ontologies to mediate the data model difference between SOA services. Similarly, semantic-aware guards could translate security vocabularies between domains based on these ontologies and enforce security policies accordingly.

We recommend that the security community should start from existing efforts to create security ontologies and, in order to ensure that others can share and reuse the ontology. We recognized the fact that it is both unlikely and undesirable that there be a single security ontology. Instead, we recommend that a suite of modular ontologies be developed, with a single core security ontology at the center. This makes it possible for different groups to extend the core security ontology to address their respective needs.

5   CDC Protocol Candidates

We see opportunities to define protocols that specify the interaction among CDC participants. These protocols will ensure interoperability among CDC participants and guards, and allow organizations to tailor security configurations based on mission needs. CDC protocol candidates include:

- CDC Application Interface: Enables interactions between mission applications and the security guard within a security domain. This interface can be specified in two levels: 1) an abstract protocol for communication with the guards that is transport-independent and 2) protocol bindings for realizing the abstract protocol with a particular transport mechanism. For web services, the mission application could potentially use WS-Addressing [20] to indicate to the security guard the ultimate destination of the message. Business processes carried out collectively by mission applications in different domains can be best understood by analyzing the interactions between applications. As such, we recommend that the security domains be configured to allow only specific application level protocols and accordingly, the guards be implemented at the application layer.

- Inter-Guard Coordination Protocol: Enables interactions among the security guards. Leveraging the security ontology, a mechanism can be defined for guards to authenticate among themselves, correlate security attributes of the source and the target applications, the activities, and the information carried in the payload. Using annotations, we can associate the application-specific metadata with the concepts in the ontology, and further associate ontology concepts with the security attributes that will be used by the guard to make runtime decisions.
- Security Monitor Interface: Defines an interface to manage CDC infrastructure, perhaps by extending the Simple Network Management Protocol (SNMP) [21].

With Inter-Guard Coordination Protocol, we are envisioning a more peer-to-peer coordination among the guards, avoiding the need a single global security system to manage multiple domains. Such system is often not practical in an inter-organizational environment and it introduces the potential of a single point of failure.

6   Road to Implementation

The CDC reference architecture can be used to guide the development of solutions that compliments and enhances existing CDC guard products to secure SOA interactions. As the first step, we see software components developed to compliment existing TOG. This component, Cross Domain Service Proxy, is associated with a particular domain and works with the domain's SOA infrastructure such as an Enterprise Service Bus (ESB) and Identify and Access Management (IdAM). Because the Proxy is an active participant of CDC workflows, applications or services always address cross domain messages to the Proxy, which can then filter the messages based on policies and inspect the content using ontologies. Through the Guard Application Interface described earlier, the Proxy can inform mission applications security decisions it takes so that the application can respond properly.   Only compliant messages are then sent out via communication link protected by the traditional guard.

This solution does introduce redundant message inspections – at the Proxy and again at the traditional cross domain guard, mainly to alleviate concerns with the new architecture. We expect that, as organizations gain confidence in the architecture, the Proxy can be either integrated into the guard products or replace the current guards.

7   Conclusion

Standardization of interactions among these CDC participants is a pre-requisite for achieving the interoperability and flexibility required by business. Due to the complex and multi-faceted nature of CDC security, standardization is only possible within a framework where interactions can be abstracted and discussed in a structured manner.

This paper represents our attempt at establishing such a framework, and we hope it will encourage further discussions within the community, resulting in more interoperable, flexible and efficient CDC solutions to serve the needs of the business.

References

[1] Swamy, N., Hicks, M.: Verified Enforcement of Security Policies for Cross-Domain Information Flows, http://www.cs.umd.edu/~mwh/papers/selinks-cpa.pdf

[2] Irvine, C.E., et al.: MYSEA: the Monterey security architecture. In: Proc. of the Workshop on Scalable Trusted Computing (ACM STC), Conference on Computer and Communications Security (CCS), pp. 39–48. Association for Computing Machinery (ACM), Chicago (2009)

[3] Atighetchi, M., et al.: XDDS: A Salable Guard-Agnostic Cross Domain Discovery Service, http://www.dtic.mil/cgi-bin/GetTRDoc?AD=ADA532504

[4] W3C, Web Services Architecture, W3C Working Group Note (February 11, 2004)

[5] Shader, M.: Cross-Domain Application Architecture: The Need for an End-to-End Approach (2012), http://yellowhouseassociates.net/download/YHA_CDAA_WP.pdf

[6] Fielding, R.: Architectural styles and the design of network-based software architectures. Diss. University of California, Irvine (2000)

[7] Intelligence Community and Department of Defense Content Discovery and Retrieval Integrated Project Team. IC/DoD Content Discovery and Retrieval Reference Architecture (February 2011)

[8] OASIS, Universal Description, Discovery and Integration v3.0.2, OASIS Standard (February 2005)

[9] Kim, A., Luo, J., Kang, M.: Security ontology for annotating resources. In: Meersman, R. (ed.) OTM 2005. LNCS, vol. 3761, pp. 1483–1499. Springer, Heidelberg (2005)

[10] Denker, G., Kagal, L., Finin, T.: Security in the Semantic Web using OWL. Information Security Technical Report 10(1), 51–58 (2005)

[11] Blanco, C., et al.: A Systematic Review and Comparison of Security Ontologies, ares. In: 2008 Third International Conference on Availability, Reliability and Security, pp. 813–820 (2008)

[12] OASIS, Web Services Security: SOAP Message Security 1.1, OASIS Standard (February 2006)

[13] Object Management Group (OMG), Business Process Model and Notation (BPMN) Version 2.0, OMG Standard (January 2011)

[14] OASIS, Web Services Business Process Execution Language 2.0, OASIS Standard (April 2007)

[15] Object Management Group (OMG), Model Driven Architecture ®, http://www.omg.org/mda/

[16] W3C, Web Services Description Language (WSDL) 1.1, W3C Note (March 15, 2001)

[17] Mundie, D.A., McIntire, D.M.: The MAL: A Malware Analysis Lexicon. CERT® Program - Carnegie Mellon University. Technical (2013)

[18] The MITRE Corporation, Science of Cyber-Security, The MITRE Corporation. Technical (2010)

[19] Zhu, W.: Semantic Mediation Bus: An Ontology-based Runtime Infrastructure for Service Interoperability. In: 2012 IEEE 16th International Enterprise Distributed Object Computing Conference Workshops (EDOCW), September 10-14, pp. 140–145 (2012)

[20] W3C, Web Services Addressing 1.0 – Core, W3C Recommendation (May 9, 2006)

[21] Harrington, D., Presuhn, R., Wijnen, B.: An Architecture for Describing Simple Network Management Protocol (SNMP) Management Frameworks. Internet Engineering Task Force RFC (December 2002)

Interoperability of Security-Aware Web Service Business Processes: Case Studies and Empirical Evaluation

Alfredo Cuzzocrea[1] and Vincenzo Rodinò[2]

[1] ICAR-CNR and University of Calabria, Italy
[2] ICAR-CNR, Italy
cuzzocrea@si.deis.unical.it, vrodino.icar@gmail.com

Abstract. In this paper, we provide significant contributions on top of a recent successful framework for *supporting the interoperability of so-called security-aware Web Service Business Processes*, i.e. Web Service Business Processes that incorporate *Access Control Policies* (ACP), via assessing and verifying its reliability on the basis of some well-suited case studies. Our evidence fully demonstrates the effectiveness as well as the robustness of the investigated framework. We complete our analytical contributions by means of a critical discussion on the advantages and possible extensions of this framework.

1 Introduction

The *Service Mosaic* project [1,2,3,4,5] identifies a *model-driven CASE platform* that aims at facilitating the development of *service-oriented applications* and the management of *Web Service lifecycle*. *Service Mosaic* allows us to model *Web Service Business Processes* via a special formalism that extends *Finite State Automata* (FSA) (e.g., [6]), augmented with time constraints, hence originating so-called *Timed FSA* [7], which represent a well-known and extensively-used formalism in the area of *real-time model checking* (e.g., [8]). Despite this, embedding time constraints into Web Service Business Processes puts severe theoretical restrictions, due to the fact that Business Processes do not originally incorporate temporal reasoning (e.g., [9]).

Service Mosaic focuses on so-called *Web Service Business Process Protocols*, i.e. graphical models that describe how a Web Service Business Process inter-operates (e.g., based on *message exchanging*) with another Web Service Business Process in distributed (Web) environments (this problem has been also investigated in [20,21]). In more details, *Service Mosaic* studies some nice properties that allow us to better support the Web Services life-cycle management, which we summarize in the following: (*i*) *compatibility*, which refers to verify if two Web Service Business Processes are fully inter-operable; (*ii*) *replaceability*, which refers to verify if two Web Service Business Processes are fully inter-changeable; (*iii*) *consistency*, which refers to verify if the implementation of a Web Service Business Process is fully compliant with its declarative section. In particular, checking the first two properties (i.e., compatibility and replaceability) shares a common step called *conversion*, which, briefly, transforms a Web Service Business Process into another one,

G. Fortino et al. (Eds.): IDCS 2014, LNCS 8729, pp. 285–299, 2014.

according to a given criterion. It would be clear enough that compatibility and replaceability are the most important properties to be studied when Web Service Business Processes are considered immersed into a reference distributed (Web) scenario. Following this main consideration, in this paper we focus on these properties, and leave the yet-relevant consistency property to further studies.

The whole paradigm proposed by *Service Mosaic* is highly flexible and prone to be extended with emerging functionalities, even not foreseen by original authors. For instance, a fortunate line of research proposes to extend Web Service Business Processes by means of *security and privacy primitives* (e.g., [10]), given the evidence stating that such processes usually inter-operate in "open" distributed environments (e.g., the Web) that naturally incur in the risk of possible *security and privacy breaches* (e.g., [11]). Within this family of processes, security issues and, in particular, *Access Control Policies* (ACP) (e.g., [12]) play a critical role, as they formalize the security policy under which two Web Service Business Processes are allowed to interact (this is also relevant in modern *Clouds* – e.g., [18,19]). As a consequence, in [13,14] authors apply the *Service Mosaic*'s paradigms to so-called *security-aware Web Service Business Process Protocols*, by deriving useful and theoretically-sound results for the protocols describing this class of processes.

In this paper, we provide significant contributions on top of the framework [13,14], via assessing and verifying its reliability on the basis of some well-suited case studies. In more details, as underlying software development tool on top of which evolving our proposed case studies, we make use of *Service Mosaic Protocol* [15], which encompasses *Service Mosaic* components and offers *a complete Java-based software suite for modeling, checking and executing Web Service Business Processes*. We complete our analytical contributions by means of a critical discussion on the advantages and possible extensions of this framework, given through the paper.

The remaining part of the paper is organized as follows. In Section 2, we provide an overview of the framework [13,14] via some illustrative examples that highlight the compatibility and replaceability properties supported by this framework. In Section 3, we provide our case study on the conversion phase. Section 4 contains our case study on the compatibility property. In Section 5, we describe our case study on the replaceability property. Finally, in Section 6, we derive conclusions and future work of our research.

2   A State-of-the-Art Framework for Checking the Compatibility and Replaceability of Security-Aware Web Service Business Processes

In order to illustrate main results of [13,14], here we provide some examples showing the compatibility and replaceability properties of security-aware Web Service Business Process Protocols. Consider Figure 1, where a Web Service Business Process Protocol P_1 is depicted. We make use of this synthetic protocol as baseline instance on top of which the compatibility and replaceability properties (and their checking) are illustrated. A common step for the checking of these properties is represented by the so-called conversion of a protocol P_i into a protocol P_i'. Basically, given a protocol P_i, conversion makes *explicit all* the *implicit transitions* in P_i. The main goal of the conversion phase is that of *preserving the time support of the target protocol* (to be converted), while leaving access control policy aspects out, being these latter useless at this stage. This is finally achieved by adding to the explicit (converted) protocol *suitable, ad-hoc time constraints*, hence achieving the definition of the so-called *Explicitly Timed Web Service Business Process Protocols assigned with ACP* [13,14].

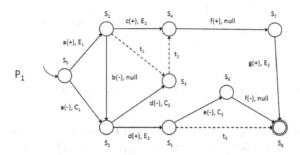

Fig. 1. Example security-aware Web Service Business Process Protocol P_1

In more details, an implicit transition occurs after that a given time constraint expires, whereas an explicit transition occurs after that a message has been sent or received, without the time constraint above. As notation, $T_{i,j,t_k}(S_i, S_j, t_k)$, such that S_i models the source state (of the protocol), S_j the destination state, and t_k a time constraint, denotes an implicit transition and states that T_{i,j,t_k} occurs after a time t_k from the time in which the protocol reaches the state S_i, by making the protocol reaching the state S_j. $T_{i,j,m,A}(S_i, S_j, m, A)$, instead, such that m models a message and A an ACP, which may be represented in terms of *credentials* if m is a sent message, or *policies* if m is a received message ([13,14]), denotes an explicit transition and states that $T_{i,j,m,A}$ occurs after m has been sent or received, being A the applied ACP's credentials or policies.

As shown in Figure 1, P_1 contains both implicit and explicit transitions. Implicit transitions, e.g. $T_{1,3,t_1}(S_1, S_3, t_1)$ and $T_{5,8,3}(S_5, S_8, t_3)$, are labeled with time constraints, whereas explicit transitions, e.g. $T_{0,1,a,E_1}(S_i, S_j, a, E_1)$ and $T_{5,6,e,C_3}(S_i, S_j, e, C_3)$, being, in particular, E_1 policies and C_3 credentials, respectively, are labeled with message specifications and an ACP. Since the presence of explicit transitions could make the Web Service Business Process whose inter-operability is described by P_1 incompatible with other processes, the conversion operation is introduced, and the explicit protocol P_1' is finally obtained (see Figure 2).

As shown in Figure 2, in order to obtain an explicit version of P_1, i.e. P_1', implicit transitions of P_1 are removed and ad-hoc time constraints have been applied to all the explicit transitions of P_1, according to the following rules:

- for each state S_i in P_1 such that an implicit transition $T_{i,j,t_k}(S_i, S_j, t_k)$ originating from it exists, update all the explicit transitions $T_{i,k,m,A}(S_i, S_k, m, A)$, such that $j \neq k$, by means of a time constraint of the form $[0, t_k[$, hence originating the new explicit transition $T_{i,k,m,A,I}(S_i, S_k, m, A, I)$, such that $I = [0, t_k[$;

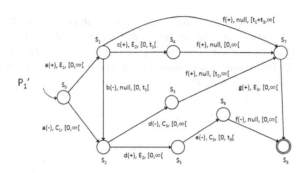

Fig. 2. Explicit version of the protocol P_1 depicted in Figure 1

- for each state S_i in P_1 such that no implicit transitions originating from it exist, update all the explicit transitions $T_{i,j,m,A}(S_i, S_j, m, A)$ by means of a time constraint of the form $[0, \infty[$, hence originating the new explicit transition $T_{i,j,m,A,I}(S_i, S_j, m, A, I)$, such that $I = [0, \infty[$;

- for each explicit transition $T_{i,j,m,A}(S_i, S_j, m, A)$ in P_1 such that a preceding implicit transition $T_{h,i,t_k}(S_h, S_i, t_k)$ or a *path of implicit/explicit transitions* $Y_{h,i,L_k}(S_h, S_i, L_k)$ to S_i exist [13,14], such that $L_k = \sum_{l=0}^{|Y_{h,i,L_k}|} t_{k_i}$ models the "cumulative" time constraint associated to the path (note that only the time constraints of implicit transitions contribute to L_k), add a new explicit transition $T_{h,j,m,A}(S_h, S_j, m, A, I)$, such that $I = [0, L_k[$.

Now, focus the attention on the compatibility checking. Compatibility leans towards verifying whether two protocols can properly interact or not. Before to introduce our running example on compatibility checking, here we introduce another synthetic protocol, namely P_2, which is shown in Figure 3. It should be noted that P_2 is already in the explicit version. In our actual running example, we study the compatibility between P_1 and P_2.

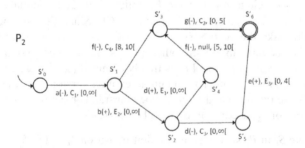

Fig. 3. Example security-aware Web Service Business Process Protocol P_2

According to [13,14], with regards to both compatibility and replaceability checking, it is convenient to express ACP in terms of *Ontologies* (e.g., [16]). In fact, Ontologies turn-out to be particularly suitable as policy specification models, due to the fact that they allow an easier policy management and an augmented protection from sensitive information leaking by avoiding malicious requests (e.g., [17]). In line with this critical finding, Figure 4 shows the Ontology used by the running example, where policies and credentials represent the Ontology concepts. example scenario.

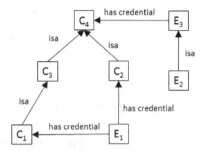

Fig. 4. Ontology on policies and credentials associated to the running example

Given two protocols P_u and P_v, the compatibility checking of P_u and P_v is carried out by means of the so-called *compatibility algorithm* [13,14], which comprises the following two steps.

- *Checking the compatibility of the two protocols in terms of message exchange* – this can be performed by constructing the so-called *product automata* A^P of the two protocols P_u and P_v [10], and checking whether (1), for each state S_x in A^P, there exist two associated states S_i and S_j in P_u and P_v, respectively, and (2) all the outgoing messages from S_i in P_u or S_j in P_v, depending on the fact that S_i corresponds to S_x, or, alternatively, S_j corresponds to S_x, respectively, can be received by the other protocol (P_v and P_u, respectively). If this is the case, then P_u and P_v in terms of message exchange, and the compatibility algorithm can move to the second step, otherwise the algorithm ends since P_u and P_v are not compatible.
- *Checking the compatibility of the two protocols in terms of ACP* – this can be performed by computing the so-called *cumulative credentials* for each transition $T_{ip,jp,mp,Ap}$ of the product automata A^P, denoted by $L_{(C)}$, which contains all the credentials associated to transitions of all the paths from the source state S_{0p} of A^P to S_{jp}, and checking the following property. If, for any interaction between two arbitrary transitions T_{i_1,j_1,m_1,A_1} and T_{i_2,j_2,m_2,A_2} of P_u and P_v, respectively, which is globally captured by $T_{ip,jp,mp,Ap}$ in A^P (hence, $T_{ip,jp,mp,Ap}$ is representative of T_{i_1,j_1,m_1,A_1} and T_{i_2,j_2,m_2,A_2}), the related ACP *policies* $A_1 \equiv E_1$ in P_u and $A_2 \equiv E_2$ in P_v, respectively, are *consistent* with the respective *credentials* in $L_{(C)}$. The consistency here is checked by also inspecting hierarchical relations in the associated Ontology (for instance, focus on the Ontology of Figure 4: E_3 is consistent with C_4 but, due to the Ontology structure, even with C_1, C_2 and C_3.)

To give an example, Figure 5 shows the product automata A^P for the two protocols P_1 and P_2 of the running example (see Figure 1 and Figure 3, respectively).

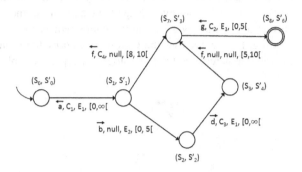

Fig. 5. Product automata of protocols P_1 of Figure 1 and P_2 of Figure 3

Now, focus the attention on the replaceability checking. Replaceability leans towards verifying whether one protocol can be replaced by the other one.

Given two protocols P_u and P_v, the replaceability checking of P_u and P_v is carried out by means of the so-called *replaceability algorithm* [13,14], which works as follows. First, the so-called *intersection automata* A^I of P_u and P_v is built [10]. Then, for each transition T_{i_I,j_I,m_I,A_I} of A^I, the so-called *cumulative policies and credentials*, denoted by $L_{\langle E,C\rangle}$, are computed, by measn of the same method provided for the product automata in the case of credentials. Finally, the following property is verified. If, for any interaction between two arbitrary transitions T_{i_1,j_1,m_1,A_1} and T_{i_2,j_2,m_2,A_2} of P_u and P_v, respectively, which is globally captured by T_{i_I,j_I,m_I,A_I} in A^I (hence, T_{i_I,j_I,m_I,A_I} is representative of T_{i_1,j_1,m_1,A_1} and T_{i_2,j_2,m_2,A_2}), the related ACP *policies or credentials* $A_1 \equiv E_1 \vee A_1 \equiv C_1$ in P_u and $A_2 \equiv E_2 \vee A_2 \equiv C_2$ in P_v, respectively, are *consistent* with the respective *credentials or policies* in $L_{\langle E,C\rangle}$, according to a similar scheme given for the compatibility checking.

To give an example, Figure 6 shows two example protocols P_3 and P_4, whereas Figure 7 shows the intersection automata A^I for such protocols.

3   Conversion of Implicit Security-Aware Web Service Business Process Protocols into Explicit Security-Aware Web Service Business Process Protocols

In this Section, we provide our case study on the conversion phase, on top of the software architecture Service Mosaic Protocol [15]. Figure 8 shows an example protocol P_i adapted from the main on described in [13,14], which is characterized by both implicit and explicit transitions.

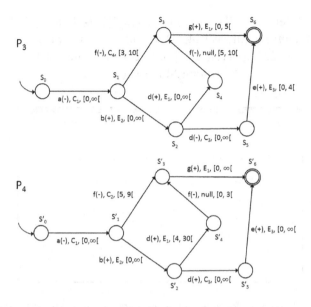

Fig. 6. Two example security-aware Web Service Business Process Protocols P_3 and P_4

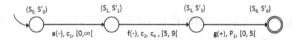

Fig. 7. Intersection automata of protocols P_3 and P_4 of Figure 6

Time constraints associated to transitions are not shown in Figure 8 in terms of labels, but they are shown in the *Properties Tab* of the *Eclipse plug-in* of Service Mosaic Protocol, as follows:

$$T_0: k < 2; T_1: k = 3; T_2: k = 1; T_3: \emptyset; T_4: k = 2; T_5: \emptyset$$

Figure 9 shows the wizard user-interface that implements the conversion process, named as *Web service business converted protocol file*, available to end-users, whereas Figure 10 shows the final result obtained from executing the conversion algorithm over the target protocol P_i, hence obtaining the converted protocol P_i'. Here, implicit transitions have been converted into ad-hoc time constraints on explicit transitions, whose temporal intervals adhere to the following pattern:

$$\text{T-Interval}([0, \infty[)$$

and the final time constraints obtained from the conversion process are the following (note that, for some P_i's implicit transitions, more P_i''s explicit transitions of kind T_h_convk have been ontained):

T_0:T-Interval($[0, 2[$); T_3:T-Interval($[0, 2[$); T_5:T-Interval($[0, \infty[$);
T_3_conv1:T-Interval($[4, 6[$); T_3_conv3:T-Interval($[4, 6[$);
T_5_conv2:T-Interval($[3, \infty[$)); T_5_conv4:T-Interval($[6, \infty[$);
T_5_conv5:T-Interval($[2, \infty[$)

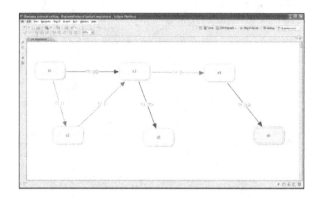

Fig. 8. The example protocol P_i with implicit and explicit transitions for the conversion case study

4   Checking the Compatibility of Security-Aware Web Service Business Process Protocols

In this Section, we provide the second case study of our research on the compatibility checking of two protocols, which we assume to be in their explicit versions, called *b1forProduct.wsprotocol* (see Figure 11) and *b2forProduct.wsprotocol* (see Figure 12).

Time constraints and ACP constraints (which represent credential or policies constraints – see Section 1) associated to transitions of *b1forProduct.wsprotocol* are the following:

$$T_0: \text{P-C}(P_1), \text{T-Interval}([0, 5[); \quad T_2: \text{P-C}(L_1); \quad T_3: \text{T-Interval}([0, 3[);$$
$$T_6: \text{P-C}(Sc_1), \text{T-Interval}([0, \infty[)$$

where, in particular, ACP rules adhere to the following pattern:

$$\text{P-C}(S_i \wedge T_j)$$

such that: (*i*) P-C stands for policy-credential; (*ii*) S_i and T_j model basic credential or policy constraints; (*iii*) $\wedge$ is the AND Boolean conjunction operator.

Fig. 9. Wizard user-interface for the conversion case study

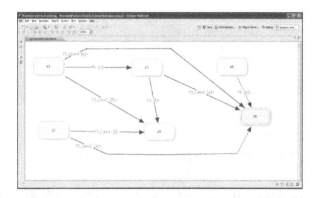

Fig. 10. The explicit version of the protocol P_i of Figure 8, P_i'

For what instead regards *b2forProduct.wsprotocol*, the set of time constrains and ACP constraints for each of the model's transitions are the following:

$$T_8: \text{T-Interval}([0,6[); \; T_{10}: \text{P-C}(L_1 \; \&\& \; P_1); \; T_{11}: \text{P-C}(J_1), \text{T-Interval}([0,3[);$$
$$T_{12}: \text{P-C}(C_1); \; T_{14}: \text{T-Interval}([0,\infty[)$$

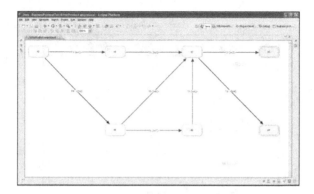

Fig. 11. The example protocol *b1forProduct.wsprotocol*

Figure 13 shows the graphical representation of the Ontology taken as reference for the actual case study, which derives from [13,14]. In more details, in Figure 13 credentials among Ontology concepts are shown as well.

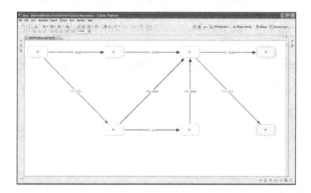

Fig. 12. The example protocol *b2forProduct.wsprotocol*

A wizard user-interface, similar to the one shown in Figure 9, allows the protocol file storing the product automata of the two protocols to be generated, named as *Web service business product protocol file*. Finally, results obtained from executing the compatibility algorithm over the two protocols, i.e. their product automata, are depicted in Figure 14. In more details, time constrains and ACP constraints obtained from the execution of the compatibility algorithm over *b1forProduct.wsprotocol* and *b2forProduct.wsprotocol* (i.e., the constraints associated to the product automata) are the following:

$$T_{24}: \text{P-C}(P_1), \text{T-Interval}([0,5[); \ T_{26}: \text{P-C}(L_1), \text{P-C}(L_1 \text{ \&\& } P_1);$$
$$T_{27}: \text{P-C}(J_1), \text{T-Interval}([0,3[); \ T_{28}: \text{P-C}(C_1); \ T_{29}: \text{P-C}(Sc_1), \text{T-Interval}([0,\infty[)$$

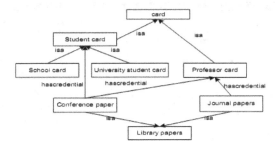

Fig. 13. Ontology adopted for the compatibility checking case study [13,14]

The provided case study clearly demonstrates that the conversion algorithm works as expected, and it also confirms the central role played by the so-called cumulative ACP (see Section 2) in the context of compatibility checking of security-aware Web Service Business Process Protocols. From Section 2, remind that, without loss of generality, given a transition T_i, cumulative ACP for T_i can be defined as the set of security rules obtained from the union of the current ACP and the set of previously-provided credentials (i.e., credentials associated to transitions preceding T_i).

Looking into details, from the provided case study, it follows that *b1forProduct.wsprotocol* requires credential L_1 on transition T_2, but *b2forProduct.wsprotocol* provides credentials L_1 and P_1 on the corresponding transition T_{10}. This is clearly showed by ACP rules on transition T_{26} of the product automata (see Figure 14). It should be noted that, if the two example protocols would be compared without the notion of cumulative ACP, then these protocols would have erroneously be considered as not compatible. Hence, the relevance of the cumulative ACP notion emerges undoubtedly.

5   Checking the Replaceability of Security-Aware Web Service Business Process Protocols

In this Section, we provide the last case study of our research on the replaceability checking of protocols, which properly refers to check whether a protocol P_i can support the same "conversations" of another protocol P_i'. In more details, we investigate the case of *security-aware full replaceability* or *replaceability in terms of intersection automata assigned with ACP* [13,14], which adhere to the class of replaceability termed as *protocol subsumption w.r.t. replaceability*, according to the classification defined by [1,2,3,4,5].

Within this conceptual framework, we introduce two example protocols, namely *b1forIntersection.wsprotocol* (see Figure 15) and *b2forIntersection.wsprotocol* (see Figure 16), respectively.

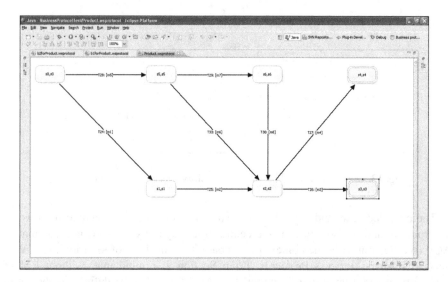

Fig. 14. Product automata obtained from the example protocols *b1ForProduct.wsprotocol* (Figure 11) and *b2ForProduct.wsprotocol* (Figure 12)

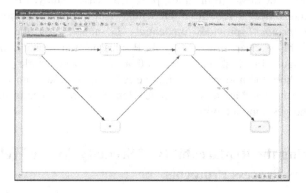

Fig. 15. The example protocol *b1forIntersection.wsprotocol*

For what regards time constraints and ACP constraints associated to transitions of *b1forIntersection.wsprotocol*, they are defined as follows:

$$T_2: \text{P-C}(L_1), \text{T-Interval}([0,5[); \ T_3: \text{P-C}(Sc_1), \text{T-Interval}([0,3[); \ T_4: \text{P-C}(P_1)$$

whereas for the case of *b2forIntersection.wsprotocol*:

$$T_6: \text{P-C}(L_1), \text{T-Interval}([0,5[); \ T_8: \text{T-Interval}([0,5[);$$
$$T_9: \text{P-C}(Sc_1), \text{T-Interval}([0,2[); \ T_{10}: \text{P-C}(P_1); \ T_{11}: \text{P-C}(L_1)$$

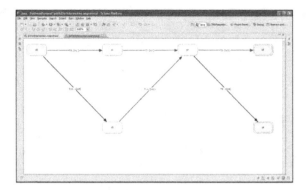

Fig. 16. The example protocol *b2forIntersection.wsprotocol*

Similarly to the case of conversion phase (see Section 3) and compatibility checking (see Section 4), we designed a suitable wizard user-interface supporting the easy construction of the intersection automata (see Section 2), which is similar to the one shown in Figure 9. Finally, Figure 17 shows the intersection automata obtained from the two example protocols. For a better understanding, here we report time constrains and ACP constraints associated to transitions of such automata:

$$T_{48}: \text{P-C}(L_1); T_{50}: \text{P-C}(L_1), \text{T-Interval}([0,5[); T_{51}: \text{P-C}(Sc_1), \text{T-Interval}([0,2[);$$
$$T_{52}: \text{P-C}(P_1); T_{53}: \text{P-C}(L_1)$$

As it follows from the results of replaceability algorithm (see Section 2), *b1forIntersection.wsprotocol* and *b2forIntersection.wsprotocol* are not compatible. Indeed, looking at the definitions of such protocols (see Figure 15 and Figure 16), they are not replaceable due to time restrictions. In fact, the time constraint associated to transition T_3 of *b1forIntersection.wsprotocol* is T-Interval($[0,3[$), whereas the one associated to transition T_9 of *b1forIntersection.wsprotocol* is T-Interval($[0,2[$). Therefore, transition T_3's time constraint is not contained neither equal to transition T_9's time constraint, so that one of the requirements of the replaceability checking is not satisfied. From this analysis, it emerges the central role of the intersection automata in the context of replaceability checking of security-aware Web Service Business Processes.

6   Conclusions and Future Work

Starting from the results of the *Service Mosaic* project [1,2,3,4,5], in this paper we have provided and critically discussed some relevant case studies on top of a successful extension of *Service Mosaic* focusing on the interoperability of so-called security-aware Web Service Business Processes, which deal with security and privacy-preserving aspects of Web Service Business Processes whose structure and functionalities have been dictated by *Service Mosaic*. In particular, our analysis has focused on three critical properties of protocols that describe how such processes

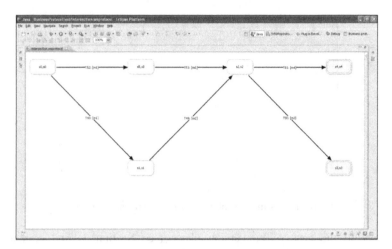

Fig. 17. Intersection automata obtained from the example protocol *b1ForIntersection.wsprotocol* (Figure 15) and *b2ForIntersection.wsprotocol* (Figure 16)

interoperate, namely conversion, compatibility and replaceability. Our results clearly show the effectiveness and the reliability of the framework [13,14]. Future work is actually oriented towards setting an experimental real-life campaign on top of which developing new case studies that aim at further corroborating the promising results obtained with this research experience mainly focusing on synthetic case studies.

References

1. Benatallah, B., Nezhad, H.R.M., Casati, F., Toumani, F., Ponge, J.: Service Mosaic: A Model-Driven Framework for Web Services Life-Cycle Management. IEEE Internet Computing 10(4), 55–63 (2006)
2. Benatallah, B., Hamid, R., Nezhad, H.R.M.: Service Mosaic Project: Modeling, Analysis and Management of Web Services Interactions. In: Proceedings of APCCM, pp. 7–9 (2006)
3. Benatallah, B., Casati, F., Toumani, F.: Representing, Analyzing and Managing Web Service Protocols. Data & Knowledge Engineering 58(3), 327–357 (2006)
4. Nezhad, H.R.M., Benatallah, B., Martens, A., Curbera, F., Casati, F.: Semi-Automated Adaptation of Service Interactions. In: Proceedings of WWW, pp. 993–1002 (2007)
5. Nezhad, H.R.M., Saint-Paul, R., Benatallah, B., Casati, F., Ponge, J., Toumani, F.: Service Mosaic: Interactive Analysis and Manipulation of Service Conversations. In: Proceedings of ICDE, pp. 1497–1498 (2007)
6. Sipser, M.: Introduction to the Theory of Computation. PWS Publishing (1997)
7. Alur, R., Dill, D.L.: A Theory of Timed Automata. Theoretical Computer Science 126(2), 183–235 (1994)
8. Bouyer, P., Markey, N., Ouaknine, J., Worrell, J.B.: On Expressiveness and Complexity in Real-Time Model Checking. In: Aceto, L., Damgård, I., Goldberg, L.A., Halldórsson, M.M., Ingólfsdóttir, A., Walukiewicz, I. (eds.) ICALP 2008, Part II. LNCS, vol. 5126, pp. 124–135. Springer, Heidelberg (2008)

 9. Ponge, J., Benatallah, B., Casati, F., Toumani, F.: Analysis and Applications of Timed Service Protocols. ACM Transactions on Software Engineering and Methodology 19(4), art. no. 11 (2010)
10. Mokhtari-Aslaoui, K., Benbernou, S., Sahri, S., Andrikopoulos, V., Leymann, F., Hacid, M.-S.: Timed Privacy-Aware Business Protocols. International Journal of Cooperative Information Systems 21(2), 85–110 (2012)
11. Hamadi, R., Paik, H.-Y., Benatallah, B.: Conceptual Modeling of Privacy-Aware Web Service Protocols. In: Krogstie, J., Opdahl, A.L., Sindre, G. (eds.) CAiSE 2007. LNCS, vol. 4495, pp. 233–248. Springer, Heidelberg (2007)
12. Samarati, P., de Vimercati, S.C.: Access Control: Policies, Models, and Mechanisms. In: Focardi, R., Gorrieri, R. (eds.) FOSAD 2000. LNCS, vol. 2171, pp. 137–196. Springer, Heidelberg (2001)
13. Elabd, E., Coquery, E., Hacid, M.-S.: Checking Compatibility and Replaceability in Web Services Business Protocols with Access Control. In: Proceedings of ICWS, pp. 409–416 (2010)
14. Elabd, E., Coquery, E., Hacid, M.-S.: From Implicit to Explicit Transitions in Business Protocols: A Semantic-Based Transformation. International Journal of Web Service Research 9(4), 69–95 (2012)
15. Ponge, J., Benatallah, B., Casati, F., Toumani, F.: Fine-Grained Compatibility and Replaceability Analysis of Timed Web Service Protocols. In: Parent, C., Schewe, K.-D., Storey, V.C., Thalheim, B. (eds.) ER 2007. LNCS, vol. 4801, pp. 599–614. Springer, Heidelberg (2007)
16. Fensel, D.: Ontologies: Silver Bullet for Knowledge Management and Electronic Commerce. Springer (2003)
17. Nejdl, W., Olmedilla, D., Winslett, M., Zhang, C.C.: Ontology-Based Policy Specification and Management. In: Gómez-Pérez, A., Euzenat, J. (eds.) ESWC 2005. LNCS, vol. 3532, pp. 290–302. Springer, Heidelberg (2005)
18. Wei, L., et al.: Security and Privacy for Storage and Computation in Cloud Computing. Information Sciences 258, 371–386 (2014)
19. Wei, L., et al.: SecCloud: Bridging Secure Storage and Computation in Cloud. In: Proceedings of ICDCS Workshops, pp. 52–61 (2010)
20. Reza Rahimi, M., et al.: MuSIC: Mobility-Aware Optimal Service Allocation in Mobile Cloud Computing. In: Proceedings of IEEE CLOUD, pp. 75–82 (2013)
21. Sheng, Q.Z., et al.: Web Services Composition: A Decade's Overview. Information Sciences 280, 218–238 (2014)
22. Duan, Q., et al.: A Survey on Service-Oriented Network Virtualization Toward Convergence of Networking and Cloud Computing. IEEE Transactions on Network and Service Management 9(4), 373–392 (2012)

Sensor Networks

A Fatigue Detect System Based on Activity Recognition

Congcong Ma, Wenfeng Li, Jingjing Cao, Shuwu Wang, and Lei Wu

School of Logistics and Engineer, Wuhan University of Technology,
Wuhan, 430077, China
macong01@126.com, {liwf,caojingjing,wangsw,wulei}@whut.edu.cn

Abstract. Fatigue is considered a key factor to accidents and illnesses in our daily life. Detecting fatigue is therefore useful to prevent accidents and keep our body healthy. It is useful to the people who usually sit many hours a day performing office jobs, it can remind people to have a rest and do some exercises, so to help them developing good working habits.

In this paper, we propose a non-invasive way to monitor people's activity. By applying Activity Recognition using Body Sensor Network technologies, we made a smart cushion to monitor people's activities; we acquire pressure data and analyze it in MATLAB to infer whether a subject is suffering fatigue. With the proposed method, we learnt that subjects are getting tired after about an hour only. Experimental results show that pressure data for left-right orientation can clearly judge whether a sitting subject is suffering fatigue.

Keywords: Activity Recognition, Body Sensor Networks, Fatigue Detection, Smart Cushion.

1   Introduction

Fatigue detection is becoming a hot topic in the smart-health domain. Increasing number of people is working in front of visual display terminals (VDTs), such as computer, smartphone or other display terminals, and, in many cases such workers feel fatigue without realizing it or properly addressing it. Fatigue is indeed often wrongly overlooked, because it can lead to mental and physical problems and negatively impact study/work efficiency and safety.

Detecting fatigue of people who always sit in front of VDTs is useful, e.g. to prevent various related illnesses.

It is possible to distinguish two kinds of fatigue: physical fatigue and mental fatigue [1]. The former is due to muscle activity when people perform manual works, the latter is caused by a variety of psychological stressors. In this paper we focused on mental fatigue.

Caused by excessively prolonged labor tasks, mental tension can negatively affect efficiency state. Mental fatigue is the origin of many diseases; if a person perform excessive or heavy overloaded mental work, he/she will undergo long-term fatigue, compromising the correct operation of physiological functions and causing a variety of diseases, and eventually leading to decreased immune system, endocrine disorders,

G. Fortino et al. (Eds.): IDCS 2014, LNCS 8729, pp. 303–311, 2014.

etc. In this case, people easily get diseases such as colds, but also seriously exposed to cardiovascular diseases [2], diabetes, etc. Therefore, fatigue prediction and early detection is of key importance to prevent various medical situations.

According to an U.S. epidemiological survey, among the adult population, about 14% of males and 20% of females suffers symptoms of fatigue performance [3]. Because of work intensity, fatigue illness and even deaths are increasing year by year. Fatigue is the main factor causing adults' body condition decline and chronic illnesses appearance.

Prolonged workload, mental stress, short time resting periods and poor physical activity cause many illnesses even suffer the dangers of karoshi. According to another survey by World Health Organization, about 35% of the world population has suffered fatigue. Since fatigue is usually not associated with other significant symptomatology it is difficult to be properly assessed using traditional clinical examination.

Body Sensor Networks (BSNs) enable to measure many important human physiological characteristics, including physical activity status [4], body temperature [5], muscle activity, heart rate, and brain activity. Based on BSN technology, we can develop many kinds of human-centered applications in diversified domains such as mobile entertainment, health care and fitness [6, 7, 8].

In this paper we formed the assumption that if a person is tired, he/she may become very quiet, or he/she might feel anxiety and conversely become unsettled. Based on this assumption, we analyzed subjects during daily working activities to investigate the difference between the condition of non-fatigue and fatigue. Specifically, we acquired data from a device with pressure sensors to monitor user posture; these data are analyzed to judge whether the user is feeling fatigue. Experimental result confirmed that if a person is tired, he/she often acts as our assumption. With this method, we can predict fatigue earlier and remind people to have a rest or perform proper stretching exercises.

2   Methodology

Activity recognition can be used to recognize basic postures such as standing, sitting, lying and squatting [9]. It can also be used in the field of fatigue detection by analyzing the data of physiological phenomena and activity behavior. Automatic fatigue detection has gained much relevance in the field of car driving; however, researches have not yet been focused on fatigue detection of office workers. The technique to detect driving attention level is essentially the same, so the methods that used in the field of monitor people's status of car driving can also be used to monitor the fatigue condition of office workers.

2.1   Related Work

Hiroshi and Masayuki developed a system to detect fatigue [10] using a camera to monitor people's activity and image processing to analyze driver's facial expressions, to observe the extent of driver's eyes closed and wide open as an alarm of fatigue. Li also proposed an image processing method to classify fatigue-related facial expressions [11]. These approaches have, however, the disadvantage to be influenced by ambient light.

Iampetch S. proposed the use of EEG signal to detect whether people was suffering fatigue [12]. This approach, however, is quite invasive as the user has to wear a device on his/her head to measure the signal of the brain activity.

Patterson used a method based on a three-axis accelerometer sensor to quantity people's activities with the aim of detecting fatigue symptoms [13]. This approach requires the user to wear smart objects too.

2.2   Proposed Method

In this paper, we propose a non-invasive way to monitor people's activity while seated. This method has advantages because it just need to place on the chair a cushion with a suit of embedded pressure sensors.

We use a FSR (Force Sensing Resistor) pressure sensor produced by Interlink Electronics [14]. It is ultra-thin, weight light, and highly accurate. Its' size is 1.75x1.5" (approximately 45x38mm).

As force is applied on the sensing areas, the resistance value of the FSR will be correspondingly altered. The more the forcing power, the smaller the resistance is. This sensor can detect a pressure power from 0 to 20kg. This pressure sensor can be easily fixed and embedded into the cushion textile or foam filling.

As the sitting pressure distribution is closely related to the person sitting posture, in this paper we design a model to distinguish fatigue and non-fatigue based on the sitting posture.

More precisely, we designed a pressure chair cushion based on four FSRs as shown in Fig. 1.

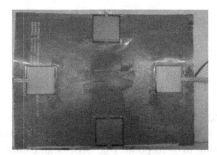

Fig. 1. FSR pressure sensor (left) and cushion equipped with FSR sensors (right)

When a person is sitting on the cushion, the FSR sensors on the cushion can detected the pressure data. If he/she slants to the right, the pressure value of the right sensor will greater than the left sensor. Use the smart cushion, we can measure the value of pressure that caused by our body weight. According to the pressure distribution, we can calculate the center of gravity of body that deviate from the center of the cushion. It can infer that people is sitting upright or swing to an orientation. The sitting posture images can be exampled as in Fig. 2.

Fig. 2. Sitting posture images with the four directions: Left, Right, Forward, Backward

As our system model indicated in Fig. 3(a), four pressure sensors was fixed on the cushion and marked as $fsr1, fsr2, fsr3, fsr4$. The four sensors was evenly placed on the cushion, they have the same distance to the center of the cushion. Pressure sensors' data are marked as F_1, F_2, F_3, F_4 , in the coordinate system we use Z axis to represent the pressure value as shown in Fig. 3(b). Here we use the sensors on X axis to explain our method, as we can indicated that the sensors on the X axis can represent the body posture   lean left and right.

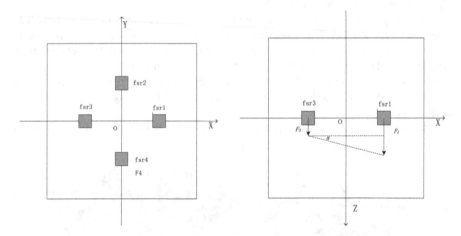

Fig. 3. (a) System model of the sensors in the chair cushion, (b) Propose Method

The minus of F_1 and F_3 can represent the body center of gravity deviate from the Y axis. When people sit on the center of the cushion, the body center of gravity is on the point of zero point. Fig. 3(b) is an example that people lean to the right side, the lean angle is a, and it can be described by the value of F_x .

$$F_x = F_1 - F_3$$

To the same case, the minus of F_2 and F_4 can represent the body center of gravity deviate from the X axis.

$$F_y = F_2 - F_4$$

2.3   System Architecture

In this section, we propose our system architecture of the posture recognition system based on Body Sensor Networks, the system architecture is depicted in Fig .4. The system is composed of several cushions with pressure sensors, the raw data was collected to the central coordinator for processing.

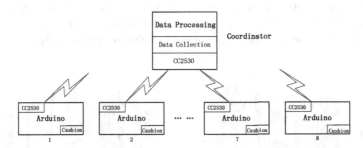

Fig. 4. Fatigue Detection System Architecture Based on BSNs

Each sensor node is composed of three modules: cushion module (we use the FSR sensors to acquire the raw data), processing module (we use Arduino board to process the data from the FSR) and transmitting module (we use CC2530 to send the signals to the coordinator).

The processing module of each sensor node is an Arduino MEGA 2560 MCU, it has the function of low energy consumption, high sampling rate and high processing speed, so it can be widely used in the field of sensor data acquisition and industrial automation. The sensor data is collected and sent to the coordinator node (i.e. a computer or smart phone acting as the BSNs coordinator) through the wireless communication use CC2530. The coordinator is in charge of further data processing and giving the results of the human posture recognition.

3   Experiments

In this paper, we mainly focused on two directions: F_x (the pressure force between left and right), F_y (the pressure force between front and back).

There is an important point of educational psychology "the adolescent can continue focus the attention about 10 to 30 minutes, adult can continue focus attention about 30 to 50 minutes", that's why there is only 45 minutes of a lesson, even the adult's classroom is not exceed an hour.

In our experiments, we found out the subject gets tired after about an hour of working activity. The experiment were carried out on 4 subjects working at computers. The average age is 24. To avoid any bias, we requested subjects to refrain from caffeine for 4 hours before taking the experiment and alcohol for 24 hours.

As the participant sits on the chair, he/she work just as usual for a whole duration of two hours. The smart cushion was placed at the center of the chair, people was sitting on it to cover every sensor, in order to make each sensor can detect the value of the pressure.

The smart cushion acquires pressure sensory data, and the sampling frequency is 20Hz. We eventually analyzed the data in MATLAB.

We have collected 66 thousand samples for analyzing. Since the cushion pressure data produced by people didn't make great changes in one second, we calculate the mean value of every 20 data, i.e., every second. In Fig. 5-Fig. 6, the axis-X utilize one second as a unit, and the axis-Y represents the force value of the pressure on the cushion, it was measured by voltage. The compared results are shown in Fig.5-Fig.6.

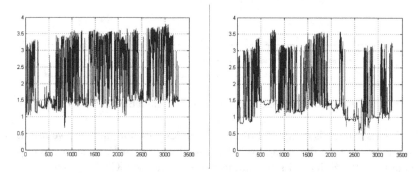

Fig. 5. Fluctuations of F_x (a) in the first hour, (b) in the second hour

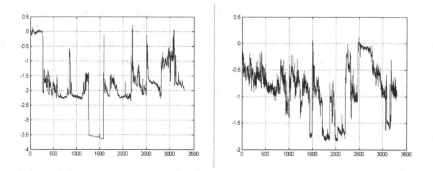

Fig. 6. Fluctuations of F_y (a) in the first hour, (b) in the second hour

Fig. 5(a) shows the lateral pressure data of every second in the first hour, we can see that at the beginning of nearly 15 minutes, people do not work in the state. Later people is working in the state, the pressure data is steady. Fig. 5(b) shows the pressure data of the second hour. After about an hour later, people has suffering a short period of fatigue. Then people still working as normal, after about 90 minutes people will suffering a bit long period of fatigue.

Fig. 6 shows the frontal pressure data of the cushion. Comparing the two figures, there are no clear signal to infer whether people is suffering fatigue.

For the sake of graphical clearness, in the following we choose data of a time segment of 5 minutes (thus containing about 6000 samples) about one person. The axis-X represent the sample data we have collected, and the axis-Y represent the value of the pressure on the cushion, it was measured by voltage.

We have interview the subject after two hours of work, he said he has great efficient at the beginning of working, after worked for an hour, he's suffering fatigue. So in the following pictures, we choose two segments of period to analyze. In each of the following figures, plots on the left are referred to the beginning of the experiment (working period from 10th minute to the 15th), while plots on the right corresponds to a working period from 70th minute to the 75th.

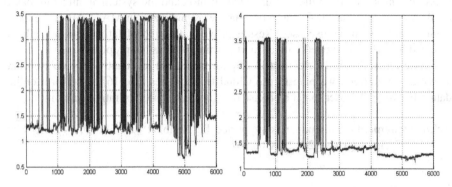

Fig. 7. Fluctuations of F_x (a) at the beginning, (b) an hour later

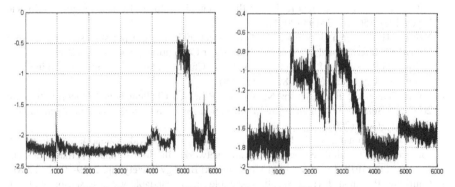

Fig. 8. Fluctuations of F_y (a) at the beginning, (b) an hour later

Specifically, Fig. 7(a) shows lateral pressure data of the cushion. Compared with Fig. 7(a), Fig. 7(b) shows the activity level after over an hour: we can see that the activity level is lower with respect to the beginning; we can infer that people is suffering fatigue.

Fig. 8 depicts frontal pressure of the cushion: in this case there are not clear changes in the signal.

Through the analysis of the two sets of data we know that the subject is initially active on the chair (pressure data fluctuates) while starts gradually to move less on the chair (pressure data are more stable to a constant value) as the fatigue appears and he/she might stay still or rely on the back of the chair.

4   Conclusion

On the basis of our results, we know that pressure data on front-back chair direction is not useful in determining user fatigue, but the pressure data from the sides of the chair can be effectively used to detect fatigue condition. The experimental results describe that when users are suffering fatigue their posture is stable and with lower activity.

In this paper, firstly, the mental fatigue experiment was designed and the hardware of smart cushion was introduced. Secondly, the proposed method was used to acquire pressure sensor data from the instrumented cushion and the system architecture based on BSNs was introduced. Furthermore, data were analyzed in MATLAB and experiment results have been discussed. Results prove that a kind of fatigue can actually be detected by a chair equipped with a smart cushion such as the proposed one.

Future research will be devoted to acquire more data to quantify people's normal activities; in addition we plan to use Cloud technologies [15, 16] to perform online data processing, in order to get a precise real-time estimation of fatigue condition.

Acknowledgments. This paper is supported by National "Twelfth Five-Year" Plan for R&D Technology (No.2012BAJ05B07).

References

1. Lal, S., Craig, A.: A critical review of the psychophysiology of driver fatigue. Biological Psychology 55(3), 173–194 (2001)
2. Nakane, H., Toyama, J., Kudo, M.: Fatigue detection using a pressure sensor chair. In: 2011 IEEE International Conference on Granular Computing, pp. 490–495 (2011)
3. Holmes, G.P., Kaplan, J.E., Gantz, N.M., et al.: Chronic fatigue syndrome: a working case definition. Ann Intern. Med., 387–389 (1988)
4. Lo, B., Yang, G.: Body Sensor Networks – Research Challenges and Opportunities. In: 2007 IET Seminar on Antennas and Propagation for Body-Centric Wireless Communications, pp. 26–32 (2007)
5. Kuroda, M., Tamura, Y., Kohno, R., Tochikubo, O.: Empirical evaluation of zero-admin authentication for vital sensors in body area networks. In: 30th Annual International Conference of the IEEE Engineering in Medicine and Biology Society, pp. 2349–2352 (2008)
6. Chulsung, P., Chou, P.H.: Eco: ultra-wearable and expandable wireless sensor platform. In: International Workshop on Wearable and Implantable Body Sensor Networks, pp. 165–168 (2006)
7. Bellifemine, F., Fortino, G., Giannantonio, R., Gravina, R., Guerrieri, A., Sgroi, M.: SPINE: A domain-specific framework for rapid prototyping of WBSN applications. Software Practice and Experience 41(3), 237–265 (2011)
8. Fortino, G., Giannantonio, R., Gravina, R., Kuryloski, P., Jafari, R.: Enabling Effective Programming and Flexible Management of Efficient Body Sensor Network Applications. IEEE Transactions on Human-Machine Systems 43(1), 115–133 (2013)
9. Li, W., Bao, J., Fu, X., Fortino, G., Galzarano, S.: Human Postures Recognition Based on D-S Evidence Theory and Multi-sensor Data Fusion. In: 2012 12th IEEE/ACM International Symposium on Cluster, Cloud and Grid Computing (CCGrid), May 13-16, pp. 912–917 (2012)

10. Ito, T., Mita, S., Kozuka, K., Nakano, T., Yamamoto, S.: Driver blink measurement by the motion picture processing and its application to drowsiness detection. In: 5th IEEE International Conference on Intelligent Transportation Systems, pp. 168–173 (2002)
11. Xing, L., Guang, H., Guangteng, M., Yanshan, C.: A new method for detecting fatigue driving with camera based on OpenCV. In: International Conference on Wireless Communications and Signal Processing, pp. 1–5 (2011)
12. Iampetch, S., Punsawad, Y., Wongsawat, Y.: EEG-based mental fatigue prediction for driving application. In: Biomedical Engineering International Conference, pp. 1–5 (2012)
13. Patterson, M., McGrath, D., Caulfield, B.: Using a tri-axial accelerometer to detect technique breakdown due to fatigue in distance runners: A preliminary perspective. In: Annual International Conference of the IEEE Engineering in Medicine and Biology Society, pp. 6511–6514 (2011)
14. http://www.interlinkelectronics.com/FSR406.php
15. Fortino, G., Di Fatta, G., Pathan, M., Vasilakos, A.V.: Cloud-Assisted Body Area Networks: State-of-the-Art and Future Challenges. ACM Wireless Networks, 1–20 (to appear, 2014)
16. Fortino, G., Parisi, D., Pirrone, V., Di Fatta, G.: BodyCloud: A SaaS Approach for Community Body Sensor Networks. Future Generation Computer Systems 35(6), 62–79 (2014)

Modelling the Performance of a WSN with Regard to the Physical Features Exhibited by the Network[*]

Declan T. Delaney and Gregory M.P. O'Hare

Clarity: Center for Sensor Web Technologies,
School of Computer Science and Informatics
University College Dublin,
Dublin, Ireland
{declan.delaney,gregory.ohare}@ucd.ie

Abstract. Wireless Sensor Networks(WSNs) have matured to a point where they present a realistic technology for monitoring non critical systems in industrial, office and domestic environments. This in turn will lead to an increased number of applications using WSN technology, each requiring a unique response from the underlying network. Due to the nature of WSN communications these different network requirements are achieved using a variety of communication tools. With ever increasing number and complexity of tools available it becomes difficult to choose which tool is best suited for an application in a given deployment.

In this paper we introduce a procedure to model the WSN network based on its physical features with the aim to give insight into the best solution for a particular deployment. We determine how each physical feature effects the ability of a communication solution to provide a quality of service for an application. We build a model of the network based on these physical features. The model is then tested to determine if it can be effectively used to compare communication solutions. We examine the model, built on simulation data, using three network solutions each based on the RPL routing protocol. Each solution differs in choice of routing metric with ETX, ETX-NH and ETT used in the comparisons. Each solution is tested over a range of physical characteristics which describe a network.

1 Introduction

WSNs presents both a cost benefit over wired solutions and a platform to develop new services for many application spaces [5,11]. This presents a technology ripe for increased industry adoption. With increasing industry attention a host of WSN applications are expected to enter the market.

However, introducing large numbers of new applications over a wide range of deployments presents a challenge using currently used processes. Due to the

---

[*] This work is supported by Science Foundation Ireland under grant 07/CE/I1147. The authors would like to thank the reviewers for their insightful comments.

G. Fortino et al. (Eds.): IDCS 2014, LNCS 8729, pp. 312–324, 2014.

complex nature of WSN dynamics, selecting the network tools which best facilitate the necessary requirements for the application is a difficult task. Current practices deal with this in one of three ways: *(i)* implementing a communication solution for the application based on previous experience but with no guarantee it will fulfil requirements for a particular deployment, *(ii)* testing each network deployment with a number of possible solutions and selecting the solution which best fits the set of requirements, or *(iii)* design of the network based on a communication solution with supervision necessary throughout the networks lifetime [18]. Most or all of these solutions require two aspects which introduce difficulties for production at scale:

- *Expert network knowledge is needed to develop applications.* The developer must understand the mechanisms involved in the communication solution and what network response they might induce for a given deployment. This need for expert knowledge is a concern expressed in [17].
- *Each deployment requires extensive testing or setup and monitoring.* Testing or monitoring each deployment introduces additional cost which may prove prohibitive for home and office applications in particular.

This paper suggests that WSN communications can be modelled using key physical characteristics of the network which define the response a communication technique elicits from the network. Basing a model on the physical features that are easily obtained from a network deployment is key to reducing the amount of testing required to characterise a deployment. The model can then be used to advise on the best communication solution for a given set of requirements in a particular deployment. The goal of this is to reduce the need for extensive knowledge for application developers and to greatly reduce the amount of testing required on individual networks before deployment. The paper presents a process for testing and evaluating WSN communication solutions in order to build a model which can be used for useful comparison. The process consists of three phases:

1. *Testing solution set.*
2. *Response modelling.*
3. *Response matching.*

The process results in a system described in figure 1, whereby the most suitable solution is obtained by simply entering a number of variables into the system.

This system is highly dependant on how well a network can be modelled. A number of challenges arise, however, when attempting to perform experiments which model a WSN for this process.

- Many physical features exist which may effect the response of a solution. We wish to build the simplest model, with the fewest features. This set should also consist of the physical features which effect the greatest influence over the response. Determining this set is in itself challenging for two reasons: *(i)* Each communication solution reacts uniquely to the physical features of the network. Defining a set that incorporates the main influences for all

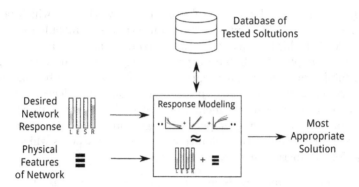

Fig. 1. The resultant system deriving from the testing process. The system requires two inputs: the network requirements(Latency, Energy efficiency, Stability, Reliability), and the physical features of the deployment we wish to find a communication solution for.

    solutions becomes more difficult. *(ii)* Removing features from the set may leave certain response types not covered by the model.

- Even with extensive testing on a given deployment it remains difficult to guarantee a level of QoS for a WSN. Determining in absolute terms how a solution will perform on a particular deployment remains difficult even with effective modelling.
- The chosen features must be those which are easily obtained from the network in order to minimise the required testing on each network before deployment.

The physical features used for testing are carefully chosen to ensure they encapsulate the main proponents determining the network response for each communication solution. In order to do this we test a number of different solutions, based on the RPL protocol, over a wide range of physical features. We evaluate the extent of the effect each feature plays in shaping the response, determining which features are most prominent.

    Using linear regression techniques over experimental data we build a model that represents the response of a network. The eventual model will present heuristics which inform the developer. The heuristics can be used in the form: *Solution A* shows *effect on metric B* for *physical scenario C*, eg. *ETX* shows *superior packet reliability* for networks with *network radius greater than 5 hops*. In summary we make the following contributions in this paper:

- Define a set of features of a physical network that are best disposed to characterise a response from the network over a number of communication solutions.
- build a model for each communication solution which presents the trends seen in the network response, in terms of latency, reliability, energy efficiency and stability, as each physical feature changes.
- Test the model and compare communication solutions so that the findings can be used to direct decision making in future deployments.

The remainder of the paper is structured with the following section detailing the work in the field relating to both WSN systems and modelling techniques. Section 3 discusses the set of physical features used to characterise the network with section 4 detailing the process involved in testing the feature set. Section 5 introduces the techniques used to model the network using physical feature data set and provides an evaluation of the models accuracy. The final section presents a conclusion to the work and furnishes possible future work for the method.

2   Related Work

Two related fields of WSN research coalesce within this paper. The first pertains to an overall system that introduces another layer of abstraction away from the network for the benefit of an application developer. The second pertains to the modelling of a WSN network. As both research fields exhibit a rich body of work the previous and related work for each are discussed separately.

WSN Systems. A huge body of work is available with regard to WSN systems. We will describe a few of the major contributions that lead us to the work presented in this paper. The advent of modular OSs such as contiki and TinyOS allowed application developers to "plug in" different network solutions based on their applications needs. Various additional layers such as chameleon [10] were introduced so that MAC layer protocol could be easily interchangeable with routing layer protocol to create highly tailored communication solutions. Despite the mechanism for implementing a highly tailored solutions becoming more feasible, the ability to choose the most appropriate solution remained difficult. Communication solutions are tested and evaluated using disparate processes leaving results that require extensive WSN knowledge to interpret and are unsuitable for comparison.

Some solutions exist that require little or no WSN knowledge. The WirelessHart [18] system however is not self organised and requires extensive network setup and network management which is only suitable for industrial applications. The Routing Protocol for Low power and lossy networks(RPL) [20] represents an industry standard solution that can be highly tailored for an applications needs. Many of RPLs capabilities as a protocol are untested leaving little scope for extensive comparison.

Network Modelling. A survey of modelling techniques is undertaken by Jacaub et. al. [13] detailing the type and scope of modelling available for WSNs. The models range from modelling node components [8,3,14], to channel modelling [19], to whole system modelling [7]. The node based techniques aim to model all components to present a layer of abstraction from particular architecture or operating systems upon which applications can be designed. The modelling approach for the entire system presented in the survey focuses again on component analysis and how each component works together without eluding to how different components can effect the overall network performance.

A number of techniques use Markov chains to model the link and route behaviour within a network [12,1] with a focus on network performance. Kamthe et. al. [12] present a fine grained model of WSN links using a multi level approach to model both long and short term dynamics on the links. Empirical data is used when building the model and the approach proves effective for modelling packet reception rates over a range of link factors including channel fading and packet frequency. Chiasserini and Garetto [1] present a network model based on Markov chains. The approach is agnostic of routing protocol used but assumes a consistent protocol throughout. The system consists of three individual components: the sensor model, the network model and the interference model. The network model is based on a queueing network where each sensor holds a buffer of packets to be forwarded. The model does not consider the possibility of dropped packets focusing solely on energy cost and time delay through each queue. The model proves effective at determining time delay of packets through the network. However, as reliability is considered a vital evaluation metric, the proposed model cannot be used for direct comparison of communication solutions.

A fundamental difference exists between the modelling suggested in the literature and the modelling undertaken in this paper. The literature describes a number of techniques to determine a generic model of a WSN usually based on component or link characteristics. The models presented are useful for higher level application development or even improving simulation precision for WSN. This paper describes a method to determine a performance model of specific communication solutions based on physical characteristics of a network. The benefit of which is to directly compare solutions without the need for extensive testing or WSN specific knowledge. With the exception of [12], all models presented in the literature are based on theoretical reasoning where as the models presented in this paper are derived explicitly from empirical testing data.

3   Physical Features

A key proponent to the success of the proposed system lies in the physical features chosen to model the network response. A large limiting factor applies to any feature which may be used. This states that any feature must be easily harvested from the network to minimise the amount of testing on each deployment. We refine this further to state that features must be available to simple packet probing contained within the networks own infrastructure negating the need for additional debugging tools. This allows the possibility of a fully functional feature set to be garnered from a connected remote location, further reducing the cost of testing a deployment. With this constraint in mind we define a feature set consisting of:

- Primary
    1. Size of network (number of nodes in the network).
    2. Network density (average over node densities).
    3. Network scale (average over individual node diameters).
    4. Channel quality.

- Secondary
  1. Network density (standard deviation).
  2. Network scale (standard deviation).

While this does not constitute an exhaustive set of features, it does satisfy our main constraint and provides results which validate the suggested system. Figure 2 illustrates these features with further discussion on each provided.

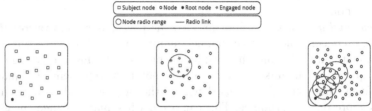

(a) Size is 22: Total number of nodes that constitute the network.

(b) Node density, 6: Number of nodes within communication range.

(c) Node diameter, 4: Minimum number of hops necessary to reach the root.

(d) Illustrating a high standard deviation in terms of network density. This scenario can occur when a number of highly sensed environments exist with sparsely sensed environments within the same network.

(e) Illustrating a high standard deviation with regard to network scale. This occurs commonly within buildings when nodes in geographically spaced rooms exist on the same network.

Fig. 2. Illustration of the manifestation of the physical features in the network

The *size*, *density* and *scale* are linked, with each feature dependant on the other two. Eg., if density and network scale are both high, the network size must be large or, high density with low number of nodes would indicate a low scale. The dependency is defined in table 1 outlying the Pearson correlation [15] between each variable. These facets also represent the main aspects of the network

Table 1. Pearson correlation between dependent variables

Variable pair	ρ
Density - Scale	-0.5493
Size - Density	8.9518e-04
Scale - Size	0.5843

topology. Depending on the application the size can greatly effect the amount of packets sent in the network. Density effects the channel contention with scale effecting hop count in the network greatly affecting latency, reliability and energy efficiency in the network. Taking the average density and scale over the whole network gives a good insight into the network topology but does not present a full picture. The scenarios shown in Figures 2d and 2e are common and cannot be expressed using node averages. The standard deviation then becomes important to determine these features. A taxonomy of the network composing of these features is easily obtained by each node sending its list of neighbours to a centralised point.

The *channel quality* is of importance to the packet reception ratio(PRR) on each link. Increasing the average channel quality across the network will increase PRR dramatically affecting the evaluation metrics. Taking an average of the channel quality of all links to a node may not fully represent the quality of the channels that actually get used within the network and as a result may not fully represent performance. This can occur when many "fringe" neighbours appear to a node, none of which are chosen for communication. A more accurate description of the used channel can be achieved by also using the best quality channel available to each node. A number of measurements are used to assess channel quality including LQI and RSSI. Such measurements are available using the CC2420 chipset synonymous with WSN communications.

4   Testing

In order to validate the proposed system and determine if physical features are fit for the purpose of modelling the response of a network a number of experiments were undertaken. The purpose of the experiments was to provide data to build a network response model for a number of different communication solutions. The goal was to present an easy form for compassion between the communication solutions. We measured the response of the network in terms of four evaluation metrics: reliability, latency, efficiency and stability. Reliability is the measure of how many sent packets get received at the root as a percentage. Latency is an average over each node in the network. The nodes latency is the average time a packet, originating from that node, takes to reach the root. Efficiency is measured in packets sent. This includes all application packets forwarded through the network. Stability is measured as the number of route changes to occur in the network during the experiment.

Experiments were conducted on the TOSSIM simulator with TinyOS used as the sensor platform for each. Each experiment was run in simulation for a network time of one hour with each node in the network sends a packet to the root each minute. The RPL routing protocol was used as the routing protocol for all experiments. RPL is fast becoming a new standard for WSN protocol and represents the state of the art for industry deployment. Three distinct solutions were implemented using RPL by using three different metrics to calculate routes: Expected Transmissions(ETX) [2], Expected Transmissions with Neighbourhood

Heuristics(ETX-NH) [4][6] and Expected Transmission Time(ETT) [9]. As neither RSSI or LQI is available in simulation to measure the channel quality across the network two different noise traces were used to vary the quality of the channel. The traces are a set of real noise traces taken from the Meyer library at Stanford University. The "Meyer light" trace represents minimal interference noise while the "Meyer heavy" trace represents a more difficult communication scenario.

Figures 3, 4, 5 and 6 display the raw data collected from the experiments. Figures 3, 4 and 5 show the network response for each solution as the density, scale and size of the network vary under the light trace. Figure 6 shows how the network response changes when the heavy trace is used. Data for the standard deviation while used in modelling is not shown for brevity.

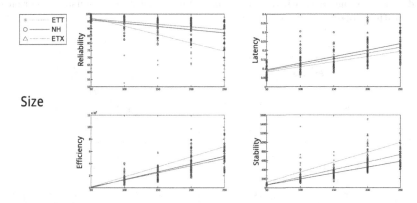

Fig. 3. Network response from each solution as size varies. Tests examined the response of the network with size 50, 100, 150, 200 and 250 nodes in the network.

Figure 3 shows all evaluation metrics following a general trend towards poorer results as size increases. Reliability and stability for both ETX and ETX-NH are well defined as size varies with latency and efficiency showing poor correlation.

Figure 4 shows a large impact on both reliability and latency effected by the change in density for all communication solutions. Neither efficiency nor stability are affected greatly by a change in density, however, density still proves a important tool for comparing each solution with regard to efficiency and stability. Each solution presents significant performance difference in terms of stability using density to compare solutions with NH presenting marked improvements over the other solutions. Both NH and ETX present an improvement over ETT with regard to network efficiency.

High correlation between scale and each metric performance is seen from figure 5. This presents scale as a good indicator of how well a solution might perform in the network. It remains difficult to distinguish between solutions at small scales however higher contrast emerges as scale increases. A particular nuance with reliability is noticed for ETT over increasing scale. ETT shows

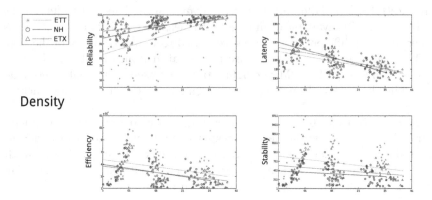

Fig. 4. The average network density is used for plotting. The density experienced during testing range from 5 to 29 nodes.

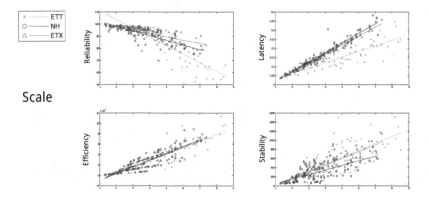

Fig. 5. Scale is measured as the average diameter for each node. The scale ranges from 1.2 to 8 hops.

improved reliability over both competitors for scale less than 4.5 hops. Over this threshold however ETT performs poorly in comparison. This may result from an error in implementation rather than a fault inherent in the metric itself. ETX handles increasing scale more gracefully with regard to reliability.

Figure 6 presents each solutions performance under light and heavy channel interference. As expected, degraded channel quality has a significant effect on network reliability. Stability and latency are also heavily effected. It is clear that there are many insights to be garnered from the data presented. Certainly, the physical features chosen present a strong case for network performance characterisation visually. It is important that the performance can be modelled efficiently using the physical features for the purpose of solution comparison.

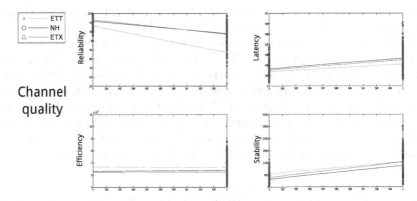

Fig. 6. The quality of the channel is determined via the noise trace used in the simulation. The noise trace represents light or heavy noise interference.

5   Modelling

The model is built with the statistical package R [16] using the data taken
from simulation. We use multiple linear regression to build each facet of the
model. For each solution we use least squares linear regression to model how
each metric responds over the set of physical features. Each physical feature
is deemed an individual predictor variable with each of the evaluation metrics
acting as response variable. Performing a T-test we determine the features that
constitute a significant role in shaping the response for each metric. Table 2
highlights these significant features.

Table 2. Showing the significant predictor variables for modelling the response of each
evaluation metric as determined by a T-test

Communication solution	Evaluation metric	Predictor variables					
		Density	Scale	Size	Density (sd)	Scale (sd)	Channel quality
NH	reliability	*	***				***
	Latency		***	**		*	***
	Efficiency		***	***	*		*
	Stability		*	**			***
ETX	Reliability	**	**	***			***
	Latency	**	***	**			***
	Efficiency		***	***	**	*	***
	Stability		**	***			***
ETT	Reliability		***	***		***	***
	Latency		**			**	***
	Efficiency		***	***		***	
	Stability		*	***			***

* p-value < 0.05, ** p-value < 0.01, *** p-value < 0.001

The table shows the importance of scale, size and the communication channel in determining the response for nearly all cases. These individual models are used to determine whether the proposed approach can reliably determine the correct solution to use in a network given a set of requirements. In order to achieve this we break the problem down into a set of smaller problems, asking whether we can determine an ordered list of performance capabilities per metric for each solution, i.e. for any given set of physical features the model determines the order of the solution performance from best to worst for each evaluation metric. Table 3 shows how accurate the model is at determining the placement for each metric on test data obtained from the TOSSIM simulator.

Table 3. Model accuracy over a test data set. The table shows the accuracy at determining the top (1), middle (2), and worst(3) performing solutions for each metric.

	Reliability	Latency	Efficiency	Stability
1	76.68%	85.7%	50.43%	78.25%
2	71.8%	61.92%	55.7%	63.25 %
3	81.39%	77.95%	59.81%	67.88%

Despite using simple regression tools to build our model, we achieve up to 85% accuracy at predicting a solutions performance with regard to the other two tested solutions. The prediction accuracy is not uniform over all metrics however, with accurately predicting efficiency proving most difficult. The results present a positive outlook for the prospect of using the physical features of the network to compare communication solutions to find the best fit for a set of requirements.

6   Conclusion and Future Work

This paper presents a case for using the physical features of a network as a basis to model the response of a communication solution in terms of reliability, latency, efficiency and stability. The purpose of the model is to provide a tool for application developers to help choose the most appropriate communication solution for a deployment without the need for extensive WSN knowledge or prior testing of the network deployment. The model uses linear regression over a set of easily extracted physical features to predict the response of the network. A linear regression model is built for each response metric desired in the network per communication solution. Using these models, direct comparison between solutions is achievable. Training and testing the model is performed on simulation data using three distinct solutions each using the RPL routing protocol. Evaluation on a test set demonstrates an accuracy of up to 85% when comparing these solutions to determine the best performance for a given evaluation metric when using the model. This research shows some promise for using physical features to model a network response. As the list of physical features used for modelling can not be considered exhaustive, future work will include testing a wider set of physical features to determine their significance on network response. Testing and evaluation on real network nodes is also necessary to provide data to build increasingly more sophisticated models for more accurate prediction.

With additional testing and increasingly more effective models in place, this method may be fit for use within a larger system aimed at realising the automatic network. The automatic network aims to adopt a suitable communication solution for a deployment without the need for extensive testing or expert knowledge with the method described in this paper providing a critical role in the system.

References

1. Chiasserini, C.F., Garetto, M.: Modeling the performance of wireless sensor networks. In: INFOCOM 2004. Twenty-third AnnualJoint Conference of the IEEE Computer and Communications Societies, vol. 1, p. 231 (March 2004)
2. De Couto, D.S.J., Aguayo, D., Bicket, J., Morris, R.: A high-throughput path metric for multi-hop wireless routing. In: Proceedings of the 9th Annual International Conference on Mobile Computing and Networking, MobiCom 2003, pp. 134–146. ACM, New York (2003)
3. Dearle, A., Balasubramaniam, D., Lewis, J., Morrison, R.: A component-based model and language for wireless sensor network applications. In: 32nd Annual IEEE International Computer Software and Applications, COMPSAC 2008, pp. 1303–1308 (July 2008)
4. Delaney, D.T., Higgs, R., O'Hare, G.M.P.: A stable routing framework for tree-based routing structures in wsns. IEEE Sensors Journal PP(99), 1–15 (2014)
5. Delaney, D.T., O'Hare, G.M.P., Ruzzelli, A.G.: Evaluation of energy-efficiency in lighting systems using sensor networks. In: BuildSys 2009, pp. 61–66. ACM, New York (2009)
6. Delaney, D.T., Xu, L., O'Hare, G.M.P.: Spreading the load in a tree type routing structure. In: Proceedings of the IEEE 22nd International Conference on Computer Communications and Networks (ICCCN 2013). IEEE (2013)
7. Diaz, M., Garrido, D., Llopis, L., Rubio, B., Troya, J.: A component framework for wireless sensor and actor networks. In: IEEE Conference on Emerging Technologies and Factory Automation, ETFA 2006, pp. 300–307 (September 2006)
8. Dietterle, D., Ryman, J., Dombrowski, K., Kraemer, R.: Mapping of high-level sdl models to efficient implementations for tinyos. In: Euromicro Symposium on Digital System Design, DSD 2004, pp. 402–406 (August 2004)
9. Draves, R., Padhye, J., Zill, B.: Routing in multi-radio, multi-hop wireless mesh networks. In: Proceedings of the 10th Annual International Conference on Mobile Computing and Networking, MobiCom 2004, pp. 114–128. ACM, New York (2004), http://doi.acm.org/10.1145/1023720.1023732
10. Dunkels, A., Österlind, F., He, Z.: An adaptive communication architecture for wireless sensor networks. In: Proceedings of the 5th International Conference on Embedded Networked Sensor Systems, SenSys 2007, pp. 335–349. ACM Press, New York (2007), http://doi.acm.org/10.1145/1322263.1322295
11. Furtado, H., Trobec, R.: Applications of wireless sensors in medicine. In: MIPRO, 2011 Proceedings of the 34th International Convention, pp. 257–261 (May 2011)

12. Kamthe, A., Carreira-Perpiñán, M.A., Cerpa, A.E.: M&M: multi-level Markov model for wireless link simulations. In: Proceedings of the 7th ACM Conference on Embedded Networked Sensor Systems, SenSys 2009, pp. 57–70. ACM, New York (2009)

13. Khalil Jacoub, J., Liscano, R., Bradbury, J.: A survey of modeling techniques for wireless sensor networks. In: SENSORCOMM 2011, The Fifth International Conference on Sensor Technologies and Applications, pp. 103–109 (2011)

14. Mozumdar, M.M.R., Gregoretti, F., Lavagno, L., Vanzago, L., Olivieri, S.: A framework for modeling, simulation and automatic code generation of sensor network application. In: 5th Annual IEEE Communications Society Conference on Sensor, Mesh and Ad Hoc Communications and Networks, SECON 2008, pp. 515–522 (June 2008)

15. Pearson, K.: Mathematical contributions to the theory of evolution. iii. regression, heredity, and panmixia. Philosophical Transactions of the Royal Society of London. Series A, Containing Papers of a Mathematical or Physical Character 187, 253–318 (1896), http://www.jstor.org/stable/90707

16. R Core Team: R: A Language and Environment for Statistical Computing. R Foundation for Statistical Computing, Vienna, Austria (2013), http://www.R-project.org/, ISBN 3-900051-07-0

17. Rubio, B., Diaz, M., Troya, J.M.: Programming approaches and challenges for wireless sensor networks. In: International Conference on Systems and Networks Communication, p. 36 (2007)

18. Song, J., Han, S., Mok, A., Chen, D., Lucas, M., Nixon, M.: Wirelesshart: Applying wireless technology in real-time industrial process control. In: Real-Time and Embedded Technology and Applications Symposium, RTAS 2008, pp. 377–386. IEEE (2008)

19. Vasilevski, M., Beilleau, N., Aboushady, H., Pecheux, F.: Efficient and refined modeling of wireless sensor network nodes using systemc-ams. In: Research in Microelectronics and Electronics, PRIME 2008. Ph.D, pp. 81–84 (June 2008)

20. Winter, et al.: RPL: Ipv6 routing protocol for low power and lossy networks. Tech. rep., IETF-ROLL (2012)

EMCR : Routing in WSN Using Multi Criteria Decision Analysis and Entropy Weights

Suman Sankar Bhunia[1], Bijoy Das[1], and Nandini Mukherjee[2]

[1] School of Mobile Computing & Communication,
[2] Department of Computer Science & Engineering,
Jadavpur University, Kolkata, India
{bhunia.suman,mantunsec}@gmail.com, nmukherjee@cse.jdvu.ac.in

Abstract. Nowadays wireless sensor networks (WSN) are widely used in diffrent applications. In any network (traditional network or WSNs), route finding is the key support for network transmission technology. In WSN, efficient routing algorithm is very important. But the realization of efficient algorithm is not so easy because of many routing parameters of the network and resource constrained nature of the sensor nodes. This paper proposes an efficient and multi-hoping routing algorithm which is able to choose an efficient route between available routes while considering multiple important criteria for taking routing decisions and at the same time providing balance in energy consumption across all the sensor nodes. This proposed scheme is based on multi-criteria decision analysis, where multiple criteria, such as residual energy, frequency (number of packets received) and hop count are taken into account. Entropy weight method is used to assign the weighted values on each criterion. The best alternative route is selected using Weighted Product Model (WPM). The scheme has been implemented using TinyOS, an event-driven operating system designed for wireless sensor network.

Keywords: WSN, Routing, Multi criteria decision analysis, Entropy.

1 Introduction

Wireless sensor network is a self-organizing wireless network system which enables densely deployment of low cost, low power nodes. These nodes collect and process data and cooperatively report them using ad-hoc network protocols and algorithms. The collected data are routed to the destination via other intermediate nodes. The features of the WSN are dynamic because of unreliable communication through wireless network, and frequent changes in topology. Hence it is required to adopt a routing algorithm which creates the routing path on-demand. Basically on-demand routing algorithm follows the following steps: starting from the source node, the next hop node is selected from the neighbours and finally the data reaches the destination.

The various constraints of the WSNs lead to set optimization problem in designing energy-efficient routing algorithms. Besides energy efficiency of the

G. Fortino et al. (Eds.): IDCS 2014, LNCS 8729, pp. 325–334, 2014.

network, there are other application goals which need to be achieved while transmitting data through the network. An example of these goals may be fast data delivery which requires using the minimum distance path from source node to the sink node. But most existing routing protocols in WSNs are proposed to solve only one of these goals. For example, EAGR [1] and GEAR [2] routing algorithms are designed to aim at finding only the shortest distance. Directed diffusion [3] routing algorithm is a fault tolerant algorithm which is suitable to handle unstable communication. There are also some routing protocols in WSN which select the next hop by considering only one criterion i.e. either energy [4][5] or distance [6]. But they cannot balance the energy consumption.

Thus, for most of the exisiting routing algorithms, next hop is selected randomly or based on residual energy, node density or distance from the sink node. If next hop is selected based on residual energy, other important performance metrics may be overlooked. For example, this node may be located far away from the sink node compared to other neighboring nodes. In this case end-to-end delay will increase as the path length (i.e. hop count) increases. Similarly, if next hop node is selected based on the shortest path (i.e. minimum hop count), then similar type of problem arises. A node near to sink node, but with low residual energy may get selected as the next hop. Hence single criterion does not always provide efficient routing decisions. So an ideal next hop selection is made based on the multiple criteria. Handling of multiple criteria to select the next hop is solved by multi-criteria decision analysis method [7].

In this paper, an algorithm is proposed which maintains balanced energy consumption among the nodes with consideration of minimum hop count using multiple criteria together. Multi criteria decision analysis (MCDA) method is used to solve decision problems with multiple criteria. MCDA method compares multiple alternatives where each alternative consists of multiple criteria and each criterion is assigned with a weighted value. There are different methods in MCDA to solve the decision problems. In our proposed scheme, Weighted Product Model (WPM) is applied for solving the decision making problem. Basically WPM method consists of m number of alternatives and n number of criterion for each alternative. To dynamically assign the weight on every criterion, this proposed scheme consider entropy weight method [8].

Remainder of the paper is organized as follows. In Section 2, multi criteria decision analysis is discussed. Subsequently, routing scheme using a multi criteria decision model is proposed in Section 3 and calculation of weights using entropy is discussed in 4. The implementation effort on TinyOS is briefed in Section 5 and evaluation of the scheme is presented in Section 6. Section 7 presents related work. Finally, we conclude the paper with a direction for future work in Section 8.

2   Multi-criteria Decision Analysis

Multi criteria decision analysis (MCDA) is a set of techniques as well an approach of *Operations Research* [9]. It is also referred as multi-criteria decision making

(MCDM). Instead of considering only a single criterion, here the decisions are made by considering multiple criteria. Criteria may be classified into *(i) benefit criteria* and *(ii) cost criteria*. A criterion is assumed to be *benefit criterion* when higher the values are, the better it is. But a *cost criterion* is one which is better when its values are lower. The decision maker takes logical and consistent decisions that do not contradict each other. Its main aim is to provide an overall ordering of options. The options are ordered from the most preferred to the least preferred. No one option is there which achieves the entire objective. So the options are ordered from the best to the worst based on the number of achieving objectives.

2.1   Weighted Product Model (WPM)

The weighted product model (WPM) is a popular multi-criteria decision analysis (MCDA) method [10]. In the proposed routing scheme, this method is used for solving the decision problem. Instead of addition, this method uses multiplication to rank the alternatives. Each alternative is compared with others by multiplying a number of ratios, one for each criterion. Each ratio is raised to the power equivalent to the relative weight of the corresponding criterion. Basically in order to compare two alternatives by using WPM, following calculation has to be done.

Suppose there are n number of criteria and m number of alternatives or options. Each alternative is denoted by A_1, A_2 and so on. Furthermore, let us assume that all the criteria are benefit criteria. Next suppose that w_j denotes the relative weight of importance of the criterion C_j and a_{ij} is the performance value of alternative A_i when it is evaluated in terms of criterion C_j. For cost criteria, relative weight is denoted by $(-w_j)$. Thus we calculate the following ratio:

$$P(A_K/A_L) = \Pi_{j=1}^{n}(a_{K}j/a_{L}j)^{w_j}, where\ K \neq L\ and\ K, L = 1, 2, 3....m \qquad (1)$$

If the ratio $P(A_K/A_L)$ is greater than or equal to the value 1, then it is concluded that A_K is more desirable than A_L .

The WPM may be illustrated in the following decision matrix in Figure 1. In this matrix, there are three alternatives (A_1, A_2, A_3) and three criteria (C_1, C_2, C_3). These criteria are assigned with three different weights (w_1, w_2, w_3). x_{11} to x_{33} are different values.

For example, if using the above decision matrix $P(A_1/A_2)$ and $P(A_2/A_3)$ are calculated as follows:

$$P(A_1/A_2) = (x_{11}/x_{21})^{w_1} \times (x_{12}/x_{22})^{w_2} \times (x_{13}/x_{23})^{w_3} > 1 \qquad (2)$$

	C_1	C_2	C_3
Alts.	w_1	w_2	w_3
A_1	x_{11}	x_{12}	x_{13}
A_2	x_{21}	x_{22}	x_{23}
A_3	x_{31}	x_{32}	x_{33}

Fig. 1. Decision Matrix

Fig. 2. A scenario for routing

$$P(A_2/A_3) = (x_{21}/x_{31})^{w_1} \times (x_{22}/x_{32})^{w_2} \times (x_{23}/x_{33})^{w_3} > 1 \qquad (3)$$

then the ranking index is: $A_1 > A_2 > A_3$

3   Proposed Routing Scheme

In this section, a routing scheme is proposed and discussed. The routing scheme is named as : Entropy weighted Multi Criteria Routing (EMCR). In EMCR, it is assumed that all the sensor nodes are deployed randomly and are not movable. The position of the sink node is known. Every node is capable of receiving and then forwarding the data to the next hop node until the data reaches its desired destination. Selection of the next hop node from amongst the neighboring nodes is an important issue for performance of the network. In Figure 2, Node N needs to select one of its neighbor nodes **x, y, z** to forward the packet towards sink node.

In this section, we present a scheme which implements WPM model of MCDA based on three different criteria i.e. residual energy, frequency of packet transmission and hop count.

Residual Energy: In WSNs, energy (i.e. battery power) is most important feature for every node. Network lifetime is fully dependent on residual energy across the nodes. More energy in nodes is always preferable.

Frequency: Here frequency means number of packets transmitted or forwarded by a node. Higher the frequency, depletion of battery power is faster. Also, chances of delay may escalate due to queuing in a busy node (ie. node with higher packet transmission frequency). It means lower frequency is desired for enhancing lifetime and faster delivery of data packets.

Hop count: A packet has to go through few intermediate nodes before reaching destination or sink node. It is denoted as number of hops. Distance from sink node may be described by number of hops. More distance implies more energy consumption to transmit a packet. Minimum hop distance must be considered to make the routing algorithm, energy efficient.

So, one benefit criterion and two cost criteria are considered in this routing algorithm. The proposed algorithm uses these three criteria to determine the *product value* applying WPM. One particular node cannot always remain the next hop node. Next hop node is changed dynamically based on this *product value*. It implies that dissipation of battery power is balanced across various nodes. Thus, network lifetime is enhanced in this proposed algorithm.

Each node maintains a neighbor table containing the four fields :*(i) Neighbor node, (ii) Residual energy, (iii) Frequency, (iv) Hop count*. The routing decision is taken based on the *neighbor table* information. Here, the above mentioned multiple parameters or criteria are used for making routing decisions. Routing decision is made through the following few steps.

Step 1: Node N applies WPM for each neighbor available in the *neighbor table*. Index value or product value $P(A_i)$ for each neighbor node is calculated using WPM. The calculation is done taking the three parameters or criteria for each of the neighbor nodes. The three criteria are residual energy (E), frequency of packet transmission (F) and hop count from sink node (H). w_1, w_2 and w_3 are the weights assigned to these three criteria respectively. So, the product value will be :

$$P(A_i) = (E)^{w_1} \times (F)^{w_2} \times (H)^{w_3} \tag{4}$$

Step 2: Now compare the product value of each neighbor node and select the next hop node which has the highest product value $P(A_i^*)$.

Step 3: After selecting the next hop node, source node sends the data packet to this node.

Weights for different criteria (w_1, w_2 and w_3) are calculated following the method as mentioned in Section 4.

4   Calculation of Weights

Instead of assigning weights arbitarily, *Entropy* method of information theory, is applied to calculate the weights in this proposed routing algorithm.

4.1   Information Theory

It is the mathematical theory which is based on statistics, concerned with the transmission, storage, methods of coding, retrieval of information, in the form of message or data. Basically, this theory defines the measure of information in terms of probability. Information can be represented by the following equation [8]:

$$I(p) = -log_b(p) \tag{5}$$

where p = probability of the event happening and b = base
There are many methods which are used to measure the information uncertainty. Entropy method is one such method which is used in information theory.

4.2   Entropy in Information Theory

The theory of entropy was founded by Clausius in 1865. Entropy is used as a useful tool in information theory as it measures the expected information content of a certain message. Entropy in information theory represents the amount of uncertainty by using the discrete probability distribution. It is concluded by using the probability distribution function that the more uncertainty is represented by broad distribution. Entropy also helps to compare various types of risk and the sources of risk [11]. Entropy is generally credited to Shannon as it is the fundamental measure in information theory. Entropy is often defined by the following equation [8].

$$H(X) = E[I(P)] = -E[log_b P(X)] = -\Sigma P(X = x)log_b P(X = x) \quad (6)$$

where H = entropy of a discrete random variable X with possible values from x_1 to x_n,
E = expected value operator,
b = base,
$P(X)$ = probability mass function,

So from Equation 6, it is clear that entropy $H(X)$ is directly proportional to the degree of uncertainty or randomness of the measured variable. Smaller the entropy implies smaller the uncertainty.

4.3   Entropy Based Weight Calculation

In the proposed routing scheme, this entropy is used to calculate the weight of each criterion. The advantage of using this method is that it reduces the risk and increases the performance. The procedure of calculating the weight of each criterion is given below.

Step 1: We assume that there are m number of alternatives and n number of criterion. Then the entropy of each criterion is calculated from the decision matrix in Figure 1. Let, E_c is the entropy of criterion C. So E_c may be derived from above-mentioned Equation 6.

$$H(X) = E_c = \sum_{i=1}^{n}(P_i)log(1/P_i) \quad (7)$$

Step 2: Higher the entropy, weight of the particular criterion is lesser and vice versa. Degree of unreliability (d_c) of a particular criterion may be calculated as:

$$d_c = 1 - E_c, \forall_c \quad (8)$$

Step 3: In order to calculate the weight(w_c) of each criterion C:

$$w_c = \frac{d_c}{\sum_{j=1}^{n} d_c}, \forall_c \quad (9)$$

So from the above calculation it may be concluded that weight is inversely proportional to entropy.

It is also observed that the weight is a function of entropy. As entropy measures the uncertainty and the weight of the criterion is inversely proportional to the entropy, the highest index value will have lowest risk and vice-versa.

5   Implementation

In order to test applicability and study the proposed EMCR routing scheme, we have used open-source TinyOS [12] and Crossbow's TelosB [13] motes as a hardware platform. Wireshark is installed on Ubuntu as packet sniffing tool. All the nodes are installed with the routing scheme and deployed in such a manner that multi-hop communication may occur. Apart from the sink node, 10 nodes are deployed.

In this proposed scheme, we have calculated the residual energy real-time. We have not followed any static mathematical derivation for this calculation. Every time to calculate the residual energy, we have called an event, *voltage.readDone()* in *nesC* language. To keep track of the packet frequency, a counter value is incremented after each packet transmission. Hop count is retrieved from the *HopsLeft* field during the neighbor discovery.

Goal of this implementation is studying efficiency of the routing scheme. So, we kept sending data packets through multiple hops to help in the observations later on. Data flow remains towards the sink node. Energy consumption is tracked throughout the experimentation in regular interval. Also, delay in sending a packet is measured.

6   Results and Discussion

In this section, evaluation of the proposed EMCR routing algorithm is presented. Results in terms of residual energy and delay, are discussed.

6.1   Residual Energy

Residual energy is fetched from the nodes in real time. Every node contains 3000 mV intially. We have performed 11 observations for each node starting from node initiation. In each observation, the residual energy value is measured after transmitting 10 packets because for each packet transmission, very small amount of energy is consumed. In Figure 3, it can be seen that during packet transmission the residual energy in each node is gradually decreasing. But more importantly it may be observed that consumption of energy across all the nodes is almost equal. It implies that packet loads are distributed among all the nodes. Therefore, it can be concluded that this method ensures balanced energy consumption which increases network lifetime.

6.2   Delay

We also measured end-to-end delay from the source node to the destination node. The delay is determined by considering the difference between *timestamps*. *Timestamps* are appended on the packets by the source node as well as the destination node. Also, *Wireshark* may be used to calculate the delay. 15 observations are performed to measure the delay. In each observation, a packet is transmitted

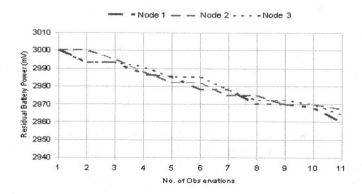

Fig. 3. Residual energy of intermediate nodes

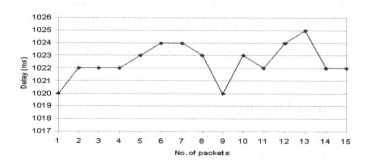

Fig. 4. Delay from source to destination through multiple hops

through multiple hops. Figure 4 represents the delay from the source to the sink node through multiple hops. In all the observations, delay is around 1 second which is minimal.

7   Related Work

This section presents some of the research works which have been carried out earlier in similar areas. In [14], the next hop node is selected in every hop based on the hop count. In [15], the next hop node is selected based on the three parameters i.e. distance, angle between two nodes and residual energy. In [16], the next node is selected based on the three parameters serially. All these papers use conventional methods for proposing routing algorithms.

Although many applications of MCDA are found in various other areas, to the best of our knowledge little application of this method has been made in the area of WSN routing. In [17], MCDA is applied in Geographical Information System (GIS) to overcome the limitation of GIS. Also, MCDA has found its application in content delivery networks [18]. Furthermore, lot of literatures are found where entropy weights are used in various MCDA applications. An entropy-based decision support system called e-FDSS is proposed in [19]. In [20], an application to the determination of weights is given when interacting criteria are considered in economics. Investment decisions are made using a MCDA method and weights are assigned using entropy in [21].

In [22], an attempt is made for a routing scheme using multiple criteria but the various weights are set static and reasons behind selection of particular weights remains unexplained. In the present paper, we explored the implementation of a multiple criteria-based routing using entropy weights in weighted product model.

8   Conclusion

In this paper, a WSN routing algorithm, EMCR, is proposed using multi criteria decision analysis. The next hop is selected based on weighted product model and the weights are calculated using entropy method of information theory. The multi criteria includes residual energy, packet transmission frequency and hop count. The main goal of this algorithm is to provide balanced energy consumption accross all the sensor nodes with minimum delay.

In future, this algorithm may be improved to provide security, recovery of faulty node in case of node failure etc. Also, we may try to involve more criteria for making the routing decisions. The algorithm may be modified incorporating node mobility. Currently, the algorithm does not take into account the application goal. A subjective MCDA method may be used to focus of specific application goals.

Acknowledgment. Research of first author is supported by TCS Research Scholarship Program. This work is partially supported by funding received from DST-NRDMS for carrying out the research project entitled "Development of an Integrated Web portal for Healthcare management based on Sensor-Grid technologies".

References

1. Zeng, K., Ren, K., Lou, W., Moran, P.J.: Energy-Aware Geographic Routing in Lossy Wireless Sensor Networks with Environmental Energy Supply. In: International Conference on Quality of Service in Heterogeneous Wired/Wireless Networks, Waterloo, Canada, August 7-9 (2006)
2. Yu, Y., Estrin, D., Govindan, R.: Geographical and energy aware routing: A recursive data dissemination protocol for wireless sensor networks. Technical report ucla/csd-tr-01-0023, UCLA Computer Science Department (2001)
3. Intanagonwiwat, C., Govindan, R., Estrin, D., Heidemann, J., Silva, F.: Directed Diffusion for wireless sensor networking. Networking 11(1), 2–16 (2003)
4. Gan, L., Liu, J., Jin, X.: Agent Based, Energy Efficient Routing in Sensor Networks. In: Third IEEE International Joint Conference on Autonomous Agents and Multiagent Systems, pp. 472–479 (2004)

5. Shah, R.C., Rabeay, J.: Energy Aware Routing for Low Energy Ad Hoc Sensor Networks. In: IEEE Wireless Communications and Networking Conference (WCNC), Orlando, USA, March 17-21 (2002)

6. Karp, B., Kung, H.T.: GPSR: Greedy perimeter stateless routing for wireless networks. In: 6th Annual International Conference on Mobile Computing and Networking, Boston, USA, pp. 243–254 (2000)

7. Hwang, C.L., Yoon, K.: Multiple Attribute Decision Making, Methods and Applications. Springer, Berlin (1981)

8. Shannon, C.E.: A Mathematical Theory of Communication. Bell System Technical Journal 27, 379–423, 623-656 (1948)

9. Triantaphyllou, E.: Multi-criteria decision making methods. Springer, US (2000)

10. Fishburn, P.C.: Additive Utilities with Incomplete Product Set: Applications to Priorities and Assignments. Operations Research Society of America (ORSA), Baltimore (1967)

11. Bushuyey, S.D., Sochney, S.V.: Entropy Measurement as a Project Control Tool. International Journal of Project management 17(6), 343–350 (1999)

12. Levis, P., Madden, S., Polastre, J., Szewczyk, R., Whitehouse, K., Woo, A., Gay, D., Hill, J., Welsh, M., Brewer, E., Culler, D.: TinyOS: An Operating System for Wireless Sensor Networks. In: Ambient Intelligence. Springer (2005)

13. TelosB-Wireless measurement system datasheet. Crossbow Inc.

14. Boukerche, A., Pazzi, R., Araujo, R.: A fast and reliable protocol for wireless sensor networks in critical conditions monitoring applications. In: 7th ACM International Symposium on Modeling, Analysis and Simulation of Wireless and Mobile Systems, Venice, Italy, pp. 157–164 (2004)

15. Huang, C.J., Wang, Y.W., Shen, H.Y., Hu, K.W.: A direction-sensitive routing protocol for underwater. Journal of Internet Technology 11, 721–729 (2010)

16. Yuanyuan, Z., Cormac, J., Sreenan, L., Sitanayah, N., Xiong, J., Park, H., Zheng, G.: An emergency-adaptive routing scheme for wireless sensor networks for building fire hazard monitoring. Sensors 11, 2899–2919 (2011)

17. Malczewski, J.: Multiple criteria decision analysis and geographic information systems. In: Trends in Multiple Criteria Decision Analysis, pp. 369–395. Springer, US (2010)

18. Bben, A., et al.: Multi-criteria decision algorithms for efficient content delivery in content networks. Annals of Telecommunications, 153–165 (2013)

19. Tang, L.C.M., Leung, A.Y.T., Wong, C.W.Y.: Entropic risk analysis by a high level decision support system for construction smes. Journal of Computing in Civil Engineering 24(1), 81–94 (2009)

20. Marichal, J.L., Roubens, M.: On the entropy of non-additive weights (2000)

21. Hsu, L.C.: Investment decision making using a combined factor analysis and entropy-based topsis model. Journal of Business Economics and Management 14(3), 448–466 (2013)

22. Rehena, Z., Roy, S., Mukherjee, N.: Efficient data forwarding techniques in Wireless Sensor Networks. In: IEEE 3rd International Advance Computing Conference (IACC), pp. 449–457 (2013)

Towards a Model-Driven Approach for Sensor Management in Wireless Body Area Networks

Ángel Ruiz-Zafra, Manuel Noguera, and Kawtar Benghazi

Departamento de Lenguajes y Sistemas Informáticos, Granada, Spain
{angelr,mnoguera,benghazi}@ugr.es

Abstract. Nowadays, new portable devices are constantly being launched with their ever greater application to an ever growing number of domains. These devices or *wearables* (from wearable computing) are present in many different areas ranging from healthcare to entertainment, and provide a series of features to enhance the quality of everyday life. When used in conjunction with other wearables, they give rise to wireless body area networks (WBAN) or body area networks (BAN). The large variety of devices along with the lack of standardized services, which means that each designer or engineer must customize the API design, forces developers to implement source code mostly from scratch in order to cope with the heterogeneity of wearables and support their integration on a wider system. The result of these drawbacks is that new device integration is hampered and the time spent on the software development process is increased and these problems are addressed in this paper. We propose a model-driven approach based on a meta-model which has been designed to define and specify interaction with sensors. Our main aim is to distance developers from specific implementation and to cope with heterogeneous designs. The resulting models, which are instances of the proposed meta-model, are specified in a custom language which we call the wearable markup language (WML). We also introduce the *coordinator*, i.e. component-based software for handling sensor models and improving the integration of new sensors.

Keywords: model driven, wearable computing, wireless body area network, component software.

1   Introduction

In recent years, progress in areas such as electronics, wireless communications and computing/software has led to the creation of portable devices which provide new functionalities. High tech devices of this type or *wearables* (from wearable computing) [1] are launched on an almost weekly basis [2]. From a simple wristwatch or GPS to state-of-the-art smart glasses, wearables are to be found in a variety of areas ranging from healthcare to entertainment or simply as service providers [15]. These new devices are becoming increasingly popular because of their potential for enhancing the quality of everyday life [3,4].

G. Fortino et al. (Eds.): IDCS 2014, LNCS 8729, pp. 335–347, 2014.
© Springer International Publishing Switzerland 2014

The use of certain devices has led to what is known as a wireless body area network (WBAN), offering numerous advantages such as a large-scale, flexible architecture and comprising sensor functionalities in order to achieve common goals. Technologists from a variety of different disciplines are involved in the creation process of such devices: e.g. electronics engineers, mathematicians, telecommunication engineers and computer engineers. Furthermore, the heterogeneity resulting from the large number and variety of devices and the lack of any standardized interface design to interact with sensors (through a customized API) results in a wide range of software components for handling each one. This lack of any standardized interface to work with the sensors restricts not only device integration and interoperability but also development efforts. Since it is necessary to develop specific source code for each sensor and for each platform, there is a resulting increase in development time.

Factors such as the dynamic nature of technology, whereby new communication protocols (e.g. Bluetooth, Wifi, ZigBee) or software solutions appear from time to time, are also involved in the device creation process. Nowadays, although most new wearables launched are wireless and are able to transmit data in real time (Bluetooth, Wifi, ZigBee), the older ones are only capable of saving information onto an internal storage medium (MMC, SDCard, Hard Drive, etc.). As a result, even two identical devices which have been designed by the same company, the same engineers and for the same purpose may very well differ significantly in terms of software development.

This paper introduces a proposal to mitigate the problems of heterogeneity and lack of any standardized interface for working with the sensors. The approach addresses the integration of wearables regardless of their characteristics (purpose, API interface, supported communication protocol, etc.) and is based on three main proposals: (1) a meta-model to define the different features to be considered in the interaction with wearables; (2) a *"coordinator"* which uses the instances of the meta-model (sensor models) to handle the devices (interaction, API use, integration); and (3) the integration process using this meta-model and coordinator. Sensor models are represented in a custom dynamic language, which we call the wearable markup language (WML), to specify the necessary elements and features to ensure interaction with the device. In this way, each wearable has a single model, as an instance of the meta-model proposed. Furthermore, the coordinator proposed has been designed and developed to handle such sensor models (meta-model instances) in an automatic and seamless way, thereby enabling interaction through a useful and easy-to-use API defined in the sensor model by the designer or engineer.

This paper is organized as follows: Section 2 describes related work; Section 3 presents a brief background on sensor development and integration; Section 4 explores our proposed approach; and finally, Section 5 summarizes our conclusions and outlines our future work.

2   Related Work

Wearable computing is an emerging field because of the increase of new technological solutions and devices. Several projects are based in the concept of WBAN, which has been applied in several areas such as healthcare or entertainment [5-7].

Other projects considered the wearables integration in a WBAN an important challenge to address, proposing design solutions based on approaches such as middleware, to improve the integration of wearables devices.

An example can be the research presented in [8], an approach to improve the ingratiation of Bluetooth based devices. Other projects such as the projects presented in [9][11] formalize a middleware oriented to e-Health environment or other research papers as the presented in [10] which makes a revision about different middleware's, exposing its features, strengths and weakness.

The main cons of these projects, which propose a software solution layer (middleware) to improve the integration of wearable devices, are that are focused in a specific scope such as to provide an approach for a specific communication protocol [9] or for a specific area as e-Health [11] (focusing on a specific functionality). Furthermore, other relevant projects presented in the review [10] intend to accomplish with certain requirements such as openness, scalability, mobility and heterogeneity, but none meets with all requirements. Also, the main cons of all of them are the non-automatic integration, the non-heterogeneity and the need to write some code to complete the integration process.

Other researches have proposed several solutions based on a model-driven approach. The projects presented in [13-14] presented an approach, in order to model a WBAN or enhance the data acquisition process from a WBAN [13-14]. The projects presented in [16-17] research about the integration process, lack of standardization and heterogeneity of WBAN, proposing a model-driven approach in order to address these challenges.

The research presented in this paper intends to solve the integration, addressing problems such as the large number of devices (heterogeneity) to integrate and the lack of the standardization in the access way to consume sensor services. To achieve this, a meta-model and a software component are proposed in this paper.

3   Background

Wearable devices are independent hardware elements which have been designed or created for a specific purpose [14]. Such devices are able to provide one or more functions from a simple global location (latitude, longitude) to simultaneously provide location, temperature and heart rate. Other devices must use all of these functions, which could even be other wearable devices such as smartphones or wristwatches.

At the present time, smartphones are extremely important in wearable computing. Thanks to their capabilities, usability and wireless support, they are gaining acceptance among wearable device users and even with central management bodies (see left-hand side of Figure 1).

Wearable devices are based on different technologies to exchange information such as wire-based communication protocol (USB) or a wireless communication protocol (Bluetooth, Wifi). Regardless of their communication protocol and whether the in formation is sent by request (packets) or stream, wearable devices are designed to serialize the information and provide the result as an array of bytes with a static or dynamic length and structure.

A custom device design might mean that the serialized result is different from other devices with the same purpose since it has been designed by other designers according to other criteria or requirements. Correspondingly, the packet length, the information provided or even the order of the information may well be different. The right-hand side of Figure 1 shows various sensors from the developer's point of view: a GPS that provides the latitude and longitude, a heart rate sensor that provides the heart rate and the RR interval and a second heart rate sensor that only provides the heart rate of the user. All of the information is sent by a sensor starting with a header (H) to identify the start of the information packet.

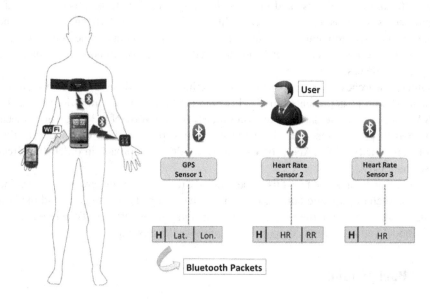

Fig. 1. Smartphone as coordinator (left) and different packets of information (right)

4   Towards a Model-Driven Approach for Sensor Management

In order to address the problem of wearable device integration, our proposed approach not only considers a meta-model to define the different wearable device features and generate the sensor models but also a coordinator as the software component to use these sensor models (meta-model instances) to interact with the devices and the proper integration process using the meta-model and the coordinator. In the following sections, we shall describe the solution in further detail.

4.1   Wearable Specification Meta-Model

The meta-model proposed in this paper has been designed to be dynamic by incorporating new features and elements so as to ensure that any wearable device can be modeled (heterogeneity) and to improve integration and ease of use for developers. The meta-model is intended to support the design interface of any wearable device.

The models generated from the meta-model (instances) are represented in a custom markup language called the wearable markup language (WML). These models contain all the required information to interact with the sensor: communication protocol used, which values and functions are provided by the sensor, marshaling information, etc.

In the design process of the meta-model, certain key features have been identified as important concerns related to wearable devices. The need to identify these concerns is crucial when proposing a meta-model which is able to cover any wearable device. The identified concerns are:

- Communication protocol is indicated in the meta-model but since the way this is handled is platform dependent, it is designed and supported by the coordinator. Wifi, Bluetooth, ZigBee or other kinds of communication protocols are standard IEEE-defined communication protocols but how these are used is also platform dependent: while BluetoothSocket and BluetoothDevice are the API proposed on the Android Platform to work with Bluetooth Protocol, CoreBluetooth is the one proposed by iOS. Both of these work with the same protocol but not in the same way from the developer's point of view.
- Wearable devices provide the information in a serialized array of bytes in two different ways: by request (synchronous packet) or by stream (asynchronous).
- Information provided by a specific wearable device could be static or dynamic (static or dynamic buffer).
- The dynamic information provided by a wearable device is specified in the same packet/stream in a static or dynamic position.
- The information provided by a wearable device, regardless of whether it is asynchronous or synchronous or not, starts with a customized header which we call the *pivot*.
- The information provided by a wearable device has a cyclic redundancy check (CRC) or other mechanism to check that the packet is valid.
- The information provided by a wearable device is divided into groups of bytes. The length and position of these groups may be static or dynamic.

The meta-model is represented in a UML diagram in Figure 2. The key features considered in the meta-model are a unique identifier that enables direct access to the model sensor (WUI) and an API comprising various services, which correspond to a specific function provided by the sensor.

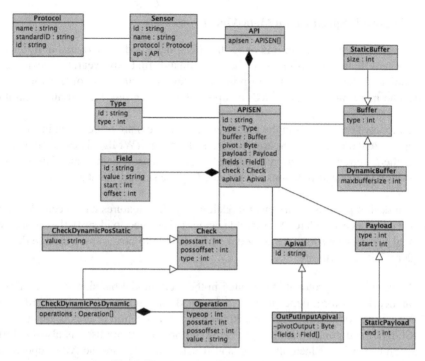

Fig. 2. Wearable specification Meta-model

According to how the information provided through a communication protocol is managed, various features have been considered and included in the meta-model in order to model a wearable device:

- Type of operation: input (stream), output or both (request)
- Pivot element: the element which indicates where the information starts
- Payload information: relevant information
- Fields which include the information from the sensor
- CRC or check method: a set of operations to validate the packet/information
- Type of buffer for each functionality: static or dynamic

One of the objectives when designing the meta-model was to make it customizable so that it would meet the present and future requirements of new sensors as they are released. In this way, it might be possible to create new customized models to cover new technologies and functions simply by defining new concepts in the meta-model to support these new features and their implementation in the coordinator.

4.2   Coordinator

The meta-model proposed in this approach has been designed to generate sensor models in order to improve the integration of wearable devices. Although these models contain the necessary information to interact with the sensors, it is also necessary for these models to represent real device use.

The software approach presented in this paper is responsible for integration models and works as a bridge between the model and developers by automating integration and making the sensors easier for the developers to use.

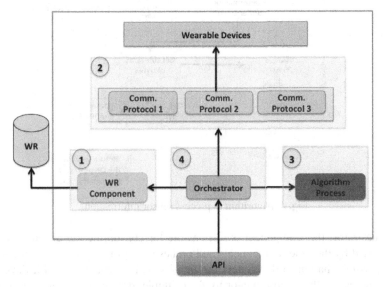

Fig. 3. Coordinator components diagram

Figure 3 shows a diagram to represent coordinator design and its different elements. There are four main elements comprising the coordinator, each with a specific purpose:

1. Wearable repository: this component is responsible for interacting with the wearable repository hosted on an external server or in the cloud where all the sensor models are. The component uses a service specifying the WUI to obtain the sensor model. Using this model, the component incorporates the new sensor into the coordinator as an internal software element.

2. Communication Protocols: in order to handle the different wearable devices, it is necessary to interact with them through different communication protocols such as Bluetooth, Wifi, ZigBee, and Serial. In order to ensure easy access to the information provided by the devices (byte arrays), a component is necessary to handle each specific communication protocol. In this part of the system (2), there are sets of components, one per communication protocol, which are used to interact with the devices. Furthermore, all the wearable devices with the same communication protocol are handled through the same component.

3. Algorithm Process: once a wearable device has sent the information, it is necessary to process this information to ensure that it is correct and to obtain the relevant information. This component is responsible for transforming the relevant information represented in arrays of bytes into understandable information using the specifications of the sensor model and ensuring the Quality of Service (QoS). The algorithm process is represented in the flowchart in Figure 4.

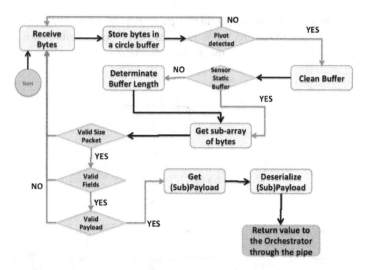

Fig. 4. Algorithm to process sensor information

4. Orchestrator: this component is responsible for consuming the different services provided by the other components and orchestrating these services to provide the proper information to developers through its API. Through the API, developers can interact with the coordinator to, for example, define which sensor to use and which values are needed, turn any device on or off, enable or disable notifications, and enable or disable automatic integration of new devices.

In order to handle the asynchronous interaction with sensors, the coordinator employs a custom software component called a *pipe*. A pipe is an event-driven software element responsible for transmitting the information from the sensors (serialized array of bits) to the developers (heart rate, RR, latitude and longitude, contextual information). In this way, when a developer uses the coordinator to handle a sensor, the coordinator returns a pipe (one pipe per sensor) to the developer. When the sensor sends the information, which is processed by the coordinator using different orchestrated services, an event/callback is sent to the developer notifying them of the relevant information related to a specific API (defined in the model).

4.3   Integration Process

The approach proposed in this paper focuses on solving the problem discussed above: the integration of any device regardless of its features (heterogeneity) and the lack of standardized access to sensor information. This approach has been designed to improve the integration of new wearable devices in wearable computing contexts, facilitate and support or automate part of the development tasks, thereby reducing implementation effort and time. In order to achieve this goal, the meta-model and the coordinator presented above are used in the integration process.

The integration process of a new wearable device supported by this approach consists of three stages and is represented in Figure 5:

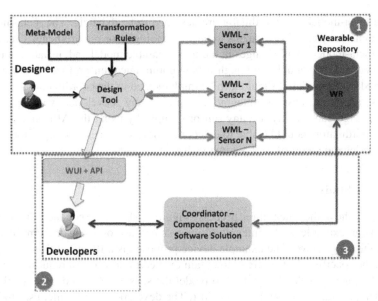

Fig. 5. Integration Process

1. *Design.* The designer uses the design tool to design the sensor model API according to its features or datasheet. During this stage, the designer uses different sensor documentation to model sensor interaction and defines a custom API to interact with the sensor to obtain the information provided by the device. The design tool uses the meta-model and the transformation rules to generate the sensor-model and this is stored in a repository.
2. *API release.* Once the design is finished, the design tool provides the designer-defined API and a unique identifier for the sensor model called the wearable unique identifier (WUI). Developers are able to access this API.
3. *Use the sensor.* With the API, the WUI and using the coordinator's, the developers are able to easily handle the device simply by using the API to obtain the information in an easy-to-understand way without the need to know about the sensor's internal workings.

This approach entails the following advantages:

- The developer can use any wearable device (heterogeneity) with no knowledge of communication protocols or how the sensor works.
- The possibility of defining a unique customized API for each sensor standardizes access to the information.
- If there is a mistake in the sensor model, the designer can redefine the model. If this redesign does not involve modifying the API, the software coordinator uses this new model transparently without affecting the developer.
- The sensor models are platform-independent and can be used by any coordinator, irrespective of platform (e.g. iOS, Android, Windows).
- Each wearable device model is designed only once.

- The meta-model and coordinator are designed to be dynamic. The meta-model is dynamic to ensure that it adapts to new technologies or requirements. Changes in the meta-model entail changes in the new wearable model and, usually, in the coordinator. For example, although a new communication protocol could be supported in the model, it should also be implemented in the coordinator.
- This approach ensures integration: firstly, any developer with no expert knowledge can quickly use any sensor (simply by using the API) and secondly, the coordinator should be able to detect new devices, access the repository to find its model and incorporate it automatically.

4.4   Case Study

In order to show the integration process, Figure 6 shows a sequence diagram that represents an example of the integration process and use of a sensor from the design stage to the usage stage. The example device proposed is a Bluetooth Heart Rate sensor with the specified API "getHR" to obtain the heart rate value in request mode.

The designer uses the design tool to model the sensor's API and generate the sensor model, providing the WUI and the API. The developer, meanwhile, uses the WUI to request the WML through the coordinator. The coordinator, in turn, uses the WR component to obtain the WML and manages this model as an internal software element to handle the sensor and a pipe is returned.

Once the device has been detected, connected and synchronized, the coordinator starts interacting with the sensor by means of the components (Figure 3) and processes the information according to the algorithm process (Figure 4). When the coordinator has a correct and understandable value, it launches an event in the corresponding pipe with the sensor information in an understandable way, returning this information to the developer who handles it in the proper way (show on the display, store in a database, process it).

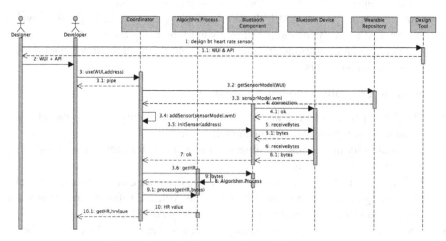

Fig. 6. Sequence diagram of integration process

Furthermore, the sensor model represented in wearable markup language (WML) and generated from the meta-model is shown in Figure 7. This sensor model contains the relevant sensor features and the customized API (getHR and getRR) and the WUI (id).

```
<sensor>
    <id>polarwearbt1</id>
    <protocol>802.15</protocol>
    <name>Polar iWL</name>
    <api>
        <apisen>
            <id>getinfo</id>
            <type>0</type>
            <maxbuffersize>16</maxbuffersize>
            <buffertype>1</buffertype>
            <pivot>0xFE</pivot>
            <payload>
                <start>5</start>
            </payload>
            <fields>
                <field>
                    <id>seq</id>
                    <value>0x06</value>
                    <start>0</start>
                    <offset>3</offset>
                </field>
                <field>
                    <id>status</id>
                    <value>0xF1</value>
                    <start>0</start>
                    <offset>4</offset>
                </field>

                    <value>
                        0xFF
                    </value>
                </val>
                <op>1</op>
                <val>
                    <type>
                        1
                    </type>
                    <value>
                        1
                    </value>
                </val>
            </ope>
        </check>
        <apival>
            <id>getHR</id>
            <start>5</start>
            <end>5</end>
            <datatype>0</datatype>
        </apival>
        <apival>
            <id>getRR</id>
            <start>6</start>
            <end>7</end>
            <datatype>0</datatype>
        </apival>
```

Fig. 7. Sensor model of the case of study represented in WML

5   Conclusions and Future Work

New wearable devices are constantly being launched. These devices are designed by a custom group of technologists (mathematicians, physicians, computer engineers). In the design process, the designers are responsible for defining the way sensor information is accessed (custom and well-defined API). This heterogeneity and lack of API standardization for using sensor services hampers the integration of these devices in already developed systems, and this in turn increases development time.

The aim of this research is to address the following main disadvantages presented in a wearable integration process in a WBAN: heterogeneity (various devices with several purposes and features) and lack of standardization in the way data from the sensors is accessed.

In order to overcome this issue, we have been working on a dynamic meta-model that is able to define the specification of any wearable device (heterogeneity), regardless of its features and also to define a custom API to access sensor information. This meta-model has been dynamically designed in order to cover the requirements and features of future-released devices. Furthermore, a software component to handle sensor models has been presented in order to facilitate the integration of new wearable devices by developers and to use the sensors in a seamless and transparent manner. We have also presented a case study to represent an example of the integration process using a meta-model instance and the coordinator.

In the future, we have a lot of hard work ahead of us: our main objective is to deploy the proposal as an open software solution so that it may be used by the developer community. Although the design phase (meta-model, wearable markup language, coordinator design) has been completed, the software solutions presented are still being developed.

We are currently working on developing and improving the usability of the design tool: an easy-to-use web platform with a user-friendly interface; and the design and implementation of transformation rules for generating sensor models from the meta-model. We are also working on the development of the coordinator to complete the implementation of the different components.

Although the coordinator has almost been developed for Android, we must conduct a hard test phase to ensure not only that it works correctly (failure monitoring, Quality of Services, efficiency) but also that it may be ported to other platforms (iOS, Windows, Linux, Windows Phone, etc.).

Acknowledgments. This research work has been partially funded by the Spanish Ministry of Economy and Competitiveness with European Regional Development Funds (FEDER), through the research project TIN2012-38600 and by the Granada Excellence Network of Innovation Laboratories (GENIL) under project PYR-2014-5. The authors would also like to acknowledge input from COST Action AAPELE (IC1303).

References

1. Mann, S.: Smart clothing: The shift to wearable computing. Communications of the ACM 39(8), 23–24 (1996)
2. Roggen, D., Perez, D.G., Fukumoto, M., Van Laerhoven, K.: ISWC 2013–Wearables Are Here to Stay. IEEE Pervasive Computing 13(1), 14–18 (2014)
3. Kleinberger, T., Becker, M., Ras, E., Holzinger, A., Müller, P.: Ambient intelligence in assisted living: enable elderly people to handle future interfaces. In: Stephanidis, C. (ed.) Universal access in HCI, HCII 2007, Part II. LNCS, vol. 4555, pp. 103–112. Springer, Heidelberg (2007)
4. Jara, A.J., Zamora, M.A., Skarmeta, A.F.: An internet of things—based personal device for diabetes therapy management in ambient assisted living (AAL). Personal and Ubiquitous Computing 15(4), 431–440 (2011)
5. Lee, Y.D., Chung, W.Y.: Wireless sensor network based wearable smart shirt for ubiquitous health and activity monitoring. Sensors and Actuators B: Chemical 140(2), 390–395 (2009)
6. Chen, C., Knoll, A., Wichmann, H.E., Horsch, A.: A review of three-layer wireless body sensor network systems in healthcare for continuous monitoring. Journal of Modern Internet of Things 2(3) (2013)
7. Zhang, Q., Su, Y., Yu, P.: Assisting an Elderly with Early Dementia Using Wireless Sensors Data in Smarter Safer Home. In: Liu, K., Gulliver, S.R., Li, W., Yu, C. (eds.) ICISO 2014. IFIP AICT, vol. 426, pp. 398–404. Springer, Heidelberg (2014)

8. Jo, T.W., You, Y.D., Choi, H., Kim, H.S.: A bluetooth-UPnP bridge for the wearable computing environment. IEEE Transactions on Consumer Electronics 54(3), 1200–1205 (2008)
9. Carr, D., O'Grady, M.J., O'Hare, G.M.P., Collier, R.: SIXTH: A Middleware for Supporting Ubiquitous Sensing in Personal Health Monitoring. In: Godara, B., Nikita, K.S. (eds.) MobiHealth. LNICST, vol. 61, pp. 421–428. Springer, Heidelberg (2013)
10. Hadim, S., Mohamed, N.: Middleware: Middleware challenges and approaches for wireless sensor networks. IEEE Distributed Systems Online 7(3), 1 (2006)
11. Castillejo, P., Martinez, J.F., Rodriguez-Molina, J., Cuerva, A.: Integration of wearable devices in a wireless sensor network for an E-health application. IEEE Wireless Communications 20(4) (2013)
12. Akbal-Delibas, B., Boonma, P., Suzuki, J.: Extensible and precise modeling for wireless sensor networks. In: Yang, J., Ginige, A., Mayr, H.C., Kutsche, R.-D. (eds.) Information Systems: Modeling, Development, and Integration. LNBIP, vol. 20, pp. 551–562. Springer, Heidelberg (2009)
13. Losilla, F., Vicente-Chicote, C., Álvarez, B., Iborra, A., Sánchez, P.: Wireless sensor network application development: An architecture-centric mde approach. In: Oquendo, F. (ed.) ECSA 2007. LNCS, vol. 4758, pp. 179–194. Springer, Heidelberg (2007)
14. Mann, S.: Wearable computing: A first step toward personal imaging. Computer 30(2), 25–32 (1997)
15. Gatzoulis, L., Iakovidis, I.: Wearable and portable eHealth systems. IEEE Engineering in Medicine and Biology Magazine 26(5), 51–56 (2007)
16. Bellifemine, F., Fortino, G., Giannantonio, R., Gravina, R., Guerrieri, A., Sgroi, M.: SPINE: a domain-specific framework for rapid prototyping of WBSN applications. Software: Practice and Experience 41(3), 237–265 (2011)
17. Fortino, G., Giannantonio, R., Gravina, R., Kuryloski, P., Jafari, R.: Enabling effective programming and flexible management of efficient body sensor network applications. IEEE Transactions on Human-Machine Systems 43(1), 115–133 (2013)

DISSN: A Dynamic Intrusion Detection System for Shared Sensor Networks

Claudio M. de Farias, Renato Pinheiro,
Rafael O. Costa, and Igor Leão dos Santos

Programa de Pós-Graduação em Informática,
Instituto Tércio Paccitti/Instituto de Matemática,
Universidade Federal do Rio de Janeiro
21941-901, Rio de Janeiro, RJ, Brasil
{cmicelifarias,renato.pinheiro,
rafaeldeoliveiracosta,igorlsantos}@gmail.com
http://www.labnet.nce.ufrj.br/

Abstract. Recent years we have witnessed the emergence of Shared Sensor Networks (SSNs) as a core component of cyber-physical systems for diverse applications. As Wireless Sensor and Actuator Networks (WSANs) design starts shifting from application-specific platforms to shared system infrastructures, a new but pressing research challenge is security. In scenarios involving unprotected hostile outdoor areas, SSNs are prone to different types of attack which can compromise reliability, integrity and availability of the sensor data traffic and sensor lifetime as well. In this work we propose a dynamic resilient security framework to be applied in the shared sensor network context. Its basic feature is the nodes neighborhood monitoring and collaboration (through the use of the byzantine algorithm) to identify an attack and enhance security. The work was experimentally evaluated in order to demonstrate the efficiency of the proposed solution.

Keywords: Intrusion detection System, security, wireless sensor networks, shared sensor networks.

1 Introduction

Recent advances in micro-electromechanical systems and wireless communication technologies have enabled the building of low-cost and small-sized sensors nodes, which are capable of sensing, processing and communicating through wireless links. Wireless Sensor Networks (WSNs) are composed of tens, hundreds or even thousands of sensor nodes. In the last few years the field of WSNs has experienced several changes, which have impacted the design and operation of such networks. One of the most noteworthy signs of these changes is the emergence of Shared Sensor and Actuator Networks (SSANs) [12], which, instead of assuming a traditional approach of application-specific network design, allow the sensing infrastructure to be shared among multiple applications, potentially belonging to different users/owners. The SSAN scenario may encompass multiple

G. Fortino et al. (Eds.): IDCS 2014, LNCS 8729, pp. 348–357, 2014.

networks with different users/owners resulting in a totally shared infrastructure, where the resources (nodes in the SSAN) are used by multiple applications, crossing the frontier of the traditional concept of specific networks/domains. Therefore, SSANs can be seen as integrated cyber-physical system infrastructures [13], which can serve a multitude of applications [5]. One of the suitable contexts to employ SSANs includes the smart spaces [14], which encompasses smart grids, smart buildings and smart cities [5]. The potential advantage of a shared WSAN design is the significant reduction in the costs of deploying the network by allowing the multiple applications to share the same nodes and networking infrastructure, thus improving the resources utilization. However, the adoption of such shared design poses new research challenges. In this paper we aim at tackling some of these challenges.

The security of SSN is a challenge that must be explored due to the limited resources of sensors (processing, memory, energy) and vulnerabilities associated with wireless communication, ad-hoc organization and the fact that the sensors are deployed in open, unprotected and often hostile areas. With that, SSNs can become targets of a large number of attacks in order to compromise the confidentiality, integrity and availability of its data or to decrease the network lifetime [9]. According to [4], a possible attack to this kind of network is a replica attack. In this attack, an adulterated sensor assumes the identity of another sensor in the network, in order to perform malicious activities, such as injecting false data capable of changing network behavior for disabling security mechanisms or shortening network lifetime. Often the target of such attack is the system responsible for ensuring application security, because, once compromised, an attacker can freely operate [7]. Thus it is necessary the system to be resilient, i.e. able to ensure the security of applications even in the presence of attacks or malfunctions [8].

One way to provide security for SSN and, consequently, for the applications running on the SSN is making use of a dynamic security system, such as a dynamic intrusion detection system (IDS). Such IDS must be able to manage the availability, integrity and confidentiality of multiple applications according to the context information collected by sensors, which by being in a highly dynamic and heterogeneous environment makes security controls to be modified in runtime. According to [6], context is any information about the execution of an application that can be used to enhance its behavior to operate in a personal, autonomous and flexible way. Therefore a system is context aware when it is able to consider environmental information to provide information or services to users. Thus, in this work we consider context information as the following information: (i) security requirements of the running applications; (ii) intruder indicator and/or attack in WSN, information provided by the IDS or other system capable of detecting an attack on the network; (iii) the amount of resources available sensors, such as available memory or residual energy. From the point of view of SSNs, it is important to note that depending on the application that is being executed, the security requirements may differ. For example, military applications require strict procedures to ensure the protection of confidential data, while other applications may not have the same kind of concern. Therefore the level of security, i.e. information that defines the security controls that should be used to meet the security requirements, should be modified as the context information change.

To overcome the challenges related to security, safety levels should be changed dynamically to mitigate vulnerabilities and extend the lifetime of the network preventing successful attacks and saving energy, because the security controls are activated only when required.

In this context, the aim of this work is to provide an efficient dynamic and resilient intrusion detection system for SSNs, called DISSN, in order to ensure the safety of the sensors, while not increasing the energy consumption. The provided IDS is dynamic and efficient because it modifies the levels of security while running according to the context, consuming less energy from the sensors. In this work, resilience is achieved through the use of the Byzantine fault algorithm, which relies on the cooperation among sensors to ensure that the security level is changed disregarding the context information sent by unreliable sensors.

The remainder of this paper is organized as follows: Related work (Section 2), description of DISSN (Section 3), tests and analysis of results (Section 4) and conclusions (Section 5).

2   Related Works

The SSAN approach has gained momentum only recently. In Efstratiou et al. [5] an extension to the traditional concept of WSANs (which aims at supporting a single application and a single user), is proposed. The proposed approach is based on decoupling the infrastructure from application ownerships. A framework is created which allows WSAN infrastructures to be shared among multiple applications, which can potentially be owned by different users. By achieving this level of decoupling, WSAN infrastructures can be viewed as an accessible resource, which can be dynamically re-purposed and re-programmed by different authorities, in order to support multiple applications.

To the best of our knowledge, no solutions were found in literature which proposed an IDS in the context of SSANs, what is a differential between our work and all the related works cited in this section. However, previous research on detection of security failures and compromising of nodes in distributed systems in general, beyond SSANs, can be grouped into two categories: resilient solutions [1,2] and non-resilient solutions [4,3].

The work of Jiang et al. [1] presents a detection system capable of identifying jamming attacks (denial of service attacks) specifically aimed against WSNs based on the IEEE 802.15.4 standard, which allows jumping between different frequencies for avoiding interference. In the work of Jiang et al. the non-compromised sensors use a resilient algorithm for key distribution, in order to establish the communication channel and maintain communication among the non-compromised sensors, even if the network jammers (sensors compromised by the jamming attack) exist. The proposal of Jiang et al. is resilient, as well as our proposal, because both are capable of supporting the continuous network operation in the presence of malicious sensors. However, unlike the proposal of Jiang et al., the resilience of our work is related to the security level of the sensors.

The work of Sundaram et al. [2] presents a solution based on iterative linear systems to counter replica attacks. In the context of WSNs, the values of the linear systems are represented by messages to be transmitted. Before sending a new message, each sensor performs a linear combination among this message to be sent and the messages received from its neighbors. As a result of this combination, if the total number neighbors of a sensor node exceeds 2f+1, where f is the number of unreliable neighbor sensors, the value received through the message is assumed to be reliable. Unlike the work of Sundaram et al., the resilience algorithm of our work is based on cooperation among the sensors through the algorithm of Byzantine failures. Thus, our resiliency solution determines if the neighbors are reliable considering the context information dynamically. Another difference is that our work is able to be resilient against different types of attacks, since context information is provided for helping to detect the malicious sensor.

The work of Conti et al. [4] proposed an algorithm that detects replica attacks in WSNs, i.e. it detects when a malicious sensor attempts to use the identity of another sensor in the network. In the work of Conti et al. the context information is the data transmitted by neighboring sensors, and each sensor uses this data in order to determine if its neighbors are malicious sensors or not. For instance, when the data collected by a neighbor about a particular phenomenon are not similar to the data collected by a given sensor, evidence that this neighbor sensor is malicious emerges. A similarity between the work of Conti et al. and our work is that both solutions proposed are aware of the context. However, unlike the work of Conti et al., our solution uses the context information for dynamically ensuring the security level of the sensors and the resilience of the IDS, while the solution of Conti et al. uses the context information only for detecting replicas, i.e. no action is taken for preventing the replica attacks.

Finally, the work of Lima and Greve [3] presents a fault detection system for distributed systems. The system of Lima and Greve uses the algorithm of Byzantine failures in order to detect failures in the communication system. As the work of Lima and Greve, our work also uses the algorithm of Byzantine failures. However, unlike the work of Lima and Greve, which uses this algorithm for discovering failures in the communication system, our work uses the algorithm of Byzantine failures for ensuring the resilience of the IDS.

3   DISSN: A Dynamic Intrusion Detection System for Shared Sensor Networks

The aim of this work is to propose a resilient dynamic intrusion detection system (IDS) for SSNs, called DISSN, capable to provide a protected environment for WSN applications, without wasting resources inappropriately, especially energy.

For this, the DISSN dynamically adjusts the WSN security controls in order to satisfy the requirements of its applications, at runtime, according to the changes in the context.

3.1 Logical Architecture

Figure 1 presents the architecture of DISSN. This architecture is composed by two subsystems: (i) Security Environment and (ii) Decision Core.

The Security Environment subsystem is formed by one or more Intrusion Detection System components, which provide information about the presence of compromised nodes or if the WSN is under attack in order to detect intrusions in the WSN or specific attacks, such as jamming attacks. The Decision Core subsystem consists of the following components: Context Manager, Dynamic Security Manager, Security Rules Manager, Resilience Manager, Adjustment Manager and Network Manager. In addition, this subsystem comprises two databases: Context Information and Security Rules. The Dynamic Security Manager component is responsible for conduct the action performed by DISSN to satisfy the security requirements of the applications according to the current context. The Context Manager component is responsible for updating the Context Information database and notify the Dynamic Security Manager when the context changes. For this, the Context Manager gathers both internal context information (such as the residual energy from the sensor) and external information (i.e. from the network, such as an intrusion warning). The Security Rules Manager component is responsible for processing the security rules in order to setting the sensor with the suitable security level for the current context. The Resilience Manager is the component responsible for the resilience of DISSN. For this, it uses the Byzantine fault algorithm in order to ensure consensus when a decision to modify the security level is taken. The Network Manager component is responsible for exchange messages between all sensors running DISSN. This component is used specifically for transmitting messages used to perform the Byzantine consensus. The Adjustment Manager is the component that sends the order for activate and deactivate the security controls in order to change the security level.

As previously mentioned, the DISSN has two databases: Context Information and Security Rules. The Context Information database stores the most recent information about the context. This is organized in the following fields: (i) The security requirement of the application (represented by an 8-bit integer); (ii) a value that identify the existence of intrusion or attacks; (iii) the residual battery power of sensors. The Security Rules database stores the rules that defines how the security level must be changed. This rules are arranged in the following format: IF <condition> THEN <security level>, allowing evaluate the current context under some predetermined threshold before taking a decision. For instance, IF Certain Security Requirement <= 7 AND no intrusion AND residual battery power > 90% THEN change the security level to 3.

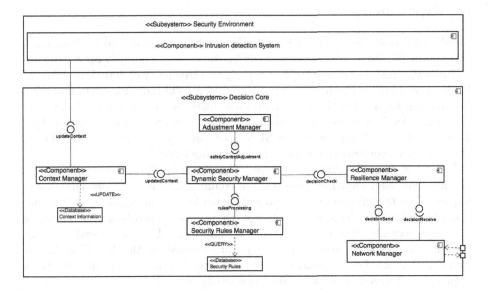

Fig. 1. DISSN Logical Architecture

3.2 DISSN Operation

Initially, the Intrusion Detection System activates the Context Manager to update the context information. Thereafter, the Context Manager waits for information from the Security Environment subsystem (external context) and periodically checks the information from the sensor (internal context). When any change occurs in the context, the Context Manager updates the Context Information database and notifies the Dynamic Security Manager that the context has changed in order to activate the other operations of the DISSN. Then the Dynamic Security Manager sends the new context information for the Security Rules Manager to determine what actions should be taken. Upon receiving the new context information, the Security Rule Manager processes it together with information from Security Rules database in order to decide what the appropriate security level for a given application. If the new recommended security level is different from current security level, the Dynamic Security Manager activates the Resilience Manager to validate the decision and changes the security controls. After receiving a decision to change the security level, the Resilience Manager request to the Network Manager to send a message to the other sensors and waits for a certain number of messages to check whether there is consensus to change the security level. If there is consensus, the Resilience Manager triggers the Adjustment Manager in order to make necessary modifications in the security controls to contemplate the new security level, which was accepted by the most sensors running DISSN.

4   Experiments

In all experiments performed with DISSN, the SSN is composed by Sun Small Programmable Object Technology (SUN Spot) sensors. The SUN Spot platform features an ARM 32-bit processor operating at a frequency of 400 MHz; 1 MB of RAM; 4 or 8 MB of Flash memory; and Chipcon 2420 radio for communication in adhering to the IEEE 802.15.4 protocol featuring 11 channels of 2.4 GHz [10]. The DISSN has been implemented using the programming language Java 2 Micro Edition (J2ME) with the SUN Spot development kit. The simulation scenarios were performed using the Solarium simulator [10].

The SUN Spot development kit provides several software components, including those that implement the stack of communication protocols. DISSN was implemented by defining new components capable to receiving context information and making the decision that changes the security controls in order to adjust (increase/decrease) the security level. Two interfaces (UpdateContext.java and SecurityListener.java) were respectively implemented by the Intrusion Detection System, i.e. the component that sends context information and the WSN applications to receive messages setting security controls.

4.1   Experiment Environment and Metrics

In our simulations, we adopted a flat network topology whose nodes are fixed. The number of sensors using DISSN was varied from 1 to 6 sensors and the number of sensors in the WSN was ranging from 6 to 12 nodes, having been arranged in the same rows equidistant from each other. During the simulation, one node was configured to act as if it was compromised at different periods in order to provide inaccurate context information. All Intrusion Detection Systems were defined to send messages every 10 seconds. Finally, we consider the confidence interval of 95% with satisfactorily strict limits after repeating 30 times each simulation.

The efficiency of DISSN was measured using the following metrics: energy consumption (measured using the number of messages due to restrictions of simulation environment), memory consumption (in Kbytes) and increased number of messages. The efficacy of DISSN was evaluated in relation to the resilience, which was measured by the consensus, showing if DISSN was able to correctly decide on the security level.

4.2   Efficiency

The efficiency of the DISSN was evaluated in three different scenarios: (i) without using DISSN and with disabled security controls, (ii) without using the DISSN and all the security controls enabled and (iii) using the DISSN to enable and disable security controls dynamically. Thus, in the first two scenarios we measured the number of messages transmitted without considering the context information, and in the third we measured the number of messages transmitted using DISSN to set appropriate levels of security according to the context information.

Regarding the quantity of messages sent/received, we can notice from that the overhead of the DISSN showed advantageous, because (i) less messages were consumed than when simply using the maximum level of security (18 messages while without using DISSN we had 50 messages) and (ii) more security is obtained than when not using any security level.

It is noteworthy that the discrepancy between the messages sent and received is due to the fact that the context information were sent using the transmission in broadcast mode, in which for every single sensor node transmission, all the other sensors account a new message reception. However we can consider that the additional overhead of our DISSN, in terms of the number of messages transmitted (sent/received), and in comparison to the scenario of disabled security controls, is negligible when compared to the advantages of using our DISSN.

With respect to memory consumption the DISSN proposed in this work consumed 26 Kbytes in size, consuming additional 50 Kbytes during its execution.

4.3 Efficacy

Two simulation experiments were conducted to evaluate if our proposed DISSN is able to properly ensure the safety of the network even in the presence of an attack. In the first experiment the resilience manager component is disabled, while in the second the component is enabled.

In both experiments one of the sensor nodes was configured as a compromised sensor node. In both experiments, during part of the nodes lifetime, this compromised node was sending incorrect information about the existence of an attack to other nodes of the SSN. Such time period (while the compromised node was sending incorrect information during the experiments) varied from 0% to 100% of the total time period of the experiment.

Table 1 shows the values of True Positives (TP), True Negatives (TN), False Positive (FP) and False Negatives (FN) in percentage, compared to the variation in the percentage of incorrect information provided by the compromised sensor node. We observe that the increasing percentage of inaccurate information makes the system less accurate in making security decisions (TP and TN are equal to 0%).

% of correct messages sent by a comproised sensor					
	100%	80%	60%	40%	20%	0%
VP	48	30	37	13	3	0
VN	52	50	23	27	7	0
FP	0	13	12	28	51	32
FN	0	7	28	32	39	68

With the use of system resiliency, even in the worst case (the compromised node sending incorrect information during 100% of the time), our DISSN was able to ensure a resilient and secure system operation, due to the Byzantine failure algorithm [8]. This fact can be seen from the results in Figure 2. DISSN counted with six sensors within the network.

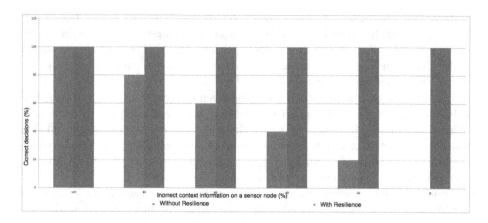

Fig. 2. Efficacy after consensus

5   Conclusion

This paper presented a resilient dynamic IDS called DISSN, whose main objective was to dynamically meet the security requirements of applications according to the execution context. With DISSN it is possible to ensure the security requirements in a dynamic and heterogeneous environment, where security controls are different depending on the current context. The use of the proposed DISSN brings the following benefits: (i) allows the security to be adjusted according to the current context where applications are executed, thereby allowing the limited resources of sensor nodes to be used efficiently, and (ii) ensures, through the consensus among the nodes in the SSN, that even in the occurrence of compromised nodes the decision of security adjustments is carried out correctly.

In future work other IDS options will be investigated, in order to analyze the relationship between energy expenditure and efficiency of the IDS resilience. We also intend to conduct tests to determine the computational impact of the IDS on the resource consumption of sensors. Finally, a comparison of the results obtained in our work to other works in literature will be performed.

References

1. Jiang, X., et al.: Compromise-resilient anti-jamming communication in wireless sensor networks. Wireless Networks 17(6), 1513–1527 (2011), http://dx.doi.org/10.1007/s11276-011-0361-8
2. Sundaram, S., Revzen, S., Pappas, G.: A control-theoretic approach to disseminating values and overcoming malicious links in wireless networks. Automatica 48(11), 2894–2901 (2012), http://dx.doi.org/10.1016/j.automatica.2012.06.072
3. de Lima, M., Greve, F.G.P.: Detectando Falhas Bizantinas em Sistemas Distribudos Dinmicos. Revista Brasileira de Redes de Computadores e Sistemas Distribudos, 9–21 (2009), http://www.lbd.dcc.ufmg.br/colecoes/rb-resd/2/1/004.pdf

4. Conti, M., Di Pietro, R., Spognardi, A.: Wireless Sensor Replica Detection in Mobile Environments. In: Bononi, L., Datta, A.K., Devismes, S., Misra, A. (eds.) ICDCN 2012. LNCS, vol. 7129, pp. 249–264. Springer, Heidelberg (2012), http://dx.doi.org/10.1007/978-3-642-25959-3_19

5. Efstratiou, C., Leontiadis, I., Mascolo, C., Crowcroft, J.: A shared sensor network infrastructure. In: Proceedings of the 8th ACM Conference on Embedded Networked Sensor Systems (SenSys 2010), pp. 367–368. ACM, New York (2010), http://dx.doi.org/10.1145/1869983.1870026

6. Hoh, S., Tan, J.S., Hartley, M.: Context-aware systems a primer for user-centred services. BT Technology Journal 24(2), 186–194 (2006), http://www.springerlink.com/content/y81x131125mr63n1/ (accessed October 5, 2012)

7. Kaur, P., Rattan, D., Bhardwaj, A.: An Analysis of Mechanisms for Making IDS Fault Tolerant. International Journal of Computer 1(24), 31–35 (2010), http://www.ijcaonline.org/journal/number24/pxc387745.pdf (accessed September 28, 2012)

8. Laprie, J.: From dependability to resilience. In: IFIP Int. Conf. on Dependable Systems and Network (2008)

9. Salmon, H.M., Farias, C.M., Loureiro, P., Pirmez, L., Rossetto, S., Rodrigues, P.H., Pirmez, R., Delicato, F.C., Carmo, L.F.R.C.: Intrusion Detection System for Wireless Sensor Networks Using Danger Theory Immune-Inspired Techniques. International Journal of Wireless Information Networks 20, 39–66 (2013)

10. SunSpotWorld, Sun SPOT World (2012), http://www.sunspotworld.com/

11. Tsai, K.-C., Sung, J.-T., Jin, M.-H.: An Environment Sensor Fusion Application on Smart Building Skins. In: 2008 IEEE International Conference on Sensor Networks Ubiquitous and Trustworthy Computing, Sutc 2008, vol. 078(2), pp. 291–295 (2008)

12. Leontiadis, I., Efstratiou, C., Mascolo, C., Crowcroft, J.: SenShare: transforming sensor networks into multi-application sensing infrastructures. In: Picco, G.P., Heinzelman, W. (eds.) EWSN 2012. LNCS, vol. 7158, pp. 65–81. Springer, Heidelberg (2012)

13. Wu, F., Kao, Y., Tseng, Y.: From wireless sensor networks towards cyber physical systems. Pervasive and Mobile Computing 7(4), 397–413 (2011) ISSN 1574-11

14. Jacobs, I.S., Bean, C.P.: Fine particles, thin films and exchange anisotropy. In: Rado, G.T., Suhl, H. (eds.) Magnetism, vol. III, pp. 271–350. Academic, New York (1963)

On the Analysis of Expected Distance between Sensor Nodes and the Base Station in Randomly Deployed WSNs

Cüneyt Sevgi[1] and Syed Amjad Ali[2]

[1] Department of Information Technologies, Işık University, Istanbul, Turkey
csevgi@isikun.edu.tr
[2] Department of Computer Technologies and Information Systems, Bilkent
University, Ankara, Turkey
syedali@bilkent.edu.tr

Abstract. In this study, we focus on the analytical derivation of the
expected distance between all sensor nodes and the base station (i.e.,
$E[d_{toBS}]$) in a randomly deployed WSN. Although similar derivations
appear in the related literature, to the best of our knowledge, our derivation, which assumes a particular scenario, has not been formulated before. In this specific scenario, the sensing field is a square-shaped region
and the base station is located at some arbitrary distance to one of the
edges of the square. Having the knowledge of $E[d_{toBS}]$ value is important
because $E[d_{toBS}]$ provides a network designer with the opportunity to
make a decision on whether it is energy-efficient to perform clustering for
WSN applications that aim to pursue the clustered architectures. Similarly, a network designer might make use of this expected value during
the process of deciding on the modes of communications (i.e., multi-hop
or direct communication) after comparing it with the maximum transmission ranges of devices. Last but not least, the use of our derivation
is not limited to WSN domain. It can be also exploited in any domain
when there is a need for a probabilistic approach to find the average
distance between any given number of points which are all assumed to
be randomly and uniformly located in any square-shaped region and at
a specific point outside this region.

Keywords: Wireless sensor networks, Optimal cluster numbers, Energy
efficiency, Random deployment, Base station location.

1 Introduction

A Wireless Sensor Network (WSN) is composed of a sheer number of *battery-
powered* sensor nodes that communicate with each other through a *wireless* channel. Moreover, these nodes have *moderate* storage and application specific sensing capabilities in addition to their *limited* on-board processing power. Although
WSNs suffer from scarcity of these resources, they offer promising potential to
operate in unattended and harsh environments where the human-interacted or

G. Fortino et al. (Eds.): IDCS 2014, LNCS 8729, pp. 358–368, 2014.

the human-controlled monitoring schemes are risky, inefficient and sometimes infeasible.

In a typical WSN application, the main objective is to deploy a multitude sensor nodes working collaboratively in order to *cover* a given sensing field and to transfer (i.e., *connectivity*) the sensed data to the base station (BS). As such, coverage and connectivity are considered as two primary performance metrics and dominating factors that achieve the optimal use of an application's scarce resources for a given deployment scenario. The sensor nodes are deployed according to either scenario: the deterministic or the random deployment. In the deterministic deployment, the locations of the sensor nodes are known in priori. Conversely, in the random deployment, the locations of the sensor nodes are not deterministic as the term also indicates. The random deployment scenarios are used more frequently than their deterministic counterparts because the randomly deployed WSNs (RDWSNs) have higher potential to be devised in real-life scenarios especially when there is a need to monitor a physical phenomenon taking place in *hostile* and *inaccessible* environments.

Since there is a lack of prior knowledge about the locations of nodes in RD-WSNs, the *connectivity* analysis is more stringent than the WSNs that adopt the deterministic deployment. In a deterministic scenario, the average distance between each node and its neighbors and similarly the average distance between each node and the BS are known in advance. However, in the random deployment scenarios, the above mentioned distances, which indeed affect the energy consumption and thus the lifetime of an application, are not known before the deployment. Therefore, it is really crucial for a network designer to estimate these distances as s/he needs to find out the modes of communication adopted by the network. These modes can be categorized as the *multi-hop* communication and the *direct* communication (a.k.a., single-hop). In a number of RDWSN applications, each sensor node is assumed to reach the BS within a single-hop. However, in those applications that adopt the direct communication, it is observed that a set of sensor nodes, which is far away from the BS, consumes a considerable amount of energy because it needs to perform long-haul transmissions. Therefore, those nodes, which are far from the BS, tend to die early and thus shorten the lifetime of the network. This is known as the *energy-hole problem*. To tackle the effects of this problem, the multi-hop communication is usually considered as more energy efficient than the direct communication. As such, in the process of making a decision on the communication modes, the network designer should need to compare the maximum transmission range with the expected value of the distance between each node and the BS ($E[d_{toBS}]$).

More importantly, $E[d_{toBS}]$ value also has an important role particularly for the *clustered* RDWSNs. In a clustering scheme, sensor nodes are basically *grouped* into clusters based on the proximity of the neighbouring nodes, the average distance to the BS, and energy levels, etc. to overcome some of the inherent challenges of WSNs. Clustering has been used as the most common technique due to its direct impact on the energy efficiency, network scalability and, more importantly, on the overall network lifetime. This is the reason why there are numerous studies on this subject in the related literature. The reader is encouraged to refer to a recent and comprehensive survey [1] for an overview of different clustering schemes. In the studies analysing clustering schemes [2] and [3], it is revealed that $E[d_{toBS}]$ value is the key determinant to find out the optimum number of clusters (k_{opt}) that maximizes the lifetime in the clustered RDWSNs. A notable work in [3] proposes a number of closed-form expressions to identify k_{opt}. Amini et. al. provide a complete theoretical framework for characterization of k_{opt} with respect to a set of parameters of the system scenario listed as follows: the number of nodes to be deployed (N), the area of sensing field (A), and $E[d_{toBS}]$. The values for N and A are definitely known before the deployment. And the only thing the network designer needs to derive the $E[d_{toBS}]$ value to find k_{opt} value which maximizes the network lifetime. As such, the derivation of $E[d_{toBS}]$ becomes one of the central concerns in the clustered RDWSNs. In [3], the authors derive various expected values for the distance with numerous powers analytically and validate them through simulations. They mainly assume two *symmetric* sensing fields: a *disc* (with radius R) and a *square* (with side length M). By considering both a disc-shaped and a square-shaped sensing fields and a single BS, they find various $E[d_{toBS}]$ values for different powers (i.e., $E[d_{toBS}]$, $E[d_{toBS}^2]$, and $E[d_{toBS}^4]$). Amini et. al. analyze the $E[d_{toBS}]$ formulations by the varying locations of the BS as follows:

– The BS is located in the center
– The BS is located on the perimeter
– The BS is located outside the (on the axis of) sensing field

However, the case that gives $E[d_{toBS}]$ ($n = 1$) when the sensing field is square and the BS is located outside the field, is *missing* and therefore there is a gap to be filled. Herein, our main contribution is to articulate this gap by deriving $E[d_{toBS}]$ for this special case.

After outlining the main motivations of this study, we introduce a review of literature devoted to this topic to identify the reasons of clustering and the importance of optimum number of clusters in a clustered architecture. Following this review, Section 3 introduces the network model employed and the pertinent assumptions used throughout the paper. Section 4 illustrates our derivation of $E[d_{toBS}]$. Section 4 also includes the validation of our formulations. And the last section presents the conclusion of our study.

2   Related Work

Lifetime maximization is usually considered as one of the most important objectives in WSN applications. Lifetime maximization objective is mainly affected by the energy-hole problem. This problem is experienced when the nodes closer to the BS are usually required to forward a large amount of traffic for devices farther from the BS. The similar problem is also observed when a set of sensor nodes, which is far away from the BS, consumes a considerable amount of energy as it needs to perform long-haul transmissions. Therefore, these nodes tend to die early which further results in energy holes. As far as the random deployment is concerned, the effects of energy-hole problem become even more serious. To minimize these effects, there are various studies which attack this problem. The most common technique to maximize lifetime in RDWSNs is to devise one clustering scheme or another. A clustering scheme typically groups sensor nodes into clusters to optimize the transmission distance for energy-efficiency and rotates the clusterheads for the evenly distribution of power loads. And the most widely-used and influential clustering scheme proposed is LEACH (Low-Energy Adaptive Clustering Hierarchy) [4].

LEACH mainly integrates the concept of energy-efficient cluster-based routing and medium access to prolong the system lifetime. It addresses the energy consumption minimization problems by making use of a distributed round-based algorithm. In each round of this distributed algorithm, it is expected that there are initially chosen number of clusters. And, after the competition of each round, clusterheads can be reelected periodically to balance the energy consumption. Thus, LEACH highly relies on the optimal number of clusters (k_{opt}) and in each round it is assumed that WSN consists of k_{opt} number of clusters. In [4], the authors describe whether there is an optimal tradeoff between the inter-cluster communication and the intra-cluster communication that balances energy consumption and they derive analytical expressions from simplifying and sound approximations. Analytical and simulation results are given to demonstrate the high performance of LEACH when compared with minimum transmission energy and static clustering. Thus, most of the studies dealing with clustering in WSN domain have been inspired by the study of LEACH. Thus, many variants of LEACH and the protocols that take the core idea from LEACH are systematically reviewed in [1].

HEED (Hybrid Energy-Efficient Distributed clustering) [5] is another protocol that aims to improve LEACH by periodically selecting clusterheads according to a hybrid of the node residual energy and a secondary parameter, such as node proximity to its neighbors or node degree.

Regardless of which clustering technique is employed or similarly which communication mode (i.e., multi-hop or single-hop) is exploited, a WSN application can only take the advantage of clustering if and only if the application is grouped with the optimum number of clusters. [3] analytically provides the optimal cluster size that minimizes the total energy expenditure in such networks, where all sensors communicate data through their elected clusterheads to the BS in a decentralized fashion. The analytical outcomes are given in the form of closed-form expressions for various widely-used network configurations. Extensive simulations are performed for the validation purposes when three cluster-based architectures namely LEACH, LEACH-Coverage, and DBS, are used.

One of the important concerns in the cluster-based architectures is the identification of k_{opt}. When portioning the WSN into clusters different from k_{opt}, the energy consumption of the WSN may become inefficient and it may degrade the network fast. Since the energy consumption of inter-cluster and intra-cluster transmissions of sensor nodes is a function of distance, k_{opt} depends on the expected distance ($E[d_{toBS}^n]$) between the sensor nodes and the BS. There can be several scenarios where the BS will be positioned relative to the sending field. A majority of these scenarios have been studied by [3] and $E[d_{toBS}^n]$ and thus k values are derived for $n=1$, $n=2$, and $n=4$ when the sensing field is a disc or a square. Authors addressed the problem of determining the k_{opt} of randomly deployed sensor nodes when the BS is located inside the field, on the perimeter and outside (on the axis of) the sensing field. It is observed that the derivation regarding one specific scenario is missing. Our contribution at this point is proposing the derivation of $E[d_{toBS}]$ of the missing scenario: when the sensing field is square and the BS is located outside the field.

3   Network Model

In this section, to facilitate the derivation of $E[d_{toBS}]$ expression, we describe the general system model and the pertinent assumptions used throughout the paper. As $E[d_{toBS}]$ value is mainly used to cluster a RDWSN with optimum number of clusters, herein we illustrate a sample RDWSN with the reduced number of devices before clustering in Figure 1(a) and after clustering in Figure 1(b). However, it should be noted once again that our derivations can also be exploited in any domain when there is a need for a probabilistic approach to find the average distance between any given number of points which are all assumed to be randomly and uniformly located in any square-shaped region and at a specific point outside this region.

For a RDWSN before clustering, let a square-shaped sensing field, with a surface area of M^2, to be covered by N sensor nodes which are deployed randomly and uniformly over this field. Figure 1(a) simply illustrates this sample network with 22 devices before the cluster formation phase. After the calculation of k_{opt} value, suppose that 6 (say $k_{opt} = 6$) of the nodes switch to *clusterhead role* and 16 of the nodes keep on playing the ordinary sensor node role as can be seen in Figure 1(b).

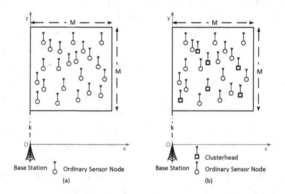

Fig. 1. A Sample Network Model (a) before clustering (b) after clustering

3.1 Assumptions

In this paper, all subsequent discussions are based on the following assumptions:

- The BS is assumed to be located at the *origin*. And the origin point is k units far away from the edge (on the axis symmetry) of the square-shaped sensing field as shown in Figure 1. The relative location of the BS is known in advance before the deployment.
- The BS is also assumed to have unlimited energy and thus there is no energy constraint associated with it. Moreover, all devices are assumed to be stationary and unattended.

4 Expected Distance between the Nodes and the BS

To derive $E[d_{toBS}]$ formulation, one should integrate the product of two functions over the entire sensing field. The first function determines the distance between a point and the BS. And the second function identifies the probability of a sensor node being at that specific point. First, we attempt to solve the problem by looking at double integrals in *Cartesian* Coordinates as shown in Figure 2(a). Recall that the infinitesimal area in the Cartesian Coordinates is $dA = dxdy$.

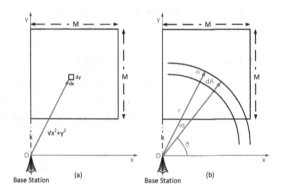

Fig. 2. Integration in the (a) Cartesian (b) Polar Coordinates

This is a rectangle with sides dx and dy. And, suppose that the probability of a sensor node being at point (x,y), which is $\sqrt{x^2 + y^2}$ units away from the BS, is $p(x, y)$. Then, the integration to find $E[d_{toBS}]$ can be written as:

$$E[d_{toBS}] = \int \int p(x, y)\sqrt{x^2 + y^2}dxdy \qquad (1)$$

Since, the probability of having a sensor node at each point inside the sensing field is identical[1], $p(x, y)$ is independent of x and y and is equal to $1/M^2$. By substituting $1/M^2$ value with $p(x, y)$ in Eqn. 1, we have:

---

[1] Due to the fact that the nodes are randomly and uniformly deployed and the sum of these probabilities is 1.

$$E[d_{toBS}] = 1/M^2 \int \int \sqrt{x^2 + y^2} dx dy \qquad (2)$$

However, it is not trivial to find the integration in Eqn. 2 in the Cartesian Coordinates. Thus, we attempt to solve the same problem by using the *Polar* Coordinates and by integrating an infinitesimal ring-shaped element $(dA = rdrd\phi)$. Before starting to integrate in the Polar Coordinates, recall that the probability of a sensor node being in the ring-shaped segment which is r radial distance from the BS is $p(r)$ as shown in Figure 2(b). Then, the integration to find $E[d_{toBS}]$ can be written in the Polar Coordinates as:

$$E[d_{toBS}] = \int \int p(r) r^2 dr d\theta \qquad (3)$$

Similar to the probability value in the Cartesian Coordinates, $p(r)$ is equal to $1/M^2$. Therefore, we have:

$$E[d_{toBS}] = 1/M^2 \int \int r^2 dr d\theta \qquad (4)$$

To be able to integrate $r^2 dr d\theta$ over the square-shaped sensing field, we need to consider two different regions with two different geometries. Thus, the sensing field is analyzed by dividing it into two separate regions as a triangle and a trapezoid as is shown in Figure 3(a) and (b) respectively.

4.1 Derivation of $E[d_{toBS-tri}]$ in a Triangle

Herein, we focus on the integration of $E[d_{toBS-tri}]$ over only the *triangular* region depicted in Figure 3(a). Boundary values for the integration are plugged in the Eqn. 4 when using the following trigonometric substitutions: $r_1 = A/cos\theta$ and $r_2 = M/cos\theta$

$$E[d_{toBS-tri}] = \frac{1}{M^2} \int_{\alpha_1}^{\alpha_2} \int_{A/cos\theta}^{M/cos\theta} r^2 dr d\theta \qquad (5)$$

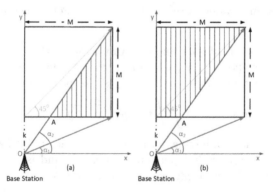

Fig. 3. (a) Shaded Triangular Region (b) Shaded Trapezoid Region

By using the similar triangles in Figure 3(a), we can denote the value of A in terms of k and M as:

$$\frac{k+M}{M} = \frac{k}{A} \quad \Rightarrow \quad A = \frac{k.M}{k+M} \tag{6}$$

Moreover, α_1 and α_2 can be expressed in terms of trigonometric identities as given in Eqn. 7 and 8 respectively.

$$\tan\alpha_1 = \frac{k}{M} \text{ and } \sec\alpha_1 = \frac{\sqrt{k^2+M^2}}{M} \tag{7}$$

$$\tan\alpha_2 = \frac{k+M}{M} \text{ and } \sec\alpha_2 = \frac{\sqrt{(k+M)^2+M^2}}{M} \tag{8}$$

Therefore, $E[d_{toBS-tri}]$ can be found as:

$$E[d_{toBS-tri}] = \frac{1}{M^2} \int_{\alpha_1}^{\alpha_2} \frac{r^3}{3}\Big|_{A/cos\theta}^{M/cos\theta} d\theta = \frac{M^3 - A^3}{3M^2} \int_{\alpha_1}^{\alpha_2} \frac{1}{\cos^3\theta} d\theta \tag{9}$$

We replace the term A in Eqn. 9 with the substitute of A in Eqn. 6. Therefore, we have:

$$E[d_{toBS-tri}] = \frac{M}{3}\left(\frac{(k+M)^3 - k^3}{(k+M)^3}\right) \int_{\alpha_1}^{\alpha_2} \frac{1}{\cos^3\theta} d\theta \tag{10}$$

In order to find the last term in Eqn. 10, we use Eqn. 11 which is from the table of integrals in [6]:

$$\int_{\alpha_1}^{\alpha_2} \frac{1}{\cos^3\theta} d\theta = \frac{1}{2}[\tan\alpha_2 \sec\alpha_2 + \ln(\sec\alpha_2 + \tan\alpha_2)] -$$

$$\frac{1}{2}[\tan\alpha_1 \sec\alpha_1 + \ln(\sec\alpha_1 + \tan\alpha_1)] \tag{11}$$

By replacing the trigonometric identities in Eqn. 7 and 8 with their substitute in Eqn. 11, we can find Eqn. 12. And finally, $E[d_{toBS-tri}]$ value for the triangular region is given in Eqn. 13.

$$\int_{\alpha_1}^{\alpha_2} \frac{1}{\cos^3\theta} d\theta =$$

$$\frac{1}{2}\left[\frac{(k+M)\sqrt{(k+M)^2+M^2}}{M^2} + \ln\left(\frac{\sqrt{(k+M)^2+M^2}}{M} + \frac{k+M}{M}\right)\right] -$$

$$\frac{1}{2}\left[\frac{k\sqrt{k^2+M^2}}{M^2} + \ln\left(\frac{\sqrt{k^2+M^2}}{M} + \frac{k}{M}\right)\right] \tag{12}$$

$$E[d_{toBS-tri}] = \frac{M}{6}\left(\frac{(k+M)^3 - k^3}{(k+M)^3}\right)$$

$$\left\{\left[\frac{(k+M)\sqrt{(k+M)^2 + M^2}}{M^2} + \ln\left(\frac{\sqrt{(k+M)^2 + M^2}}{M} + \frac{k+M}{M}\right)\right] - \left[\frac{k\sqrt{k^2 + M^2}}{M^2} + \ln\left(\frac{\sqrt{k^2 + M^2}}{M} + \frac{k}{M}\right)\right]\right\} \quad (13)$$

4.2   Derivation of $E[d_{toBS-trap}]$ in a Trapezoid

Herein, we concentrate on the integration of $E[d_{toBS-trap}]$ over the *trapezoidal* region depicted in Figure 2(b). A trapezoidal region can be typically expressed by subtracting an area of a larger triangle from a smaller one. While the first term in the Eqn. 14 represents the larger triangle, the second one represents the smaller triangle.

$$E[d_{toBS-trap}] = \frac{1}{M^2}\left[\int_{\alpha_2}^{\frac{\pi}{2}}\int_0^{M+k/\sin\theta} r^2 dr d\theta - \int_{\alpha_2}^{\frac{\pi}{2}}\int_0^{A/\sin\theta} r^2 dr d\theta\right] \quad (14)$$

$$E[d_{toBS-trap}] = \frac{1}{M^2}\left[\int_{\alpha_2}^{\frac{\pi}{2}} \frac{r^3}{3}\Big|_0^{M+k/\sin\theta} d\theta - \int_{\alpha_2}^{\frac{\pi}{2}} \frac{r^3}{3}\Big|_0^{A/\sin\theta} d\theta\right] \quad (15)$$

$$E[d_{toBS-trap}] = \frac{1}{M^2}\left[\frac{(M+k)^3}{3} - \frac{A^3}{3}\right]\left[\int_{\alpha_2}^{\frac{\pi}{2}} \frac{1}{\sin^3\theta} d\theta\right] \quad (16)$$

Again by using the table of integrals in [6], the last term (B) in Eqn. 16 can be rewritten as:

$$\int_{\alpha_2}^{\frac{\pi}{2}} \frac{1}{\sin^3\theta} d\theta = \frac{1}{2}\left[-\cot\theta\csc\theta + \ln|\csc\theta - \cot\theta|\right]\Big|_{\alpha_2}^{\frac{\pi}{2}} = B \quad (17)$$

From Figure 3, we can easily find the following trigonometric identities:

$$\cot\frac{\pi}{2} = 0 \text{ and } \csc\frac{\pi}{2} = 1 \quad (18)$$

After $B = B' - B''$ substitution, we have:

$$B' = \frac{1}{2}\left[-\cot\frac{\pi}{2}\csc\frac{\pi}{2} + \ln|\csc\frac{\pi}{2} - \cot\frac{\pi}{2}|\right] = 0 \quad (19)$$

$$B'' = \frac{1}{2}\left[-\cot\alpha_2\csc\alpha_2 + \ln|\csc\alpha_2 - \cot\alpha_2|\right] \quad (20)$$

$$B = \frac{1}{2}\left[\frac{M}{k+M}\frac{\sqrt{(k+M)^2+M^2}}{k+M}\right] - \frac{1}{2}\ln\left|\frac{\sqrt{(k+M)^2+M^2}}{k+M} - \frac{M}{k+M}\right| \quad (21)$$

$$E[d_{toBS-trap}] = \frac{1}{M^2}\left[\frac{(M+k)^3}{3} - \frac{A^3}{3}\right]B \quad (22)$$

By replacing the terms A and B in Eqn. 22 with their substitutes in Eqn. 6 and 21 respectively, we have the following:

$$E[d_{toBS-trap}] = \frac{1}{2M^2}\left[\frac{(M+k)^3}{3} - \frac{(\frac{k.M}{k+M})^3}{3}\right]$$

$$\left[\frac{M}{k+M}\frac{\sqrt{(k+M)^2+M^2}}{k+M} - \ln\left|\frac{\sqrt{(k+M)^2+M^2}}{k+M} - \frac{M}{k+M}\right|\right] \quad (23)$$

4.3 Derivation of $E[d_{toBS}]$ in a Square

Finally, to find $E[d_{toBS}]$, we add $E[d_{toBS-tri}]$ and $E[d_{toBS-trap}]$ expressions both for the triangle (Eqn. 13) and for the trapezoid (Eqn. 23). And, the formulation for our research problem is given in Eqn. 24

$$E[d_{toBS}] = \frac{M}{6}\left(\frac{(k+M)^3-k^3}{(k+M)^3}\right)$$

$$\left\{\left[\frac{(k+M)\sqrt{(k+M)^2+M^2}}{M^2} + \ln\left(\frac{\sqrt{(k+M)^2+M^2}}{M} + \frac{k+M}{M}\right)\right] - \right.$$

$$\left.\left[\frac{k\sqrt{k^2+M^2}}{M^2} + \ln\left(\frac{\sqrt{k^2+M^2}}{M} + \frac{k}{M}\right)\right]\right\} +$$

$$\frac{1}{2M^2}\left[\frac{(M+k)^3}{3} - \frac{(\frac{k.M}{k+M})^3}{3}\right]$$

$$\left[\frac{M}{k+M}\frac{\sqrt{(k+M)^2+M^2}}{k+M} - \ln\left|\frac{\sqrt{(k+M)^2+M^2}}{k+M} - \frac{M}{k+M}\right|\right] \quad (24)$$

4.4 Validation

In order to validate our $E[d_{toBS}]$ formulation given in Eqn. 24, we compared it with Eqn. 42 in [3]. While the latter one assumes that the BS is located on the edge of the square-shaped sensing field, our derivation in Eqn. 24 assumes that the BS in arbitrarily located units outside the field. To adapt Eqn. 24 in this study to the one in [3], in other words, to move the BS from k units outside the field to the edge of the sensing field, we assign $k = 0$ into Eqn. 24. After substituting 0 for k in Eqn. 24, we have the following expressions:

$$E[d_{toBS}] = \frac{M}{6} \{ \left[\sqrt{2} + \ln\left(\sqrt{2}+1\right) \right] - [0 + \ln(1+0)] \} +$$
$$\frac{1}{2M^2} \left[\frac{(M)^3}{3} \right] \left[\sqrt{2} - \ln\left|\sqrt{2}-1\right| \right] \quad (25)$$

$$E[d_{toBS}] = \frac{M}{3} \left[\sqrt{2} + \ln\left(\sqrt{2}+1\right) \right] \quad (26)$$

The fact that Eqn. 26 is exactly the same as the Eqn. 42 in [3] validates our finding.

5   Conclusion

We have formulated $E[d_{toBS}]$ when sensor nodes are deployed randomly and uniformly over a square-shaped sensing field and the BS is located outside the field. This expected value is required not only for the calculation of the optimum number of clusters in the clustered RDWSNs but also for the decision whether multi-hop or direct communication should be devised. One of the limitations of our derivation in this paper is that the BS is assumed to be located on the axis of (outside) the sensing field. Our future work will focus on this limitation and explore $E[d_{toBS}]$ when the BS is located at any *arbitrary* point *outside* the sensing field rather than at a specific point on the axis of the sensing field.

References

1. Tyagi, S., Kumar, N.: A systematic review on clustering and routing techniques based upon LEACH protocol for wireless sensor networks. Journal of Network and Computer Applications 36(2), 623–645 (2013)
2. Amini, N., Vahdatpour, A., Dabiri, F., Noshadi, H., Sarrafzadeh, M.: Joint consideration of energy-efficiency and coverage-preservation in microsensor networks. Wireless Communications and Mobile Computing 11(6), 707–722 (2011)
3. Amini, N., Vahdatpour, A., Xu, W., Gerla, M., Sarrafzadeh, M.: Cluster size optimization in sensor networks with decentralized cluster-based protocols. Computer Communications 35(2), 207–220 (2012)
4. Heinzelman, W., Chandrakasan, A., Balakrishnan, H.: An application-specific protocol architecture for wireless microsensor networks. IEEE Transactions on Wireless Communications 1(4), 660–670 (2002)
5. Younis, O., Fahmy, S.: HEED: a hybrid, energy-efficient, distributed clustering approach for ad hoc sensor networks. IEEE Transactions on Mobile Computing 3(4), 366–379 (2004)
6. Dwight, H.B., Hedrick, E.R.: Tables of Integrals and Other Mathematical Data, 3rd edn. The Macmillan Company (1956)

Performability Modelling and Analysis of Clustered Wireless Sensor Networks with Limited Storage Capacities

Fredrick A. Omondi[1], Enver Ever[2], Purav Shah[1], Orhan Gemikonakli[1], and Leonardo Mostarda[1]

[1] Middlesex University, The Burroughs, NW4 4BT, London, United Kingdom
{f.adero,p.shah,o.gemikonakli,l.mostarda}@mdx.ac.uk
[2] Middle East Tech. University, North Cyprus Campus, Guzelyurt, Mersin 10, Turkey
eever@metu.edu.tr

Abstract. Wireless Sensor Network (WSN) technology has seen an increasing demand for use in various application areas including multimedia sensor networks, smart agriculture and industrial automation. The applications demand for optimum results are dictated by the complexity of their deployment environment, hence the need for improved performance, availability and reliability. Packet loss due to limited memory capacity has become a major drawback in some areas of WSN applications like Multimedia Wireless Sensor Networks (WMSN). Most of the existing studies consider performance and availability evaluation separately. Considering systems for pure performance evaluation may cause overestimation of systems ability to perform. On the other hand focussing only on the availability may be too conservative since various levels of performance are not considered. In this paper, we propose an analytical modelling approach for bounded WSN queues where cluster-tree architecture is considered and integrated performance and availability measures analysed in the presence of failures, repairs/replacement and restoration. Open queuing network is used to model the behaviour of the cluster head as an $M/M/1/L$ queuing system and using spectral expansion method, the system is solved and validated against simulation results. Both analytical and simulation results presented are in good agreement and are further used to analyse the trade-off between the arrival rate and buffer size for optimum performance and availability.

Keywords: Wireless Sensor Networks, Modelling, Performance, Availability, Reliability, Performability, Queue Capacity.

1 Introduction

The use of WSN technology has become promising and interesting with application areas including seismic, acoustic, chemical and physiological sensing as well as ambient assisted living. For applications involving large number of nodes, the deployment strategy for sensor nodes play a vital role in extending the overall

G. Fortino et al. (Eds.): IDCS 2014, LNCS 8729, pp. 369–382, 2014.
© Springer International Publishing Switzerland 2014

network lifetime whilst providing good quality of service and reliable performance. Performance of WSNs is continuously hindered by limited sensor node resources and failures categorised as node, cluster and network failures [1].

Significant independent studies have been reported on performance and availability/reliability of WSNs to address issues hindering WSN quality of service (QoS). The concerns of independent performance and availability studies have remained unresolved and require attention in order to improve WSNs QoS. Another concern in WSNs is limited storage memory (buffer) both for operating systems and temporary data storage. This means sensor nodes can only offer limited buffer space for temporary storage of data being processed.Any packets arriving when the buffer is full are lost. The constraint is worsened when a node is used as cluster head (CH) processing and transmitting all internally and externally generated data towards the sink. Studies have also indicated use of cluster tree as a preferred topology for deployment of WSNs in many application areas following implementation of mechanisms like use of back-up CH (BCH) or secondary CH (SCH) and CH rotation which prevent central point of failure at the cluster head [2] . This increases traffic to the CH and may result to more packet loss.

WSN designers ought to consider fault tolerance, scalability, operating environment, energy efficiency, network topology as well as complying with the limited sensor node resources. Much work has been done to improve the lifetime of sensor nodes by using mechanisms for extending the battery life, replacement of failed/dead nodes and use of clustering algorithm to improve WSN lifetime [3]. Proposals for saving node energy include altering operations between active and sleep modes are presented in [4],[5]. Even though independent work on performance and availability/reliability has also been reported [4], [6], to the best of our knowledge there is no previous integrated performance and availability studies for clustered wireless sensor network that also considers CH limited buffer capacity.

The novelty of this study is therefore to develop a mathematical model integrating performance and availability studies while at the same time considering the effects caused by restricting node buffer sizes. The study also incorporates the possibility of cluster head failures, repairs/replacement and restoration during operations. The model is then used to analyse cluster and CH performance and availability related issues. The rest of the paper is organised as follows: Section 2 reviews related works, Section 3 describes the system under study, Sections 4 presents the queuing model for the system, section 5 presents a two dimensional representation of the proposed model, Section 6 presents numerical results and finally section 7 concludes the current work and provides future directions.

2   Related Work

Performance modelling and analysis is important in supporting research as well as design, development and optimization of computer and communication systems and applications. The use of WSNs in various application areas has also brought with it the need for performance and availability modelling for optimization of WSN networks. In [4], a Markov model for WSNs whose nodes may enter sleep mode was presented and investigated against the system performance in terms of energy consumption, network capacity, data delivery and delay. This model presented a trade-off which exists between performance metrics and sensor dynamics in sleep/active modes. In [7], a new evaluation method for optimising packet buffer capacity of nodes using queuing network model was presented to improve the transmission QoS. However, the effects of node failures on network performance were not considered.

In order to improve WSNs availability, use of BCH and SCH has been proposed in [2] as a form of redundancy when a cluster head fails. However performance degradation due to replacement and transfer delays between failing CH and BCH in the event of failure is not considered. Performance of star topology has also been enhanced by cluster-tree deployment which provide redundancy through use of BCH, SCH and CH rotation thereby alleviating central point of failure at the CH, improve performance, and prolong WSN lifetime [2]. Robots have also been proposed in [9],[10] for repair of nodes and broken network connections. It is therefore evident that failing nodes can be repaired through software reconfigurations and replacement using mobile nodes in cases of complete failure.

Originally, WSNs were meant for low to medium rate applications hence memory was not a major concern. However, the introduction of video and image sensors in addition to bursty high data rate applications has caused additional challenges [11]. Data intensive applications that send results to a central server are particularly constrained due to the large buffer size required to queue sensed data [12]. This becomes more challenging in clustered networks where the cluster head has to queue lots of data from internal and external sources for onward transmission to the sink.

In summary, it is evident there is need for a planning and deployment tool that takes into account the limited storage capacity of sensor nodes acting as CHs. In addition, it should incorporate an integrated performance and availability modelling and evaluation in order to reduce any effects that may result from independent studies. For clustered WSNs, this tool may also be used for performance tuning and upgrades once the network is operational.

3   System Description

A cluster system with one CH coordinating cluster operations is considered based on earlier work in [4] and [13]. The cluster is assumed to be part of a wider network with K clusters. In this arrangement, the cluster head operation is rotated among strategically deployed full function nodes. The choice of the CH is based on node energy levels and other metrics deemed appropriate [2], [4], and [5]. To conserve energy, CHs rotationally go to sleep after transferring operations to the next CH. For this purpose, use of the best energy saving protocols like UHEED [3] is assumed. The system is assumed to have redundant sensor nodes deployed at inception but kept inactive until the need to replace a failing node arises [6]. It is further assumed that all nodes are equipped with omnidirectional antennas with same radius (d) and can communicate directly with the CH based on the Zigbee 802.15.4 standards. Reduced Function (RF) nodes far away from the CH may transmit their data through Full Function (FF) nodes to the CH. To reduce the energy consumption further, the nodes are able to choose an arbitrary transmission power level as long as the radius does not exceed d.

Information sensed and aggregated at the nodes (FF and RF) are forwarded to the CH which finalises cluster data aggregation. The CHs also generate data packets based on their observations. The total information is then transmitted by the CH to the sink directly or through intermediary CHs. It is assumed that at least one path exists towards the sink[4]. Like other communication networks, this system is subject to failures which may result from hardware, software and channel link errors of failures. Figure 1 shows the system scenario in consideration.

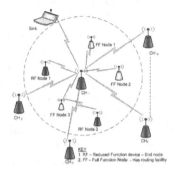
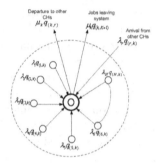

Fig. 1. Topology of the reference scenario   **Fig. 2.** Single CH Queueing Model

4   System Modelling

4.1   Choosing Preferred Model

In a cluster based WSN topology, the CH is the central point of communication between the cluster nodes and the sink. All cluster nodes are assumed connected directly to the CH. The CH connects either directly or through other CHs to the sink forming an overall cluster tree network. The nodes independently monitor their habitat and contend with others for channel availability to relay their observed data to the cluster head. It is assumed that the CH is not aware of the next arrival source until the arrival actually occurs. Due to limited memory capacity of the CH, it is assumed that any data arriving when the CH buffer is full is not allowed in the system and automatically dropped. Packets arrival at the CH is assumed to follow Poisson distribution with mean rate λ and service time assumed exponentially distributed with rate μ [14]. Service priority is based on first come first served (FCFS).

In this model, the total arriving data at the CH originate from within the cluster (internal sources) and externally from other cluster heads (external sources) forwarding their data to the sink. From IEEE 802.15.4/Zigbee standards, a maximum of 36 nodes is recommended per cluster for better performance. This is confirmed in [9] where performance measure were analysed by varying arrival rates and sensor node density per cluster. In this scenario, more than 30 nodes inclusive of the CH are considered. Since we have relatively large number of independent Poisson streams, the resulting superposition of all the arriving jobs at the CH from both internal and external sources follow Poisson distribution [15] with rate λ_k where k stands for the CH (node k).

From the preceding discussions, the CHs operation is similar to an open queuing network with input and output entries. When operating at steady state, average flows entering the CH queue is same us the flow leaving the queue. The behaviour and operations at each cluster head is similar and may be independently modelled using an M/M/1/L queuing system following Jacksons theorem that treats each node in an open queue network as a single server.

4.2   Queueing Model for the System

The resulting job arrivals at the cluster head is a collection of jobs from the cluster nodes, the sensed information by the cluster head itself and the forwarded data from other cluster heads. The jobs are assumed to be independent and identically distributed random variables with rate λ. The operation is assumed similar at all other CHs. For this study, it is assumed there are K CHs ($k = 1, 2, \ldots K$) through which the sink may be reached. The behaviour of a single CH, node k is modelled as an open queue network using M/M/1/L queueing system. The CH is assumed to have a total of N nodes, ($n = 1, 2, \ldots N$). Since the number of cluster nodes plus CHs are taken to be more than 30, it is possible to assume that the resulting superposition of all the job arrivals at node k from internal (N) and external (K) sources (where $N + K \geq 30$) follow Poisson distribution with mean arrival rate λ_k [21]

Figure 2 shows the proposed queuing model for analysing the single CH behaviour. $\lambda_n q_{n,k}$ and $\lambda_r q_{r,k}$ represent the internal and external arrivals at node k (CH) respectively. Once the jobs are processed at node k, they are transmitted directly or forwarded upward to the sink through node r. Here node r represents the next CH towards the sink. The operation at the forwarding node r is similar to that at node k. Since the nodes are prone to failures, it is assumed that when a node fails it is taken into repair process immediately [2], [9]. This could be through software reconfiguration or replacement of failing nodes. Service times, failure times, and repair times are all assumed to be exponentially distributed with rates μ_k , ξ_k and η_k respectively. A finite queue length (L) is introduced and jobs arriving when the queue is full are blocked and assumed lost. The interruption policy is such that service is resumed from the point of interruption or repeat with re-sample.

Jobs leaving node k are rerouted to node r with the probability $q_{k,r}$ for service at node r. If jobs are not routed to node r then $q_{k,r} = 0$. It is assumed without loss of generality that as far as the queue length distributions are concerned $q_{k,k} = 0, (k = 1, 2, \ldots, K)$. Also $q_{k,K+1} = 1 - \sum_{r=1}^{K} q_{k,r}$ is the exit probability from the system after a job is serviced at node k. The exit probability $q_{k,K+1}$, is assumed to be non zero for at least one value of k. Q is the routing probability matrix of size $K \times K$, such that, $Q_{k,r} = q_{k,r}; (1 \leq k, r \leq K)$. To analyse the performability of this system, steady state conditions are considered. The total arrival rate (λ_k) at CH node k as the sum of external and internal traffic rates can then be expressed as:

$$\lambda_k = \sigma_k + \sum_{r=1}^{K} \lambda_r q_{r,k}; \qquad k = 1, 2, \ldots, K \tag{1}$$

Here σ_k is the sum of all internal arrivals and may be expressed as;

$\sigma_k = \sum_{n=1}^{N} \lambda_n q_{n,k} \qquad n = 1, 2, \ldots, N$

The term $\sum_{r=1}^{K} \lambda_r q_{r,k}$ represents the externally arriving jobs from other CHs as mentioned earlier. The blocking probability when the queue is full, the effective arrival rate ($\lambda_{k,e}$) at the CH (node k) and the rate at which the jobs are lost ($\lambda_{k,l}$) due to blocking can be calculated using equations 2 3 and 4 respectively.

$$P_B = \sum_{i=0}^{N} P_{i,L} \tag{2}$$

Where: $P_{i,L}$ is the probability of being in the operative state i when the buffer if full and L is the maximum buffer capacity.

$$\lambda_{k,e} = \lambda_k (1 - P_B) \tag{3}$$

$$\lambda_{k,l} = \lambda_k P_B \tag{4}$$

In order to define the total arrival rates for each node, the row vectors $\lambda = (\lambda_1, \lambda_2, \ldots, \lambda_N)$ and $\sigma = (\sigma_1, \sigma_2, \ldots, \sigma_N)$ can be employed. Let also E_k be the unit matrix of size $K \times K$ then;

$$\lambda(E_k - Q) = \sigma \tag{5}$$

Letting the effective average service rate at the CH be $\hat{\mu}_k$, and taking into account the losses resulting from failures and repairs it can be shown that $\hat{\mu}_k$ is given by equation 6,[18], [19].

$$\hat{\mu}_k = \mu_k . \eta_k / (\eta_k + \xi_k) \tag{6}$$

For steady state, the effective service rate must be greater than the effective arrival rate at the CH. Thus $\hat{\mu}_k > \lambda_{k,e}; k = 1, 2, \ldots K$ is the condition for steady state analysis.

5   Two Dimensional Markov Representation of the Proposed Model

In this system since all the sensor nodes forward their information to the CH, the matrix Q has a special form and the total amount of arrivals to CH can be calculated as $\lambda_k = C \times \lambda$, where C is the number of sensor nodes in the WSN cluster and λ is the average packet generation rate of the sensor nodes [8].

Similar studies using M/M/1/L have been conducted before [20], [15] though no records of the same is known for WSN systems. The state transition diagram for the cluster head is given in figure 3. The operative states F and R represent failed and fully active states respectively.

The model treats sleep and breakdown states as short and long breakdown periods respectively since data will continue to arrive in both of the states. However, service is only possible when the server is fully operational. The system state at time t may be described using a pair of integer valued random variable $I(t)$ and $J(t)$ specifying the cluster head operative states and the number of jobs in the system respectively. The operative states $I(t)$ in this case represents the assumed failed and working periods of the CH. $Z = [I(t), J(t)]; t \geq 0$ is an irreducible Markov process on a lattice strip (QBD process), that models the system. Its state space is $(0, 1) \times (0, 1, \ldots, L)$. Similar models [20], [21] are analysed for exact performability evaluation of various Multi sever systems with single repairman and for both finite and infinite L for some repair strategies. It is possible to extend the exact solution methodology for performability evaluation of WSNs. Since the possible operative states of the CH and the number of data

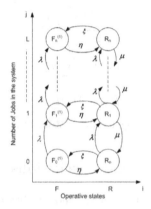

Fig. 3. State transition diagram for CH performability

arrivals are represented in the horizontal and vertical directions of the lattice respectively, the transition matrices can be derived as:

i A is the matrix of instantaneous transition rates from (i, j) to state (l, j),($i = 0, 1; l = 0, 1; i \neq l; j = 0, 1, \ldots, L$), with zeros in the leading diagonal, caused by a change in the state [21]. These are the purely lateral transitions of the model Z. A clearly depends on parameters ξ and η. The state transition matrices A and A_j are of size $(2) \times (2)$ and can be given as shown below.

ii Matrices B and C are transition matrices for one step upward and one step downward transitions respectively [21]. When there is no job in the system, the elements of matrix C are zero. The transition rate matrices do not depend on j for $j \geq M$, where M is a threshold having an integer value [21]. The respective transition matrices are shown below:

$$A = A_j = \begin{bmatrix} 0 & \eta \\ \xi & 0 \end{bmatrix} \text{ and } B = B_j = \begin{bmatrix} \lambda & 0 \\ 0 & \lambda \end{bmatrix} \text{ and } C = C_j = \begin{bmatrix} 0 & 0 \\ 0 & \mu \end{bmatrix}$$

Elements of matrix B are dependent on the data arrival rate (λ) at the CH while elements of matrix C depend on the CH service rate (μ).

Once the state transition matrices are established, spectral expansion solution technique is then employed to derive steady state probabilities for the model. The details of how Spectral Solution technique works may be found in [20], [18]. From the state probabilities, a number of steady-state availability, reliability, performability measures can be computed quite easily. For illustration, we have concentrated on the blocking probability described by 2, the mean queue length (MQL), throughput (γ), utilization (u), and response time (R_T) which may be computed using equations 7 through 10 respectively. From the model service is only possible when there are jobs in the system.

$$MQL = \sum_{j=0}^{L} j \sum_{i=0}^{N} P_{i,j} \tag{7}$$

$$\gamma = \sum_{j=1}^{L} \sum_{i=1}^{N} \mu P_{i,j} \tag{8}$$

$$u = 1 - \sum_{i=0}^{N} P_{i,0} \tag{9}$$

$$R_T = MQL/\gamma \tag{10}$$

where, L and N are queue length and system states respectively as shown in figure 3.

6   Numerical Results and Discussions

In this section, numerical results for the model obtained using Spectral Expansion solution approach are presented. The results are verified using a dedicated event driven simulation software for the actual system developed in C++ language and validated using well known mathematical solutions. The simulation software has also been verified to exactly match the M/M/1/L system performance as presented in [23], [20]. Finally, the steady state results are compared with results obtained from a similar study but with an infinite queue [13] in order to understand the effects of limited memory capacity in sensor nodes acting as CHs. Table 1 bellow lists a summary of steady state performance metrics used in this study.

6.1   Parameter Choice

In this section, parameter choices are discussed and a summary of simulation parameters used are presented in Table 2. The parameters shown in Table 2 are considered throughout the evaluation of the system, unless otherwise stated. In

Table 1. Performance Metrics Explained

Performance Metrics	Brief Description
Effective arrival rate ($\lambda_{k,e}$)	Rate of packets arrival at CH excluding blocked packets
Rate of jobs lost ($\lambda_{k,l}$)	Rate data packets are lost due to blocking
Mean Queue Length (MQL)	Average number of packets in the queue at steady state
Throughput (γ)	Departing packets from CH per unit time after service
Utilization (u)	The fraction of time the server is busy during operation
Response time (R_T)	Total time data packet take in the system
Blocking Probability (P_B)	Probability arriving packet finds buffer is full

choosing the input parameters, a generic system was considered. From IEEE 802.15.4/Zigbee standards, a maximum number of 36 nodes is recommended for for optimal CH operation. Though in most research work, arrival rates of 1 packet/second is used, variation of arrival rates between 1 to 10 packets/second has also been recorded [24]. In other areas, mean arrival rates have been varied between $\lambda = 1 - 15$ packets/hr [25].

Assuming a full capacity cluster operation for monitoring moisture content in an agricultural farmhouse. Configured with the same mean arrival rate of $\lambda = 8$ packets/hr from each cluster node ($\lambda_1 = \lambda_2 = \lambda_3 =,\ldots,= \lambda_C$), the effective arrival at the CH becomes $\lambda_k = C \times \lambda = 288$ packets/hr. For stability, the CH requires a slightly higher mean service rate per hour. Considering that the CH has in addition, internal data and control processes, a service rate of $\mu_k = 300$ packets/hr was arbitrarily chosen in order to ensure steady state condition is reached when the CH is operating in full capacity. Arrival rates following Poisson distribution are varied between $1 - 8$ packets/hr from each node to ensure the system remains stable. An arbitrary queue length of $L = 50$ packets was also chosen for this study throughout the experiments.

Sensors are usually attached with a 2×AA battery pack of $2.7 - 3.3$ volts capable of continuous operation for 3.25 days as given in the CC2420 transceiver data sheet. In this study, it is assumed that good mechanism for availability are put in place and battery depletion is not the cause of failures. Use of backup for CHs and solar charging systems [6], [25] are just but a few example of such mechanisms. In order to model these systems, mean failure (ξ) and repairs (η) rates were assumed to be $\xi = 0.001/hr$ and $\eta = 0.5/hr$ translating to mean failure and repair occurring after every 1000hrs and 2hrs respectively. These values are maintained during the experiment except where specified.

6.2   Results and Discussions

In figure 4, the MQL is presented as a function of arrival rate λ. For every run, a fixed number of nodes is chosen and the arrival rate λ is varied between 0 to 14 packets/hr. It is observed that for steady state operations the MQL

Table 2. Simulation parameters and values

No.	Parameter Type	Parameter Values
1.	Arrival rate λ	0 - 14
2.	Service rate μ	300
3.	Failure rate ξ	0.001 - 0.01
4.	Repair rate η	0.5
5.	Queue capacity L	10, 30, 50, 100, 500, 1000

is kept below 5 jobs after which the system becomes unstable and the MQL shoots up. This is contrary to the infinite system studied in [13] which indicate a slightly higher MQL value (10 jobs) before the system becomes unstable. The results indicate that when the CH is configured for low arrival rates, in this case $\lambda = 5$packets/hr then many cluster nodes $(20 - 36)$ may be accommodated. On the other hand, setting high arrival rates of $\lambda = 10$packets/hr results into the system getting saturated with fewer nodes between $20 - 28$.

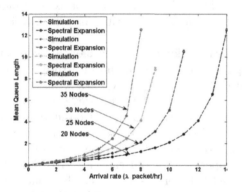

Fig. 4. MQL vs Arrival rate

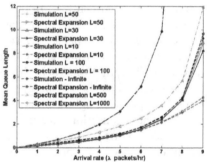

Fig. 5. MQL vs Arrival Rates

Assuming an infinite buffer for WSN CH may therefore impact negatively on system performance hence the need to optimise operations using the available resources. In both finite and infinite scenarios, it is confirmed that fewer nodes are able to accommodate higher arrival rates as opposed to many nodes which saturate the system at lower arrival rates. This confirms a trade off when coverage and optimum performance are of concern as highlighted in [13].

In figure 5, the effects of varying queue capacity is compared. The number of nodes is maintained at 30 throughout the experiment. The following buffer sizes were used; $L = 10, 30, 50, 100, 500, 1000$. During each run, the arrival rate is varied from 1 to 9 packets/hr and the MQL is recorded appropriately. It is observed that when queue capacity is low, then MQL is very low resulting into more jobs being lost. However, as the queue capacity (L) is increased, a limit is approached beyond which further increases do not cause any meaningful change to MQL.

In figure 6, the average response time for a finite system is noted to be much less compared to the infinite systems [13] since only a few packets may wait in the queue at any given time, while the rest of the packets are blocked. Though these results are generic, the response times may easily be customised for particular WSN application requirements for purposes of deployment planning and operation management.

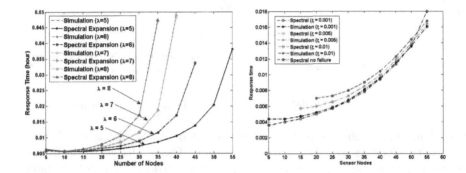

Fig. 6. Varying Nodes vs Response Time   **Fig. 7.** Failure Rate Vs Response Time

In figure 7, the response time is given as a function of number of nodes for various failure rates. For this experiment queue length value of $L = 10$ is used. Arrival rate (λ) is constant but overall arrivals to the cluster head is increasing due to increasing number of nodes. It can be observed that response time is higher when the system exhibits high failure rates. As the nodes are increased, the arrival rate also increases followed by gradual increase in response time. As the nodes are increased, a level of arrival rate is reached after which any additional nodes results into rapid increase in response time. For optimum operation at higher failure rates it is preferable to maintain above 20 active nodes per cluster but not more than desired maximum of 36 nodes. From figures 6 and 7 it can be deduced that preferable response time for better performance falls below 0.025hrs. Systems configured for much lower response times are mostly preferable for WSNs.

Figure 8 shows system blocking probability increasing with increase in arrival rates. It is noted that blocking probability is minimal at low failure rates but shoots up at higher failure rates. Also worth acknowledging is the exponential growth of blocking probability until a steady state is reached after which further increase of arrival rate only results to system oscillating around the steady state. From the observation, it is noted that high failure rates may result into system being highly unreliable hence more data losses. This can be used as a WSN system calibration tool for setting acceptable failure limits, continuous monitoring and prediction of future system behaviour.

From figure 9, it is observed that for $L = 10$, the blocking probability is higher at low arrival rates but remains steady and sharply increases as the arrival rate increases past 6 to 9 packets/hr. For a queue length of $L = 500$, the blocking

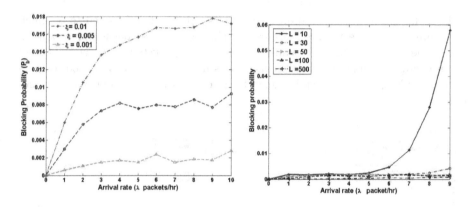

Fig. 8. P_B vs Arrival Rate   **Fig. 9.** P_B vs. Arrival rate

probability approaches zero, thus confirming that as the queue length tends to infinity, blocking probability approaches zero. The results shown in figure 9 shows the performance of realistic WSN systems which do not have infinite buffer length. From figures 5 and 9, it is possible to recommend buffer sizes for various applications which are dependent on the volume of data generated and whether they are mission critical. In table 3, generalised buffer size recommendations for various applications are given. To maximise the performance of the system, the system utilisation was maintained between 0.1 to a maximum of 0.9, which is below the maximum possible 0.998 required for system stability.

Table 3. Proposed Buffer sizes for various application categories

Application Categories	Buffer Sizes	Application Types
Low data intensive	10 − 30	Smart Agriculture
Medium data intensive	30 − 50	Body Area Networks (BANs)
Data intensive	50 − 100	Volcanic eruption, wild forest fire
High data intensive	100 − 500	Video & Data; e.g. Intelligent Transport Syst.
Very high data intensive	500	Real time multi-media applications

7   Conclusions and Future Directions

In this paper, a solution technique is presented for modelling and performability analysis of clustered WSNs with bounded queues. The study is focused around the behaviour of the CH as it receives and processes internal and external job arrivals while at the same time, prone to possible breakdowns, repairs/replacement, and restoration during operations. The CH is successfully modelled using an M/M/1/L open queuing network and its steady state probabilities derived using spectral expansion solution technique. To the best of our knowledge, this is the first attempt to model and analyse integrated performance and availability measures for clustered WSNs under bounded queues.

Numerical results are presented comparatively with results obtained from simulation runs for various performability measures. The results which are in good agreement with discrepancies under 2% clearly show the effects of bounded CH queues and confirm the importance of performability modelling for wireless networks [13]. From the result, it is deduced that finite queues limit acceptable data packets at the CH at any given time and results to loss of packets arriving when the queue is full. Variations in required buffer capacities are application dependent with data intensive (multimedia) applications demanding more storage as highlighted in table 3.

This study can be further extended to model intra and inter cluster traffic with consideration to priority queues for mission critical applications in a mixed application environment. An example of this may be monitoring the spread of pests in the agricultural farm where other applications like temperature, humidity, fire and intrusion detection are also of interest. It is also possible to classify and include in the model, other CH operative states like sleep mode, channel failure, reduced operation state and others. Furthermore, the effects of performance and availability measures on energy consumption can also be incorporated in optimisation studies.

References

1. Dong, S.K., Ghosh, R., Trivedi, K.S.: A Hierarchical Model for Reliability Analysis of Sensor Networks. In: 2010 IEEE 16th Pacific Rim International Symposium on Dependable Computing (PRDC), pp. 247–248 (December 2010)
2. Hashmi, S.U., Rahman, S.M.M., Mouftah, H.T., Georganas, N.D.: Reliability Model for Extending Cluster Lifetime using Backup Cluster Heads in Cluster-Based Wireless Sensor Networks. In: 2010 IEEE 6th International Conference on Wireless and Mobile Computing, Networking and Communications (WiMob), pp. 479–485 (October 2010)
3. Enver, E., Luchmun, R., Leonardo, M., Alfredo, N., Purav, S.: UHEED - An Unequal Clustering Algorithm for Wireless Sensor Networks. In: SENSORNETS, pp. 185–193 (2012)
4. Chiasserini, C.-F., Garetto, M.: Modeling the performance of wireless sensor networks. In: 2004 INFOCOM 23rd Annual Joint Conference of the IEEE Computer and Communications Societies, vol. 1 (March 2004)
5. Li, W.W.: Several characteristics of active/sleep model in wireless sensor networks. In: 2011 4th IFIP International Conference on New Technologies, Mobility and Security (NTMS), pp. 1–5 (February 2011)
6. Munir, A., Gordon-Ross, A.: Markov modeling of fault-tolerant wireless sensor networks. In: 2011 Proceedings of 20th International Conference on Computer Communications and Networks (ICCCN), July 31-August 4, pp. 1–6 (2011)
7. Qiu, T., Feng, L., Xia, F., Wu, G., Zhou, Y.: A Packet Buffer Evaluation Method Exploiting Queueing Theory for Wireless Sensor Networks. Journal of Computer Science and Information Systems 8(4), 1028–1049 (2011)
8. Wang, Z., Yang, K., Hunter, D.: Modelling and Analysis of Convergence of Wireless Sensor Network and Passive Optical Network using Queueing Theory. In: 2011 IEEE 7th International Conference on Wireless and Mobile Computing, Networking and Communications (WiMob), pp. 37–42 (October 2011)

9. Liu, X., Feng, Y., Lv, Q., Zhao, T.: Cascaded movement strategy for repairing coverage holes in wireless sensor networks. In: 2011 International Conference on Information Technology, Computer Engineering and Management Sciences (ICM), vol. 2, pp. 108–111 (September 2011)

10. Zhang, J., Song, G., Qiao, G., Li, Z., Wang, A.: A Wireless Ssensor Nnetwork System with a Jumping Node for Unfriendly Environments. International Journal of Distributed Sensor Networks 2012 (2012)

11. Akkaya, K., Younis, M.: An Energy-Aware QoS Routing Protocol for Wireless Sensor Networks. In: 2003 IEEE Proceedings of the 23rd International Conference on Distributed Computing Systems Workshops, pp. 710–715 (2003)

12. Chang, S., Kirsch, A., Lyons, M.: Energy and storage reduction in data intensive wireless sensor network applications. Technical report, Harvard University (2007)

13. Omondi, F.A., Ever, E., Shah, P., Gemikonakli, O.: Modelling wireless sensor networks for performability evaluation. In: Cichoń, J., Gębala, M., Klonowski, M. (eds.) ADHOC-NOW 2013. LNCS, vol. 7960, pp. 172–184. Springer, Heidelberg (2013)

14. Zhang, Y., Li, W.: Modeling and Energy Cconsumption Evaluation of a Stochastic Wireless Sensor Network. EUROSIP Journal on Wireless Communications and Networking, 1–11 (2012)

15. Chakka, R., Ever, E., Gemikonakli, O.: Joint-State Modeling for Open Queuing Networks with Breakdowns, Repairs and Finite Buffers. In: MASCOTS 2007. 15th International Symposium on Modeling, Analysis, and Simulation of Computer and Telecommunication Systems, pp. 260–266 (October 2007)

16. Wang, Y., Vuran, M.C., Goddard, S.: Cross-layer analysis of the end-to-end delay distribution in wireless sensor networks. IEEE/ACM Transactions on Networking (TON) 20(1), 305–318 (2012)

17. Chiasserini, C., Garetto, M.: An analytical model for wireless sensor networks with sleeping nodes. IEEE Transactions on Mobile Computing 5(12), 1706–1718

18. Thomas, N., Mitrani, I.: Routing among different nodes where servers break down without losing jobs. In: Proceedings of the International Computer Performance and Dependability Symposium, pp. 246–255 (April 1995)

19. Sheng-li, L., Jing-bo, L., De-quan, Y.: The M/M/1 repairable queueing system with variable breakdown rates. In: Chinese Control and Decision Conference (CCDC), pp. 2635–2637 (June 2009)

20. Chakka, R.: Spectral Expansion Solution for some Finite capacity Queues. Annals of Operations Research 79, 27–44 (1998)

21. Ever, E., Kirsal, Y., Gemikonakli, O.: Performability modelling of handoff in wireless cellular networks and the exact solution of system models with service rates dependent on numbers of originating and handoffr calls. In: International Conference on Computational Intelligence, Modelling and Simulation, CSSim 2009, pp. 282–287 (September 2009)

22. Mitrany, I.L., Avi-Itzhak, B.: A many-server queue with service interruptions. Journal of Operations Research 16(3), 628–638 (1968)

23. Cassandras, C.G.: Introduction to Discrete Event Systems, 2nd edn. Springer

24. Zhou, H., Luo, D., Gao, Y., Zuo, D.C.: Modeling of node energy consumption for wireless sensor networks. Wireless Sensor Network 3(1), 18–23 (2011)

25. Li, Z., Peng, Y., Zhang, W., Qiao, D.: J-roc: A Joint Routing and Charging Scheme to Prolong Sensor Network Lifetime. In: 2011 IEEE 19th International Conference on Network Protocols (ICNP), pp. 373–382 (2011)

Discovery of Hidden Correlations between Heterogeneous Wireless Sensor Data Streams

Francesco Cauteruccio[1], Giancarlo Fortino[2],
Antonio Guerrieri[2], and Giorgio Terracina[1]

[1] Dipartimento di Matematica e Informatica,
[2] Dipartimento di Ingegneria Informatica, Modellistica, Elettronica e Sistemistica,
Università della Calabria, I87036 - Rende (CS) - Italy
`f.cauteruccio@gmail.com`, `g.fortino@unical.it`,
`aguerrieri@deis.unical.it`, `terracina@mat.unical.it`

Abstract. This paper proposes a novel approach for monitoring heterogeneous wireless sensor networks and to identify hidden correlations between sensors. The technique is tested in an experimental environment based on the Building Management Framework. Results show that the proposed approach is actually capable of identifying hidden correlations, is robust to environment variations and is sensitive to sensors faults.

1 Introduction

Recent technological and software improvements allowed a widespread diffusion of Wireless Sensor Networks and related applications [1,2]. This led to a significant increase in the amount of produced sensor data and in the complexity of sensor networks. Significant effort has been spent in the last few years on the definition of frameworks for a flexible and efficient management of Wireless Sensor and Actuator Networks (WSANs) [3,4]; this includes intelligent sensing/actuation techniques, as well as data abstractions for improved data analysis.

The complexity of WSANs is constantly growing. In fact, a growing number of networks include heterogeneous sensors, i.e. devices producing different kinds of signals/measures/messages. As an example, sensors in the network may produce not only differently scaled real value data, but also text messages, discrete signals, symbolic alerts, etc.

While sensors network management and the development of robust data acquisition layers received much attention in the literature, one big open challenge in WSANs is anomaly detection [5,6], i.e. the detection of unexpected behavior in incoming data. Anomalies can be generated either by malfunctioning in the sensors or by deviations in the environment. In most cases, it is a challenging task being able to distinguish between the two.

Most of the approaches for anomaly detection concentrate on the analysis of data produced by each *single* device [7]. This is mainly done by fairly complex mathematical analysis of data streams; however, these approaches can be usually applied on numerical data only. Other approaches compare incoming data

G. Fortino et al. (Eds.): IDCS 2014, LNCS 8729, pp. 383–395, 2014.

packets to fixed patterns identifying known behavioral models [8]; typical applications of this kind of techniques are fraud detection for credit cards [9] and intrusion detection in security [10]. Neural networks are often applied also in this setting [6]. However, all these techniques are not well suited for heterogeneous sensor networks.

In this paper, we propose a novel approach specifically conceived for monitoring heterogeneous WSANs. In particular, we propose to identify (hidden) correlations between sensors and to exploit such knowledge to monitor the behaviour of sensors during their working life. As an example, assume we are able to identify that the behavior of two different and heterogeneous sensors is, for some not necessarily obvious reason, correlated. The observation of significant variations of this correlation during time may allow us to suspect that some anomaly is occurring. In fact, it may happen that for two sensors measuring light and temperature, values of temperature are actually influenced by (e.g., sun) light or vice versa (think for example to sensors near incandescent objects).

Obviously, this correlation measure should be robust enough to endorse reasonable variations like time shifts and value drifts, but to identify spikes and noises in the signals.

In order to find correlations between heterogeneous sequences of data, we resort to a solution that stems from classical sequence alignment techniques [11]. Here, the optimal alignment between two sequences defined over the same alphabet of symbols provides a measure of the edit distance, indicating their similarity/dissimilarity[1]. Observe that the best alignment may shift elements to best fit symbol correspondences.

Example 1. Let $s_1 = $ AAABCCDCAC and $s_2 = $ AADBCBBDCC be two sequences. The best alignment is shown next, where the minimum edit distance is 4.

$$s_1 : \text{AAABCCDDCAC} \rightarrow \text{AAABCCDDCAC}$$
$$s_2 : \text{AADBCBBDCC} \ \ \rightarrow \text{AADBCBBDC-C}$$
$$\text{** **   ** *}$$

However, as previously pointed out, when dealing with heterogeneous data streams, generated sequences may come from very different contexts and may be represented with different symbols/metrics. In this context, if the mapping from one symbol set to the other is not known a-priori, a "blind" alignment must be carried out; this means that finding the best mapping between symbols in order to compute the optimal alignment becomes part of the problem. Moreover, in order to accommodate possible drifts, it is necessary to provide the flexibility of mapping some symbol of the first sequence into more than one symbol of the second sequence (and vice versa) so that *many-to-many* mappings can be considered. This is also needed, for example, to accommodate different discretization metrics of numerical sequences.

---

[1] In the classical definition of edit distance, allowed transformations are insertions, deletions and substitutions of symbols, which are the ones we consider in this paper.

In this paper we provide an algorithm to derive "blind" alignments, where insertions, deletions, and substitutions of symbols are allowed and where the best many-to-many mappings between symbols are automatically inferred. The best alignment is then used to derive a correlation index between the two sequences.

The technique is tested in an experimental environment based on the Building Management Framework (BMF) [12]. Results show that the proposed approach is actually capable of identifying hidden correlations, is robust enough to acceptable environment variations and is capable to identify potential sensors faults.

To the best of our knowledge there is no approach in the literature facing all the problems outlined above.

A seminal work on a related topic has been introduced by Baker [13], which computes similarities over parameterized strings, i.e. strings where some of the symbols act as parameters which can be properly substituted at no cost. The work considers *bijective global* transformation functions allowing *exact p-matches* only. Thus, the two strings to be matched must have the same length n: no substitutions or insertions are allowed. Mismatches are allowed in [14] where it has been considered the problem of finding all locations in a string t for which there exists a *global bijection* π mapping a pattern p into the appropriate substring of t minimizing the Hamming distance. *Injective* functions instead of bijective ones are considered in [15]. In [16], the notion of p-edit distance has been introduced where allowed edit operations are *insertions*, *deletions*, and *exact p-matches*. Note that mismatches are not allowed. Moreover, two substrings that participate in two distinct exact p-matches are independent of each other, so that mappings have *local* validity over substrings not broken by insertions and deletions. In particular, within each such substring, the associated mapping function is required to be *bijective*. [17] extends the approach in [16] requiring the transformation function to have *global* validity, but still limits the set of allowed edit operations (substitutions are not allowed).

The plan of the paper is as follows. Section 2 formally introduces the statement of the problem and proposes a solution; Section 3 describes the case study we exploited in the experiments, which are presented in Section 4, where obtained results are also discussed. Finally, in Section 5 we draw our conclusions.

2   Problem Statement and Solution

In this section we first formally introduce the Multi-Parameterized Edit Distance, which is used in this paper to discover hidden correlations between heterogeneous wireless sensor data streams. Then we provide an efficient heuristic for computing the correlation.

2.1   Problem Statement

Let each stream of data be represented as an ordered sequence of symbols (a string), where some of the symbols may play the role of parameters, i.e. their matching with other symbols is not regulated by symbol identity. Let then Σ,

Π_1, and Π_2 be disjoint alphabets of symbols (Σ) and parameters (Π_1, and Π_2). Throughout the following sections, we assume that two strings s_1 over $\Sigma \cup \Pi_1$ and s_2 over $\Sigma \cup \Pi_2$ are given. The length of the string s_i ($i \in \{1, 2\}$), i.e., the number of symbols in it, will be denoted by $len(s_i)$. Moreover, for each position $1 \leq j \leq len(s_i)$, the j-th symbol of s_i will be identified by $s_i[j]$.

Let $-$ be a symbol not included in $\Sigma \cup \Pi_1 \cup \Pi_2$. Then, a string $\bar{s}_i$ over $\Sigma \cup \Pi_i \cup \{-\}$ is a *transposition* of s_i if this latter string can be obtained from s_i by deleting all the occurrences of $-$. The set of all the possible transpositions of s_i is denoted by $\mathcal{TR}(s_i)$. An *alignment* for the strings s_1 and s_2 is a pair $\langle \bar{s}_1, \bar{s}_2 \rangle$ where $\bar{s}_1 \in \mathcal{TR}(s_1)$ and $\bar{s}_2 \in \mathcal{TR}(s_2)$ and where $len(\bar{s}_1) = len(\bar{s}_2)$. Here, $-$ is meant to denote an insertion/deletion operation performed on s_1 or s_2.

Definition 1 (π-partition). *Given an alphabet Π and an integer π such that $0 < \pi \leq |\Pi|$, a π-partition is a partition Φ^π of Π such that $0 < |\phi_v| \leq \pi$, for all $\phi_v \in \Phi^\pi$.*

Definition 2 (Matching Schema). *Given two alphabets Π_1 and Π_2, and two integers π_1 and π_2, a $\langle \pi_1, \pi_2 \rangle$-matching schema is a function $M_{\langle \pi_1, \pi_2 \rangle} : \Phi_1^{\pi_1} \times \Phi_2^{\pi_2} \rightarrow \{\text{true}, \text{false}\}$, where $\Phi_i^{\pi_i}$ ($i \in \{1, 2\}$) is a π_i-partition of Π_i and, for each $\phi_v \in \Phi_1^{\pi_1}$ there is at most one $\phi_w \in \Phi_2^{\pi_2}$ (and respectively, for each $\phi_w \in \Phi_2^{\pi_2}$ there is at most one $\phi_v \in \Phi_1^{\pi_1}$) such that $M(\phi_v, \phi_w) = \text{true}$; this means that all symbols in ϕ_v match with all symbols in ϕ_w. $M(\phi_v, \phi_w) = \text{false}$ indicates that all symbols in ϕ_v mismatch with all symbols in ϕ_w.*

Definition 3 (Match and distance). *Let $\langle \bar{s}_1, \bar{s}_2 \rangle$ be an alignment for s_1 and s_2, let $M_{\langle \pi_1, \pi_2 \rangle}$ be a $\langle \pi_1, \pi_2 \rangle$-matching schema over π-partitions $\Phi_1^{\pi_1}$ and $\Phi_2^{\pi_2}$, and let j be a position with $1 \leq j \leq len(\bar{s}_1) = len(\bar{s}_2)$. We say that $\langle \bar{s}_1, \bar{s}_2 \rangle$ has a match at j if either:*

- $s_1[j], s_2[j] \in \Sigma$ *and* $s_1[j] = s_2[j]$*, or*
- $s_1[j] \in \phi_v, s_2[j] \in \phi_w, \phi_v \in \Phi_1^{\pi_1}, \phi_w \in \Phi_2^{\pi_2}$ *and* $M_{\langle \pi_1, \pi_2 \rangle}(\phi_v, \phi_w) = \text{true}$.

The distance between $\bar{s}_1$ and $\bar{s}_2$ under $M_{\langle \pi_1, \pi_2 \rangle}$ is the number of positions at which $\langle \bar{s}_1, \bar{s}_2 \rangle$ does not have a match.

Given the previous definitions, we introduce the notion of *multi-parameterized edit distance* between two strings s_1 and s_2 which will be the formal basis for the computation of our correlation factor.

Definition 4 (Multi-Parameterized Edit Distance). *Given two integers π_1 and π_2 such that $0 < \pi_1 \leq |\Pi_2|$ and $0 < \pi_2 \leq |\Pi_1|$ the $\langle \pi_1, \pi_2 \rangle$-multi-parameterized edit distance between s_1 and s_2 ($\mathcal{L}_{\langle \pi_1, \pi_2 \rangle}(s_1, s_2)$ for short) is the minimum distance that can be obtained with any $\langle \pi_1, \pi_2 \rangle$-matching schema and any alignment $\langle \bar{s}_1, \bar{s}_2 \rangle$.*

Observe that, in order to properly compute $\mathcal{L}_{\langle \pi_1, \pi_2 \rangle}(s_1, s_2)$ several components play a crucial role: (*i*) π_1 and π_2, which determine the (maximum) size of each partition; (*ii*) π-partitions $\Phi_1^{\pi_1}$ and $\Phi_2^{\pi_2}$, in fact there can be many π-partitions for the same set of π_1, π_2, Π_1, and Π_2; (iii) matching schemas $M_{\langle \pi_1, \pi_2 \rangle}$, which determine the way partitions of different sets can be combined via matching; (iv) alignments, in fact there can be many possible alignments between two strings.

Example 2. Let $\Sigma = \emptyset$, $\Pi_1 = \{$A,B,C,D$\}$ and $\Pi_2 = \{$E,F,G,H$\}$. Let $s1 =$ AAABCCDCAA and $s2 =$ EEFGHGGFHH. For $\pi_1 = \pi_2 = 1$, the best alignment $\langle \bar{s}_1, \bar{s}_2 \rangle$ is the following (obtained matching $\{$A$\}$-$\{$E$\}$, $\{$B$\}$-$\{$G$\}$, $\{$C$\}$-$\{$H$\}$, and $\{$D$\}$-$\{$F$\}$):

$$s_1 : \text{AAABCCDDCAA} \rightarrow \text{AAABCCDDCAA}$$
$$s_2 : \text{EEFGHGGFHH} \rightarrow \text{EEFGHGGFH-H}$$
$$\text{** ** \quad **}$$

which gives $\mathcal{L}_{\langle 1,1 \rangle}(s_1, s_2) = 5$. For $\pi_1 = \pi_2 = 2$, the best alignment is the following (obtained with the matching $\{$B,A$\}$-$\{$E,H$\}$, and $\{$C,D$\}$-$\{$G,F$\}$):

$$s_1 : \text{AAABCCDDCAA} \rightarrow \text{AAABCCDDCAA}$$
$$s_2 : \text{EEFGHGGFHH} \rightarrow \text{-EEFGHGGFHH}$$
$$\text{** * *****}$$

which gives $\mathcal{L}_{\langle 2,2 \rangle}(s_1, s_2) = 3$.

Definition 5 (Multi-Parameterized Correlation Index $I_{\langle \pi_1, \pi_2 \rangle}(s_1, s_2)$).
Given two integers π_1 and π_2 such that $0 < \pi_1 \leq |\Pi_2|$ and $0 < \pi_2 \leq |\Pi_1|$ the Multi-Parameterized Correlation Index ($I_{\langle \pi_1, \pi_2 \rangle}(s_1, s_2)$ for short) is defined as:

$$I_{\langle \pi_1, \pi_2 \rangle}(s_1, s_2) = \frac{|\bar{s}_1| - \mathcal{L}_{\langle \pi_1, \pi_2 \rangle}(s_1, s_2)}{|\bar{s}_1|}$$

where $\bar{s}_1$ (or equivalently $\bar{s}_2$) is the length of the optimal alignment computed for $\mathcal{L}_{\langle \pi_1, \pi_2 \rangle}(s_1, s_2)$.

Observe that $I_{\langle \pi_1, \pi_2 \rangle}(s_1, s_2) \in [0..1]$ and can be expressed as a percentage of similarity.

2.2   Heuristic Solution

A Naïve approach to the computation of $\mathcal{L}_{\langle \pi_1, \pi_2 \rangle}(s_1, s_2)$ may simply consist in the generation of all the valid matching schemas $M_{\langle \pi_1, \pi_2 \rangle}$ and, for each of them, in the computation of the standard edit distance between s_1 and s_2. This approach is clearly unfeasible; in fact, while the computation of the edit distance, given a matching schema, can be carried out in $O(|s_1| \times |s_2|)$, the number of possible matching schemas is exponential in Π_1 and Π_2. In fact, it is possible to prove that the overall problem is NP-Complete. Therefore, the definition of a heuristic solution is necessary.

Since computing the edit distance, given a matching schema, is an easy task, the heuristic proposed in this paper concentrates on the identification of an optimal matching schema. In what follows, in order to simplify the presentation, we will refer to the computation of the standard edit distance with classic algorithms, based on dynamic programming. However, the approach is modular in such a way that more efficient algorithms for the standard edit distance computation can be applied.

The approach is based on a *random-restart steepest ascent hill climbing algorithm*, which works by iterative refinements of the matching schema. Intuitively, at step 0, a valid matching schema M^0 is first chosen, and a global edit distance computed. At each iteration i, neighbors of the current matching schema M^i are considered, and the edit distance obtainable with it is computed. The one allowing to obtain the lowest edit distance is set as the matching schema M^{i+1} for the next step. This phase stops when the edit distance cannot be further improved in the current step and the edit distance obtained with the current matching schema is returned as the result. A neighbor of a matching schema is a perturbation exchanging only one pair of symbols in the same partition.

In order to increase the chances of finding the optimal alignment, a certain number of random restarts, with a new randomly selected matching schema, are subsequently carried out.

The algorithm BLINDALIGNMENT shows how to compute $\mathcal{L}_{\langle \pi_1, \pi_2 \rangle}(s_1, s_2)$ where, for the sake of presentation, we assume that Σ is empty. $I_{\langle \pi_1, \pi_2 \rangle}(s_1, s_2)$ can then be computed straightforwardly.

3   Case Study

As a case study, ambient data have been sensed from a set of wireless sensor nodes deployed in an indoor building environment, specifically at DIMES, Department of Informatics, Modelling, Electronics and Systems, University of Calabria, as shown in Figure 1. In particular, the node tagged as *(a)* has been positioned in an air conditioned and artificially illuminated laboratory; node *(b)* has been located in a corridor without windows and with air conditioning system; node *(c)* has been placed in an office room far from the direct sunlight; nodes *(d)* and *(e)* have been placed both in the same room as node c, but with their sensors leant against a window.

Nodes organized in a multi-hop wireless sensor network have been effectively and efficiently managed through the Building Management Framework (BMF) [4]. The BMF is a domain-specific framework designed for the flexible and efficient management of WSANs deployed in buildings. It offers features such as fast prototyping of WSAN applications, intelligent sensing/actuation techniques, and abstractions for capturing the floor plan of a building.

BMF enables the use of heterogeneous WSANs managed by a basestation, which acts both as a network configurator and a data collector. Basestation and nodes communicate through the BMF Communication Protocol, an application level protocol built on top of multi-hop networks protocols (Dissemination and Collection Tree Protocols [18,19]) An example of BMF network is

Input   : String s_1 and s_2 over Π_1 and Π_2 and three integers π_1, π_2 and T
Output: $\mathcal{L}_{\langle \pi_1, \pi_2 \rangle}(s_1, s_2)$
Data   : M, M': two $\Pi_1 \times \Pi_2$ boolean matrices representing matching
        schemas; *improved*: boolean; t, *mindist*, *globaldist*: integer
begin
  $t = 0$;
  initialize(M);
  mindist $=$ *editdistance*(s_1, s_2, M);
  globaldist $=$ *mindist*;
  improved $=$ TRUE;
  while improved **do**
      improved $=$ FALSE;
      $n =$ neighbors(M);
      foreach M' *in* n **do**
          if *editdistance*(s_1, s_2, M') $<$*mindist* **then**
              mindist $=$ *editdistance*(s_1, s_2, M');
              improved $=$ TRUE;
              $M = M'$;
          end
      end
      if *not improved* **then**
          if *mindist* $<$ *globaldist* **then**
              globaldist $=$ *mindist*;
              improved $=$ TRUE;
              $t = 0$;

          else if $t < T$ **then**
              $t = t + 1$;
              improved $=$ TRUE;
              $M = randomSelect(M)$;
              mindist $=$ *editdistance*(s_1, s_2, M);

      end
  end
  return *globaldist*
end

Algorithm 1. BLINDALIGNMENT

shown in Figure 2, where the BMF high-level layered architecture for both the BMF basestation and node sides is shown. In particular, on the basestation-side, the BMF architecture is split in layers comprehending: (i) support for heterogeneous sensor platforms (e.g. TelosB, Tyndall, Shimmer, SunSPOT), (ii) a network management layer that allows to flexibly manage the BMF network through configuration packets sent over the air, (iii) a Basestation Core providing a set of functionalities to manage/configure the network (e.g. group nodes,

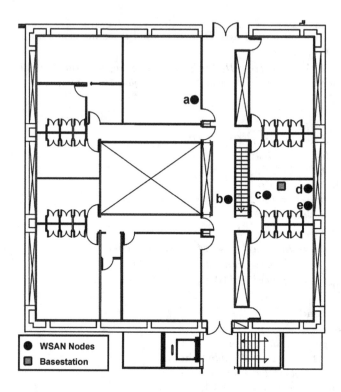

Fig. 1. Wireless sensor nodes deployed at DIMES

create periodic sensing or actuation requests to the network), and (iv) a set of applications that can be run on top of the Basestation Core; on the node-side the BMF layers comprehend: (i) a set of platform-specific components to allow the use of different type of nodes in a BMF network, (ii) a network management layer to allow communication among nodes and with the basestation, and (iii) a platform-independent core to implement the node specific functionalities, such as signal processing and multi-request scheduling on the nodes functionalities.

For the case study, BMF nodes have been configured to send to the basestation synthetic data every minute. In particular, every node in the deployment collects data from light and temperature sensors every second and every minute sends to the basestation the mean computed over the samples read. To provide the algorithm (explained in Section 2) with a complete input, the BMF basestation has been improved with a filter that removes redundant packets received from the network and purposely masks data losses.

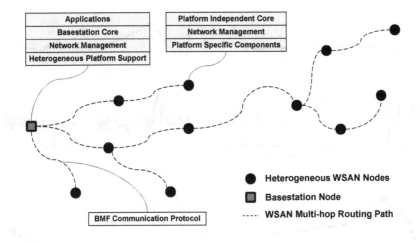

Fig. 2. A BMF Network

4   Experiments and Result Analysis

In this section, we report results for a number of tests carried out to assess the effectiveness of our technique. Tests have been carried out collecting one whole day data from different wireless sensor nodes (see Section 3).

Collected numerical data have been discretized in order to produce one string for each pair node-sensor; for each string s_i, $len(s_i) = 500$ and $\Pi_i = 20$. We then concentrated on comparing light and temperature data coming from each node. The BLINDALIGNMENT algorithm has been executed on a server equipped with an Intel Xeon X3430 processor and 4 GB of RAM running the Ubuntu Linux kernel 2.6.26-2-686-bigmem SMP i686 GNU/Linux operating system.

We carried out three kinds of tests, which are detailed next.

4.1   Hidden Correlation for Different Positioning of the Sensors Nodes

In this test, we considered only the nodes a-d. Figure 3 plots the raw data collected from considered nodes; observe that it is hard to state, from the figures only, some degree of correlation between measured temperature and light.

We first measured $I_{\langle \pi_1, \pi_2 \rangle}$ for the four sensors nodes and using different configurations, namely $I_{\langle 1,1 \rangle}$, $I_{\langle 2,2 \rangle}$, and $I_{\langle 3,3 \rangle}$; moreover, we computed the same measures on randomly generated string pairs (having the same lengths and alphabets as the test ones) and averaged obtained values. Results are shown in Table 1. From the analysis of this table, it is possible to observe that the most correlated measures are those obtained from nodes *(a)* and *(d)*. Obtained results confirmed our intuition for *(d)* since intuitively temperature is significantly dependent on sunlight; however results for *(a)* where not so obvious but they can

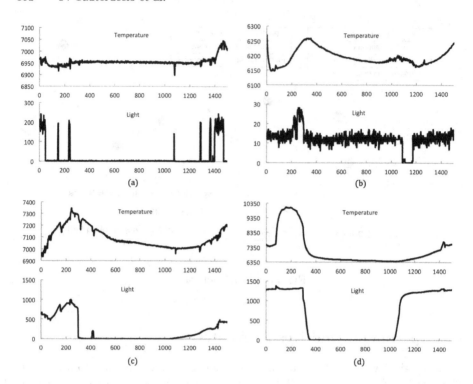

Fig. 3. Plot of (T)emperature and (L)ight collected from nodes a, b, c, d

Table 1. BLINDALIGNMENT and Std Correlation

Node	$I_{\langle 1,1 \rangle}(T, L)$	$I_{\langle 2,2 \rangle}(T, L)$	$I_{\langle 3,3 \rangle}(T, L)$	Std Corr.
a	62.00%	75.00%	81.80%	0.49
b	30.40%	45.80%	54.40%	0.22
c	41.40%	52.60%	69.60%	0.54
d	55.50%	72.00%	80.80%	0.61
expected random	27,57%	41,80%	49,90%	0.016

be motivated by the fact that temperature and light are kept almost constant by artificial illumination and conditioning (see Figure 3).

In order to have a comparison meter for these results, we also computed the standard mathematical correlation degree between numerical sequences (see Table 1), which basically confirmed the trends measured with BLINDALIGNMENT. Observe, however, that computing this measure is possible only between pairs of numerical data; as an example, we could have not computed it if one of the sensors produced labelled messages; on the contrary, $I_{\langle \pi_1, \pi_2 \rangle}$ is a more general measure which may compare heterogeneous sequences, and can take into account both temporal and amplitude shifts.

Table 2. Day span

Node	$I_{\langle 1,1 \rangle}(T,L)$		$I_{\langle 2,2 \rangle}(T,L)$		$I_{\langle 3,3 \rangle}(T,L)$	
	Day 1	Day 2	Day 1	Day 2	Day 1	Day 2
d	51.72%	51.01%	64.94%	67.20%	72.77%	75.85%
e	49.04%	43.17%	63.54%	66.91%	71.67%	75.46%

4.2   Robustness of the Measure

In a second series of experiments, we verified the robustness of the approach to natural and artificial variations in the measurement context. Specifically, we considered nodes d-e from which we collected the stream of Temperature and Light for two consecutive days. Moreover, the second day of observation, one of the nodes has been covered with an opaque sheet in order to simulate a "cloudy" day. Obtained results for $I_{\langle \pi_1, \pi_2 \rangle}$ are shown in Table 2. The analysis of this table shows that *(i)* correlation results remain stable throughout the days and that *(ii)* the proposed measure is robust to context variations. In fact, the correlation computed for node *(e)* does not significantly change over the two days even if this was the one covered by the opaque sheet.

4.3   Sensitivity to Sensor Faults

In the third series of experiments, we checked the sensitivity of the approach to possible faults of node sensors. In particular, we simulated faults in one of the sensors of a node introducing randomly generated out-of-scale noise in the stream. Then, we computed $I_{\langle \pi_1, \pi_2 \rangle}$ for different percentage of noisy values. Obtained results are illustrated in Figure 4 where it is possible to observe that the correlation index correctly decreases for an increasing amount of noise. From the analysis of this graph it is possible to conclude that our approach could be possibly able to identify potential sensor faults when observing significant variations in the correlation index.

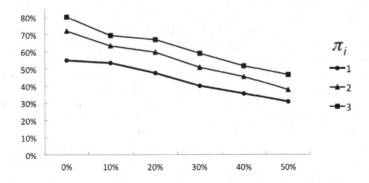

Fig. 4. Sensitivity to sensor faults, Node *(d)*

5   Conclusion

In this paper we presented a novel approach for monitoring heterogeneous wireless sensor networks. The approach showed to be general enough to handle various kind of variabilities in input streams of data, such as data scales and formats, data drifts, time shifts, noises, environment changes, etc. Experimental validation on a real use case provided numerical validation of these properties and, more generally, of the capability to handle heterogenous data streams. Presented work is a first step towards monitoring of different kind of sensors in complex networks. As far as future work is concerned, we plan to further improve the approach both in terms of efficiency and in terms of practical applicability. In particular, several extensions could be devised in order to include domain specific notions about potential symbol correlations, or in order to restrict time-based alignments to represent cause-effect measures. Another line of extensions aim to design automatic control flows in wireless sensor networks using the proposed approach. Finally, we plan to conduct a more extensive testing with more heterogeneous sensor data and positioning.

References

1. Akyildiz, I.F., Su, W., Sankarasubramaniam, Y., Cayirci, E.: Wireless sensor networks: a survey. Computer Networks: The International Journal of Computer and Telecommunications Networking 38, 393–422 (2002)
2. Fortino, G., Giannantonio, R., Gravina, R., Kuryloski, P., Jafari, R.: Enabling Effective Programming and Flexible Management of Efficient Body Sensor Network Applications. IEEE Transactions on Human-Machine Systems 43(1), 115–133 (2013)
3. Stankovic, J.: When sensor and actuator cover the world. Electronics and Telecommunications Research Institute (ETRI) Journal 30(5), 627–633 (2008)
4. Fortino, G., Guerrieri, A., O'Hare, G., Ruzzelli, A.: A flexible building management framework based on wireless sensor and actuator networks. Journal of Network and Computer Applications 35, 1934–1952 (2012)
5. Bosman, H., Liotta, A., Iacca, G., Wörtche, H.: Anomaly detection in sensor systems using lightweight machine learning. In: IEEE International Conference on Systems, Man, and Cybernetics (SMC), pp. 7–13 (2013)
6. Bosman, H., Liotta, A., Iacca, G., Wörtche, H.: Online extreme learning on fixed-point sensor networks. In: IEEE 13th International Conference on Data Mining Workshops (ICDMW), pp. 319–326 (2013)
7. Zhang, Y., Jiang, J.: Bibliographical review on reconfigurable fault-tolerant control systems. Annual Reviews in Control 32(2), 229–252 (2008)
8. Ahmed, T., Coates, M., Lakhina, A.: Multivariate online anomaly detection using kernel recursive least squares. In: 26th IEEE International Conference on Computer Communications (INFOCOM), pp. 625–633 (2007)
9. Phua, C., Lee, V.C.S., Smith-Miles, K., Gayler, R.W.: A comprehensive survey of data mining-based fraud detection research. CoRR abs/1009.6119 (2010)
10. Garcia-Teodoro, P., Díaz-Verdejo, J.E., Maciá-Fernández, G., Vázquez, E.: Anomaly-based network intrusion detection: Techniques, systems and challenges. Computers & Security 28(1-2), 18–28 (2009)

11. Levenshtein, V.: Binary codes capable of correcting deletions, insertions, and reversals. Soviet Physics-Doklady 10(8), 707–710 (1966)
12. Guerrieri, A., Fortino, G., Ruzzelli, A., O'Hare, G.: A WSN-based building management framework to support energy-saving applications in buildings. In: Advancements in Distributed Computing and Internet Technologies: Trends and Issues, pp. 258–273 (2011)
13. Baker, B.S.: Parameterized pattern matching: Algorithms and applications. Journal of Computer and System Sciences 52, 28–42 (1996)
14. Hazay, C., Lewenstein, M., Sokol, D.: Approximate parameterized matching. ACM Transactions on Algorithms 3(3), art. 29 (2007)
15. Apostolico, A., Erdős, P., Lewenstein, M.: Parameterized matching with mismatches. Journal of Discrete Algorithms 5(1), 135–140 (2007)
16. Baker, B.: Parameterized diff. In: Proc. of the 10th Annual ACM-SIAM Symposium on Discrete Algorithms (SODA), pp. 854–855. Society for Industrial and Applied Mathematics, Philadelphia (1999)
17. Keller, O., Kopelowitz, T., Lewenstein, M.: On the longest common parameterized subsequence. Theoretical Computer Science 410(51), 5347–5353 (2009)
18. Levis, P., Patel, N., Culler, D., Shenker, S.: Trickle: a self-regulating algorithm for code propagation and maintenance in wireless sensor networks. In: Proceedings of the 1st conference on Symposium on Networked Systems Design and Implementation, NSDI 2004, vol. 1. USENIX Association, Berkeley (2004)
19. Gnawali, O., Fonseca, R., Jamieson, K., Kazandjieva, M., Moss, D., Levis, P.: CTP: An Efficient, Robust, and Reliable Collection Tree Protocol for Wireless Sensor Networks. ACM Transactions on Sensors Networks 10(1), 16:1–16:49 (2013)

A Learning-Based MAC for Energy Efficient Wireless Sensor Networks

Stefano Galzarano[1,2], Giancarlo Fortino[2], and Antonio Liotta[1]

[1] Department of Electrical Engineering,
Eindhoven University of Technology (TU/e), Eindhoven, The Netherlands
{s.galzarano,a.liotta}@tue.nl
[2] Department of Informatics, Modelling, Electronics and Systems (DIMES),
University of Calabria (UNICAL), Rende, Italy
g.fortino@unical.it

Abstract. Designing energy-efficient communication protocols is one of the main challenges in wireless sensor networks. This work presents an adaptive radio scheduling schema employing a reinforcement learning algorithm for reducing the energy consumption while preserving the other network performances. By means of a decentralized on-line approach, each nodes determines the most beneficial radio schedule by dynamically adapting to its own traffic load and to the neighbors' communication activities. We compare our approach with other learning-based MAC protocols as well as conventional MAC approaches and show that, under different simulating scenarios and traffic conditions, our protocol achieves better trade-offs in terms of energy consumption, latency and throughput.

Keywords: Wireless Sensor Networks (WSN), Media Access Control (MAC), energy-efficient protocol, reinforcement learning.

1 Introduction

Wireless Sensor Networks (WSNs) are typically composed of small embedded devices providing sensing and computing capabilities for supporting a wide range of distributed applications [1]. Unless external energy power sources are available, which however sacrifice size, weight and flexibility, sensor nodes are typically battery-powered systems. Thus, energy constraint is one of the main limitation of WSNs due to the difficulties in recharging or replacing batteries once the WSN has been deployed.

The usual approach for extending the network lifetime is then adopting energy-efficient mechanisms for managing the node's tasks and keeping the energy consumption to a minimum. Specifically, handling the radio activities is the most demanding requirements in WSNs, since wireless communication and sensing are the most energy-consuming tasks. As a consequence, the MAC protocol has a significant impact on the whole network performance because it is responsible for coordinating the access to the radio channel, thus affecting directly not only

G. Fortino et al. (Eds.): IDCS 2014, LNCS 8729, pp. 396–406, 2014.

the energy consumption but also other metrics like throughput and latency. A well conceived MAC layer should guarantee an energy-efficient radio management by firstly addressing the main sources of energy waste such as overhearing, idle listening, packet collisions and excessive retransmissions and, at the same time, ensuring the successful delivery of packets to destination.

Since a WSN is usually deployed as an unstructured network in which nodes randomly form ad-hoc connections to each other, the MAC protocol can rely neither on a fixed duty cycle nor on a centralized orchestrator in charge of controlling the optimal allocation of communication slots among nodes. On the contrary, a distributed and decentralized approach capable of adapting to the changing network conditions is more suitable [2]. The need for such an adaptive behavior encouraged us to explore computational intelligence methods [3] for sensor networks, thanks also to the fact that some machine learning approaches can be viable solutions even in the context of lightweight sensor system [4,5].

In this paper, a contention-based MAC protocol for WSNs is described and evaluated. Based on Reinforcement Learning (RL) [6], the protocol aims at efficiently managing the node's sleep and active periods to reduce energy consumption by taking into consideration the current traffic load of the node and of its neighborhood. Moreover, since both MAC [7] and network protocols [8] contribute to the network performance, our protocol benefits from a cross-layer interaction with the network layer, so as to better understand the communication patterns to significantly reduce energy consumption due to both idle listening and overhearing. The proposed approach is inherently distributed and thanks to its very low computational complexity, it is suitable for practical deployments in real resource-constrained sensor platforms.

The rest of this paper is organised as follows. In Sect. 2, we report some of the most representative MAC approaches proposed for WSNs. A detailed description of our approach is provided in Sect. 3. In Sect. 4 our protocol is compared with other learning-based MAC protocol through simulation and the performance results are discussed. Finally, in Sect. 5, conclusions are drawn.

2   Related Work

MAC protocols for WSNs are usually divided into two main categories, contention-based and schedule-based (or contention-free). In a contention-based approach, the node does not rely on pre-scheduled transmissions but has to contend for the access to the radio channel whenever it has data to send. On the contrary, in schedule-based approaches, the channel is handled through reservation and one or more transmission slots are assigned to each node.

A typical contention-free protocol relies on a time division multiple access (TDMA) [9] which adopts a fixed time-based schedule for avoiding packet collisions. However, the small slot duration needs an extremely exact timing in order to avoid critical behaviors, whereas maintaining a deterministic schedule in an ad-hoc environment is a complex task.

S-MAC [10] is a contention-based MAC protocol aiming at reducing energy consumption and collisions. It divides time into large frames, and each frame into two time portions (a sleeping phase and an active phase). Compared to the TDMA approach, S-MAC requires much looser synchronization among neighboring nodes. However, due to a fixed duty cycle it is not able to adapt to changing network traffic conditions.

The Timeout-MAC (T-MAC) protocol [11] is an improvement of S-MAC as it uses an adaptive duty cycle. In particular, by means of a time-out mechanism it detects possible activities in its vicinity. If no activity is detected during the time-out interval, the node goes to sleep for a certain period of time. Such a mechanism occurs every time a communication between two nodes is over. Although T-MAC outperforms S-MAC, its performance degrades under high traffic loads.

In the P-MAC [12] protocol the sleep-wakeup schedules of the sensor nodes are adaptively determined on the basis of a node's own traffic and that of its neighbors. The idle listening periods, which are source of energy wastage, are minimized by means of some kind of matching algorithm among patterns of schedules in the neighboring. However, the high computational complexity limits its use in real resource-constrained sensor platforms.

Other adaptive MAC protocols have been proposed in the literature and few of them employ online machine learning approaches such as reinforcement learning [13,14].

The RL-MAC protocol proposed in [13] tackles the problem of adjusting the sleeping and active periods over the frame by actively inferring the state of other nodes with the aim of increasing throughput and saving energy. In its active period, the node can transmit data messages only during a specific reserved slot. Moreover, at the beginning of this reserved slot, the node exchanges some control information as well as the reward for the other nodes, depending on the number of waiting messages and the number of successfully transmitted messages during the reserved slot. It achieves higher throughput and lower energy expenditure compared to S-MAC.

In [14], the authors address the problem of high latency and high energy expenditure in random topology for data aggregation applications. They first define a specific energy efficiency function to be locally computed by each node over each time frame. Then, the proposed algorithm computes the average energy efficiency by considering the node's neighborhood and use the result as reward signal in order to determine the optimal start and duration of the sleep period for the next frame. The proposed decentralized algorithm is reported to achieve better results in terms of energy expenditure and latency, with respect to a non-learning approach (fixed sleep duration).

3   RL-Based Protocol Design

The proposed protocol has been designed to allow each node to independently determine a good sleep/active scheduling policy over the time by not only taking into consideration its own traffic load but also learning at runtime the neighborhood's behavior and then adapting to the changing local traffic conditions.

The basic underlying structure of our protocol is similar to most other MAC protocols: it divides the time into small discrete units, called *frames*, which are further divided into smaller time units, the *slots*. Both frame length and slot number depend on the specific application and, thus, they are considered parameters of the algorithm and remain unchanged at runtime. On top of this frame-based structure, a simple asynchronous CSMA-CA approach is employed. Setting the optimal length of the frame or the amount of time slots within the frame will not be discussed in this paper due to space restrictions.

The main aim of the algorithm is to learn the most beneficial wake-up schedule in order to limit the number of slots in which the node's radio will be turned on and prevent the main source of energy waste such as overhearing and idle listening. This non-fixed schedule reduces energy consumption over the time while preserving the network performances in terms of throughput and latency, as discussed in Sect. 4.

Specifically, a Reinforcement Learning (RL) algorithm has been employed. This is concerned with how an agent (i.e. each node in our specific case) takes actions so as to maximize some kind of long-term reward. In particular, the agent explores its environment by selecting at each step a specific action and receiving a corresponding reward from the environment. Since the best action is never known a-priori, the agent has to learn from its experience, by means of the execution of a sequence of different actions and deducing what should be the best behavior based on the obtained corresponding rewards.

In particular, the popular Q-Learning algorithm has been chosen as the basis for our protocol. It does not need the environment to be modeled whereas its actions depend on a so called *Q-function*, which evaluates the quality of a specific action at a specific agent's state. However, differently from the traditional Q-learning, the notion of states is not used in our approach.

On each node, a specific Q-function is computed on every slot within the frame and the resulting Q-values are stored and updated frame by frame. Each of these Q-values specifies how beneficial it is for the node to stay awake on a specific slot of the frame. Thus, this set of values determines the wake-up pattern of the node over the current frame. As a consequence, the actions available to each agent/node consist in deciding whether it should stay in active or in sleep mode during each single time slot, whereas the Q-values are updated based on specific events occurring during the same slot at each frame (e.g. sent, received or overheard packet, as will be discussed later on) and on some state information coming from the node's neighbors. In particular, on a certain node i, the quality value of a specific slot is updated by means of the following update rule:

$$Q^i_{s,f+1} \leftarrow (1 - \lambda)Q^i_{s,f} + \lambda R^i_{s,f} \tag{1}$$

where $Q^i_{s,f} \in [0,1]$ is the Q-value associated to the slot s of the current frame f, $Q^i_{s,f+1}$ is the updated Q-value of the same slot s but for the next frame, $\lambda \in [0,1]$ is the learning rate and $R^i_{s,f}$ is the obtained reward during the slot of the current frame. The new set of $Q^i_{s,f+1}$ values will be then considered for determining the radio schedule pattern to be employed during the next frame.

It is worth noting that, at startup, all the Q-values on every node are set to "1", meaning that all nodes have their radio transceiver ON in every slot (i.e. for the entire frame). During the learning process, the Q-values changes over the time accordingly to the new obtained rewards. In order to properly set the state for the radio transceiver on the basis of the Q-values, our protocol relies on a specific parameter, T_{ON}, representing a threshold value:

$$Radio_{[slot\ s]} = \begin{cases} On & \text{if } Q^i_{s,f} \geq T_{ON} \\ Off & \text{otherwise} \end{cases}$$

If the quality value of a specific slot s is below this threshold value, the node will put itself in sleep mode for the duration of the whole slot. Otherwise, it will stay in active mode because most likely there will be communication activities directly involving the node.

In such a decentralized learning approach, the main challenge is defining a suitable reward function for the individual node that will implicitly lead to a coordinated-group behavior. Thus, it should consider the current condition of both the node and its neighborhood. Specifically, a certain node i will consider as reward signals for a specific slot s the following information:

- **Received packets**: the total amount of packets correctly received by the node from its neighbors during the slot;
- **Transmitted packets**: the amount of packets the node has successfully transmitted to the intended receiver during the slot. In case of unicast communication in the MAC layer, successful data reception is directly acknowledged with an ACK packet.
- **Over-heard packets**: the amount of over-heard packets received during the same slot, i.e. the packets received but actually not intended for the node itself. Again, in unicast communication the MAC layer is able to directly detect such packets;
- **Expected received packets**: the amount of packets a specific neighboring node has sent to node i during the slot; this is the only information explicitly exchanged by the protocol and is necessary when the node is in sleep mode during the slot and cannot perceive the communication activities of its neighborhood. Thanks to this information, the node is then able to figure out when it would be better to turn on the radio again during the slot because of a new packet traffic pattern. It is also used to check the amount of packets not successfully received due to collisions.

The transmission of the MAC packets may also take place in broadcast mode, so that a node is not able to figure out whether each single received packet is actually destined for itself or not and the ACK packet cannot be sent back. In this case, it is necessary to get some extra information from the upper layers. This is why our MAC protocol employs an effective cross-layer communication: every received broadcast packet is decapsulated and delivered to the network layer, which in turns checks whether or not the packet is intended for the node. In case the packet is discarded, the network layer signals the MAC protocol about the reception of a overheard packet, and the reward function is updated accordingly.

Moreover, if the radio is turned off at a specific slot but the node needs to send a packet, we prefer to buffer it and postpone its transmission on the next available slot (i.e. the first one in which the node is in active mode).

4 Simulations and Results

In this section we proceed with the experimental comparison between our protocol and other similar learning-based approaches, in particular the ones proposed in [14], which we will rename as EE-MAC here for easy reference, and the RL-MAC proposed in [13]. For each comparison, different simulation scenarios and settings have been considered, since we have decided to employ the same experimental setup described in the original reference papers. Our protocol has been implemented, simulated and evaluated in Castalia[1], a plugin for OMNET++ specifically designed for simulating WSNs.

4.1 Comparison with EE-MAC

As described in [14], networks characterized by a random topology and different sizes (10 and 50 nodes) have been considered. As for the communication pattern, a nodes-to-sink data gathering application has been employed in our simulations, since data-collection is one of the most typical use cases of a WSN in real contexts. In particular, the sensor data acquired by each node is sent to a sink, which is centered in the middle of the simulation area. In both scenarios (i.e. small and large networks), the packet rate is set to 2 packets per second, with a data payload of 32 bytes, whereas the simulation time for the learning process is 500 seconds (the time needed by the setup phase described later on is not included).

Since the sink is not in the transmission range of every node, a multipath ring routing has been used as network layer protocol. Once the nodes are deployed, an initial setup phase is first triggered by the sink, which broadcasts a specific packet with a counter set to 0. When the packet is received by a one-hop distance node, it sets its own level/ring number to 0, increments the counter and rebroadcasts the packet. This process goes further on until all nodes set their own ring level. During this setup phase, the learning algorithms are not running because we are only interested in the traffic pattern generated by the actual sensor data. Once the setup phase is over, every node has a ring number representing the hop distance to the sink. When a node has data to send, it broadcasts a data packet by attaching its ring number. Only the neighbors with a smaller ring number process the packet and rebroadcast it by replacing the previous value for the ring number with its own ring number. This process continues until the data packet reaches the sink.

---

[1] http://castalia.research.nicta.com.au

The following performance criteria have been considered and measured in the experiments:

- *Average latency*, which measures the mean time a message takes to be delivered to the sink from the sending node.
- *Standard deviation of the average latency.*
- *The maximum latency of the network*, i.e. the latency of the packet that took the most time to reach the sink.
- *Total number of packets received* by the sink within the simulation time.
- *Average improvement of the remaining battery*, which measures the mean increment, in percentage, of the remaining battery at the end of the simulation by using the learning algorithm instead of a fixed sleep duration.

The results provided by the simulations are reported in Tab. 1.

Table 1. Comparison results

Performance metric - 10 nodes	EE-MAC	Our QL-based MAC
Latency - mean (sec)	3.937	0.045
Latency - std. dev. (sec)	3.348	0.024
Latency - max (sec)	18.975	0.14
Packets arrived at Sink	2167	6679
Remaining battery improvement - mean	10.4%	26.2%
Performance metric - 50 nodes	**EE-MAC**	**Our QL-based MAC**
Latency - mean (sec)	5.823	0.246
Latency - std. dev. (sec)	5.850	0.137
Latency - max (sec)	50.892	0.872
Packets arrived at Sink	2296	23722
Remaining battery improvement - mean	1.9%	12.7%

As it can be seen, in both small and large network and for all the performance metrics our approach provides a better performance. In particular, it is worth noting the differences in latency. It is evident how our learning algorithm guarantees a latency below 1 second even in the large network, where, by adopting the EE-MAC algorithm, a data packet may even take a few tens of seconds before being delivered to the sink. Another significant difference is related to the packet delivery, since our approach is able to successfully deliver a greater number of packets to the sink, in both networks. In particular, the EE-MAC shows very poor performance when dealing with the large network, by delivering almost the same amount of packets as in the small network although. This means that most of the data packets are actually lost during the data gathering process probably due to a high collision rate. Finally, as for the energy efficiency, our algorithm provides a higher increment in the remaining battery after the end of the simulation.

4.2   Comparison with RL-MAC

In order to further evaluate the performance of the proposed MAC protocol, several other simulations have been carried out in comparison to RL-MAC, the reinforcement learning-based MAC protocol described in [13]. Moreover, the performance of a non-learning protocol, S-MAC, has been also taken into consideration. Three scenarios have been simulated having different network topology: star, linear and mesh. For each scenario, the data packet inter-arrival time has been varied and the following performance metrics have been considered: data throughput, latency, and energy efficiency. The energy efficiency represents the energy cost per-byte of the goodput (i.e. excluding any overhead from the data throughput). As for the radio setting, the parameters in Tab. 2 have been used for all the simulations.

Table 2. Radio parameters used in the simulations

Radio Parameter	Value
Transmission power:	0.5 W
Receiving power:	0.3 W
Idle listening power:	0.05 W
Radio transmission rate:	20 kbps

A first set of simulations are related to the star topology, with a receiving sink node in the middle and all other nodes sending data packets with a varying inter-arrival time, from 1 to 10 seconds (the theoretical generating throughput is between 20 and 200 byte/sec). A second set of simulations focus on a linear topology network consisting of 10 nodes. The traffic is generated from one edge node to the other one, with 200-byte long packet sent with the same varying inter-arrival time, i.e. from 1 to 10 seconds and thus generating throughput between 20 and 200 byte/sec.

Fig. 1 shows that our protocol can achieve a considerably higher throughput with respect to both RL-MAC and S-MAC when traffic load is heavy (i.e. at low data packet inter-arrival time). In particular, it is able to always achieve the maximum theoretical throughput both in the star topology, Fig. 1(a), and in the linear one, Fig. 1(b), since it is able to effectively adapt to any traffic load without incurring any packet loss. On the contrary, when traffic load is high (200 byte/sec), the RL-MAC throughput can achieve 80% of the generated traffic in the star topology and only 35% in the linear one.

As illustrated in Fig. 2, the proposed protocol clearly outperforms both RL-MAC and S-MAC in term of packet latency. Specifically, the values are constantly much lower than 1 second, meaning that such a metric is not influenced at all by the traffic load of the network and all the packets are successfully delivered to destination with very negligible delay. RL-MAC, instead, with respect to the S-MAC, provides better results at higher traffic load, i.e. with less than 5-second and 8-second inter-arrival time for the star and linear topology.

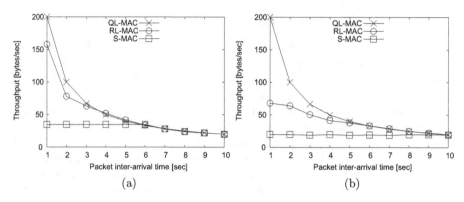

Fig. 1. Data throughput versus packet inter-arrival time on star (a) and linear (b) topologies

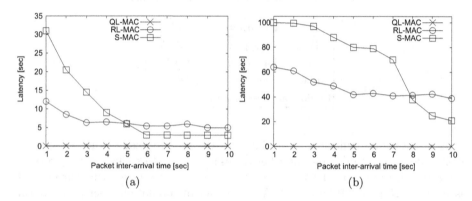

Fig. 2. Latency versus packet inter-arrival time on star (a) and linear (b) topologies

In term of energy efficiency, as it can be seen in Fig. 3(a), for the star topology, our protocol offers up to 40% of energy savings when compared to RL-MAC and up to 80% when compared to S-MAC. Much more evident is the energy savings achieved in the liner topology, Fig. 3(b). In fact, differently from RL-MAC and S-MAC, the energy efficiency of the proposed protocol does not change so much between the star and the linear topology because, in both scenarios, the nodes are kept in active mode during the same slots of the frame over the time. Moreover, in all the algorithms, the energy spent per-byte decreases (or the energy efficiency increases) as the traffic load increases because more energy is used in transmission and reception rather than idle listening.

In the last set of simulations, a mesh network consisting of 100 nodes (having a transmission range of 20 meters) uniformly distributed over a 100x100 meters area is adopted. The sink is placed in one of the corner of the simulation area, whereas a subset of nodes are selected for generating the data traffic to the sink. Again, the inter-arrival time has been varied from 1 to 10 sec.

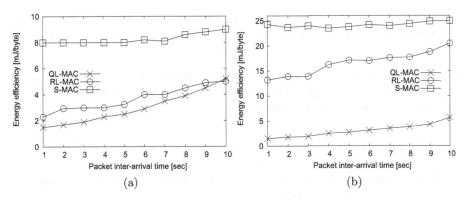

Fig. 3. Energy efficiency versus packet inter-arrival time on star (a) and linear (b) topologies

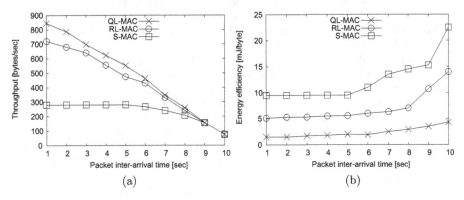

Fig. 4. Throughput (a) and Energy efficiency (b) versus packet inter-arrival time on mesh topology

In Fig. 4, the data throughput and the energy efficiency of the three protocols are depicted. In particular, the proposed protocol achieves the higher throughput, especially when the traffic load is heavy and, at the same time, is able to better manage the average energy expenditure of the network.

5   Conclusion

In this paper, a Q-Learning based MAC protocol is proposed. The decentralized learning algorithm is employed to dynamically adapt the radio scheduling to both the node's traffic load and the traffic load of its neighbors, in order to reduce the energy consumption while preserving the network performance. The simulation results show that, compared to other reinforcement learning-based MAC protocols for WSNs, the adaptive behavior of our protocol guarantees higher network performance in terms of throughput, latency and packet delivery and lower average energy consumption. Moreover, the learning approach requires minimal overhead and very low computational complexity, so that the protocol is suitable for practical deployments in real resource-constrained sensor platforms.

Acknowledgments. This work has been partially supported by ARTEMIS project DEMANES (Design, Monitoring and Operation of Adaptive Networked Embedded Systems, contract 295372).

References

1. Yick, J., Mukherjee, B., Ghosal, D.: Wireless sensor network survey. Computer Networks 52, 2292–2330 (2008)
2. Liotta, A.: Farewell to deterministic networks. In: 2012 IEEE 19th Symposium on Communications and Vehicular Technology in the Benelux (SCVT), pp. 1–4 (2012)
3. Liotta, A.: The Cognitive Net is Coming. IEEE Spectrum 50, 26–31 (2013)
4. Bosman, H.H.W.J., Liotta, A., Iacca, G., Wortche, H.: Online extreme learning on fixed-point sensor networks. In: 2013 IEEE 13th International Conference on Data Mining Workshops, pp. 319–326 (2013)
5. Bosman, H.H.W.J., Liotta, A., Iacca, G., Wortche, H.: Anomaly detection in sensor systems using lightweight machine learning. In: 2013 IEEE International Conference on Systems, Man, and Cybernetics (SMC), pp. 7–13 (2013)
6. Kaelbling, L.P., Littman, M.L., Moore, A.P.: Reinforcement Learning: A Survey. Journal of Artificial Intelligence Research 4, 237–285 (1996)
7. Galzarano, S., Liotta, A., Fortino, G.: QL-MAC: A Q-Learning Based MAC for Wireless Sensor Networks. In: Aversa, R., Kołodziej, J., Zhang, J., Amato, F., Fortino, G. (eds.) ICA3PP 2013, Part II. LNCS, vol. 8286, pp. 267–275. Springer, Heidelberg (2013)
8. Galzarano, S., Savaglio, C., Liotta, A., Fortino, G.: Gossiping-based AODV for Wireless Sensor Networks. In: Proceedings of the 2013 IEEE International Conference on Systems, Man, and Cybernetics (SMC), pp. 26–31 (2013)
9. Havinga, P.J., Smit, G.J.: Energy-efficient TDMA medium access control protocol scheduling. In: Asian International Mobile Computing Conf., AMOC, pp. 1–10 (2000)
10. Ye, W., Heidemann, J., Estrin, D.: An Energy-Efficient MAC Protocol for Wireless Sensor Networks. In: Proc. 21st International Annual Joint Conference of the IEEE Computer and Communications Societies, New York, USA (2002)
11. Dam, T.V., Langendoen, K.: An Adaptive Energy-Efficient MAC Protocol for Wireless Sensor Networks. In: Proceedings of the 1st International Conference on Embedded Networked Sensor Systems, SenSys (2003)
12. Zheng, T., Radhakrishnan, S., Sarangan, V.: PMAC: An adaptive energy-efficient MAC protocol for wireless sensor networks. In: Proceedings of the 19th IEEE International Parallel and Distributed Processing Symposium, p. 8 (2005)
13. Liu, Z., Elhanany, I.: RL-MAC: A reinforcement learning based MAC protocol for wireless sensor networks. International Journal of Sensor Networks 1, 117–124 (2006)
14. Mihaylov, M., Tuyls, K., Nowé, A.: Decentralized learning in wireless sensor networks. In: Taylor, M.E., Tuyls, K. (eds.) ALA 2009. LNCS (LNAI), vol. 5924, pp. 60–73. Springer, Heidelberg (2010)

Smart Energy Systems

Equilibria in Concave Non-cooperative Games and Their Applications in Smart Energy Allocation

Maciej Drwal[1], Weronika Radziszewska[2], Maria Ganzha[2,3],
and Marcin Paprzycki[2]

[1] Institute of Computer Science, Wroclaw University of Technology, Wroclaw, Poland
[2] Systems Research Institute, Polish Academy of Sciences, Warsaw, Poland
[3] Institute of Informatics, University of Gdansk, Gdansk, Poland

Abstract. Game theory is often applied to modeling interactions of non-cooperative decision makers. Such interaction appear, among others, in the case of energy management. In this context we formulate the problem of energy allocation for a group of electric vehicles in a smart grid. Subsequently, we formulate a game-theoretic model of interactions of agents controlling vehicle charging schedules. An algorithm for computing pure Nash equilibrium in such game is presented. Moreover, we introduce a solver, which is specifically designed to find equilibria in concave games. The core of the proposed solver is based on the primal-dual interior-point method for nonlinear programming. Experimental results of applying the solver are compared with a centralized solution.

Keywords: game theory, smart energy, demand side management, convex optimization, charging electric vehicles, energy allocation.

1 Introduction

Electric vehicles have a long history [1], but only now their popularity is rising. This is, among others, due to the availability of cheaper and more ecological energy from renewable power sources. Electric vehicles are pollution free and "almost silent." Their range and speed is often not worse than those of conventional models (especially in cities, where traveled distances are limited and speed is reduced by the traffic). Their main limitations are the capacity and the physical properties of batteries, which tend to be heavy, not very durable and, constrained by the speed of charging. Furthermore, the infrastructure for battery-recharge (or exchange) is still insufficient. However, there are many ongoing country-level projects that fund construction of charging stations, for example the UK government dedicated £37 million to building charging stations [6]. Furthermore, the pressure on decreasing the emission levels (in particular in the cities) is helping speed-up the development of infrastructure for electric cars.

In this context, need for solving the problem of charging a group of electric vehicles, is no longer a futuristic one. Note that, a sudden peak in the power

G. Fortino et al. (Eds.): IDCS 2014, LNCS 8729, pp. 409–421, 2014.

grid, caused by multiple electric vehicles that are to be charged, has to be quickly compensated by the existing power production. While currently, charging electric vehicles takes only a fraction of the power of the network, with the increasing number of cars this fraction will increase fast. This might cause serious power peaks, as fast-charging vehicles can take large amounts of power in a very short time, which might destabilize the currently existing power grid. Control over maximum power usage can help avoiding such power peaks. Therefore, it can be assumed that charging stations will have limitations on the amount of power available to connected cars. Optimizing discharge of available power, becomes important, to allow owners to "optimally" use their vehicles. Furthermore, stable power consumption allows contracting energy for long term. Such long-term deals are much more beneficial both both the supplier (planning power production) and the consumer (who pays less). Note that deviations from the contracted power consumption are additionally charged.

Therefore, we consider charging a group of electric vehicles in a charging station placed within a smart grid. Following one of the major approaches to the development of smart grids, we assume that electric cars are controlled by software agents (one per vehicle) [3, 12]. One of the main ideas underlying the smart grid is that vehicles can be flexibly charged, according to their current needs (e.g. the distance of the next anticipated travel or the time when the car/motorbike will be needed again). In this scenario, a game-theoretic model of interactions between agents controlling the process of charging the vehicles can be applied. Here, allocation decisions are made independently by each agent in a distributed manner [13, 18].

1.1 Detailed Problem Description

Problems faced by the power grid are varied: balancing power, power peaks, failures, unpredictability of usage and of production, etc. Here, we consider a small subclass of the Demand Side Management (DSM) problem: allocation of energy to a group of electric vehicles to be charged at a charging station, placed within a smart grid environment. This problem concerns distribution of scarce resources and thus it is assumed that agents representing individual vehicles are selfish, as cooperation requires existence of common goals and communication. While there can be a common goal (e.g. shaving the power peaks or reducing the cost of electricity by signing a long-term contract with the provider), such goals are placed within policies of the charging station, and their management is out of the scope of our work. Therefore, agents representing cars compete for power and a game theoretic approach becomes appropriate.

Let us now describe our use case scenario. We assume that a "charging station" has a limited number of charging slots and a limit on the total amount of power it can draw at one time. Such limit is the effect of long-term deals with the energy suppliers as well as the actual power infrastructure within and outside of the station. Each car has a software agent installed, which is responsible, among others, for vehicle's battery charge/exchange planning. These plans are to match the user's needs. Note that the "special" situation, when batteries are to be exchanged/replaced, is omitted from the current contribution. The charging station allows the vehicles, to charge with an appropriate speed (related to the throughput of the slot and battery limitations) in a sequence of fixed time periods. Car agents define their strategies concerning how much power needs to be charged in a given time period for "their vehicle." The minimal goal is to reach the minimal required charge level, e.g. to complete the next trip (the ultimate goal is to reach the total capacity of the battery). If there are too many vehicles with large power requirements, it is not possible to charge them concurrently at high rates. As a result, the actual charging speeds are decided by the charging station; when the vehicles with their proclaimed demands arrive and connect to the charging slots. We assume that all vehicles arrive once per day (we plan to relax this restriction in the future), and are supposed to be left at the charging station for up to a fixed number of hours (e.g., 10 hours at a time).

Here, it is assumed that agents in vehicles arriving at the station for charging are not aware of other agents demands. Thus charging plans need to be negotiated among agents representing all vehicles. This can be interpreted as a non-cooperative game. Here, we omit a situation when charging schedule negotiations involve also selection of the charge station. In other words, the individual charging schedule involves its power needs and the limited power output of the selected station. Consequently, in order to achieve the highest charging efficiency, agents should construct charging schedules, which correspond to the Nash equilibria of an allocation game (defined in Section 4). Proposed approach can be extended to consider the changing prices of electric energy, battery exchange, number of charging periods during the day, selection of the charging stations among these that are available, etc.).

The paper is organized as follows. In Section 2 we present an overview of the related works. We follow, in Section 3, with the definition of the needed mathematical notation. Next, in Section 4, we formulate the decision making problem. Section 5 contains details of software developed to solve the problem. In Section 6 we summarize the results of an experimental study. Finally, in Section 7 we summarize the paper and outline future research directions.

2   Related Works

Considered problem is typically called the Demand Side Management (DSM) or the Demand Response (DR). A comprehensive review of the literature of this topic can be found in [3]. There are two main approaches to the solution of the DSM: (a) planning and scheduling power usage [10], and (b) dynamically shifting consumption towards a better moment [21]. Research in the DSM includes contributions from mathematics, game theory and social psychology [19].

In power management, some devices can be automatically delayed or interrupted. However, when an operated by a human device might be of little importance, the user might refuse to switch it off. Separately, power storage units allow compensating for sudden peaks of energy consumption and, consequently, may limit the daily variability of power use [22]. In considered problem, devices are electric cars equipped with batteries. Such batteries can, in theory, be used as a general power storage. However, their main use is to power the electric vehicle. Therefore, the key problem is to charge the car in a limited time, without over-loading the power grid. Car batteries have relatively high capacity. Therefore, while a single car is not causing a big charging load, a large number of cars can result in a serious load for the grid. The effect of using plug-in electric vehicle (PHEV) on the power grid, including the influence on its stability, is discussed in [9]. Here, author analyses the charging patterns of batteries and shows that electric vehicle can be considered a Flexible AC Transmission System and can help improve the power quality in the energy network. In [11] the decentralized control method of charging electric vehicle is presented. In that work, the large number of electric cars is considered and the charging control goal is to shift the power usage by cars to off-peak time and, by doing that, reduce the cost of sup-ping power supply. Separately, in [17], the state of the art concerning charging electric vehicles and its effect on power prices is considered. Authors show that the electric/hybrid vehicles are much cheaper on average. In [4, 24] the amount of power used during charging and the payoff were considered. However, other aspects, such as the order, speed and/or time of charging, were omitted. While these aspects can be simplified in theory (resulting in an easier model), in the actual power systems they have to be considered.

The analysis of battery operation, found in [22], considers the amount of charged or discharged power, in a time interval of a predefined length. This publication provides foundation for the game model, proposed in our paper.

2.1   Game-Theoretic Approach

Most of work in non-cooperative game theory concerns games with a finite sets of strategies. In such games decision makers choose among a predefined sets of actions. Here, only mixed-strategy Nash equilibria are guaranteed to exist (see, for instance, [5]). Furthermore, the complexity class PPAD (Polynomial Parity Arguments on Directed Graphs; [15]) captures the inherent combinatorial difficulty of this type of problems. It is conjectured that *no* polynomial-time algorithms exist for solving them.

Concave games, in contrast, are computationally less demanding. By allowing the decision makers to choose from a continuum of decisions, and by exploiting properties of strategy space, it is possible to reach an equilibrium in polynomial time. It has to be stressed that such games still model decision making problems of practical importance. For instance, in a packet-based computer network, a sender may wish to select the transmission speed in a channel of limited capacity (shared with other transmissions) [8,20]. Financial institutions may select prices of their assets and expect yields depending on all prices of assets available on the market. Users of smart energy grids may use only some of their deices – when the supply of energy, for all users, is limited – and energy has to be shared.

Recently, we have developed a software package aimed at efficiently solving concave games. There exist a number of packages for convex programming, us-ing highly efficient implementations of primal-dual interior-point method. Our work aims at providing a similar functionality for the non-cooperative game theory. The tool under development will allow easy description of the input, while efficiently computing the equilibria.

Here, note that a centralized solution can be found for the considered problem. However, it requires providing information about the level of battery charge, required battery level, and other data, which might be considered a violation of privacy by the owner of the vehicle. Furthermore, as was mentioned in [11], the owners of vehicles are reluctant to give away the control over the charging procedure. Furthermore, solutions where the agent of a car suggests strategies for charging its vehicle allow the system to consider special constraints (e.g. controlling the number of charge cycles) that might prolong the life of the battery.

3   Definitions

Strategic (mathematical) games are used to model situations of conflict (or cooperation) between two or more players. Each player decides on its *strategy* (also called *action*), and receives a *payoff*, which, in general, depends on strategies of other players. It is assumed that each player is rational, and wants to maximize its payoff. For more details, see [14]. Now, let $\mathcal{N} = \{1, \ldots, N\}$, $N \geq 2$, be the set of players. A *non-cooperative game* is defined by specifying sets of strategies $\{S_i\}_{i \in \mathcal{N}}$ and payoff functions $\{u_i\}_{i \in \mathcal{N}}$ that are to be maximized (alternatively, *cost functions* $c_i = -u_i$ can be defined, and the goal of each player would be to minimize them). The set S_i is called the set of *pure strategies* of ith player, or its *strategy space*. Vector $\mathbf{x} = (x_1, x_2, \ldots, x_N)$, where $x_i \in S_i$, is called *strategy profile* of the game, and consists of strategies x_i of all players. Value of $u_i(\mathbf{x})$ defines the *payoff* of ith player, resulting from a strategy profile $\mathbf{x}$. The following notation is conventionally used for the strategy profile:

$$\mathbf{x}_{-i} = (x_1, \ldots, x_{i-1}, x_{i+1}, \ldots, x_N).$$

It denotes a vector of all strategies, except that of the ith player. The notation $\mathbf{x} = (x_i, \mathbf{x}_{-i})$ is often used to distinguish the ith player's strategy. Assuming that players make decisions *independently* and are characterized by *selfishness*, the best outcome of the game would be the one in which each player realizes the best response to all other players' strategies. A (*pure*) *Nash equilibrium* of a game is such strategy profile $\bar{\mathbf{x}}$ that:

$$\forall i \in \mathcal{N}, \ \ \forall x_i : \ \ u_i(\bar{x}_i, \bar{\mathbf{x}}_{-i}) \geq u_i(x_i, \bar{\mathbf{x}}_{-i}).$$

If each player decided on a strategy $\bar{x}_i$, such that $\bar{\mathbf{x}}$ is a Nash equilibrium, then no player has an incentive to change its strategy, as such change is not going to improve its payoff. Thus, such strategy profile can be seen as the "socially best profile." Therefore, non-cooperative, rational, selfish agents should prefer to use strategies resulting in a Nash equilibrium.

Let us now consider *concave* non-cooperative games. Here, the strategy of each player is a vector in the Euclidean space $\mathbf{x}_i \in \mathbb{R}^{m_i}$, $i = 1, \ldots, N$. Each strategy space set S_i is a convex set. The payoff function u_i is continuous in $\mathbf{x}$, and is concave in $\mathbf{x}_i$, for each fixed value $\mathbf{x}_{-i}$. Alternatively, consider cost functions c_i, continuous in $\mathbf{x}$, and convex in $\mathbf{x}_i$, for each fixed value $\mathbf{x}_{-i}$. It is well-known that pure Nash equilibrium always exists in concave games [16]. An equilibrium point is a solution of a system of nonlinear equations, similar to the Karush-Kuhn-Tucker (KKT) conditions, in standard optimization. Assume that the strategy space of ith player can be defined by a set of differentiable functions:

$$S_i = \{\mathbf{x}_i : h_{i1}(\mathbf{x}_i) \geq 0, h_{i2}(\mathbf{x}_i) \geq 0, \ldots, h_{ik_i}(\mathbf{x}_i) \geq 0\}.$$

Finally, in the considered game, an equilibrium point $\mathbf{x}$ must satisfy the feasibility conditions of all strategy spaces, i.e.:

$$\forall i \in \mathcal{N}, \ \forall j \in \{1, \ldots, k_i\} : \quad h_{ij}(\mathbf{x}_i) \geq 0, \tag{1}$$

as well as the complementary slackness conditions:

$$\forall i \in \mathcal{N}, \ \forall j \in \{1, \ldots, k_i\}, \ \exists \lambda_{ij} \geq 0 : \quad \lambda_{ij} h_{ij}(\mathbf{x}_i) = 0, \tag{2}$$

and the stationarity conditions of Lagrange functions:

$$\nabla_{\mathbf{x}_i} u_i(\mathbf{x}) - \sum_{j=1}^{k_i} \lambda_{ij} \nabla_{\mathbf{x}_i} h_j(\mathbf{x}_i) = 0, \forall i \in \mathcal{N}. \tag{3}$$

4   Problem Formulation

Let us now consider an optimization problem representing the vehicle charging scenario. Let $\mathcal{N}$ denote the set of electric vehicles (EVs), where $|\mathcal{N}| = N$. Each of them has an energy demand $D_n > 0$, as well as a battery capacity $C_n > 0$, $n = 1, \ldots, N$. The total charging time of all N vehicles is divided into a fixed number of T discrete intervals (e.g., 1-hour intervals). Each vehicle needs to formulate a charging plan $\mathbf{x}_n = [x_{n,1}, \ldots, x_{n,T}]^{\mathsf{T}}$, where $x_{n,t}$ is the n-th vehicle's requested charging rate for t-th time interval, while $x_{n,t}$ represents the requested speed of charging n-th vehicle's battery during t-th time interval. Observe that it is *not* assumed that vehicles arrive at the charging station at the same time, but the access time to the charging slots is discretized: a vehicle may set its requested rates to 0 for some of T charging periods, which means that it does not have to be connected to the charging station then. In order for the n-th vehicle to satisfy its demand, it must receive the total energy allocation equal to $\sum_{t=1}^{T} x_{n,t}$, which must reach at least the amount of energy needed for the next expected travel (but it cannot be greater than the capacity of its battery):

$$\forall n \in \mathcal{N} \quad D_n \leq \sum_{t=1}^{T} x_{n,t} \leq C_n. \tag{4}$$

Additionally, in order for a vehicle to be operational, it is required that its energy level never falls below a minimum energy reserve threshold. To assure this, for each charging interval t there is a rate lower bound $L_{n,t}$ given by:

$$\forall n \in \mathcal{N} \ \forall t \in \{1, \ldots, T\} \ x_{n,t} \geq L_{n,t}. \tag{5}$$

Note that values $L_{n,t}$ do not have to be positive, as we may allow, in a given time interval t, for discharging the battery (negative values of $x_{n,t}$ are interpreted as discharging rates). However, here we consider only the case when $L_{n,t} \geq 0$. Nevertheless, this generalizes to include discharging. The reserve threshold is not explicitly given in the input data, as it is enough to provide values of $L_{n,t}$.

Although user agents may select any rate requests satisfying (4)–(5), the actual charging rate is allocated by the charging station, taking into account the total requestes from all N vehicles. In each t-th time interval, each n-th vehicle receives a fraction ρ_t of its requested rate $x_{n,t}$, where $\rho_t = f(\sum_{j=1}^{N} x_{j,t})$; the function $f : \mathbb{R} \to [0,1]$ is a nonincreasing function of a total of requested rates. It is selected in order to prevent the station overcharge. In general, if the station has a fixed supply S units of energy for one charging period t, then for the aggregate demand $d > S$, $f(d) < 1$ must be selected so that $\sum_{j=1}^{N} x_{j,t} f(d) < S$. The faster the function f decreases, the more the station penalizes the aggregate demands that are too high. Here, we restrict f to linear functions, leaving choice of other functions for future investigations. The total energy that the n-th vehicle receives from the station in the time period consisting of T-intervals is equal to:

$$u_n(\mathbf{x}_n) = \sum_{t=1}^{T} x_{n,t} f(\sum_{j=1}^{N} x_{j,t}). \tag{6}$$

We can now define the following energy-allocation game. Let us assume that $\mathcal{N}$ players have feasible strategies defined as the set of all vectors $\mathbf{x}_n = [\mathbf{x}_1, \ldots, \mathbf{x}_T]^\mathsf{T}$ satisfying (4)–(5). Here, the goal of each player is to maximize the payoff function defined as in (6). In other words, each player must select the charging rate resulting in fastest charging, but must take into consideration the fact that requesting too high charging rate by many players will be penalized by the reduced energy flow from the station. Thus, each player should individually balance its request between fast charging and keeping charging rates low, to prevent the station overcharge (which would penalize all players).

5   Software Solver

5.1   Representation of Games

Let us now describe in more detail the software that we have developed for solving convex/concave non-cooperative games. To solve a game, we first need to pass it as an input to the solver. The developed software uses a relatively simple syntax, which is presented in Example 1, and stores game descriptions as a text file.

Example 1. Input file representing a simple two-player instance of the considered game.

```
N 2
S1 (x11, x12) {
   10 - x11 - x12
}
S1 {
   x11 + x12 - 5
}
S2 (x21, x22) {
   20 - x21 - x22
}
S2 {
   x21 + x22 - 10
}
P1 {
   set y = 1 - x11 - x21 - x12 - x22
   x11 * y + x12 * y
}
P2 {
   set y = 1 - x11 - x21 - x12 - x22
   x21 * y + x22 * y
}
```

Here, the first line defines the number of players, indicated by the integer after symbol N (two players in this case). Following are definitions of the strategy spaces of each player. A strategy space is defined in the form:

$$h_{ij}(\mathbf{x}_i) \geq 0,$$

where h_{ij} is the jth constraint of the ith player's strategy space. User must provide formulas for h_{ij}, for each player, which is accomplished in constraint blocks, denoted by the symbol S, immediately followed by the index of the player. Names of player's decision variables must be given in parentheses before the first constraint block (and can be omitted in each subsequent block). The body of the function itself must be contained within brackets. In Example 1, there are two constraints defining the strategy space of *Player 1*: $h_{11}(\mathbf{x}_1) = 10 - x_{11} - x_{12}$, and $h_{12}(\mathbf{x}_1) = x_{11} + x_{12} - 5$, where $\mathbf{x}_1 = (x_{11}, x_{12})$.

Subsequently, the payoff functions are defined in function blocks, starting with the symbol P, followed by the index of the player. The value of the payoff can depend on all decision variables of all other players. Thus any subset of decision variables of all players may appear in the block defining payoff function.

The value of the last expression in each block is the payoff. Observe that computations can be simplified using **set** expressions, which define the auxiliary variables. For instance the variable y defined at the beginning of both payoff functions, above. Here, variable y appears multiple times in the second line of the payoff function, but the expression is evaluated only once.

The input syntax supports arithmetic operations on floating point numbers, as well as all standard mathematical functions (min/max, logarithms, exponentiation, trigonometric functions).

5.2 Optimization Algorithm

The core solver is based on the primal-dual interior-point method from nonlinear programming. The method seeks to find a solution to the relaxed KKT conditions, which define a system of equations (1)–(3). Such solution approximates pure Nash equilibrium in the convex/concave non-cooperative game. By regulating the relaxation parameter one may obtain the approximation with an arbitrary accuracy (bounded only by the use of floating-point arithmetic). For each player $n \in \mathcal{N}$ we can formulate the KKT conditions corresponding to its problem of maximizing the concave function. The primal-dual variant of the interior-point algorithm relaxes the slackness conditions (2) to the form:

$$\forall i \in \mathcal{N} \; \forall j \in \{1, \ldots, k_i\} \quad \lambda_{ij} h_{ij}(\mathbf{x}_i) = 1/t, \tag{7}$$

where $t > 0$ is a parameter. Feasibility conditions (1) are changed from the inequality to the equality, by introducing the vector of slack variables $\mathbf{s} = [s_{11}, \ldots, s_{ij}, \ldots, s_{Nk_N}]^\mathsf{T}$:

$$\forall i \in \mathcal{N} \; \forall j \in \{1, \ldots, k_i\} \quad h_{ij}(\mathbf{x}_i) - s_{ij} = 0. \tag{8}$$

After user selects the accuracy $\epsilon > 0$ and the parameter $\alpha > 0$, the solver starts from a small value of $t = t_0$ and "any" feasible solution $\mathbf{x} = \mathbf{x}_0$. Next, it forms a set of linear equations (1), (3) and (7), by substituting $\mathbf{x}_0$ into them. Based on these equations, the solver computes a Newton step $\Delta\mathbf{x}$, which indicates the direction of maximization. The Newton step is computed from the solution of the system of the following primal-dual equations [23]:

$$\begin{bmatrix} \nabla_x^2 \mathcal{L}_1 & \ldots & \nabla_x^2 \mathcal{L}_N & \mathbf{0} & -\mathbf{H}^\mathsf{T}(\mathbf{x}) \\ \mathbf{0} & \ddots & \mathbf{0} & \Lambda & \mathbf{S} \\ h_1(\mathbf{x}_1) & \ldots & h_N(\mathbf{x}_N) & -\mathbf{I} & \mathbf{0} \end{bmatrix} \begin{bmatrix} \Delta\mathbf{x}_1 \\ \vdots \\ \Delta\mathbf{x}_N \\ \Delta\mathbf{s} \\ \Delta\boldsymbol{\lambda} \end{bmatrix} = \begin{bmatrix} \nabla u_1(\mathbf{x}) - \boldsymbol{\lambda}_1^\mathsf{T} h_1(\mathbf{x}_1) \\ \vdots \\ \nabla u_N(\mathbf{x}) - \boldsymbol{\lambda}_N^\mathsf{T} h_N(\mathbf{x}_N) \\ \mathbf{S}\boldsymbol{\lambda} - \mathbf{e}/t \\ \mathbf{H}(\mathbf{x}) - \mathbf{s} \end{bmatrix}, \tag{9}$$

where $\mathcal{L}_n = u_n(\mathbf{x}) - \boldsymbol{\lambda}_n^\mathsf{T}(h_n(\mathbf{x}_n) - \mathbf{s}_n)$ is the Lagrangian associated with n-th player's payoff function, $\boldsymbol{\lambda}$ is the vector of all dual variables, $\mathbf{H}(\mathbf{x})$ is the Jacobian matrix of all constraints $h(\mathbf{x})$, matrix Λ is a diagonal matrix of all dual variables, $\mathbf{S}$ is a diagonal matrix of all slack variables, and $\mathbf{I}$ and $\mathbf{e}$ are unit matrix and vector, respectively. The actual step (in both primal $\mathbf{x}$ and dual $\boldsymbol{\lambda}$ variables) is computed using appropriately selected parameters α. Then, the solution is updated as follows: $\mathbf{x} \leftarrow \mathbf{x} + \alpha\Delta\mathbf{x}$. If the change in either the value of solution or the right hand side of (9) is smaller than ϵ, the solver halts.

The algorithm has has been implemented in C++, using BLAS/LAPACK libraries for efficient matrix computations [2]. Note that use of BLAS may allow efficient use of multicore processors. This may be of value when solving large problems. Observe that solving system (9) requires computing Jacobian and Hessian of the system of equations resulting from KKT conditions. This requires calculating derivatives, which, if done numerically, can be moderately time consuming for some functions. In order to alleviate this, the solver allows the user to provide analytically derived expressions for derivatives.

6   Experimental Study

In the computational experiments we used randomly generated problem instances, defined by the number of players N and the number of charging time intervals T (of constant duration). Table 1 presents the results for $N = 10$ and $T = 5$. For each n-th player, energy consumption demands D_n were randomly generated using uniform distribution from the interval $[0, 0.05]$, while battery capacities C_n were randomly generated using uniform distribution from the $[D_n, 0.1]$ interval. Minimal threshold values $L_{n,t}$ were selected from the $[0, 0.01]$ interval, again, using uniform distribution. Function f was $f(x) = 1 - x$.

Table 1. Detailed computational results for instance with $N = 10$ and $T = 5$

player	$t = 1$	$t = 2$	$t = 3$	$t = 4$	$t = 5$	demand	payoff (charge)
1	0.00819	0.00916	0.01222	0.00916	0.01127	0.022	0.045
2	0.00781	0.01079	0.01279	0.01379	0.00481	0.006	0.044
3	0.01107	0.00594	0.01392	0.01092	0.00918	0.046	0.046
4	0.00620	0.01524	0.00924	0.01213	0.00720	0.035	0.045
5	0.00704	0.01416	0.01516	0.00705	0.00704	0.045	0.045
6	0.01112	0.00896	0.00696	0.01086	0.01212	0.038	0.045
7	0.01156	0.01252	0.01044	0.00850	0.00754	0.046	0.046
8	0.00465	0.01372	0.01172	0.01172	0.00875	0.046	0.046
9	0.00899	0.00994	0.00913	0.00908	0.01317	0.044	0.045
10	0.00892	0.00678	0.01074	0.01274	0.01082	0.015	0.044

It took the solver 18 iterations to find a Nash equilibrium for $\epsilon = 0.001$, and 6 iterations for $\epsilon = 0.01$. Table 1 contains values of $x_{n,t}$, D_n and u_n, for each player from the final iteration. Observe that each player receives approximately the same payoff, which means that the station assigns, in total, approximately the same amount of energy to each vehicle. However, in each time period t the charging rates vary significantly for each car. Overall, all demands are satisfied and allocation is well balanced.

In the second experiment we considered the performance of the proposed algorithm for an increasing number of players N. For convenience, we normalized the units of energy to the capacity of the charging station. Hence, the demand of each client was inversely proportional to the total number of clients. Specifically, no car would claim more than $1/2$ unit of energy in each charging interval. Moreover, we assumed that if the total demand in the charging period exceeded one unit, then no charging took place. Thus, functions in equations (6) were:

$$u_n(\mathbf{x}) = \sum_{t=1}^{T} x_{n,t} \left(1 - \sum_{m=1}^{N} x_{m,t} \right).$$

Table 2 compares results of applying our solver with allocations obtained by solving the concave quadratic problem centrally, assuming that all clients' demands are known in advance by a central authority (e.g. they have all been submitted to the charging station that establishes the charging schedule based on its preferences). The first column represents the number of clients N. The second column, (**min.sol.**), presents the smallest amount of energy that any player receives in the equilibrium solution, while the column **max.sol.**, states the largest amount of energy that any player receives in the equilibrium solution. In comparison, columns denoted **min.central** and **max.central** contain info about minimal and maximal allocations computed centrally. They have been obtained as a solution to a problem of finding vector $\mathbf{x}$ that maximizes the objective function:

$$U(\mathbf{x}) = \frac{1}{N} \sum_{n=1}^{N} u_n(\mathbf{x}) \tag{10}$$

subject to constraints (4)–(5). This constitutes the average players' payoff, and can be considered as a measure of "social" quality of the solution [13]. These values were obtained using the state-of-the-art CPLEX [7] software, which applies the barrier interior-point algorithm to solve concave quadratic problems (see, [7] for all details concerning the centralized solution method).

Table 2. Comparison of solutions computed for different number of players N

instance N	min.sol.	max.sol.	min.central	max.central	iterations	time
10	0.061	0.13	0.021	0.15	8	6 s.
15	0.040	0.092	0.014	0.16	12	39 s.
20	0.029	0.076	0.006	0.21	9	55 s.
25	0.015	0.061	0.004	0.21	10	116 s.
30	0.012	0.048	0.003	0.193	11	216 s.
35	0.006	0.031	0.001	0.2	11	334 s.
40	0.002	0.027	0	0.202	11	492 s.
50	0.004	0.100	0	0.221	10	846 s.

The solution computed centrally typically allocates large amount of energy to a specific car (e.g., the first client that arrived at the station), while leaving only very little energy for other cars (they are charged just as much as needed to satisfy their minimal demands). This can be seen as an *unfair allocation*. In contrast, the equilibrium solutions (found using the proposed method) tend to balance allocations among clients (differences between the client with the smallest allocated charge and the one with the largest one are relatively small). This can be seen as a *fair allocation* that reduces negative effects of selfishness (due to the threat of loss of payoff that each player takes into consideration). As a result, each client usually receives significantly more than the requested minimum, while no client dominates others in its total allocation. Here, the drawback is that the corresponding values $U(\mathbf{x})$ (average allocated energy) are strictly less than the optimal average values computed centrally. This global performance loss is the price paid for balancing allocations. An interesting question opens here: what is better "unfair optimality" or "fair suboptimality." However, this question cannot be answered on the basis of computational optimization itself.

Moreover, Table 2 lists numbers of iterations needed to reach Nash equilibrium when the requested accuracy was $\epsilon = 0.01$, and the computation time. The number of iterations is almost constant, regardless of the problem size. However, the computational cost of a single iteration raises quickly with increasing N, thus computing the charging plans for a large number of cars can become expensive.

7 Concluding Remarks

In the paper we have demonstrated practical application of theory of non-cooperative concave games to smart energy allocation (charging electric vehicles). The presented approach is distributing power "fairly though suboptimally." In this case, fairness means that the differences between the total amount of allocated energy (to each car) are relatively small. Note that, when human decision-making is considered, fairness is very often considered to be of great value. Moreover, we have described a solver for computing equilibria in non-cooperative convex/concave games with the use of primal-dual interior-point algorithm. We have evaluated its performance for the considered vehicle charging scenario and the results are encouraging.

Across the paper we have indicated a number of directions, which we plan to explore. Some of them are related to the vehicle charging scenario itself, others to the solver. We will disclose our findings in subsequent reports.

References

1. Anderson, C.D., Anderson, J.: Electric and Hybrid Cars: A History, 2nd edn. McFarland, Incorporated, Publishers (2004)
2. Anderson, E., Bai, Z., Bischof, C., Blackford, S., Demmel, J., Dongarra, J., Du Croz, J., Greenbaum, A., Hammarling, S., McKenney, A., Sorensen, D.: LAPACK Users' Guide, 3rd edn. SIAM, Philadelphia (1999)
3. Balijepalli, V.S.K.M., Pradhan, V., Khaparde, S.A., Shereef, R.M.: Review of demand response under smart grid paradigm. In: 2011 IEEE PES Innovative Smart Grid Technologies - India (ISGT India), pp. 236–243 (December 2011)
4. Chau, C., Elbassioni, K., Khonji, M.: Truthful mechanisms for combinatorial ac electric power allocation. arXiv preprint arXiv:1403.3907 (2014)

5. Deng, X., Papadimitriou, C., Safra, S.: On the complexity of equilibria. In: Proceedings of the 34th Annual ACM Symposium on Theory of Computing, pp. 67–71. ACM (2002)
6. The Rt Hon Michael Fallon MP Department for Transport, The Rt Hon Norman Baker MP and Office for Low Emission Vehicles. Hundreds of new chargepoints for electric cars (2013)
7. Users Manual for CPLEX 12.2. IBM ILOG (2010)
8. Gąsior, D., Drwal, M.: Pareto-optimal Nash equilibrium in capacity allocation game for self-managed networks. Computer Networks 57(14), 2675–2868 (2013)
9. Islam, F.: Impact and Utilization of Emerging PHEV in Smart Power Systems. PhD thesis, University of New South Wales - UNSW Canberra. Engineering & Information Technology (2013)
10. Kim, T., Poor, H.V.: Scheduling power consumption with price uncertainty. IEEE Transactions on Smart Grid 2(3), 519–527 (2011)
11. Ma, Z., Callaway, D., Hiskens, I.: Decentralized charging control of large populations of plug-in electric vehicles. IEEE Trans. Contr. Sys. Techn. 21(1), 67–78 (2013)
12. Mohsenian-Rad, A., Wong, V., Jatskevich, J., Schober, R., Leon-Garcia, A.: Autonomous demand-side management based on game-theoretic energy consumption scheduling for the future smart grid. IEEE Transactions on Smart Grid 1(3), 320–331 (2010)
13. Nisan, N.: Algorithmic Game Theory. Cambridge University Press (2007)
14. Osborne, M.J., Rubinstein, A.: A course in game theory. MIT Press (1994)
15. Papadimitriou, C.: On the complexity of the parity argument and other inefficient proofs of existence. Journal of Computer and System Sciences 48(3), 498–532 (1994)
16. Rosen, J.B.: Existence and uniqueness of equilibrium points for concave n-person games. Econometrica: Journal of the Econometric Society, 520–534 (1965)
17. Rotering, N., Ilic, M.: Optimal charge control of plug-in hybrid electric vehicles in deregulated electricity markets. IEEE Transactions on Power Systems 26(3), 1021–1029 (2011)
18. Saad, W., Han, Z., Poor, H., Basar, T.: Game-theoretic methods for the smart grid: An overview of microgrid systems, demand-side management, and smart grid communications. IEEE Signal Processing Magazine 29(5), 86–105 (2012)
19. Schultz, P.W., Nolan, J.M., Cialdini, R.B., Goldstein, N.J., Griskevicius, V.: The constructive, destructive, and reconstructive power of social norms. Psychological Science 18(5), 429–434 (2007)
20. Turowska, M., Gąsior, D., Drwal, M.: Allocation-pricing game for multipath routing in virtual networks. In: Swiątek, J., Grzech, A., Swiątek, P., Tomczak, J.M. (eds.) Advances in Systems Science. AISC, vol. 240, pp. 553–563. Springer, Heidelberg (2014)
21. Vandael, S., Boucké, N., Holvoet, T., De Craemer, K., Deconinck, G.: Decentralized coordination of plug-in hybrid vehicles for imbalance reduction in a smart grid. In: The 10th International Conference on Autonomous Agents and Multiagent Systems, vol. 2, pp. 803–810 (2011)
22. Vytelingum, P., Voice, T.D., Ramchurn, S.D., Rogers, A., Jennings, N.R.: Theoretical and practical foundations of large-scale agent-based micro-storage in the smart grid. J. Artif. Int. Res. 42(1), 765–813 (2011)
23. Wright, S., Nocedal, J.: Numerical optimization. Springer, New York (1999)
24. Yu, L., Chau, C.: Complex-demand knapsack problems and incentives in ac power systems. In: Proceedings of the 2013 International Conference on Autonomous Agents and Multi-agent Systems, pp. 973–980. International Foundation for Autonomous Agents and Multiagent Systems (2013)

A Distributed System
for Smart Energy Negotiation

Alba Amato[1], Beniamino Di Martino[1], Marco Scialdone[1],
Salvatore Venticinque[1], Svein Hallsteinsen[2], and Shanshan Jiang[2]

[1] Second University of Naples, Dep. of Industrial and Information Engineering,
Aversa, Italy
[2] SINTEF ICT, Throndeim, Norvey
{alba.amato,beniamino.dimartino,marco.scialdone,
salvatore.venticinque}@unina2.it,
{Svein.Hallsteinsen,Shanshan.Jiang}@sintef.no

Abstract. Distributed energy production by Solar Panels is really wide-spread today. However the mismatch between production and consumption during the day, and expensiveness of energy storages, limits an high rate of self-consumption. In fact the overall overproduction is currently reversed into the power grid and delivered to the energy provider. In this context the CoSSMic project aims at developing a distributed software architecture that allows for the collaboration among neighbors, both to schedule the consumptions and the exchange of energy, in order to maximize the self-consumption of micro grids. This paper focus on the architecture design, scouting of technology and preliminary demonstrator.

Keywords: Multi-Agent Systems, Smart Grid, Smart Energy.

1 Introduction

Rooftop PV panels may play a central role in the transition to an energy supply system based on renewable energy sources. However the fluctuating nature of the energy production from such panels limits the achievable levels of self-consumption and self-sufficiency of building micro-grids with local PV production, and therefore also causes challenges for the public grid. Coordinating load shifting, use of storage, and exchange of excess power between the buildings in a neighbourhood could alleviate this situation and bring significant benefits in terms of reduced power bills for the house owners, reduced peak loads on the public grid and in turn reduced need for fossil fuel based backup production capacity. To exploit this potential, the CoSSMic project is developing an innovative autonomic ICT based system, able to control the energy usage and storage and the exchange with the public grid of clusters of collaborating micro-grids. The system is governed by preferences and constraints set by the building inhabitants, using modern interaction devices such as smartphones and touchpads, and is exploiting pricing signals and other demand side guidance provided by the electric power retailers and public grid operators. Storage can be provided by dedicated batteries, and also by battery powered units connected temporarily

G. Fortino et al. (Eds.): IDCS 2014, LNCS 8729, pp. 422–434, 2014.

for charging, e.g. electric cars. Weather forecasts will be used to predict power needs and thus enable near optimal coordination. The economic benefits will be shared among the neighbours according to reward based business models ensuring sufficient rewards to the users willing to share resources and collaborate to optimise the overall working of the power grid.

In this paper we outline the architecture of the intended system and discuss the design choices made. In addition to the functional requirements inherent in the functionality outlined above, the architecture has been shaped by the wish to provide a low threshold and low cost solution that can be installed and maintained by common people without special technical skills, and foster the emergence of neighbourhoods with coordinated energy management without command by a central authority, the need establish organisational structures, nor to invest in central equipment. This has resulted in a highly distributed peer-to-peer oriented architecture with a flexible deployment model able to leverage on cloud resources if desirable.

The paper is structured as follows. Section 2 gives a brief overview of related work. Then Section 3 details the requirements and objectives. In sections 4-6 we present and discuss the architecture from different viewpoints in accordance with the IEEE Recommended Practice for Architectural Description for Software-Intensive Systems[1], and in Section 7 we give an overview of the ongoing implementation. Finally, some preliminary conclusions are drawn.

2   Related Work

Several different Smart Grid Architectures are promoted and various standards for Smart Grid exist. The various regional and international initiatives for Smart Grid standardization outline the importance of standards in the Smart Grid domain [10]. In the context of the European Commission's Standardization Mandate M/490, an holistic viewpoint of an overall architecture named Smart Grid Architecture Model (SGAM) [5] is developed. The layers of the SGAM are [10]: *Business Layer*, regarding strategic and tactical goals and processes as well as regulatory aspects; *Function Layer*, IT-oriented, technology independent description of use cases, functions and service; *Information Layer*, Business objects and data models of the Function Layer to enable interoperability; *Communication Layer*, Specification of protocols and procedures for the data exchange between components based on the Information Layer; *Component Layer*, Physical and technical view on Smart Grids components. Power-system related infrastructure and equipment, ICT-infrastructure and -systems are also considered.

IntelliGrid architecture[9], created by the Electric Power Research Institute (EPRI), provides tools and recommendations for standards and technologies for utility use in designing IT-based systems, such as advanced metering, distribution automation, and demand response. Several utilities have applied IntelliGrid architecture including Southern California Edison, Long Island Power Authority, Salt River Project, and TXU Electric Delivery.

---

[1] http://standards.ieee.org/findstds/standard/1471-2000.html

Grid 2030 [6] is a joint vision statement for the U.S. electrical system developed by the electric utility industry, equipment manufacturers, information technology providers, federal and state government agencies, interest groups, universities, and national laboratories. It covers generation, transmission, distribution, storage, and enduse. The National Electric Delivery Technologies Roadmap is the implementation document for the Grid 2030 vision. The Roadmap outlines the key issues and challenges for modernizing the grid and suggests paths that government and industry can take to build Americas future electric delivery system.

The SmartHouse/SmartGrid[2] project sets out to validate and test how ICT-enabled collaborative technical-commercial aggregations of Smart Houses provide an essential step to achieve the needed radically higher levels of energy efficiency in Europe. The three main goals that the SmartHouse/SmartGrid project is heading towards are: improving energy efficiency, increasing the penetration of renewable energies, and diversifying and decentralising Europe's energy mix.

The CossMic project is based on 1471-2000 standard, an IEEE Recommended Practice for Architectural Description for Software-Intensive Systems. It is an approved and proposed IEEE smart grid-related standard that addresses the activities of the creation, analysis, and sustainment of architectures of software-intensive systems, and the recording of such architectures in terms of architectural descriptions. CoSSMic [1] is overcoming the limitations of current solutions by coordinating local energy production and storage resources of neighbourhoods of individual houses, thereby balancing the energy flow and consumption and reducing the fluctuations towards the central power grid, and improving the predictability of consumer behaviour.

3   Requirements and Objectives

Optimizing the use of energy leads to increased utilisation of energy produced by local renewable resources. As a result, there is an economic return and also less pollution due to the decrease of the consumption of electricity from non-renewable sources such as fossil fuels. To achieve this goal the CoSSMic project will enable the exchange of energy between producers and consumers to limit the need of storage and the delivery of energy across the grid when there is a peak of production. Moreover, to minimize the overlapping of overproductions among households, the CoSSMic framework will plan the optimal schedule of load by controlling the appliance using weather forecast, monitoring information and according to user's constraints and preferences. An ICT platform has been designed to support producers (which in our case are users who have installed solar panels) for selling energy to their neighbors, and buying when there is a power need. The user thus becomes at the same time producer and consumer (*prosumer*). The energy exchange will be made by intelligent agents that act on user's behalf autonomously, according to high level policy set by prosumers.

---

[2] http://www.smarthouse-smartgrid.eu/index.php?id=43

Agents based networks to support users' activities [7] and negotiation/brokering of Service Level Agreements (SLA) [3] have been investigated in different application fields. Main objective of the agents, here, will be the optimal negotiation strategy. In both cases, the agents will enter into a virtual market [2]. If agents fail to sell/buy all the energy required, they must contact the electricity company (GenCo). Then software agents represent the main actors of the ICT platform. They will take the role of *Consumers* when they manage an appliance that absorbs energy, such as refrigerators, computers, ovens, washing machines, etc, but also storages when they absorb energy. *Producers* will manage solar panels, but also energy storages with available energy. *Gencos* will be represented by agents that are always ready to receive or deliver energy. The important requirements that have contributed to shape the architecture are the possibility to implement the foreseen functionality. To achieve this aim we need to integrate a variety of devices such that they can be monitored and controlled. We also need to keep installation complexity and cost low (low threshold technology), to support wireless communication with devices, to support "plug-and-play" style of installation, to allow deployment on cheap commonly available hardware, offloading resource demanding computations to the cloud if necessary, to use already available communication infrastructure to communicate between buildings and with the public grid, to use already available user interaction devices, such as smart phones and touch pads. Besides, to enable easy and sustainable emergence of neighbourhoods we need that can be created without setting up central resources so that new houses can join dynamically and the system is robust to the failing or withdrawal of individual houses.

The framework must also provide functionalities for the management of devices, like electric cars, allowing to turn them on/off by an interactive control or according to preferences and constraints set by user. For example, the system must allow the user to specify earliest and latest start time for appliance, charging policy for energy storages, etc.

4   CoSSMic Architecture

The CoSSMic architecture design follows the model defined by ARCADE architecture description[3]. ARCADE is based on the standard 1471-2000 - *IEEE Recommended Practice for Architectural Description for Software-Intensive Systems*[4] and proposes an understanding of architecture as covering both the system and the organisational and business environment it is going to operate within, and both architectural level requirements and architectural and technological choices. A central element is the meta-model for architecture descriptions introducing concepts such as stakeholders, concerns and views. A stakeholder is an individual, team, or organization (or classes thereof) with interests in, or concerns relative to, a system. A view is a representation of a whole system from the

---

[3] http://www.arcade-framework.org/
[4] http://standards.ieee.org/findstds/standard/1471-2000.html

perspective of a related set of concerns. The CoSSMic architecture is described using five views with respective models:

Context View. The models in the context view provide a description of the environment, in particular the main stakeholders and their concerns. The main stakeholders include user, installer, electricity supplier/retailer, equipment vendor, Distributed System Operator (DSO), public authorities, the CoSSMic trial and evaluation team and software developer. This view also describes the activities of the system with regard to the stakeholders (i.e., use cases) and the equipment and external services that the system interfaces.

Requirements View. Architectural requirements have been collected and derived from various sources, including user centric workshops held at the two trial sites, business model analysis, technology survey and analysis. One design decision coming from the requirements is that the system needs a computing device (as called home gateway in this paper) with capacity to firstly, act as a gateway for communication, and secondly, execute the intelligence based on distributed computing. Another requirement concerning the flexibility of the deployment of software components sets constraints for the distribution view and deployment models.

Component View. This view identifies and documents specific physical or logical components, including information elements and data model, interfaces and interactions between components. We have identified main components for device integration , user and neighbourhood management, as well as components for planning and optimisation.

Distribution View. This describes the logical distribution of software and hardware components. It shows if some components cannot be separated and if any must be separated. The distribution view is further discussed in the next section.

Deployment View. The realisation view shows how the logical components of the CoSSMic software system are realised as "'physical" components and deployed into the environment. It also describes the architectural and technological choices. Four deployment models have been proposed based on the distribution view. More details about these models are described in the next Sections.

4.1   Components View

In Figure 1 the main components of CoSSMic System are shown. Functionalities and interfaces are defined. The user interface supports interactive control and configuration of the system. Cloud services provide information about energy tariff and predicted PV production. They provide remote resources to offload computation and data when necessary resources are not available locally, and support communication over distributed infrastructures. Using the Cloud, users can access CoSSMic services outside their household. The Mediator provides APIs for storing and management of smartgrid information. Mediator services are accessed by the drivers to store measures and by agents to collect information about energy production and consumption of the household. The same APIs are used to store the results of negotiation. The allocation of energy to devices is modeled as task schedule with power and time constraints carried out by soft-

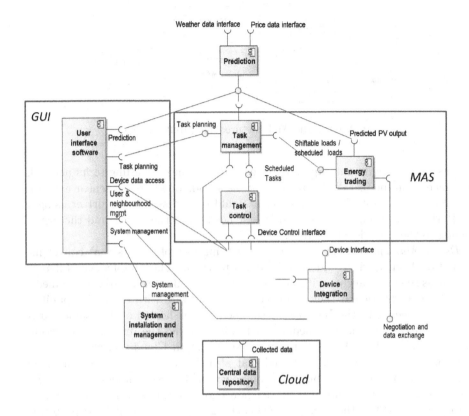

Fig. 1. CoSSMic Architecture - Components View

ware agents. The Multi Agent System (MAS) includes both agents platforms and application that use optimization techniques and negotiation mechanisms for management and exchange of green energy. The agents, acting on behalf of the user, invoke the mediator to obtain information about energy production/consumption. They schedule and control tasks, switching smart plugs or controlling more complex appliances. Agents use the mediator also to store results of negotiation in terms of energy and credits exchanged with the CoSSMic neighborhood. They negotiate the energy exchanges exploiting neighborhood management facilities, for sharing information about the scheduled loads and over energy productions, but also for implementing the negotiation protocol.

4.2 Distribution View

In Figure 2 we complement the previous figure with devices and drivers, and identify those packages which cannot be distributed.

Devices: They are hardware devices with any kind of wireless/wired network interface. These devices (inside home/office/building) are connected to a device

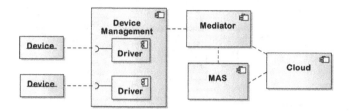

Fig. 2. CoSSMic Architecture - Distribution View

drivers. According to the capability of each device and according to its network interface it can be installed standalone or as a node of a wireless sensor network (WSN). For example, in the first case it could be accessed by its driver using a TCP/IP connection. In the second case it needs that the device and the driver belong to the same local network.

Device Management: It is composed of a number of drivers that collect information from devices and send controls to them. They implement different interfaces to communicate with devices and a uniform interface to use the mediator APIs. In particular they can execute on hardware with reduced capability that is connected to the Internet. If the mediator is hosted on the same hardware the drivers invoke the mediator APIs locally and the Internet connection is eventually used by the mediator or by MAS exploit Cloud services.

CoSSMic Mediator: It is preferred that also the mediator runs on the same node. In fact to develop a pure p2p microgrid of CoSSMic nodes we plan the execution of a mediator instance in each household. In this way users devices and data are bounded to the local area network and there will be limited problems about privacy and routing.

MAS: Software agents implement negotiation and task schedule. They can be hosted on the same node of the mediator if the computational capabilities support its execution. Otherwise agents will execute in Cloud accessing the mediator API via Internet if it executes at different locations.

Cloud Services: As we will see in the next section, the agents, except for one configuration (All In Cloud), reside on the home gateway and use the Cloud only to exchange information.

4.3   Deployment View

As possible configurations we have taken into account the heterogeneity of users and what could be their needs and their priorities. We have, for example, considered the need to access the platform from remote. Whether the communication of private information outside the household is another criteria. The market type and its boundary can be an additional requirement (es. the whole neighborhood or just the buildings in a campus or in a park). Starting from the general view of Figure 2, we modeled four configurations for deployment(Figure 3).

All In Home: All Software resides on a home gateway and the cloud is only used by agents to negotiate energy. In this configuration, the entire system resides

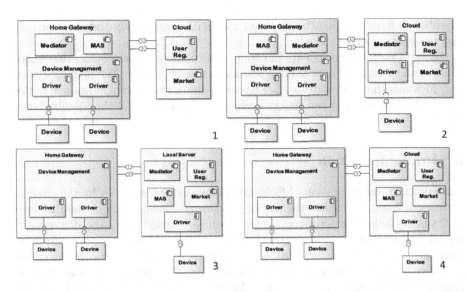

Fig. 3. Framework Configurations: 1. All in home, 2. Hybrid, 3. All Private, 4. All in Cloud

inside the home. Everything is managed by a home gateway that encapsulates the functions of device management, mediator and MAS. The various devices in the home, using special driver, connect to the home gateway. The connect to the web GUI, hosted at the home gateway in order to control and manage the system. Cloud services are only used by agents to exchange info about energy. The optimization is performed inside the home and the energy exchange occurs within the neighborhood.

Hybrid: Conceptually, it is similar to *All in Home* but it is more complete. In fact, it gives the possibility to access the system from the outside through mobile devices. In this configuration, on the home gateway only the front end (client side) of the mediator is present, that syncs with the mediator (server side) in the cloud. As All In Home, the optimization is performed inside the home and the energy exchange occurs within the neighborhood. In the previous case, the measurement data reside in the home gateway while in this case they reside in the cloud.

All Private: There are no public Cloud services. The software is distributed between a home gateway and a local server. This configuration favors privacy. In this configuration, that can represent the case of an industry or a campus or a homepark, the privacy is the most important thing. In fact, through this configuration, the data never go outside, so much so that cloud services are not present. In place of the cloud there is a local server where there are the mediator and the MAS. All the home gateway of the campus connect to this local server. The energy is exchanged only locally, namely the industry/campus works as a neighborhood itself and therefore it does not exchanges energy with other neighbors but only among the gateways within its organization and consequently also the optimization is local.

All In Cloud: All services are in Cloud. This configuration requires that there is always access to the network and less assurance of privacy. The home gateway only forwards the information of devices to mediator that is in cloud as well as the MAS. The optimization and energy exchange are performed at the neighborhood level.

5   Implementation

The current implementation of CoSSMic demonstrator is driven by the characteristics of trials selected at the city of Kostanz (Germany) and at the Province of Caserta (Italy). Experimental activities have started using the deployment model "All in Home". Real devices are currently monitored in each household, including smart meters for solar panels and for the global consumption, but also smart plugs to monitor and control heaters, air conditioners, washing machines and other common appliances. Meters are connected to a local gateway through heterogeneous wireless interface. In particular WIFI, UHF 800Ghz and zigbee radio are supported and applied according to the specific requirements of the trial site. Virtual devices are used for testing and simulation purpose. The local gateway is hosted on a Raspberry Pi, that is a credit-card-sized single-board computer equipped with an SD memory, an ARM processor, 512 RAM. A derivative of Linux based Debian distribution is used as Operating System. In the current deployment model the gateway runs drivers, the mediator, the multi agent system and a web GUI. Drivers are developed from scratch for the specific meter/connection technology. They use the mediator APIs to store monitoring information and to receive control actions for the managed devices. The mediator implementation is based on EmonCMS[5], an open-source web-app for processing, logging and visualising energy, temperature and other environmental data. EmonCMS has been extended to provide facilities to drivers for the management of devices. Both the user GUI and software agents use the REST APIs of the mediator, to run related interactive and autonomous monitoring and control actions on energy resources. In particular agents provide information about the energy exchange with the neighborhood, which is represented itself as an additional device. A fine grain control of the Mediator is also available by the extended web interface of EmonCMS that is shown in Figure 4, but it is hidden to the final user. Moreover by the GUI the user can also set constraints about the utilization of his appliances such as earliest and latest start time. Such a policy is enforced by software agents that are delegated to negotiate the energy exchanges with other agents of the neighborhood, eventually shifting their loads to improve the global optimization of self-consumption.

The JADE[6] agent platform has been used to develop a preliminary prototype of the multi agent system. JADE [4] is a free software framework for agents

---

[5] http://emoncms.org/
[6] http://jade.tilab.com/

Inputs

⊖ Node 0

Node:	name	Description	Process list	last updated	value			
0	powerout		kwh hist	inactive	8.09	✎	🗑	⚲
0	powerin			inactive	200	✎	🗑	⚲
0	power			5 hours ago	8.86	✎	🗑	⚲

⊖ Node 1

Node:	name	Description	Process list	last updated	value			
1	powerin		log kwh	inactive	50.0	✎	🗑	⚲

⊖ Node 30

Node:	name	Description	Process list	last updated	value			
30	powerout			inactive	2250	✎	🗑	⚲

Fig. 4. EmonCMS Input View

development and management totally written in Java. JADE is also fully compliant with FIPA specifications. The current Architecture of the MAS is shown in Figure 5. A Control Agent is responsible for the energy scheduling and negotiation of his own device. Solar panels are represented by producer agents, whereas appliances by consumer agents. An energy storage is handled by a couple of producer and consumer. Schedule strategy is driven by weather forecast,

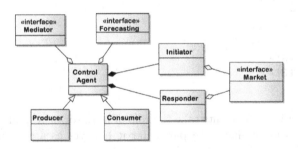

Fig. 5. Architecture of MAS

user constraints, device information and market availability. The goal is always the optimization of self-consumption that will improve the individual's utility by a fair distribution of the global savings.

Market APIs allowed the implementation of the negotiation protocol over a peer to peer overlay, which supports sharing of their energy schedule in terms of energy offers and requests. A distributed solution is in fact preferred to a centralized that is also investigated by research efforts on Cloud and Big data technologies [8].

The SLA template shown in Listing 1 includes agent id, date, needed power (Watt), price (Eur), duration, Earliest and Latest Start Time (EST, LST).

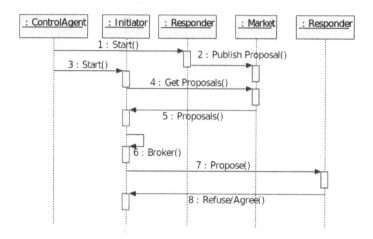

Fig. 6. Sequence diagram of negotiation

```
<?xml version ="1.0" encoding ="UTF-8"?>
<SLA>
<AId> Agent_1 </AgentId>
<Date> 04/15/2014 </Date>
<Power> 3000 </Power>
<Price> 0.2 </Price>
<Last> 02:55 </Last>
<IP>ContractNet </IP>
<EST> 15:05 </EST>
<LST> 16:05 </LST>
</SLA>
```

As shown in Figure 6, agents take the role of initiator or responder in a many to many negotiation scenario. In particular it behaves as a responder when it has published its own proposal and is contacted by another agent. In this case it will accept or refuse the incoming request. Agents behave as initiator when they broker the best composite SLA, choosing the best set of published proposals that satisfy its energy needs, and contacting other agents to close the agreements. For the communication of agents across the neighborhood we are investigating two different technologies. An XMPP (Extensible Messaging and Presence Protocol) communication infrastructure, based on the Tigase[7] solution at server side and on Smack APIs[8] at client side is already available. We have also investigated the adoption a server-less infrastructure based on Retroshare[9] for the market implementation.

---

[7] http://www.tigase.org/

[8] http://www.igniterealtime.org/projects/smack/

[9] http://retroshare.sourceforge.net/

The current prototype allows the users to access the GUI by a web browser. The user is asked to edit an APIKEY at the startup, when the CoSSMic smart pack is installed and it needs to demonstrate the ownership of the equipment. After that the first user is registered and the GUI is used to define other users and authorization policies. In Figure 7 a snapshot of the preliminary implementation of the GUI is shown. The GUI connects device instances to mediator

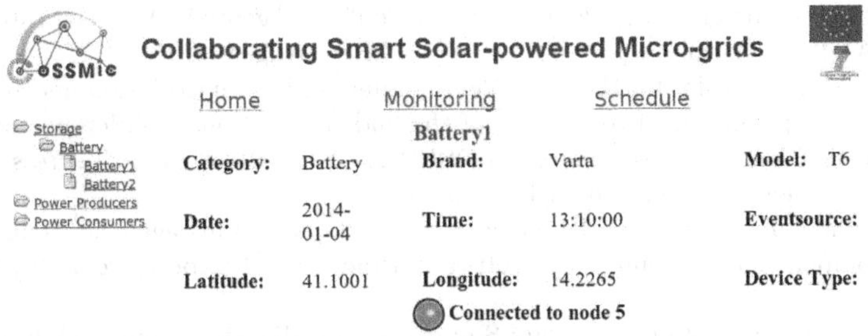

Fig. 7. GUI snapshot

nodes handled by drivers. Households, individual devices and neighborhood are monitored and controlled by specific dialogs, defined by a user-centric approach during project meeting. In fact user trials have been actively involved in the design process since the beginning of the project. Cloud services are also planned to be designed and developed for supporting remote access by the user and also to monitor mobile equipment such electric cars.

6   Conclusion

In this paper we presented design and technologies for the development of an ICT platform to enable the collaboration among neighbors, who consume and produce energy by renewable sources. Distributed scheduling and negotiation of green energy by intelligent software agents are exploited to address the fluctuating nature of decentralized energy production by solar panels and to increase the rate of self-consumption of the neighborhood. Ongoing activities focus on development of all the software components and on their integration. Numerical simulation using synthetic and real data have been used to tune the optimization strategy. Experimental activities have been started in the city of Konstanz (Germany) and in the Province of Caserta (Italy), which have been selected as trials sites.

Acknowledgements. This paper is partially supported by the EU CoSSMic project FP7-608806-Smart Cities-2013 and by PRIST 2009, Fruizione assistita e context aware di siti archelogici complessi mediante terminali mobile, founded by Second University of Naples.

References

1. Amato, A., Aversa, R., Di Martino, B., Scialdone, M., Venticinque, S., Hallsteinsen, S., Horn, G.: Software agents for collaborating smart solar-powered micro-grids. In: Caporarello, L., Di Martino, B., Martinez, M. (eds.) Smart Organizations and Smart Artifacts. Lecture Notes in Information Systems and Organisation, vol. 7, pp. 125–133. Springer International Publishing (2014)
2. Amato, A., Di Martino, B., Scialdone, M., Venticinque, S.: An agent-based approach for smart energy grids. In: 6th Int. Conf. on Agents & Artificial Intelligence (ICAART 2014), vol. 2, pp. 164–171. SciTePress, Angers (2014)
3. Amato, A., Liccardo, L., Rak, M., Venticinque, S.: SLA negotiation and brokering for sky computing. In: Proceedings of the 2nd International Conference on Cloud Computing and Services Science, CLOSER 2012, pp. 611–620. SciTePress, Science and Technology Publications, PRT (2012)
4. Bellifemine, F., Poggi, A., Rimassa, G.: Developing multi-agent systems with a fipa-compliant agent framework. Software: Practice and Experience 31(2), 103–128 (2001)
5. Bruinenberg, J., Colton, L., et al.: Smart grid coordination group technical report reference architecture for the smart grid version 1.0 (draft) 2012-03-02. Tech. rep. (2012)
6. Department of Energy: 2030: A National Vision for Electricity's Second 100 Years (2003)
7. Di Martino, B., Venticinque, S., Aversa, R.: Distributed agents network for ubiquitous monitoring and services exploitation. In: 7th IEEE/IFIP International Conference on Embedded and Ubiquitous Computing (EUC 2009), vol. 1, pp. 197–204. IEEE Computer Society, Washington, DC (2009),
http://dx.medra.org/10.1109/CSE.2009.122
8. Esposito, C., Ficco, M., Palmieri, F., Castiglione, A.: A knowledge-based platform for big data analytics based on publish/subscribe services and stream processing. Knowledge-Based Systems (2014)
9. Hughes, J.: Intelligrid architecture concepts and iec61850. In: 2005/2006 IEEE PES Transmission and Distribution Conference and Exhibition, pp. 401–404 (May 2006)
10. Uslar, M.: Introduction and smart grid basics. In: Standardization in Smart Grids. Power Systems, pp. 3–12. Springer, Heidelberg (2013)

Social Networks and Applications

Recommending Users in Social Networks by Integrating Local and Global Reputation

Pasquale De Meo[1], Fabrizio Messina[2], Domenico Rosaci[3], and Giuseppe M.L. Sarné[4]

[1] DICAM, University of Messina, Italy
pdemeo@unime.it
[2] DMI, University of Catania, Italy
messina@dmi.unict.it
[3] DIIES, University Mediterranea of Reggio Calabria, Italy
domenico.rosaci@unirc.it
[4] DICEAM, University Mediterranea of Reggio Calabria, Italy
sarne@unirc.it

Abstract. A central research theme in the Online Social Network (OSN) scenario consists of predicting the trustworthiness a user should assign to the other OSN members. Past approaches to predict trust relied on global reputation models: they were based on feedbacks about the actions performed by the user in the past and provided for the entire OSN. These models have shown an evident limitation in considering the effects of malicious and fraudulent behaviors, thus making unreliable the feedbacks themselves. In this paper, we propose to integrate global reputation models with a local reputation, computed on the user ego-network. Some experiments, performed on real datasets show that the global reputation is useful only if the size of the user ego-network is small, as for a newcomer. Besides, the integrated usage of global and local reputations leads to predict the expected trust with a very high level of precision.

1 Introduction

A relevant research issue in Online Social Networks (OSNs) is that to design recommender systems capable to provide a user with suggestions about the trustworthiness to assign to other users with which he/she has not interacted in the past. This capability would avoid the user to be involved with unreliable users also to avoid risks and harmful interactions. This issue emerged in large online e-Commerce communities, for instance eBay, and it is largely discussed in many OSNs in which users are allowed to create and share contents and opinions with other users. This is the case, for example, of OSNs like EPINIONS (www.epinions.com) and CIAO (www.ciao.it), in which users provide reviews about commercial products falling in different categories, but also of more generalist OSNs like Facebook (www.facebook.com) and Twitter (www.twitter.com).

Almost all of these platforms face such an issue by adopting a reputation system. Reputation is a form of indirect trust, in which a user takes advantage from

G. Fortino et al. (Eds.): IDCS 2014, LNCS 8729, pp. 437–446, 2014.

the recommendations of other users in order to evaluate the probable trustworthiness of an interlocutor. Generally, in the traditional online social contexts[22, 21], the reputation of a user is evaluated by averaging the feedbacks provided by all the users of the community. For instance, in CIAO and in EPINIONS, each user can post a review that can be evaluated by the other users, and a value of *helpfulness* is associated with each review. Such a form of reputation will be called *global reputation*, to highlight that it has been generated by leveraging on the feedbacks issued from the entire community. Global reputation has also been largely used in past recommender systems for OSNs [2–4] but its effectiveness in estimating trustworthiness of unknown users is limited by the uncertainty about the reliability of the recommendations.

In this paper, we propose to integrate the traditional use of the global reputation with another form of reputation, called *local reputation*, based on suggestions only coming by the entourage of the user (friends, friends of friends and so on) and thus probably more reliable than completely unreferenced recommendations. Our contribution consists in proposing a model to integrate local and global reputation in an OSN, depending on three main parameters, namely: (*i*) the importance given to local vs global reputation; (*ii*) the threshold of reputation under which a user is considered unreliable; (*iii*) the size of the ego-network associated with a target user, i.e., the subgraph of the social graph containing all the OSN members that are connected to the user via a path of trust links. We evaluate our model on a dataset extracted from the above mentioned social network CIAO, obtaining two main results: i) the role of the global reputation is relevant only for those users having an ego-network small enough; ii) the use of the sole local reputation is the best choice for minimising the average error in predicting the trust, with respect to consider all the users of the OSN.

The paper is organised as follows. Section 2 illustrates some related work on recommending users in OSNs. In Section 3 we synthetically describe the scenario which we deal with, while Section 4 presents the approach we propose for predicting the trust of a user in another user. Section 5 describes some experiments we performed for evaluating our proposal and, finally, in Section 6 we draw our final conclusions.

2   Related Work

Due to their exponential growth in popularity, OSNs permeate many aspects of the human life [10]. However, social interactions and decision processes carried out on OSNs can be potentially risky, as much as the OSN size is large [13], for the presence of malicious behaviors performed by unreliable partners [6].

In the OSN trust systems, the three main aspects are identifiable in: (*i*) informative sources [1]; (*ii*) aggregation rules [5]; (*iii*) trust inference along the SN [16, 31]. More in detail, the informative sources at disposal of a user are the direct opinions, derived by own personal past experiences, and/or the indirect information, consisting of the opinions provided by other users. They are known as the reliability and the reputation of a user, respectively [11, 20, 28]. In an OSN scenario, reputation is often predominant since a user usually interacts with a narrow portion of affiliated and, therefore, a trustworthy opinion about someone could be difficult to obtain without to rely on the opinions provided by others. As a consequence, different proposals exist in the literature to aggregate such informative sources, often in a unique global synthetic trust measure [26, 27].

Trust computational models rely on a local or a global point of view, independently of the fact that a trust model is implemented in a centralised or distributed fashion. This means that a user can have a partial vision of trust of other OSN members (e.g., some of his/her peers) or, vice versa, the computation of trust is based on parameters/metrics defined over the whole OSN. Massa and Aversani [19] investigated both advantages and disadvantages of local and global metrics and the main outcome of their study is that local trust metrics can be more accurate than global ones if based on the personal users' point of views. Conversely, the computation of local trust values is surely more time-expensive than the computation of global trust metrics, although, it depends on the user's neighbor horizon adopted to discovery a *trust* chain linking two users [31]. If we model an OSN as a directed graph (*trust network*) whose vertices are users and edges encode trust relationships, we can use some topological concepts from graph theory – like the concept of path or the concept of shortest path – to infer[24, 23, 25] trust relationships among pairs of unknown users. See, for instance [7, 17, 14, 16].

The TidalTrust algorithm [7] infers trust values in trust networks. In Tidal-Trust, trust values are continuous values in a fixed interval. TidalTrust performs a modified Breadth First Search on the trust network to find all the shortest path linking two users (not directly connected) in an incremental way and computing the user's trust rating as a weighted average of trust ratings from the source to the target users. This algorithm relies on the assumption that closer neighbors provide more accurate trust predictions about a trustworthy user than other OSN users. MoleTrust [18] differs from TidalTrust for the opportunities to specify a maximum depth in the search-tree and to perform a backward exploration. MoleTrust computes the trust score of all the users at each depth in the path between two users. In particular, (i) the trust score of a user at depth x only depends on trust scores of users at depth $x - 1$ (already computed) and (ii) predicted users' trust values only consider the average of all incoming trust edges coming from users having a predicted trust score greater than a threshold weighted by the trust score of the user who has issued the trust statement.

Sparsity problems might force trust-based systems to consider ratings provided by indirect and poor reliably neighbors with a strong risk to decrease in precision. To address such an issue, Jamali and Ester proposed in [12] a random walk model called TrustWalker, which considers both ratings of the target item and those of similar items. The random walker searches in the trust network, while the other component considers ratings on similar items to limit depth search in the network. TrustWalker improves the precision by preferring raters at a nearer distance and improves the coverage by considering similar items as well as the exact target item (with probability increasing with the walk length).

The algorithm proposed in [9] combines trust and distrust and propagates them through an OSN. Even though this approach provides interesting results in predicting trust and distrust between unknown users, distrust rates are not always available in an OSN. SWTrust [13] is a framework incorporable in different trust models to generate small trusted subgraphs of large OSNs. Authors developed, both in centralised and distributed version, a breadth-first search algorithm to preprocess large SNs based on the *weak ties* theory [8] on the spread of information in SNs and by inferring trust values. The two algorithms return a *trust* network where trusted knowledge chains allow trust evaluations to be performed. This algorithm has been validated by using the real data set EPINIONS .

Finally, a model integrating in a single measure the propagation of local trust and global influence [15] within an OSN is presented in [30]. Both [15] and [30] assume that each link connecting OSN users may express an interest to a content or the trust into a user and that trust between each pair of users belonging to the same neighbor is already known (either explicitly or implicitly). This model analyses the graph to discover trustful, influential or interesting nodes into the OSN by incorporating the notion of influence with the freshness of the trust connections between users.

3   The Social Network Scenario

Our scenario deals with an OSN S composed by a set of users U. We represent such a network as a directed unlabelled graph $G_S = \langle N, A \rangle$, where N is the set of nodes and A is the set of arcs. Each node $n \in N$ is associated with a user $u_n \in U$, while each arc $a \in A$ is a pair (a, b), with $a, b \in N$ representing a trust link between the users u_a and u_b (i.e. a trusts b). We denote by $n(u)$ the node of the graph corresponding to the user u.

We define the *ego-network* of a user u the sub-graph of G_S, denoted by $G_u = \langle T, P \rangle$, where T is a set of nodes containing $n(u)$ and all the nodes $n(k) \in U$ that are connected to $n(u)$; P contains all the arcs belonging to the paths existing between $n(u)$ and $n(k)$, for each $k \in T$. In words, G_u represents both all the users in which u directly trusts and all the users *indirectly trusted* by u; we say that u indirectly trusts a user v if either (i) there exists a user k which directly trusts v and u directly trusts k or (ii) there exists a user k which trusts in v, and u, in turn, indirectly trusts k. Hereafter, we will informally say that a user v belongs to the ego-network of u if the node $n(v)$ belongs to G_u.

In the context above, we define *local trust* a relation LT defined on $U \times U$, such that an ordered pair of users $t = [u, v]$ belongs to LT if and only if the node $n(v)$ belongs to the ego-network G_u of u. For all the nodes $n(u)$, $n(v)$ such that $[u, v] \in LT$ we define a local reputation measure $\lambda(u, v)$, that represents how much the users belonging to the ego network of u trusts v. More in particular, we propose to compute the local reputation by suitably summing the contributions (in terms of trust in v) of all the users k ($k \neq u$) belonging to the ego-network of u which are also connected with v. We denote by $s(u, v)$ this sum, and we call *local network* $L(u, v)$ the set of contributors, i.e., $L(u, v) = \{z : z \in G_u \wedge \exists(z, v) \in G_u\}$.

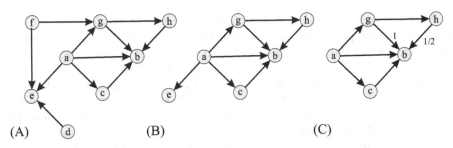

Fig. 1. (A) An example of social network; (B) The ego-network of node a; (C) The nodes involving in the computation of $\lambda(a,b)$ - links label the contributions.

If $k \in L(u,v)$ is a user in which u directly trusts, then there exists an arc $(n(u), n(k))$ in G_u; in this case, the contribution of k to $s(u,v)$ will be equal to 1. Instead, if k is indirectly trusted by u, then there is at least one path in G_u connecting u and k. We consider the shortest path between $n(u)$ and $n(k)$ in G_u and suppose it has length $l_{u,k}$. In this case, the contribution carried in by k to the trust computation will be equal to $1/2^{l_{u,k}-1}$. This choice corresponds to consider as exponentially less important the contributions coming from users more distant from u in the ego-network of u for computing the local reputation of v. We normalise $s(u,v)$ dividing it by the maximum value of the analogous sums $s(u,z)$, for all $z \in U$. More formally, the formula for computing $\lambda(u,v)$ is:

$$\lambda(u,v) = \frac{\sum_{k \in L(u,v), k \neq u,v} \frac{1}{2^{l_{u,k}-1}}}{\max_{z \in U, z \neq u,v} \left(\sum_{h \in L(u,z), h \neq u,z} \frac{1}{2^{l_{u,h}-1}} \right)} \tag{1}$$

An important characteristic of $\lambda(u,v)$ is represented by the number of nodes that contribute to its computation, that is the cardinality $\|L(u,v)\|$. If $\|L(u,v)\|$ is very small, then u will not have a sufficient information about v from his/her ego-network. A simple example of the above scenario is graphically depicted in Figure 1-(A), representing a social network with 8 nodes. In Figure 1-(B) is represented the ego-network of the node a, while in Figure 1-(A) we can observe that, in order to compute $\lambda(a,b)$, the nodes contributing to the sum appearing at the numerator of Equation 3 are g,c and h. The contributions of g and c to the sum are equal to 1, because g and c are directly connected with a, while the contribution of h is equal to $1/2$, since the length of the shortest path between a and h is 2. The sum of these three contributions equals $(1+1+1/2)=2.5$ and also represents the maximum value of the other sums considered when computing the maximum in the denominator of Formula 3. For this reason, we conclude that $\lambda(a,b)$ is equal to 1. Instead, we note that, in order to compute $\lambda(a,h)$, the unique contribution to the sum appearing at the numerator of Equation 3 is that of the node g, that is equal to 1. Then we can conclude that $\lambda(a,h) = 1/2.5 = 0.4$.

Moreover, in our scenario we suppose that users can make *actions*, and each action can be evaluated by the other users by means of a *feedback*. For instance, in Facebook each user can post a content, and the other user can use features like *I like it*, thus providing a positive evaluation of that content. In other social networks, as in EPINIONS or in CIAO, each can provide reviews of some items, and the other users can evaluate the helpfulness of the reviews.

Generally, we define the *global reputation* of a user u, denoted by $\gamma(u)$, as the average of all the feedbacks related to all the actions made by u. More formally, if $a_u^1, a_u^2, ...a_u^p$ are the p actions performed by u, $f(k, a_u^i)$ is the feedback provided by the user k about the i-th action a_u^i of u and $\|U\|$ is the cardinality of the set of users U of the OSN, therefore the global reputation is defined as follows:

$$\gamma(u) = \frac{\sum_{i=1,..,p} \sum_{k \in U, k \neq u} f(k, a_u^i)}{p \cdot \|U\| - 1} \tag{2}$$

4   Suggesting Trust

In this section, we present our approach for suggesting to a user u if he/she should trust or not in another user v of a given social network. To this aim, if v is the user that must be evaluated from u, we propose to assign to v a synthetic *score*, denoted by $\sigma(u, v)$ to take into account both local and global reputations we defined in Section 3. More in particular, we propose to use a weighted mean of $\lambda(u, v)$ and $\gamma(v)$, weighting the importance of $\lambda(u, v)$ with respect to $\gamma(v)$ by a parameter ω, where ω is a real value ranging in $[0...1]$. Formally,

$$\sigma(u, v) = \omega \cdot \lambda(u, v) + (1 - \omega) \cdot \gamma(v) \tag{3}$$

Now, we suggest the user u to trust in v if the score $\sigma(u, v)$ is greater than a threshold τ. More formally, let $st(u, v)$ be a variable, whose value is 1 if u has to trust in v, 0 otherwise. Then:

$$st(u, v) = \begin{cases} 1 & \text{if } \sigma(u, v) > \tau \\ 0 & \text{otherwise} \end{cases} \tag{4}$$

In order to find suitable values for ω and τ, we propose to examine a training-set $TR = \langle U*, A*, F*, T* \rangle$, where: (*i*) $U* \subset U$ is a subset of the users of S; (*ii*) $A*$ is a set of actions performed by the users of $U*$; (*iii*) $F*$ is a set of feedbacks provided by the users of U^* related to the actions contained in $A*$; (*iv*) $T*$ contains the trust values $t(u, v)$, for all $u, v \in U^*$. Then, given two values ω and τ, we can compute the suggested trust $st(u, v)$, and then determining the difference, in the absolute value, between $st(u, v)$ and the actual trust $t(u, v)$. Moreover, we will compute the mean of these differences for all the pair (u, v), obtaining the global error $\epsilon = \epsilon(\omega, \tau)$:

$$\epsilon(\omega, \tau) = \frac{\sum_{u, v \in U, u \neq v} |st(u, v) - t(u, v)|}{(\|U\| - 1)^2} \tag{5}$$

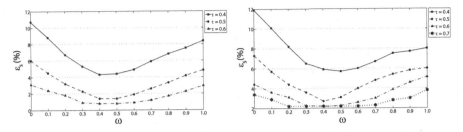

Fig. 2. Average error vs ω: A) node 101, local dimension $\rho = 733$; B) node 1, local dimension $\rho = 2560$

We will use the values for ω^* and τ^* minimising $\epsilon(\omega, \tau)$, i.e.:

$$\epsilon(\omega^*, \tau^*) = \min \frac{\sum_{u,v \in U, u \neq v} |st(u,v) - t(u,v)|}{(\|U\| - 1)^2} \tag{6}$$

5 Experiments

In this Section, we describe some experiments to validate our approach. We used as test-bed some real data extracted from the well-known CIAO social network. The dataset has been crawled in the context of the research described in [29], and it is publicly available at `http://www.public.asu.edu/~jtang20/datasetcode/truststudy.htm`. First, we examined how the global error $\epsilon(\omega, \tau)$ depends on the mean $\|L(u, v)\|$ of the user u, i.e. on the following parameter, denoted by ρ_u and computed as $\rho_u = \sum_{v \in U} \frac{\lambda(u,v)}{|L(u,v)|}$.

In Figures 2-3 the relationship $\epsilon = \epsilon(\omega, \tau)$ is reported for different values of ω and τ, and for 4 users having different values of ρ_u. We observe for all the users the error generally decreases with the parameter τ, obtaining the best results in correspondence of $\tau = 0.6$. For values of τ higher than 0.6, the error increases, thus we have only represented the curves corresponding to some values of $\tau > 0.6$.

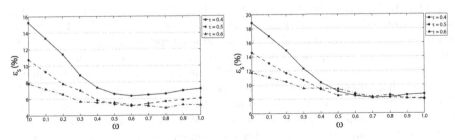

Fig. 3. Average error vs ω: A) node 13, local dimension $\rho = 7360$; B) node 339, local dimension $\rho = 14599$

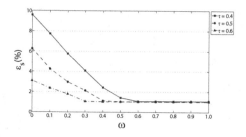

Fig. 4. Average error vs ω for the whole CIAO social network dataset

We also note that user with ID equal to 101, having a relatively small value of ρ_u (i.e, $\rho_u = 733$) presents an error that has a minimum in correspondence of the pair $(\omega, \tau) = (0.5, 0.6)$. Therefore, for this type of user, it is important to merge both local and global reputations in equal measure, due to the fact that the local ego-network is not sufficiently large to suggest a correct trust without the help of the global reputation. User with ID equal to 1, having $\rho = 2560$, again presents a minimum error in $(0.5, 0.6)$, but the difference from using high values of ω is less important (if we would set $\omega = 1$. Thus, by exploiting only the local reputation, we will obtain an increment of the error lesser than 2%).

Figures 3 A-B are related with users having very high values of ρ_u, and show that the influence of the global reputation is almost negligible. The result reported in Figure 4 is finally related to the entire CIAO dataset, and represents the global error averaged on all the 2600 users composing the dataset. This result shows that for obtaining the minimum average error for the entire community, it is possible also to use $\omega = 1$, avoiding to consider the global trust.

6   Conclusion

In this paper, we propose a model integrating local and global reputation in an OSN. We considered three important parameters for characterising the model: (i) ω represents the importance given to local vs global reputation; (ii) τ is the reputation threshold under which a user is considered unreliable; (iii) ρ represents the dimension of the user ego-network, containing all the OSN members connected to him/her via a path of trust links. Some experiments on a real dataset extracted from the social network CIAO, show that the size of user ego-networks has a discriminatory effect: in fact, global reputation is relevant only for those users having an ego-network small enough but in the case of users having large ego-networks, local reputation is sufficient for predicting trustworthiness with a very high precision. Besides, our experiments show that the use of the sole local reputation is the best choice to minimise the average error in predicting the trust, by considering all the users of the OSN. We argue that these results are particularly important in designing a recommender system for OSNs having large ego-networks for most of the users, since in this case we can avoid to use a global reputation mechanism, as usually implemented by many OSNs.

In our ongoing research, we plan to better study the influence of several parameters characterising the ego-network of the user.

Acknowledgements. This work is a part of the research project **PRISMA**, code **PON04a2_A/F**, funded by the Italian Ministry of University within the **PON 2007-2013** framework program.

References

1. De Meo, P., Ferrara, E., Rosaci, D., Sarnè, G.M.L.: How to improve group homogeneity in online social networks. In: Proc. of the 14th WOA 2013. CEUR Workshop Proceedings, vol. 1099. CEUR-WS.org (2011)
2. De Meo, P., Nocera, A., Quattrone, G., Rosaci, D., Ursino, D.: Finding reliable users and social networks in a social internetworking system. In: Proc. of the 2009 Int. Database Engineering & Applications Symposium, pp. 173–181. ACM (2009)
3. De Meo, P., Nocera, A., Rosaci, D., Ursino, D.: Recommendation of reliable users, social networks and high-quality resources in a social internetworking system. AI Communications 24(1), 31–50 (2011)
4. De Meo, P., Quattrone, G., Rosaci, D., Ursino, D.: Dependable recommendations in social internetworking. In: Web Intelligence and Intelligent Agent Technologies, 2009, pp. 519–522. IET (2009)
5. Dellarocas, C.: Designing reputation systems for the social web. SSRN Electronic Journal (2010)
6. Fogel, J., Nehmad, E.: Internet social network communities: Risk taking, trust, and privacy concerns. Computers in Human Behavior 25(1), 153–160 (2009)
7. Golbeck, J.A.: Computing and applying trust in web-based social networks (2005)
8. Granovetter, M.: The strength of weak ties: A network theory revisited. Sociological Theory 1(1), 201–233 (1983)
9. Guha, R., et al.: Propagation of trust and distrust. In: Proc. of the 13th International Conference on World Wide Web, pp. 403–412. ACM (2004)
10. Heidemann, J., Klier, M., Probst, F.: Online social networks: A survey of a global phenomenon. Computer Networks 56(18), 3866–3878 (2012)
11. Huynh, T.D., Jennings, N.R., Shadbolt, N.R.: An integrated trust and reputation model for open multi-agent systems. Autonomous Agents and Multi-Agent Systems 13(2), 119–154 (2006)
12. Jamali, M., Ester, M.: Trustwalker: A random walk model for combining trust-based and item-based recommendation. In: Proc. of the 15th ACM SIGKDD Int. Conf. on Knowledge Discovery and Data Mining, pp. 397–406. ACM (2009)
13. Jiang, W., Wang, G., Wu, J.: Generating trusted graphs for trust evaluation in online social networks. Future Generation Computer Systems 31, 48–58 (2014)
14. Jøsang, A., Gray, E., Kinateder, M.: Simplification and analysis of transitive trust networks. Web Intelligence and Agent Systems 4(2), 139–161 (2006)
15. Kempe, D., Kleinberg, J., Tardos, E.: Maximizing the spread of influence through a social network. In: Proc. of the 9th ACM SIGKDD International Conference on Knowledge Ddiscovery and Data Mining, pp. 137–146. ACM (2003)
16. Kim, Y., Song, H.S.: Strategies for predicting local trust based on trust propagation in social networks. Knowledge-Based Systems 24(8), 1360–1371 (2011)
17. Lesani, M., Montazeri, N.: Fuzzy trust aggregation and personalized trust inference in virtual social networks. Computational Intelligence 25(2), 51–83 (2009)

18. Massa, P., Avesani, P.: Trust-aware recommender systems. In: Proc. of the 2007 ACM Conference on Recommender Systems, pp. 17–24. ACM (2007)
19. Massa, P., Avesani, P.: Trust metrics on controversial users: Balancing between tyranny of the majority. IJSWIS 3(1), 39–64 (2007)
20. Messina, F., Pappalardo, G., Rosaci, D., Santoro, C., Sarné, G.M.L.: A trust-based approach for a competitive cloud/grid computing scenario. In: Intelligent Distributed Computing VI, pp. 129–138 (2013)
21. Messina, F., Pappalardo, G., Rosaci, D., Santoro, C., Sarné, G.M.L.: HySoN: A distributed agent-based protocol for group formation in online social networks. In: Klusch, M., Thimm, M., Paprzycki, M. (eds.) MATES 2013. LNCS, vol. 8076, pp. 320–333. Springer, Heidelberg (2013)
22. Messina, F., Pappalardo, G., Rosaci, D., Santoro, C., Sarné, G.M.L.: A distributed agent-based approach for supporting group formation in p2p e-learning. In: Baldoni, M., Baroglio, C., Boella, G., Micalizio, R. (eds.) AI*IA 2013. LNCS (LNAI), vol. 8249, pp. 312–323. Springer, Heidelberg (2013)
23. Messina, F., Pappalardo, G., Santoro, C.: Complexsim: An smp-aware complex network simulation framework. In: 2012 Sixth International Conference on Complex, Intelligent and Software Intensive Systems (CISIS), pp. 861–866. IEEE (2012), doi:10.1109/CISIS.2012.102
24. Messina, F., Pappalardo, G., Santoro, C.: Exploiting gpus to simulate complex systems. In: 2013 Seventh International Conference on Complex, Intelligent, and Software Intensive Systems (CISIS), pp. 535–540. IEEE (2013), doi:10.1109/CISIS.2013.97
25. Messina, F., Pappalardo, G., Santoro, C.: Complexsim: A flexible simulation platform for complex systems. International Journal of Simulation and Process Modelling 8(4), 202–211 (2013), doi:10.1504/IJSPM.2013.059417
26. Pinyol, I., Sabater-Mir, J.: Computational trust and reputation models for open multi-agent systems: A review. Artificial Intelligence Review 40(1), 1–25 (2013)
27. Rosaci, D., Sarné, G.M.L., Garruzzo, S.: Integrating trust measures in multiagent systems. International Journal of Intelligent Systems 27(1), 1–15 (2012)
28. Sabater, J., Sierra, C.: Regret: reputation in gregarious societies. In: Proc. of the 5th Int. Conference on Autonomous Agents, pp. 194–195. ACM (2001)
29. Tang, J., Hu, X., Gao, H., Liu, H.: Exploiting local and global social context for recommendation. In: IJCAI, pp. 2712–2718. AAAI Press (2013)
30. Varlamis, I., Eirinaki, M., Louta, M.: Application of social network metrics to a trust-aware collaborative model for generating personalized user recommendations. In: The Influence of Technology on Social Network Analysis and Mining. LNSN, vol. 6, pp. 49–74. Springer (2013)
31. Ziegler, C.N., Lausen, G.: Spreading activation models for trust propagation. In: EEE 2004, pp. 83–97. IEEE (2004)

A Carpooling Open Application with Social Oriented Reward Mechanism

Simone Bonarrigo, Vincenza Carchiolo, Alessandro Longheu, Mark Loria,
Michele Malgeri, and Giuseppe Mangioni

Dip. Ingegneria Elettrica, Elettronica e Informatica - Università degli Studi di Catania - Italy
simone.bonarrigo@hotmail.it,
{vincenza.carchiolo,alessandro.longheu,michele.malgeri,
giuseppe.mangioni}@dieei.unict.it,mark.loria@gmail.com

Abstract. Carpooling is currently getting more and more attractive thanks both to an increasing emphasis placed on environmental issues and to the huge use of web based social networks. They indeed (1) allow to spread all information for an effective service (2) compensate the lack of confidence among carpooling users (3) promote carpooling companies via viral marketing (4) act as a basis for trust based users recommendation system. CORSA is an open source solution for a real time ride sharing (RTRS) carpooling service, with high accessibility, high usability, and effectiveness and efficiency in finding a riding solution for users. This proposal also endorses the role of social networks using a virtual credits reward mechanism.

Keywords: carpooling, RTRS, ride sharing, social networks virtual credits.

1 Introduction

The transport system based on sharing private cars, simply known as *carpooling* is an innovative yet quite old idea whose first proposals date back to more than thirty years ago [10] [22]. The renewal of the interest for carpooling is due to the increasing emphasis placed on the reduction in the number of vehicles, the expenses for gas and in energy consumption and pollution.

An additional factor that is encouraging the intensive adoption of carpooling comes from the massive use of web based social networks [12] [20]. They indeed represent a well-established tool:

- to share all information for an effective carpooling service (users personal profiles, ongoing position, preferred routes etc.)
- to leverage social relationships to remedy the lack of confidence among users that currently limits the use of carpooling,
- to encompass the traditional forms of marketing and advertising for instance endorsing carpooling companies by viral marketing [9]
- to provide feedback mechanisms as users/service rating and recommendation useful to build an overlay trust network [4] that can consolidate the relationship of carpooling users [8] and allow to safely add new users, e.g. persons could choose only trusted people for sharing their routes [5].

G. Fortino et al. (Eds.): IDCS 2014, LNCS 8729, pp. 447–456, 2014.

– to exploit hidden relationships, for instance if a community of people that lives and/or work at close places is discovered [3], the system can put them into contact for sharing common routes

The work presented in this paper, named CORSA (Carpooling Open source Ride Sharing Application) [17], is a solution for a carpooling service accessible anytime from anywhere with high usability, effectiveness and efficiency in automatically providing users with helpful solutions. In addition to these features, in our proposal we also endorse the role of social networks. Indeed, we reward users with virtual credits to promote carpooling and to spend such credits, an ecosystem of business or public institutions affiliated with the platform is needed; for this mechanism to be successful, we push users to publicize it to their friends belonging to the same social netwkork acting as in a competition where the greater score you earn, the more credits you can spend on the platform, according to the viral marketing paradigma [16].

To exploit social networks from the very beginning, the initial set of users involved in the testing phase consists of students attending the same university, so a (possibly strong connected) virtual social network is already present. Finally, the work was developed using only open sources libraries, to spread its adoption.

The paper is organized as follows. In section 2 we briefly compare our approach with others, whereas in section 3 the application model and its architecture are discussed. In section 4 we introduce some use cases to show how the application works, providing concluding remarks and future works in section 5.

2   Related Work

In literature, two carpooling services exist, the Daily Car Pooling Problem [1], where each day a number of users declare their availability for picking up colleagues, and the Long-term Car Pooling Problem, where the goal is to define pools where each user will (in turn) pick up the remaining pool members on different days [19]. Our proposal falls into the former, in particular belongs to the so-called real time ride sharing (or RTRS) family problems [15] [13] [11], where trips are planned just before they occur.

Considering other (even commercial) solutions, there are several characteristics that differentiate RTRS platforms: user registration and management, with special attention to drivers; payment methods; Gamification mechanisms to encourage the usage of the service; feedback and ranking system to manage trust and reputation of users; route management, in particular pick up and dropoff points of passengers.

Six companies are taken into consideration: Lyft [18], Uber [24], SideCar [21], Wingz [25], BlaBlacar [2] and Carma [6]. The first four offer services comparable to the ones of a taxi in which passengers contact drivers asking to dropped off in a certain destination. Registered users can become drivers if they successfully pass the companys approval process and meet security requirements such as: no criminal record, minimum age 23 years old, at least three years of driving, a car that meets specific safety standards, no DUI. In addition, all drivers must have insurance coverage. The remaining companies, BlaBlaCar and Carma, are traditional carpooling, where drivers actually share their car for journeys they are doing. In all six cases, passenger pay a monetary compensation for the service.In the case of BlaBlaCar the payment is made in cash, in all other cases with cardcredit. The compensation fee is divided with different percentages between the driver and the company. For example Lyft retains 20 % of the fees for each ride while Carma 15%.

All systems provide a method for calculating the right compensation according to the duration and length of the ride. Costs for the first four companies are higher. In Uber the price can vary also with the type of car.

All companies have adopted a policy of incentives that rewards frequent users and all those who invite new users to join the community. The rewards are provided in the form of coupons, credits that can be used inside the platform itself and free rides. All these companies developed a feedback system that allows drivers and passengers to rate each other at the end of each trip. Each user can view a log of the completed trips with their scores and comments that determine their reliability within the community. To increase the trust factor, most of the platforms integrate to a certain degree with popular social networks, such as Facebook.

Following the analysis of the various realtime ridesharing companies, Carma emerges as the most interesting as it is able to target micro mobility with soft real time capabilities without falling into the a taxi model. This is also reflected in the lower rates that are closer to expense compensation rather than a profit.

3 The Development of the RTRS Service

3.1 Requirements

Most carpooling platforms don't face two questions, the former related to the *real time* requirement and the latter to the so-called *micro carpooling*. The fact that a micro carpooling system targets short range trips means that the definition of pickup points is a crucial aspect. Whereas long distance carpooling can easily make use of points of interest such as bus stations, airports, ecc micro carpooling requires finding a pickup point in the proximity of starting locations of driver and rider. The real time factor reinforces this problem since pickup points must be reached quickly by both users. Automatic selection of pickup points requires considerable work to determine in advance which would be convenient. This would limit the spread of the app as it would only be usable in towns that the system targets. A workaround is to let users freely decide pickup points by chatting before the ride.

3.2 Technical Issues

From a technical view point the challenges that a real time ride sharing platform implies derive mainly from the constraints on usability and response time of the system. We can describe these constraints with three concepts:

- *Automatically* - The usage scenario of a real time ride sharing app implies that the system must make all the possible choices for the end user. Many carpooling websites and services closely resemble a bulletin board where the user must find a compatible ride. The short span of useful time and the limited display screen create the need for an intelligent behind the scenes selection of compatible rides to display. Ideally the system must be able to show a limited selection of compatible rides, as an excess of options would consume useful time.

- *Immediately* - The aspect of immediacy resides not only in the name but in the nature of the use cases of such system. Short range travelers that make use of public transportation might want the ability to make choices very quickly in order to make decisions regarding the rest of their journey. A system that provides such slow performances would be useless for users, representing a waste of time and not allowing them to effectively make use of the system by integrating it with the all ready present transportation network. Operational speed and quick response time translate in optimization of ride lookup and reducing network data transfer to the bare minimum.
- *Easily* - The expected context of use is on the go, the app (we propose to adopt) for a real time ride sharing system must be usable in the simplest of ways. This aspect has more to do with the usability of the user interface but also with how well the use cases represent the effective desired usage.

3.3   Virtual Credits and Social Networks

The majority of carpooling platforms often resemble a bulletin board with a number of proposed journeys the user can choose from, usually proposed according to the compatibility of start and finish point only. The platforms that allow searching of intermediate journeys provide this feature by letting the driver insert during the creation of the route in between stops that he plans to do. This is a time consuming operation that can be easily automated by a system that considers compatibility between rides on the basis of the actual scheduled route. This solution however forces the developer to face a new set of challenges, mainly related to performance as the lookup is a more resource intensive operation. In order to ensure extremely fast response time vertical and horizontal scalability might not always represent the ideal solution. We further discuss lookup optimization and the problems we have encountered in the next paragraph.

The innovation of our carpooling idea is to use virtual credits as the sole source of reimbursement for the service. The purpose of carpooling is to share a resource in order to obtain various benefits for the environment, social interaction and urban mobility. Our aim is not to create a money making platform for the driver, by creating an alternative to taxis or Transportation Network Companies. In short distance micro-carpooling the payment procedure needs to be addressed differently than a long distance carpooling. The short distances involved indeed would lead to ridiculously low reimbursements that cannot guarantee the coverage of costs implied by the extra mileage. The usage of virtual credits seems to be the best for several reasons:

- In a micro carpooling context the resulting compensation is minimal. The driver might not be inclined to share their time and resources for a low fee. The idea of rewarding the driver with credits reusable in different scenarios, might be an incentive for the driver to be an active member of the community.
- By using virtual credits, institutions and retail companies would be directly involved in creating campaigns that would generate economic, cultural and social benefits.

– By using virtual credits it is easy to implement fun and engaging recreational initiatives, incentivizing users to be active carpoolers.

Integration with social networks is a key feature of the platform. The first benefit is the increase in mutual trust between users. Secondly, by creating a community around the platform users can create events, which involve other people, even strangers, but with whom they share the same interests. As an example a user may share with the community the intention of reaching the city centre for a concert. By sharing rides users not only save money, but also enlarge their social network by reaching people they shares interests with and spend quality time with. Tight integration with social networks allows the carpooling platform to add social interactions to the list of environmental and financial benefits. Also government institutions and retail companies can benefit from the use of our system and social network. By promoting events and activities, they can reward users to reach their facilities by ridesharing. Institutions and companies would benefit from users actively promoting them through the social network. Users would benefit by gaining extra virtual credits that can be spent within the market. The implementation of such system is very simple. By accessing a dedicated interface, institutions and retail companies can create promotional campaigns with associated locations. These locations, called hot spots, can be markers or polygons that represent a place of interest. When users check-in or check-out their position is controlled by the server. If there is an associated promotional campaign to their location they receive the reward. The most interesting aspect of the carpooling is that it allows to improve transportation and environmental sustainability by reducing traffic. Micro-carpooling is especially interesting since cities are highly polluted areas, due to the high traffic density. CORSA is a valuable tool to address such problems. By creating campaigns and associated hotspots it allows institutions to influence urban mobility in a way that is engaging and fun for the end user. Secondly, by analyzing long term data, government institutions could study accurate commuter flows allowing them to create effective campaigns or redefine parts of the public transport network.

4   Using CORSA

The system we propose is composed of three main components (see fig 1): a mobile frontend, a server backend with real time bidirectional communication capabilities and a path mangment system accessed through an API. The app and the real time server communicate through web sockets, while calls to the path managment api are done through http. In both cases data is transferred by JSON[14].

The mobile solution, coming from the real time requirement, could be developed as a native implementation or as a hybrid solution. Both have strengths and weaknesses with the main trade off being between performance and platform coverage [23]. These are both key aspects for our platform, but a lot of the performance concerns are tied to network communication and server interaction. Going native would only speed up part of the process. On the other hand, fast prototyping and spread of the applications are key aspects we did not want to compromise on.

Morevoer, a common problem in developing mobile apps that require heavy interaction with a server is to establish whether first developing the app and then the server

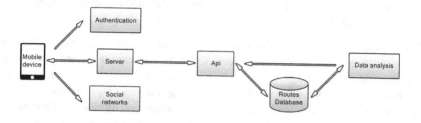

Fig. 1. Application architecture - Components of the CORSA platform

or conversely developing both of them side by side. What emerged pretty quickly was that usability was so important that use cases would need to be tested for usability constraints on a device or emulator. Graphical mockups didn't aid the purpose, since the lack of navigation structures in mobile apps is substituted by gestures. Because of all of this we decided to use a web application as a mockup. To compensate the absence of the api we created static JSON files to inject data into the app. At the end a testing stage where we evaluated usability of the UI and use cases, the static JSON files actually described what data the path management API had to provide and it's structure. With a well defined structure, we were able to concentrate on algorithms and query optimization during the API implementation stage.

4.1   Mobile Application

The system front end is a hybrid mobile app made by two main components: a native wrapper and a web application. While the codebase can be written from scratch, we used existing frameworks to speed up the development of the app. Mobile web frameworks differ firstly on the level of integration they offer. On one side of the spectrum we have fully integrated solutions such as JQuerymobile that combine elements of logic, navigation and UI. On the other side we have limited frameworks that target specific needs leaving the developer to decide which ones to use and how to integrate them. Integrated solutions are useful as they allow the developer to have a running app soon. Heavy customization can however become problematic. We went for the second approach using AngularJS, a javascript MVC framework, and Topcoat as a css library. We preferred separating the two elements to have more flexibility for later customization of the application. As a native wrapper we used Apache Cordova [7]. In the following, some use cases of the mobile app are described.

Searching for a driver or passenger - A user simply needs to specify his desired destination (see fig 2) and the app will show a list of compatible rides. Alternatively he can specify a departure and arrival address, time of depature and number of seats required or available. If not specified the former will be set to the default values, that can be customized from a settings dashboard. For each proposed ride the user can view the route on a map, view profile details (e.g. rating). A real time chat allows the passenger and driver to negotiate pickup and drop-off locations. Once the user finds a travel com-

Fig. 2. Mobile app - Creating a journey and searching for a driver

panion that suits him he has the ability to propose a journey. If the proposed journey is accepted by the other user, the ride contract is established.

Direct contact - The system provides a means of direct contact between users to aid commuters and groups of friends organize journeys. This feature allows to formalize rides with people a user already knows and gain reputation and virtual credits within the platform.

Handshake - The system provides a means for formalizing the start and finish of the journey with a virtual handshake. This can be implemented in a number of ways, such as tapping a feature on the apps GUI or by scanning a qrcode. With a simple calculation on the distance between pickup and drop-off points the system can then calculate the number of credits that need to be charged. This stage is crucial for the rewarding system in order to determine stat and finish locations.

User and journey feedback - Once the journey has ended the app allows to review the passenger or driver. Feedback can be generic, to reflect the general level of satisfaction or specific, for instance ride quality, punctuality or similar.

4.2 Paths Management

Calculating distance between objects and paths on the earths surface is a complex operation and rarely encompasses all the various irregularities that such surface present. The majority of applications will use a degree of approximation that can be accepted by the specific use case. For a real time ride sharing app that is oriented to short distance travels the approximation of the earths surface to a plane is acceptable. One of the most common ways of build a route is to store a number of intermediate points that are virtually connected by segments. To simplify the process we focused on nodes since they represent the geographical location really crossed by the driver, whereas segments will not necessarily approximate curves in the path.

If nodes are too far from each other the system can provide additional nodes to provide a better fitting to the actual route and better intermediate sampling. A passengers and a drivers route are said to be compatible if the nodes of the former fall within the neighborhood of two nodes of the drivers route. To simplify the process we used square bounding boxes centered on the starting and arrival points transforming the problem of compatibility into a simple problem of elements within a numerical range (see fig 3).

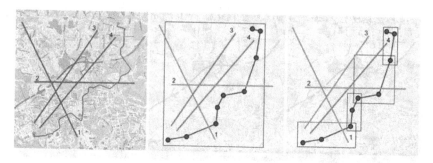

Fig. 3. Path matching

The compatibility analysis between the routes of a passenger and a driver would require in a full scan approach the calculation of 2*n distances between points, where n represents the number of nodes crossed by a driver. While this could be feasible in a small environment, for an app that goes viral with usage heavily concentrated over peak commuter hours it could significantly affect performance.

We considered the lookup procedure as a stratified process made up of two sets of quering algorithms. Each level of the lookup process contributes to the main procedure by pushing data to the mobile device as it finds it. The general idea is to try to find results with limited queries based on assumptions made on statistics and analysis of the typical usage and fall back on the brute force if the amount or quality of data found is not ideal. If the system is able to find the minimum amount of rides required with an average level of compatibility it stops, otherwise it passes to the next query. If all the targeted queries fail the system terminates the execution for that ride. With this approach some compatible rides can be lost, but it's a compromise that is acceptable and that is flexible.

The first algorithm will try to match routes based on start and finish nodes just as other carpooling platforms. The rate of success of this query depends a lot on the nature of usage of the system. We create a bounding box around the departure and arrival points and search for corresponding nodes that fall within it. These represent the best answers usually as no pick up point needs to be agreed on, since the car is already parked, so ideally if the system manages to provide an acceptable number of such rides the search algorithm terminates successfully.

The idea of bounding boxes is to iterate over the set of rides by further narrowing the subset of rides to take into consideration. We first filter the rides based on a bounding box that contains the ride for which we are searching passengers or drivers for. These will not be minimum bounding boxes, but always buffered since minimum bounding boxes tend to a segment if the route is orientated along the horizontal o vertical axis. We repeat this procedure by increasing the number of bounding boxes that cover sub-portions of the path, with every iteration better fitting the path. The objective of this phase is to filter the paths memorized in memory until we reach a number we can handle. The result is that the bounding box approach will return a subset that contains the best rides but isn't able to filter out all the bad ones. Just as an example, this technique would still consider compatible a ride that closely follows our path but in an opposite direction. When the subset has shrunk to an acceptable size, determined by computational power and system load, the system must run the compatibility algorithm to ensure validity of the result. Running only on a small subset this can happen very quickly.

4.3 Server and Asymmetric Data

One of the main problems we faced when evaluating the results of queries described above, is that there is no guarantee that drivers and passengers will be able to see data symmetrically. The work around we implemented was to accept this as a normal behavior and shift the app structure to respond to events. Leveraging the potential of web sockets, apps can virtually communicate to each other. If a passenger tries to contact a driver, and the latter is unaware of such journey, the app will be notified and pull data from the server quering only a specific trip.

5   Conclusions

An open source solution for a real time ride sharing (RTRS) has been introduced, named CORSA. Our proposal comes with high accessibility, high usability, and effectiveness and efficiency in finding a riding solution for users. Here we also described how social networks can endorse effect and benefits of the virtual credits reward mechanism CORSA is based on. We also analyzed some of RTRS platform related questions, both from a functional and a technical point of view. The overall architecture was described, in particular the mobile app acting as the user front-end, and the paths management mechanism.

We are going to consider further questions, as

- how the use of social network can improve the proposed carpooling service
- to discover and exploit hidden relationships, for instance communities among users sharing trips
- to gather data on users and rides for further analysis.

This work was developed under the projecty "S.R.S. - Progetto di formazione integrato SINERGREEN (Smart Intelligent Energy Green), RES-NOVAE, SEM" supported by MIUR (Minister of Education, University and Research).

References

1. Baldacci, R., Maniezzo, V., Mingozzi, A.: An exact method for the car pooling problem based on lagrangean column generation. Oper. Res. 52(3), 422–439 (2004),
   http://dx.doi.org/10.1287/opre.1030.0106
2. Blablacar, https://www.blablacar.it/
3. Carchiolo, V., Longheu, A., Malgeri, M., Mangioni, G.: Search for overlapped communities by parallel genetic algorithms. CoRR abs/0912.0913 (2009),
   http://dblp.uni-trier.de/db/journals/corr/
   corr0912.html#abs-0912-0913

4. Carchiolo, V., Longheu, A., Malgeri, M., Mangioni, G.: Trust assessment: A personalized, distributed, and secure approach. Concurr. Comput. Pract. Exper. 24(6), 605–617 (2012), http://dx.doi.org/10.1002/cpe.1856

5. Carchiolo, V., Longheu, A., Malgeri, M., Mangioni, G.: Users' attachment in trust networks: Reputation vs. Int. J. Bio-Inspired Comput. 5(4), 199–209 (2013), http://dx.doi.org/10.1504/IJBIC.2013.055450

6. Carma, https://www.carmacarpool.com/

7. Cordova, http://cordova.apache.org/

8. Diewald, S., Möller, A., Roalter, L., Kranz, M.: MobiliNet: A Social Network for Optimized Mobility. In: Adjunct Proceedings of the 4th International Conference on Automotive User Interfaces and Interactive Vehicular Applications (AutomotiveUI 2012), pp. 145–150 (October 2012)

9. Domingos, P.: Mining social networks for viral marketing. IEEE Intelligent Systems 20(1), 80–82 (2005)

10. Fagin, R., Williams, J.H.: A fair carpool scheduling algorithm. IBM J. Res. Dev. 27(2), 133–139 (1983), http://dx.doi.org/10.1147/rd.272.0133

11. Ghoseiri, K., Haghani, A., Hamedi, M., Center, M.A.U.T.: of Transportation, P.D., of Transportation. Research, U.S.D., Administration, I.T.: Real-time Rideshare Matching Problem. Mid-Atlantic Universities Transportation Center (2011), http://books.google.it/books?id=l3YFtwAACAAJ

12. Golbeck, J.: The dynamics of web-based social networks: Membership, relationships, and change. First Monday 12(11) (2007), http://firstmonday.org/ojs/index.php/fm/article/view/2023

13. Huang, Y., Jin, R., Bastani, F., Wang, X.S.: Large scale real-time ridesharing with service guarantee on road networks. CoRR abs/1302.6666 (2013)

14. JSON, http://tools.ietf.org/html/rfc7159

15. Kamar, E., Horvitz, E.: Collaboration and shared plans in the open world: Studies of ridesharing. In: Proceedings of the 21st International Jont Conference on Artifical Intelligence, IJCAI 2009, pp. 187–194. Morgan Kaufmann Publishers Inc., San Francisco (2009), http://dl.acm.org/citation.cfm?id=1661445.1661476

16. Leskovec, J., Adamic, L.A., Huberman, B.A.: The dynamics of viral marketing. ACM Trans. Web 1(1) (May 2007), http://doi.acm.org/10.1145/1232722.1232727

17. Loria, M., Bonarrigo, S.: Rtrs: A social oriented proposal. Tech. rep., DIEEI - Universita' di Catania (2014)

18. Lyft - On demand ridesharing, https://www.lyft.me/

19. Maniezzo, V., Carbonaro, A., Hildmann, H.: An ants heuristic for the long term car pooling problem. In: Onwubolu, G.C., Babu, B.V. (eds.) New Optimization Techniques in Engineering. STUDFUZZ, vol. 141, pp. 411–430. Springer, Heidelberg (2004), http://dx.doi.org/10.1007/978-3-540-39930-8_15

20. Mika, P.: Social Networks and the Semantic Web, Semantic Web and Beyond, vol. 5. Springer, Berlin (2007)

21. Sidecar, https://www.side.cr/

22. Teal, R.F.: Carpooling: Who, how and why. Transportation Research Part A: General 21(3), 203–214 (1987), http://www.sciencedirect.com/science/article/pii/0191260787900148

23. Tradeoff, http://tech.pro/blog/1355/when-to-go-native-mobile-web-or-cross-platformhybrid

24. Uber, https://www.uber.com/

25. Wingz, https://www.wingz.me/

Author Index